# CANNON COUNTY, TENNESSEE

# MARRIAGE RECORDS

## BOOKS A, A-1, B, C, D, E, AND F

## 1838-1899

### VOLUME 1

Helen L. Rogers

Heritage Books
2024

# HERITAGE BOOKS

*AN IMPRINT OF HERITAGE BOOKS, INC.*

**Books, CDs, and more—Worldwide**

For our listing of thousands of titles see our website
at
www.HeritageBooks.com

A Facsimile Reprint
Published 2024 by
HERITAGE BOOKS, INC.
Publishing Division
5810 Ruatan Street
Berwyn Heights, MD 20740

International Standard Book Number
Paperbound: 978-0-7884-9066-8

# CANNON COUNTY, TENNESSEE

# MARRIAGE RECORDS

## Books A, A-1, B, C, D, E, and F

## 1838 - 1899

## Volume I

by

## Helen L. Rogers

# EXPLANATION OF THE BOOK

Cannon County is located in Middle Tennessee. It was organized January 31, 1836 when the General Assembly of the State of Tennessee passed an Act establishing the County of Cannon with Woodbury as the county seat. The county was established from parts of Rutherford, Smith, Wilson, and Warren Counties. The county was named for Governor Newton Cannon of Williamson County, Tennessee.

The Cannon County marriage records are recorded in the County Court Clerk's Office in the Courthouse at Woodbury. The original records have suffered materially from lack of care, lack of finances, and constant handling. Some of the records have been lost. Many marriages during the Civil War era are missing. There were no marriages for the year 1861 and only sixteen during 1862. In several instances, it is known that marriages took place during this time; however, no record has been found for these marriages. Duplications are numerous, and entries were not always found in chronological order.

The records contained in this book were taken directly from a microfilmed copy of the original county marriage books. Every effort has been made to copy entries exactly as written. The orginal books have also been checked. A debt of gratitude is owed to Grace Swider who sat with me for many hours deciphering and transcribing records both from the microfilm and from the original record.

The records are presented in alphabetical order with the groom and bride's name in the left column. The next column gives the name of that person's spouse. This is followed by the name of the book and page number where the record is found. The last two entries include the date when the license was purchased and the date of the marriage or return. Other important information found in the records is also listed here.

| Groom or Bride | Groom or Bride | Book/Page | Date of License | Date of Marriage |
|---|---|---|---|---|
| ----, E. J. Miss | Stacy, Joseph | A2/76 | September 3, 1855 | September 4, 1855 |
| ----, ------- | Nichols, Holms | F/88 | June 28, 1896 | June 10, 1896 |
| ----, Lucinda Miss | Vasser, William | A2/73 | May 3, 1852 | May 4, 1852 |
| ----, Malinda Miss | Medford, Henry | A2/47 | March 22, 1856 | March 22, 1856 |
| ----, Margarett Miss | Sullins, Zacriah | A2/36 | October 26, 1854 | No Return |
| ----, Simeon | Bryant, Lillie | F/10 | June 22, 1893 | June 28, 1893 |
| Acres, Meredith | Pallett, Miss Elizabeth | A/45 | December 25, 1841 | December 25, 1841 |
| Adams, Armenty A. | Summars, C. B. | C/304 | February 13, 1884 | February 13, 1884 |
| Adams, A. T. | Preston, Helen | E/214 | September 20, 1889 | September 20, 1889 |
| Adams, Alexander | Turner, Miss Martha | B/12 | December 21, 1867 | December 21, 1867 |
| Adams, Annie | Stanley, J. N. | F/136 | November 6, 1897 | November 7, 1897 |
| Adams, Bennie | Deberry, Nannie | C/448 | November 1, 1891 | November 1, 1891 |
| Adams, G. W. | Barrett, Mollie | D/101 | | February 16, 1882 |
| Adams, Henry | Talley, Laura | C/394 | July 9, 1887 | July 10, 1887 |
| Adams, John | Daniel, Miss Ann Eliza | A/42 | October 16, 1841 | October 18, 1841 |
| Adams, John | Walls, Sarah | C/208 | December 23, 1878 | No Return |
| Adams, Mary | Hancock, Joseph | B/10 | October 6, 1866 | October 7, 1866 |
| Adams, Mary (col.) | Neal, Tom (col.) | F/158 | October 14, 1898 | October 16, 1898 |
| Adams, Mary, (col) | Neal, Tom (col) | E/386 | October 14, 1898 | |
| Adams, Minnor | Merritt, Laura | C/396 | August 6, 1887 | August 7, 1887 |
| Adams, Mintie | Davenport, E. H. | F/92 | August 8, 1896 | August 8, 1896 |
| Adams, Nancy Miss | Jones, A. F. | A2/15 | February 13, 1852 | February ??, 1852 |
| Adams, Peter | Estes, Miss Rachel | B/76 | December 30, 1868 | December 31, 1868 |
| Adams, Robert J. | Boly, Harriet | C/180 | December 13, 1877 | December 13, 1877 |
| Adams, Sarah E. | Bryson, Thos. T. | C/290 | September 3, 1883 | September 5, 1883 |
| Adams, Tempy | Hancock, James | B/8 | September 30, 1865 | September 30, 1865 |
| Adams, W. F. | Smith, Sarah | C/60 | July 8, 1873 | July 9, 1873 |
| Adams, W. F. | Wilcher, Tina | C/216 | June 22, 1879 | June 22, 1879 |
| Adams, Wm | Preston, Mary | E/210 | September 9, 1889 | September 9, 1889 |
| Adams, Wm. J. | Smith, Miss E. N. | A2/32 | March 2, 1854 | March 2, 1854 |
| Adamson, Alse | Snow, Samuel | B/98 | January 18, 1870 | January 18, 1870 |
| Adamson, Francis | Odom, C. C. | C/282 | May 27, 1883 | April 29, 1883 |
| Adamson, Helen | Adamson, T. W. | F/20 | October 8, 1893 | October 8, 1893 |
| Adamson, Malissa | Owen, S. E. H. | B/86 | September 18, 1869 | September 19, 1869 |
| Adamson, Nancy M. | Walker, Leonard | A/54 | September 12, 1842 | No Return |
| Adamson, Presley A. | Hale, Miss Nancy C. | B/38 | January 25, 1867 | January 31, 1867 |
| Adamson, Prestly L. | Warren, Miss Mary Frances | A/82 | July 28, 1845 | July 29, 1845 |
| Adamson, T. W. | Adamson, Helen | F/20 | October 8, 1893 | October 8, 1893 |
| Adcock, America Ann Miss | McCabe, Wm. B. | A2/26 | June 7, 1853 | June 9, 1853 |
| Adcock, Katharine | Parker, Adam | A/32 | September 9, 1840 | September 9, 1840 |
| Adcock, Leonard | Wood, Miss Sarah | A/43 | October 30, 1841 | October 30, 1841 |
| Addams, N. A. | Stroud, F. R. | C/270 | January 5, 1881 | No Return |
| Adonis, Peggey G. Miss | Barrett, Simon | A2/25 | May 22, 1853 | May 22, 1853 |
| Airs, Paralee | Hicks, W. R. | C/154 | February 3, 1877 | February 4, 1877 |
| Aken, B. H. | Fletcher, Miss May | A/105 | November 13, 1847 | November 14, 1847 |
| Akers, N. J. | Moore, Jacob | C/38 | September 17, 1872 | September 19, 1872 |

| Groom or Bride | Groom or Bride | Book/Page | Date of License | Date of Marriage |
|---|---|---|---|---|
| Akers, T. P. Miss | Lorance, R. C. | B/100 | February 23, 1870 | February 24, 1870 |
| Akins, W. B. | Wilson, L. J. | F/22 | November 18, 1893 | November 18, 1893 |
| Alden, Manerva Ann Miss | Cummings, William | A/84 | November 6, 1845 | November 6, 1845 |
| Aldridge, Millia | Thomas, John, A. | A/7 | October 2, 1838 | October 2, 1838 |
| Alexander, ? ? | Pinkerton, Richard | E/184 | June 22, 1889 | June ??, 1889 |
| Alexander, A. O. | Sand?, Miss Martha Frances | A/102 | October 5, 1847 | October 5, 1847 |
| Alexander, A. W. | Wilson, C. N. | F/152 | August 1, 1898 | August 3, 1898 |
| Alexander, Abner D. | Sands, Miss Nancy | A/49 | May 25, 1842 | May 25, 1842 |
| Alexander, Ada | Carter, J. N. | D/12 | | February 23, 1882 |
| Alexander, Addi | Hudeston, Marshal | F/8 | May 1, 1893 | May 2, 1893 |
| Alexander, Adre (col.) | Jerrett, Wesley (col.) | F/102 | November 30, 1896 | November 30, 1896 |
| Alexander, B. C. | Devenport, N. E. | C/44 | October 22, 1872 | October 22, 1872 |
| Alexander, Benjamin T. | Barkley, Miss Mary Isabella | A2/11 | September 12, 1851 | September 18, 1851 |
| Alexander, Bob | Meares, Alta | F/156 | September 27, 1898 | September 27, 1898 |
| Alexander, Cresia | Carney, Granville | E/130 | January 29, 1889 | January 31, 1889 |
| Alexander, Dellar | Shelton, J. B. | F/106 | December 19, 1896 | December 20, 1896 |
| Alexander, Donnie | Simpson, Rocindy | F/108 | January 9, 1897 | January 10, 1897 |
| Alexander, Dora | Richardson, Willis | D/12 | | March 12, 1882 |
| Alexander, Dora | Thurston, W. J. | F/58 | February 2, 1895 | February 3, 1895 |
| Alexander, Dora | Frazier, Zach | C/82 | February 4, 1874 | February 16, 1874 |
| Alexander, E. E. | Campbell, Mary | F/148 | March 19, 1898 | March 20, 1898 |
| Alexander, E. Miss | Keel, T. M. | A2/51 | December 4, 1856 | No Return |
| Alexander, Elisabeth Miss | Mears, Thomas J. | A2/75 | December 30, 1854 | December 30, 1854 |
| Alexander, Ella | Smith, A. A. | F/172 | March 13 1899 | March 15, 1899 |
| Alexander, Fannie | Wilson, Mike | F/56 | January 12, 1895 | January 13, 1895 |
| Alexander, Florance | Cash, W. A. | C/198 | September 3, 1878 | September 4, 1878 |
| Alexander, Francis M. | Hayes, Mary R. | C/130 | December 30, 1875 | December 30, 1875 |
| Alexander, Geo H. | McBroom, Mary F. | C/134 | February 4, 1876 | February 4, 1876 |
| Alexander, Geo. | McAdoo, N. C. | C/48 | December 31, 1872 | December 31, 1872 |
| Alexander, Hattie | Pinkerton, J. F. | F/6 | February 28, 1893 | March 2, 1893 |
| Alexander, Helan Miss | Moore, Robert D. | B/78 | February 1, 1869 | February 4, 1869 |
| Alexander, J. G. | Ward, Miss Caroline | A2/21 | December 21, 1852 | December 30, 1852 |
| Alexander, J. M. | Tassey, Miss Bettie Jane | B/68 | August 12, 1868 | August 13, 1868 |
| Alexander, James | Harris, Virginia | F/154 | August 20, 1898 | August 21, 1898 |
| Alexander, James A. | Hay, Miss Anliza | A2/93 | January 1, 1860 | January 3, 1860 |
| Alexander, John | Young, Miss C. | B/122 | December 28, 1870 | December 29, 1871 |
| Alexander, John D. | Davenport, Miss Margaret S. | B/108 | August 23, 1870 | August 25, 1870 |
| Alexander, John Mc. | Bragg, Miss Mary N. | B/46 | July 15, 1867 | July 16, 1867 |
| Alexander, M. (col.) | Davis, Ona | C/450 | December 5, 1891 | December 6, 1891 |
| Alexander, M. A. | Sullivan, J. B. | A2/105 | October 23, 1862 | October 23, 1862 |
| Alexander, M. E. | Jones, C. B. | C/460 | July 14, 1892 | July 17, 1892 |
| Alexander, M. P. | Tenpenny, John | A2/74 | November 3, 1853 | November 3, 1853 |
| Alexander, M. P. Miss | Tenpenny, John | A2/74 | November 3, 1853 | November 3, 1853 |
| Alexander, Madison | McKnight, Laura | C/324 | January 28, 1885 | January 28, 1885 |
| Alexander, Margarett A. Miss | Witherspoon, John K. | A/117 | November 21, 1848 | No Return |
| Alexander, Marshal | Rucker, Casie | C/302 | January 23, 1884 | No Return |

| Groom or Bride | Groom or Bride | Book/Page | Date of License | Date of Marriage |
| --- | --- | --- | --- | --- |
| Alexander, Martha L. | Wood, Thos. O. | A2/113 | April 19, 1864 | April 19, 1864 |
| Alexander, Martin | Hollandsworth, Nova | E/365 | January 15, 1920 | |
| Alexander, Mary | Williams, Dennis | C/178 | November 30, 1877 | December 2, 1877 |
| Alexander, Mary M. | Givens, J. W. | C/124 | November 27, 1875 | November 28, 1875 |
| Alexander, Mary A. | Ready, C. C. | C/6 | August 4, 1871 | August 15, 1871 |
| Alexander, Mary Adaline Miss | Crane, John W. | A/91 | September 15, 1846 | September 17, 1846 |
| Alexander, N. J. T. | Tenpenny, Daniel | C/24 | February 20, 1872 | February 20, 1872 |
| Alexander, N. M. | Northcutt, J. M. | C/228 | October 1, 1874 | October 1, 1879 |
| Alexander, Nancy | Bryson, Daniel | A/10 | January 17, 1839 | January 23, 1839 |
| Alexander, Nancy A. | McBroom, D. T. | D/9 | | December 29, 1881 |
| Alexander, Nancy Miss | George, John A. | A/46 | January 20, 1842 | January 20, 1842 |
| Alexander, Neomi | Travis, John A. | A2/110 | December 30, 1863 | December 31, 1863 |
| Alexander, Osin | Fisher, Marian | A2/116 | October 4, 1864 | October 7, 1864 |
| Alexander, Rachel | Barkley, Morgan | B/2 | August 21, 1865 | No Return |
| Alexander, Roxanna Miss | McBroom, John | A/117 | November 15, 1848 | November 16, 1848 |
| Alexander, Sandy | Woodard, Lucy | E/155 | November 17, 1888 | November 18, 1888 |
| Alexander, Sarah E. Miss | Cook, Stephen | A/94 | December 22, 1846 | December 23, 1846 |
| Alexander, Sarah Jane Miss | Crieson, James C. | A2/7 | November 7, 1850 | No Return |
| Alexander, Sissie | Keith, John | E/88 | October 17, 1888 | October 18, 1888 |
| Alexander, T. A. | Wilson, W. N. | F/52 | December 12, 1894 | December 13, 1894 |
| Alexander, W. T. | Conley, Emley T. | C/22 | February 1, 1872 | February 1, 1872 |
| Alexander, W. T. | Tenpenny, Miss Sibbie | C/414 | August 6, 1890 | August 6, 1890 |
| Alexander, W. T. | Vandell, Bettie | F/8 | April 13, 1893 | April 13, 1893 |
| Alexander, Will | Talley Mary (col) | E/29 | April 15, 1888 | April 15, 1888 |
| Alexander, William | Finley, Miss Tenn | C/372 | November 6, 1886 | No Return |
| Alexander, William T. | Mingle, Miss Better | C/386 | March 23, 1887 | March 23, 1887 |
| Alexander, Wm. | Bailey, Francis | C/256 | September 1, 1880 | September 1, 1880 |
| Alford, Elizabeth Miss | Rogers, James | A2/49 | August 11, 1856 | August 12, 1856 |
| Alford, John | Sullivan, Drucilla | A2/121 | March 6, 1865 | March 6, 1865 |
| Alford, Malinda | Morgan, Anderson | A2/133 | December 15, 1865 | December 15, 1865 |
| Alford, Mary | Moss, W. D. | A2/93 | January 24, 1860 | No Return |
| Alford, Wm. C. | Duncan, Miss Sarah Ann | A2/40 | April 30, 1855 | May 16, 1855 |
| Allen, A. G. | Miller, Visey A. | C/302 | January 18, 1884 | January 20, 1884 |
| Allen, Alice | Brison, Timothy | C/192 | May 8, 1878 | May 9, 1878 |
| Allen, Babe | Pitts, Thomas | E/126 | January 4, 1889 | January 13, 1889 |
| Allen, Benjamin F. | Young, Miss Youffey | A/38 | April 13, 1841 | April 13, 1841 |
| Allen, Charley | Bryson, Margeret | C/366 | September 11, 1886 | September 12, 1886 |
| Allen, Clemmsy | Rogers, Wilburn | C/92 | August 19, 1874 | August 30, 1874 |
| Allen, E. R. | Todd, Martha | F/138 | November 27, 1897 | November 28, 1897 |
| Allen, G. R. | Lowrance, M. N. | C/52 | February 13, 1873 | February 13, 1873 |
| Allen, Isabeller | Mahather, James | C/310 | July 16, 1884 | July 16, 1884 |
| Allen, J. G. | Prater, Eliza B. | C/170 | September 5, 1877 | September 6, 1877 |
| Allen, James | Smith, Emeline | C/46 | December 13, 1872 | December 13, 1872 |
| Allen, James L. | Carrick, Sarah E. | A2/132 | November 16, 1865 | November 16, 1865 |
| Allen, Jenie | Gannon, Samuel L. | C/310 | July 26, 1884 | No Return |
| Allen, Jesse | Ware, A. A. | D/17 | | December 4, 1882 |

| Groom or Bride | Groom or Bride | Book/Page | Date of License | Date of Marriage |
|---|---|---|---|---|
| Allen, Joe | Edwards, Lillia | C/314 | September 20, 1884 | September 20, 1884 |
| Allen, John | Pitts, Julia A. E. | C/184 | January 3, 1878 | January 3, 1878 |
| Allen, John | Pickerson, Jane | D/101 | | January 8, 1882 |
| Allen, John D. | Lorance, Martha A. | C/172 | September 27, 1877 | September 27, 1877 |
| Allen, John M. | Hancock, Mon. A. | A2/39 | February 14, 1855 | No Date |
| Allen, John M. | Hancock, A. T. | A2/39 | February 14, 1855 | No Return |
| Allen, Maud | Petty, Willie | E/364 | November 26, 1898 | |
| Allen, Maud | Petty, Willey | F/160 | November 26, 1898 | November 27, 1898 |
| Allen, Minnie | Barrett, Milas | F/112 | February 2, 1897 | February 21, 1897 |
| Allen, Nancy V. Miss | Young, Tilford M. | A2/90 | November 16, 1859 | No Return |
| Allen, Rebeca Miss | Clendennen, Robert W. | A/122 | June 4, 1849 | June 6, 1849 |
| Allen, Samuel | Burch, Miss Mary Ann | B/86 | September 2, 1869 | September 2, 1869 |
| Allen, Samuel B. | West, Miss Manerva Ann | A/45 | December 10, 1841 | December 10, 1841 |
| Allen, W. B. | Deberry, Rebecca J. | C/110 | February 26, 1975 | February 26, 1875 |
| Allen, Wm | Merriman, Sarah J. | C/210 | January 10, 1879 | January 10, 1879 |
| Allison, H. E. Miss | Barrett, A. | B/58 | December 5, 1867 | December 9, 1867 |
| Allison, Jane | McMahan, Brownlow | C/202 | October 30, 1878 | October 30 1878 |
| Allman, Polema | Lasiter, J. L. | F/128 | August 25, 1897 | August 29, 1897 |
| Allmon, E. H. | McGill, P. T. | A2/115 | July 13, 1864 | July 13, 1864 |
| Alman, Armenta | Shaver, J. N. | C/78 | January 3, 1874 | January 4, 1874 |
| Alman, Lidie | Todd, John | C/328 | March 26, 1885 | No Return |
| Alman, Mollie | Hayes, Pink | C/298 | December 27, 1883 | No Return |
| Almon, Ann Miss | Duke, Alexander | B/80 | March 16, 1869 | March 18, 1869 |
| Almon, Sarah E. Miss | Thompson, Taylor | B/66 | June 10, 1868 | June 11, 1868 |
| Alread, Elizabeth | Elkins, J. P. | F/10 | May 13, 1893 | May 18, 1893 |
| Alread, J. S. | Womack, D. G. | C/286 | July 6, 1883 | July 8, 1883 |
| Amos, Saray | Elam, Henry | C/428 | January 8, 1891 | January 10, 1891 |
| Amos, W. A. | Sparks, Mariah C. | C/372 | October 23, 1886 | No Return |
| Amus, Sarah | Gann, Robt. | C/40 | September 19, 1872 | No Return |
| Anders (?), Betty | Ford, D. S. | C/242 | October 29, 1879 | January 7, 1880 |
| Anderson, Asa | Ellie, Miss Mary Ann | A/46 | December 30, 1841 | December 30, 1841 |
| Anderson, Elijah | Taylor, Miss Elizabeth | A/37 | April 6, 1841 | April 6, 1841 |
| Anderson, Geol | Nelson, Martha | C/148 | November 15, 1876 | November 24, 1876 |
| Anderson, J. G. | McGill, Miss Martha | A2/143 | August 22, 1866 | August 26, 1866 |
| Anderson, J. M. | Good, N. C. | C/34 | August 14, 1872 | No Return |
| Anderson, James | Ashford, Miss Ann Eliza | A/57 | December 22, 1841 | December 22, 1841 |
| Anderson, Jane Miss | Taylor, George L. | A/93 | November 2, 1846 | November 2, 1846 |
| Anderson, John | Hargus, Miss Jerusha | A/63 | July 13, 1843 | July 14, 1843 |
| Anderson, John | Northcut, Lockey | C/356 | April 9, 1886 | April 11, 1886 |
| Anderson, Lucinda | Ensey, W. S. | C/62 | July 14, 1873 | July 14, 1873 |
| Anderson, Martha | Keaton, Lee | F/76 | November 23, 1895 | November 27, 1895 |
| Anderson, Martha Miss | Pealer, Leny | A/77 | March 8, 1845 | March 9, 1845 |
| Anderson, Mary | Pealer, King | A/25 | February 25, 1840 | February 25, 1840 |
| Anderson, Stephen A. | Evans, Nancy A. | A2/108 | August 13, 1863 | No Return |
| Anderson, Rebeca | Foard, D. S. | C/226 | October 29, 1879 | No Return |
| Anderson, Sarah | Lemmons, W. A. | C/204 | November 12, 1878 | November 17, 1878 |

| Groom or Bride | Groom or Bride | Book/Page | Date of License | Date of Marriage |
|---|---|---|---|---|
| Anderson, T. A. | Sisom, Josie | E/107 | December 7, 1888 | December 9, 1888 |
| Anderson, W. C. | Hipp, E. C. | C/192 | June 22, 1878 | June 23, 1878 |
| Anderson, W. H. | Sullens, Susie Ann | F/72 | October 19, 1895 | October 20, 1895 |
| Anderson, William | McCoy, Catherine | E/261 | January 10, 1890 | No Return |
| Anderson, William W. | Taylor, Miss Martha L. | B/44 | April 6, 1867 | April 7, 1867 |
| Andrew, Mary F. Miss | McKnight, S. H. A. | A/104 | November 9, 1847 | November 11, 1847 |
| Andrews, Eleanor F. Miss | McKnight, G. D. A. | A/126 | September 5, 1849 | No Return |
| Andrews, Elizabeth | Smith, C. G. O. | A2/9 | January 7, 1851 | No Return |
| Andrews, J. M. | McKnight, Miss Sarah J. | A/93 | October 31, 1846 | November 24, 1846 |
| Angles, Melinda Jane | Sissom, Jesse | A/7 | October 13, 1838 | No Return |
| Anos, Henry | Partin, Eliza | A/35 | January 1, 1841 | January 7, 1841 |
| Aread, S. H. | Colvart, Lena | C/464 | September 20, 1892 | September 2, 1892 |
| Armstrong, Allen | Wright, Etta | B/18 | August 3, 1870 | No Return |
| Armstrong, John | Campbell, Miss Mahaly | A2/57 | September 3, 1857 | August 3, 1857 |
| Armstrong, John | Ramsey, Miss Caroline | B/74 | December 5, 1868 | December 6, 1868 |
| Armstrong, Knox | Rigsby, Florance | C/202 | October 16, 1878 | October 17, 1878 |
| Armstrong, M. C. | Travis, D. D | C/230 | November 16, 1879 | November 30, 1879 |
| Armstrong, Mahala Miss | Vance, Thomas | B/40 | February 14, 1867 | February 14, 1867 |
| Armstrong, N. Miss | Hays, S. F. | A2/61 | December 24, 1857 | December 24, 1857 |
| Armstrong, Pernina S. Mrs. | Campbell, Thomas | A2/11 | February 17, 1851 | February 18, 1851 |
| Armstrong, Richard | Dennis, Elizabeth | A/70 | June 15, 1844 | June 25, 1844 |
| Armstrong, Samuel P. | Blanks, Miss Sarah C. | C/408 | November 17, 1887 | November 18, 1887 |
| Arnet, James | Hendrix, Sarah | A2/122 | March 20, 1865 | No Return |
| Arnett, James | Motley, Ann | C/400 | September 3, 1887 | September 4, 1887 |
| Arnett, Elijah D. | Melton, Ochey K. | C/336 | September 7, 1885 | September 10, 1885 |
| Arnett, J. E. | Melton, R. C. | C/242 | February 21, 1880 | No Return |
| Arnett, James | Motley, Ann | C/400 | September 3, 1887 | September 4, 1887 |
| Arnett, Jas. E. | Grizzell, Izzan | A2/102 | September 11, 1860 | No Return |
| Arnett, Joe | Melton, Zanie | E/360 | December 2, 1898 | |
| Arnett, Joe E. | Melton, Janie | F/162 | December 24, 1898 | August 11, 1898 |
| Arnett, M. J. | Mathis, J. H. | C/432 | March 26, 1891 | March 29, 1891 |
| Arnett, Nannie | Campbell, Albert | F/72 | October 17, 1895 | November 1, 1895 |
| Arnett, Pinkney | Vaughn, Martha | C/28 | June 1, 1872 | June 2, 1872 |
| Arnett, Susan | Murphy, John | C/228 | October 1, 1079 | October 5, 1879 |
| Arnold, America | Herold, Miss Issabella | A/122 | January 12, 1849 | January 13, 1849 |
| Arnold, Emmar | Wilson, Wm. | C/282 | May 7, 1883 | February 6, 1884 |
| Arnold, Elizabeth Miss | Beechboard, Robert | A2/8 | November 30, 1850 | December 1, 1850 |
| Arnold, Harvy | Bush, Miss M. E. | B/82 | July 3, 1869 | July 4, 1869 |
| Arnold, Howey (Harvey) | Herald, Miss Jenetta | A2/13 | December 26, 1851 | December 28, 1851 |
| Arnold, Mariah Miss | Vasser, William | A2/37 | November 29, 1854 | November 30, 1854 |
| Arnold, N. C. | Cotheren, S. A. | A2/102 | September 15, 1860 | No Return |
| Arnold, W. J. | Tolbert, Miss P. J. | B/110 | September 15, 1870 | September 18, 1870 |
| Arnold, William | Cantrell, Miss Lucinda | A2/50 | August 30, 1856 | August 30, 1856 |
| Arnold, William Jefferson | Sagely, Miss Mariah Elvina | A/106 | December 25, 1847 | December 25, 1847 |
| Aronheart, Nancy Ann | Simpson, Thomas | F/48 | November 16, 1894 | November 18, 1874 |
| Arrington, F. M. | Bynum, Miss Martha | A2/137 | February 5, 1866 | February 6, 1866 |

| Groom or Bride | Groom or Bride | Book/Page | Date of License | Date of Marriage |
|---|---|---|---|---|
| Arvin, William | Mullins, Martha | A2/125 | August 3, 1865 | August 10, 1865 |
| Ase, Sarah Ann Miss | Knight, James | A2/63 | March 4, 1858 | March 4, 1858 |
| Ashfor, Nola | Stewart, Hugh | F/14 | August 17, 1893 | No Return |
| Ashford, A. E. | Bogle, F. R. | C/366 | September 16, 1886 | September 19, 1886 |
| Ashford, Ann Eliza Miss | Anderson, James | A/57 | December 22, 1841 | December 22, 1841 |
| Ashford, Antaliza Miss | Mathews, Walter | A/51 | July 21, 1842 | April 20, 1842 |
| Ashford, Baxel | Rigsby, Miss Jane | A2/67 | September 17, 1858 | September 27, 1858 |
| Ashford, Bettie | Vance, John D. | F/22 | November 21, 1893 | November 22, 1893 |
| Ashford, Compton | McPhearson, Miss Margarett E. | A/44 | November 24, 1841 | November 25, 1841 |
| Ashford, Elizabeth | Johns, Thomas | C/308 | June 14, 1884 | June 14, 1884 |
| Ashford, Elizabeth Miss | Gann, Russel | A2/81 | July 29, 1857 | July 29, 1857 |
| Ashford, Ella | Prater, Granville | F/134 | October 9, 1897 | October 10, 1897 |
| Ashford, George | Mullen, Nancy | A2/16 | February 3, 1852 | February 3, 1852 |
| Ashford, George | Hammons, Miss Sarah P. | B/64 | December 31, 1867 | December 31, 1867 |
| Ashford, Mallisa | Melton, Richard | A/39 | July 24, 1841 | July 25, 1841 |
| Ashford, Mary Miss | Young, Alexander | A/61 | April 6, 1843 | No Return |
| Ashford, Nancy | Mullens, Joseph | A/5 | August 14, 1838 | August 16, 1838 |
| Ashford, Nancy Jane Miss | Hale, Creed W. | A/122 | May 8, 1849 | May 8, 1849 |
| Ashford, Polk | Collins, Sarah | A2/130 | October 19, 1865 | October 20, 1865 |
| Ashford, Polly | Ledbetter, Eli | A/2 | April 25, 1838 | |
| Ashford, Richard | Milligan, Miss Ruthy | A2/85 | May 5, 1859 | No Return |
| Ashford, William | Blackwell, Hilder | C/466 | September 26, 1892 | September 27, 1892 |
| Ashford, Handsom | Melton, Josh | F/98 | October 18, 1896 | October 18, 1096 |
| Ashley, D. J. | Hill, Agnis | C/122 | October 23, 1875 | October 24, 1875 |
| Ashley, John R. | Duncan, Miss Clarissa | A/126 | August 11, 1849 | August 16, 1849 |
| Ashley, Mary | Webber, Benjamin | A2/112 | February 1, 1864 | No Return |
| Ashley, Wm. S. | Holt, Malisa | C/132 | January 22, 1876 | January 23, 1876 |
| Ashly, William C. | Spry, Miss Mary M. | A2/1 | March 9, 1850 | March 9, 1850 |
| Ashworth, Thomas C. | Smith, Jane | A/55 | November 4, 1842 | November 4, 1842 |
| Atcheley, Nannie? Miss | Eason, R. F. | B/68 | July 30, 1868 | July 30, 1868 |
| Atchley, Margaret E. | Barrett, Houston | A2/129 | October 3, 1865 | October 8, 1865 |
| Atnip, J. H. | Moore, Idella | C/474 | December 29, 1892 | December 29, 1892 |
| Aushus, J. H. | Pack, N. M. | C/234 | December 24, 1879 | December 25, 1879 |
| Ausment, Mary | Burch, William P. | A2/132 | November 22, 1865 | Executed No Date |
| Austin, J. W. | Barrett, Miss M. J. | A2/66 | July 24, 1858 | No Return |
| Auston, Sarah Miss | Phins, Wm. M. | A2/58 | October 9, 1857 | October 10, 1857 |
| Auton, Elizabeth Miss | Earls, Nathan | A2/55 | April 9, 1857 | Arpil 10, 1857 |
| Avent, Logie | Chambers, Jacob | C/388 | May 14, 1887 | No Return |
| Avert, Albert | Patz, Addie H. | E/66 | August 31, 1888 | September 4, 1888 |
| Babbett, S. F. | Garis, W. G. D. | A2/72 | February 18, 1859 | February 18, 1859 |
| Babbit, S. F Miss | Garis, W. G. D. | A2/67 | September 27, 1858 | September 27, 1858 |
| Babel, S. F. Miss | Garris, William G. D. | A2/84 | February 18, 1859 | February 18, 1859 |
| Bagett, Rosanar H. | Spry, J. H. | C/218 | July 23, 1879 | July 24, 1879 |
| Bailey, Ada | Sullens, J. | E/388 | October 12, 1898 | |
| Bailey, Aline | Lawrence, Robert | C/426 | December 20, 1890 | December 21, 1890 |

| Groom or Bride | Groom or Bride | Book/Page | Date of License | Date of Marriage |
|---|---|---|---|---|
| Bailey, Andrew J. | Sullivan, Miss Laura Ann | A2/11 | April 21, 1852 | No Return |
| Bailey, Anna Miss | Warren, Wm. | C/450 | December 9, 1891 | December 9, 1891 |
| Bailey, C. J. | Gunter, Miss Josie | F/82 | January 9, 1896 | January 9, 1896 |
| Bailey, Dillard | Stone, Ruth A. | C/20 | January 13, 1872 | January 14, 1872 |
| Bailey, E. J. | Melton, Ida | C/472 | December 27, 1892 | December 27, 1892 |
| Bailey, E. J. | Sullins, Miss Marietta | E/10 | January 21, 1888 | ??? |
| Bailey, Elizabeth | Cox, J. L. | C/282 | May 3, 1883 | No Return |
| Bailey, Ferdelia Miss | Elkins, S. J. | E/19 | February 16, 1888 | February 16, 1888 |
| Bailey, France | Summars, Asaline | F/88 | June 17, 1896 | June 21, 1896 |
| Bailey, Francis | Alexander, Wm. | C/256 | September 1, 1880 | September 1, 1880 |
| Bailey, Francis | Mullican, Josie | C/340 | October 24, 1885 | October 25, 1885 |
| Bailey, H. L. | Turpin, Sarah J. | C/334 | August 13, 1885 | August 13, 1884 |
| Bailey, Helen | Masey, James | C/446 | October 3, 1891 | October 3, 1891 |
| Bailey, Ida | Hoover, J. L. | C/470 | December 17, 1892 | December 18, 1892 |
| Bailey, Ida | Sullins, J. | F/158 | October 12, 1898 | October 13, 1898 |
| Bailey, Isaac | Lorrance, Miss Bettie | C/412 | December 21, 1887 | December 21, 1887 |
| Bailey, J. N. | Gilley, Lucinda | C/130 | December 31, 1875 | January 2, 1876 |
| Bailey, Jacob | Markum, Miss Calafornia | B/108 | August 25, 1870 | August 24, 1870 |
| Bailey, James | Cox, Elizabeth | C/142 | August 12, 1876 | No Return |
| Bailey, Jim B. | Markum, Mary E. | C/206 | November 30, 1878 | November 31, 1878 |
| Bailey, John R. | St. John, Lidelia | C/170 | September 13, 1877 | September 13, 1877 |
| Bailey, Joseph | Preston, Miss Sallie | B/56 | November 25, 1867 | December 8, 1867 |
| Bailey, Joseph A. | Evans, Miss Sallie | B/108 | August 31, 1870 | August 31, 1870 |
| Bailey, Josephine Miss | Cummins, Warren | A2/135 | January 13, 1866 | January 14, 1866 |
| Bailey, L. A. Miss | Hipp, A. R. | B/34 | December 26, 1866 | December 26, 1866 |
| Bailey, M. A. | Underhill, J. H. | F/60 | March 15, 1895 | March 17, 1895 |
| Bailey, M. F. | Good, M. E. | C/232 | December 4, 1879 | December 4, 1879 |
| Bailey, M. J. Miss | Turner, W. H. | A2/67 | September 29, 1858 | September 29, 1858 |
| Bailey, Mack | Higdon, Maggie | E/326 | December 31, 1898 | |
| Bailey, Malessie | Rains, J. B. | C/338 | October 8, 1885 | October 8, 1885 |
| Bailey, Malissa Miss | Owen, Abraham | B/60 | December 26, 1867 | December 26, 1867 |
| Bailey, Manerva Miss | Sullivan, Samuel C. | A/50 | June 30, 1842 | June 30, 1842 |
| Bailey, Martha E. | Campbell, J. D. | A2/110 | November 10, 1863 | No Return |
| Bailey, Mary J. | Young, Calvin | C/216 | March 30, 1879 | March 30, 18779 |
| Bailey, Mary J. Miss | Conley, A. J. | B/82 | July 17, 1869 | July 17, 1869 |
| Bailey, Miss H. L. | Winnett, T. J. | F/90 | June 29, 1896 | June 29, 1896 |
| Bailey, Mollie | Lawrence, James T. | E/116 | December 29, 1888 | No Return |
| Bailey, Mollie S. | Williams, W. H. | D/23 | | April 17, 1883 |
| Bailey, Nancy | Mears, Elijah | A/28 | April 22, 1840 | April 24, 1840 |
| Bailey, R. A. Miss | Melton, Elias R. | A2/70 | November 18, 1858 | No Return |
| Bailey, Robert | Stone, Miss Issabella | A/63 | July 18, 1843 | July 20, 1843 |
| Bailey, Robert | Rains, Miss Rhoda | A/129 | December 14, 1849 | December 19, 1849 |
| Bailey, Robert | Cumings, Miss T. P. | A2/44 | December 8, 1855 | December 9, 1855 |
| Bailey, Robert | Higdon, Miss Allie | C/464 | September 8, 1892 | September 8, 1892 |
| Bailey, Ruth | Gilley, Joseph D. | C/400 | September 10, 1887 | September 10, 1887 |
| Bailey, Rutha A. Miss | Melton, Elias R. | A2/82 | November 18, 1858 | November 18, 1858 |

| Groom or Bride | Groom or Bride | Book/Page | Date of License | Date of Marriage |
|---|---|---|---|---|
| Bailey, Sallie | Melton, Oakly | F/106 | December 16, 1896 | December 20, 1896 |
| Bailey, Sarah N. Miss | Shirley, Alfred | A2/136 | January 30, 1866 | January 30, 1866 |
| Bailey, Wade | Higdon, Maggie | F/164 | December 31, 1898 | January 1, 1899 |
| Bailey, Wiley | Melton, Jennie | F/102 | November 17, 1896 | November 19, 1896 |
| Bailey, William M. | Neely, Miss Elizabeth | A2/1 | March 22, 1850 | No Date |
| Bailey, Wm. | Melton, Miss Martha E. | A2/89 | September 20, 1859 | No Return |
| Baily, Bettie | Davis, Benj. | C/44 | October 24, 1872 | October 24, 1872 |
| Baily, Hugh L. | Cummings, Parasade | A2/109 | October 19, 1863 | No Return |
| Baily, John N. | Stone, Mary | A/3 | May 23, 1838 | June 3, 1838 |
| Baily, Margaret E. Miss | Shirley, John W. | A2/93 | December 28, 1859 | No Return |
| Baily, Mary A. Miss | Wood, B. F. | A2/59 | November 3, 1857 | November 5, 1857 |
| Baily, Robert | Neely, Miss Caroline | A2/56 | June 5, 1857 | June 7, 1857 |
| Baily, Vinson | Campbell, Paralee | C/42 | October 19, 1872 | October 20, 1872 |
| Bain, Frances Ann | Covington, W. L. | A2/79 | October 6, 1856 | October 6, 1856 |
| Baine, Isaiah | Stanton, Miss Rebecca | A/67 | January 16, 1844 | January 18, 1844 |
| Bains, A. D. | St. John, Syntha | C/250 | July 8, 1880 | July 8, 1880 |
| Baird, Henry | Clark, Mary | B/10 | February 22, 1867 | February 22, 1867 |
| Baird, J. A. | Wiley, Miss Frances Ann | A/72 | August 30 1844 | September 1, 1844 |
| Baird, Mary Miss | Wheeler, N. T. | B/116 | November 10, 1870 | November 10, 1870 |
| Bairns, Euhley | Muse, J. L. | C/224 | September 25, 1879 | September 25, 1879 |
| Baker, Bill (col.) | Todd, Nettie (col.) | F/84 | February 22, 1896 | February 29, 1896 |
| Baker, John W. | Prior, Sarah | A2/12 | November 11, 1851 | November 13, 1851 |
| Baley, J. A. | Stewart, Bethany | C/152 | January 3, 1877 | January 4, 1877 |
| Baley, James | Ferrell, Cennine | C/44 | October 31, 1872 | October 31, 1872 |
| Baley, Martha A. Miss | Seals, James | B/130 | April 12, 1871 | April 12, 1871 |
| Baley, S. F. Miss | Lening, N. J. | B/122 | December 28, 1870 | December 28, 1870 |
| Baltimore, Ader | Lynn, George | F/12 | July 7, 1893 | July 11, 1893 |
| Baltimore, G. H. | Cunningham, Rebeca | C/372 | October 23, 1886 | October 24, 1886 |
| Baltimore, Joseph | Simpson, Miss Jane | A2/30 | December 19, 1853 | December 20, 1853 |
| Baltimore, Mary A. | Webber, J. G. | C/120 | September 16, 1875 | September 17, 1875 |
| Baltimore, P. J. | McCuller, Miss R. S. | B/112 | September 28, 1870 | September 29, 1870 |
| Baltimore, Philip J. | Simpson, Miss Mary Elizabeth | A/116 | November 7, 1848 | November 7, 1848 |
| Baltimore, Roxie | Lynn, Richard | F/34 | March 28, 1894 | April 14, 1894 |
| Baly, John S. | Marcum, Miss Melvina J. | A2/91 | November 25, 1859 | No Return |
| Baly, Martha H. | Maxey, P. P. | A2/111 | January 6, 1864 | January 7, 1864 |
| Baly, Mary | Smith, T. B. | A2/98 | June 20, 1860 | June 20, 1860 |
| Bank, Lucy P. Miss | Smithson, Joshua C. | A2/36 | October 17, 1854 | October 17, 1854 |
| Banks, Arrenea | Parker, John | A2/36 | November 9, 1854 | November 9, 1854 |
| Banks, Dennis | Hays, Miss Maranda M. | A2/49 | August 11, 1856 | August 12, 1856 |
| Banks, Edgar | Duke, Dora | F/72 | October 19, 1895 | October 20, 1894 |
| Banks, Elizabeth Miss | Stroud, Jessee | A2/66 | August 7, 1858 | No Return |
| Banks, Lethie J. | Spangler, Samuel | A2/44 | November 29, 1855 | November 29, 1855 |
| Bankston, James M. | Wiser, Miss Julian J. | A2/157 | June 15, 1866 | June 17, 1866 |
| Bankston, John | Moten, Miss Margarett | A2/24 | March 26, 1853 | March 27, 1853 |
| Barett, Abraham | Elkins, Miss Martha | A2/24 | March 19, 1853 | March 29, 1853 |
| Barett, Martha Miss | Willson, W. A. | A2/59 | November 10, 1857 | November 11, 1857 |

| Groom or Bride | Groom or Bride | Book/Page | Date of License | Date of Marriage |
| --- | --- | --- | --- | --- |
| Barker, Donalson | Neeley, Miss Mary | A2/138 | February 27, 1866 | March 1, 1866 |
| Barkley, Charley H. | McKnight, Bella J. | D/9 | | December 22, 1881 |
| Barkley, Franklin | McKnight, Aimey | B/2 | August 21, 1865 | August 26, 1865 |
| Barkley, Hattie | Murry, Samuel | D/4 | | August 9, 1881 |
| Barkley, Lidia | Knight, John | C/376 | November 23, 1886 | November 24, 1886 |
| Barkley, Mariah | Taylor, Thomas | C/158 | March 2, 1877 | March 2, 1877 |
| Barkley, Mary Isabella Miss | Alexander, Benjamin T. | A2/11 | September 12, 1851 | September 18, 1851 |
| Barkley, Morgan | Alexander, Rachel | B/2 | August 21, 1865 | No Return |
| Barkley, Nancy Ann Miss | Warren, Alexander | A2/9 | January 6, 1851 | January 7, 1851 |
| Barnes, Alex | Trimble, Tennie | C/58 | June 14, 1873 | June 15, 1873 |
| Barnes, Alex (col.) | Pinkerton, Sallie | C/458 | March 25, 1892 | March 25, 1892 |
| Barnes, Bill | Smith, Laura | C/338 | September 27, 1885 | September 27, 1885 |
| Barnes, Della | Wheeler, Thomas R. | C/188 | March 12, 1878 | March 12, 1878 |
| Barnes, Dosia Miss | Rushing, Frank | B/128 | March 10, 1871 | March 10, 1871 |
| Barnes, Harrett Miss | Sullens, James | A2/18 | July 20, 1852 | July 21, 1852 |
| Barnes, Harriett | Wood, John | F/18 | October 9, 1893 | October 9, 1893 |
| Barnes, Henry | Rushing, Emily | B/14 | August 15, 1868 | August 18, 1868 |
| Barnes, J. A. | Burger, S. | A2/45 | November 27, 1855 | No Return |
| Barnes, James | Murry, Alice | C/286 | July 17, 1883 | July 17, 1883 |
| Barnes, Jessee | Burgner, Susan J. | A2/43 | November 27, 1855 | November 27, 1855 |
| Barnes, Laura | Keele, James M | C/190 | April 3, 1874 | April 4, 1878 |
| Barnes, Lula | Gilley, J. C. | C/464 | August 16, 1892 | August 17, 1892 |
| Barnes, Lula | Bush, Thomas | C/442 | August 8, 1891 | No Return |
| Barnes, Lutisia | McFerrin, Zeke | C/66 | September 20, 1873 | September 22, 1873 |
| Barnes, Mary C. | Morgan, James | F/86 | March 23, 1896 | No Return |
| Barnes, Mary J. | Todd, Wilson | A2/103 | October 20, 1960 | No Return |
| Barnes, Rachal | Keele, Thomas | C/190 | April 3, 1878 | April 4, 1878 |
| Barnes, Robert | Vernon, Ann | C/454 | February 1, 1892 | February 1, 1892 |
| Barnes, Stephen (col.) | Vernon, Eda | F/6 | March 18, 1893 | March 18, 1893 |
| Barnes, Stephens | Martin, Josie | C/110 | March 15, 1875 | March 15, 1875 |
| Barnet, James | Espy, W. J. | F/54 | December 24, 1894 | December 25, 1894 |
| Barns, Asbery | McDougal, Malisa | C/232 | December 9, 1879 | December 9, 1879 |
| Barns, Polley | Webb, Jacob | D/4 | | September 11, 1881 |
| Barrat, Richard | Phillips, Elizabeth | A/45 | December 18, 1841 | December 19, 1841 |
| Barratt, Lucy | King, John M. | C/146 | September 30, 1876 | October 1, 1876 |
| Barratt, A. B. | Morgan, Catharine | A2/102 | September 15, 1860 | No Return |
| Barratt, Eli B. | Moon, Miss Isabella Moon | A/73 | September 23, 1844 | September 23, 1844 |
| Barratt, George | Morgan, Staly | C/214 | March 12, 1879 | No Return |
| Barratt, J. W. | Escue, Perline | C/50 | January 11, 1873 | January 12, 1873 |
| Barratt, James N. | Herriman, Nancy A. | C/154 | February 3, 1877 | February 3, 1877 |
| Barratt, Jessee | Evans, Miss Nancy C. | A/84 | November 22, 1845 | November 27, 1845 |
| Barratt, Martha J. | Williams, Joseph O. | A2/120 | February 18, 1865 | February 19, 1865 |
| Barratt, Mary J. | Cates, A. W. | A2/108 | May 20, 1863 | May 28, 1863 |
| Barratt, Polly Miss | Smith, Greenberry | A/114 | September 26, 1848 | October 5, 1848 |
| Barratt, Samuel | Phillips, Laura | C/162 | June 15, 1877 | June 15, 1877 |
| Barratt, Samuel | Moody, Sue | C/190 | March 27, 1878 | March 27, 1878 |

| Groom or Bride | Groom or Bride | Book/Page | Date of License | Date of Marriage |
|---|---|---|---|---|
| Barratt, Sarah Miss | Fann, Francis | A/85 | December 17, 1845 | December 17, 1845 |
| Barratt, W. H. | Gannon, Susen | C/160 | March 24, 1877 | March 25, 1877 |
| Barratt, Ward, Jr. | Preston, Miss Elizabeth | A/73 | September 18, 1844 | September 18, 1844 |
| Barret Levi | Travis, Sal | C/460 | July 9, 1892 | July 17, 1892 |
| Barret, B. F. | Welch, M. E. | A2/130 | October 4, 1865 | October 11, 1865 |
| Barret, Exie | Hays, Jim | F/132 | September 22, 1897 | September 23, 1897 |
| Barret, James P. | Kenser, Rebecca Ann | A2/123 | May 5, 1865 | May 7, 1865 |
| Barret, M. L. | Watson, Joseph | E/34 | May 11, 1888 | May 22, 1888 |
| Barret, Wm. | Herriman, Susan | C/278 | April 16, 1881 | April 17, 1881 |
| Barrett, A. | Allison, Miss H. E. | B/58 | December 5, 1867 | December 9, 1867 |
| Barrett, A. B. | Hipp, Sallie B. | C/30 | July 17, 1872 | No Return |
| Barrett, A. Miss | Manus, D. E. | A2/70 | December 16, 1858 | December 17, 1858 |
| Barrett, Alsie C. | Star, Joseph | C/366 | September 8, 1886 | No Return |
| Barrett, Annis | Morgan, William | A2/129 | September 23, 1865 | September 24, 1865 |
| Barrett, Armandy | Goins, Samuel | C/462 | July 16, 1892 | July 17, 1892 |
| Barrett, Babe | McKnight, Ed | C/46 | December 14, 1872 | December 15, 1872 |
| Barrett, Bettie | White, Wm. | E/159 | December 30, 1888 | December 30, 1888 |
| Barrett, Canzade | Parker, W. C. | C/344 | December 17, 1885 | No Return |
| Barrett, Charity M. | Hibdon, William C. | A2/79 | September 19, 1856 | September 19, 1856 |
| Barrett, Charles A. | Cummings, Edney C. | D/14 | | August 11, 1882 |
| Barrett, Clem | Walker, Bob | F/106 | December 24, 1896 | December 24, 1896 |
| Barrett, Cressy | Litter, George | C/218 | July 14, 1879 | July 14, 1879 |
| Barrett, Dillard | Travis, Nancy | D/15 | | September 3, 1882 |
| Barrett, E. A. | Malard, Eugene | D/12 | | March 23, 1882 |
| Barrett, E. C. Miss | Mitchel, G. W. P. | A2/42 | October 2, 1855 | October 4, 1855 |
| Barrett, E. L. | King, Wm | E/102 | November 20, 1888 | November 20, 1888 |
| Barrett, Edna Miss | Davenport, J. J. | C/408 | November 15, 1887 | November 15, 1887 |
| Barrett, Elender | Moody, William | A2/36 | October 4, 1854 | October 4, 1854 |
| Barrett, Eli B. | Gannon, Mary Ann | C/36 | September 7, 1872 | September 7, 1872 |
| Barrett, Eliza Tennessee Gowen Miss | Smith, William A. | B/36 | December 28, 1866 | January 2, 1867 |
| Barrett, Elizabeth Miss | Carrol, Willis F. | A/35 | November 11, 1840 | November 12, 1840 |
| Barrett, Elizabeth Miss | Wheeling, Bennett | A/131 | December 19, 1849 | December 20, 1849 |
| Barrett, Ella | Herriman, George | F/90 | July 8, 1896 | July 10, 1896 |
| Barrett, Fanny B. | Higgins, J. H. | C/436 | May 2, 1891 | May 3, 1891 |
| Barrett, Foster | Bullard, Rena | E/4 | January 12, 1888 | |
| Barrett, Frances L. Miss | Vinson, Robert | B/94 | December 2, 1869 | December 2, 1869 |
| Barrett, Frank | Mooneyham, Mandy | C/334 | August 27, 1885 | No Return |
| Barrett, George | Smith, Nellie | F/4 | February 23, 1893 | February 24, 1893 |
| Barrett, Harm | Jonsen, Miss Margarett | A2/45 | December 22, 1855 | December 23, 1855 |
| Barrett, Houston | Atchley, Margaret E. | A2/129 | October 3, 1865 | October 8, 1865 |
| Barrett, J. H. | Moody, S. L. | C/360 | July 15, 1886 | July 15, 1886 |
| Barrett, J. H. | Travis, Iser | C/448 | October 12, 1891 | No Return |
| Barrett, J. M. | Blaire, Miss Elvira | B/56 | December 2, 1867 | December 5, 1867 |
| Barrett, J. M. | Berryhill, Miss Sarah | B/130 | April 12, 1871 | April 12, 1871 |
| Barrett, J. M. | Bogle, E. L. | C/50 | February 3, 1873 | February 4, 1873 |

| Groom or Bride | Groom or Bride | Book/Page | Date of License | Date of Marriage |
| --- | --- | --- | --- | --- |
| Barrett, J. W. | Valentin, Miss Mary | B/86 | September 9, 1869 | September 9, 1869 |
| Barrett, James | Lang, Margarett | A2/81 | March 1, 1858 | March 1, 1858 |
| Barrett, James | Travis, Plem | C/446 | September 25, 1891 | September 25 1891 |
| Barrett, James | Holland, Ella | F/100 | November 7, 1896 | November 9, 1896 |
| Barrett, James P. | Jones, Miss Nancy P. | A2/145 | September 18, 1866 | September 18, 1866 |
| Barrett, Jno B. | Deberry, Bellzora | C/182 | December 24, 1877 | December 25, 1877 |
| Barrett, John | Sapp, Jane | A/16 | August 20, 1839 | August 11, 1839 |
| Barrett, John | Cathy, Miss Milly | A2/48 | May 10, 1856 | May 10, 1856 |
| Barrett, John W. | Lance, Miss Manerva | A2/1 | March 14, 1850 | March 14, 1850 |
| Barrett, John W. | Vinson, Sarah | A/120 | February 20, 1849 | February 20, 1849 |
| Barrett, Johnevie | Fann, S. A. | F/50 | December 8, 1894 | December 9, 1894 |
| Barrett, Joseph H. | Ward, Miss Nancy A. | A2/22 | December 23, 1852 | December 23, 1852 |
| Barrett, L. J. | Ready, J. F. | C/144 | September 21, 1876 | September 21, 1876 |
| Barrett, Levi | Jaco, Mary C. | C/30 | July 12, 1872 | July 14, 1872 |
| Barrett, Lillie | Bogle, Nathan | E/226 | October 26, 1889 | October 27, 1889 |
| Barrett, Lisby Miss | Gunter, John L. | B/62 | January 13, 1868 | January 14, 1868 |
| Barrett, M. E. | Smithson, J. J. | C/246 | April 26, 1880 | May 5, 1880 |
| Barrett, M. J. | Bogle, Jno A. | C/140 | August ??, 1876 | August 28, 1876 |
| Barrett, M. J. Miss | Austin, J. W. | A2/66 | July 24, 1858 | No Return |
| Barrett, M. Miss | Lemay, T. P. | A2/26 | July 9, 1853 | No Return |
| Barrett, Margaret Ann | Barrett, R. L. | A2/132 | November 15, 1865 | November 16, 1865 |
| Barrett, Martha | Cotter, John L. | C/278 | April 13, 1881 | April 13, 1881 |
| Barrett, Martha C | Reed, W. A | C/180 | December 6, 1877 | December 6, 1877 |
| Barrett, Mary | Hollandsworth, N. | C/56 | April 22, 1873 | April 23, 1873 |
| Barrett, Mary | Watson, Joel | C/348 | January 11, 1886 | January 11, 1886 |
| Barrett, Mary | Crank, S. B. | C/216 | May 6, 1879 | No Return |
| Barrett, Mary Miss | Bogle, Mayord | F/68 | August 21, 1895 | August 25, 1895 |
| Barrett, Milas | Allen, Minnie | F/112 | February 2, 1897 | February 21, 1897 |
| Barrett, Missie | Webb, Jacob | C/446 | September 20, 1891 | No Return |
| Barrett, Mollie | Adams, G. W. | D/101 | | February 16, 1882 |
| Barrett, Nancy E. | Summar, Samuel | C/112 | April 29, 1875 | May 2, 1875 |
| Barrett, Nathan | Vinson, Miss Mary | A2/11 | March 18, 1851 | March 18, 1851 |
| Barrett, Phobe | Biles, J. T. | F/88 | May 5, 1896 | No Return |
| Barrett, R. L. | Barrett, Margaret Ann | A2/132 | November 15, 1865 | November 16, 1865 |
| Barrett, Rutha Miss | Miles, Telford | A2/31 | December 29, 1853 | December 29, 1853 |
| Barrett, S. A. Miss | Henderson, M. G. | B/52 | September 24, 1867 | No Return |
| Barrett, S. D. | Nichol, Bnea | F/110 | January 12, 1897 | January 12, 1897 |
| Barrett, Sallie | Mingle, L. K. | F/30 | January 30, 1894 | No Return |
| Barrett, Sallie | Gannon, William | C/420 | October 25, 1890 | October 26, 1890 |
| Barrett, Simon | Adonis, Miss Peggey G. | A2/25 | May 22, 1853 | May 22, 1853 |
| Barrett, Sylvia | Jennings, J. W. | E/137 | February 8, 1889 | February 10, 1889 |
| Barrett, Tennie | Murphy, James A. | C/324 | January 19, 1885 | No Return |
| Barrett, Thos | Gann, Viney | C/194 | July 17, 1878 | July 17, 1878 |
| Barrett, Thos. | Hollandsworth, Mary | C/30 | June 25, 1872 | June 26, 1872 |
| Barrett, Thos. J. | Saffle, Margrett C. | C/82 | February 18, 1874 | February 19, 1874 |
| Barrett, Ward Jr. | Hammonds, Miss Joice V. | A/116 | November 9, 1848 | November 9, 1848 |

| Groom or Bride | Groom or Bride | Book/Page | Date of License | Date of Marriage |
|---|---|---|---|---|
| Barrett, William | Fitch, Miss Parlie | A/118 | January 4, 1849 | January 4, 1849 |
| Barrett, William C. | Denton, Miss Frances | B/58 | December 23 1867 | December 24, 1867 |
| Barrett, Wm. | Hollandswoth, Susan | C/28 | May 23, 1872 | May 24, 1872 |
| Barrutt, Henry | Fuston, Sarah | A2/111 | January 1, 1864 | January 1, 1864 |
| Barry, John | Cowen, Miss Matilda B. | A2/5 | September 24, 1850 | No Return |
| Barry, Matilda B. Mrs. | Sullivan, T. G. | B/84 | July 26, 1869 | July 27, 1869 |
| Barthen, Sarah | Willson, G. W. | A2/20 | November 19, 1852 | November 19, 1852 |
| Barton, Albert | Glaspler, Ater | C/256 | May 22, 1880 | May ??, 1880 |
| Barton, Alf | Moore, Florence | C/54 | March 13, 1873 | March 13, 1873 |
| Barton, Ann | Woods, Jack | F/1 | January 7, 1893 | January 7, 1893 |
| Barton, Dan | McBroom, Linner | E/250 | December 26, 1889 | December 26, 1889 |
| Barton, Daniel | McBroom, Rachel | B/10 | December 24, 1866 | March 4, 1867 |
| Barton, Dave | Gross, Mary | C/94 | August 22, 1874 | August 27, 1874 |
| Barton, Edman (col) | McCrary, Hattie (col) | E/370 | November 21, 1898 | |
| Barton, Exeakie | Martin, Nancy | F/56 | December 27, 1895 | December 30, 1895 |
| Barton, Ezekiel | Ferrell, Miss Laura | C/2 | June 7, 1871 | No Return |
| Barton, Florance | McKnight, James | D/7 | | November 24, 1881 |
| Barton, James S. | Hare, Miss Bettie H. | A2/44 | December 6, 1855 | December 6, 1855 |
| Barton, Jane | Tenpenny, John | B/18 | December 23, 1869 | No Return |
| Barton, Joannah | Pinkerton, Richard | C/162 | May 31, 1877 | May 31, 1877 |
| Barton, Jordan | Lyon, Snow | E/390 | October 11, 1898 | |
| Barton, Jordan (col.) | McCray, Hattie (col) | F/160 | November 21, 1898 | November 22, 1898 |
| Barton, Lizzie | Jordan, E. L. Jr. | C/358 | May 5, 1886 | No Return |
| Barton, Mary | Taylor, Wesley | B/6 | August 28, 1865 | September 3, 1865 |
| Barton, Mary | Biles, Park | C/338 | September 30, 1885 | September 30, 1885 |
| Barton, Mary C. Miss | Jetton, Jamie R. | C/430 | February 24, 2891 | February 25, 1891 |
| Barton, Robert | Daniel, Margaret | B/12 | December 14, 1867 | December 15, 1867 |
| Barton, Sopha Miss | Milton, Sandy | B/118 | December 7, 1870 | December 15, 1870 |
| Barton, Susan | Johnson, John | C/244 | March 19, 1880 | March 19, 1880 |
| Barton, William Jr. | McBroom, Sarah J. | A/8 | November 1, 1838 | November 1, 1838 |
| Basham, A. G. | Finley, Nanie | C/342 | December 5, 1885 | December 6, 1885 |
| Basham, Amandy | Wilson, John | D/7 | | November 30, 1881 |
| Basham, Bettie | Wilson, Marshall | E/158 | December 27, 1888 | December 27, 1888 |
| Basham, Elizabeth Miss | Gann, James A. | A2/47 | March 4, 1856 | March 4, 1856 |
| Basham, Isaiah | Wilson, Tennie | C/470 | December 17, 1892 | December 18, 1892 |
| Basham, James H. | Wilson, Betti | D/3 | | September 8, 1881 |
| Basham, James, M. | Stafford, Mary A. | A2/86 | June 30, 1859 | No Return |
| Basham, Jenny | Wilson, Willie | C/430 | January 26, 1891 | January 26, 1891 |
| Basham, John | Hiet, Mary | A/57 | December 7, 1842 | December 13, 1842 |
| Basham, Mattie | Todd, Jaco | F/152 | August 6, 1898 | August 6, 1898 |
| Basham, Mollie | McBroon, R. L. | E/97 | November 3, 1888 | November 4, 1888 |
| Basham, Nannie | Duke, P. P. | F/146 | February 17, 1898 | February 20, 1898 |
| Basham, T. G. | Wood, Susan E. | C/268 | January 3, 1881 | January 6, 1881 |
| Basham, Wm. | Owen, Miss H. D. | A2/66 | August 15, 1858 | August 15, 1858 |
| Bashham, William | Prator, Miss M. E. | A2/65 | June 24, 1858 | Handed in no Return |
| Bass, A. M. | Hawkins, Mary | C/326 | February 18, 1885 | February 19, 1885 |

| Groom or Bride | Groom or Bride | Book/Page | Date of License | Date of Marriage |
| --- | --- | --- | --- | --- |
| Bass, Ann | Ewing, Munroe | E/154 | November 24, 1888 | November 25, 1888 |
| Bass, Thos | Taylor, Nicey | C/172 | October 11, 1877 | No Return |
| Bassham, Adam | Scott, Rachel | F/34 | September 20, 1894 | September 20, 1894 |
| Bassham, Alvis | Wilson, S. A. | C/78 | December 31, 1873 | December 31, 1873 |
| Bassham, M. E. Miss | Couch, J. W. | C/8 | September 2, 1871 | September 3, 1871 |
| Bassham, T. G. | Gaither, Miss M. E. | B/116 | November 18, 1870 | No Return |
| Bates, Abagail Miss | Seawell, Frances M. | A/58 | January 5, 1842 | January 5, 1842 |
| Bates, Abbie | Withrowe, Allen | C/398 | August 16, 1887 | August 17, 1887 |
| Bates, Alvin | St. Johns, Miss Marry C. | A2/34 | August 14, 1854 | August 14, 1854 |
| Bates, Carril | Mooneyham, Robert | C/436 | April 25, 1891 | April 26, 1891 |
| Bates, Emma | Mooneyham, John | C/290 | August 25, 1883 | No Return |
| Bates, Lou Miss | Shacklett, John L. | B/32 | December 13, 1866 | December 14, 1866 |
| Bates, Lucy Mrs. | James, Samuel R. | A2/5 | August 10, 1850 | August 11, 1850 |
| Bates, Martha Jane Miss | St. John, Harmon | A/88 | April 29, 1846 | April 30, 1846 |
| Batimore, J. W. | Spry, Harriett | C/186 | February 19, 1878 | February 21, 1878 |
| Batson, Elizabeth M. | Maxey, Richard | A/18 | October 26, 1839 | October 29, 1839 |
| Batson, Jane Miss | Williams, Joshua | A/98 | March 30, 1847 | March 31, 1847 |
| Batson, Meranda Jane Miss | Bryant, David | A/113 | July 31, 1848 | July 31, 1848 |
| Batton, Angie Miss | Tyree, William H. | B/92 | November 19, 1869 | November 24, 1869 |
| Batton, Mary E. | Burger, A. H. | C/100 | November 10, 1874 | November 10, 1874 |
| Batton, P. D. | Wood, M. A. | C/66 | August 30, 1873 | September 2, 1873 |
| Baty, Andy | Todd, Mary J. | C/358 | April 24, 1886 | April 24, 1886 |
| Baxter, J. A. | Donnell, S. A. | C/148 | November 2, 1876 | November 12, 1876 |
| Baxter, Mary Miss | Baxter, R. F. | A2/136 | January 31, 1866 | February 1, 1866 |
| Baxter, R. F. | McKnight, C. R. | C/80 | January 17, 1874 | January 29, 1874 |
| Baxter, R. F. | Baxter, Miss Mary | A2/136 | January 31, 1866 | February 1, 1866 |
| Baxter, R. M. | Odom, L. C. | C/422 | November 22, 1890 | No Return |
| Baxter, Richard | Cook, Charlott | A2/130 | October 5, 1865 | October 5, 1865 |
| Bay, Alford | Bell, Jane | C/210 | January 14, 1879 | January 15, 1879 |
| Beadon, S. E. Miss | Sawles, J. D. | B/114 | November 5, 1870 | November 7, 1870 |
| Bearden, M. J | Simmons, W. M. | C/184 | January 23, 1878 | January 23, 1878 |
| Bearden, Mary E. | Parker, J. W. | C/214 | March 23, 1879 | March 30, 1879 |
| Bearden, P. A. | Sissom, W. F. | C/268 | December 11, 1880 | December 12, 1880 |
| Bearder, Andrew | Moon, Jennie | E/185 | June 22, 1889 | June 22, 1889 |
| Bearding, H. | Griffa, Elvina | C/118 | August 27, 1875 | August 29, 1875 |
| Beargin, Thomas | Gordon, Miss Amanda | B/50 | August 26, 1867 | August 27, 1867 |
| Beashears, Rebecca | Malone, John J. | A/51 | July 13, 1842 | No Return |
| Beason, J. H. | Duke, Miss S. H. | B/128 | March 9, 1871 | March 15, 1871 |
| Beaty, A. J. | Gooding, Radid? | A/16 | August 3, 1839 | No Return |
| Beaty, Allen | Davis, Miss Margaret | A/71 | July 26, 1844 | July 26, 1844 |
| Beaty, Andy (col.) | Todd, Bettie (col.) | F/168 | January 21, 1899 | January 22, 1899 |
| Beaty, J. A. | Miller, Eliza | C/156 | February 12, 1877 | February 15, 1877 |
| Beaty, James | Bivins, Miss Nancy | B/32 | November 20, 1866 | November 20, 1866 |
| Beaty, Jane | Todd, Bud (col.) | F/136 | November 3, 1897 | No Return |
| Beaty, Jane Miss | Brown, Richard | A/40 | August 20, 1841 | August 20, 1841 |
| Beaty, Mary | Kuykendall, Norris | A/75 | December 3, 1844 | December 3, 1844 |

| Groom or Bride | Groom or Bride | Book/Page | Date of License | Date of Marriage |
|---|---|---|---|---|
| Beaty, Philip D. | Greear, Miss Polly Ann | A/44 | December 4, 1841 | December 5, 1841 |
| Beaty, Sissy | Reed, Eleazon? | A/34 | October 17, 1840 | October 17, 1840 |
| Beaty, Thomas H. | Gooding, Susanah | A/22 | January 14, 1840 | Solemnized, No Date |
| Beckton, G. N. | Taylor, M. H. | C/252 | August 12, 1880 | August 2, 1880 |
| Bedden, Magie | Ready, J. H. | C/200 | October 5, 1878 | October 6, 1878 |
| Beechboard, Robert | Arnold, Miss Elizabeth | A2/8 | November 30, 1850 | December 1, 1850 |
| Beeson, Margarett J. Miss | Mullins, John A. | A/104 | October 17, 1847 | October 18, 1847 |
| Belk, John | Burnet, Piley | A/13 | May 8, 1839 | May 8, 1839 |
| Bell, Emaline | Jamison, William | A/30 | June 18, 1840 | No Return |
| Bell, Annie Miss | Earles, Willey | F/172 | March 18, 1899 | March 19, 1899 |
| Bell, G. H. | Taylor, Laura | C/360 | July 3, 1886 | July 4, 1886 |
| Bell, J. H. | Mason, May | F/140 | December 18, 1897 | December 20, 1897 |
| Bell, J. T. | Young, Miss R. A. | A2/70 | November 24, 1858 | November 25, 1858 |
| Bell, J. T. | Miller, Ruby | E/340 | December 22, 1888 | |
| Bell, J. T. | Miller, Ruby | F/164 | December 22, 1898 | December 22, 1898 |
| Bell, James | Moore, Nancy | A/16 | August 27, 1839 | August 29, 1839 |
| Bell, James H. | Fisher, Miss Sarah E. | A2/39 | January 1, 1855 | January 1, 1855 |
| Bell, Jane | Bay, Alford | C/210 | January 14, 1879 | January 15, 1879 |
| Bell, Jane Ann Miss | Gilley, Charles | A/48 | April 1, 1842 | March 15, 1842 |
| Bell, Jane E. | Petty, Wm | D/101 | | February 1, 1882 |
| Bell, John | Davis, Mary | E/81 | September 19, 1888 | September 20, 1888 |
| Bell, John B. | Summar, Lillian | F/22 | November 25, 1893 | November 26, 1893 |
| Bell, Josie | Davis, William | E/28 | April 14, 1888 | April 14, 1888 |
| Bell, Lewis | Woods, Sarah A. | D/101 | | February 19, 1882 |
| Bell, Lusalina E. | Tenpenny, Joseph W. | C/210 | January 4, 1879 | January 5, 1879 |
| Bell, M. E. Miss | Todd, J. H. | A2/96 | May 18, 1860 | May 20, 1860 |
| Bell, Mary J. | Pulliam, B. H. | C/180 | December 13, 1877 | December 13, 1877 |
| Bell, Mary W. | Cook, T. | C/156 | February 23, 1877 | February 23, 1877 |
| Bell, N. A. | Herrell, H. G. | C/224 | September 11, 1879 | September 11, 1879 |
| Bell, R. T. | Davenport, ? ? | E/129 | January 26, 1889 | January 27, 1889 |
| Bell, Rebecca C. | Stamper, James | A2/133 | December 2, 1865 | December 3, 1865 |
| Bell, S. J. | Mason, N. F. | A2/100 | July 18, 1860 | July 19, 1860 |
| Bell, Sallie | Bell, Wm | C/340 | October 14, 1885 | October 14, 1885 |
| Bell, Sallie | Bivens, B. R. | F/98 | October 13, 1896 | October 13, 1896 |
| Bell, Susan | Petty, Ambus | C/220 | August 6, 1879 | No Return |
| Bell, Susan | Petty, Ambrose | C/232 | August 6, 1879 | August 7, 1879 |
| Bell, W. E. | Coleman, Miss Hattie | C/386 | March 10, 1887 | March 10, 1887 |
| Bell, W. W. | Kell, Rebeca C. | A2/34 | August 16, 1854 | August 16, 1854 |
| Bell, William C. | Bryson, Miss Susan J. | A2/145 | October 6, 1866 | October 7, 1866 |
| Bell, Wm | Bell, Sallie | C/340 | October 14, 1885 | October 14, 1885 |
| Benfon, Mary E. Miss | Warren, John | A/95 | December 26, 1846 | December 27, 1846 |
| Bennet, J. D. | Jones, Mattie L. | C/14 | November 16, 1871 | November 16, 1871 |
| Bennett, C. O. | Coleman, Levina | C/38 | September 12, 1872 | September 12, 1872 |
| Bennett, Elizabeth M. Miss | Gann, John H. | A2/41 | September 18, 1855 | September 18, 1855 |
| Berks, Mary Miss | Moore, Samuel A. | A/108 | February 14, 1848 | February 14, 1848 |
| Berrett, E. M. Miss | Moses, R. R. | A2/55 | April 20, 1857 | No Return |

| Groom or Bride | Groom or Bride | Book/Page | Date of License | Date of Marriage |
|---|---|---|---|---|
| Berrett, Samuel | Nichols, Miss Pheba J. | A2/56 | April 29, 1857 | April 30, 1857 |
| Berryhill, Charlie | Sullins, Sadie | C/150 | December 8, 1876 | December 8, 1876 |
| Berryhill, M. J. | Sullins, Alex | C/190 | April 4, 1878 | No Return |
| Berryhill, M. J. Miss | Vickers, R. L. | C/4 | August 3, 1871 | August 4, 1871 |
| Berryhill, P. I | Moss, Thomas | C/312 | August 4, 1884 | August 4, 1884 |
| Berryhill, Sarah Miss | Barrett, J. M. | B/130 | April 12, 1871 | April 12, 1871 |
| Beshears, M. A. | Youngblood, W. J. | C/434 | April 1, 1891 | April 2, 1891 |
| Beshears, Margrett A | Hollandsworth, J. F | C/178 | November 20, 1877 | November 20, 1877 |
| Beshers, Elijah | Keath, Miss Sarah E. | C/2 | May 24, 1871 | May 25, 1871 |
| Besheas, Mary E. | Hibdon, A. J. | C/308 | April 15, 1884 | April 15, 1884 |
| Bess, A. M. | Millikin, Miss Parlee | B/94 | November 13, 1869 | November 13, 1869 |
| Bethel, B. J. | Eason, Miss Jane | A2/53 | January 21, 1857 | No Return |
| Bethel, Caroline | Bethel, Isaac | B/6 | August 28, 1865 | August 29, 1865 |
| Bethel, Green W. | Marcum, Miss Eliza | A2/11 | March 22, 1851 | No Return |
| Bethel, Henry | Bethel, Sally | B/6 | August 28, 1865 | August 29, 1865 |
| Bethel, Idie Miss | Quarles, J. T. | C/46 | November 25, 1872 | No Return |
| Bethel, Isaac | Bethel, Caroline | B/6 | August 28, 1865 | August 29, 1865 |
| Bethel, J. L. | Kirby, Ada | C/100 | November 18, 1874 | November 19, 1874 |
| Bethel, Nannie | Brown, James | F/118 | May 20, 1897 | May 22, 1897 |
| Bethel, Polley | Elkins, John B. | D/1 | | July 15, 1881 |
| Bethel, Sally | Bethel, Henry | B/6 | August 28, 1865 | August 29, 1865 |
| Bethel, T. J. | Foster (?), J. P. | C/238 | January 17, 1880 | January 18, 1880 |
| Bethell, C. F. | Smith, Mrs. S. C. | B/70 | October 2, 1868 | October 2, 1868 |
| Bethell, India C. | Covington, John A. | A2/122 | March 16, 1865 | March 16, 1865 |
| Bethell, Lafayette | Gann, Miss Tennessee | A2/91 | November 26, 1859 | No Return |
| Bethell, Len | Woodsides, J. H. | C/124 | November 29, 1875 | December 2, 1875 |
| Bethell, Lydia H. Miss | Kennedy, J. W. | B/76 | January 12, 1869 | January 14, 1869 |
| Bethell, M. E. Miss | Tatum, R. F. | B/40 | February 6, 1867 | February 7, 1867 |
| Bethell, Mark | Donnell, Miss Isabella | B/96 | December 15, 1859 | No Return |
| Bethell, T. N. | McKnight, W. M. | B/74 | December 23, 1868 | December 25, 1868 |
| Bethell, Tennie L. Miss | Rushing, John R. | A2/136 | January 31, 1866 | January 31, 1866 |
| Bether, Susan | Laugthery, J. N. | C/238 | January 19, 1880 | January 22, 1880 |
| Betherl, C. D. | Higgins, Alta | D/20 | | May 14, 1882 |
| Beverly, Jane Miss | Todd, Robert | A2/72 | January 17, 1859 | No Return |
| Beverly, Jane Miss | Todd, Robert | A2/83 | January 17, 1859 | No Return |
| Bevins, Cynthia A. | Heatherly, Geo. | C/50 | February 1, 1873 | February 4, 1873 |
| Bevins, Lizzie | Martin, Mat | C/408 | November 26, 1887 | November 26, 1887 |
| Bewrey, Elizabeth Miss | Conley, George W. | A2/17 | May 20, 1852 | May 20, 1852 |
| Biles, Ellen | Saffley, Jerry | F/94 | September 23, 1896 | September 13, 1896 |
| Biles, J. T. | Barrett, Phobe | F/88 | May 5, 1896 | No Return |
| Biles, Park | Barton, Mary | C/338 | September 30, 1885 | September 30, 1885 |
| Binem, Martha | Wimberly, Jonathan | A2/100 | July 14, 1860 | July 15, 1860 |
| Binges, Caroline Miss | Patterson, Robert | A/38 | May 12, 1841 | May 13, 1841 |
| Bivens, Alford | Laseter, Mary | C/12 | October 5, 1871 | No Return |
| Bivens, B. R. | Bell, Sallie | F/98 | October 13, 1896 | October 13, 1896 |
| Bivens, Lizzy (col.) | Lyon, Stephen (col.) | F/172 | March 15, 1899 | No Return |

| Groom or Bride | Groom or Bride | Book/Page | Date of License | Date of Marriage |
|---|---|---|---|---|
| Bivins, L. M. S. | Zumbro, Elizabeth S. | A2/106 | December 27, 1862 | December 28, 1862 |
| Bivins, Nancy Miss | Beaty, James | B/32 | November 20, 1866 | November 20, 1866 |
| Bivvans, A. J. | Bryant, Miss M. A. | A2/63 | March 2, 1858 | March 2, 1858 |
| Black, Sarah | Thompson, Daniel | B/4 | August 23, 1865 | August 28, 1865 |
| Blackburn, David | Gilley, Nettie | E/255 | December 31, 1880 | December 6, 1889 |
| Blackburn, John | Brown, Sarah A. | A2/98 | June 29, 1860 | No Return |
| Blackburn, Tennessee | Swanger, John | C/424 | December 10, 1890 | December 11, 1890 |
| Blackwell, Eliza A. | Woods, Alexander H. | C/214 | March 5, 1879 | March 5, 1879 |
| Blackwell, Hilder | Ashford, William | C/466 | September 26, 1892 | September 27, 1892 |
| Blackwell, J. G. | St. John, E. A. | C/78 | January 3, 1874 | January 3, 1874 |
| Blades, Huldy | Holland, Geo | C/90 | June 2, 1874 | June 3, 1877 |
| Blain, Jonathan T. | York, Eliza | A2/104 | November 19, 1860 | No Return |
| Blair, Alley | Neal, Jim | C/230 | November 8, 1879 | November 9, 1879 |
| Blair, Bobillo Miss | Melton, Hugh | C/452 | December 16, 1891 | December 24, 1891 |
| Blair, Dell F. | Hayes, J. L. | E/123 | January 2, 1889 | January 2, 1889 |
| Blair, H. T. | Motley, Saphrona | C/398 | August 20, 1887 | August 21, 1887 |
| Blair, Isaac P. | Warren, Miss Elvira | A/72 | September 7, 1844 | September 8, 1844 |
| Blair, J. R. | Bullard, Mary R. | C/110 | March 2, 1875 | March 21, 1875 |
| Blair, James | Melton, Jane Caroline | A/56 | November 25, 1842 | No Return |
| Blair, John | Stewart, Sarah E. | C/374 | November 10, 1886 | November 11, 1886 |
| Blair, John | Turner, Ider | C/470 | December 10, 1892 | December 11, 1892 |
| Blair, Parealee | Hancock, A. U. | F/46 | October 20, 1894 | October 21, 1894 |
| Blair, Polly Miss | Summar, Baldy H. | A/74 | November 4, 1844 | November 5, 1844 |
| Blair, Rilda Miss | Parsley, James | C/384 | February 27, 1887 | February 27, 1887 |
| Blair, Sarah | Tate, J. B. | F/6 | March 6, 1893 | March 7, 1893 |
| Blair, Sarah C. Miss | Marcum, Charles | A2/48 | May 15, 1856 | No Return |
| Blaire, Elvira Miss | Barrett, J. M. | B/56 | December 2, 1867 | December 5, 1867 |
| Blaire, Millia | York, Antney | B/18 | July 29, 1870 | No Return |
| Blaire, Olley | Gates, G. W. | B/8 | October 9, 1865 | October 14, 1865 |
| Blaire, W. B. | Ford, Miss Martha C. | B/68 | July 27, 1868 | July 28, 1868 |
| Blancet, Calvin | Cantrell, Miss Issabella | A/85 | December 13, 1845 | December 14, 1845 |
| Blancet, Eliza Miss | Owen, Thomas | A2/32 | February 2, 1854 | February 2, 1854 |
| Blancet, M. J. Miss | Edwards, M. L. | A2/50 | November 5, 1856 | No Return |
| Blancett, Jordan | Reed, Miss Amanda | A2/96 | April 23, 1860 | April 26, 1860 |
| Blanch, Bettie | Elkins, Wm. | E/101 | November 17, 1888 | November 17, 1888 |
| Blank, William | Summer, W. A. | A2/68 | October 8, 1858 | No Return |
| Blanks | Vance, David | E/151 | December 17, 1888 | December 20, 1888 |
| Blanks, Jim | Davenport, Ollie | F/68 | August 30, 1895 | September 1, 1895 |
| Blanks, John C. | Vance, S. A. | C/424 | December 10, 1890 | December 11, 1890 |
| Blanks, Julia Ann Miss | Leech, John C. | A/86 | December 28, 1845 | January 12, 1846 |
| Blanks, L. A. | Wilson, Mike | C/332 | July 30, 1880 | August 30, 1885 |
| Blanks, M. A. | Davenport, J. B. | F/66 | July 20, 1895 | July 21, 1895 |
| Blanks, Mary Ann Miss | Owens, Claiborne | A/58 | December 31, 1842 | January 1, 1843 |
| Blanks, S. B. | Gaither, Miss S. C. | F/88 | June 8, 1896 | June 9, 1896 |
| Blanks, Sarah C. Miss | Armstrong, Samuel P. | C/408 | November 17, 1887 | November 18, 1887 |
| Blansett, Miss Lavisa | Todd, John R. | A2/23 | January 29, 1853 | January 30, 1853 |

| Groom or Bride | Groom or Bride | Book/Page | Date of License | Date of Marriage |
|---|---|---|---|---|
| Blanton, Hannah | Gilley, William | A/2 | April 14, 1838 | April 15, 1838 |
| Blanton, James | Bray, Mary | D/4 | | August 4, 1882 |
| Blanton, Jane | Wale, J. H. | A2/97 | May 29, 1860 | May 29, 1860 |
| Blanton, John | St. John, M. C. | D/2 | | August 18, 1882 |
| Blanton, M. J. | Phillips, E. M. | C/22 | January 26, 1872 | January 28, 1872 |
| Blanton, R. C. | Garmon, Samuel | C/180 | December 22, 1877 | No Return |
| Blanton, Vinson | Rigsby, Miss Martha | A/88 | April 4, 1846 | April 26, 1846 |
| Blanton, William | Patterson, Miss Frances | B/66 | May 15, 1868 | May 18, 1868 |
| Blay, Mary | McAdoo, Richard | E/94 | October 25, 1888 | October 28, 1888 |
| Blew, John | Webb, Samantha | B/16 | May 1, 1869 | May 1, 1869 |
| Blue, Andrew | Todd, Rachel | C/220 | August 29, 1879 | August 31, 1879 |
| Blue, Bettie | Enais, Hagser | D/12 | | April 16, 1882 |
| Blue, Florence | Parseley, Columbus | F/106 | December 28, 1896 | December 24, 1896 |
| Blue, John | Hunter, Mary A. | A2/82 | August 28, 1858 | August 30, 1858 |
| Blue, Judy | Glimes, Jack | C/362 | August 11, 1886 | No Return |
| Blue, Lewis (col.) | Roberts, Amandy | C/298 | December 6, 1883 | No Retrun |
| Blue, N. J. | Mosey, Miss Doretha | A2/69 | October 28, 1858 | October 28, 1858 |
| Blue, Rachel (col.) | Roberts, Joe (col.) | F/90 | July 8, 1896 | July 8, 1896 |
| Blue, Tenne | Lyons, Frank | C/336 | September 18, 1885 | September 18, 1885 |
| Blue, Sarah C. Miss | Marcum, Charles | A2/79 | May 15, 1856 | May 15, 1856 |
| Bluer, Munroe | Grizzell, Martha | E/202 | August 24, 1889 | No Return |
| Bly, Dick | Dixon, Ella | C/354 | March 6, 1886 | March 7, 1886 |
| Bly, William | McNelly, Yonan | C/394 | July 16, 1887 | July 17, 1887 |
| Bodkins, Rachael C. Miss | Todd, Milton | A/84 | November 10, 1845 | November 10, 1845 |
| Bogle, A. C. Miss | Young, E. M. | B/120 | December 14, 1870 | December 14, 1870 |
| Bogle, Allen | Young, Caroline | A2/121 | March 1, 1865 | March 1, 1965 |
| Bogle, B. A. | Womack, I. Y. | F/12 | July 21, 1893 | July 24, 1893 |
| Bogle, Bunter Miss | Travis, Wm. | E/06 | November 30, 1888 | November 30, 1888 |
| Bogle, Burter | Bogle, F. M. | C/436 | May 8, 1891 | May 10, 1891 |
| Bogle, C. E. | Travis, S. P. | C/96 | October 10, 1874 | October 11, 1874 |
| Bogle, C. L. | Brandon, D. F. | D/22 | | March 11, 1883 |
| Bogle, Caroline | Parris, J. B. Jr. | C/30 | July 22, 1872 | July 22, 1872 |
| Bogle, Charlotta | Milligan, Joel | C/90 | July 25, 1874 | July 26, 1874 |
| Bogle, Catherin | Bogle, Thos | C/296 | November 6, 1883 | November 7, 1883 |
| Bogle, Daniel | Smith, Miss Polly Ann | A/37 | February 27, 1841 | February 28, 1841 |
| Bogle, Delia | Pattrick, Isaac | C/422 | November 3, 1890 | November 3, 1890 |
| Bogle, Dona | Burkett, Aud | F/78 | December 16, 1895 | December 16, 1895 |
| Bogle, E. E. | Tenpenny, Jesse A. | D/7 | | November 21, 1881 |
| Bogle, E. E. Miss | Wamack, J. S. | A2/59 | October 29, 1857 | No Return |
| Bogle, E. L. | Barrett, J. M. | C/50 | February 3, 1873 | February 4, 1873 |
| Bogle, Ednie F. | Partrick, Isaac | C/112 | March 27, 1875 | March 28, 1875 |
| Bogle, Elizabeth | Thompson, Sam | C/354 | March 5, 1886 | March 15, 1886 |
| Bogle, Eliza E. Miss | Hernden, M. F. | A2/69 | October 23, 1858 | October 24, 1858 |
| Bogle, Eliza J. | Odom, Armsted J. | A/103 | October 14, 1847 | October 15, 1847 |
| Bogle, F. L. | Davenport, Elizabeth | C/398 | August 27, 1887 | August 28, 1887 |
| Bogle, F. M. | Bogle, Burter | C/436 | May 8, 1891 | May 10, 1891 |

| Groom or Bride | Groom or Bride | Book/Page | Date of License | Date of Marriage |
|---|---|---|---|---|
| Bogle, F. P. | Keeton, M. E. | C/326 | February 26, 1885 | March 1, 1885 |
| Bogle, F. R. | Ashford, A. E. | C/366 | September 16, 1886 | September 19, 1886 |
| Bogle, G. B. | Taylor, Dedie | F/154 | August 20, 1898 | August 21, 1898 |
| Bogle, G. W. | Mullingax, Miss Sarah E. | A2/54 | February 2, 1857 | No Return |
| Bogle, G. W. | Preston, M. J. | C/108 | February 18, 1875 | February 18, 1875 |
| Bogle, George | Davenport, Miss Pelina | B/96 | December 23, 1869 | December 28, 1869 |
| Bogle, George R. | Todd, Miss Locky Jane | A/110 | April 7, 1848 | No Return |
| Bogle, H. M. | Pearce, Miss Malinda J. | B/64 | February 6, 1868 | February 9, 1868 |
| Bogle, H. M. | Davenport, M. M. | C/284 | June 26, 1883 | June 25, 1883 |
| Bogle, H. S. | Davenport, Parilee | D/21 | | August 6, 1883 |
| Bogle, Hattie | Todd, James | F/172 | March 12, 1899 | No Return |
| Bogle, Hattie | Hollandsworth, Cole | C/260 | November 4, 1880 | No Return |
| Bogle, Isaac | Ledbetter, Bettie | C/330 | July 4, 1885 | July 4, 1885 |
| Bogle, Isaac | Taylor, Sallie | E/260 | January 10, 1890 | No Return |
| Bogle, J. M. | Willson, Miss E. | A2/68 | October 20, 1858 | October 20, 1858 |
| Bogle, J. Q. | Davenport, Miss M. E. | B/112 | October 14, 1870 | October 14, 1870 |
| Bogle, J. R. | Womack, Miss Lizzie | E/179 | June 8, 1889 | June 9, 1889 |
| Bogle, J. W. | Powell, Miss Francis | C/414 | October 16, 1887 | October 18, 1887 |
| Bogle, James | Sauls, Miss Charity E. | A2/146 | October 18, 1866 | October 18, 1866 |
| Bogle, James | Summar, Medie | C/298 | December 27, 1883 | No Return |
| Bogle, James | Warren, Sallie A. | F/2 | February 4, 1893 | February 5, 1893 |
| Bogle, Jas | Jaco, Samanther M. J. | C/134 | March 1, 1876 | March 2, 1876 |
| Bogle, Jas. G. | Tittle, Miss Mollie | C/456 | March 12, 1892 | March 2, 1892 |
| Bogle, Jno A. | Barrett, M. J. | C/140 | August ??, 1876 | August 28, 1876 |
| Bogle, John | Keaton, Miss Charlotte | A/118 | December 21, 1848 | December 22, 1848 |
| Bogle, John | Milligan, Hattie | F/46 | October 11, 1894 | October 11, 1894 |
| Bogle, John | Milligan, Hattie | F/52 | October 11, 1894 | October 11, 1894 |
| Bogle, John E. | Wilcher, Miss Delila E. | B/104 | July 4, 1870 | No Return |
| Bogle, John F. | Willson, Miss Lucy | A2/71 | January 3, 1859 | January 5, 1959 |
| Bogle, Joseph Y. | Sullins, Miss A. M. P. | A2/64 | March 29, 1858 | March 29, 1858 |
| Bogle, Josephine | Odom, Samuel C. | C/40 | September 21, 1872 | September 22, 1872 |
| Bogle, Josiah F. | Willson, Lusey | A2/83 | January 3, 1859 | No Return |
| Bogle, Julia | Bogles, Snowe | F/14 | August 11, 1893 | No Return |
| Bogle, L. F. | Jones, Miss M. T. | A2/38 | March 3, 1855 | No Return |
| Bogle, Lamartha | Rigsby, J. M. | C/208 | December 28, 1878 | December 29, 1878 |
| Bogle, Layfayette | Jones, Miss July A. | A2/12 | October 1, 1851 | October 9, 1851 |
| Bogle, Leand | Hast, Willie B. | C/464 | September 24, 1892 | September 25, 1892 |
| Bogle, Leanthe | Markin, T. T. | C/402 | September 17, 1887 | September 18, 1887 |
| Bogle, Letley | Bragg, Spence | E/21 | February 25, 1888 | February 26, 1888 |
| Bogle, M. C. | Womack, M. J. | E/134 | February 7, 1889 | February 13, 1889 |
| Bogle, Margarett Miss | Night, Calvin | A2/54 | February 16, 1857 | February 18, 1857 |
| Bogle, Margret | Cooper, Abram | A/22 | November 4, 1839 | November 8, 1839 |
| Bogle, Martha | Sauls, William | A/57 | December 8, 1842 | December 8, 1842 |
| Bogle, Martha E. Miss | King, William J. | A2/147 | November 1, 1866 | November 1, 1866 |
| Bogle, Mary J. | Stiles, Wm. H. | C/240 | February 4, 1880 | February 5, 1880 |
| Bogle, Mary J. | Elkins, Wm. | C/330 | March 25, 1885 | March 26, 1885 |

| Groom or Bride | Groom or Bride | Book/Page | Date of License | Date of Marriage |
|---|---|---|---|---|
| Bogle, Mayord | Barrett, Miss Mary | F/68 | August 21, 1895 | August 25, 1895 |
| Bogle, Michael | Ferrell, Susan J. | A2/119 | January 5, 1865 | January 5, 1865 |
| Bogle, Mickey | Wilson, S. H. | C/138 | April 27, 1876 | April 28, 1876 |
| Bogle, Media Miss | Harris, Philmon | C/386 | March 17, 1887 | No Return |
| Bogle, Mollie | Womack, James | C/438 | June 25, 1891 | June 25, 1891 |
| Bogle, Sallie Miss | Elkins, Thomas | C/386 | March 7, 1887 | March 7, 1887 |
| Bogle, N. C. | Moore, B. H. | C/74 | December 4, 1873 | December 5, 1873 |
| Bogle, N. S. | King, M. E. | C/68 | October 11, 1873 | October 19, 1873 |
| Bogle, Nancy Ann | Todd, John | F/14 | August 19, 1893 | |
| Bogle, Nancy M. | See, Andrew | A2/115 | July 21, 1864 | No Return |
| Bogle, Nancy M. Miss | Stone, Thos. D. | B/126 | February 11, 1871 | February 12, 1871 |
| Bogle, Nancy Miss | Scott, Sam | B/122 | December 26, 1870 | December 26, 1870 |
| Bogle, Nathan | Barrett, Lillie | E/226 | October 26, 1889 | October 27, 1889 |
| Bogle, Peny | Shirley, R. L. | F/144 | January 19, 1898 | January 19, 1898 |
| Bogle, R. B. | Ready, M. J. | C/158 | February 24, 1877 | March 1, 1877 |
| Bogle, R. M. | Robinson, Joseph | A2/37 | November 4, 1854 | November 5, 1854 |
| Bogle, Robert | Gann, Eliza | A/33 | September 22, 1840 | September 22, 1840 |
| Bogle, Robert | Crabtree, Miss Nancy | A2/42 | October 18, 1855 | October 21, 1855 |
| Bogle, Robert | Womack, Parlee | C/272 | February 26, 1881 | February 27, 1881 |
| Bogle, S. C. | Gilley, Isaac G. | B/108 | August 20, 1870 | No Return |
| Bogle, S. F. | Davenport, Parelle | C/288 | August 6, 1883 | No Return |
| Bogle, S. L. | Wilson, W. A. | D/15 | | September 27, 1882 |
| Bogle, Sallie | Davis, Luke | E/332 | December 28, 1898 | |
| Bogle, Sallie | Davis, Mate | F/164 | December 28, 1898 | No Return |
| Bogle, Sarah | Latymoore, George | C/200 | October 5, 1878 | October 6, 1878 |
| Bogle, Sarah A. Miss | Keeny, R. A. | A2/59 | November 4, 1857 | November 4, 1857 |
| Bogle, Sarah C. | George, Tilman | C/242 | February 14, 1880 | February 14, 1880 |
| Bogle, Susie E. | Brandon, W. C. | F/136 | November 16, 1897 | November 17, 1897 |
| Bogle, T. A. | Stanley, Mattie | C/346 | December 24, 1885 | December 24, 1885 |
| Bogle, T. L. | Spurlock, Miss A. T. | B/118 | December 7, 1870 | December 7, 1870 |
| Bogle, Thos | Bogle, Catherin | C/296 | November 6, 1883 | November 7, 1883 |
| Bogle, Tolbert | Summar, Verin | F/104 | December 12, 1896 | December 21, 1896 |
| Bogle, W. M. | Keeton, Eliza A. | D/14 | | August 10, 1882 |
| Bogle, W. R. | Wamack, Nancy M. | C/20 | September 25, 1871 | September 27, 1871 |
| Bogle, William | Sumers, Sarah | A/19 | November 12, 1839 | November 14, 1839 |
| Bogle, William | Gann, Margaret | C/460 | June 10, 1892 | No Return |
| Bogles, Mathew S. | Cleveland, Miss Mary E. | A2/12 | October 11, 1851 | October 12, 1851 |
| Bogles, Snowe | Bogle, Julia | F/14 | August 11, 1893 | No Return |
| Bolen, Ella | Gowen, Jackson | F/70 | September 5, 1895 | September 8, 1895 |
| Bolen, Martha Miss | Meers, Gabriel | A2/142 | August 2, 1866 | Executed No Date |
| Boles, Isiah J. | Todd, Mary A. | C/124 | November 17, 1875 | November 18, 1870 |
| Boley, Clay J. | Ferrell, Wm. | C/78 | December 31, 1873 | January 1, 1874 |
| Bolin, John | Fry, Miss Nancy | A2/15 | February 26, 1852 | February 26, 1852 |
| Bolt, C. R. | Lowe, Sarah | F/96 | September 26, 1896 | September 27, 1896 |
| Boly, Harriet | Adams, Robert J. | C/180 | December 13, 1877 | December 13, 1877 |
| Bomer, Wm. | Brogon, Miss Lucy | A2/17 | May 29, 1852 | No Return |

| Groom or Bride | Groom or Bride | Book/Page | Date of License | Date of Marriage |
|---|---|---|---|---|
| Bond, Barthena | Wilson, Stephen | C/42 | October 16, 1872 | October 20, 1872 |
| Bond, James A. | Garner, Miss Matilda J. | A2/135 | January 15, 1866 | January 17, 1866 |
| Bond, Lewis W. | Hollis, Elizabeth | A/15 | July ??, 1839 | July 29, 1839 |
| Bond, R. J. | Mathews, Miss Sarah C. | A2/8 | November 18, 1850 | November 19, 1850 |
| Bond, William | Cooper, Sarah L. | A/56 | November 19, 1842 | December 12, 1842 |
| Bonds, Richard J. | Cooper, Alaminta | A/55 | October 13, 1842 | October 14, 1842 |
| Bonds, William | Reynolds, Margarett | A/17 | September 18, 1839 | No Return |
| Boners, Giles S. | Northcut, Visa E. | A2/111 | December 31, 1863 | December 31, 1863 |
| Bonn, A. | Waldon, R. E. | A2/95 | March 5, 1860 | No Return |
| Boren, A. J. | Dodd, Sallie | C/190 | March 28, 1878 | March 28, 1878 |
| Boren, Barthena J. | Russel, M. W. | A2/111 | January 28, 1864 | January 31, 1864 |
| Boren, Calvin | Gorden, Mary A. | C/284 | June 11, 1883 | June 11, 1883 |
| Boren, Calvin | Mitchell, Sallie | C/462 | July 28, 1892 | July 30, 1892 |
| Boren, M. J. | McFarland, D. J. | F/112 | February 10, 1897 | February 14, 1897 |
| Boren, Sarah E. | Smithson, John M. F. | B/72 | October 7, 1868 | October 11, 1868 |
| Bornet, Lou Miss | Pitts, Jno. A. | C/452 | December 26, 1891 | December 27, 1891 |
| Borren, Brazell | Vasser, Anney | A2/42 | September 9, 1855 | Returns Missing |
| Botkins, Issabella B. | Duncan, James | A/61 | March 16, 1843 | March 16, 1863 |
| Botten, George J. | Hale, Miss Mary D. | A2/88 | September 3, 1859 | No Return |
| Bottom, Andrew | Lasiter, Maggie | C/402 | September 22, 1887 | September 22, 1887 |
| Bottom, L. M. | Good, Bettie F. | C/372 | October 30, 1886 | October 31, 1886 |
| Bottom, Sallie | Davenport, Robert | C/376 | December 22, 1886 | December 23, 1886 |
| Bottoms, Bettie | Wilson, J. E. | E/240 | December 16, 1889 | December 18, 1889 |
| Bottoms, Munroe | Thursten, Bettie Jane | C/212 | February 8, 1879 | No Return |
| Bottoms, S. H. | Good, Mary P. | C/344 | December 15, 1885 | December 15, 1885 |
| Bounds, Ellen | Moore, Marshack | E/113 | December 22, 1888 | December 23, 1888 |
| Bounds, Lissie? | Higgins, Pleas (col.) | C/420 | October 16, 1890 | October 16, 1890 |
| Bounds, Wesley | Covington, Malisa | C/48 | December 25, 1872 | December 26, 1872 |
| Bowe, W. M. | Sauls, Jerush | D/13 | | July 15, 1882 |
| Bowen, A. S. | Grimes, Susan | C/284 | June 21, 1883 | June 21, 1883 |
| Bowen, Abner B. | Gaither, Miss Martha | A/65 | September 12, 1843 | September 12, 1843 |
| Bowen, Amandy | Nichol, J. J. | C/254 | August ??, 1880 | No Return |
| Bowen, Amandy | Nichol, J. Y. | C/274 | August 20, 1880 | No Return |
| Bowen, D. C. Miss | Parrett, Hyram | B/110 | September 9, 1870 | September 11, 1870 |
| Bowen, Emaliza Miss | Martin, Thomas S. | A/74 | October 24, 1844 | October 24, 1844 |
| Bowen, J. R. | Branden, Miss Sarah | C/408 | November 15, 1887 | November 15, 1887 |
| Bowen, John | Rogers, Ary Ursula | A/55 | October 28, 1842 | October 28, 1842 |
| Bowen, M. A. | Carnahan, J. C. | F/68 | September 14, 1895 | September 15, 1895 |
| Bowen, Mary Frances Miss | Lasiter, Peyton | A2/142 | August 16, 1866 | August 17, 1866 |
| Bowen, Mary Frances Miss | Laseter, Peyton | A2/143 | August 16, 1866 | August 17, 1866 |
| Bowen, Mary Miss | Haley, George | A2/54 | February 20, 1857 | No Return |
| Bowen, Mary Miss | Bradford, Jernesry | A2/70 | November 20, 1858 | November 21, 1858 |
| Bowen, R. J. Miss | Bradford, J. C. | A2/56 | May 21, 1857 | May 21, 1857 |
| Bowen, S. T. Miss | Thomason, J. A. | B/116 | November 10, 1870 | November 11, 1870 |
| Bowen, Samuel | Vinson, Miss Ursula Ann | A/103 | October 26, 1847 | October 28, 1847 |
| Bowen, Samuel | Pitts, Miss Mandy M. | A2/37 | December 7, 1854 | December 7, 1854 |

| Groom or Bride | Groom or Bride | Book/Page | Date of License | Date of Marriage |
|---|---|---|---|---|
| Bowen, Wm. | Richards, Mandy | C/64 | August 20, 1873 | August 21, 1873 |
| Bowenen, Rich | Simpson, Nancy | F/64 | July 22, 1895 | July 22, 1895 |
| Bowers, A. J. | St. John, Callie | D/17 | | November 30, 1882 |
| Bowers, Francis | Lafevers, Miss Sary | A2/73 | March 8, 1859 | No Return |
| Bowers, Francis | Lafevers, Miss Sary | A2/84 | March 8, 1859 | March 10, 1859 |
| Bowers, Francis | Pendleton, Sarah | A2/104 | November 14, 1860 | No Return |
| Bowers, H. S. | Pendleton, Miss Rachel | B/72 | November 27, 1868 | No Return |
| Bowers, William | Winaham, Miss Elizabeth | A/79 | May 28, 1845 | May 28, 1845 |
| Bowk, J. D. | Gaither, Leve | C/474 | December 31, 1892 | December 31, 1892 |
| Bowland, Vina | Pindkerton, Richard | F/62 | April 10, 1895 | April 16, 1895 |
| Bowland, William | Gawing, Lavinda | F/98 | October 12, 1896 | October 18, 1896 |
| Bowley, Y. | Cooper, Amandy | C/248 | May 29, 1880 | May 29, 1880 |
| Bowlin, John B. | Richardson, Miss Agness | A/131 | January 30, 1850 | January 30, 1850 |
| Bowlin, Mattie | Smith, Brown (col.) | C/440 | July 11, 1891 | No Return |
| Bowlin, Polk | Sullins, Sallie | C/292 | September 8, 1883 | No Return |
| Bowlin, Richard | Gowens, Sarah | A2/117 | October 15, 1864 | No Return |
| Bowlin, Saml | Davis, Eliza | C/104 | December 24, 1874 | December 24, 1874 |
| Bowlin, Z. | Keath, L. | C/62 | July 17, 1873 | July 20, 1873 |
| Bowman, Elehue | Good, Exser | F/96 | September 16, 1896 | September 17, 1896 |
| Bowman, John F. W. | Caffey, Miss Sarah Jane | A/43 | October 28, 1841 | October 28, 1841 |
| Bowren, C. L. | York, Bertha | F/110 | January 9, 1897 | January 10, 1897 |
| Bowren, Joseph | Young, Delpha | A2/19 | September 22, 1852 | September 22, 1852 |
| Bowren, Zeb | Gunter, Miss A. | B/116 | November 12, 1870 | November 13, 1870 |
| Boxley, Westley | Harris, Miss Dorcas | A/118 | November 30 1848 | December 1, 1848 |
| Boyd, Elizabeth | Litteral, Saunder | A/6 | September 14, 1838 | September 14, 1838 |
| Boyd, John B. | Smith, Miss Sophia Ann | A2/74 | February 2, 1854 | February 2, 1854 |
| Boyle, Reia M. | Robinson, Joseph W. | A2/36 | November 4, 1854 | November 5, 1854 |
| Boyles, Ater | Gilley, George | C/346 | December 21, 1885 | December 21, 1885 |
| Brackon, S. F Miss | Fann, W. A. | C/462 | August 10, 1892 | August 11, 1892 |
| Bradberry, Cullen | Kincaid, Nancy | A/12 | March 23, 1839 | March 24, 1839 |
| Bradford, J. C. | Bowen, Miss R. J. | A2/56 | May 21, 1857 | May 21, 1857 |
| Bradford, James | Patton, Katharin | A/10 | February 20, 1839 | February 20, 1839 |
| Bradford, Jernesry | Bowen, Miss Mary | A2/70 | November 20, 1858 | November 21, 1858 |
| Bradley, Louisa | Gribble, John | C/128 | December 23, 1875 | December 23, 1875 |
| Brady, John | Cope, Miss Maggie | F/74 | October 26, 1895 | October 17, 1895 |
| Brage, Miss Georgia | Taylor, J. B. | F/62 | April 16, 1895 | May 4, 1895 |
| Bragg, Bettie | Byrn, A. B. | C/418 | September 16, 1890 | September 16, 1890 |
| Bragg, D. F. | Pitar, Miss Sarah Jane | A2/55 | February 24, 1857 | No Return |
| Bragg, Ellen E. | Good, C. L. | C/98 | October 13, 1874 | October 14, 1874 |
| Bragg, Elizabeth Miss | Denton, Jessee | A/52 | August 11, 1842 | August 11, 1842 |
| Bragg, Frances | Sullivan, Andrew | A/77 | February 25, 1845 | February 25, 1845 |
| Bragg, George | Kittrell, Elen | F/144 | January 12, 1898 | January 12, 1898 |
| Bragg, Henry M. | Sullivan, Miss Bettie | C/412 | December 31, 1887 | January 1, 1888 |
| Bragg, J. S. | Franses, Minnie | F/94 | August 29, 1896 | August 30, 1896 |
| Bragg, James | Roberson, Lahama E. | B/104 | July 20, 1870 | July 21, 1870 |
| Bragg, Jennie | Graham, Earle | F/76 | December 10, 1895 | December 11, 1895 |

| Groom or Bride | Groom or Bride | Book/Page | Date of License | Date of Marriage |
|---|---|---|---|---|
| Bragg, Julian Miss | Todd, William F. | B/60 | January 13, 1868 | January 14, 1868 |
| Bragg, Lavica Miss | Carter, Jesse | A/103 | October 15, 1847 | October 5, 1847 |
| Bragg, Lizy Miss | Tucker, Jackson | A2/17 | May 9, 1852 | May 9, 1852 |
| Bragg, Lizzie | Powell, Wm. | C/58 | June 11, 1873 | June 12, 1873 |
| Bragg, Lorena Miss | Campbell, Amos | B/68 | August 27, 1868 | August 27, 1868 |
| Bragg, M. E | Hutcheson, J. F. | C/208 | December 27, 1878 | January 1, 1879 |
| Bragg, M. E. | Todd, J. B. | D/18 | | December 20, 1882 |
| Bragg, Margaret | Faulkenberry, James | A/28 | May 5, 1840 | May 5, 1840 |
| Bragg, Margarett | Sullivan, Thomas G. | A/53 | September 6, 1842 | September 6, 1842 |
| Bragg, Margart | Hays, Wm. B. | A2/20 | November 15, 1852 | November 16, 1852 |
| Bragg, Mary N. Miss | Alexander, John Mc. | B/46 | July 15, 1867 | July 16, 1867 |
| Bragg, Miss M. E. | Kittrell, J. J. | F/48 | November 7, 1894 | November 7, 1894 |
| Bragg, N. C. | Tennerson, Hiram | C/104 | December 24, 1874 | December 25, 1874 |
| Bragg, Nancy | Denton, John | A/25 | February 26, 1840 | February 26, 1840 |
| Bragg, Nancy J. Miss | Peden, Monford | A2/4 | August 17, 1850 | August 18, 1850 |
| Bragg, Nancy Miss | Davenport, James B. | A/116 | November 14, 1848 | November 14, 1848 |
| Bragg, Rebecca J. | Gaither, Silas | A2/131 | November 2, 1865 | November 2, 1865 |
| Bragg, S. E. | McBroom, Miss Elizabeth | B/72 | November 11, 1868 | November 12, 1868 |
| Bragg, S. E. Miss | Gaither, Isaac | B/128 | April 3, 1871 | April ?, 1871 |
| Bragg, Sarah Miss | Whitlock, John | A2/6 | October 24, 1850 | October 24, 1850 |
| Bragg, Sarah Miss | Smithson, H. | A2/42 | October 2, 1855 | October 4, 1855 |
| Bragg, Spence | Bogle, Letley | E/21 | February 25, 1888 | February 26, 1888 |
| Bragg, Susa | Harris, R. H. | F/132 | September 21, 1897 | September 22, 1897 |
| Bragg, Susan Miss | Miller, Joseph | A2/77 | January 19, 1856 | Executed--No Date |
| Bragg, T. M. | Finley, Zenobo | F/64 | July 3, 1895 | July 3, 1895 |
| Bragg, Thomas | Keele, Mary E. | C/350 | January 19, 1886 | January 19, 1886 |
| Bragg, Thomas D. | Roberson, Miss Mary P. | B/42 | February 27, 1867 | February 28, 1867 |
| Bragg, W. J. | Bryson, S. E. | E/225 | October 22, 1889 | October 23, 1889 |
| Bragg, W. M. | Mitchell, Miss Callie | C/16 | December 2, 1871 | December 2, 1871 |
| Bragg, W. M. | Harris, Lizie | F/70 | September 25, 1895 | September 25, 1895 |
| Bragg, William M | Davenport, Miss Laurena S. | A/95 | December 28, 1846 | December 28, 1846 |
| Bragg, William O. | Brandon, Miss N. M. | B/80 | February 10, 1869 | February 11, 1869 |
| Brailer, J. A. | Linch, Miss L. B. | A2/90 | November 8, 1859 | No Return |
| Bralley, Margarett | Philips, David H. | A/53 | September 10, 1843 | September 11, 1842 |
| Bralley, Nancy Miss | Given, William C. | A/58 | December 24, 1842 | December 24, 1842 |
| Bralley, Sarah A. | Philips, Samuel R. | A/59 | February 3, 1843 | February 5, 1843 |
| Bramer, C. P. | Spurlock, Miss C. J. F. | A2/53 | January 8, 1857 | No Return |
| Branatt, Munro | Womack, Martha | C/50 | January 11, 1873 | January 12, 1873 |
| Branden, Beckey J. | Grimes, David | C/210 | January 18, 1879 | January 20, 1879 |
| Branden, James | Frances, Media | F/20 | October 14, 1893 | October 15, 1893 |
| Branden, Sarah Miss | Bowen, J. R. | C/408 | November 15, 1887 | November 15, 1887 |
| Brandon, A. G. | Cates, Miss A. B. | B/102 | May 18, 1870 | May 19, 1870 |
| Brandon, A. J | Wilson, Laura A. | C/50 | February 3, 1873 | February 4, 1873 |
| Brandon, A. T. | Brandon, Miss M. J. | A2/54 | February 12, 1857 | February 12, 1857 |
| Brandon, A. T. | Simpson, Miss R. | B/110 | September 6, 1870 | September 6, 1870 |
| Brandon, Abraham | Helton, Nancy F. | A/128 | November 20, 1849 | November 20, 1849 |

| Groom or Bride | Groom or Bride | Book/Page | Date of License | Date of Marriage |
|---|---|---|---|---|
| Brandon, Adam | Byfor, Josie | C/450 | December 1, 1891 | December 2, 1891 |
| Brandon, B. B. | Lowe, T. J. | F/94 | August 29, 1896 | August 30, 1896 |
| Brandon, Becca | Thompson, Robert | C/226 | October 28, 1879 | No Return |
| Brandon, C. A. | Hollis, N. C. | F/28 | January 17, 1894 | January 11, 1894 |
| Brandon, Cornelius | Summars, Mary | A/34 | October 23, 1840 | No Return |
| Brandon, Crida Miss | Gann, John | B/76 | January 6, 1869 | January 6, 1869 |
| Brandon, D. C. | Duggin, T. E. | C/164 | July 20, 1877 | July 21, 1877 |
| Brandon, D. F. | Bogle, C. L. | D/22 | | March 11, 1883 |
| Brandon, David G. | Patton, Miss Elizabeth | A/74 | November 18, 1844 | November 19, 1844 |
| Brandon, Dollie | Haley, Isaac | E/382 | October 29, 1898 | |
| Brandon, Dollie | Haley, Isaac | F/158 | October 29, 1898 | October 30, 1898 |
| Brandon, E. T. | Mitchel, Syntha | A2/110 | November 14, 1863 | November 15, 1863 |
| Brandon, Elizabeth | Harris, Zephaniah | A/34 | October 27, 1840 | No Return |
| Brandon, George | Ivie, Ellar | C/220 | July 22, 1879 | July 24, 1879 |
| Brandon, Hiram | Harris, Amanda | A/11 | February 26, 1839 | February 26, 1839 |
| Brandon, J. A. | Todd, Miss M. E. | B/118 | December 14, 1870 | December 14, 1870 |
| Brandon, J. M. | Smith, Miss O. J. | C/2 | July 5, 1871 | July 13, 1871 |
| Brandon, J. T. | Haley, Salley | C/322 | January 5, 1885 | No Return |
| Brandon, James | Todd, Miss Mary Jane | C/412 | December 2, 1887 | December 2, 1776 |
| Brandon, Jesse | Maxey, Mary | C/316 | October 22, 1884 | No Return |
| Brandon, Jesse | Macey, Mary | D/23 | | October 26, 1884 |
| Brandon, Jesse B. | Simpson, Miss Martha A. | A/94 | December 2, 1846 | December 2, 1846 |
| Brandon, John | Gannon, Miss Roxanna | A/114 | September 7, 1848 | September 7, 1848 |
| Brandon, John | Gannon, Bettie | C/300 | January 16, 1884 | No Return |
| Brandon, John E. | McCray, Nancy | A/13 | May 16, 1839 | May 16, 1839 |
| Brandon, John F. | Womack, Miss M. A. A. | A2/80 | March 14, 1857 | March 15, 1857 |
| Brandon, Jonathan | Orrand, Miss Joannah | A2/153 | May 24, 1866 | May 24, 1866 |
| Brandon, Jonathan J. | Lowe, Miss Harriet | A2/9 | January 3, 1851 | No Return |
| Brandon, Jonnathan | Reed, Sarah | C/12 | October 28, 1871 | October 30, 1871 |
| Brandon, K. T. | Roberson, Miss Josephine | B/64 | March 28, 1868 | March 29, 1868 |
| Brandon, Lavisa Miss | Gorden, George H. | A/41 | October 6, 1841 | No Return |
| Brandon, Lillie | Perry, W. H. | F/96 | September 22, 1896 | September 23, 1896 |
| Brandon, Linda | Rogers, Will | F/98 | October 7, 1896 | October 14, 1896 |
| Brandon, Lucinda Miss | Gann, John | B/60 | January 9, 1868 | February 8, 1868 |
| Brandon, M. C. | Sullivan, M. G. | C/240 | January 27, 1880 | January 29, 1880 |
| Brandon, M. J. Miss | Irvin, H. A. | B/62 | February 10, 1868 | February 18, 1868 |
| Brandon, Margaret E. Miss | Gaither, R. L. | A2/136 | January 30, 1866 | February 1, 1866 |
| Brandon, Margaret E. | Petty, James A. | A2/133 | December 2, 1865 | December 3, 1865 |
| Brandon, Mary A. | Brandon, Wm. A. | C/70 | October 19, 1873 | October 19, 1873 |
| Brandon, Mary Mrs. | Summar, Cantrell B. | A/75 | November 21, 1844 | November 21, 1844 |
| Brandon, Mathew | Vane, Mary A. | A2/36 | October 26, 1854 | October 26, 1854 |
| Brandon, Monroe | Shelton, Zettie | F/116 | April 29, 1897 | April 29, 1897 |
| Brandon, N. E. | Todd, L. M. | C/186 | February 21, 1878 | No Retrun |
| Brandon, N. M. Miss | Bragg, William O. | B/80 | February 10, 1869 | February 11, 1869 |
| Brandon, Nancy | Ward, M. L. | C/262 | November 13, 1880 | November 14, 1880 |
| Brandon, Nitha Jane | Rodgers, W. B. | C/446 | September 9, 1891 | September 10, 1891 |

| Groom or Bride | Groom or Bride | Book/Page | Date of License | Date of Marriage |
|---|---|---|---|---|
| Brandon, R. | Byford, M. M. | A2/33 | June 29, 1854 | June 29, 1854 |
| Brandon, Rebecca Miss | Godwin, Benjamin A. | A/62 | May 4, 1843 | May 4, 1843 |
| Brandon, Rena | Thompson, Robert | C/234 | October 28, 1879 | October 28, 1879 |
| Brandon, Robert B. | Bryson, Miss Malinda F. | B/68 | August 1, 1868 | August 2, 1868 |
| Brandon, S. D. | Brown, J. L. | C/404 | September 28, 1887 | No Return |
| Brandon, S. S. | Jones, Miss Christeney | B/40 | February 15, 1867 | February 17, 1867 |
| Brandon, Sabella | Gooden, William | A/8 | November 21, 1838 | No Return |
| Brandon, Sallie C. | Bryson, G. P. | C/318 | November 12, 1884 | November 13, 1884 |
| Brandon, Sallie C. | Bryson, G. B. | C/318 | November 12, 1884 | No Return |
| Brandon, Sarah | Summars, Robert H. | D/1 | | June 4, 1881 |
| Brandon, W. C. | Bogle, Susie E. | F/136 | November 16, 1897 | November 17, 1897 |
| Brandon, William | Burk, Miss Elizabeth | A2/51 | December 12, 1856 | No Return |
| Brandon, Wm. | Sheres, Miss Jane | A2/38 | February 27, 1855 | No Return |
| Brandon, Wm. A. | Brandon, Mary A. | C/70 | October 19, 1873 | October 19, 1873 |
| Branon, Calvin C. | Sullivan | A/72 | August 29, 1844 | No Return |
| Brant, Melvina | Stacy, Jonnie | E/196 | July 31, 1889 | July 31, 1889 |
| Brantley, Franklin | McKnight, Sylva | B/2 | August 21, 1865 | August 26, 1865 |
| Brantley, Ross | Flowers, Louella | F/118 | May 28, 1897 | May 30, 1897 |
| Brantly, Maggie | Bryson, Sam | C/144 | September 21, 1876 | September 22, 1876 |
| Brasheares, William | Nokes, Nancy | A/57 | December 10, 1842 | December 13, 1842 |
| Brashears, Alexander | Skurlock, Miss Lucinda | A/112 | July 26, 1848 | July 26, 1848 |
| Brashears, Alexr. | Hutchens, Vina C. | A2/112 | March 20, 1864 | March 20, 1864 |
| Brashears, Nelly | Taylor, Richard | A/78 | May 9, 1845 | May 9, 1845 |
| Brashears, Ruth Miss | Moore, Samuel Jr. | A/79 | June 2, 1845 | June 5, 1845 |
| Brashears, William | Herrin, Miss Sally | A/84 | November 1, 1845 | November 3, 1845 |
| Brasher, Thomas J. | Fuston, Esteller | C/328 | March 11, 1885 | March 12, 1885 |
| Brashers, J. L. | Scurlock, America | A2/46 | February 5, 1856 | February 6, 1856 |
| Braswell, Joe | Zuarles, Joe | F/154 | August 30, 1898 | August 31, 1898 |
| Braton, Wm | Kirsey, Miss Frances | A2/35 | September 13, 1854 | September 13, 1854 |
| Bratton, Delia | Ledbetter, Tiff | C/422 | November 20, 1890 | November 20, 1890 |
| Bratton, M. F. | Williams, B. A. | C/202 | October 18, 1878 | November 19, 1878 |
| Bratton, Nancy | Hancock, R. T. | E/211 | September 10, 1889 | September 10, 1889 |
| Brawley, Wm | Rawlings, Manervy | C/22 | February 13, 1872 | February 13, 1872 |
| Braxton, Catherine | Gilley, J. B. | E/73 | September 17, 1888 | September 20, 1888 |
| Braxton, Eliza | Daniel J. C. | E/104 | November 29, 1888 | December 2, 1888 |
| Braxton, J. M. | Parker, Mary | C/78 | December 20, 1873 | January 1, 1874 |
| Braxton, John | Wilson, Della | F | August 21, 1893 | No Return |
| Braxton, Patrick | Shirley, Angeline | C/162 | June 4, 1877 | No Return |
| Bray, Mary | Blanton, James | D/4 | | August 4, 188 |
| Brazel, Laura | Williams, James M. | C/330 | June 16, 1885 | June 18, 1885 |
| Brazwell, Elixabeth V. | Craddock, J. T. | C/84 | March 2, 1874 | February 5, 1874 |
| Breis, James F. | Carter, Sallie | D/12 | | February 23, 1882 |
| Brents, J. J. | Fugitt, Lemma | C/236 | January 7, 1880 | January 7, 1880 |
| Brents, Solomon | Brownfield, Elizabeth | A/3 | May 31, 1838 | May 31, 1838 |
| Brevard, Th. | Ferrill, Miss M. R. | A2/27 | August 24, 1853 | August 24, 1854 |
| Brevard, Thomas B. | Fugitt, Jane W. | A/104 | November 2, 1847 | November 2, 1847 |

| Groom or Bride | Groom or Bride | Book/Page | Date of License | Date of Marriage |
|---|---|---|---|---|
| Brevard, W. F. | Smith, Minnie | D/9 | | December 29, 1881 |
| Brewer, A. G. | Elledge, Mattie | C/350 | January 19, 1886 | January 19, 1886 |
| Brewer, Bettie Miss | Vance, D. B. | B/72 | November 22, 1868 | November 23, 1868 |
| Brewer, Caty | Teele, Charle | C/336 | September 29, 1885 | No Return |
| Brewer, Fannie | Keile, Samm | C/318 | November 2, 1884 | November 2, 1884 |
| Brewer, Hattie E. | High, C. J. | F/48 | November 13, 1894 | November 15, 1894 |
| Brewer, James | Wilson, Elisabeth | C/262 | November 12, 1880 | No Return |
| Brewer, Jesse | Weedon, Martha E. | A/61 | March 23, 1843 | March 23, 1843 |
| Brewer, Joel | Spangler, Mary E. | A2/94 | February 22, 1860 | No Return |
| Brewer, Joel | Shipp, Margrett E. | C/322 | January 24, 1885 | January 25, 1885 |
| Brewer, John L. | Stephens, Miss Martha F. | B/94 | December 9, 1869 | December 9, 1869 |
| Brewer, Lucy | Davis, Samuel | C/276 | March 18, 1881 | No Return |
| Brewer, M. J. | Todd, W. C. | C/194 | July 23, 1878 | July 24, 1878 |
| Brewer, Martha Miss | Miller, William C. | A2/18 | July 25, 1852 | July 25, 1852 |
| Brewer, Mattie | Stephen, D. R. | E/346 | December 21, 1898 | |
| Brewer, Mattie | Warrick, H. D. | F/98 | October 3, 1896 | October 4, 1896 |
| Brewer, N. H. | Owenby, H. M. | D/14 | | August 21, 1882 |
| Brewer, Nancy A. | Edwards, C. C. | C/230 | November 14, 1879 | November 18, 1879 |
| Brewer, S. A. | Turner, Miss M. E. | B/120 | December 19, 1870 | December 22, 1870 |
| Brewer, Sarah R. | Gay, Wm. | A2/21 | December 7, 1852 | December 8, 1852 |
| Brewer, Thomas J. | Hall, Miss Mary | A/120 | February 14, 1849 | February 15, 1849 |
| Brewer, W. M. | Gower, Miss Bettie | B/118 | November 24, 1870 | November 24, 1870 |
| Brewies, A. E. | Odom, J. H. | C/44 | October 23, 1872 | October 25, 1872 |
| Brewin (?), L. J. Miss | Odom, R. L | C/6 | August 5, 1871 | August 6, 1871 |
| Brewis, Media | Young, J. A. | F/26 | December 26, 1893 | December 28, 1893 |
| Brewis, Tammie | McAffry, S. L. | C/380 | December 28, 1886 | January 2, 1886 |
| Briant, Frances | Webber, F. M. | A2/124 | July 31, 1865 | August 5, 1865 |
| Brien, James W. | Turner, M. M. C. | A2/47 | April 28, 1856 | No Return |
| Bright, James R. | Maney, Miss Priscilla | A/104 | November 2, 1847 | No Return |
| Brim, Columbus | Pitz, Mattie | C/382 | January 26, 1887 | No Return |
| Brim, Cyntha | McGregar, Isaac | C/244 | March 15, 1880 | March 15, 1880 |
| Brim, Osias D. | Spurlock, Julian | B/90 | October 28, 1869 | October 28, 1869 |
| Brim, Sarah | Goff, L. P. | C/72 | November 21, 1873 | November 21, 1873 |
| Brim, Surmantha | Merriman, Wm. F. | C/186 | February 5, 1878 | February 5, 1878 |
| Brinkley, Nancy J. | Thomason, John A. | C/178 | December 1, 1877 | December 2, 1877 |
| Brison, B. D. | Brison, Miss E. | A2/69 | November 11, 1858 | November 11, 1858 |
| Brison, E. Miss | Brison, B. D. | A2/69 | November 11, 1858 | November 11, 1858 |
| Brison, Martha M. | West, A. W. | A2/98 | June 26, 1860 | No Return |
| Brison, Timothy | Allen, Alice | C/192 | May 8, 1878 | May 9, 1878 |
| Brnum, Amandy | Jernigan, Newton | D/7 | | December 8, 1881 |
| Brnum, Callie | Morgan, Ed | E/187 | July 6, 1889 | No Return |
| Brnum, Caroline | Pendleton, Samuel | C/188 | December 19, 1877 | December 20, 1877 |
| Brogon, Lucy Miss | Bomer, Wm. | A2/17 | May 29, 1852 | No Return |
| Brooks, Elracy | Robison, John | C/372 | October 26, 1886 | No Return |
| Brooks, Isaac | Duke, Miss Elizabeth | A/113 | August 5, 1848 | August 6, 1848 |
| Brooks, John R. | Wimberley, Miss Martha | A/97 | January 25, 1847 | February 7, 1847 |

| Groom or Bride | Groom or Bride | Book/Page | Date of License | Date of Marriage |
|---|---|---|---|---|
| Brooks, July | Gannon, James | C/250 | July 7, 1880 | July 7, 1880 |
| Brooks, Martha | Gaither, Ivory | C/136 | April 11, 1876 | April 11, 1876 |
| Brooks, Mattie | Owen, Thos J. | C/210 | January 16, 1879 | January 18, 1870 |
| Brooks, Tennie W. | Gannon, James P. | C/68 | October 11, 1873 | October 12, 1873 |
| Brooks, Wm. | William, Miss Julie A. | B/112 | September 24, 1870 | September 25, 1870 |
| Brown, A. J. | Bruce, Miss Nancy E. | A2/137 | February 17, 1866 | February 18, 1866 |
| Brown, Ann | Miller, L. D. | C/322 | December 25, 1884 | December 26, 1884 |
| Brown, Ann Miss | Fugitt, Townsend | A2/29 | September 19, 1853 | September 19,1853 |
| Brown, Brit | Markum, Lizzie | F/130 | September 17, 1897 | September 18, 1897 |
| Brown, C. C. | Coleman, Miss Ann E. | B/76 | January 21, 1869 | January 21, 1869 |
| Brown, Calvin | Higgins, Miss Lucy | B/122 | January 6, 1871 | January 8, 1871 |
| Brown, Claudia | Hancock, Walter | E/352 | December 14, 1898 | |
| Brown, D. S. | Mullins, Sallie | D/13 | | May 25, 1882 |
| Brown, E. W. | Odom, C. | C/316 | November 17, 1884 | November 17, 1884 |
| Brown, Elizabeth H. | Marchbanks, James | A/19 | November 1, 1839 | November 2, 1839 |
| Brown, Elizabeth Miss | Wrather, Farmer D. | A/120 | February 15, 1849 | February 15, 1849 |
| Brown, Elmore | Woolard, Ella | F/112 | February 13, 1897 | February 13, 1897 |
| Brown, Elvira | Roach, J. L | C/102 | December 12, 1874 | December 14, 1874 |
| Brown, Fannie Miss | Parker, Silas | B/44 | April 9, 1867 | April 11, 1867 |
| Brown, J. H. | Bynum, M. E. | C/238 | January 15, 1880 | January 15, 1880 |
| Brown, J. L. | Brandon, S. D. | C/404 | September 28, 1887 | No Return |
| Brown, J. N. | Williams, Parialee | F/114 | March 5, 1897 | No Return |
| Brown, J. N. | Williams, Paralee | F/148 | March 5, 1898 | March 8, 1898 |
| Brown, James | Deberry | B/128 | March 25, 1871 | March 28, 1871 |
| Brown, James | Bethe., Nannie | F/118 | May 20, 1897 | May 22, 1897 |
| Brown, James W. | Lewis, Margaret | A2/125 | August 4, 1865 | August 6, 1865 |
| Brown, Jane | Pearson, Richard | A2/108 | July 9, 1863 | No Return |
| Brown, Jane Miss | Daniel, Robert C. | A2/77 | January 7, 1856 | January 7, 1856 |
| Brown, Jesse | Richards, F. C. | E/221 | October 15, 1889 | October 16, 1889 |
| Brown, John | Smith, Miss Feriba | B/34 | December 19, 1866 | December 20, 1866 |
| Brown, John | Stacy, Miss Sarah Adaline | B/112 | October 7, 1870 | October 9, 1870 |
| Brown, John A. J. | Watson, Miss A. C. | B/102 | May 28, 1870 | May 29, 1870 |
| Brown, Joseph M. | Mills, Mollie | F/138 | December 3, 1897 | December 4, 1897 |
| Brown, Josey | Johnson, Wm. | C/264 | December 23, 1880 | December 23, 1880 |
| Brown, Lucinda Miss | Moore, Wm. N. | A2/59 | November 3, 1857 | November 5, 1857 |
| Brown, M. A. E | Gowen, H. N. | C/50 | January 7, 1873 | January 7, 1873 |
| Brown, Martha A. | Rogers, J. H. | C/114 | June 4, 1875 | June 4, 1875 |
| Brown, Manerva J. Miss | Witt, Martin M. | A/125 | July 30, 1849 | July 30, 1849 |
| Brown, Martin | Sellars, Miss Salina | A/120 | February, 13, 1849 | February 13, 1849 |
| Brown, Mary | Gross, Harrison | A2/53 | June 2, 1866 | June 3, 1866 |
| Brown, Mary | Jones, John | C/396 | July 23, 1887 | July 24, 1887 |
| Brown, Mary A. | Williams, David | C/40 | September 21, 1872 | September 22, 1872 |
| Brown, Mary D. Miss | Dill, Adison | A2/50 | August 14, 1856 | August 14, 1856 |
| Brown, Matilda | Pitts, James | E/108 | December 15, 1888 | December 16, 1888 |
| Brown, Mattie | Stephen, D. R. | F/162 | December 21, 1898 | December 21, 1898 |
| Brown, Miss Claudia | Hancock, Walter | F/162 | December 14, 1898 | December 14, 1898 |

| Groom or Bride | Groom or Bride | Book/Page | Date of License | Date of Marriage |
|---|---|---|---|---|
| Brown, Nancy | Duggan, Aaron | A/27 | April 2, 1840 | April 2, 1840 |
| Brown, Nancy Mrs. | Sullivan, John R. | A2/1 | March 5, 1850 | March 5, 1850 |
| Brown, Nellie | Henderson, Nat | F/138 | November 20, 1897 | No Return |
| Brown, Newton | Spurlock, Fannie | C/320 | December 24, 1884 | December 24, 1884 |
| Brown, Oma Ann Miss | Cox, Cabele | A/125 | July 16, 1849 | July 16, 1849 |
| Brown, Richard | Beaty, Miss Jane | A/40 | August 20, 1841 | August 20, 1841 |
| Brown, Robt. | Markum, Helen | F/118 | May 29, 1897 | No Return |
| Brown, Sarah | Gilley, James | C/332 | July 15, 1885 | July 16, 1885 |
| Brown, Sarah | Campbell, Cal | C/196 | August 29, 1878 | August 29, 1878 |
| Brown, Sarah A. | Blackburn, John | A2/98 | June 29, 1860 | No Return |
| Brown, Sarah A. | Williams, Lewis | D/16 | | October 3, 1882 |
| Brown, Sarah P. Mrs. | Wells (Webb), John | A/61 | April 11, 1843 | April 11, 1843 |
| Brown, Silas N. | Whittemore, Sarah | F/144 | January 14, 1898 | January 15, 1898 |
| Brown, Susan Ann Miss | Byford, John H. | A/100 | June 26, 1847 | Return Not Executed |
| Brown, T. J. | Summers, Miss M. A. | A2/61 | December 24, 1857 | December 24, 1857 |
| Brown, Tempa Caroline | Gray, Wm. P. | A2/31 | December 27, 1853 | December 27, 1853 |
| Brown, Thomas | Burger, Sarah C. | F/76 | December 9, 1895 | December 11, 1895 |
| Brown, W. E. | Whitfield, M. J. | C/94 | September 11, 1874 | September 17, 1874 |
| Brown, W. M. | Hall, Miss Mary E. | A2/158 | June 18, 1866 | No Return |
| Brown, Wm | Pitts, M. J. | D/19 | | December 28, 1882 |
| Brownfield, Elizabeth | Brents, Solomon | A/3 | May 31, 1838 | May 31, 1838 |
| Broyles, J. A. | Tittle, N. P. | C/418 | September 16, 1890 | September 18, 1890 |
| Broyles, J. H. | Rollins, Maggie T. | C/292 | September 5, 1883 | No Return |
| Broyles, J. H. | Rollins, Maggie | C/390 | September 5, 1883 | No Return |
| Bruce, Nancy E. Miss | Brown, A. J. | A2/137 | February 17, 1866 | February 18, 1866 |
| Bruce, Robert | Young, Rebeca | C/406 | October 29, 1887 | October 29, 1887 |
| Bruster, Vina | Davenport, J. B. | F/14 | July 24, 1893 | August 21, 1893 |
| Bryan, Fannie | Price, J. D. | C/324 | January 15, 1885 | January 15, 1885 |
| Bryan, J. V. | Summar, Miss Bette | C/380 | January 3, 1887 | No Return |
| Bryan, L. P. | Todd, Miss Lizzie | C/382 | January 18, 1887 | January 19, 1887 |
| Bryan, Manson | McAdoo, Lizie | C/398 | August 29, 1887 | August 29, 1887 |
| Bryan, Spence | Stacy, Susanna | F/84 | February 15, 1896 | February 16, 1896 |
| Bryan, T. M. | Hancok, Hattie | C/422 | November 1, 1890 | November 2, 1890 |
| Bryan, W. R. | Davenport, Nancy | F/72 | October 12, 1895 | October 13, 1895 |
| Bryans, Irving | Whitlock, Allice | F/106 | December 16, 1896 | No Return |
| Bryant, Amandy J. | Lewis, Geo W. | C/142 | August 19, 1876 | August 20, 1876 |
| Bryant, B. L. Miss | Bush, Berry | A2/67 | August 25, 1858 | No Return |
| Bryant, Bell | Vasser, B. F. | C/342 | November 27, 1885 | November 29, 1885 |
| Bryant, Beet Miss | Wilson, William | E/44 | June 28, 1888 | July 1, 1888 |
| Bryant, D. J. | Simmons, A. N. | E/2 | January 10, 1888 | January 15, 1888 |
| Bryant, David | Batson, Miss Meranda Jane | A/113 | July 31, 1848 | July 31, 1848 |
| Bryant, Elizabeth Miss | Holt, William | B/50 | August 17, 1867 | August 17, 1867 |
| Bryant, Ira J. | Hale, Miss Nancy E. | A2/27 | September 1, 1853 | No Return |
| Bryant, J. T. | Holt, Clem | C/290 | August 13, 1883 | August 14, 1883 |
| Bryant, James | West, Mary J. | C/286 | July 13, 1883 | July 15, 1883 |
| Bryant, James W. | Polock, Miss Elizabeth Ann | A/94 | December 3, 1846 | No Return |

| Groom or Bride | Groom or Bride | Book/Page | Date of License | Date of Marriage |
|---|---|---|---|---|
| Bryant, Jas. | West, Martha | C/176 | November 9, 1877 | November 11, 1877 |
| Bryant, John | Owens, Cindy | D/3 | | July 10, 1881 |
| Bryant, John M. | Dukes, Miss Dollie | C/388 | May 17, 1887 | May 18, 1887 |
| Bryant, Lillie | Freeman, Sun | F/2 | January 22, 1893 | No Return |
| Bryant, Lillie | ----, Simeon | F/10 | June 22, 1893 | June 28, 1893 |
| Bryant, Lizzie | Hawkins, Roman Treser | C/336 | September 19, 1885 | September 20, 1885 |
| Bryant, Lizzie | Stacy, G. C. | C/440 | July 25, 1891 | July 30, 1891 |
| Bryant, M. A. Miss | Bivvans, A. J. | A2/63 | March 2, 1858 | March 2, 1858 |
| Bryant, M. E. | Jewell, S. T. | C/140 | July 21, 1876 | No Return |
| Bryant, Matildy | Hill, G. W. | F/152 | July 22, 1898 | July 17, 1898 |
| Bryant, Sarah | Sullivan, J. V. | F/66 | August 10, 1895 | August 11, 1895 |
| Bryant, Spence | McCollough, Angeline | C/296 | November 24, 1883 | November 25, 1883 |
| Bryant, Thomas | Lewis, Minnie | F/110 | February 8, 1897 | February 28, 1897 |
| Bryant, Wesley | Cooper, Tennessee | C/18 | December 23, 1871 | December 24, 1871 |
| Bryant, Wm. S. | Stacy, Susanna | C/36 | August 23, 1872 | August 25, 1862 |
| Bryant, Zachariah T. | Dodd, Miss Rachel P. | B/98 | December 7, 1869 | December 9, 1869 |
| Brynum, John | Hoover, Elizabeth | A/9 | December 6, 1838 | December 6, 1838 |
| Brynum, Mary Elizabeth Jane Miss | Stacy, John A. | B/66 | April 4, 1868 | April 5, 1868 |
| Brynum, Sallie A. Miss | Todd, L. A. | B/42 | February 28, 1867 | March 3, 1867 |
| Bryson, ---- | Davenport, ---- | F | September 2, 1893 | |
| Bryson, A. J. | Tucker, E. D. | C/166 | August 11, 1877 | August 12, 1877 |
| Bryson, B. M. | Higdon, Edna | C/382 | January 22, 1887 | January 23, 1887 |
| Bryson, Beth (col.) | Pinkerton, Ada | C/444 | August 26, 1891 | August 27, 1891 |
| Bryson, Bethell | Grooms, Amanda | F/18 | October 14, 1893 | October 14, 1893 |
| Bryson, Charles | Clark, Tildy | F/56 | January 10, 1895 | January 10, 1895 |
| Bryson, D. Z | Davenport, M. E. | E/362 | November 26, 1898 | |
| Bryson, D. Z. | Davenport, M. E. | F/162 | November 26, 1898 | November 17, 1898 |
| Bryson, Daniel | Alexander, Nancy | A/10 | January 17, 1839 | January 23, 1839 |
| Bryson, Daniel | Hubbard, Nancy | A2/105 | October 18, 1862 | October 21, 1862 |
| Bryson, Daniel | Knight, Liddie | C/90 | May 26, 1874 | No Return |
| Bryson, E. D. | Wilson, M. L. | A2/125 | August 4, 1865 | August 6, 1865 |
| Bryson, Elisabeth | Francis, Harris | C/274 | February 8, 1881 | February 8, 1881 |
| Bryson, Elizabeth Miss | Summer, B. D. | A2/60 | November 22, 1857 | November 20?, 1857 |
| Bryson, Emley F. | Mears, W. T. | C/16 | December 2, 1871 | December 3, 1871 |
| Bryson, Fatomy Miss | Cooper, A. D. | A2/89 | October 6, 1859 | No Return |
| Bryson, Francis A. | Travis, J. | C/162 | April 26, 1877 | No Return |
| Bryson, G. B. | Brandon, Sallie C. | C/318 | November 12, 1884 | No Return |
| Bryson, G. P. | Brandon, Sallie C. | C/318 | November 12, 1884 | November 13, 1884 |
| Bryson, H. H. | Davenport, M. A. | C/226 | October 10, 1879 | No Return |
| Bryson, Hannah | Dow, Henry | C/194 | July 22, 1878 | July 27, 1878 |
| Bryson, J. A. | Moore, Miss Nancy | A2/88 | August 30, 1859 | No Return |
| Bryson, J. D. | Bryson, Nancy J. | C/172 | September 22, 1877 | September 23, 1877 |
| Bryson, J. J. | Sumer, Miss Cindy L. H. | A2/41 | August 14, 1855 | Returns Missing |
| Bryson, J. J. | Fann, M. M. | F/132 | September 28, 1897 | September 29, 1897 |
| Bryson, J. W. | Duggin, Florance | F/158 | September 27, 1898 | September 28, 1898 |

| Groom or Bride | Groom or Bride | Book/Page | Date of License | Date of Marriage |
|---|---|---|---|---|
| Bryson, James H. | Jones, Miss Sarrah M. | A2/57 | September 7, 1857 | No Return |
| Bryson, John | Rich, Julia A. | C/380 | December 27, 1886 | December 28, 1886 |
| Bryson, L. C. | Odom, Edney A. | C/286 | July 16, 1883 | July 19, 1883 |
| Bryson, L. M. | Davenport, John R. | C/306 | March 9, 1884 | No Return |
| Bryson, Laura | Mingles, S. H. | C/328 | March 5, 1885 | March 5, 1885 |
| Bryson, Loely P. Miss | Cooper, John M. | A/92 | October 27, 1846 | October 27, 1846 |
| Bryson, Louisa | Davenport, T. W. | E/140 | February 21, 1889 | February 21, 1889 |
| Bryson, M. A. | Mingle, W. F. | C/250 | July 23, 1880 | July 23, 1880 |
| Bryson, M. L. | Davenport, W. B. | C/222 | August 11, 1879 | August 13, 1879 |
| Bryson, Malinda F. Miss | Brandon, Robert B. | B/68 | August 1, 1868 | August 2, 1868 |
| Bryson, Margarett Ann | Gann, John | F/84 | February 10, 1896 | February 14, 1896 |
| Bryson, Margeret | Allen, Charley | C/366 | September 11, 1886 | September 12, 1886 |
| Bryson, Martha | Wilson, Michael | A/8 | October 16, 1838 | October 16, 1838 |
| Bryson, M. O Miss | Gannon, George | C/452 | December 12, 1891 | December 12, 1891 |
| Bryson, Mary J. | Milligan, John P. | C/56 | March 22, 1873 | March 23, 1873 |
| Bryson, Mary M. Miss | Francis, M. H. | B/54 | October 21, 1867 | October 21, 1867 |
| Bryson, Mahaly T. Miss | Ready, John S. | C/4 | July 27, 1871 | July 27, 1871 |
| Bryson, Nancy J. | Bryson, J. D. | C/172 | September 22, 1877 | September 23, 1877 |
| Bryson, Nancy Miss | Gillam, J. M. | A2/99 | July 2, 1860 | No Return |
| Bryson, Nathan | Smith, Lou | C/90 | August 6, 1874 | August 6, 1874 |
| Bryson, Nathan | Smith, Lou | C/92 | August 6, 1874 | No Return |
| Bryson, Parthena Miss | Summar, Z. T. | B/78 | January 28, 1869 | January 28, 1869 |
| Bryson, Polly Miss | Davenport, William | A/82 | July 24, 1845 | July 24, 1845 |
| Bryson, R. T. | Davenport, L. E. | C/182 | December 25, 1877 | December 30, 1877 |
| Bryson, Robert | Summers, Miss | A2/57 | August 6, 1857 | August 20, 1857 |
| Bryson, S. E. | Bragg, W. J. | E/225 | October 22, 1889 | October 23, 1889 |
| Bryson, S. S. | Smith, A. M. | C/72 | November 18, 1873 | No Return |
| Bryson, Sam | Brantly, Maggie | C/144 | September 21, 1876 | September 22, 1876 |
| Bryson, Samuel H. | McKnight, Miss Sarah M. | B/104 | July 7, 1870 | July 7, 1870 |
| Bryson, Sarah Miss | Harris, John L. | A/82 | August 5, 1845 | August 5, 1845 |
| Bryson, Sarah J. | Salers, J. D. | C/202 | October 16, 1878 | October 16, 1878 |
| Bryson, T. J. | Peden, L. A. | D/7 | | November 20, 1881 |
| Bryson, Thos. T. | Adams, Sarah E. | C/290 | September 3, 1883 | September 5, 1883 |
| Bryson, W. B. | Wallace, Virginia | F/156 | September 5, 1898 | September 5, 1898 |
| Bryson, W. D. | Davenport, Fanie | F/22 | November 11, 1893 | November 13, 1893 |
| Bryson, W. K | Ramsey, E. J. | C/268 | January 5, 1881 | No Return |
| Bryson, William | West, Sally | A/5 | August 15, 1838 | August 15, 1838 |
| Bryson, Wm. B. | Moore, Miss M. L. | A2/30 | December 10, 1853 | December 11, 1853 |
| Bucher, Joshua | Gan, Miss Allaminta | A2/50 | September 13, 1856 | Return not Executed |
| Bucy, Asaline | Porterfield, Edgar | F/124 | August 4, 1897 | August 8, 1897 |
| Bucy, Dosier | Parker, Dona | F/84 | February 15, 1896 | February 16, 1896 |
| Bucy, George W. | Mears, Miss Sarah | A2/10 | January 11, 1851 | January 12, 1851 |
| Bucy, Josh | Harris, Tennie | F/124 | August 4, 1897 | August 8, 1897 |
| Bucy, Sarah J. Mrs. | Richards, Jessee | B/124 | January 17, 1871 | January 17, 1871 |
| Bullard, Charity Miss | Fergason, F. M. | B/114 | October 31, 1870 | November 3, 1870 |
| Bullard, Elizabeth | Hendrickson, John | A2/96 | April 27, 1860 | April 27, 1860 |

| Groom or Bride | Groom or Bride | Book/Page | Date of License | Date of Marriage |
|---|---|---|---|---|
| Bullard, J. T. | Mahaffa, Susan J. | C/166 | August 15, 1877 | August 16, 1877 |
| Bullard, Mary R. | Blair, J. R. | C/110 | March 2, 1875 | March 21, 1875 |
| Bullard, Morgan | Tucker, Ida | C/328 | March 21, 1885 | March 21, 1885 |
| Bullard, Nathan | Rogers, Lucinda | C/246 | April 10, 1880 | April 10, 1880 |
| Bullard, Paralee | Vandergriff, John D. | C/150 | December 20, 1876 | December 20, 1876 |
| Bullard, Rena | Barrett, Foster | E/4 | January 12, 1888 | |
| Bullard, Willey | Tate, Ada | F/52 | October 27, 1894 | October 27, 1894 |
| Bullen, J. W. | Watson, Miss Nancy A. | A2/72 | January 15, 1859 | No Return |
| Bullen, Mahulda Miss | Rogers, Wilbern | A/95 | January 4, 1847 | January 10, 1847 |
| Bullen, Sarah Ann Miss | Martin, Wm. | B/130 | April 1, 1871 | April 1, 1871 |
| Bulling, Polly Miss | Rogers, John Jr. | A/89 | June 17, 1846 | June 17, 1846 |
| Bunch, Malinda Mrs. | Goad, William | B/80 | March 31, 1869 | March 31, 1860 |
| Bunch, Nancy Miss | Sullins, John J. | B/80 | May 1, 1869 | May 1, 1869 |
| Burch, Clementine Miss | Denis, Thomas | B/88 | September 30, 1869 | September 30, 1869 |
| Burch, J. G. | Mason, Rena | E/191 | July 13, 1889 | July 14, 1889 |
| Burch, J. M. | Holland, Amandy A. | C/60 | July 5, 1873 | No Return |
| Burch, Jane | Wimberley, J. C. | A2/122 | March 10, 1865 | March 10, 1865 |
| Burch, Mary Ann Miss | Allen, Samuel | B/86 | September 2, 1869 | September 2, 1869 |
| Burch, Nora | Parton, James | F/92 | August 22, 1896 | August 23, 1896 |
| Burch, William P. | Ausment, Mary | A2/132 | November 22, 1865 | Executed No Date |
| Burchett, A. J. | Sissom, M. C. | C/434 | April 4, 1891 | April 5, 1891 |
| Burchett, F. J. | Wilson, Emma | C/334 | August 3, 1885 | August 5, 1885 |
| Burchett, M. G. L. | Stacy, S. H | C/166 | August 1, 1877 | August 2, 1877 |
| Burchett, Thomas | Millikin, Miss Parthena | A2/62 | January 7, 1858 | No Return |
| Burger, A. H. | Batton, Mary E. | C/100 | November 10, 1874 | November 10, 1874 |
| Burger, F. E. | Hawkins, J. I. | C/102 | December 15, 1875 | December 16, 1874 |
| Burger, Isaac | Gunter, Miss Adaline | B/38 | January 26, 1867 | No Return |
| Burger, Josephine Miss | Hodge, James L. | B/52 | September 12, 1867 | September 12, 1867 |
| Burger, M. J. Miss | Reaves, A. H. | A2/23 | January 1, 1853 | January 4, 1853 |
| Burger, Mary | Jones, Enoch | A2/31 | February 8, 1854 | February 8, 1854 |
| Burger, Pelina J. Miss | Grizzle, Richard | B/42 | February 27, 1867 | February 19, 1867 |
| Burger, R. J. | Gunter, Miss Mattie | C/454 | February 8, 1892 | February 11, 1892 |
| Burger, Rutha | Melton, John W. | A2/16 | March 11, 1852 | March 11, 1852 |
| Burger, S. | Barnes, J. A. | A2/45 | November 27, 1855 | No Return |
| Burger, S. P. Miss | Jetton, T. J. | A2/34 | July 31, 1854 | July 31, 1854 |
| Burger, Sam | Vanhooser, Nancy | E/220 | October 14, 1889 | No Return |
| Burger, Sara | Patterson, T. E. | C/312 | September 7, 1884 | September 9, 1884 |
| Burger, Sarah C. | Brown, Thomas | F/76 | December 9, 1895 | December 11, 1895 |
| Burger, Susan | Owens, Alford | C/106 | January 14, 1875 | January 14, 1875 |
| Burger, W. O. | Jones, H. J. | A2/94 | January 30, 1860 | No Return |
| Burger, W. O. | Smith, Eliza J. | C/468 | November 22, 1892 | November 24, 1892 |
| Burgett, Jane | Holt, Lee | F/62 | April 9, 1895 | April 11, 1895 |
| Burgett, Martha A. Miss | Lambert, J. E. | A2/46 | March ?, 1856 | March 2, 1856 |
| Burgner, Susan J. | Barnes, Jessee | A2/43 | November 27, 1855 | November 27, 1855 |
| Burk, C. Miss | Richerson, Franklin | A2/86 | June 11, 1859 | No Return |
| Burk, D. T. W. | Burk, Nancy | A2/119 | January 13, 1865 | January 13, 1865 |

| Groom or Bride | Groom or Bride | Book/Page | Date of License | Date of Marriage |
|---|---|---|---|---|
| Burk, Elizabeth Miss | Brandon, William | A2/51 | December 12, 1856 | No Return |
| Burk, Isabella | Gaithen, Baswell | A2/120 | February 1, 1865 | February 1, 1865 |
| Burk, Jane C. Miss | Greer, John C. | A2/17 | January 7, 1852 | January 11, 1852 |
| Burk, John | Peydan, Nancy | A2/20 | November 18, 1852 | November 18, 1852 |
| Burk, N. J. | Hailey, Miss S. A. | A2/67 | September 2, 1858 | Handed in No Return |
| Burk, Nancy | Burk, D. T. W. | A2/119 | January 13, 1865 | January 13, 1865 |
| Burk, Nancy Ann Miss | Hays, B. | A2/30 | December 21, 1853 | December 22, 1853 |
| Burk, Samuel | Todd, Minnie | C/380 | January 1, 1887 | January 2, 1887 |
| Burk, Samuel | Gaither, Emma | F/18 | September 23, 1893 | September 23, 1893 |
| Burk, Sara Miss | Hailey, Caphus C. | A2/45 | January 5, 1856 | January 5, 1856 |
| Burk, Sarah Miss | Thompson, A. | A2/63 | February 13, 1858 | No Return |
| Burk, Sarah F. | Meeks, Isaac | C/324 | January 21, 1885 | January 21, 1885 |
| Burke, Daniel | Pedon, Miss Sarah | A2/49 | August 2, 1856 | August 2, 1856 |
| Burke, G. C. | Tolbert, Miss Parlee | B/70 | September 30, 1868 | No Return |
| Burke, J. D. | Ford, Florance C. | C/344 | December 19, 1885 | No Return |
| Burke, J. R. | Todd, Mary | C/344 | December 19, 1885 | December 20, 1885 |
| Burke, N. J. | Sullivan, A. E. | A2/147 | November 10, 1866 | November 10, 1866 |
| Burkee, James | Eades, Miss Sally | A/44 | November 16, 1841 | November 17, 1841 |
| Burkes, Belle | Parker, J. L. | C/440 | July 18, 1891 | July 18, 1891 |
| Burket, James | Gilly, Miss Mary A. | A2/46 | January 17, 1856 | January 17, 1856 |
| Burket, Martha | Young, William | A2/118 | December 18, 1864 | No Return |
| Burket, Mary  Miss | Hall, James | A2/57 | August 1, 1857 | August 3, 1857 |
| Burkett, A. J. | Derryberry, Nancy Jane | A2/6 | October 19, 1850 | No Return |
| Burkett, Aud | Bogle, Dona | F/78 | December 16, 1895 | December 16, 1895 |
| Burkett, David | Ferrell, Miss Fannie | B/56 | November 27, 1867 | November 28, 1867 |
| Burkett, J. M. | Rigsby, Caroline | C/34 | August 22, 1872 | August 22, 1872 |
| Burkett, James | Elkins, Amand E. | F/120 | July 24, 1897 | July 25, 1897 |
| Burkett, Job | Richards, Miss Nancy A. | B/86 | September 16, 1869 | September 16, 1869 |
| Burkett, John | Marcum, Miss Paulina | A/121 | March 10, 1849 | March 11, 1849 |
| Burkett, M. C. | Ford, S. J. | C/72 | November 12, 1873 | November 13, 1873 |
| Burkett, Matilda Miss | Markum, Berry | A/64 | August 26, 1843 | August 26, 1843 |
| Burkett, Margrett | Porter, Solom | C/28 | May 17, 1872 | May 17, 1872 |
| Burkett, Mary | Patterson, Lee | C/260 | October 27, 1880 | No Return |
| Burkette, Joanna | Watson, E. | C/468 | November 16, 1892 | November 17, 1892 |
| Burks, H. E. | Foster, P. E. | C/234 | December 22, 1879 | December 24, 1879 |
| Burks, Mary C. | Tenpenny, M. A. | C/240 | January 22, 1880 | January 22, 1880 |
| Burks, Mary L | Earls, Larcan W. | E/391 | December 20, 1919 | |
| Burks, Richard (col.) | Gasaway, Nancy (col.) | F/166 | December 20, 1898 | December 21, 1898 |
| Burks, Richard, (col) | Gasaway, Nancy | E/350 | December 20, 1898 | |
| Burks, Roeevans | Hetherly, Luella | C/448 | October 7, 1891 | No Return |
| Burnet, Pulley | Belk, John | A/13 | May 8, 1839 | May 8, 1839 |
| Burnett, James | Moore, Liza | C/128 | December 23, 1875 | December 23, 1875 |
| Burnett, Jimmie | Lowe, John | C/164 | June 30, 1877 | July 1, 1877 |
| Burnett, M. L. F. | Burnett, S. A. | C/152 | January 4, 1877 | January 4, 1877 |
| Burnett, Matilda Miss | Flemming, Albert M. | A/39 | July 24, 1841 | July 25, 1841 |
| Burnett, Matilda | Meeks, J. W. | C/60 | July 5, 1873 | No Return |

| Groom or Bride | Groom or Bride | Book/Page | Date of License | Date of Marriage |
| --- | --- | --- | --- | --- |
| Burnett, S. A. | Davenport, Miss Sarah S. | B/98 | February 1, 18k70 | February 1, 1870 |
| Burnett, S. A. | Burnett, M. L. F. | C/152 | January 4, 1877 | January 4, 1877 |
| Burroughs, J. S. | Jones, Claudie | D/19 | | December 14, 1882 |
| Burry, Margart Miss | Tenpenny, James | A2/89 | September 17, 1859 | No Return |
| Burt, Sarah Miss | Spray, J. M. | A2/19 | August 23, 1852 | No Return |
| Busey, T. J. | Fann, Miss Mary J. | C/6 | August 9, 1871 | August 10, 1871 |
| Busey, Thomas J. | Reed, Miss Malissa C. | B/36 | January 7, 1867 | January 8, 1867 |
| Busey, William H. | Gibson, Miss Elizabeth A. | B/106 | July 20, 1870 | July 21, 1870 |
| Bush, Arnettie | Hillis, Daniel | F/60 | February 12, 1895 | February 12, 1895 |
| Bush, Amanda J. | Perry, John L. | C/168 | August 25, 1877 | August 28, 1877 |
| Bush, Barbery | Lambert, Robert | C/124 | December 6, 1875 | December 12, 1876 |
| Bush, Berry | Bryant, Miss B. L. | A2/67 | August 25, 1858 | No Return |
| Bush, Daisy | Roger, Polk | F/120 | June 9, 1897 | June 13, 1897 |
| Bush, E. J. | Williams, H. C. | C/226 | October 29, 1879 | October 30, 1879 |
| Bush, Elizabeth Miss | Ewell, John | A/96 | January 7, 1847 | January 7, 1847 |
| Bush, Emily Mariah Miss | Rodgers, William | B/58 | December 16, 1867 | December 17, 1867 |
| Bush, Grant | Cawthon, Anna | E/53 | August 3, 1888 | August 9, 1888 |
| Bush, H. L. | Hooker, Miss Elizabeth | B/58 | December 18, 1867 | December 19, 1867 |
| Bush, Harvy | Bynum, Miss Emaline | A/93 | December 1, 1846 | December 3, 1846 |
| Bush, Henry L. | Todd, Sarah J. | A2/23 | January 4, 1853 | January 6, 1853 |
| Bush, J. B. | Frances, Bula | F/82 | January 14, 1896 | January 14, 1896 |
| Bush, J. W. | Lemmons, Mary | C/168 | August 20, 1877 | September 16, 1877 |
| Bush, James L. | Gilley, Mary E. | C/234 | December 26, 1879 | December 25, 1879 |
| Bush, Jeremiah | Dereberry, Miss Elizabeth A. | A/107 | January 27, 1848 | January 27, 1848 |
| Bush, Jess. H. | Perry, Sarah J. | C/178 | November 29, 1877 | No Return |
| Bush, John H. | Spry, Nancy | C/366 | July 23, 1886 | July 25, 1886 |
| Bush, L. P. | Williams, Miss Frances | B/74 | December 12, 1868 | December 13, 1868 |
| Bush, L. P. | Patton, Mary H. | C/314 | October 9, 1884 | No Return |
| Bush, Lillie | Stacy, H. B. | F/104 | December 7, 1896 | December 10, 1896 |
| Bush, Linnie | Gilley, William | C/284 | May 28, 1883 | May 28, 1883 |
| Bush, Lucinda Miss | Cawthon, Wm. | A2/28 | October 17, 1853 | October 20, 1853 |
| Bush, M. C. Miss | Bynum, Allen | A2/28 | September 28, 1853 | September 29, 1853 |
| Bush, M. E. | Duke, J. J. | C/108 | March 3, 1875 | March 3, 1875 |
| Bush, M. E. Miss | Arnold, Harvy | B/82 | July 3, 1869 | July 4, 1869 |
| Bush, Malinda | Frasure, Robert | A2/16 | Omitted | September 14, 1851 |
| Bush, Mariah | Thompson, Allen | A2/97 | June 7, 1860 | No Return |
| Bush, Mariah | Thomas, A. | A2/103 | November 11, 1860 | No Return |
| Bush, Mary E. Miss | Ross, William S. | B/54 | October 30, 1867 | October 30, 1867 |
| Bush, Mary M. | Cowthern, Wm | C/204 | November 16, 1878 | December 26, 1878 |
| Bush, Nancy Jane | Stacy, William J. | C/426 | December 19, 1890 | December 28, 1890 |
| Bush, Pate | Lewis, Janie | C/422 | November 8, 1890 | November 9, 1890 |
| Bush, Peterson | Roberts, Manervia | C/104 | December 26, 1874 | December 27, 1874 |
| Bush, Rebecca Anne | Lamberth, Anderson | A/32 | August 26, 1840 | August 27, 1840 |
| Bush, Sallie | Wilson, John H. | C/136 | March 30, 1876 | March 30, 1876 |
| Bush, Samuel D. | Ford, Miss Lavisa H. | A2/6 | October 19, 1850 | October 20, 1850 |
| Bush, Sarah | Perry, E. | C/252 | July 31, 1880 | August 1, 1880 |

| Groom or Bride | Groom or Bride | Book/Page | Date of License | Date of Marriage |
|---|---|---|---|---|
| Bush, Sarah | Gilley, J. R. Y. | A2/91 | February 8, 1860 | No Return |
| Bush, Sarah Jane Miss | Bynum, James Ira | A/95 | December 30, 1846 | January 1, 1847 |
| Bush, Thomas | Barnes, Lula | C/442 | August 8, 1891 | No Return |
| Bush, Thomas | Duke, Mary | F/6 | April 8, 1893 | April 9, 1893 |
| Bush, Uriah | Lambirth, Mary Ann | A/15 | July 22, 1839 | July 22, 1839 |
| Bush, Uriah | Johnson, Miss Miariah | A/78 | May 6, 1845 | May 6, 1845 |
| Bush, W. H. | Smith, Miss Jennie | C/392 | June 30, 1887 | No Return |
| Bush, W. J. | Stacy, Susan A. | A2/134 | January 2, 1866 | No Return |
| Bush, Willis | Trigg, Miss Amanda | A/72 | September 18, 1844 | September 19, 1844 |
| Bush, Wm. H. | Lemmon, Sarah L. | D/8 | | December 14, 1881 |
| Bush, Z. | Todd, Miss E. J. | A2/62 | January 28, 1858 | No Return |
| Bushs, N. L. | Haley, N. J. | C/342 | December 5, 1885 | December 5, 1885 |
| Busy, Jenetta | Davis, Joshua | A/57 | December 29, 1842 | December 29, 1842 |
| Butcher, Marthy | Campbell, Isaac | A2/52 | December 27, 1856 | Return not Executed |
| Butcher, R. J. | Vinson, Malissie | F/62 | March 20, 1895 | March 21, 1895 |
| Butcher, Ruthy Miss | Hollandsworth, James F. | A2/139 | March 13, 1866 | March 15, 1866 |
| Butter, J. W. | Watson, Nancy A. | A2/83 | January 15, 1859 | No Return |
| Byfor, Josie | Brandon, Adam | C/450 | December 1, 1891 | December 2, 1891 |
| Byfor, Prilee | Markum, Wm | D/19 | | December 24, 1882 |
| Byford, C. A. | Spry, May | C/366 | September 16, 1886 | September 19, 1886 |
| Byford, E. B. | Hurst, H. H. | E/268 | July 4, 1904 | No Return |
| Byford, Elizabeth Miss | Inglis, Evan A. | A/72 | September 14, 1844 | September 17, 1844 |
| Byford, G. W. | Foster, E. A. | C/110 | March 9, 1875 | March 11, 1875 |
| Byford, J. R. | Byford, Miss Nancy E. | A2/64 | April 5, 1858 | April 7, 1858 |
| Byford, J. W. | Wilson, Cynthia A. | C/152 | January 17, 1877 | January 18, 1877 |
| Byford, James | Millikeen, Virginia | C/154 | January 20, 1877 | January 21, 1877 |
| Byford, James Hardy | Soape, Miss Elizabeth Ann | A/110 | April 13, 1848 | April 13, 1848 |
| Byford, John | Cooper, Miss Susanah | B/64 | March 2, 1868 | May 8, 1868 |
| Byford, John H. | Brown, Miss Susan Ann | A/100 | June 26, 1847 | Return Not Executed |
| Byford, L. E. Miss | Millikin, A. G. | A2/160 | June 21, 1866 | June 21, 1866 |
| Byford, Leander | Simmons, Miss Mary E. | B/60 | December 28, 1867 | December 31, 1867 |
| Byford, M. M. | Brandon, R. | A2/33 | June 29, 1854 | June 29, 1854 |
| Byford, Mary A. Miss | Pitt, Reuben | A2/43 | November 26, 1855 | November 27, 1855 |
| Byford, Mary J. Miss | Hatfield, J. W. | A/103 | October 14, 1847 | No Return |
| Byford, Matilda J. Miss | Simmons, James | B/70 | September 11, 1868 | September 12, 1868 |
| Byford, Nancy E. Miss | Byford, J. R. | A2/64 | April 5, 1858 | April 7, 1858 |
| Byford, Nora | Parker, N. J. | F/148 | April 6, 1898 | April 6, 1898 |
| Byford, Partheny O. Miss | Millikin, John | A2/74 | January 2, 1854 | January 3, 1854 |
| Byford, Thomas | Lenox, Nancy K. | A/12 | April 13, 1839 | No Return |
| Byler, Caroline | Dickins, I. F. | A2/28 | October 13, 1853 | October 16, 1853 |
| Bynnum, Sallie | Taylor, Ambus | C/208 | January 2, 1870 | January 2, 1870 |
| Bynuim, Gettie | Jernigan, W. H. | F/164 | December 22, 1898 | December 22, 1898 |
| Bynum, Allen | Bush, Miss M. C. | A2/28 | September 28, 1853 | September 29, 1853 |
| Bynum, B. I. | Tolbert, July A. | C/66 | September 3, 1873 | September 4, 1873 |
| Bynum, Elizabeth | Tolbert, L. J. | A2/134 | January 1, 1866 | January 4, 1866 |
| Bynum, Emaline Miss | Bush, Harvy | A/93 | December 1, 1846 | December 3, 1846 |

33

| Groom or Bride | Groom or Bride | Book/Page | Date of License | Date of Marriage |
|---|---|---|---|---|
| Bynum, F. G. | Jernigan, Ann | D/4 | | September 1, 1881 |
| Bynum, J. F. | Thompson, F. E. | D/10 | | December 25, 1881 |
| Bynum, James Ira | Bush, Miss Sarah Jane | A/95 | December 30, 1846 | January 1, 1847 |
| Bynum, John | King, Mary F. | D/2 | | July 31, 1881 |
| Bynum, Louisa J. Miss | Shelton, Thomas W. | B/96 | December 21, 1869 | December 21, 1869 |
| Bynum, Lucinda | McCaslin, C. E. | C/62 | July 30, 1873 | July 31, 1873 |
| Bynum, Lucinda Miss | Gilley, Jesse N. | B/90 | October 5, 1869 | No Return |
| Bynum, M. E. | Brown, J. H. | C/238 | January 15, 1880 | January 15, 1880 |
| Bynum, M. L. | Earp, G. W. | C/24 | March 6, 1872 | March 7, 1872 |
| Bynum, Martha Miss | Arrington, F. M. | A2/137 | February 5, 1866 | February 6, 1866 |
| Bynum, Mary | Johnson, John C. | C/206 | December 18, 1878 | December 22, 1878 |
| Bynum, Mary C. Miss | Williams, J. B. | B/72 | December 1, 1868 | December 2, 1868 |
| Bynum, Mary J. | Curlee, James | C/334 | August 20, 1885 | August 20, 1885 |
| Bynum, Nancy E. | Donnel, Austin | A2/119 | January 10, 1865 | January 11, 1865 |
| Bynum, Red | Hutchens, Ruth S. | C/240 | January 30, 1880 | January 30, 1880 |
| Bynum, Roxey | Stacy, Harvy | C/258 | October 14, 1880 | October 14, 1880 |
| Bynum, S. W. | Miss Jane Law | A2/80 | October 17, 1857 | October 17, 1857 |
| Bynum, William | Sagely, Miss Mary Ann | A/95 | December 30, 1846 | December 31, 1846 |
| Bynum, Wm | Stacy, Lucinda | A2/117 | November 8, 1864 | November 11, 1864 |
| Bynum, Wm. | Webber, Miss Martha L. | A2/90 | November 2, 1859 | No Return |
| Byran, Bettie | Jernigan, W. H. | E/342 | December, 22, 1898 | |
| Byres, F. B. | Preston, Jane | E/265 | January 30, 1890 | No Return |
| Byron, Miss Minnie | Sullivan, Jesse | C/404 | October 6, 1887 | No Return |
| Byrum, Nancy P. | Gilley, Jesse | C/396 | July 22, 1887 | July 24, 1887 |
| Byrn, A. B. | Bragg, Bettie | C/418 | September 16, 1890 | September 16, 1890 |
| Byrn, Eliza | Odom, John | C/222 | August 14, 1879 | August 14, 1879 |
| Byrn, John | Reddy, Miram | B/10 | June 20, 1867 | June 21, 1867 |
| Byrn, L. C. | Hardcastle, L. C. | C/258 | October 14, 1880 | October 14, 1880 |
| Byrn, Mollie | McAdoo, J. C. | C/244 | March 10, 1880 | March 10, 1880 |
| Byrn, Susan | Kenedy, H. H. | C/228 | October 1, 1879 | October 1, 1879 |
| Byrn, W. B | Miller, Rebecca J. | C/168 | August 14, 1877 | No Return |
| Byrn, Wm. | Maney, M. E. | C/370 | October 18, 1886 | October 18, 1886 |
| Byrne, James H. | McKnight, Sarah E | A/76 | February 16, 1845 | February 20, 1845 |
| Byrns, Tennessee Miss | Stephens, H. G. | B/94 | December 13, 1869 | December 15, 1869 |
| Byron, Sallie | Patton, J. A. | E/103 | November 28, 1888 | November 28, 1888 |
| Byrum, Fannie | Hill, J. W. | E/237 | December 3, 1889 | No Return |
| Byrum, Fannie | Guy, Thomas | E/242 | December 19, 1889 | December 19, 1889 |
| Byrum, Redmon | Jones, Miss Martha Jane | A/35 | November 18, 1840 | November 23, 1840 |
| Cabbage, J. F. | Long, Nancy J. | C/112 | April 23, 1875 | April 25, 1875 |
| Caffey, Sarah Jane Miss | Bowman, John F. W. | A/43 | October 28, 1841 | October 28, 1841 |
| Caffy, Daisey | Williams, C. H. | F/32 | February 15, 1894 | February 25, 1894 |
| Cagle, John | Cagle, Sallie | F/106 | December 7, 1896 | December 13, 1896 |
| Cagle, Sallie | Cagle, John | F/106 | December 7, 1896 | December 13, 1896 |
| Cagwell, Martha | Wallace, James | A/31 | July 21, 1840 | July 21, 1840 |
| Callico, Jack | McClennen, Fannie | C/152 | January 17, 1877 | No Return |
| Cambel, William | Young, Miss Dora | A2/56 | April 6, 1857 | Return not Executed |

| Groom or Bride | Groom or Bride | Book/Page | Date of License | Date of Marriage |
|---|---|---|---|---|
| Cambell, Sallie | Young, Thomas | F/30 | January 28, 1894 | January 28, 1894 |
| Campbell, A. J. | Grizzle, E. A | C/224 | September 6, 1879 | September 7, 1879 |
| Campbell, A. G. | Faiestar, Miss N. H. | A/100 | August 4, 1847 | August 4, 1847 |
| Campbell, A. J. | Grizzle, E. A. | C/224 | September 6, 1879 | September 7, 1879 |
| Campbell, Albert | Arnett, Nannie | F/72 | October 17, 1895 | November 1, 1895 |
| Campbell, Amos | Bragg, Miss Lorena | B/68 | August 27, 1868 | August 27, 1868 |
| Campbell, Amos | Morgan, Larena | B/72 | October 21, 1868 | October 22, 1868 |
| Campbell, Betsey J. | Genty, Wm. | C/82 | February 16, 1874 | February 18, 1874 |
| Campbell, Bettie Miss | Richards, I. G. | C/424 | December 17, 1890 | December 17, 1890 |
| Campbell, Cal | Brown, Sarah | C/196 | August 29, 1878 | August 29, 1878 |
| Campbell, Catherine L. | Wilson, H. W. | C/204 | November 13, 1878 | November 14, 1878 |
| Campbell, Charles T. | Hipp, Jennie | E/78 | September 18, 1888 | September 19, 1888 |
| Campbell, Dealy | Scott, John S. | C/350 | January 16, 1886 | January 17, 1886 |
| Campbell, Della | Murphey, J. K. | E/374 | October 5, 1898 | |
| Campbell, Della | Murphy, James | F/160 | November 5, 1898 | November 6, 1898 |
| Campbell, Docia | Smithson, D. C. | C/106 | January 19, 1875 | January 19, 1875 |
| Campbell, Dovey Mrs. | Grizzel, William | B/106 | August 15, 1870 | August 17, 1870 |
| Campbell, Edna | Ferrel, Richard | E/87 | October 10, 1888 | October 10, 1888 |
| Campbell, Elizbeth | Evins, Alexander | C/370 | October 1, 1886 | October 3, 1886 |
| Campbell, Ella | Davis, G. H. | F/100 | October 17, 1896 | October 18, 1896 |
| Campbell, G. L. | Ready, C. H. | F/70 | September 10, 1895 | September 11, 1895 |
| Campbell, G. R. | Spurlock, Miss Elixabeth | A2/19 | September 14, 1852 | September 14, 1852 |
| Campbell, G. W. | Smithson, Miss Lennie | F/82 | February 1, 1896 | February 2, 1896 |
| Campbell, H. U. | Moore, J. A. | C/122 | October 16, 1875 | October 21, 1875 |
| Campbell, Hallie | Laner, Lee | C/466 | October 17, 1892 | October 17, 1892 |
| Campbell, Hattie Miss | Seals, B. F. | C/454 | February 10, 1892 | February 11, 1892 |
| Campbell, Henry | Melton, Miss Cythian | A2/57 | August 29, 1857 | Return not Exectued |
| Campbell, Henry V. | McDougal, Mary | D/5 | | October 9, 1881 |
| Campbell, Ida | Parsley, Ferrell | F/126 | August 18, 1897 | August 19, 1897 |
| Campbell, Isaac | Butcher, Marthy | A2/52 | December 27, 1856 | Return not Executed |
| Campbell, J. A. | Sullivan, Lillie | F/144 | January 22, 1898 | January 23, 1898 |
| Campbell, J. C. | Pedon, Amanda | C/38 | September 13, 1872 | September 13, 1872 |
| Campbell, J. D. | Haily, Ann E. | A2/115 | July 19, 1864 | No Return |
| Campbell, J. D. | Bailey, Martha E. | A2/110 | November 10, 1863 | No Return |
| Campbell, J. D. | Mason, Mary | C/166 | August 1, 1877 | August 2, 1877 |
| Campbell, J. D. | King, Emeline | C/416 | September 13, 1890 | September 14, 1890 |
| Campbell, J. D. | Powell, N. C. | D/1 | | July 20, 1881 |
| Campbell, J. D. | Reed, Isie | F/104 | December 9, 1896 | December 10, 1896 |
| Campbell, J. E. | Rewed, Miss M. J. | F/160 | October 1, 1898 | October 2, 1898 |
| Campbell, J. H. | Tittle, Anna Lee | C/404 | October 13, 1887 | October 13, 1887 |
| Campbell, J. H. | Tittle, Anna Lee | C/404 | October 13, 1887 | October 13, 1887 |
| Campbell, J. H. | Sissom, Mary C. | C/442 | July 28, 1891 | July 29, 1891 |
| Campbell, J. R. | Tober, Ida S. | F/130 | September 11, 1897 | September 12. 1897 |
| Campbell, J. W. | Morgan, Miss Serecia E. | B/40 | January 30, 1867 | January 31, 1867 |
| Campbell, J. W. | Wheeler, Alice | C/52 | February 13, 1873 | February 13, 1873 |
| Campbell, J. W. | Tenpenny, Frances | F/10 | June 15, 1893 | June 15, 1893 |

| Groom or Bride | Groom or Bride | Book/Page | Date of License | Date of Marriage |
|---|---|---|---|---|
| Campbell, James | Gilley, Miss Sarah E. | A2/89 | September 18, 1859 | No Return |
| Campbell, Jas. A. | Harriman, J. A. | F/70 | September 29, 1895 | September 29, 1895 |
| Campbell, Jesse | Harrris, Tixie | F/12 | July 7, 1893 | July 9, 1893 |
| Campbell, John D. | Melton, Zeruna (?) | C/10 | September 30, 1871 | October 1, 1871 |
| Campbell, John D. | King, Annie | F/130 | September 16, 1897 | September 19, 1897 |
| Campbell, M. E. | Muncy, L. J. | C/322 | January 10, 1884 | January 11, 1885 |
| Campbell, Mahaly Miss | Armstrong, John | A2/57 | September 3, 1857 | August 3, 1857 |
| Campbell, Marian F. | Young, Sarah F. | C/300 | January 21, 1884 | January 31, 1884 |
| Campbell, Martha | Ferrell, William | E/71 | September 6, 1888 | September 6, 1888 |
| Campbell, Mary | Stewart, Booker | E/30 | April 20, 1888 | April 22, 1888 |
| Campbell, Mary | Alexander, E. E. | F/148 | March 19, 1898 | March 20, 1898 |
| Campbell, Mary Miss | Dobbs, John | B/46 | May 10, 1867 | May 12, 1867 |
| Campbell, Mattie | Kirby, James | E/67 | September 28, 1888 | September 30, 1888 |
| Campbell, Mattie | Kirby, James | E/84 | September 28, 1888 | September 28, 1888 |
| Campbell, Nancy Miss | Tassey, Alexander | A/92 | October 8, 1846 | No Return |
| Campbell, Nancy J. | Gann, Robt | C/318 | November 22, 1884 | November 22, 1884 |
| Campbell, Noley | Owen, J. S. | C/354 | February 23, 1886 | February 24, 1886 |
| Campbell, O. P. | Powell, Sallie | F/86 | March 11, 1896 | March 11, 1896 |
| Campbell, Paralee | Baily, Vinson | C/42 | October 19, 1872 | October 20, 1872 |
| Campbell, R. C. | Covington, Pearle | C/472 | December 22, 1892 | December 22, 1892 |
| Campbell, Rhoda | Vandergriff, W. J. | A2/132 | November 23, 1865 | November 23, 1865 |
| Campbell, Sarah | Evans, Alexander | C/418 | September 15, 1890 | September 15, 1890 |
| Campbell, Sarah Miss | Melton, E. R. | B/48 | July 31, 1867 | August 1, 1867 |
| Campbell, Susan Miss | Vandergriff, Marion | A2/87 | July 16, 1859 | No Reutrn |
| Campbell, T. A. | Duggin, Vella | F/8 | May 6, 1893 | May 7, 1893 |
| Campbell, T. C. | Daniel, W. R. | F/28 | December 28, 1893 | December 31, 1893 |
| Campbell, T. D. | Ferrell, J. T. | F/14 | August 2, 1893 | August 24, 1893 |
| Campbell, Thomas | Moon, Mrs. Nancy | A2/8 | December 19, 1850 | December 20, 1850 |
| Campbell, Thomas | Armstrong, Mrs. Pernina S. | A2/11 | February 17, 1851 | February 18, 1851 |
| Campbell, Thos | Perry, Miss Jennie | B/112 | October 1, 1870 | October 2, 1870 |
| Campbell, Vincent | Pitman, Sarah Ann | A2/109 | September 26, 1863 | Solemnized, No date |
| Campbell, W. D. | Webber, Polley | C/14 | November 27, 1871 | November 27, 1871 |
| Campbell, W. F. | Ferrell, Sarah | F/6 | March 14, 1893 | March 15, 1893 |
| Campbell, W. G. | Freece, Mary F. | C/338 | October 14, 1885 | October 14, 1885 |
| Campbell, W. H. | Young, Emma L. | F/48 | November 5, 1894 | No Return |
| Campbell, W. R. | Weedon, Miss Jo | B/124 | January 24, 1871 | January 25, 1871 |
| Campbell, W. T. | Lafevers, Mamie | F/142 | December 26, 1897 | December 26, 1897 |
| Campbell, Wm | Patterson, Miss Susan | A2/30 | December 24, 1853 | No Return |
| Campbell, Wm | Gilley, Terisian | A2/95 | April 14, 1860 | No Return |
| Campell, Elma Miss | Ring, Layfayett | A2/22 | December 22, 1852 | December 23, 1852 |
| Can, Maggie | Miller, John | F/140 | December 22, 1897 | December 23, 1897 |
| Canes, A. B. | Davis, Miss Elizabeth | A2/68 | October 19, 1858 | October 20, 1858 |
| Canes, Wm. L. | Wilson, Mattie J. | C/352 | February 15, 1886 | February 15, 1886 |
| Cannahan, N. C. | Gaither, C. G. F. | C/192 | June 20, 1878 | June 20, 1878 |
| Cannon, Henry | Taylor, Agness | A/3 | May 15, 1838 | May 15, 1838 |
| Cannon, Rayford | Hillis, Miss Elizabeth Jane | A/64 | August 17, 1843 | August 19, 1843 |

| Groom or Bride | Groom or Bride | Book/Page | Date of License | Date of Marriage |
|---|---|---|---|---|
| Cantrell, Agness | Evans, J. W. | C/424 | December 3, 1890 | December 4, 1890 |
| Cantrell, Bertha | Roberts, J. B. | F/32 | February 20, 1894 | February 25, 1894 |
| Cantrell, Easter Miss | Parker, Thomas | A/119 | January 4, 1849 | January 4, 1849 |
| Cantrell, Elizabeth Miss | Mullins, William S. | A/118 | December 7, 1848 | December 7, 1848 |
| Cantrell, Issabella Miss | Blancet, Calvin | A/85 | December 13, 1845 | December 14, 1845 |
| Cantrell, James | Hanons, Miss Elizabeth | A2/13 | December 31, 1851 | December 31, 1851 |
| Cantrell, James W. | Summar, Miss Martha | B/58 | December 21, 1867 | December 28, 1867 |
| Cantrell, Janette Miss | Mullins, Henry B. | A/97 | February 16, 1847 | February 16, 1847 |
| Cantrell, Lucinda Miss | Arnold, William | A2/50 | August 30, 1856 | August 30, 1856 |
| Cantrell, Mary | Walker, J. T. | F/90 | July 15, 1896 | July 15, 1896 |
| Cantrell, Mary J. | Murphy, Robt | D/20 | | January 14, 1883 |
| Cantrell, Nora Bell | Spicer, William | C/416 | September 10, 1890 | No Date |
| Cantrell, P. P. | Patterson, O. E. | C/80 | January 26, 1874 | January 26, 1874 |
| Cantrell, Roda | Merrimon, Thomas | B/88 | September 29, 1869 | September 29, 1869 |
| Cantrell, Sarah (col.) | Higgins, Alex (col.) | F/142 | January 1, 1898 | January 3, 1898 |
| Cantrell, Stephen | Mullins, Miss Lucinda | A/87 | March 19, 1846 | March 19, 1846 |
| Cantrell, Thomas | Gaither, Ann | A/23 | January 20, 1840 | January 21, 1840 |
| Cantrell, Watson | Gunter, Mattie | F/152 | July 16, 1898 | July 17, 1898 |
| Cantrell, Will (col.) | Odom, Myrtle (col.) | F/144 | January 24, 1898 | January 24, 1898 |
| Capps, Ann Miss | Neely, Isaacah | A/69 | April 20, 1844 | April 24, 1844 |
| Capps, Elizabeth | Merriman, Ezekiel | A/12 | March 23, 1839 | March 24, 1839 |
| Capps, Ruthy | Maness, George W. | A2/15 | February 8, 1852 | February 8, 1852 |
| Capshaw, H. L. W. | Fletcher, Miss Louisa | A2/49 | July 17, 1856 | July ??, 1856 |
| Capshaw, J. J. C. | Rigsby, Miss Malinda C. | B/104 | July 12, 1870 | |
| Capshaw, Truly | Heriman, Josiah | A/13 | April 12, 1838 | April 12, 1838 |
| Caric, T. J. | Jimerson, Miss E. | A2/57 | August 6, 1857 | August 6, 1857 |
| Carick, N. E. | Elrod, J. M. | C/294 | October 27, 1883 | October 31, 1883 |
| Carick, Thomas A. | Shirley, Manervey | C/290 | September 1, 1883 | September 4, 1883 |
| Carmichael, Anna E. Miss | Miller, Wm. H. | B/98 | February 3, 1870 | February 3, 1870 |
| Carmichael, Malissa J. | Spurlock, Joseph | A2/123 | May 3, 1865 | May 4, 1865 |
| Carmichael, William G. | West, Miss Malissa J. | A2/6 | June 4, 1850 | June 4, 1850 |
| Carmon, Samuel | Middleton, Patience | A/26 | March 28, 1840 | March 28, 1840 |
| Carnahan, A. L. | Gilley, Ella | F/86 | March 11, 1896 | March 11, 1896 |
| Carnahan, Andy | Gaither, M. E. | C/198 | September 5, 1878 | September 5, 1878 |
| Carnahan, J. C. | Bowen, M. A. | F/68 | September 14, 1895 | September 15, 1895 |
| Carnahan, James M. | Elledge, Roxex | C/350 | January 23, 1884 | January 24, 1886 |
| Carnahan, Jane R. | Hoover, Wm. | C/32 | July 22, 1872 | July 22, 1872 |
| Carnahan, John H. | Teague, Miss Sarah A. | B/74 | December 2, 1868 | December 3, 1868 |
| Carnahan, Loe | Knox, J. B. | C/376 | December 20, 1886 | December 22, 1886 |
| Carnahan, Sallie E. | Paschal, N. T. | C/58 | May 14, 1873 | No Return |
| Carnes, E. M. | McBroom, Thomas | C/142 | August 10, 1876 | August 10, 1876 |
| Carnes, J. E. | Neely, Nanie | C/352 | February 8, 1886 | April 26, 1886 |
| Carney, Granville | Alexander, Cresia | E/130 | January 29, 1889 | January 31, 1889 |
| Caroll, Charlotte Miss | Stephens, Simeon D. | A/122 | December 7, 1848 | December 7, 1848 |
| Carr, Allice | Miller, George | F/126 | August 22, 1897 | August 22, 1897 |
| Carr, Ann | Jennings, Jim | C/248 | July 1, 1880 | July 1, 1880 |

| Groom or Bride | Groom or Bride | Book/Page | Date of License | Date of Marriage |
|---|---|---|---|---|
| Carr, Isabella M. | Davis, G. Y. | C/234 | December 26, 1879 | January 1, 1880 |
| Carr, O. C. | Wilson, Elizabeth | D/6 | | October 27, 1881 |
| Carrack, T. F. | Mitchell, A. L. | A2/122 | March 11, 1865 | No Return |
| Carrell | Hughs, L. | A2/20 | November 4, 1852 | November 4, 1852 |
| Carric, Thomas A. | Hollis, Elsie | F/150 | June 11, 1898 | No Return |
| Carrick, A. J. | Elam, M. A. | C/190 | April 1, 1878 | April 4, 1878 |
| Carrick, Eliza | Scurlock, H. N. | C/430 | January 26, 1891 | January 19, 1891 |
| Carrick, Esther C. Miss | Gooding, Richard | B/34 | December 22, 1866 | December 27, 1866 |
| Carrick, Florence | Hill, James | F/158 | September 30, 1898 | October 2, 1898 |
| Carrick, James | King, Nancy | D/7 | | December 8, 1881 |
| Carrick, James T. | Young, Mary | F/10 | May 15, 1893 | May 16, 1893 |
| Carrick, Joseph N. | Young, Miss E. J. | A2/82 | September 9, 1858 | September 8, 1858 |
| Carrick, Mary E. Miss | Creson, James | B/36 | January 7, 1867 | January 7, 1867 |
| Carrick, Nancy A. | Dickson, T. F. | D/15 | | September 14, 1882 |
| Carrick, Sarah A. | Sissom, Thomas | C/80 | January 19, 1874 | January 25, 1874 |
| Carrick, Sarah E. | Allen, James L. | A2/132 | November 16, 1865 | November 16, 1865 |
| Carrick, Smith | More, Fannie | F/28 | December 28, 1893 | December 28, 1893 |
| Carrick, T. A. | Young, Miss Sarah F. | B/72 | November 13, 1868 | November 14, 1868 |
| Carrick, Thomas | Hill, Eliza | C/42 | October 19, 1872 | October 20, 1872 |
| Carrick, Thomas A. | Miller, Rachel | F/154 | August 16, 1898 | August 18, 1898 |
| Carrick, Thomas M. | Young, Nicy C. | C/252 | August 2, 1880 | August 2, 1880 |
| Carrol, John F. | Summers, Emma D. | C/432 | March 26, 1891 | No Return |
| Carrol, Willis F. | Barrett, Miss Elizabeth | A/35 | November 11, 1840 | November 12, 1840 |
| Carroll, Martha | Milligan, Joel | C/192 | June 17, 1878 | June 17, 1878 |
| Carson, Green | McGill, Mary A. | C/132 | February 1, 1876 | March 19, 1876 |
| Carson, John | Ferrell, Hattie | C/228 | October 20, 1879 | January 27, 1880 |
| Carson, Mary Ann Miss | Cooper, James | A/98 | February 24, 1847 | February 28, 1847 |
| Carter, Amanda J. Miss | Hogwood, James R. | B/70 | September 23, 1868 | September 24, 1868 |
| Carter, Bettie | Harris, B. D. | F/28 | January 4, 1894 | January 4, 1894 |
| Carter, D. R. | McKnight, Miss Nannie A. | B/70 | September 16, 1868 | September 16, 1868 |
| Carter, D. R. | McKnight, M. H. | C/302 | January 22, 1884 | January 23, 1884 |
| Carter, Elizabeth Miss | Wilcher, J. A. | B/62 | February 13, 1868 | February 13, 1868 |
| Carter, Emma | Sullens, J. D. | F/60 | March 14, 1895 | No Return |
| Carter, J. N. | Alexander, Ada | D/12 | | February 23, 1882 |
| Carter, J. T. | McBrum, M. A. | C/108 | February 10, 1875 | February 11, 1875 |
| Carter, James | Jones, Miss Katharine | A/91 | September 11, 1846 | September 11, 1846 |
| Carter, James | Sullivan, L. C. | A2/116 | October 4, 1864 | October 6, 1864 |
| Carter, James R. | McBroom, Miss Bettie | B/52 | September 12, 1867 | September 12, 1867 |
| Carter, Jess M. | Todd, Mary | F/134 | October 2, 1897 | October 3, 1897 |
| Carter, Jesse | Bragg, Miss Lavica | A/103 | October 15, 1847 | October 5, 1847 |
| Carter, Luiza F. Miss | Edward, J. W. | A2/86 | June 6, 1859 | No Return |
| Carter, M. L. | McKnight, E. A. | C/264 | December 23, 1880 | December 23, 1880 |
| Carter, Mahaly | Jones, Aaron F. | A2/18 | August 5, 1852 | August 5, 1852 |
| Carter, Mattie J. | Haywood, John F. | C/324 | January 14, 1885 | January 14, 1885 |
| Carter, Miss Nannie | Rudy, Wm. | F/150 | June 12, 1898 | June 12, 1898 |
| Carter, Nettie | Ready, F. M. | C/442 | August 5, 1891 | August 5, 1891 |

| Groom or Bride | Groom or Bride | Book/Page | Date of License | Date of Marriage |
|---|---|---|---|---|
| Carter, R. R. | Youree, W. E. | C/72 | November 13, 1873 | November 13, 1873 |
| Carter, R. A. | Dowing, Bettie | C/204 | November 13, 1878 | November 13, 1878 |
| Carter, Roda L. | Williams, Freelin | C/184 | January 12, 1878 | January 13, 1878 |
| Carter, S. E. | Darnel, M. A. | C/270 | January 18, 1881 | January 20, 1881 |
| Carter, Sallie | Breis, James F. | D/12 | | February 23, 1882 |
| Carter, Sarah E. | Hagwood, H. B. | C/78 | December 24, 1873 | December 25, 1873 |
| Carter, Thos. | Smith, Lizzie | C/68 | October 8, 1873 | October 9, 1873 |
| Carter, Vicey | Turney, J. F. | C/292 | September 15, 1883 | September 18, 1883 |
| Carter, W. A. | Ramsey, J. C. | C/164 | July 24, 1877 | July 24, 1877 |
| Carter, W. P. | McNight, Miss Mary F. | B/128 | March 16, 1871 | March 16, 1871 |
| Caruther, S. A. E. Miss | Gaither, W. P. | A2/78 | March 3, 1856 | March 4, 1856 |
| Caruthers, John | Reed, Miss Jane | B/54 | November 16, 1867 | November 19, 1867 |
| Caruthers, May E. | Jarrett, Isaac L. | A2/33 | June 21, 1854 | June 22, 1854 |
| Caruthers, R. J. Miss | Oglesby, J. H. | B/78 | February 24, 1869 | February 25, 1869 |
| Cash, W. A. | Alexander, Florance | C/198 | September 3, 1878 | September 4, 1878 |
| Catcart, Bascomb | Gray, Matte | F/12 | June 28, 1893 | June 28, 1893 |
| Cates, A. B. | Cates, Miss J. E. | B/82 | July 17, 1869 | July 18, 1869 |
| Cates, A. B. Miss | Brandon, A. G. | B/102 | May 18, 1870 | May 19, 1870 |
| Cates, A. H. | Cates, W. D. | C/164 | July 28, 1877 | July 29, 1877 |
| Cates, A. W. | Barratt, Mary J. | A2/108 | May 20, 1863 | May 28, 1863 |
| Cates, Caroline | Hollis, J. E. | A2/117 | November 14, 1864 | November 14, 1864 |
| Cates, Florence | Parker, R. S. | E/205 | September 3, 1889 | September 4, 1889 |
| Cates, J. A. Miss | Taylor, W. H. | C/228 | October 4, 1879 | October 4, 1879 |
| Cates, J. E. Miss | Cates, A. B. | B/82 | July 17, 1869 | July 18, 1869 |
| Cates, James | Taylor, Emma | C/164 | July 1, 1877 | July 1, 1877 |
| Cates, Joseph M. D. | Taylor, Miss Mary Jane | A/113 | September 5, 1848 | September 5, 1848 |
| Cates, M. E. | Cates, W. J. | C/50 | January 19, 1873 | January 19, 1873 |
| Cates, Mary Miss | Taylor, W. N. | B/84 | August 26, 1869 | August 26, 1869 |
| Cates, Mollie | McMahan, T. V. | F/102 | November 24, 1896 | November 25, 1896 |
| Cates, W. D. | Cates, A. H. | C/164 | July 28, 1877 | July 29, 1877 |
| Cates, W. J. | Cates, M. E | C/50 | January 19, 1873 | January 19, 1873 |
| Cathcart, Ada | Grizzle, Elze | C/270 | January 24, 1881 | January 26, 1881 |
| Cathcart, W. A. | Rushing, Miss Martha | B/124 | January 11, 1871 | No Return |
| Catherine, Miss Annie | Simmons, Willey | F/58 | February 3, 1895 | February 3, 1895 |
| Cathey, Alice Miss | Mingle, William J. | A2/11 | February 10, 1851 | February 10, 1851 |
| Cathey, Jane Rutherford | Faulkenbery, John | A/18 | October 23, 1839 | October 27, 1839 |
| Cathey, Lucy Miss | Finley, Thomas | A/98 | April 10, 1847 | April 10, 1847 |
| Cathey, Mary | Mullins, Dosune | A/25 | February 26, 1840 | February 16, 1840 |
| Cathey, Robert | Standly, Angaline | A/130 | January 9, 1850 | January 9, 1850 |
| Cathy, E. W. | Owen, William B. | A/27 | April 5,1840 | April 5,1840 |
| Cathy, Milly Miss | Barrett, John | A2/48 | May 10, 1856 | May 10, 1856 |
| Cathy, Sarah S. Miss | Thompson, Wm. | A2/50 | October 10, 1856 | October 10, 1856 |
| Cathy, William C. | Finley, Miss Nancy | A/102 | September 26, 1847 | September 26, 1847 |
| Cawthan, David | Decke, Miss Matilda C. | A2/50 | August 29, 1856 | No Return |
| Cawthan, David | McBride, Martha | C/332 | July 11, 1885 | July 11, 1885 |
| Cawthan, Sarah | Haithcock, James | D/5 | | October 9, 1881 |

| Groom or Bride | Groom or Bride | Book/Page | Date of License | Date of Marriage |
|---|---|---|---|---|
| Cawthen, Sarah | Herrell, E. F. | C/254 | August 18, 1880 | August 18, 1880 |
| Cawthen, Sarah | Lemmons, John W. | C/258 | October 12, 1880 | October 14, 1880 |
| Cawthers, Mahaley | Knapper, John | C/214 | March 1, 1879 | March 2, 1879 |
| Cawthon, Adaline | Parker, John | F/86 | March 11, 1896 | March 13, 1896 |
| Cawthon, Anna | Bush, Grant | E/53 | August 3, 1888 | August 9, 1888 |
| Cawthon, Burt | Williams, Mary M. | C/428 | January 5, 1891 | January 18, 1891 |
| Cawthon, C. R. | Jernigan, W. H. | E/193 | July 25, 1889 | No Return |
| Cawthon, E. M. J. | Reed, J. B. | C/84 | March 17, 1874 | March 17, 1874 |
| Cawthon, Harvey | Daughtery, Alsey A. | C/26 | May 6, 1872 | May 6, 1872 |
| Cawthon, Helen Miss | Gilley, James | C/388 | May 4, 1887 | No Return |
| Cawthon, Hyram | Williams, Julia | F/14 | August 7, 1893 | August 27, 1893 |
| Cawthon, J. B. | Gilley, Emma | C/446 | September 30, 1891 | October 1, 1891 |
| Cawthon, Mary Miss | McCullar, Samuel | B/112 | October 7, 1870 | October 18, 1870 |
| Cawthon, Mollie | Talbert, J. C | C/314 | October 18, 1884 | October 26, 1884 |
| Cawthon, N. E | Stacy, J. A. J. | C/104 | January 4, 1875 | January 8, 1875 |
| Cawthon, Parlee | Lemmons, H. B. | C/354 | March 6, 1886 | No Return |
| Cawthon, W. M. | Woods, Newton | C/364 | August 18, 1886 | September 2, 1886 |
| Cawthon, Wm. | Bush, Miss Lucinda | A2/28 | October 17, 1853 | October 20, 1853 |
| Cawthone, A. J. | Sissom, Bettie | D/19 | | December 28, 1882 |
| Cawthorn, Amanda | Simmons, Adam | F/86 | March 4, 1896 | March 5, 1896 |
| Cawthorn, C. R. Miss | Jernigan, W. H. | C/412 | July 25, 1889 | July 25, 1889 |
| Cawthorn, Novella | Collens, C. C. | F/94 | September 7, 1896 | September 11, 1896 |
| Chaffen, Geo | Miller, Annica | C/134 | February 25, 1876 | No Return |
| Chambers, Jacob | Avent, Miss Logie | C/388 | May 14, 1887 | No Return |
| Chambers, Jakes | Hancock, Mary | C/144 | September 28, 1876 | September 29, 1876 |
| Chambers, Manerva | Hill, Gilbert | B/18 | July 11, 1870 | July 11, 1870 |
| Chambers, Sam | Hancock, Elizabeth | C/42 | October 16, 1872 | October 17, 1872 |
| Chambly, David | Hancock, Rebecca F. | A2/120 | January 23, 1865 | January 24, 1865 |
| Chapell, T. A. Miss | Jetton, Granville | A2/38 | December 30, 1854 | January 4, 1855 |
| Chapin, Lawyer | Ivy, Miss Amanda | C/386 | April 2, 1887 | April 3, 1887 |
| Chapman, E. P. | Graham, Miss D. | A2/96 | May 5, 1860 | May 5, 1860 |
| Cherry, Elizabeth Miss | Coop, John M. | A2/69 | October 26, 1858 | October 28, 1858 |
| Cherry, Emaline Miss | Sherrril, John A. | A2/76 | September 20, 1855 | September 20, 1855 |
| Cherry, Margaret Miss | Simpson, John A. | A/83 | September 11, 1845 | September 12, 1845 |
| Cherry, Martha Miss | Parker, John | A/36 | February 25, 1841 | February 25, 1841 |
| Cherry, Milley Miss | Pealer, Page | A/90 | July 28, 1846 | July 30, 1846 |
| Childress, Stephen | Mitchel, Jane | A/56 | November 16, 1842 | November 17, 1842 |
| Childress, Stephen P. | Standly, Miss Elizabeth | A/74 | October 17, 1844 | October 17, 1844 |
| Chumbey, Pleasant | Oconner, Caroline | A2/82 | March 1, 1859 | March 3, 1858 |
| Chumley, Sarah Miss | Evans, Charles E. | A2/39 | January 4, 1855 | January 4, 1855 |
| Chumly, Caroline | Tally, Richard | A2/105 | October 6, 1862 | October 7, 1862 |
| Church, Elizabeth | Philips, Benjamin H. F. | A/54 | September 24, 1842 | September 24, 1842 |
| Church, Franklin | Thompson, Miss Caroline | A/109 | March 21, 1848 | March 21, 1848 |
| Cinly, Dovy Miss | Walls, Daniel | A2/90 | November 12, 1859 | No Return |
| Clar, Emma | Hayes, Joce (col.) | E/118 | December 24, 1888 | December 24, 1888 |
| Clark, A. E. (col.) | Lyon, D. S. (col.) | D/17 | | October 23, 1882 |

| Groom or Bride | Groom or Bride | Book/Page | Date of License | Date of Marriage |
|---|---|---|---|---|
| Clark, Annie E. | Smithson, Albert | F/18 | September 23, 1893 | September 23, 1893 |
| Clark, Eliza J. | Mason, T. P. | C/108 | February 19, 1875 | February 21, 1875 |
| Clark, Joseph M. | Long, Miss Hanah P. | B/44 | April 6, 1867 | April 7, 1867 |
| Clark, Mary | Baird, Henry | B/10 | February 22, 1867 | February 22, 1867 |
| Clark, Mary C. | Prater, P. T. | C/434 | April 6, 1891 | April 7, 1891 |
| Clark, Ortime | Gowen, Laborn | A2/40 | July 18, 1855 | Returns Missing |
| Clark, Tildy | Bryson, Charles | F/56 | January 10, 1895 | January 10, 1895 |
| Clark, W. F. | Patton, S. J. | D/14 | | July 27, 1882 |
| Clark, W. J. | Peeler, Mary A. | C/66 | September 20, 1873 | September 21, 1873 |
| Classie Woodley | Woods, George | B/16 | August 20, 1869 | August 20, 1869 |
| Clay, Henry | Fugett, Frances | B/14 | June 12, 1868 | June 13, 1868 |
| Clements, Elizabeth Miss | Price, William | A/75 | November 19, 1844 | November 19, 1844 |
| Clements, Martha Jane Miss | Gullett, Samuel | A/64 | July 25, 1843 | July 25, 1843 |
| Clements, Meeky H. Miss | Craft, Joseph H. | A/89 | June 27, 1846 | No Return |
| Clemments, Sarah | Laseter, Hardy | A/7 | October 3, 1838 | October 3, 1838 |
| Clemmets, Permelia Ann Miss | Lord, Mitchel | A/34 | October 15, 1840 | October 15, 1840 |
| Clendenen, Paul | Espey, Sarah L. | C/10 | September 18, 1871 | September 21, 1871 |
| Clendennan, P. C. | Swanger, Tilda | C/450 | November 24, 1891 | November 24, 1891 |
| Clendennen, Robert W. | Allen, Miss Rebeca | A/122 | June 4, 1849 | June 6, 1849 |
| Clendin, Fatt | Young, Eliza J. | F/70 | September 6, 1895 | September 6, 1895 |
| Cleveland, Mary E. Miss | Bogles, Mathew S. | A2/12 | October 11, 1851 | October 12, 1851 |
| Clifford, John H. | Hayes, Miss Mary M. | B/52 | September 8, 1867 | September 13, 1867 |
| Clifford, L. S. Miss | Hayes, W. M. | B/46 | June 5, 1867 | June 6, 1867 |
| Clore, Nancy J. Miss | Wilcher, William | A/38 | May 14, 1841 | May 16, 1841 |
| Coarcy, Elizabeth | Haley, Eli | F/96 | September 18, 1896 | September 29, 1896 |
| Cobert, Valentine | Hargis, Lidia | A/14 | June 1, 1839 | June 1, 1839 |
| Cock, John | Wood, Miss Nancy Ann | A2/37 | December 20, 1854 | December 21, 1854 |
| Coleman, Ann E. Miss | Brown, C. C. | B/76 | January 21, 1869 | January 21, 1869 |
| Coleman, Barbary | Harvey, Francis M. | A2/132 | November 27, 1865 | November 29, 1865 |
| Coleman, Franklin | Thompson, Miss Sarah C. | A/33 | September 30, 1840 | October 1, 1840 |
| Coleman, Hattie Miss | Bell, W. E. | C/386 | March 10, 1887 | March 10, 1887 |
| Coleman, Levina | Bennett, C. O. | C/38 | September 12, 1872 | September 12, 1872 |
| Coleman, Mary Miss | Earvin, John W. | B/40 | February 19, 1867 | February 19, 1867 |
| Coleman, Mattie | Dillons, Z. T. | C/92 | June 28, 1874 | June 28, 1874 |
| Coleman, N. M. | Miller, Flora C. | D/9 | | December 22, 1881 |
| Collans, M. J. | Evans, John | C/252 | August 11, 1880 | August 11, 1880 |
| Collens, C. C. | Cawthorn, Novella | F/94 | September 7, 1896 | September 11, 1896 |
| Collins, A. R. Miss | Womack, Thomas J. | B/110 | September 14, 1870 | September 15, 1870 |
| Collins, Edna | Merriman, Alek | F/46 | October 20, 1894 | October 21, 1894 |
| Collins, F. M. | Prater, Miss Dona | C/382 | January 15, 1887 | January 16, 1887 |
| Collins, Flora | Elkins, Silas | F/158 | September 29, 1898 | September 29, 1898 |
| Collins, Frances | Davanport, George | A2/111 | January 21, 1864 | January 29, 1864 |
| Collins, Frances | Watson, Nancy A. | C/166 | August 8, 1877 | August 9, 1877 |
| Collins, G. W. | Ranson, S. H. | D/22 | | January 4, 1883 |
| Collins, Jeremiah | Keaton, Mary P. | A2/125 | August 6, 1865 | August 6, 1865 |
| Collins, Lavina Miss | Gann, M. C. | B/32 | November 17, 1866 | November 18, 1866 |

| Groom or Bride | Groom or Bride | Book/Page | Date of License | Date of Marriage |
|---|---|---|---|---|
| Collins, M. M. | McKnight, Elim | A2/33 | May 18, 1854 | May 18, 1854 |
| Collins, Mary Miss | Perry, Edmond | A2/62 | January 31, 1858 | January 31, 1858 |
| Collins, Nora | Prater, William E. | F/2 | February 2, 1893 | February 4, 1893 |
| Collins, Sarah | Ashford, Polk | A2/130 | October 19, 1865 | October 20, 1865 |
| Collins, Tennessee Miss | Prater, Moses | C/384 | February 12, 1887 | February 13, 1887 |
| Collins, William | Milligan, Julie A. | C/16 | December 15, 1871 | December 17, 1871 |
| Collins, Wm. | Deberry, Margarette | C/416 | September 6, 1890 | September 8, 1890 |
| Colvart, Lena | Aread, S. H. | C/464 | September 20, 1892 | September 2, 1892 |
| Colvert, James L. | Mathews, Miss Johanna E. | A/88 | April 1, 1846 | April 1, 1846 |
| Colvert, William A. | Johnson, Miss Elizabeth M. | A/80 | July 10, 1845 | July 10, 1845 |
| Colvert, William A. | Johnson, Miss Elizabeth M. | A/81 | July 10, 1845 | July 10, 1845 |
| Colwell, Andrew J. | Whit, Miss Martha Anne | A/31 | July 22, 1840 | July 22, 1840 |
| Colwell, Nancy Miss | Whitt, Jonathan | A/64 | August 4, 1843 | August 7, 1843 |
| Combs, J. B. | Summare, Miss Rosa | F/174 | April 22, 1899 | April 23, 1899 |
| Comer, James M. | Hendrickson, Miss Elizabeth | A2/4 | August 10, 1850 | August 15, 1850 |
| Comer, Lon | Culwell, Mary | F/64 | July 7, 1895 | July 8, 1895 |
| Conley, A. J. | Bailey, Miss Mary J. | B/82 | July 17, 1869 | July 17, 1869 |
| Conley, Emley T. | Alexander, W. T. | C/22 | February 1, 1872 | February 1, 1872 |
| Conley, George W. | Bewrey, Miss Elizabeth | A2/17 | May 20, 1852 | May 20, 1852 |
| Conley, Isah | Sullins, Matilda | A2/108 | September 2, 1863 | No Return |
| Conley, James G. | Walls, Miss Caroline | A/33 | October 6, 1840 | October 6, 1840 |
| Conley, John | Kersey, Mary J. | A2/129 | September 21, 1865 | September 21, 1865 |
| Conley, N. C. | Sullins, Miss V. A. | B/82 | May 21, 1869 | May 21, 1869 |
| Conley, Thomas | Knox, Ada | F/104 | December 1, 1896 | December 2, 1896 |
| Conley, Zachariah | Finley, Miss Margaret P. | B/90 | October 18, 1869 | October 18, 1869 |
| Conn, Alley | Martin, Lewis G. | A/11 | March 4, 1839 | March 4, 1839 |
| Connelly, Elizabeth | Walls, Daniel | A/129 | December 6, 1849 | December 6, 1849 |
| Conner, William O. | Rogers, Mrs. Leanah | A/112 | July 27, 1848 | July 27, 1848 |
| Conoley, George E. | Pelham, John | E/8 | January 21, 1888 | January 22, 1888 |
| Conty, Martha Miss | Fowler, Burrell | A2/37 | November 15, 1854 | November 15, 1854 |
| Cook, Charlotte | Baxter, Richard | A2/130 | October 5, 1865 | October 5, 1865 |
| Cook, Elizabeth Ann Miss | Willson, Andrew | A2/39 | March 29, 1855 | March 29, 1855 |
| Cook, Elizabeth S. Miss | Mitchell, Isaac S. | A2/61 | December 31, 1857 | December 31, 1857 |
| Cook, J. W. | Gooding, Miss Emeline | A2/42 | November 27, 1855 | December 2, 1855 |
| Cook, John W. | Lea, Mat | A2/104 | November 17, 1860 | November 17, 1860 |
| Cook, Manerva Miss | Jones, John | A/132 | January 19, 1850 | January 19, 1850 |
| Cook, Martha R. Miss | Stephens, James H. | B/98 | January 13, 1870 | January 13, 1870 |
| Cook, Mary | Gunter, C. Y. | C/60 | June 28, 1873 | June 29, 1873 |
| Cook, Nancey H. Miss | Tenpenny, Richard | C/8 | August 31, 1871 | August 31, 1871 |
| Cook, Samuel | Warren, Miss Rebecca J. | A2/90 | November 15, 1859 | Executed No Date |
| Cook, Stephen | Alexander, Miss Sarah E. | A/94 | December 22, 1846 | December 23, 1846 |
| Cook, Stephen | Todd, Sallie | C/282 | May 22, 1883 | May 22, 1883 |
| Cook, T. | Bell, Mary W. | C/156 | February 23, 1877 | February 23, 1877 |
| Cook, William | Todd, Miss Minnie | C/394 | July 13, 1887 | July 13, 1887 |
| Coop, John M. | Cherry, Miss Elizabeth | | October 26, 1858 | October 28, 1858 |
| Cooper, A. A. | Finley, Tennie | C/348 | January 8, 1886 | No Return |

| Groom or Bride | Groom or Bride | Book/Page | Date of License | Date of Marriage |
|---|---|---|---|---|
| Cooper, A. D. | Bryson, Miss Fatomy | A2/89 | October 6, 1859 | No Return |
| Cooper, A. H. | Odom, Jetter | E/166 | April 1, 1889 | No Return |
| Cooper, Abram | Bogle, Margret | A/22 | November 4, 1839 | November 8, 1839 |
| Cooper, Alaminta | Bonds, Richard J. | A/55 | October 13, 1842 | October 14, 1842 |
| Cooper, Amandy | Bowley, Y. | C/248 | May 29, 1880 | May 29, 1880 |
| Cooper, Anna | Ford, J. P. | A2/119 | January 12, 1865 | January 27, 1865 |
| Cooper, Berry | Young, Miss Charity | A/132 | February 23, 1850 | February 23, 1850 |
| Cooper, Betty | McCaslin, Logan | A2/102 | September 12, 1860 | September ?, 1860 |
| Cooper, Branchford | Raker, Miss Ella | F/66 | August 12, 1895 | No Return |
| Cooper, Christopher | Davenport, Miss Harriet M. | A/98 | March 10, 1847 | March 11, 1847 |
| Cooper, D. T. | Mingle, Taylor | C/430 | January 31, 1891 | February 1, 1891 |
| Cooper, Emeline | Gains, J. B. | A2/91 | February 1, 1860 | No Return |
| Cooper, Emma | Fann, J. F. | C/440 | July 23, 1891 | July 23, 1891 |
| Cooper, G. W. | Ford, Miss Harrette | A2/23 | January 13, 1853 | January 13, 1853 |
| Cooper, H. J. | Layman, Miss Nancy | A2/41 | September 18, 1855 | September 18, 1855 |
| Cooper, Hollis | Espey, Miss Jemima | A2/90 | October 26, 1859 | No Return |
| Cooper, Isaiah | Sissom, Miss Delila C. | B/42 | March 14, 1867 | March 14, 1867 |
| Cooper, J. A. | King, Miss Margaret E. | B/84 | August 27, 1869 | August 27, 1869 |
| Cooper, J. M. | Gilley, M. C. | C/142 | August 5, 1876 | August 6, 1876 |
| Cooper, James | Carson, Miss Mary Ann | A/98 | February 24, 1847 | February 28, 1847 |
| Cooper, James | Gilley, Miss Mary | F/170 | February 3, 1899 | February 4, 1899 |
| Cooper, Jemima Malissa Miss | Finley, James | A2/10 | January 30, 1851 | No Return |
| Cooper, John | Thompson, Miss Martha Ann | A/80 | July 3, 1845 | July 3, 1845 |
| Cooper, John | Thompson, Miss Martha Ann | A/81 | July 3, 1845 | July 3, 1845 |
| Cooper, John | Stacey, Sarah M. C. | C/132 | January 27, 1976 | January 27, 1876 |
| Cooper, John D. | McAdow, Miss Azaline | B/98 | January 7, 1870 | January 12, 1870 |
| Cooper, John M. | Bryson, Miss Loely P. | A/92 | October 27, 1846 | October 27, 1846 |
| Cooper, L. M. F. | Mears, W. S. | C/434 | April 10, 1891 | April 12, 1891 |
| Cooper, M. D. L. | Slendly, Miss Sarah | A2/63 | February 3, 1858 | February 3, 1858 |
| Cooper, M. E. Miss | Francis, A. A. | B/120 | December 15, 1870 | December 15, 1870 |
| Cooper, M. P. | Masey, J. R. | F/28 | January 8, 1894 | January 8, 1894 |
| Cooper, Martha J. | Thompson, F. G. | A2/31 | February 20, 1854 | February 20, 1854 |
| Cooper, Martha L. | Sauls, Henry | B/90 | October 6, 1869 | October 10, 1869 |
| Cooper, Martha Miss | Taylor, Barry K. | A2/10 | February 3, 1851 | February 7, 1851 |
| Cooper, Mary | Sissom, Jesse | C/202 | October 12, 1878 | October 13, 1878 |
| Cooper, Mary C. Miss | Knox, William | A2/50 | August 30, 1856 | No Return |
| Cooper, Mary J. | Lynn, D. B. | C/170 | September 19, 1877 | September 20, 1877 |
| Cooper, Melia J. | Owen, Geo | C/114 | June 5, 1875 | June 6, 1875 |
| Cooper, N. C. | Harris, B. C. | C/320 | December 17, 1884 | No Return |
| Cooper, Naney Miss | Ensey, Eligia A. | A2/24 | February 7, 1853 | February 10, 1853 |
| Cooper, Nealie | Hitson, William | F/98 | October 3, 1896 | October 4, 1896 |
| Cooper, P. G. | Summers, Amanda J. | B/56 | November 25, 1867 | November 26, 1867 |
| Cooper, P. Y. | Tinley, H. B. | C/370 | October 23, 1886 | No Return |
| Cooper, Peyton L. | Hatfield, Miss Mary | A/110 | April 5, 1848 | April 5, 1848 |
| Cooper, Philip | Sullens, Miss Margaret | A2/17 | May 6, 1852 | May 6, 1852 |
| Cooper, Phillip | Lollin, Miss Margarett | A2/17 | May 6, 1852 | May 6, 1852 |

| Groom or Bride | Groom or Bride | Book/Page | Date of License | Date of Marriage |
|---|---|---|---|---|
| Cooper, Phillip | Sullens, Miss Margaret | A2/18 | May 6, 1852 | May 6, 1852 |
| Cooper, Rachiel | West, John A. | A2/104 | November 8, 1860 | No Return |
| Cooper, Rutha Miss | Lanier, Wm. J. | A2/68 | October 14, 1858 | No Return |
| Cooper, S. L. | Lewis S. H. | C/72 | November 18, 1873 | November 19, 1873 |
| Cooper, Sara E. | Sissom, H. A. | C/36 | September 6, 1872 | September 13, 1872 |
| Cooper, Sarah L. | Bond, William | A/56 | November 19, 1842 | December 12, 1842 |
| Cooper, Susanah Miss | Byford, John | B/64 | March 2, 1868 | May 8, 1868 |
| Cooper, T. E. | Odum, Willie | F/142 | January 10, 1898 | January 13, 1897 |
| Cooper, Tennessee | Bryant, Wesley | C/18 | December 23 1871 | December 24, 1871 |
| Cooper, Tennie | Gather, Bill | F/48 | November 20, 1894 | No Return |
| Cooper, Thomas | Todd, Sarah | A2/80 | December 5, 1857 | December 5, 1857 |
| Cooper, Thomas J. | Sissom, Miss Sarah E. | B/40 | February 20, 1867 | February 21, 1867 |
| Cooper, W. C. | Davenport, Francis | C/140 | June 29, 1876 | June 29, 1876 |
| Cooper, W. D. | Milligan, Asezeline | F/1 | January 11, 1893 | No Return |
| Cooper, William | Forcana, Miss Katherin | A2/74 | January 1, 1854 | January 1, 1854 |
| Cooper, William B. | Owen, Miss Drucilla | A/98 | March 11, 1847 | No Return |
| Cooper?, James W. | Sissoms, Miss Mary A. C. | B/116 | November 20, 1870 | November 20, 1870 |
| Cope, Elizabeth | Gilly, T. F. | C/102 | November 28, 1874 | December 2, 1874 |
| Cope, G. P. | Right, Jesie | C/306 | March 3, 1884 | March 6, 1885 |
| Cope, Maggie Miss | Brady, John | F/74 | October 26, 1895 | October 17, 1895 |
| Cope, Mary Miss | Patterson, J. C. | B/120 | December 21, 1870 | December 22, 1870 |
| Cope, Sam | Ferrell, Harriett | F/80 | January 3, 1896 | January 5, 1896 |
| Copland, Arnold | Petrill, Miss Martha | A2/28 | September 6, 1853 | No Return |
| Corn, Sarah E. Mrs. | Jetton, Granville | A2/14 | January 29, 1852 | January 29, 1852 |
| Corner, Isabella | Mason, Taylor | C/430 | February 5, 1891 | February 5, 1891 |
| Cos, Mary M. | Jones, B. F. | A2/114 | July 25, 1864 | August 4, 1864 |
| Cosbey, Mary E. | Lorance, M. W. | C/64 | August 23, 1873 | August 24, 1873 |
| Cotheren, S. A. | Arnold, N. C. | A2/102 | September 15, 1860 | No Return |
| Cothran, Plesant | Parker, Miss Angeline | A2/22 | January 12, 1853 | January 18, 1853 |
| Cothran, W. P. | Neal, Lou G. | C/76 | December 18, 1873 | December 24, 1873 |
| Cotter, John L. | Barrett, Martha | C/278 | April 13, 1881 | April 13, 1881 |
| Cotter, T. G. | Taylor, Miss S. E. | B/122 | December 29, 1870 | December 29, 1870 |
| Cotter, Willie | Williams, Amandy | C/246 | April 4, 1880 | No Return |
| Couch, Alie | Hawkins, Sam E. | F/140 | December 15, 1897 | December 19, 1897 |
| Couch, Florence Miss | Odom, E. H. | C/400 | August 30, 1887 | September 2, 1887 |
| Couch, J. M. | Odom, Miss S. M. | B/100 | February 24, 1870 | February, 24, 1870 |
| Couch, J. W. | Bassham, Miss M. E. | C/8 | September 2, 1871 | September 3, 1871 |
| Couch, Lizzie | Johnson, David | F/54 | January 5, 1895 | January 6, 1895 |
| Couch, M. M. Miss | Elrod, J. M. | B/92 | October 30, 1869 | October 31, 1869 |
| Couch, Tennessee | Johnson, F. H. | C/382 | January 19, 1887 | January 20, 1887 |
| Couch, Tennie | Reed, Ezekiel | F/122 | July 29, 1897 | July 29, 1897 |
| Couch, Willis F. | Walls, Miss Martha | A/123 | June 15, 1849 | June 15, 1849 |
| Couch, Wm. H. | Luster, Katharine | A/36 | February 8, 1841 | February 10, 1841 |
| Coughanour, E. C. | Todd, Wm. C. | A2/109 | September 17, 1863 | September 20, 1863 |
| Coughanour, J. A. | Rawlins, Mary | A2/110 | December 25, 1863 | December 29, 1863 |
| Coulter, Malinda | Travis, James | A/55 | October 29, 1842 | October 29, 1842 |

| Groom or Bride | Groom or Bride | Book/Page | Date of License | Date of Marriage |
|---|---|---|---|---|
| Course, Tennie | Haley, John | D/22 | | April 22, 1883 |
| Course, Tennie | Haley, John | C/282 | April 16, 1883 | No Return |
| Cousley, Marinda A. | Higgenbottom, James | A2/62 | January 21, 1858 | January 25, 1858 |
| Couthen, Martha J. Miss | Jarnegin, Wm. A. | A2/64 | May 5, 1858 | No Return |
| Covington, Edmond | Silvertooth, Miss Elizabeth | A2/13 | December 15, 1851 | December 19, 1851 |
| Covington, Frances Miss | Henderson, J. T. | A2/123 | April 9, 1865 | April 9, 1865 |
| Covington, Hattie Miss | Martin, Charles | B/16 | December 28, 1868 | December 30, 1868 |
| Covington, John A. | Bethell, India C. | A2/122 | March 16, 1865 | March 16, 1865 |
| Covington, Leath | Mullins, David | A/29 | May 20, 1840 | June 4, 1840 |
| Covington, Malisa | Bounds, Wesley | C/48 | December 25, 1872 | December 26, 1872 |
| Covington, Mary Miss | Wood, William T. | A2/146 | October 8, 1866 | October 9, 1866 |
| Covington, Pearle | Campbell, R. C. | C/472 | December 22, 1892 | December 22, 1892 |
| Covington, W. C. | Jones, Miss Mary | C/376 | December 22, 1886 | December 22, 1886 |
| Covington, W. L. | Bain, Frances Ann | A2/79 | October 6, 1856 | October 6, 1856 |
| Covington, William L. | George, Mariah | A/18 | October 8, 1839 | October 8, 1839 |
| Cowen, Matilda B. Miss | Barry, John | A2/5 | September 24, 1850 | No return |
| Cowthern, Wm | Bush, Mary M. | C/204 | November 16, 1878 | December 26, 1878 |
| Cowthron, Hugh | Stacy, Miss Adline | A2/15 | March 11, 1852 | March 11, 1852 |
| Cox, C. A. | Watson, Geneva | C/20 | December 27, 1871 | December 27, 1871 |
| Cox, Cabele | Brown, Miss Oma Ann | A/125 | July 16, 1849 | July 16, 1849 |
| Cox, Caroline | Fagan, James H. | A/126 | August 11, 1849 | August 12, 1849 |
| Cox, Charles A. | Evans, Miss Julia Ann | B/82 | July 20, 1869 | July 20, 1869 |
| Cox, Christena | Stanly, Robert M. | A2/120 | February 18, 1865 | February 21, 1865 |
| Cox, D. F. Miss | Morgan, J. S. | A2/87 | August 19, 1859 | No Return |
| Cox, Eleanor | Rich, William | A/77 | February 26, 1845 | February 27, 1845 |
| Cox, Elizabeth | Bailey, James | C/142 | August 12, 1876 | No Return |
| Cox, Henry | Mullins, Louisa | A2/107 | February, 9, 1863 | February 15, 1863 |
| Cox, J. L. | Bailey, Elizabeth | C/282 | May 3, 1883 | No Return |
| Cox, J. S. H. Miss | Patrick, Jessee | A2/70 | November 27, 1858 | November 30, 1858 |
| Cox, Jemima Miss | Todd, James S. | A/92 | October 16, 1846 | October 16, 1846 |
| Cox, Lavina Ann Sophia Miss | McGee, William | A/40 | July 23, 1841 | July 29, 1841 |
| Cox, Mary A. Miss | Gaither, Bazel | A/124 | February 14, 1849 | February 14, 1849 |
| Cox, Mary N. Miss | Wilsher, Charles M. | A/40 | August 25, 1841 | August 26, 1841 |
| Cox, Miss Celia | Jones, James A. | A2/135 | January 13, 1866 | January 13, 1866 |
| Cox, Salina Jane Miss | Knox, James B. | A/132 | January 5, 1850 | January 16, 1850 |
| Cox, Susannah | Todd, Micajah F. | A/5 | August 22, 1838 | August 22, 1838 |
| Cox, Thomas | Marshall, Eliza Jane | A2/7 | November 16, 1850 | November 16, 1850 |
| Cox, William H. | Seates, Alisold | A/26 | March 4, 1840 | No Return |
| Crabtree, Dorcas | Milligan, John | A/12 | April 5, 1839 | April 21, 1839 |
| Crabtree, Eligah | Gilly, Miss Isza | A2/31 | January 18, 1854 | January 18, 1854 |
| Crabtree, Elijah | Gilley, Miss Izza | A2/74 | February 18, 1854 | February 19, 1854 |
| Crabtree, Eliza J. Miss | Hollandsworth, John | B/68 | July 23, 1868 | July 23, 1868 |
| Crabtree, Malisa | Hollandsworth, Robert | C/96 | October 10, 1874 | October 13, 1874 |
| Crabtree, Nancy Miss | Bogle, Robert | A2/42 | October 18, 1855 | October 21, 1855 |
| Crabtree, Sarah E. | Jones, A. A. B. | C/144 | September 1, 1876 | September 3, 1876 |
| Craddock, J. T. | Brazwell, Elixabeth V. | C/84 | March 2, 1874 | February 5, 1874 |

| Groom or Bride | Groom or Bride | Book/Page | Date of License | Date of Marriage |
|---|---|---|---|---|
| Craddock, Simeon | Denton, Margrett | C/32 | August 8, 1872 | September 5, 1872 |
| Craft, Bird | Watters, L. | C/294 | October 15, 1883 | No Return |
| Craft, Chatata | Goins, John B. | A2/45 | December 28, 1855 | December 28, 1855 |
| Craft, Elisabeth Miss | West, Henry H. | A2/98 | June 29, 1860 | July 1, 1860 |
| Craft, Frances Miss | Wilson, Walter | B/102 | May 2, 1870 | May 3, 1870 |
| Craft, Hessie Ann Miss | Petty, William E. | A2/143 | August 14, 1866 | August 15, 1866 |
| Craft, J. J. | Petty, Miss Aseah | B/104 | June 5, 1870 | June 5, 1870 |
| Craft, James L. | Essary, Miss Rebecca E. | A/85 | November 29, 1845 | November 30, 1845 |
| Craft, Johathan | Helton, Nancy | C/256 | July 31, 1880 | July 31, 1880 |
| Craft, Johathan | Helton, Nancy | C/274 | July 31, 1880 | No Return |
| Craft, Jonathan A. | Turner, Nancy | A2/97 | May 26, 1860 | May 28, 1860 |
| Craft, Joseph H. | Clements, Miss Meeky H. | A/89 | June 27, 1846 | No Return |
| Craft, Mary | Peeler, K. S. | C/112 | May 4, 1875 | May 5, 1875 |
| Craft, Rositta | Wilson, Walter, Jr. | C/126 | December 18, 1875 | December 19, 1875 |
| Crafte, Martha Miss | Travis, James | A2/15 | February 29, 1852 | No Return |
| Crage, S. W. | Youree, W. H. | D/22 | | February 12, 1883 |
| Craig, Sue Miss | Whitaker, B. A. | E/47 | July 11, 1888 | July 12, 1888 |
| Crain, Henry | Perry, Miss Malisa | A2/39 | March 20, 1855 | March 20, 1855 |
| Cramner, Robert | Know, Miss Mary | B/8 | November ??, 1870 | No Return |
| Crane, A. M. | Sapp, Miss E. S. | A2/56 | June 6, 1857 | June 7, 1857 |
| Crane, A. W. | McDanel, Miss Roda A. | A2/152 | May 23, 1866 | May 23, 1866 |
| Crane, Elisabeth | Sullins, Eli | D/2 | | August 4, 1881 |
| Crane, John W. | Alexander, Miss Mary Adaline | A/91 | September 15, 1846 | September 17, 1846 |
| Crane, Mary E. | Hendrix, William M. | A/121 | March 15, 1849 | March 15, 1849 |
| Crank, G. W. | Stephens, Miss Marry | A2/24 | February 10, 1853 | February 10, 1853 |
| Crank, James A. | Rucker, Angie | C/288 | July 22, 1883 | July 22, 1883 |
| Crank, S. B. | Barrett, Mary | C/216 | May 6, 1879 | No Return |
| Crawford, John | Goings, Miss Roda | A2/144 | September 12, 1866 | September 13, 1866 |
| Craye, Jennie | Mitchell, Robty | D/16 | | September 21, 1881 |
| Creson, Benjamin F. | Sissom, Miss Sarah | A/86 | January 3, 1846 | January 3, 1846 |
| Creson, Elizabeth | Parker, J. E. | C/132 | February 2, 1876 | February 2, 1876 |
| Creson, H. J. | Perry, Ed | C/20 | January 11, 1872 | January 11, 8172 |
| Creson, J. F. | Simons, Emiline | C/132 | February 2, 1876 | February 2, 1876 |
| Creson, James | Carrick, Miss Mary E. | B/36 | January 7, 1867 | January 7, 1867 |
| Creson, James | McGill, Bettie | F/156 | September 2, 1898 | No Return |
| Creson, Joshua | Leigh, Miss Elizabeth W. | A/94 | December 17, 1846 | December 17, 1846 |
| Creson, M. B. | Todd, T. J. | D/10 | | December 29, 1881 |
| Creson, Mary Miss | Hollis, J. B. | A2/137 | February 17, 1866 | February 18, 1866 |
| Creson, Martha Miss | Perry, J. B. | C/380 | January 1, 1887 | January 3, 1887 |
| Creson, Sarah Miss | Leigh, Ware | A/92 | October 22, 1846 | October 22, 1846 |
| Crieson, James C. | Alexander, Miss Sarh Jane | A2/7 | November 7, 1850 | No Return |
| Crockett, Kitty | Simons, Joseph | C/120 | September 27, 1875 | September 28, 1875 |
| Crocker, Eugenia Miss | Goodloe, B. R. | B/44 | April 9, 1867 | April 9, 1867 |
| Cronk, G. W. | Maxwell, Matilda | C/134 | February 15, 1876 | February 15, 1876 |
| Crop, Martha | Travis, Franklin W. | A/14 | June 15, 1839 | No Return |
| Cross, Eliza Issabella Miss | Tucker, John | A/121 | October 19,1848 | October 19,1848 |

| Groom or Bride | Groom or Bride | Book/Page | Date of License | Date of Marriage |
|---|---|---|---|---|
| Crouch, C. G. Miss | Shelton, Charles | C/458 | May 28, 1892 | May 29, 1892 |
| Crouch, J. B. | Foster, Miss Lucinda | C/10 | September 7, 1871 | September 10, 1871 |
| Crouch, J. B. | Grizzle, Elisabeth | C/256 | October 4, 1880 | October 17, 1880 |
| Crouch, J. B. | Grear, Miss Mary | C/458 | April 28, 1892 | No Return |
| Crouch, S. B. | Mayfield, Queen | C/148 | November 24, 1876 | November 24, 1876 |
| Crouch, Tinnie | Owen, Luther | F/90 | July 19, 1896 | July 19, 1896 |
| Croughonour, Maleda Miss | Todd, M. F. | A2/79 | May 12, 1856 | May 13, 1856 |
| Crow, Martha Jane Miss | Smith, Lorenzo D. | A/87 | February 26, 1846 | February 26, 1846 |
| Culwell, Mary | Comer, Lon | F/64 | July 7, 1895 | July 8, 1895 |
| Cumings, T. P. Miss | Bailey, Robert | A2/44 | December 8, 1855 | December 9, 1855 |
| Cumins, Julina Miss | Stine, W. G. | A2/91 | December 14, 1859 | No Return |
| Cumins, Matilda | St. John, Floyd | A/121 | March 8, 1849 | March 8, 1849 |
| Cumins, N. B. | Preston, Ruth | C/292 | September 15, 1883 | September 16, 1883 |
| Cummings, A. H. | Melton, Miss Mary | A2/24 | March 30, 1853 | March 20, 1853 |
| Cummings, A. J. | McCabe, Tina | E/378 | October 29, 1898 | |
| Cummings, Cyrena Miss | Keeny, James | A/63 | July 16, 1843 | July 20, 1843 |
| Cummings, Edney C. | Barrett, Charles A. | D/14 | | August 11, 1882 |
| Cummings, Francis Miss | Walls, James J. | C/406 | November 2, 1887 | November 2, 1887 |
| Cummings, John | Mullinex, John A. | C/312 | August 22, 1884 | August 24, 1884 |
| Cummings, John M. | Land, Lular | C/298 | December 28, 1883 | December 28, 1883 |
| Cummings, Mary E. Miss | Elkins, Dillard S. | A/73 | October 2, 1844 | October 2, 1844 |
| Cummings, Matilda P. | Sullins, James | D/12 | | February 28, 1882 |
| Cummings, Media | Stewart, Hoyt | E/376 | October 30, 1898 | |
| Cummings, Media | Stewart, Hoyt | F/160 | October 30, 1898 | October 30, 1898 |
| Cummings, Miss Dovie | Preston, Mr. W. D. | F/64 | June 26, 1895 | June 26, 1895 |
| Cummings, Nancy | Young, Isaac | D/19 | | December 17, 1882 |
| Cummings, O. J. | McCabe, Tina | F/160 | October 29, 1898 | October 30, 1898 |
| Cummings, P. D. | Mears, Melvina | A2/131 | November 9, 1865 | November 12, 1865 |
| Cummings, Parasade | Baily, Hugh L. | A2/109 | October 19, 1863 | No Return |
| Cummings, Rebecca J. Miss | Leigh, William J. | B/76 | December 25, 1868 | January 7, 1869 |
| Cummings, Sarah | Moore, H. E. | D/18 | | December 24, 1882 |
| Cummings, Thomas | Mullican, Mary Ann | F/38 | June 17, 1896 | June 21, 1896 |
| Cummings, Warren | Sullivan, Dove | A/11 | March 5, 1839 | March 6, 1839 |
| Cummings, William | Rains, Delphia | A/2 | March 27, 1838 | March 27, 1838 |
| Cummings, William | Aldern Miss Manerva Ann | A/84 | November 6, 1845 | November 6, 1845 |
| Cummins, Adaline Miss | Young, Joseph | A2/22 | December 22, 1852 | January 3?, 1852 |
| Cummins, Adaline Miss | Ferrell, Young | B/34 | December 19, 1866 | December 20, 1866 |
| Cummins, Benjamin | Melton, Miss Sarah Jane | A/49 | April 28, 1842 | April 23, 1842 |
| Cummins, Bettie | Lafever, Wm. | D/1 | | July 14, 1881 |
| Cummins, Dallas | Mason, Lillie | D/13 | | June 30, 1882 |
| Cummins, Dove Mrs. | Sullens, William | A/121 | March 18, 1849 | March 18, 1849 |
| Cummins, Elizabeth Miss | Kincaid, Thomas | A2/6 | September 5, 1850 | September 6, 1850 |
| Cummins, J. P. | Elledge, T. B. | C/70 | October 28, 1873 | October 29, 1873 |
| Cummins, James | Foster, Miss Ann | A/127 | September 20, 1849 | September 20, 1849 |
| Cummins, John | Melton, Anne | A/28 | May 5, 1840 | No Return |
| Cummins, L. L. C. | Hopkins, Miss Lucy Ann | B/72 | October 17, 1868 | October 18, 1868 |

| Groom or Bride | Groom or Bride | Book/Page | Date of License | Date of Marriage |
|---|---|---|---|---|
| Cummins, L. T. | Worley, Miss Matilda P. | A2/146 | October 24, 1866 | October 25, 1866 |
| Cummins, Lucy E. Miss | Lawrence, James T. | B/90 | October 6, 1869 | October 7, 1869 |
| Cummins, M. Miss | Melton, J. A. | A2/90 | October 28, 1859 | No Return |
| Cummins, Margaret Miss | Melton, H. P. | B/36 | May 9, 1867 | May 14, 1867 |
| Cummins, Mary J. Miss | Woods, G. D. | B/126 | February 10, 1871 | No Return |
| Cummins, Rebecca A. | McFerrin, Alford | C/44 | November 16, 1872 | November 17, 1872 |
| Cummins, Sallie | Young, T. M. | C/148 | November 24, 1876 | November 26, 1876 |
| Cummins, Sarah | Neely, W. R. | C/152 | January 13, 1877 | January 14, 1877 |
| Cummins, W. B. | Preston, Miss Frances C. | B/86 | September 8, 1869 | September 9, 1869 |
| Cummins, W. B. | Markum, Martha | C/224 | September 6, 1879 | No Return |
| Cummins, W. G. | Shachelford, Fannie | F/114 | March 6, 1897 | March 8, 1897 |
| Cummins, Warren | Bailey, Miss Josephine | A2/135 | January 13, 1866 | January 14, 1866 |
| Cummins, Wm (col.) | Simmons, Bettie | C/370 | October 22, 1886 | No Return |
| Cuningham, J. | Rogers, Miss Elizabeth | A2/14 | February 2, 1852 | February 2, 1852 |
| Cunningham, F. P. | Maxey, J. J. | C/80 | January 5, 1874 | No Return |
| Cunningham, Jane Miss | Moss, Charles D. | A2/85 | April 3, 1859 | April 3, 1859 |
| Cunningham, Mary | Petty, Micagah | A2/76 | September 28, 1855 | September 29, 1855 |
| Cunningham, Pate | Good, Dora | F/30 | February 5, 1894 | No Return |
| Cunningham, Rebeca | Baltimore, G. H. | C/372 | October 23, 1886 | October 24, 1886 |
| Cuper, Thomas | Heron, Miss Margaret | C/460 | July 7, 1892 | No Return |
| Curdon, Mary Miss | Warren, Benjamin | A2/21 | December 14, 1852 | December 14, 1852 |
| Curis, Ann Miss | Mares, William | A/48 | April 11, 1842 | April 11, 1842 |
| Curlee, Amanda | Gaither, John W. | A2/143 | August 27, 1866 | August 28, 1866 |
| Curlee, Burt | Davis, Ruth | C/468 | October 20, 1892 | October 20, 1892 |
| Curlee, Burt | Davis, Ruth | C/468 | October 20, 1892 | October 20, 1892 |
| Curlee, D. E. | Smith, John | F/32 | February 15, 1894 | No Return |
| Curlee, E. M. | Hoover, C. C. | C/276 | March 17, 1881 | March 17, 1881 |
| Curlee, Eliza | Sellars, Jordan B. | A/30 | June 26, 1840 | June 28, 1840 |
| Curlee, Fannie | Hollis, Dennie | C/294 | October 5, 1883 | October 7, 1883 |
| Curlee, Henretta | Gaither, C. C. | C/400 | September 3, 1887 | September 4, 1887 |
| Curlee, James | Bynum, Mary J. | C/334 | August 20, 1885 | August 20, 1885 |
| Curlee, James P. | McBroom, Anelyn | C/232 | December 4, 1879 | December 4, 1879 |
| Curlee, James P. | Patton, Addie L. | E/232 | November 13, 1889 | November 13, 1889 |
| Curlee, Maggie | McBroom, W. B. | F/14 | August 19, 1893 | September 11, 1893 |
| Curlee, P. B. | Gaither, Miss Mary H. | A2/74 | September 26, 1853 | September 27, 1853 |
| Curlee, P. B. | Gaither, Miss Elizabeth F. | A2/77 | October 10, 1855 | October 11, 1855 |
| Curlee, Peyton B. | Ferrell, Miss Roxanah | A2/81 | January 13, 1858 | January 13, 1858 |
| Curlee, R. C. | Owenby, Sallie | F/48 | November 20, 1894 | November 28, 1894 |
| Curlee, T. B. | Foster, Bettie P. | C/44 | October 24, 1872 | October 24, 1872 |
| Curlee, T. G. | Thomas, Miss A. D. | B/56 | November 19, 1867 | November 20, 1867 |
| Curry, Amand | Mason, J. W. | E/80 | September 20, 1888 | September 20, 1888 |
| Curtis, Silas R. | Kuykendall, Miss Easter J. | A/94 | December 22, 1846 | December 22, 1846 |
| Dabbs, J. T. | Tedder, Sarah | C/64 | August 19, 1873 | August 21, 1873 |
| Dabbs, John T. | Hettson, Miss Mary | A2/62 | January 12, 1858 | January 12, 1858 |
| Dabbs, L. M. | Davenport, J. M. | A2/116 | August 30, 1864 | September 4, 1864 |
| Dabbs, Mary Miss | Taylor, G. W. | C/408 | November 14, 1887 | November 14, 1887 |

| Groom or Bride | Groom or Bride | Book/Page | Date of License | Date of Marriage |
|---|---|---|---|---|
| Daniel, Lindy | White, Melton | C/134 | February 25, 1876 | February 27, 1876 |
| Daniel J. C. | Braxton, Eliza | E/104 | November 29, 1888 | December 2, 1888 |
| Daniel, Ann Eliza Miss | Adams, John | A/42 | October 16, 1841 | October 18, 1841 |
| Daniel, Boregard (col.) | McKnight, Hattie (col.) | D/14 | | July 2, 1882 |
| Daniel, E. A. Miss | Justice, H. A. | A2/69 | November 4, 1853 | November 4, 1853 |
| Daniel, Ellen | Wood, W. J. | E/233 | November 23, 1889 | November 24, 1889 |
| Daniel, Geo. | Smith, Eliza | C/26 | April 24, 1872 | April 25, 1872 |
| Daniel, George | Pinkerton | B/4 | August 22, 1865 | August 27, 1865 |
| Daniel, James | Rucker, Mandy | D/12 | | March 16, 1882 |
| Daniel, Margaret | Barton, Robert | B/12 | December 14, 1867 | December 15, 1867 |
| Daniel, Martha Miss | Pelham, Levi | A/97 | January 25, 1847 | February 3, 1847 |
| Daniel, Nancy | Parsley, Brice | A/5 | August 16, 1838 | August 16, 1838 |
| Daniel, R. T. | Young, Miss Mary A. | A2/92 | December 17, 1859 | No Return |
| Daniel, Robert | Wood, Josie | E/147 | March 27, 1889 | March 28, 1889 |
| Daniel, Robert C. | Brown, Miss Jane | A2/77 | January 7, 1856 | January 7, 1856 |
| Daniel, Sallie | Hays, Luther E. | F/96 | September 14, 1896 | No Return |
| Daniel, Sam | People, Miss Jennie | C/8 | September 7, 1871 | September 7, 1871 |
| Daniel, Tenne | Herrell, George | E/142 | February 28, 1889 | February 28, 1889 |
| Daniel, W. R. | Campbell, T. C. | F/28 | December 28, 1893 | December 31, 1893 |
| Danning?, George | Mitchell, Sopha | C/236 | January 1, 1880 | January 1, 1880 |
| Daraberry, Cindy R. Miss | Kerklin, Isaac | A2/24 | September 27, 1852 | November 27, 1852 |
| Darbery, Eliza Miss | Prater, John | B/126 | March 4, 1871 | March 5, 1871 |
| Darnel, M. A. | Carter, S. E. | C/270 | January 18, 1881 | January 20, 1881 |
| Darnell, Martha E. | Parker, Joseph | D/16 | | September 21, 1882 |
| Darnell, W. C. | Elander, Miss Sarah | A2/31 | December 26, 1853 | No Return |
| Dass, Shelby | Robertson, Fannie | F/34 | September 18, 1894 | September 18, 1894 |
| Daugherty, Jennie | Odom, John H. | F/132 | September 14, 1897 | September 16, 1897 |
| Daughety, J. R. | Vantres, Florance | C/320 | December 20, 1884 | December 21, 1885 |
| Daughtery, Alsey A. | Cawthon, Harvey | C/26 | May 6, 1872 | May 6, 1872 |
| Daughtry, H. B. | Lambert, A. J. | C/174 | October 23, 1877 | October 26, 1877 |
| Daughtry, Mary | Jetton, Robert | C/378 | December 25, 1886 | December 26, 1886 |
| Daules (Daubs), Judie | Wood, Jerry | C/70 | November 6, 1873 | November 6, 1873 |
| Davanport, George | Collins, Frances | A2/111 | January 21, 1864 | January 29, 1864 |
| Davanport, J. B. | Moore, Margaret | A2/112 | March 3, 1864 | No Return |
| Davenport | Bell, R. T. | E/129 | January 26, 1889 | January 27, 1889 |
| Davenport, ---- | Bryson, ---- | F | September 2, 1893 | |
| Davenport, ---- | Summar, ---- | F | August 26, 1893 | |
| Davenport, A. A. | Davenport, Martha | A2/125 | August 19, 1865 | August 20, 1865 |
| Davenport, A. H. | Odom, Lizzy | F/124 | August 2, 1897 | August 4, 1897 |
| Davenport, A. L. | Jones, J. F. | C/378 | December 25, 1886 | December 26, 1886 |
| Davenport, Authy | Harrison, Joseph | C/442 | August 1, 1891 | August 2, 1891 |
| Davenport, B. D. | Willird, Miss D. L. | A2/65 | August 2, 1858 | August 2, 1858 |
| Davenport, B. L. | McKnight, Lue | F/120 | July 3, 1897 | July 4, 1897 |
| Davenport, Davey | Mingles, G. W. | D/20 | | January 10, 1883 |
| Davenport, E. H. | Womack, Sara S. | E/22 | February 27, 1888 | March 1, 1888 |
| Davenport, E. H. | Adams, Mintie | F/92 | August 8, 1896 | August 8, 1896 |

| Groom or Bride | Groom or Bride | Book/Page | Date of License | Date of Marriage |
|---|---|---|---|---|
| Davenport, Elizabeth | Bogle, F. L. | C/398 | August 27, 1887 | August 28, 1887 |
| Davenport, F. J. | Leech, W. N. | C/110 | March 8, 1875 | No return |
| Davenport, Fanie | Bryson, W. D. | F/22 | November 11, 1893 | November 13, 1893 |
| Davenport, Fannie | Ready, J. S. | F/66 | July 15, 1895 | July 16, 1895 |
| Davenport, Fanny | Sloan, W. A. | C/198 | September 21, 1878 | No Return |
| Davenport, Fanny E. Miss | Smith, Neil H. | A/106 | December 21, 1847 | December 22, 1847 |
| Davenport, Francis | Cooper, W. C. | C/140 | June 29, 1876 | June 29, 1876 |
| Davenport, G. L. | Milligan, Henry | E/92 | October 25, 1888 | October 2, 1888 |
| Davenport, Gawen | Womack, Julia | C/428 | January 2, 1891 | January 4, 891 |
| Davenport, Geo. | Preston, Rebecca | C/68 | October 3, 1873 | November 2, 1873 |
| Davenport, H. M. | Willard, Virginia | C/454 | February 1, 1892 | February 3, 1892 |
| Davenport, Hardy | Strong, Julie | C/46 | December 5, 1872 | December 5, 1872 |
| Davenport, Hardy | Williams, Mary | C/256 | September 7, 1880 | September 7, 1880 |
| Davenport, Harriet M. Miss | Cooper, Christopher | A/98 | March 10, 1847 | March 11, 1847 |
| Davenport, Henry | Pedigo, Sarah | A/7 | October 3, 1838 | October 5, 1838 |
| Davenport, Henry | Summar, Maggie | F/84 | February 18, 1896 | February 19, 1896 |
| Davenport, J. A. | Jones, AnEliza | E/200 | August 17, 1889 | August 18, 1889 |
| Davenport, J. B | Merritt, Miss Nancy | A2/42 | October 13, 1855 | No Return |
| Davenport, J. B. | Duncan, Martha S. | A2/110 | July 11, 1863 | No Return |
| Davenport, J. B. | Preston, Mary | C/172 | October 3, 1877 | October 4, 1877 |
| Davenport, J. B. | Payton, Margarett | C/196 | August 14, 1878 | August 14, 1878 |
| Davenport, J. B. | Wimberly, Lyda | D/18 | | November 7, 1882 |
| Davenport, J. B. | Bruster, Vina | F/14 | July 24, 1893 | August 21, 1893 |
| Davenport, J. B. | Blanks, M. A. | F/66 | July 20, 1895 | July 21, 1895 |
| Davenport, J. H. | Farler, Sarah J. | C/326 | February 19, 1885 | No Return |
| Davenport, J. J. | Barrett, Miss Edna | C/408 | November 15, 1887 | November 15, 1887 |
| Davenport, J. M. | Dabbs, L. M. | A2/116 | August 30, 1864 | September 4, 1864 |
| Davenport, J. M. | Tedder, Miss Melvina | B/82 | July 5, 1869 | July 18, 1869 |
| Davenport, J. M. | Reed, Mary | C/146 | September 30, 1876 | October 1, 1876 |
| Davenport, J. M. | Sowls, Allie | F/58 | February 12, 1895 | No Return |
| Davenport, J. M. | Davenport, Virginia | F/62 | April 6, 1895 | April 7, 1895 |
| Davenport, J. P. | Vasser, Sissie | C/348 | January 11, 1886 | January 11, 1886 |
| Davenport, James B. | Bragg, Miss Nancy | A/116 | November 14, 1848 | November 14, 1848 |
| Davenport, James H. | Davenport, Ruth | C/236 | January 9, 1880 | January 9, 1880 |
| Davenport, Jas. H. | Payton, Callie | C/96 | September 26, 1874 | September 28, 1874 |
| Davenport, Jennie | Parton, Isaac | C/444 | August 15, 1891 | August 16, 1891 |
| Davenport, Jessie | McKnight, Miss Mattie | C/452 | December 26, 1891 | December 27, 1891 |
| Davenport, Joe B. | Davenport, Nancy C. | C/352 | February 18, 1886 | February 18, 1886 |
| Davenport, John | Smith, Miss Sarah | B/116 | November 10, 1870 | November 10, 1870 |
| Davenport, John C. | Jones, Susan | A2/101 | September 1, 1860 | No Return |
| Davenport, John F. | Gan, Calidonia | A2/110 | December 24, 1863 | December 27, 1863 |
| Davenport, John R | Bryson, L. M. | C/306 | March 9, 1884 | No Return |
| Davenport, Kerry | Smith, Nancy M. | C/354 | March 7, 1886 | March 11, 1886 |
| Davenport, L. C. | Womack, L. D. | D/15 | | September 10, 1882 |
| Davenport, L. E. | Bryson, R. T. | C/182 | December 25, 1877 | December 30, 1877 |
| Davenport, L. M. | Poterfield, W. F. | C/116 | July 28, 1875 | July 29, 1875 |

| Groom or Bride | Groom or Bride | Book/Page | Date of License | Date of Marriage |
|---|---|---|---|---|
| Davenport, L. N. | Harris, G. W. | C/304 | February 9, 1884 | No Return |
| Davenport, Laurena S. Miss | Bragg, William M. | A/95 | December 28, 1846 | December 28, 1846 |
| Davenport, M. | Hickey, Ben | C/296 | November 3, 1883 | November 3, 1883 |
| Davenport, M. A. | Bryson, H. H. | C/226 | October 10, 1879 | No Return |
| Davenport, M. B. | Tittle, Ader | D/16 | | October 22, 1882 |
| Davenport, M. E. | Bryson, D. Z. | E/362 | November 26, 1898 | |
| Davenport, M. E. | Bryson, D. Z. | F/162 | November 26, 1898 | November 17, 1898 |
| Davenport, M. E. Miss | Bogle, J. Q. | B/112 | October 14, 1870 | October 14, 1870 |
| Davenport, M. M. | Bogle, H. M. | C/284 | June 26, 1883 | June 25, 1883 |
| Davenport, Margaret S. Miss | Alexander, John D. | B/108 | August 23, 1870 | August 25, 1870 |
| Davenport, Martha | Davenport, A. A. | A2/125 | August 19, 1865 | August 20, 1865 |
| Davenport, Martha Miss | Roberson, Foster M. | B/96 | December 22, 1869 | December 26, 1869 |
| Davenport, Mary | Davenport, W. C. | C/334 | August 20, 1885 | August 20, 1885 |
| Davenport, May | Fann, Sam | F/154 | August 31, 1898 | August 31, 1898 |
| Davenport, Medie | Ford, Bill | F/100 | October 24, 1896 | No Date |
| Davenport, Mollie | Sutton, John | C/250 | July 8, 1880 | No Return |
| Davenport, Nancy | Kirkland, J. H. | C/336 | September 1, 1885 | September 1, 1885 |
| Davenport, Nancy | Bryan, W. R. | F/72 | October 12, 1895 | October 13, 1895 |
| Davenport, Nancy C. | Davenport, Joe B. | C/352 | February 18, 1886 | February 18, 1886 |
| Davenport, Nancy M. Miss | Orrand, Thomas A. | B/54 | October 19, 1867 | October 20, 1867 |
| Davenport, Nancy Miss | Parten, Henry | A2/95 | April 3, 1860 | April 3, 1860 |
| Davenport, Nathan | Tennpenny, Colister | E/234 | November 24, 1889 | November 24, 1889 |
| Davenport, Ollie | Blanks, Jim | F/68 | August 30, 1895 | September 1, 1895 |
| Davenport, Ona | Vance, James | F/98 | October 3, 1896 | October 6, 1896 |
| Davenport, Parelle | Bogle, S. F. | C/288 | August 6, 1883 | No Return |
| Davenport, Parilee | Bogle, H. S. | D/21 | | August 6, 1883 |
| Davenport, Pelina Miss | Bogle, George | B/96 | December 23, 1869 | December 28, 1869 |
| Davenport, R. | Milligan, Lotty | C/168 | September 1, 1877 | September 2, 1877 |
| Davenport, R. B. F. | Preston, Mary L. | C/112 | May 15, 1875 | No Return |
| Davenport, R. B. F. | Long, Miss H. J. | F/58 | January 26, 1895 | January 27, 1895 |
| Davenport, R. H. | Wilson, Rosie | C/196 | August 28, 1878 | August 29, 1878 |
| Davenport, Reuben | Mathews, Miss Sarah | A/99 | May 4, 1847 | May 4, 1847 |
| Davenport, Riley | Womack, Martha F. | C/200 | September 27, 1878 | September 28, 1878 |
| Davenport, Robert | Leech, M. J. | A2/114 | July 13, 1864 | July 14, 1864 |
| Davenport, Robert | Bottom, Sallie | C/376 | December 22, 1886 | December 23, 1886 |
| Davenport, Ruth | Davenport, James H. | C/236 | January 9, 1880 | January 9, 1880 |
| Davenport, S. A. | Reed, G. P. | C/210 | January 21, 1870 | January 23, 1870 |
| Davenport, S. L | Jones, R. B. | C/462 | July 26, 1892 | July 26, 1892 |
| Davenport, S. M. | Summer, R. H. | F/72 | October 19, 1895 | October 20, 1895 |
| Davenport, Sam | Hollandsworth, Mary E. | F/18 | September 14, 1893 | September 14, 1893 |
| Davenport, Sam | Richards, Miss Ida | F/152 | July 2, 1898 | July 3, 1898 |
| Davenport, Sam B. | Preston, Martha J. | C/70 | November 1, 1873 | November 2, 1873 |
| Davenport, Sarah S. Miss | Burnett, S. A. | B/98 | February 1, 1870 | February 1, 1870 |
| Davenport, Susan | Jones, Mennie | F/2 | January 14, 1893 | No Return |
| Davenport, T. B. | Dobbs, Miss A. P. | F/56 | December 8, 1894 | December 9, 1894 |
| Davenport, T. W. | Bryson, Louisa | E/140 | February 21, 1889 | February 21, 1889 |

| Groom or Bride | Groom or Bride | Book/Page | Date of License | Date of Marriage |
|---|---|---|---|---|
| Davenport, Thomas W. | Jones, Miss Mary E. | A2/4 | August 20, 1850 | August 20, 1850 |
| Davenport, Virginia | Davenport, J. M. | F/62 | April 6, 1895 | April 7, 1895 |
| Davenport, W. A. | Francis, Nannie | F/34 | March 22, 1894 | March 22, 1894 |
| Davenport, W. B. | Bryson, M. L. | C/222 | August 11, 1879 | August 13, 1879 |
| Davenport, W. C. | Davenport, Mary | C/334 | August 20, 1885 | August 20, 1885 |
| Davenport, W. C. | Whirley, Etna | C/472 | December 17, 1892 | December 18, 1892 |
| Davenport, W. I. | Graham, Cornelia A. | F/28 | December 27, 1893 | December 27, 1783 |
| Davenport, W. R. | Summer, Miss Pitson | B/70 | September 19, 1868 | September 20, 1868 |
| Davenport, W. S. | Peyden, Miss Barbara A. | A2/27 | August 12, 1853 | August 12, 1853 |
| Davenport, Warren | Smith, Miss Ann F. | B/66 | July 9, 1868 | July 9, 1868 |
| Davenport, Warren | Winnett, Julia A. | C/80 | January 10, 1874 | January 11, 1874 |
| Davenport, William | Bryson, Miss Polly | A/82 | July 24, 1845 | July 24, 1845 |
| Davenport, Wm. | Smith, Corddie | E/79 | September 20, 1888 | September 20, 1888 |
| Davenport, Wm. A. | Hibdon, Susan | A2/115 | July 28, 1864 | August 2, 1864 |
| Davenport, Wm. C. | Stanley, Eliza | A2/45 | January 1, 1856 | No Return |
| Davis Andy | Stanly, Susan C. | C/52 | February 17, 1873 | No Retrun |
| Davis, Anderson | Tucker, Lucretia | A2/3 | August 3, 1850 | August 4, 1850 |
| Davis, Anderson | Tucker, Lucretia | A2/4 | August 3, 1850 | August 4, 1850 |
| Davis, Andy | McNeely, Mary Ann | F/88 | June 13, 1896 | June 13, 1896 |
| Davis, Annie Miss | Keaton, H. L. | B/124 | January 2?, 1871 | January 29, 1871 |
| Davis, Ark | Sullins, Saml | C/124 | November 8, 1875 | November 11, 1875 |
| Davis, Benj. | Baily, Bettie | C/44 | October 24, 1872 | October 24, 1872 |
| Davis, Bettie | Tittle, Sam | C/274 | March 4, 1881 | March 4, 1881 |
| Davis, Charles | Martin, Nannie | E/95 | October 31, 1888 | October 31, 1888 |
| Davis, Charley | Thomas, Nancy | C/348 | January 12, 1886 | January 14, 1886 |
| Davis, Cintha Miss | Rogers, John Jr. | A/79 | June 6, 1845 | June 6, 1845 |
| Davis, D. K. Miss | Ford, W. J. | B/122 | December 28, 1870 | December 29, 1870 |
| Davis, David | Moore, Lotty | C/66 | September 11, 1873 | September 11, 1873 |
| Davis, Drew (col.) | Sims, James (col.) | D/4 | | October 9, 1881 |
| Davis, E. H. | Winnette, Telia | C/474 | December 29, 1892 | January 1, 1893 |
| Davis, Eliza | Bowlin, Saml | C/104 | December 24, 1874 | December 24, 1874 |
| Davis, Elizabeth | Davis, Thomas | C/192 | April 28, 1878 | April 28, 1878 |
| Davis, Elizabeth | Romine, James | C/164 | July 14, 1877 | July 15, 1877 |
| Davis, Elizabeth Miss | Canes, A. B. | A2/68 | October 19, 1858 | October 20, 1858 |
| Davis, Ester | Tittle, T. D. | C/170 | September 15, 1877 | September 15, 1877 |
| Davis, F. M. | Fowler, Martha | C/322 | January 10, 1885 | January 11, 1885 |
| Davis, Fannie E. | Underwood, Wm. B. | D/22 | | April 1, 1883 |
| Davis, G. H | Campbell, Ella | F/100 | October 17, 1896 | October 18, 1896 |
| Davis, G. Y. | Carr, Isabella M. | C/234 | December 26, 1879 | January 1, 1880 |
| Davis, Geo | Fite, N. A. | C/146 | October 2, 1876 | October 5, 1876 |
| Davis, George | Hancock, Darthuly | C/362 | July 26, 1886 | July 28, 1886 |
| Davis, J. A. | Thomas, Maud | E/253 | December 27, 1889 | December 27, 1889 |
| Davis, J. E. | Travis, Miss S. D | E/109 | December 18, 1888 | December 18, 1888 |
| Davis, J. J. | Doakes, Miss Mary H. | B/36 | December 31, 1866 | January 1, 1867 |
| Davis, J. M. | Prater, Bettie | F/84 | February 26, 1896 | February 27, 1896 |
| Davis, Jacob | Moon, Miss Charlotte | A/70 | July 10, 1844 | July 11, 1844 |

| Groom or Bride | Groom or Bride | Book/Page | Date of License | Date of Marriage |
|---|---|---|---|---|
| Davis, James | Hollis, Harriet | E/14 | August 23, 1868 | No Return |
| Davis, James | Parker, Bettie | C/124 | November 12, 1875 | November 14, 1875 |
| Davis, James | Walker, Mary | E/61 | August 16, 1888 | August 16, 1888 |
| Davis, John | Young, Nancy Emaline | A/83 | September 10, 1845 | September 10, 1845 |
| Davis, John | Rigsly, Miss Ruthey | A2/64 | March 25, 1858 | No Return |
| Davis, John | Wooton, Doshie | F/92 | August 3, 1896 | August 5, 1896 |
| Davis, Joseph | Finch, Miss Katharine E. | A/109 | March 2, 1848 | March 2, 1848 |
| Davis, Joshua | Busy, Jenetta | A/57 | December 29, 1842 | December 29, 1842 |
| Davis, Joshua | Duncan, Elizabeth | A2/123 | June 28, 1865 | June 29, 1865 |
| Davis, Lewis | Rogers, Miss Zilpha | A/109 | March 14, 1848 | March 14, 1848 |
| Davis, Lottie | Wilson, Walter | F/146 | February 14, 1898 | February 14, 1898 |
| Davis, Luke | Bogle, Sailie | E/332 | December 28, 1898 | |
| Davis, M. A. | Sowells, Wm. | F/128 | August 25, 1897 | August 26, 1897 |
| Davis, M. E. Miss | Thomas, J. W. | B/102 | April 4, 1870 | April 7, 1840 |
| Davis, Manervia | Parsley, James | A/1 | March 1, 1838 | March 1, 1838 |
| Davis, Margaret Miss | Beaty, Allen | A/71 | July 26, 1844 | July 26, 1844 |
| Davis, Martha A. E. | Sparkman, P. M. | D/17 | | November 2, 1882 |
| Davis, Mary | Bell, John | E/81 | September 19, 1888 | September 20, 1888 |
| Davis, Mary Miss | Womack, Benjamin | C/386 | March 3, 1887 | March 3, 1887 |
| Davis, Mary E. | Duke, J. M. | C/112 | April 14, 1875 | April 18, 1875 |
| Davis, Mary E. Miss | Mathews, John W. | A2/79 | May 3, 1856 | May 26, 1870 |
| Davis, Mate | Bogle, Sallie | F/164 | December 28, 1898 | No Return |
| Davis, Nancy D. | Parton, Thomas | C/244 | February 27, 1880 | No Return |
| Davis, Parisade | Sullens, Balam | C/88 | July 21, 1874 | July 21, 1874 |
| Davis, Parisade | Sullen, Balane | C/92 | July 21, 1874 | No Return |
| Davis, Ona | Alexander, M. (col.) | C/450 | December 5, 1891 | December 6, 1891 |
| Davis, Paralee Miss | West, Jourden | A2/82 | August 9, 1858 | August 11, 1858 |
| Davis, Parlee | Nokes, Sam | C/272 | February 14, 1881 | February 15, 1881 |
| Davis, R. M. | Wommack, Y. J. | C/122 | October 16, 1875 | No Date |
| Davis, Rebecca | Stanly, Mort | C/58 | June 24, 1873 | No Return |
| Davis, Robert | Higgins, Miss Julian | B/102 | May 28, 1870 | May 29, 1870 |
| Davis, Ross | Reed, Jane | C/434 | April 9, 1891 | April 9, 1891 |
| Davis, Ruth | Curlee, Burt | C/468 | October 20, 1892 | October 20, 1892 |
| Davis, S. C. | Tedder, J. C. | F/74 | November 23, 1895 | November 24, 1895 |
| Davis, Samuel | Brewer, Lucy | C/276 | March 18, 1881 | No Return |
| Davis, Samuel A. | Moon, Margaret | A2/134 | December 30, 1865 | December 31, 1865 |
| Davis, Sarah | Gooding, James | C/126 | December 18, 1875 | No Return |
| Davis, Sarah | Rigsby, John K. | A/75 | December 25, 1844 | December 26, 1844 |
| Davis, Sarah J. | Reed, James | F | August 22, 1893 | No Return |
| Davis, Simeon | McBroom, Minnie | E/82 | September 22, 1888 | September 23, 1888 |
| Davis, T. J. | Womack, Mary E. | C/12 | October 21, 1871 | October 21, 1871 |
| Davis, T. Y. | Petty, Miss Nannie D. | B/76 | December 26, 1868 | No Return |
| Davis, Thomas | Davis, Elizabeth | C/192 | April 28, 1878 | April 28, 1878 |
| Davis, Thomas Y. | Petty, Mary E. | D/1 | | May 22, 1881 |
| Davis, Tom | Meares, Myrtle | F/176 | May 5, 1899 | May 7, 1899 |
| Davis, W. V. | Young, M. A. | C/326 | February 4, 1885 | February 5, 1885 |

| Groom or Bride | Groom or Bride | Book/Page | Date of License | Date of Marriage |
|---|---|---|---|---|
| Davis, William | Bell, Josie | E/28 | April 14, 1888 | April 14, 1888 |
| Davis, Wm. | Higdon, Allice | C/356 | April 22, 1886 | April 22, 1886 |
| Davis, Wm. H. | Petty, Mariar F. | A2/121 | March 1, 1865 | March 25, 1865 |
| Davis, Wm. P. | Preston, Josie | C/12 | October 6, 1871 | October 11, 1871 |
| Ddom, Miss Nannie | Odom, W. D. | F/68 | September 17, 1895 | September 22, 1895 |
| Dean, Noah | Williams, Elizabeth | A/12 | March 22, 1839 | March 22, 1839 |
| Deanboise, Elizabeth | Espy, Robert | A/1 | March 23, 1838 | March 27, 1838 |
| Dearley, Martha (col.) | Keele, Joe (col.) | F/90 | July 13, 1896 | July 14, 1896 |
| Deberry | Brown, James | B/128 | March 25, 1871 | March 28, 1871 |
| Deberry, Angeline | Scott, Martin | C/420 | October 18, 1890 | October 19, 1890 |
| Deberry, Bellzora | Barrett, Jno B. | C/182 | December 24, 1877 | December 25, 1877 |
| Deberry, Charles | Thomas, Della | C/468 | November 19, 1892 | November 20, 1892 |
| Deberry, Ise | Foster, Robert | C/448 | October 14, 1891 | October 15, 1891 |
| Deberry, Jacob | Turner, Ellen | E/96 | November 3, 1888 | November 4, 1888 |
| Deberry, Jane Miss | Delong, Levi | C/378 | December 25, 1886 | December 27, 1886 |
| Deberry, Margarette | Collins, Wm. | C/416 | September 6, 1890 | September 8, 1890 |
| Deberry, Molley | Melton, John | E/39 | May 19, 1888 | May 19, 1888 |
| Deberry, Mry | Scot, James | C/368 | September 28, 1886 | No Return |
| Deberry, Nannie | Adams, Bennie | C/448 | November 1, 1891 | November 1, 1891 |
| Deberry, Rebecca J. | Allen, W. B. | C/110 | February 26, 1975 | February 26, 1875 |
| Debery, Bill | Rigsby, Mary L. | C/326 | February 21, 1885 | February 22, 1885 |
| Debonk, Miss Minervy | Devenport, J. B. | A2/89 | October 15, 1859 | No Return |
| Decke, Miss Matilda C. | Cawthan, David | A2/50 | August 29, 1856 | No Return |
| Delang, David | Sherley, Miss Emily | A2/80 | March 14, 1857 | March 15, 1857 |
| DeLoach, Jno | Turpentine, Peggy Ann | C/194 | August 12, 1878 | August 15, 1878 |
| Deloach, Lousanna Miss | Elkins, Shaderick W. | A/113 | August 19, 1848 | No Return |
| DeLoach, Martha Miss | Hollis, William C. | A/39 | June 28, 1841 | June 28, 1841 |
| Delong, Levi | Deberry, Miss Jane | C/378 | December 25, 1886 | December 27, 1886 |
| Delong, Wm. | Odom, Etter | C/364 | August 17, 1886 | September 30, 1886 |
| Delony, Watser | Stoner, Miss Norvena | A2/55 | February 16, 1859 | No Return |
| Dement, Mattie E. | Hogwood, D. I. | D/9 | | December 22, 1881 |
| Dement, Vina | Weedon, Wesley | C/32 | August 12, 1872 | August 12, 1872 |
| Dement, W. M. | McKnight, Annie | F/78 | December 17, 1895 | December 18, 1895 |
| Denby, Hariett | Edge, Elisha | A/10 | January 30, 1839 | February 1, 1839 |
| Denby, William | Patterson, Ann | A/79 | June 28, 1845 | No Return |
| Denis, Emerline Miss | Hutcheans, David | A2/85 | April 13, 1859 | May 2, 1859 |
| Denis, Thomas | Burch, Miss Clementine | B/88 | September 30, 1869 | September 30, 1869 |
| Denley, John | Patterson, Mary | C/272 | January 25, 1881 | January 30, 1881 |
| Dennis, Charlotte | Hollinsworth, John | A/31 | July 10, 1840 | July 10, 1840 |
| Dennis, Eliza Miss | Murfrey, B. F. | A/124 | August 2, 1849 | August 2, 1849 |
| Dennis, Elizabeth | Armstrong, Richard | A/70 | June 15, 1844 | June 25, 1844 |
| Dennis, John | Esque, Eliza | A/65 | November 21, 1843 | November 21, 1843 |
| Dennis, John N. | Grizzel, Miss Martha N. | B/92 | November 11, 1869 | November 14, 1869 |
| Dennis, Laurel | Hollandsworth, Tilford | C/442 | August 4, 1891 | |
| Dennis, M. K. | Hayes, Cedy | C/190 | April 20, 1878 | No Return |
| Dennis, Mary Miss | Markum, Alfred | B/92 | November 11, 1869 | November 14, 1869 |

| Groom or Bride | Groom or Bride | Book/Page | Date of License | Date of Marriage |
|---|---|---|---|---|
| Dennis, Mat | Tarleton, Susan | A2/122 | March 23, 1865 | No Return |
| Dennis, Mathew | Reeves, Salena | A/67 | February 8, 1844 | February 8, 1844 |
| Dennis, R. A. | King, Della | F/28 | January 15, 1894 | January 18, 1894 |
| Dennis, T. M. | Thomas, H. L. | F/30 | January 24, 1894 | NO Return |
| Dennis, Thos | Paterson, Fannie | C/140 | July 31, 1876 | No Return |
| Dennis, William | Higgins, Peggy | A/13 | May 8, 1839 | May 15, 1839 |
| Denny, J. A. | Wilson, M. J. | E/330 | December 28, 1898 | |
| Denton, Frances Miss | Barrett, William C. | B/58 | December 23 1867 | December 24, 1867 |
| Denton, J. E. | Reed, Amandy | C/32 | July 30, 1872 | August 1, 1872 |
| Denton, J. S. | Reed, Amandy | A2/32 | July 30, 1856 | August 1, 1872 |
| Denton, Jessee | Bragg, Miss Elizabeth | A/52 | August 11, 1842 | August 11, 1842 |
| Denton, John | Bragg, Nancy | A/25 | February 26, 1840 | February 26, 1840 |
| Denton, Margaret Miss | Miller, Richard | A2/77 | January 12, 1856 | January 13, 1856 |
| Denton, Margrett | Craddock, Simeon | C/32 | August 8, 1872 | September 5, 1872 |
| Denton, Smith J. | Pinkerton, Mary F. | E/37 | May 14, 1888 | May 14, 1888 |
| Denton, William | Mullins, Margret | A/23 | February 4, 1840 | February 4, 1840 |
| Deraberry, Pelina A. Miss | Lewis, William C. | B/100 | April 2, 1870 | April 2, 1870 |
| Dereberry, Elizabeth A. Miss | Bush, Jeremiah | A/107 | January 27, 1848 | January 27, 1848 |
| Derryberry, Barbary Miss | Smith, John R. | A2/7 | November 6, 1850 | No Endorsement |
| Derryberry, Jacob | Lasater, Miss Cinderella | A/114 | September 29, 1848 | October 1, 1848 |
| Derryberry, Nancy Jane | Burkett, A. J. | A2/6 | October 19, 1850 | No Return |
| Derting, S. L. | Knight, Mary F. | C/246 | March 26, 1880 | March 28, 1880 |
| Dethcart, Rebecca Miss | Hays, William B. | A/101 | August 9, 1847 | August 9, 1847 |
| Devanport, A. H. | Willson, Miss S. S. | A2/50 | October 10, 1856 | No Return |
| Devanport, Joseph | Gan, Miss Sarah | A2/23 | February 16, 1853 | February 16, 1853 |
| Devanport, William | Willson, Miss M. E. | A2/81 | January 15, 1858 | January 15, 1858 |
| Devenport, Eliza Miss | James, F. M. | A2/71 | January 5, 1859 | No Return |
| Devenport, Eliza Miss | Jones, B. M. | A2/83 | January 5, 1859 | January 6, 1859 |
| Devenport, George | Givens, Miss Fordy | B/118 | December 1, 1870 | December 6, 1870 |
| Devenport, H. G. | Pedon, Miss M. J. | C/8 | September 7, 1871 | September 7, 1871 |
| Devenport, Henry W. | Mingle, Sarah J. | C/16 | December 13, 1871 | December 13, 1871 |
| Devenport, J. B | Merrett, Miss Nancy | A2/73 | October 13, 1852 | October 15, 1852 |
| Devenport, J. B. | Dabonk, Miss Minervy | A2/80 | October 15, 1859 | No Return |
| Devenport, John S. | Winnett, Sarah E. | C/40 | October 2, 1872 | October 3, 1872 |
| Devenport, N. E. | Alexander, B. C. | C/44 | October 22, 1872 | October 22, 1872 |
| Dickens, Deley A. | Ivey, Philip | B/6 | September 1, 1865 | No Return |
| Dickens, Elizabeth | Haley, James | A/33 | September 19, 1840 | September 20, 1840 |
| Dickens, Fanny Dickens Miss | Gotcher, W. M. | A/104 | November 2, 1847 | November 3, 1847 |
| Dickens, Henry (col.) | Woods, Anna (col.) | D/18 | | November 10, 1882 |
| Dickens, John | Martin, Paralee | C/58 | June 13, 1873 | June 15, 1873 |
| Dickens, Nancy M. A. Miss | Kipp, G. B. | A2/61 | January 5, 1857 | No Return |
| Dickens, Sis | Jennings, Wesley | C/256 | September 8, 1880 | September 8, 1880 |
| Dickins, I. F. | Byler, Caroline | A2/28 | October 13, 1853 | October 16, 1853 |
| Dickins, N. C. | Todd, J. A. | C/184 | January 14, 1878 | February 6, 1878 |
| Dickson, T. F. | Carrick, Nancy A. | D/15 | | September 14, 1882 |
| Disheus, Rebecca | Woods, Joe (col.) | C/454 | February 13, 1892 | No Return |

| Groom or Bride | Groom or Bride | Book/Page | Date of License | Date of Marriage |
|---|---|---|---|---|
| Diehl, A. R. | Summar, Florence | C/432 | March 7, 1891 | March 8, 1891 |
| Dill, Adison | Brown, Miss Mary D. | A2/50 | August 14, 1856 | August 14, 1856 |
| Dill, Ann W. | Franks, S. B. | C/204 | November 17, 1878 | November 18, 1878 |
| Dill, W. C. | Odom, Miss A. L. | B/32 | November 27, 1866 | November 28, 1866 |
| Dillard, Lizzie | Gilley, Joe (col.) | C/420 | October 16, 1890 | October 17, 1890 |
| Dillon, Henry | Preston, Ann | C/378 | December 25, 1886 | December 26, 1886 |
| Dillen, Joseph | Stephens, Miss M. J. | A2/127 | September 14, 1865 | September 14, 1865 |
| Dillian, Phebe | Vandergriff, William | A/9 | December 13, 1838 | December 15, 1838 |
| Dillon, Charles | Odom, Juda Ann | B/8 | January 27, 1866 | No Return |
| Dillon, Charles | Odom, Fanny | B/10 | July 19, 1866 | July 20, 1866 |
| Dillon, Charles | Odom, Fanny | B/10 | July 19, 1866 | July 20, 1866 |
| Dillon, E. T. | Fugitt, Sallie | C/10 | September 18, 1871 | September 21, 1871 |
| Dillon, Eliza Miss | Massie, W. M. | B/96 | December 14, 1869 | December 14, 1869 |
| Dillon, Frances E. Miss | Phalon, E. H. | A2/127 | September 11, 1865 | September 12, 1865 |
| Dillon, Henry | Preston, Ann | C/378 | December 25, 1886 | December 26, 1886 |
| Dillon, Miss Fannie | Gribble, Cling | F/32 | February 1, 1894 | February 1, 1894 |
| Dillon, S. J. | Elgin, Mary A. | A2/118 | December 20, 1864 | December 21, 1864 |
| Dillons, Z. T. | Coleman, Mattie | C/92 | June 28, 1874 | June 28, 1874 |
| Dirting, John | Tittle, Miss Salena | A/68 | March 5, 1844 | March 28, 1844 |
| Distin, Clarissa Miss | Keaton, Henry | A/91 | September 17, 1846 | September 20, 1846 |
| Dixon, A. J. | Smithson, S. V. | F/176 | May 4, 1899 | May 7, 1899 |
| Dixon, Armsted | Morris, Mary | F/34 | October 6, 1894 | No Return |
| Dixon, Cally | George, Bill | C/354 | March 6, 1886 | March 7, 1886 |
| Dixon, Ella | Bly, Dick | C/354 | March 6, 1886 | March 7, 1886 |
| Dixon, James | Yates, Joesie | C/444 | August 27, 1891 | August 27, 1891 |
| Dixon, Joseph | Moore, Lizzie | F/6 | March 11, 1893 | March 12, 1893 |
| Dixon, Mattie L. | Rodgers, Willie | C/318 | November 3, 1884 | No Return |
| Dixon, Wash | Low, Mary | F/46 | October 20, 1894 | October 21, 1894 |
| Doak, John | Stephen, Willie | C/264 | May 23, 1880 | May 23, 1880 |
| Doak, Miss Birtha | Youree, J. F. | F/110 | February 8, 1897 | February 8, 1897 |
| Doak, R. D. | Preston, M. J. | C/120 | September 15, 1875 | September 16, 1875 |
| Doak, T. C. | Preston, H. L. | A2/127 | September 7, 1865 | September 7, 1865 |
| Doakes, Mary H. Miss | Davis, J. J. | B/36 | December 31, 1866 | January 1, 1867 |
| Doaks, Pheivia | Youree, R. S. | F/138 | December 7, 1897 | December 7, 1897 |
| Dobbs, A. S. | Vance, James | E/262 | January 15, 1890 | No Return |
| Dobbs, Clotie | Keaton, Alonzo | F/122 | July 28, 1897 | No Return |
| Dobbs, Elija | Higgins, Nettie | F/176 | May 11, 1899 | May 14, 1899 |
| Dobbs, J. T. | Walls, Jane | D/17 | | November 25, 1882 |
| Dobbs, James | Nokes, Mollie | C/88 | May 15, 1874 | May 16, 1874 |
| Dobbs, John | Campbell, Miss Mary | B/46 | May 10, 1867 | May 12, 1867 |
| Dobbs, John L. | Duggin, F. M. | F/4 | February 14, 1893 | February 16, 1893 |
| Dobbs, Miss A. P. | Davenport, T. B. | F/56 | December 8, 1894 | December 9, 1894 |
| Dodd, A. A.Miss | Williams, J. M. | A2/58 | October 22, 1857 | October 22, 1857 |
| Dodd, Albert | Sullivan | A2/130 | October 5, 1865 | October 5, 1865 |
| Dodd, Demaries E. Miss | Sullivan, William L. | A2/136 | January 17, 1866 | January 18, 1866 |
| Dodd, H. L. W. | Hancock, S. F. | E/212 | September 12, 1889 | September 12, 1889 |

| Groom or Bride | Groom or Bride | Book/Page | Date of License | Date of Marriage |
|---|---|---|---|---|
| Dodd, J. J. | Knight, Miss Lou | C/458 | April 26, 1892 | April 26, 1892 |
| Dodd, J. W. | Hancock, Miss And | F/84 | July 6, 1895 | No Return |
| Dodd, James H. | King, Miss Nancy E. | A2/24 | January 5, 1853 | January 5, 1853 |
| Dodd, John A. | Sullivan, Miss Ann E. | B/84 | August 25, 1869 | August 25, 1869 |
| Dodd, Joseph Y. | Hancock, Analiza | D/7 | | November 20, 1861 |
| Dodd, Mary Miss | Mathews, John W. | A/46 | January 19, 1842 | January 20, 1842 |
| Dodd, Mollie | Nelson, J. S. | C/110 | March 11, 1875 | March 11, 1875 |
| Dodd, Rachel P. Miss | Bryant, Zachariah T. | B/98 | December 7, 1869 | December 9, 1869 |
| Dodd, S. A. | Moore, M. P. | D/6 | | November 3, 1881 |
| Dodd, Sallie | Boren, A. J. | C/190 | March 28, 1878 | March 28, 1878 |
| Dodd, Smithy J. Miss | Givan, Bluford, H. | A2/72 | February 2, 1859 | No Return |
| Dodd, W. A. | Owen, B. A. | C/418 | October 11, 1890 | October 12, 1890 |
| Dodd, William | Matthews, Miss Charlotte | A/48 | March 12, 1842 | March 18, 1842 |
| Dodson, Carrol | Shirley, Sarah | C/278 | May 12, 1881 | No Return |
| Dom (Odom), James H. | Owin, Miss Susan M. | A2/35 | September 12, 1854 | September 12, 1854 |
| Donel, M. M. | McAdoo, R. F. | C/208 | December 2, 1878 | December 23, 1878 |
| Donnel, Austin | Bynum, Nancy E. | A2/119 | January 10, 1865 | January 11, 1865 |
| Donnell, Isabella Miss | Bethell, Mark | B/96 | December 15, 1869 | No Return |
| Donnell, James | Talley, Harriet | B/18 | February 2, 1870 | February 2, 1870 |
| Donnell, Jas. W. | McCasline, Roxannah | C/152 | January 17, 1877 | January 19, 1877 |
| Donnell, S. A. | Baxter, J. A. | C/148 | November 2, 1876 | November 12, 1876 |
| Donnell, Sarah E. Miss | Summar, J. N. | B/42 | March 15, 1867 | March 15, 1867 |
| Donnelle, William C. | Lansden, Miss Sarah P. | A/97 | February 8, 1847 | February 23, 1847 |
| Donoho, Edward | Maney, Miss Virginia | A/112 | June 27, 1848 | June 27, 1848 |
| Dood, Mary E. Miss | Hale, Thomas | B/92 | November 22, 1869 | November 23, 1869 |
| Dood, Sinthy J. Miss | Geons, Bluford H. | A2/33 | February 2, 1859 | No Return |
| Dougherty, D. Miss | Byrn, W. M. | B/92 | November 23, 1869 | November 24, 1869 |
| Dougherty, Martha A. Miss | Maney, H. J. | B/80 | March 15, 1869 | March 16, 1869 |
| Douglas, James T. | Sparks, Miss Mary F. | C/4 | August 5, 1871 | August 6, 1871 |
| Douglass, James I. | Martin, Roslin L. | A2/121 | February 21, 1865 | February 22, 1865 |
| Dow, Henry | Bryson, Hannah | C/194 | July 22, 1878 | July 27, 1878 |
| Dowing, Bettie | Carter, R. A. | C/204 | November 13, 1878 | November 15, 1878 |
| Downing, A. L. | Mitchell, Roxey | C/320 | December 10, 1884 | December 10, 1884 |
| Downing, George R. | Hoover, Mary | C/322 | December 27, 1884 | December 28, 1884 |
| Downing, Jennie | Hoover, J. P. | F/150 | June 4, 1898 | June 5, 1898 |
| Downing, July | Hoover, J. I. | C/302 | January 22, 1884 | January 22, 1884 |
| Downing, W. A. | Northcut, H. J. | C/342 | December 3, 1885 | December 13, 1885 |
| Downing, W. R. | Hoover, Beatrice | F/18 | September 16, 1893 | September 16, 1893 |
| Dozier, John H. | Dozier, Miss Martha A. | A/123 | July 26, 1849 | July 26, 1849 |
| Dozier, Jonathan | Hollis, Miss Louisa Caroline | A/101 | August 12, 1847 | August 12, 1847 |
| Dozier, Martha A. Miss | Dozier, John H. | A/123 | July 26, 1849 | July 26, 1849 |
| Dozier, Peter | Elkins, Polly | A/76 | January 7, 1845 | January 7, 1845 |
| Drennen, J. C. | McBroom, Epple | F/140 | December 22, 1897 | December 22, 1897 |
| Driver, Aldona | Murphy, Robt. T. | C/62 | July 30, 1873 | July 30, 1873 |
| Driver, Elizabeth | Farless, Robt | C/158 | March 1, 1877 | March 1, 1877 |
| Dubirth, Nancy | Golahah, Robert | A/16 | August 2, 1839 | August 2, 1839 |

| Groom or Bride | Groom or Bride | Book/Page | Date of License | Date of Marriage |
|---|---|---|---|---|
| Dubois, Martha Miss | Helton, James | A/125 | July 19, 1849 | July 19, 1849 |
| Duboise, James P. | Tenpenny, Miss Julian | B/48 | July 25, 1867 | July 25, 1867 |
| Duboise, John Irvin | Hollis, Miss Susan Jane | A/68 | March 8, 1844 | March 14, 1844 |
| Duboise, Mary A. Miss | Elkins, Charles | A/111 | April 29, 1848 | April 30, 1848 |
| Duboys, James M. | Hays, Miss Nancy | A2/53 | January 1, 1857 | January 15, 1857 |
| Dugan, Roy | Smithson, Milley | E/380 | October 29, 1898 | |
| Duggam, Prestley | Hancock, Miss Mary | A/70 | June 18, 1844 | June 18, 1844 |
| Duggan, Aaron | Brown, Nancy | A/27 | April 2, 1840 | April 2, 1840 |
| Duggan, Henry S. | McKnight, Miss Sarah E. | A/105 | December 20, 1847 | December 21, 1847 |
| Duggan, Susan | Higgins, James | A/10 | January 22, 1839 | January 24, 1839 |
| Duggen, Henry S. | Tittle, Selina | A/14 | June 6, 1839 | June 6, 1839 |
| Duggin, Delie | Harris, Billey | F/124 | August 4, 1897 | August 5, 1897 |
| Duggin, F. M | Dobbs, John L. | F/4 | February 14, 1893 | February 16, 1893 |
| Duggin, Florance | Bryson, J. W. | F/158 | September 27, 1898 | September 28, 1898 |
| Duggin, Henry | Sawles, Allice | F/156 | September 9, 1898 | September 9, 1898 |
| Duggin, J. W. | Harris, Sallie | F/132 | September 28, 1897 | September 30, 1897 |
| Duggin, James C. | Leech, Caldonia | C/132 | January 27, 1876 | January 27, 1876 |
| Duggin, Juliann Miss | Sauls, David | A2/84 | March 21, 1859 | No Return |
| Duggin, Lonney | Pitman, Lvie | F/128 | August 23, 1897 | August 24, 1897 |
| Duggin, M. C. L. | Travis, Sallie | C/400 | September 5, 1887 | No Return |
| Duggin, N. E. | Roper, Walter | F/50 | November 22, 1894 | November 25, 1894 |
| Duggin, S. A. | Leech, A. L. | C/126 | December 23, 1875 | December 23, 1875 |
| Duggin, T. E. | Brandon, D. C. | C/164 | July 20, 1877 | July 21, 1877 |
| Duggin, Thos. | Jones, Eunice | C/74 | November 26, 1873 | November 27, 1863 |
| Duggin, Vella | Campbell, T. A. | F/8 | May 6, 1893 | May 7, 1893 |
| Duggin, W. H. | Summar, E. A. | C/102 | December 16, 1874 | December 17, 1874 |
| Duggin, W. P. | McKnight, Mary J. | C/64 | July 31, 1873 | July 31, 1873 |
| Duggins, J. T. | Odom, Ednie A. | C/230 | November 10, 1879 | November 12, 1879 |
| Duke, Alexander | Almon, Miss Ann Almon | B/80 | March 16, 1869 | March 18, 1869 |
| Duke, Ann | Williams, John | C/312 | August 27, 1884 | August 27, 1884 |
| Duke, B. Harry | Edwards, Miss Melinda | A/106 | December 23, 1847 | December 23, 1847 |
| Duke, Bettie | Rains, I. W. | C/436 | May 4, 1891 | May 7, 1891 |
| Duke, C. J. | McMahan, Rebecca J. | C/144 | September 15, 1876 | September 17, 1876 |
| Duke, C. P. | Simmons, Sallie | D/8 | | December 25, 1881 |
| Duke, Calvin | Swanger, Mollie | F/76 | December 14, 1895 | December 14, 1895 |
| Duke, Della | Stacy, William | F/156 | September 15, 1898 | September 17, 1898 |
| Duke, Dora | Banks, Edgar | F/72 | October 19, 1895 | October 20, 1894 |
| Duke, Elizabeth Miss | Brooks, Isaac | A/113 | August 5, 1848 | August 6, 1848 |
| Duke, G. A. | Williams, Jane F. | C/102 | December 18, 1874 | December 20, 1874 |
| Duke, Gideon | King, Betsy | A/24 | February 12, 1840 | February 13, 1840 |
| Duke, I. J. | Edwards, Miss Marry | A2/28 | August 29, 1853 | August 30, 1853 |
| Duke, I. N. | Haley, Janie | D/20 | | January 26, 1883 |
| Duke, J. J. | Bush, M. E. | C/108 | March 3, 1875 | March 3, 1875 |
| Duke, J. M. | Lynn, Rachal | A2/133 | December 6, 1865 | December 7, 1865 |
| Duke, J. M. | Davis, Mary E. | C/112 | April 14, 1875 | April 18, 1875 |
| Duke, J. W. | Duncan, Mary A. | E/141 | February 23, 1889 | February 24, 1889 |

| Groom or Bride | Groom or Bride | Book/Page | Date of License | Date of Marriage |
|---|---|---|---|---|
| Duke, James | Parker, Omy M. | C/124 | December 6, 1875 | December 5, 1875 |
| Duke, James | Duke, Ome | C/254 | August 25, 1880 | August 25, 1880 |
| Duke, Jno ? | Duke, Miss Mary | C/454 | January 22, 1892 | January 22, 1892 |
| Duke, John | Parker, Miss Nancy | B/44 | April 17, 1867 | April 18, 1867 |
| Duke, John A. | Haley, Vicy C. | A2/20 | October 15, 1852 | October 16, 1852 |
| Duke, M. J. Miss | Duke, W. J. | E/241 | December 17, 1889 | December 19, 1889 |
| Duke, Malinda | Orr, J. B. | D/6 | | November 17, 1881 |
| Duke, Marcel | Hawkins, Malinda | C/204 | November 5, 1878 | November 7, 1878 |
| Duke, Martha A. | Parker, John M. | C/350 | January 29, 1886 | January 31, 1886 |
| Duke, Mary | Bush, Thomas | F/6 | April 8, 1893 | April 9, 1893 |
| Duke, Mary Miss | Duke, Jno ? | C/454 | January 22, 1892 | January 22, 1892 |
| Duke, Mary A. | Williams, Jno. R. | C/96 | October 5, 1874 | October 11, 1874 |
| Duke, Mary J. | Roberson, Wm. | F/60 | March 9, 1895 | March 10, 1895 |
| Duke, Mary Miss | Duke, Jno ? | C/454 | January 22, 1892 | January 22, 1892 |
| Duke, Matilda | Swanger, W. S. | C/394 | July 16, 1887 | July 16, 18878 |
| Duke, Monroe | Lynn, Miss Sarah | B/50 | August 31, 1867 | September 1, 1867 |
| Duke, Mordecai M. | Rhea, Miss Eleanor | A/98 | March 17, 1847 | March 17, 1847 |
| Duke, N. R. J. | Haley, Venturian | A2/103 | October 24, 1860 | No Return |
| Duke, Nancy | Smithson, J. A. | F/112 | February 23, 1897 | February 27, 1897 |
| Duke, Ome | Duke, James | C/254 | August 25, 1880 | August 25, 1880 |
| Duke, P. P. | Basham, Nannie | F/146 | February 17, 1898 | February 20, 1898 |
| Duke, S. C. | Haley, W. V. | C/162 | May 30, 1877 | May 30, 1877 |
| Duke, S. H. Miss | Beason, J. H. | B/128 | March 9, 1871 | March 15, 1871 |
| Duke, Sarah Ann Miss | Haley, David | A/106 | January 11, 1848 | January 11, 1848 |
| Duke, Sarah Miss | Smithson, Gardner | C/452 | December 30, 1891 | December 31, 1891 |
| Duke, Sarah P. Miss | Lewis, Jesse G. | B/90 | October 5, 1869 | October 10, 1869 |
| Duke, Tom | St.John Miss Rosie | F/122 | July 27, 1897 | July ??, 1897 |
| Duke, Tilda E. | Lemmons, J. B. | C/160 | March 21, 1877 | March 22, 1877 |
| Duke, W. C. | Parker, Annie | F/132 | September 21, 897 | September 24, 1897 |
| Duke, W. J. | Duke, Miss M. J. | E/241 | December 17, 1889 | December 19, 1889 |
| Duke, Willey | Stone, Doscha | C/204 | November 26, 1878 | November 26, 1878 |
| Duke, William | Morgan, Cynthia | A/1 | March 19, 1838 | March 22, 1838 |
| Dukes, Calvin | Parker, Mahala | C/144 | August 26, 1876 | September 17, 1876 |
| Dukes, Dollie Miss | Bryant, John M. | C/388 | May 17, 1887 | May 18, 1887 |
| Dukin, J. F. | Prator, Miss M. J. | A2/69 | October 27, 1858 | October 28, 1858 |
| Duncan, Clarissa Miss | Ashley, John R. | A/126 | August 11, 1849 | August 16, 1849 |
| Duncan, Eliza A. | Simmons, Jese | A2/134 | December 22, 1865 | December 24, 1865 |
| Duncan, Elizabeth | Davis, Joshua | A2/123 | June 28, 1865 | June 29, 1865 |
| Duncan, L. G. | Pendleton, W. G. | C/12 | October 10, 1871 | No Return |
| Duncan, J. D. | Ensey, Rebecca A. | C/38 | September 10, 1872 | September 10, 1872 |
| Duncan, J. H. | Moore, V. H. | E/230 | November 4, 1889 | No Return |
| Duncan, James | Botkins, Issabella B. | A/61 | March 16, 1843 | March 16, 1863 |
| Duncan, Jane | McFerrin, Edmund | B/4 | August 24, 1865 | No Return |
| Duncan, L. H. | Williams, Mary M. | C/310 | August 2, 1884 | August 3, 1884 |
| Duncan, L. L. | Finley, Henry | A2/129 | September 27, 1865 | September 27, 1865 |
| Duncan, L. T. | Scott, Miss Mary E. | B/44 | April 9, 1867 | No Return |

| Groom or Bride | Groom or Bride | Book/Page | Date of License | Date of Marriage |
|---|---|---|---|---|
| Duncan, M. R. | Saddler, Sarah M. N. | C/302 | January 25, 1884 | January 27, 1884 |
| Duncan, Manerva Miss | Lemons, Isaac | A/84 | October 25, 1845 | Executed--No Date |
| Duncan, Martha S. | Davenport, J. B. | A2/110 | July 11, 1863 | No Return |
| Duncan, Mary A. | Duke, J. W. | E/141 | February 23, 1889 | February 24, 1889 |
| Duncan, Mary Ann Miss | Whitamore, William | A2/9 | January 10, 1851 | January 12, 1851 |
| Duncan, Matisa | Todd, Ranson | A2/21 | November 20, 1852 | November 21, 1852 |
| Duncan, N. J. R. | Gilley, W. T. | C/310 | July 22, 1884 | July 23, 1884 |
| Duncan, P. B. | Williams, Bettie | E/239 | December 11, 1889 | December 15, 1889 |
| Duncan, P. J. | Sadler, A. J. | C/308 | June 2, 1884 | June 8, 1884 |
| Duncan, Peter B. | Sissam, Lisa A. | A2/78 | March 3, 1856 | March 4, 1856 |
| Duncan, Polly | Williams, Jesse | A/33 | September 22, 1840 | September 22, 1840 |
| Duncan, Rebecca A. | Wright, T. R. | C/60 | July 10, 1873 | No Return |
| Duncan, Sarah Ann Miss | Alford, Wm. C. | A2/40 | April 30, 1855 | May 16, 1855 |
| Duncan, W. B. D. | Rains, Miss R. D. | A2/32 | March 18, 1854 | January 17, 1854 |
| Duncan, W. J. | Parker, Margrett | C/296 | November 24, 1883 | November 25, 1883 |
| Dunkin, Owen | Wyly, Miss Nancy S. | A2/24 | March 9, 1853 | March 10, 1853 |
| Dunlap, Delor | Green, George | C/414 | July 19, 1890 | July 20, 1890 |
| Dunlap, E. F. | Parker, W. F. | C/334 | August 8, 1885 | August 9, 1885 |
| Dunlap, W. S. | Tolbert, Miss Sallie | E/25 | March 8, 1888 | March 8, 1888 |
| Dunn, Annie (col.) | Martin, Bob (col.) | F/148 | April 3, 1898 | April 3, 1898 |
| Dunn, Daniel (col.) | Taylor, Nannie | C/408 | November 26, 1887 | November 27, 1887 |
| Dunn, Irving | Gaither, Lizie | F/74 | November 13, 1895 | November 13, 1895 |
| Dunn, Wm. J. | Knox, Miss Nancy C. | A/108 | February 14, 1848 | February 17, 1848 |
| Durrett, Rhamy Miss | Prator, Marcus | A2/75 | January 3, 1855 | January 4, 1855 |
| Dyer, Charlie | Lorance, Josie | C/300 | January 12, 1884 | January 12, 1884 |
| Eades, Sally Miss | Burkee, James | A/44 | November 16, 1841 | November 17, 1841 |
| Eads, Mathew W. | Espey, Miss Vina A. | A2/79 | June 18, 1856 | June 19, 1856 |
| Eads, Samuel | Moore, Miss Permela | A2/17 | March 2, 1852 | No Return |
| Eagleton, Adell | New, W. R. | E/259 | January 8, 1890 | No Return |
| Eagleton, Elvira | Mathews, Cephas | F/144 | January 20, 1898 | January 20, 1898 |
| Eakes, George | Ekins, Rebecca | A2/65 | July 2, 1858 | July 14, 1858 |
| Earles, Eva | Youngblood, Joe | E/348 | December 21, 1898 | |
| Earles, Eva | Youngblood, Joe | F/162 | December 21, 1898 | December 25, 1898 |
| Earles, G. A. | Robinson, Rose Ann | C/448 | October 5, 1891 | October 12, 1891 |
| Earles, Willey | Bell, Miss Annie | F/172 | March 18, 1899 | March 19, 1899 |
| Earls, Larcan W. | Burks, Mary L. | E/391 | December 20, 1919 | |
| Earls, Nathan | Auton, Miss Elisabeth | A2/55 | April 9, 1857 | April 10, 1857 |
| Earls, Sallie | Ford, James | C/360 | July 21, 1886 | No Return |
| Earnhart, Harriman | Stone, Mary V. | C/312 | August 22, 1884 | August 22, 1884 |
| Earp, Alice | Tolber, William | F/132 | September 18, 1897 | September 23, 1897 |
| Earp, G. W. | Bynum, M. L. | C/24 | March 6, 1872 | March 7, 1872 |
| Earvin, John W. | Coleman, Miss Mary | B/40 | February 19, 1867 | February 19, 1867 |
| Earwood, Caroline | Wood, B. F. | D/10 | | December 4, 1881 |
| Eason, Emily | McFerrin, Alfred | B/2 | August 23, 1865 | August 25, 1865 |
| Eason, Harriet Miss | Givens, William J. | A2/10 | January 20, 1851 | January 21, 1851 |
| Eason, Jane Miss | Bethel, B. J. | A2/53 | January 21, 1857 | No Return |

| Groom or Bride | Groom or Bride | Book/Page | Date of License | Date of Marriage |
|---|---|---|---|---|
| Eason, R. F. | Atcheley, Miss Nannie? | B/68 | July 30, 1868 | July 30, 1868 |
| Eatherly, Elizabeth | Miller, James | C/302 | January 30, 1884 | January 30, 1884 |
| Edding, Plesant | Merritt, Nancy | A2/19 | September 25, 1852 | No Return |
| Eddings, Wm. R. | Muncy, Elizabeth | A2/21 | December 8, 1852 | December 8, 1852 |
| Eddington, Hugh | Osment, Martha I. | A2/106 | October 21, 1862 | October 22, 1862 |
| Edge, Elisha | Denby, Hariett | A/10 | January 30, 1839 | February 1, 1839 |
| Edge, Mary C. | Prater, W. C. | C/406 | November 9, 1887 | November 9, 1887 |
| Edge, Mollie | Gowens, Wm. | C/396 | August 4, 1887 | August 11, 1887 |
| Edward, J. W. | Carter, Miss Luiza F. | A2/86 | June 6, 1859 | No Return |
| Edward, Nancy | Philips, Wm. C. | A2/85 | May 23, 1859 | Execution not Clear |
| Edwards, Alford | Lewin, Miss Jane | A2/60 | December 19, 1857 | No Return |
| Edwards, C. C. | Brewer, Nancy A. | C/230 | November 14, 1879 | November 18, 1879 |
| Edwards, Charity Miss | Moon, John | A2/43 | October 22, 1855 | October 29, 1855 |
| Edwards, Elizabeth | Hollis, George W. | A/16 | August 1, 1839 | No Return |
| Edwards, Lillia | Allen, Joe | C/314 | September 20, 1884 | September 20, 1884 |
| Edwards, M. L. | Blancet, Miss M. J. | A2/50 | November 5, 1856 | No Return |
| Edwards, Martha E. | Moon, John | C/52 | February 1, 1873 | February 2, 1873 |
| Edwards, Mary E. Miss | Turner, G. T. | B/86 | September 18, 1869 | September 19, 1869 |
| Edwards, Mary Miss | Hopkins, Joseph W. | A/117 | November 24, 1848 | November 21, 1848 |
| Edwards, Mary Miss | Duke, I. J. | A2/28 | August 29, 1853 | August 30, 1853 |
| Edwards, Melinda Miss | Duke, B. Harry | A/106 | December 23, 1847 | December 23, 1847 |
| Edwards, Nancy A. Miss | Reed, John H. | A2/86 | June 25, 1859 | No Return |
| Edwards, Nancy Miss | Lanier, James H. | A2/68 | October 21, 1858 | October 21, 1858 |
| Edwards, Sarah F. | Pitts, Isaac F. | D/16 | | October 15, 1882 |
| Edwards, Susannah | Hollis, Lewis J. | A/15 | July 9, 1839 | July 11, 1839 |
| Edwards, Uphey | St. John, John | A2/54 | January 29, 1857 | January 29, 1857 |
| Edwards, W. H. | Stacy, M. J. | D/1 | | June 9, 1881 |
| Edwards, William | Payne, Eliza | A/54 | September 27, 1842 | September 27, 1842 |
| Edwards, Wm. H. | Stacy, Sarah E. | A2/114 | May 3, 1864 | No Return |
| Ekens, Liza Jane Miss | Prater, M. M. | A2/51 | December 1, 1856 | No Return |
| Ekins, Rebecca | Eakes, George | A2/65 | July 2, 1858 | July 14, 1858 |
| Elam, Fate | Perry, Mary | C/260 | November 4, 1880 | November 4, 1880 |
| Elam, Flora Miss | Nokes, Nelson | A/63 | June 3, 1843 | June 4, 1843 |
| Elam, Francis | Wileyford, John | C/62 | July 28, 1873 | July 31, 1873 |
| Elam, Henry | Pendleton, Elizabeth | A/34 | October 22, 1840 | October 24, 1840 |
| Elam, Henry | Amos, Saray | C/428 | January 8, 1891 | January 10, 1891 |
| Elam, J. B. | Shelton, R. A. | C/270 | January 20, 1881 | January 20, 1881 |
| Elam, J. M. | McMahan, Sarah J. | C/92 | August 18, 1874 | August 20, 1874 |
| Elam, Jackline | Kirby, R. S. | C/226 | October 9, 1879 | October 9, 1879 |
| Elam, M. A. | Carrick, A. J. | C/190 | April 1, 1878 | April 4, 1878 |
| Elam, M. R. | Spangler, M. D. | C/108 | February 18, 1875 | February 19, 1875 |
| Elam, Mary Ann Miss | Wilson, John | A2/154 | May 25, 1866 | May 25, 1866 |
| Elam, N. B. | Inglish, Sallie | C/256 | September 16, 1880 | No Return |
| Elam, Reuben | Lance, Miss Polly | A/66 | December 24, 1843 | December 27, 1843 |
| Elams, Rubin L. | Teele, Lou | C/468 | November 23, 1892 | November 23, 1892 |
| Elander, Sarah Miss | Darnell, W. C. | A2/31 | December 26, 1853 | No Return |

61

| Groom or Bride | Groom or Bride | Book/Page | Date of License | Date of Marriage |
|---|---|---|---|---|
| Elder, Edward | Orand, Miss Elizabeth | A2/38 | January 9, 1855 | January 9, 1855 |
| Eledge, Clannatin Miss | Inglish, Alex | C/402 | September 145, 1887 | September 15, 1887 |
| Eledge, Martha Miss | Gilley, Samuel | B/114 | October 15, 1870 | October 16, 1870 |
| Elgin, Mary A. | Dillon, S. J. | A2/118 | December 20, 1864 | December 21, 1864 |
| Elkin, Robt. L. | Foster, Eliza T. | C/32 | August 10, 1872 | August 10, 1872 |
| Elkins, Allice | Stephens, J. F. | C/338 | October 15, 1885 | October 15, 1885 |
| Elkins, Amand E. | Burkett, James | F/120 | July 24, 1897 | July 25, 1897 |
| Elkins, Angeline | McMahan, J. T. | C/96 | October 1, 1874 | October 1, 1874 |
| Elkins, Ann | Melton, Willie | E/177 | May 10, 1889 | May 10, 1889 |
| Elkins, Arta M. | Morgan, Gordon | A/6 | September 7, 1838 | September 10, 1838 |
| Elkins, Bettie | Merriman, Wesley | C/464 | August 29, 1892 | No Return |
| Elkins, Bezie | Rucker, Wiley | F/108 | December 27, 1896 | December 27, 1896 |
| Elkins, C. Miss | Thomas, William | A2/61 | December 24, 1857 | December 24, 1857 |
| Elkins, Calidonia | Smith, Isaac | A2/114 | May 18, 1864 | May 18, 1864 |
| Elkins, Charles | Duboise, Miss Mary A. | A/111 | April 29, 1848 | April 30, 1848 |
| Elkins, D. L | Walkup, Miss Emily | A2/7 | November 29, 1850 | December 1, 1850 |
| Elkins, D. L. | Elkins, Elizabeth T. | A2/105 | October 6, 1862 | October 7, 1862 |
| Elkins, Dillard S. | Cummings, Miss Mary E. | A/73 | October 2, 1844 | October 2, 1844 |
| Elkins, Dona | Haley, W. H. | F/98 | October 3, 1896 | October 4, 1896 |
| Elkins, Dosia E. | Sowell, William F. | B/42 | March 20, 1867 | March 20, 1867 |
| Elkins, Eliza | Young, Polk | F/20 | November 1, 1893 | November 1, 1893 |
| Elkins, Eliza A. | Taylor, John | C/274 | February 28, 1881 | March 1, 1881 |
| Elkins, Elizabeth T. | Elkins, D. L. | A2/105 | October 6, 1862 | October 7, 1862 |
| Elkins, H. R. | Higgins, Eliza Ann | B/62 | February 4, 1868 | February 4, 1868 |
| Elkins, H. R. | Neely, Miss R. E. | A2/86 | July 9, 1859 | July 10, 1859 |
| Elkins, Hampton | Gooding, Miss Mary | A2/32 | March 2, 1854 | No Return |
| Elkins, Hariett Miss | Neely, N. L. | A2/30 | March 30, 1854 | March 30, 1854 |
| Elkins, J. D. | Pitman, Vicy J. | C/110 | March 3, 1875 | March 7, 1875 |
| Elkins, J. P. | Parris, Miss Harriett | A2/71 | January 6, 1859 | January 6, 1859 |
| Elkins, J. P. | Parris, Miss Harriett | A2/83 | January 6, 1859 | January 6, 1859 |
| Elkins, J. P. | Alread, Elizabeth | F/10 | May 13, 1893 | May 18, 1893 |
| Elkins, J. T. | Jones, Miss Lizzie | E/12 | January 21, 1888 | ?? |
| Elkins, J. W. | Mason, Miss Ann | C/450 | December 7, 1891 | December 8, 1891 |
| Elkins, James | Lewis, Miss Jane | A2/86 | July 4, 1859 | No Return |
| Elkins, Jennie Miss | Maney, William L. | C/390 | June 2, 1887 | June 2, 1887 |
| Elkins, John | Lowrance, Mandy | C/54 | February 27, 1873 | February 30, 1873 |
| Elkins, John B. | Bethel, Polley | D/1 | | July 15, 1881 |
| Elkins, John D. | Tittle, Julia Ann | A/17 | September 4, 1839 | September 5, 1839 |
| Elkins, John W. | Exque, Lucinda | A2/3 | June 29, 1850 | June 30, 1850 |
| Elkins, Leona | Gilley, John | F/54 | January 6, 1895 | January 6, 1895 |
| Elkins, Leroy Lafayette | Young, Miss Mary Caroline | A2/79 | April 5, 1856 | April 6, 1856 |
| Elkins, Lilley | West, Willey | F/80 | January 4, 1896 | January 4, 1896 |
| Elkins, Lora | Todd, W. A. | F/142 | December 30, 1897 | December 30, 1897 |
| Elkins, Lucinda | Prater, C. L. | C/62 | July 17, 1873 | No Return |
| Elkins, Lucy Ann | Pitman, Stanford | B/34 | December 25, 1866 | December 25, 1866 |
| Elkins, M. G. | Vandagriff, Miss Mary Jane | A2/37 | December 7, 1854 | December 7, 1854 |

| Groom or Bride | Groom or Bride | Book/Page | Date of License | Date of Marriage |
|---|---|---|---|---|
| Elkins, M. J. Miss | Parris, J. B. | A2/87 | August 13, 1859 | No Return |
| Elkins, M. S. | Foster, R. C. | F/136 | November 15, 1897 | November 15, 1897 |
| Elkins, Malissa Caroline Miss | Melton, Bemjamin | A/86 | January 28, 1846 | January 28, 1846 |
| Elkins, Margaret | Todd, Walter L. | A2/123 | June 15, 1865 | June 15, 1865 |
| Elkins, Margarett E. Miss | Prater, James | A/132 | February 18, 1850 | February 18, 1850 |
| Elkins, Martha Miss | Barett, Abraham | A2/24 | March 19, 1853 | March 29, 1853 |
| Elkins, Martha Virginia Miss | Fowler, Jacob B. | A/89 | May 21, 1846 | May 21, 1846 |
| Elkins, Mary C. Mrs. | Merritt, Thomas | C/2 | May 2, 1871 | May 3, 1871 |
| Elkins, Mary J. Miss | Foster, John R. | B/112 | September 6, 1870 | September 27, 1870 |
| Elkins, Mary M. J. | Worley, Osiah | C/126 | December 17, 1875 | December 17, 1875 |
| Elkins, Minnie | Phillips, J. | F/154 | August 6, 1898 | August 7, 1898 |
| Elkins, Minnie Miss | Mathis, Willie | F/176 | May 20, 1899 | No Return |
| Elkins, Mollie | Hall, J. P. | F/22 | November 16, 1893 | November 16, 1893 |
| Elkins, N. A. | Markum, Wm | C/22 | January 24, 1872 | January 25, 1872 |
| Elkins, Nancy | Mears, James | A/50 | July 2, 1842 | July 3, 1842 |
| Elkins, Polly | Dozier, Peter | A/76 | January 7, 1845 | January 7, 1845 |
| Elkins, Rachell J. Miss | Youngblood, Andrew | A2/56 | April 22, 1857 | April 22, 1857 |
| Elkins, S. J. | Bailey, Miss Ferdelia | E/19 | February 16, 1888 | February 16, 1888 |
| Elkins, S. W. | Spicer, Vester | F/46 | October 20, 1894 | October 21, 1894 |
| Elkins, Sandy J. | Elledge, Malissa | A2/119 | January 23, 1865 | January 24, 1865 |
| Elkins, Sarah Ann Miss | Tittle, John | A2/30 | December 22, 1853 | December 22, 1853 |
| Elkins, Sarah F. | Elrod, S. D | C/178 | November 19, 1877 | November 20, 1877 |
| Elkins, Shaderick W. | Deloach, Miss Lousanna | A/113 | August 19, 1848 | No Return |
| Elkins, Silas | Thomas, Miss Sarah F. | B/126 | March 4, 1871 | No Return |
| Elkins, Silas | Collins, Flora | F/158 | September 29, 1898 | September 29, 1898 |
| Elkins, Stacy C. | Young, John A. | A/56 | November 23, 1842 | November 23, 1842 |
| Elkins, Susannah | Manus, Daniel | A/29 | June 11, 1840 | June 11, 1840 |
| Elkins, T. D. | Foster, Miss Mary Ann | A2/142 | August 6, 1866 | August 7, 1866 |
| Elkins, Tennie | Gunter, Jesse | D/12 | | March 19, 1882 |
| Elkins, Thomas | Sullins, Ruth | C/190 | April 18, 1878 | April 18, 1878 |
| Elkins, Thomas | Bogle, Miss Sallie | C/386 | March 7, 1887 | March 7, 1887 |
| Elkins, W. J. | Knox, Emeline | D/8 | | December 16, 1881 |
| Elkins, Wm. | Hollis, Francis | C/192 | May 11, 1878 | May 12, 18878 |
| Elkins, Wm. | Bogle, Mary J. | C/330 | March 25, 1885 | March 26, 1885 |
| Elkins, Wm. | Blanch, Bettie | E/101 | November 17, 1888 | November 17, 1888 |
| Elladge, Wm. C. | McClain, Mary | A/94 | December 23, 1846 | December 24, 1846 |
| Elledge, Charles | Ready, Callie | B/122 | December 28, 1870 | December 30, 1870 |
| Elledge, Eliza J. | Sissom, Wm. T. | C/168 | August 21, 1877 | August 23, 1877 |
| Elledge, George | Wood, Susan C. | C/204 | November 16, 1878 | No Return |
| Elledge, James B. | Mayfield, Edny S. | C/66 | September 20, 1873 | September 21, 1873 |
| Elledge, Malissa | Elkins, Sandy J. | A2/119 | January 23, 1865 | January 24, 1865 |
| Elledge, Mattie | Brewer, A. G. | C/350 | January 19, 1886 | January 19, 1886 |
| Elledge, Roxex | Carnahan, James M. | C/350 | January 23, 1884 | January 24, 1886 |
| Elledge, Sarah Ann Miss | Vance, Samuel | A/44 | November 13, 1841 | November 14, 1841 |
| Elledge, Sarah E. | Turner, Jno E. | C/74 | November 26, 1873 | November 26, 1873 |
| Elledge, Sarah F. | Mears, T. B. | C/136 | April 9, 1876 | April 9, 1876 |

| Groom or Bride | Groom or Bride | Book/Page | Date of License | Date of Marriage |
|---|---|---|---|---|
| Elledge, Susan Miss | Turner, J. E. | B/122 | December 24, 1870 | December 25, 1870 |
| Elledge, T. B. | Cummins, J. P. | C/70 | October 28, 1873 | October 29, 1873 |
| Elledge, William F. | Wood, Nancy Ann | A/18 | October 3, 1839 | October 4, 1839 |
| Ellidge, Paompey | Jones, Mary | C/24 | February 29, 1872 | February 29, 1872 |
| Ellie, Mary Ann Miss | Anderson, Asa | A/46 | December 30, 1841 | December 30, 1841 |
| Elliott, A. C. | McCullough, Miss Mary A. | C/6 | August 29, 1871 | August 30, 1871 |
| Ellison, Joseph M. | Mitchell, Mollie | B/16 | December 24, 1868 | December 25, 1868 |
| Ellison, Martha Miss | Jones, Lafayette | B/104 | June 24, 1870 | June 26, 1870 |
| Elrod, A. T. | Justic, Miss Susan | B/124 | January 12, 1871 | January 12, 1871 |
| Elrod, Adam | Lowing, Jane | A/5 | August 2, 1838 | August 2, 1838 |
| Elrod, B. F. | Milligin, Miss Annie | C/8 | September 6, 1871 | September 6, 1871 |
| Elrod, Daisey | Wooton, W. E. | F/72 | October 21, 1895 | October 21, 1895 |
| Elrod, Eliza B. | Ferrel, Wm. B. | A/17 | August 29, 1839 | August 29, 1839 |
| Elrod, Elizabeth Miss | Mitchel, James H. | A/105 | November 20, 1847 | November 20, 1847 |
| Elrod, J. M. | Couch, Miss M. M. | B/92 | October 30, 1869 | October 31, 1869 |
| Elrod, J. M. | Carick, N. E. | C/294 | October 27, 1883 | October 31, 1883 |
| Elrod, Luda, Miss | Northcut, James M. | C/408 | November 14, 1887 | November 14, 1887 |
| Elrod, Margaret A. Miss | Ferrel, John | A/72 | August 24, 1844 | August 25, 1844 |
| Elrod, Martha T. | Hanes (Davis), Joseph T. | A2/13 | December 20, 1851 | December 23, 1851 |
| Elrod, Miss I. J. | Justice W. E. | A2/61 | December 23, 1857 | No Return |
| Elrod, Nannie A. | Lorance, F. J. | A2/120 | February 8, 1865 | February 8, 1865 |
| Elrod, Nannie D. | Summers, J. H. | F/50 | December 8, 1894 | No Return |
| Elrod, S. D | Elkins, Sarah F. | C/178 | November 19, 1877 | November 20, 1877 |
| Elrod, S. E. | Walkup, G. E. | D/6 | | October 19, 1881 |
| Elrod, S. H. | Jones, Mary | A2/104 | October 24, 1860 | No Return |
| Elrod, Thomas | Moss, Sallie | C/328 | February 10, 1885 | February 12, 1885 |
| Elroy, A. B. | Knox, Emma | C/418 | September 29, 1890 | No Return |
| Emery, Elizabeth Selah Miss | Romine, Jeremiah | A/113 | August 4, 1848 | August 8, 1848 |
| Enais, Hagser | Blue, Bettie | D/12 | | April 16, 1882 |
| Enas, Hayes | Hawkins, Nancy | C/316 | October 25, 1884 | October 26, 1884 |
| English, Andrew | Teague, Miss Roxie | A2/146 | April 20, 1866 | April 22, 1866 |
| English, John D. | Martin, Mary J. | A2/14 | January 10, 1852 | January 12, 1852 |
| English, Nancy Miss | Esque, John | A/47 | February 3, 1842 | February 3, 1842 |
| English, Sarah | Martin, W. A. | C/34 | August 19, 1872 | August 21, 1872 |
| Ennevvey, William | Fish, Josie | E/189 | July 6, 1889 | No Return |
| Ennie, Isabella Miss | Hopkins, Harmon H. | A/48 | February 19, 1842 | February 20, 1842 |
| Enos, Henry | Kinnamon, Miss Nelly | A/115 | October 12, 1848 | October 12, 1848 |
| Ensey, Eligia A. | Cooper, Miss Naney | A2/24 | February 7, 1853 | February 10, 1853 |
| Ensey, James A. H. | Ferrell, Miss Margarett Ann | B/62 | March 9,. 1868 | March 12, 1868 |
| Ensey, Rebecca A. | Duncan, J. D. | C/38 | September 10, 1872 | September 10, 1872 |
| Ensey, W. S. | Anderson, Lucinda | C/62 | July 14, 1873 | July 14, 1873 |
| Epsey, James R. | Leigh, Marry L. | A2/34 | July 27, 1854 | July 29, 1854 |
| Ersry, Wm. L. | Parker, Mary J. | A2/21 | November 19, 1852 | November 22, 1852 |
| Ervin, Nancy E. Miss | Pallett, G. W. D. | A/130 | October 25, 1849 | October 25, 1849 |
| Ervin, Wm. | Lance, R. L. | C/94 | September 16, 1874 | September 19, 1874 |
| Erving, Charles | Nelson, Mary | C/320 | December 23, 1884 | December 24, 1884 |

| Groom or Bride | Groom or Bride | Book/Page | Date of License | Date of Marriage |
|---|---|---|---|---|
| Escue, Charles | Gilliam, Miss Malissa | A2/144 | August 30, 1866 | August 28, 1866 |
| Escue, George | Tenpenny, Nicy J. | C/202 | October 16, 1878 | October 16, 1878 |
| Escue, M. L. | Travis, Martha | C/278 | May 15, 1881 | May 15, 1881 |
| Escue, Nancy Miss | Gooding, William | A2/74 | March 28, 1854 | March 30, 1854 |
| Escue, Perline | Barratt, J. W. | C/50 | January 11, 1873 | January 12, 1873 |
| Eskhue, G. G | Good, Nancy R. | A2/81 | July 24, 1857 | July 26, 1857 |
| Espey, Charles | Finly, Miss Katherine | A2/49 | June 11, 1856 | June 11, 1856 |
| Espey, Eliabeth | Finley, John | A/59 | February 8, 1843 | February 9, 1843 |
| Espey, Geo. W. | McCullough, Elvira | C/162 | June 3, 1877 | June 3, 1877 |
| Espey, Henrietta | Todd, Hiram | A/32 | August 13, 1840 | August 13, 1840 |
| Espey, Jemima Miss | Cooper, Hollis | A2/90 | October 26, 1859 | No Return |
| Espey, Sarah L. | Clendenen, Paul | C/10 | September 18, 1871 | September 21, 1871 |
| Espey, Vina A. Miss | Eads, Mathew W. | A2/79 | June 18, 1856 | June 19, 1856 |
| Espey, W. J. | Turner, Amandy M. | C/98 | October 19, 1874 | October 20, 1874 |
| Espy, Charles | Herald, Susan A. | C/30 | July 11, 1872 | July 12, 1872 |
| Espy, John L. | Whittemore, M. E. | C/296 | Novembver 10, 1883 | November 18, 1883 |
| Espy, M. J. | St. John, J. W. | C/46 | December 16, 1872 | December 22, 1872 |
| Espy, Nancy Miss | Ring, William | A/90 | September 4, 1846 | September 6, 1846 |
| Espy, Narcissa | Jamison, Robert | A2/40 | July 12, 1855 | July 12, 1855 |
| Espy, Robert | Deanboise, Elizabeth | A/1 | March 23, 1838 | March 27, 1838 |
| Espy, W. J. | Barnet, James | F/54 | December 24, 1894 | December 25, 1894 |
| Esque, Charles | Gannon, Miss Mary | A/104 | October 30, 1847 | October 31, 1847 |
| Esque, Eliza | Dennis, John | A/65 | November 21, 1843 | November 21, 1843 |
| Esque, John | English, Miss Nancy | A/47 | February 3, 1842 | February 3, 1842 |
| Essary, Martha F. Miss | Price, Peter | A/131 | January 12, 1850 | January 12, 1850 |
| Essary, Rebecca E. Miss | Craft, James L. | A/85 | November 29, 1845 | November 30, 1845 |
| Estep, Edward | Lewis, Ella | E/174 | April 30, 1889 | April 30, 1889 |
| Estes, Edward | Parker, Miss Mary Ann | A/112 | December 8, 1847 | December 8, 1847 |
| Estes, Margarett Ann | Thompson, Gideon | A/76 | December 26, 1844 | December 26, 1844 |
| Estes, Martha | Smithson, J. F. | C/358 | May 10, 1886 | May 10, 1886 |
| Estes, Rachel Miss | Adams, Peter | B/76 | December 30, 1868 | December 31, 1868 |
| Estes, W. R. | Melton, Helen | C/434 | April 16, 1891 | April 16, 1891 |
| Estragre, Mary F. | Melton, W. L. | E/16 | January 30, 1888 | January 30, 1888 |
| Etherly, John | Sparks, Miss Better | C/384 | February 26, 1887 | No Return |
| Evans, Alexander | Campbell, Sarah | C/418 | September 15, 1890 | September 15, 1890 |
| Evans, C. C. | Stor, Mary | C/40 | September 28, 1872 | September 29, 1872 |
| Evans, C. E. Miss | Woods, Thomas J. | A2/26 | August 3, 1853 | August 3, 1853 |
| Evans, Charles E. | Chumley, Miss Sarah | A2/39 | January 4, 1855 | January 4, 1855 |
| Evans, David | Melton, Miss Eliza | A/110 | April 20, 1848 | No Return |
| Evans, E. A. Miss | Worley, D. B. | B/112 | October 13, 1870 | October 16, 1870 |
| Evans, E. L. | Markum, Healen | C/98 | October 31, 1874 | November 1, 1874 |
| Evans, J. W. | Marrs, M. A. | C/350 | January 15, 1886 | January 17, 1886 |
| Evans, J. W. | Cantrell, Agness | C/424 | December 3, 1890 | December 4, 1890 |
| Evans, James M. | Stone, Elizabeth | A/57 | December 22, 1842 | December 23, 1842 |
| Evans, James M. | Mullins, Miss Julia | A2/131 | November 9, 1865 | November 9, 1865 |
| Evans, Jno. C. | Gunter, Miss Fannie | C/454 | February 2, 1892 | February 2, 1892 |

| Groom or Bride | Groom or Bride | Book/Page | Date of License | Date of Marriage |
|---|---|---|---|---|
| Evans, John | Collans, M. J. | C/252 | August 11, 1880 | August 11, 1880 |
| Evans, John C. | Williams, May J. | C/246 | March 31, 1880 | March 31, 1880 |
| Evans, Julia Ann Miss | Cox, Charles A. | B/82 | July 20, 1869 | July 20, 1869 |
| Evans, Lemuel D. | Kirsey, Miss Ethalinda | A2/4 | August 27, 1850 | August 27, 1850 |
| Evans, Nancy | Hibdon, J. F. | C/356 | April 8, 1886 | April 11, 1886 |
| Evans, Nancy A. | Anderson, Stephen A. | A2/108 | August 13, 1863 | No Return |
| Evans, Nancy C. Miss | Barratt, Jessee | A/84 | November 22, 1845 | November 27, 1845 |
| Evans, Polly E. Miss | Ferrell, E. G. | B/38 | January 14, 1867 | January 16, 1867 |
| Evans, R. D. | Lynch, L. J. | F/66 | July 27, 1895 | July 28, 1895 |
| Evans, Sallie Miss | Bailey, Joseph A. | B/108 | August 31, 1870 | August 31, 1870 |
| Evans, Sarah Miss | Gunter, Campbell | A2/38 | March 7, 1855 | March 9, 1855 |
| Evans, W. J. | Mason, Angie | E/263 | January 15, 1890 | No Return |
| Everett, Malissie Mrs. | Vinson, B. F. | C/388 | April 29, 1887 | May 1, 1887 |
| Evins, Alexander | Campbell, Elizbeth | C/370 | October 1, 1886 | October 3, 1886 |
| Evon, Elizabeth Miss | Neely, Isaah | A2/14 | January 12, 1852 | January 12, 1852 |
| Ewel, Laten | Williams, Milly | A2/112 | February 22, 1864 | No Return |
| Ewell, John | Bush, Miss Elizabeth | A/96 | January 7, 1847 | January 7, 1847 |
| Ewell, Sarah | Todd, Wm | A/14 | June 18, 1839 | June 21, 1839 |
| Ewing, Anna | Thompson, Frank (col) | C/462 | August 5, 1892 | August 5, 1892 |
| Ewing, John (col.) | Flories, Mattie (col.) | D/14 | | August 11, 1882 |
| Ewing, John L. | McAdoo, Mary Jane | A/20 | December 9, 1839 | December 19, 1839 |
| Ewing, Munroe | Bass, Ann | E/154 | November 24, 1888 | November 25, 1888 |
| Ewing, Nancy M. Miss | Thompson, John B. | A2/137 | February 13, 1866 | February 14, 1866 |
| Ewing, Rufus (col) | Hoppins, Annie | C/416 | September 7, 1890 | September 7, 1890 |
| Ewing, Tennie | Roberson, Samuel | C/30 | July 17, 1872 | No Return |
| Exque, Lucinda | Elkins, John W. | A2/3 | June 29, 1850 | June 30, 1850 |
| Exque, Mary R. Miss | Tucker, James M. | A2/7 | November 2, 1850 | November 3, 1850 |
| Fagan, Albert T. | Keter, Miss Issabella Elizbeth Ann | A/48 | March 19, 1842 | March 19, 1842 |
| Fagan, Eliza Miss | McGill, William | A/83 | August 15, 1845 | August ?, 1845 |
| Fagan, Elizabeth A. Miss | Smith, J. C. | A/119 | January 26, 1849 | January 28, 1849 |
| Fagan, Granville | McFaddan, Miss Ann M. | A2/75 | September 18, 1854 | September 18, 1854 |
| Fagan, I. N. Miss | McBroom, J. W. | B/128 | April 4, 1871 | April 5, 1871 |
| Fagan, James H. | Cox, Caroline | A/126 | August 11, 1849 | August 12, 1849 |
| Fagan, M. J. Miss | Gaither, T. A. | A2/145 | March 31, 1866 | April 1, 1866 |
| Fagan, Mollie E. Miss | House, Hartwell | B/48 | July 23, 1867 | July 25, 1867 |
| Fagan, Robert L. | Gaither, Miss Cynthia | A/87 | February 16, 1846 | February 16, 1846 |
| Faiestar, N. H. Miss | Campbell, A. G. | A/100 | August 4, 1847 | August 4, 1847 |
| Falkenbery, Isabella Miss | Sullivan, R. F. | B/32 | November 29, 1866 | November 29, 1866 |
| Fan, Alexander | Harris, Martha A. | A2/113 | April 21, 1864 | April 21, 1864 |
| Fanen, Rebecca | Powel, John | A2/113 | March 26, 1864 | March 25, 1864 |
| Fann, Alford | Hibdon, Miss M. S. | A2/15 | February 28, 1852 | February 28, 1852 |
| Fann, Amanda | Mullins, Wm. | C/368 | September 25, 1886 | September 26, 1886 |
| Fann, Behtel | Gann, May | F/152 | July 27, 1898 | July 27, 1898 |
| Fann, Bettie | Nichols, James | F/138 | December 1, 1897 | December 1, 1897 |
| Fann, Emaline | Richardson, Brice M. | A/28 | April 15, 1840 | April 15, 1840 |

| Groom or Bride | Groom or Bride | Book/Page | Date of License | Date of Marriage |
|---|---|---|---|---|
| Fann, Francis | Barratt, Miss Sarah | A/85 | December 17, 1845 | December 17, 1845 |
| Fann, G. | Sneed, Miss T. H. | A2/57 | September 26, 1857 | September 26, 1857 |
| Fann, Geriah F. | Hayes, Adam | E/229 | November 2, 1889 | No Return |
| Fann, Grundy | Sauls, Miss Caroline | A/68 | March 5, 1844 | March 10, 1844 |
| Fann, Grundy | Harris, M. B. | A2/99 | July 12, 1860 | No Return |
| Fann, H. D. | Tucker, Frances | E/192 | July 24, 1889 | July 25, 1889 |
| Fann, Hardy | Latemore, Huldy | C/240 | February 2, 1880 | February 3, 1880 |
| Fann, J. F. | Cooper, Emma | C/440 | July 23, 1891 | July 23, 1891 |
| Fann, J. Q. | Gaither, Miss Elizabeth | B/126 | February 23, 1871 | February 27, 1871 |
| Fann, James | Harris, Miss Sarah J. | B/84 | September 1, 1869 | September 2, 1869 |
| Fann, Jemima | Reed, William | A/7 | October 4, 1838 | October 4, 1838 |
| Fann, Jane | Reed, David | C/78 | January 5, 1874 | January 11, 1874 |
| Fann, Jemima Miss | Gannon, Henry | C/412 | December 17, 1887 | December 18, 1887 |
| Fann, Jno. A. | Gann, Mary C. | C/70 | October 28, 1873 | October 29, 1873 |
| Fann, Joe | Northcutt, Eliza | F/70 | September 4, 1895 | September 6, 1895 |
| Fann, John L. | Tenpenney, H. M. | F/26 | December 21, 1893 | December 21, 1893 |
| Fann, Julie Q. | Tucker, Samuel | C/32 | August 12, 1872 | August 13, 1872 |
| Fann, Levi | Thomas, Lucy Jane | E/59 | August 11, 1888 | August 11, 1888 |
| Fann, Levie | Latymore, Elizabeth | C/290 | August 18, 1883 | August 19, 1883 |
| Fann, M. M. | Bryson, J. J. | F/132 | September 28, 1897 | September 29, 1897 |
| Fann, Maggie | Gaither, James | F/142 | December 25, 1897 | December 26, 1897 |
| Fann, Malissa Miss | Reed, D. B. | A/105 | November 29, 1847 | November 30, 1847 |
| Fann, Mary Ann | West, Frank | E/372 | October 5, 1898 | |
| Fann, Mary E. | Tucker, Thomas | E/54 | September 18, 1888 | September 18, 1888 |
| Fann, Mary E. | Tucker, Thomas | E/74 | September 18, 1888 | September 18, 1888 |
| Fann, Mary J. Miss | Busey, T. J. | C/6 | August 9, 1871 | August 10, 1871 |
| Fann, Melissa Miss | Smith, Jesse | A/100 | July 13, 1847 | Return Not Executed |
| Fann, Pelina | Gann?, Nathaniel | A2/134 | December 21, 1865 | December 28, 1865 |
| Fann, S. A. | Barrett, Johnevie | F/50 | December 8, 1894 | December 9, 1894 |
| Fann, Sam | Davenport, May | F/154 | August 31, 1898 | August 31, 1898 |
| Fann, Sarah A. | Tedder, D. H. | C/32 | July 31, 1872 | July 31, 1872 |
| Fann, W. A. | Brackon, Miss S. F. | C/462 | August 10, 1892 | August 11, 1892 |
| Fann, W. T. | Mullins, Miss Maggie | C/454 | January 4, 1892 | January 4, 1892 |
| Fann, Wm. | Wilson, Martha | A2/114 | June 25, 1864 | June 25, 1864 |
| Fare, D. L. Miss | McKnight, A. G. | A2/59 | November 3, 1857 | November 3, 1857 |
| Fare, Mary A. | McKnight, Moses W. | A2/41 | September 24, 1855 | Returns Missing |
| Farler, Henry | Hart, Lucinda | A/36 | February 12, 1841 | February 14, 1841 |
| Farler, Mahala | Merriman, Thomas | A/68 | February 5, 1844 | No Return |
| Farler, Mary Miss | Thomas, Daniel | A/71 | August 1, 1844 | August 1, 1844 |
| Farler, Patton | Philips, Miss Haney | A/67 | January 30, 1844 | February 2, 1844 |
| Farler, Sarah J. | Davenport, J. H. | C/326 | February 19, 1885 | No Return |
| Farler, Tabitha Miss | Waters, Edward | B/48 | August 3, 1867 | August 4, 1867 |
| Farless, Margrett | Stacy, S. P. | C/184 | Janaury 17, 1878 | No Return |
| Farless, Robt | Driver, Elizabeth | C/158 | March 1, 1877 | March 1, 1877 |
| Farley, John Jefferson | Thomas, Miss Sarah | A/98 | March 6, 1847 | March 7, 1847 |
| Farley, Letty Miss | Prater, Thomas M. | A/92 | October 26, 1846 | October 26, 1846 |

| Groom or Bride | Groom or Bride | Book/Page | Date of License | Date of Marriage |
|---|---|---|---|---|
| Farley, Nancy J. Miss | Waters, Cravin | B/120 | December 22, 1870 | December 23, 1870 |
| Farley, Patton | Walls, Dovey | C/20 | January 1, 1872 | January 1, 1872 |
| Farley, Tebipha Miss | Prator, W. R. J. | A2/76 | January 22, 1855 | January 22, 1855 |
| Farley, Thos H. | Youngblood, Arthelia | C/196 | August 14, 1878 | August 15, 1878 |
| Farly, Charles | Prater, Miss Martha C. | A2/75 | January 4, 1855 | January 5, 1855 |
| Farrell, Harrison W. | Ferrell, Miss Sarah Jane | B/64 | March 17, 1868 | March 17, 1868 |
| Farrell, Sarah Jane Miss | Murfrey, Robert S. | A/83 | October 3, 1845 | No Return |
| Farrell, W. H. | Mason, Daisie | E/344 | December 21, 1898 | |
| Farris, Birdie (col.) | Lawrence, Hiram (col.) | F/110 | January 30, 1897 | January 31, 1897 |
| Faulkam, James | Millikin, Parthana | A2/81 | February 7, 1858 | February 7, 1858 |
| Faulkenberg, Benjamin | Waters, Miss Delitha | A2/1 | January 24, 1850 | No Return |
| Faulkenberry, James | Bragg, Margaret | A/28 | May 5, 1840 | May 5, 1840 |
| Faulkenbery, John | Cathey, Jane Rutherford | A/18 | October 23, 1839 | October 27, 1839 |
| Ferbush, Lizzie | Kep, Charley | C/464 | September 1, 1892 | September 1, 1892 |
| Fergason, F. M. | Bullard, Miss Charity | B/114 | October 31, 1870 | November 3, 1870 |
| Ferrel, Elizabeth J. Miss | Whorton, Thomas | B/108 | August 24, 1870 | August 25, 1870 |
| Ferrel, James | St. John, Martha | A2/127 | September 16, 1865 | September 16, 1865 |
| Ferrel, John | Elrod, Miss Margaret A. | A/72 | August 24, 1844 | August 25, 1844 |
| Ferrel, Jordon | Taylor, Julia | B/4 | August 22, 1865 | August 28, 1865 |
| Ferrel, Margaret | McBroom, John | A2/109 | October 5, 1863 | October 5, 1863 |
| Ferrel, Richard | Campbell, Edna | E/87 | October 10, 1888 | October 10, 1888 |
| Ferrel, Wm. B. | Elrod, Eliza B. | A/17 | August 29, 1839 | August 29, 1839 |
| Ferrell, Alex | Fowler, Sarah J. | C/176 | September 8, 1877 | September 9, 1877 |
| Ferrell, Amanda | Vandergriff, John A. | E/93 | October 25, 1888 | October 25, 1888 |
| Ferrell, C. | Sullens, Miss M. | A2/86 | July 16, 1859 | No Return |
| Ferrell, Caroline | Warren, Joe | E/57 | August 8, 1888 | August 8, 1888 |
| Ferrell, Cennine | Baley, James | C/44 | October 31, 1872 | October 31, 1872 |
| Ferrell, E. E. | McLea?, Margarette | E/256 | January 1, 1890 | No Return |
| Ferrell, E. G. | Evans, Miss Polly E. | B/38 | January 14, 1867 | January 16, 1867 |
| Ferrell, E. G. | Pattrick, Miss Mary E. | B/88 | September 23, 1869 | September 23, 1860 |
| Ferrell, E. T. | Witter, J. W. | E/64 | August 29, 1888 | August 29, 1888 |
| Ferrell, Eliza Ann Miss | Weedon, John F. | A/128 | November 12, 1849 | November 13, 1849 |
| Ferrell, Eliza P. | Hart, Em | C/76 | December 10, 1873 | December 11, 1873 |
| Ferrell, Elizabeth Miss | Gasaway, C. H. | A2/29 | December 3, 1853 | No Return |
| Ferrell, Enoch | Sullins, Miss Susanah | A2/92 | December 20, 1859 | No Return |
| Ferrell, Enoch | Melton, Isabell | E/145 | March 20, 1889 | March 20, 1889 |
| Ferrell, Fannie Miss | Burkett, David | B/56 | November 27, 1867 | November 28, 1867 |
| Ferrell, Harriett | Cope, Sam | F/80 | January 3, 1896 | January 5, 1896 |
| Ferrell, Hattie | Carson, John | C/228 | October 20, 1879 | January 27, 1880 |
| Ferrell, J. A. | Melton, Liza | C/352 | February 1, 1886 | February 7, 1886 |
| Ferrell, J. B. | Rigsby, Fances A. | C/36 | August 31, 1872 | September 1, 1872 |
| Ferrell, J. B. | Moon, Josie | C/300 | January 3, 1884 | January 3, 1884 |
| Ferrell, J. G. | Todd, Miss Sarah | F/170 | February 10, 1899 | February 12, 1899 |
| Ferrell, J. H. | Miller, S. T. | E/252 | December 27, 1889 | December 29, 1889 |
| Ferrell, J. T. | Campbell, T. D. | F/14 | August 2, 1893 | August 24, 1893 |
| Ferrell, James W. | Moore, Miss Delila | B/102 | May 13, 1870 | May 15, 1870 |

| Groom or Bride | Groom or Bride | Book/Page | Date of License | Date of Marriage |
|---|---|---|---|---|
| Ferrell, Jesse | Hopp, Fannie | F/6 | March 13, 1893 | March 15, 1893 |
| Ferrell, John | Spurlock, Sarah | A/67 | February 15, 1844 | February 15, 1844 |
| Ferrell, John | Murphy, Emma | F/132 | September 28, 1897 | September 30, 1897 |
| Ferrell, Laura | McDougle, T. B | C/174 | October 24, 1877 | October 24, 1877 |
| Ferrell, Laura Miss | Barton, Ezekiel | C/2 | June 7, 1871 | No Return |
| Ferrell, M. L. | Sullivan, W. H. | C/24 | March 7, 1872 | March 7, 1872 |
| Ferrell, Malisa A. | Tate, John A. | C/36 | August 31, 1872 | September 1, 1872 |
| Ferrell, Margarett Ann | Ensey, James A. H. | B/62 | March 9, 1868 | March 12, 1868 |
| Ferrell, Marinda Miss | Spurlock, William | A/110 | April 28, 1848 | April 30, 1848 |
| Ferrell, Martha Miss | Taylor, James D. | B/118 | November 28, 1870 | December 1, 1870 |
| Ferrell, Mary | Mitchell, Andy | C/52 | February 18, 1873 | February 18, 1873 |
| Ferrell, Mary | Mitchell, Andy | C/172 | October 4, 1877 | October 7, 1877 |
| Ferrell, Mary Elizabeth Miss | Pendleton, William T. | B/50 | August 8, 1867 | August 11, 1867 |
| Ferrell, Mary Jane | Weedon, John F. | A/59 | January 31, 1843 | January 31, 1843 |
| Ferrell, Mary Miss | Spurlock, John A. | A/130 | December 27, 1849 | No Return |
| Ferrell, P. A. | Parker, J. Y. | D/5 | | October 13, 1881 |
| Ferrell, Polk | Hipp, Mary | C/94 | September 25, 1874 | September 27, 1874 |
| Ferrell, Roxanah Miss | Curlee, Peyton B. | A2/81 | Janaury 13, 1858 | January 13, 1858 |
| Ferrell, Ruth Miss | Sullins, Samuel | B/54 | October 1, 1867 | October 3, 1867 |
| Ferrell, Sallie | Stacy, Stephen | C/276 | March 30, 1881 | March 30, 1881 |
| Ferrell, Sallie B. | Warren, J. K. | F/80 | January 3, 1896 | January 5, 1896 |
| Ferrell, Samantha Miss | Smithson, D. S. | E/143 | March 13, 1889 | March 15, 1889 |
| Ferrell, Sarah | Campbell, W. F. | F/6 | March 14, 1893 | March 15, 1893 |
| Ferrell, Sarah Jane Miss | Farrell, Harrison W. | B/64 | March 17, 1868 | March 17, 1868 |
| Ferrell, Sue | Reed, C. P. | F/148 | April 23, 1898 | April 24, 1898 |
| Ferrell, Susan J. | Bogle, Michael | A2/119 | January 5, 1865 | January 5, 1865 |
| Ferrell, T. A. | Perry, Eliva | F/176 | May 10, 1899 | No Return |
| Ferrell, T. E. | Turner, Allice | C/292 | September 17, 1883 | September 20, 1883 |
| Ferrell, W. G. | Sullivan, Tomary | A2/113 | March 27, 1864 | March 27, 1864 |
| Ferrell, W. H. | Mason, Daisie | F/164 | December 21, 1898 | December 22, 1898 |
| Ferrell, W. M. | Patterson, Miss Bettie | C/392 | June 18, 1887 | June 19, 1887 |
| Ferrell, William | Young, Miss Sarah | A/64 | August 1, 1843 | August 1, 1843 |
| Ferrell, William | Rideout, Manca | C/68 | October 3, 1873 | October 4, 1873 |
| Ferrell, William | Campbell, Martha | E/71 | September 6, 1888 | September 6, 1888 |
| Ferrell, Wm. | Boley, Clay J. | C/78 | December 31, 1873 | January 1, 1874 |
| Ferrell, Young | Cummins, Miss Adaline | B/34 | December 19, 1866 | December 20, 1866 |
| Ferrell, Young | Harrald, Mary | F/104 | December 1, 1896 | December 6, 1896 |
| Ferrill, E. W. | Hare, Miss J. W. | A2/63 | February 10, 1858 | February 10, 1858 |
| Ferrill, M. R. Miss | Brevard, Th. | A2/27 | August 24, 1853 | August 24, 1854 |
| Fields, Martin | Goins, Miss Scyntha | B/44 | March 28, 1867 | March 28, 1867 |
| Fight, Obediah | McCullough, Miss Sarah A. | B/100 | February 9, 1870 | February 16, 1870 |
| Finch, Katharine E. Miss | Davis, Joseph | A/109 | March 2, 1848 | March 2, 1848 |
| Finetta, John | Martin, Martha | F/140 | December 8, 1897 | December 9, 1897 |
| Fingers, C. M. | Henegar | D/16 | | October 12, 1882 |
| Finley, A. F. | Sullivan, M. E. | C/364 | September 4, 1886 | September 5, 1886 |
| Finley, Aleathy Miss | Owen, Jeremiah J. | A2/10 | November 21, 1850 | November 21, 1850 |

| Groom or Bride | Groom or Bride | Book/Page | Date of License | Date of Marriage |
|---|---|---|---|---|
| Finley, Annaliza | Thurston, G. W. | C/72 | November 17, 1873 | November 17, 1873 |
| Finley, Alexander | Leigh, Miss Manerva J. | A2/1 | March 7, 1850 | March 7, 1850 |
| Finley, Cristeney C. Miss | Herrall, Legrand | A2/136 | January 22, 1866 | January 25, 1866 |
| Finley, E. E. | Owens, W. B. Jr. | C/150 | December 22, 1876 | December 22, 1876 |
| Finley, Effa Miss | Webber, John A. | A/87 | February 20, 1846 | February 22, 1846 |
| Finley, Fannie | Hayes, Albert | C/362 | July 31, 1886 | August 1, 1886 |
| Finley, Foster | Henne, Mattie | C/128 | December 23, 1875 | December 23, 1875 |
| Finley, Frances Miss | Smith, W. J. | A2/144 | June 30, 1866 | July 1, 1866 |
| Finley, Geo. | Gaither, Miss Marener | B/128 | March 14, 1871 | March 14, 1871 |
| Finley, Geo. W. | Lynn, Martha J. | C/64 | August 4, 1873 | August 7, 1873 |
| Finley, Henry | Duncan, L. L. | A2/129 | September 27, 1865 | September 27, 1865 |
| Finley, Henry M. | Lewis, Minervie J. | E/194 | July 25, 1889 | No Return |
| Finley, J. A. | Williams, Lillie | F/120 | July 19, 1897 | July 24, 1897 |
| Finley, J. C. | Gaither, Miss E. | B/116 | November 7, 1870 | November 8, 1870 |
| Finley, James | Cooper, Miss Jemima Malissa | A2/10 | January 30, 1851 | No Return |
| Finley, Jane P. | Taylor, J. G. | C/24 | March 7, 1872 | March 7, 1872 |
| Finley, John | Espey, Eliabeth | A/59 | February 8, 1843 | February 9, 1843 |
| Finley, Josie | Stroud, N. E. | C/288 | July 27, 1883 | July 29, 1883 |
| Finley, M. C. | Smith, J. B. | C/306 | March 15, 1884 | March 16, 1884 |
| Finley, Malinda | Whittamore, J. H. | C/198 | September 18, 1878 | September 19, 1878 |
| Finley, Manerva J. | Lewis, Peter J. | B/74 | December 12, 1868 | December 12, 1868 |
| Finley, Margaret P. Miss | Conley, Zachariah | B/90 | October 18, 1869 | October 18, 1869 |
| Finley, Mary A. | Parker, George | A2/125 | August 9, 1865 | August 9, 1865 |
| Finley, Mary L | Sullivan, Aesen H. | C/272 | February 19, 1881 | No Return |
| Finley, Nancy Miss | Cathy, William C. | A/102 | September 26, 1847 | September 26, 1847 |
| Finley, Nancy Miss | Whittemore, William B. | A2/145 | September 22, 1866 | September 23, 1866 |
| Finley, Nanie | Basham, A. G. | C/342 | December 5, 1885 | December 6, 1885 |
| Finley, Rebecca | Williams David | A2/12 | November 11, 1851 | November 11, 1851 |
| Finley, Rebecca | Parker, Jessee | C/188 | March 19, 1878 | March 29, 1878 |
| Finley, Sarah A. | Hayes, B. F. | C/150 | November 29, 1876 | November 29, 1876 |
| Finley, Sarah E. | Shelton, B. F. | C/364 | August 28, 1886 | August 29, 1886 |
| Finley, Sarah Jane Miss | Ham, Bradley | B/34 | December 24, 1866 | December 25, 1866 |
| Finley, Tenn Miss | Alexander, William | C/372 | November 6, 1886 | No Return |
| Finley, Tennie | Cooper, A. A. | C/348 | January 8, 1886 | No Return |
| Finley, Thomas | Cathey, Miss Lucy | A/98 | April 10, 1847 | April 10, 1847 |
| Finley, Thomas | Sissom, Lillie | F/142 | December 31, 897 | January 2, 1898 |
| Finley, Wiley | Howeth, Nancy | F/52 | December 22, 1894 | December 23, 1894 |
| Finley, Zenobo | Bragg, T. M. | F/64 | July 3, 1895 | July 3, 1895 |
| Finly, Alex | West, Malinda | C/62 | July 21, 1873 | No Return |
| Finly, Catharine Jane Miss | Parker, John A. | A2/50 | September 13, 1856 | September 14, 1856 |
| Finly, E. | Sullivan, T. C. | A2/103 | September 25, 1860 | No Return |
| Finly, Elenor Miss | Simpson, Andrew S. | A2/53 | January 1, 1857 | No Return |
| Finly, Elizabeth | Haithcock, James H. | A/68 | February 23, 1844 | February 25, 1844 |
| Finly, Katherine Miss | Espey, Charles | A2/49 | June 11, 1856 | June 11, 1856 |
| Fish, Josie | Ennevvey, William | E/189 | July 6, 1889 | No Return |
| Fisher, A. N. | Weedan, Miss Tennessee E. | A2/78 | January 22, 1856 | January 22, 1856 |

| Groom or Bride | Groom or Bride | Book/Page | Date of License | Date of Marriage |
|---|---|---|---|---|
| Fisher, John | Porterfield, Miss Mariah E. | A/74 | November 20, 1844 | November 21, 1844 |
| Fisher, Marian | Alexander, Osin | A2/116 | October 4, 1864 | October 7, 1864 |
| Fisher, Marian E. | McFerin, Wm | A2/108 | August 17, 1863 | No Return |
| Fisher, R. E. | Jones, Lizzie | E/152 | December 17, 1888 | December 17, 1888 |
| Fisher, Tina Mai Miss | Hayes, Robert Rush | C/460 | June 1, 1891 | June 1, 1892 |
| Fisher, Sarah E. Miss | Bell, James H. | A2/39 | January 1, 1855 | January 1, 1855 |
| Fitch, Parlie Miss | Barrett, William | A/118 | January 4, 1849 | January 4, 1849 |
| Fite, Daniel | Sutton, Miss Margarett Jane | A2/8 | December 23, 1850 | December 25, 1850 |
| Fite, F. M. | Groom, Miss Beoda | C/458 | April 4, 1892 | No Return |
| Fite, J. C. | Odom, Miss Sarah L. | C/6 | August 28, 1871 | September 3, 1871 |
| Fite, John A. | Paty, Miss H. A. | B/126 | February 7, 1871 | February 9, 1871 |
| Fite, Moses G. | Partrick, Annie L. | C/130 | January 17, 1876 | No Return |
| Fite, N. A. | Davis, Geo | C/146 | October 2, 1876 | October 5, 1876 |
| Fite, Nannie | Melton, E. T. | F/76 | December 13, 1895 | December 22, 1895 |
| Fitspatrick, Susan | Preston, Wm. L. | C/12 | October 17, 1871 | October 18, 1871 |
| Flaners, Mary | Seay, Wm | C/364 | August 19, 1886 | August 19, 1886 |
| Fleming, S. H. | McMahan | D/16 | | September 14, 1882 |
| Flemming, Albert M. | Burnett, Miss Matilda | A/39 | July 24, 1841 | July 25, 1841 |
| Flemmings, Robert L. | Good, Cyntha A. | C/374 | November 11, 1886 | November 11, 1886 |
| Fletcher, John | Thompson, Sarah | C/98 | October 31, 1874 | November 29, 1874 |
| Fletcher, Hariett | Medlock, Thomas | C/18 | December 27, 1871 | December 28, 1871 |
| Fletcher, Louisa Miss | Capshaw, H. L. W. | A2/49 | July 17, 1856 | July ??, 1856 |
| Fletcher, Mary | Talley, Joe | C/252 | August 12, 1880 | August 12, 1880 |
| Fletcher, Mary, Miss | Smith, William | C/378 | December 24, 1886 | December 24, 1886 |
| Fletcher, May Miss | Aken, B. H. | A/105 | November 13, 1847 | November 14, 1847 |
| Flories, Mattie (col.) | Ewing, John (col.) | D/14 | | August 11, 1882 |
| Flower, Willie | Keneiday, Annie | C/366 | September 18, 1886 | No Return |
| Flowers, Cora | Mingle, J. D. | C/174 | October 23, 1877 | October 24, 1877 |
| Flowers, Louella | Brantley, Ross | F/118 | May 28, 1897 | May 30, 1897 |
| Floyd, Fan | Scrugs, Ed | C/304 | December 8, 1884 | December 8, 1884 |
| Floyd, R. F. | Odom, Ida | C/100 | November 4, 1874 | November 5, 1874 |
| Floyd, S. E. Miss | Odom, M. M. | C/8 | August 30, 1871 | August 31, 1871 |
| Foard, D. S. | Anderson, Rebeca | C/226 | October 29, 1879 | No Return |
| Foard, Harris | Melton, Lucy J. | C/222 | August 21, 1879 | August 19, 1879 |
| Forcana, Katherine Miss | Cooper, William | A2/74 | January 1, 1854 | January 1, 1854 |
| Ford, Amanda T. Miss | Underhill, George W. | B/66 | June 13, 1868 | June 14, 1868 |
| Ford, Bill | Davenport, Medie | F/100 | October 24, 1896 | No Date |
| Ford, D. S. | Makum, Miss P. D. | A2/90 | October 31, 1859 | November 9, 1859 |
| Ford, D. S. | Rigsby, Mary E | C/16 | December 16, 1871 | December 17, 1871 |
| Ford, D. S. | Anders (?), Betty | C/242 | October 29, 1879 | January 7, 1880 |
| Ford, Daniel S. | Spurlock, Parmelia A. | A/10 | February 22, 1839 | No Return |
| Ford, Easter L. Miss | Pitman, William | A/123 | June 27, 1849 | June 27, 1849 |
| Ford, Ellen | Hays, James | C/242 | February 17, 1880 | February 17, 1880 |
| Ford, Florance C. | Burke, J. D. | C/344 | December 19, 1885 | No Return |
| Ford, Gorley T. S. | Manking, Miss Isabella | A2/88 | September 13, 1859 | No Return |

| Groom or Bride | Groom or Bride | Book/Page | Date of License | Date of Marriage |
|---|---|---|---|---|
| Ford, Harrette Miss | Cooper, G. W. | A2/23 | January 13, 1853 | January 13, 1853 |
| Ford, Harry E. | Gunthe, Miss Sarah | A2/34 | July 27, 1854 | July 17, 1854 |
| Ford, J. P. | Cooper, Anna | A2/119 | January 12, 1865 | January 27, 1865 |
| Ford, James | Earls, Sallie | C/360 | July 21, 1886 | No Return |
| Ford, James W. | Todd, Jemima M. | A2/130 | October 20, 1865 | November 1, 1865 |
| Ford, Larkin | Jimmerson, Miss R. C. | B/118 | November 24, 1870 | November 24, 1870 |
| Ford, Lavisa H. Miss | Bush, Samuel D. | A2/6 | October 19, 1850 | October 20, 1850 |
| Ford, Luanna J. Miss | Sissom, Joseph H. | B/114 | October 15, 1870 | October 16, 1870 |
| Ford, Martha C. Miss | Blaire, W. B. | B/68 | July 27, 1868 | July 28, 1868 |
| Ford, Mary | Olivar, Thomas | A/76 | February 19, 1845 | February 19, 1845 |
| Ford, Mary | Smith, Wm. | A2/114 | May 13, 1864 | May 15, 1864 |
| Ford, Nancy | McMickley, William | A/6 | September 4, 1838 | September 4, 1838 |
| Ford, Nancy E. Miss | Jameson, John A. | B/52 | September 23, 1867 | October 3, 1867 |
| Ford, O. H. | Fox, T. C. | C/452 | December 10, 1891 | December 10, 1891 |
| Ford, Orvell H. | Know, Miss P. | A2/127 | September 14, 1865 | September 21, 1865 |
| Ford, S. J. | Burkett, M. C. | C/72 | November 12, 1873 | November 13, 1873 |
| Ford, Thomas | Hancock, Miss ??? | A2/8 | December 23, 1850 | No Return |
| Ford, Thomas | Raney, Miss Eliza J. | A2/35 | December 21, 1854 | December 21, 1854 |
| Ford, W. J. | Davis, Miss D. K. | B/122 | December 28, 1870 | December 29, 1870 |
| Ford, Wm. J. | Urp, Willie A. | C/330 | May 23, 1885 | May 24, 1885 |
| Foreman, Rachael M. | Sullivan, Andy | C/154 | January 30, 1877 | January 30, 1877 |
| Fortenberry, Mary E. | Gannon, Wm. H. | C/124 | November 27, 1875 | November 28, 1875 |
| Foster, Ann Miss | Cummins, James | A/127 | September 20, 1849 | September 20, 1849 |
| Foster, Eliza T. | Elkin, Robt. L. | C/32 | August 10, 1872 | August 10, 1872 |
| Foster, Francis | Grizzle, Wm. | C/270 | January 19, 1881 | January 19, 1881 |
| Foster, Hannah | Webb, Jesse | C/402 | September 15, 1887 | September 15, 1887 |
| Foster, J. P. | Bethel, T. J. | C/238 | January 17, 1880 | January 18, 1880 |
| Foster, Bettie P. | Curlee, T. B. | C/44 | October 24, 1872 | October 24, 1872 |
| Foster, E. A. | Byford, G. W. | C/110 | March 9, 1875 | March 11, 1875 |
| Foster, Hanah Miss | Foster, Wm. N. | A2/51 | November 22, 1856 | No Return |
| Foster, Isaac | York, Miss Syrilda | B/66 | June 9, 1868 | June 14, 1868 |
| Foster, J. D. | Markum, Miss M. A. | A2/87 | August 27, 1859 | No Return |
| Foster, John R. | Elkins, Miss Mary J. | B/112 | September 6, 1870 | September 27, 1870 |
| Foster, Katharine Miss | Tackett, John O. | A/62 | May 29, 1843 | May 29, 1843 |
| Foster, Lucinda Miss | Crouch, J. B. | C/10 | September 7, 1871 | September 10, 1871 |
| Foster, Mary Ann Miss | Elkins, T. D. | A2/142 | August 6, 1866 | August 7, 1866 |
| Foster, Mary J. | Hollensworth, D. A. | C/200 | October 5, 1878 | October 6, 1878 |
| Foster, P. E. | Burks, H. E. | C/234 | December 22, 1879 | December 24, 1879 |
| Foster, Polly Ann Miss | Stone, William J. | A/120 | February 15, 1849 | February 15, 1849 |
| Foster, Porter | Stone, Miss Margarett A. | A/41 | September 9, 1841 | September 9, 1841 |
| Foster, R. C. | Elkins, M. S. | F/136 | November 15, 1897 | November 15, 1897 |
| Foster, R. D. | Thursten, George | C/214 | March 9, 1879 | March 9, 1879 |
| Foster, Richard | Lorancer, Malissa | E/246 | December 23, 1889 | December 24, 1889 |
| Foster, Robert | Deberry, Ise | C/448 | October 14, 1891 | October 15, 1891 |
| Foster, Robert M. | Soape, Miss Zenobia F. | A2/8 | December 5, 1850 | December 5, 1850 |
| Foster, Samm | Smithe, Stella | F/104 | December 7, 1896 | December 10, 1896 |

| Groom or Bride | Groom or Bride | Book/Page | Date of License | Date of Marriage |
|---|---|---|---|---|
| Foster, Sarah Jane | Preston, Samuel | A2/2 | May 27, 1850 | June 8, 1850 |
| Foster, W. L. | Paterson, Emily K. | A2/124 | July 24, 1865 | July 26, 1865 |
| Foster, W. R. | Smith, M. A. | C/100 | November 28, 1874 | December 3, 1874 |
| Foster, Wm. N. | Foster, Miss Hanah | A2/51 | November 22, 1856 | No Return |
| Fouston, Ann Miss | Keaton, John | A/51 | July 12, 1842 | July 14, 1842 |
| Fowler, Burrell | Conty, Miss Martha | A2/37 | November 15, 1854 | November 15, 1854 |
| Fowler, Jacob B. | Elkins, Miss Martha Virginia | A/89 | May 21, 1846 | May 21, 1846 |
| Fowler, James M. | Lance, Frances E. | B/74 | December 7, 1868 | December 7, 1868 |
| Fowler, Jessee | Winnett, Miss Charlotte | A2/138 | February 20, 1866 | February 21, 1866 |
| Fowler, John | Youngblood, M. F. | C/68 | October 16, 1873 | October 16, 1873 |
| Fowler, Josephine | Smith, Thomas | A2/106 | November 12, 1862 | No Return |
| Fowler, Laura A. | Hart, William | A2/117 | November 5, 1864 | November 8, 1864 |
| Fowler, Lerd | Stile, Sarah | E/15 | January 28, 1888 | January 18, 1888 |
| Fowler, Martha | Davis, F. M. | C/322 | January 10, 1885 | January 11, 1885 |
| Fowler, Mary B. | Phillips, H. B. | C/114 | June 9, 1875 | June 10, 1875 |
| Fowler, Nancy Miss | Kuykendall, Jacob | A2/33 | June 6, 1854 | No Return |
| Fowler, Patton | Prator, Miss Nancy E. | A2/40 | June 13, 1855 | June 13, 1855 |
| Fowler, Sarah | Logan, J. M. | C/348 | January 4, 1886 | No Return |
| Fowler, Sarah J. | Ferrell, Alex | C/176 | September 8, 1877 | September 9, 1877 |
| Fowler, Thomas | Hollis, Mollie | C/400 | September 8, 1887 | September 8, 1887 |
| Fowler, W. J. | Youngblood, Elizabeth C. | C/82 | February 12, 1874 | February 12, 1874 |
| Fowller, F. L. | Spicer, Sarah | D/19 |  | December 27, 1882 |
| Fox, C. R. | Jernigan, R. B | E/65 | August 29, 1888 | August 29, 1888 |
| Fox, James M. | Know, Miss Martha P. | A2/136 | January 19, 1866 | January 23, 1866 |
| Fox, Mollie | Milligan, B. B. | F/116 | April 29, 1897 | April 29, 1897 |
| Fox, T. C. | Ford, O. H. | C/452 | December 10, 1891 | December 10, 1891 |
| Frances, Bula | Bush, J. B. | F/82 | January 14, 1896 | January 14, 1896 |
| Frances, Jimm | Willard, Alta | F/68 | September 17, 1895 | September 15, 1895 |
| Frances, Media | Branden, James | F/20 | October 14, 1893 | October 15, 1893 |
| Frances, Malissa Miss | Willard, D. B. | B/76 | January 23, 1869 | January 24, 1869 |
| Francis, A. A. | Cooper, Miss M. E. | B/120 | December 15, 1870 | December 15, 1870 |
| Francis, A. F. | McAdoo, V. P. | C/74 | December 3, 1873 | December 4, 1873 |
| Francis, A. L. | Paschal, J. F. | E/90 | October 18, 1888 | October 18, 1888 |
| Francis, Armsted | Summar, Elizabeth | A/34 | October 14, 1840 | No Return |
| Francis, C. C. | Summar, Miss Lavis | B/62 | March 9, 1868 | March 9, 1868 |
| Francis, C. J. Miss | McAdoe, J. N. | B/34 | December 24, 1866 | December 25, 1866 |
| Francis, Dalton | Keele, Emma | F/136 | November 17, 1897 | November 17, 1897 |
| Francis, E. P. Miss | Hancock, R. T. | B/86 | September 9, 1869 | September 9, 1869 |
| Francis, Harris | Bryson, Elisabeth | C/274 | February 8, 1881 | February 8, 1881 |
| Francis, J. D. | Summer, Miss P. E. | A2/46 | January 30, 1856 | January 31, 1856 |
| Francis, L. S. | Gaither, I. R. | C/186 | February 4, 1878 | No Return |
| Francis, Lucinda Miss | Johnson, P. P. | A/73 | October 1, 1844 | October 2, 1844 |
| Francis, M. C. | Summar, Miss L. J. | A2/63 | February 26, 1858 | February 28, 1858 |
| Francis, M. C. | Smith, Mat | C/348 | January 9, 1886 | January 10, 1886 |
| Francis, M. H. | Bryson, Miss Mary M. | B/54 | October 21, 1867 | October 21, 1867 |
| Francis, Malinda Miss | Vandagriff, Richard | A2/70 | December 22, 1858 | December 22, 1858 |

| Groom or Bride | Groom or Bride | Book/Page | Date of License | Date of Marriage |
|---|---|---|---|---|
| Francis, Martha Miss | Wilson, James W. | A2/8 | December 5, 1850 | No Return |
| Francis, Mary Ann | Owen, Jos. D. | A2/112 | March 10, 1864 | March 15, 1864 |
| Francis, N. H. | McNabb, G. R. | C/122 | September 29, 1875 | September 30, 1875 |
| Francis, Nannie | Davenport, W. A. | F/34 | March 22, 1894 | March 22, 1894 |
| Franklin, Ed | McAdoo, Tennie | E/181 | June 11, 1889 | No Return |
| Franklin, Peter F. | Wade, Miss Elizabeth | A/128 | October 11, 1849 | October 31, 1849 |
| Franks, Hettie | Sewell, Burt | C/350 | January 14, 1886 | Janaury 14, 1886 |
| Franks, L. B. | New, Miss Fanny | A2/159 | June 18, 1866 | June 21, 1866 |
| Franks, S. B. | Dill, Ann W. | C/204 | November 17, 1878 | November 18, 1878 |
| Franses, Minnie | Bragg, J. S. | F/94 | August 29, 1896 | August 30, 1896 |
| Frasure, Robert | Bush, Malinda | A2/16 | Omitted | September 14, 1851 |
| Frazier, Margaret C. | Hill, Wm. G. | C/222 | August 20, 1879 | August 20, 1879 |
| Frazier, Zach | Alexander, Dora | C/82 | February 4, 1874 | February 16, 1874 |
| Freece, Mary F. | Campbell, W. G. | C/338 | October 14, 1885 | October 14, 1885 |
| Freeman, Avander | Todd, Almarinda | A2/48 | June 6, 1856 | June 15, 1866 |
| Freeman, Ellar | Swindell, W. G. | C/226 | October 30, 1879 | October 30, 1879 |
| Freeman, J. H. | Wood, Miss Mattie J. | A2/67 | September 21, 1858 | No Return |
| Freeman, Jake | Jones, Hannah J. | C/66 | September 16, 1873 | September 22, 1873 |
| Freeman, Marthie | Parker, J. A. | E/243 | December 20, 1889 | December 10, 1889 |
| Freeman, Nancy A. E. Miss | Vasser, W. J. | B/128 | March 6, 1871 | March 7, 1871 |
| Freeman, Simeon | Stacy, Prudence | C/144 | August 31, 1876 | September 3, 1876 |
| Freeman, Sun | Bryant, Lillie | F/2 | January 22, 1893 | No Return |
| Freeman, William | Vasser, Nancy A. | C/208 | January 1, 1879 | January 1, 1879 |
| Freeman, William | Williams, Mineva | F/24 | November 28, 1893 | November 28, 1893 |
| Freemon, Elizabeth | James, Robert G. | A/23 | January 20, 1840 | January 20, 1840 |
| Freeze, Emaline | Gray, Abraham | A2/134 | January 1, 1866 | January 4, 1866 |
| Freeze, Hiram | Jones, Sarah | A/75 | December 26, 1844 | December 26, 1844 |
| Freeze, John | Hogwood, Miss Mattie A. | B/54 | October 19, 1867 | October 20, 1867 |
| Freeze, Mary E | Lynn, J. B. | C/170 | September 19, 1877 | September 20, 1877 |
| Freeze, Sarah | Parker, Thomas | C/272 | January 28, 1881 | January 29, 1881 |
| French, John M. | Green, Miss Mary E. | B/60 | January 7, 1868 | January 8, 1868 |
| French, Lona | Patton, James R. | C/468 | October 22, 1892 | October 23, 1892 |
| French, Susie (col.) | Robertson, Bill (col.) | F/118 | May 28, 1897 | May 29, 1897 |
| Frigiter | Jetten, Robert | E/157 | December 25, 1888 | December 25, 1888 |
| Fry, Elizabeth | Wheeling, James M. | A2/18 | August 18, 1852 | August 19, 1852 |
| Fry, Nancy Miss | Bolin, John | A2/15 | February 26, 1852 | February 26, 1852 |
| Fugett, Frances | Clay, Henry | B/14 | June 12, 1868 | June 13, 1868 |
| Fugett, Horace | Novil, Beulia | F/112 | February 10, 1897 | February 10, 1897 |
| Fugett, Lucindy | Spurlock, Mon | C/276 | January 19, 1881 | January 19, 1881 |
| Fugett, Sam | Webb, Bettie | C/170 | September 15, 1877 | No Return |
| Fugett, Susan | Hare, Washington | B/10 | January 31, 1867 | January 31, 1867 |
| Fugett, Washington | Taylor, Elvira | B/8 | December 8, 1865 | December 8, 1865 |
| Fugett, Wat | Motone, Mariah | C/214 | March 1, 1879 | March 2, 1879 |
| Fugette, Jane | McFerrin, Joe | F/6 | March 18, 1893 | March 18, 1893 |
| Fugitt, Elizabeth | Smith, Wm. | C/180 | December 13, 1877 | No Return |
| Fugitt, Emley | Johnson, Jake | C/264 | August 5, 1880 | August 5, 1880 |

| Groom or Bride | Groom or Bride | Book/Page | Date of License | Date of Marriage |
|---|---|---|---|---|
| Fugitt, Emily | Fugitt, Martin | B/4 | August 24, 1865 | August 24, 1865 |
| Fugitt, Irvin | Stewart, Jane | C/272 | February 11, 1881 | February 11, 1881 |
| Fugitt, Jane W. | Brevard, Thomas B. | A/104 | November 2, 1847 | November 2, 1847 |
| Fugitt, Lemma | Brents, J. J. | C/236 | January 7, 1880 | January 7, 1880 |
| Fugitt, Martin | Fugitt, Emily | B/4 | August 24, 1865 | August 24, 1865 |
| Fugitt, Nath | Keele, Sarah J. | D/22 | | January 1899, 1883 |
| Fugitt, Nathan | Webb, Sarah | C/138 | May 31, 1876 | June 1, 1876 |
| Fugitt, Sallie | Dillon, E. T. | C/10 | September 18, 1871 | September 21, 1871 |
| Fugitt, Sam | Wilson, Margrett A. | C/338 | October 17, 1885 | October 18, 1885 |
| Fugitt, Saml. (Col) | Wood, Josephine | C/54 | February 22, 1873 | February 22, 1873 |
| Fugitt, Townsend | Brown, Miss Ann | A2/29 | September 19, 1853 | September 19,1853 |
| Fugitt, Wash | Taylor, Mariah | C/250 | July 1, 1880 | July 1, 1880 |
| Fugitt, Wm | Glasper, Lucinda | C/76 | December 11, 1873 | December 11, 1873 |
| Fugitte, Addie | Mitchell, Jackson | C/146 | September 28, 1876 | September 28, 1876 |
| Fugitte, Dora | Miller, Charlie | C/158 | March 8, 1877 | March 8, 1877 |
| Fuller, J. N. Jr. | Prater, Stacy A. | C/116 | July 27, 1875 | July 27, 1875 |
| Fuller, James | Givens, Miss Elizabeth C. | B/46 | July 11, 1867 | July 11, 1867 |
| Fuller, Landers | Phillips, Tennie | C/308 | April 26, 1884 | April 27, 1884 |
| Fuller, Robert | Parker, Nancy | F/148 | April 6, 1898 | April 7, 1898 |
| Fuller, Robert | Smithson, Susan | C/198 | September 19, 1878 | September 22, 1878 |
| Fuller, Susan | McKnight, Abner | B/14 | December 28, 1867 | December 28, 1867 |
| Furbus, Callie | Parton, Isaac | E/161 | March 2, 1889 | March 4, 1889 |
| Furgerson, Ella | Wivite, Robert (col) | C/380 | January 5, 1887 | January 5, 1887 |
| Furgerson, Malissa | Wright, Yandell | E/120 | December 26, 1888 | December 26, 1888 |
| Furman, Ann E. Miss | Henderson, Pleasant T. | A/79 | May 26, 1845 | May 28, 1845 |
| Fuston, Elizabeth Miss | Keetan, William | A2/76 | March 17, 1855 | March 20, 1855 |
| Fuston, Esteller | Brasher, Thomas J. | C/328 | March 11, 1885 | March 12, 1885 |
| Fuston, G. N | Keaton, Catherine | C/102 | December 12, 1874 | December 13, 1874 |
| Fuston, H. T. | McMahan, M. J. | C/138 | May 30, 1876 | May 30, 1876 |
| Fuston, H. D. | Summar, John P. | C/266 | December 28, 1880 | December 30, 1880 |
| Fuston, Hatty A. | Sessoms, T. A. | C/406 | October 29, 1887 | October 29, 1887 |
| Fuston, John | Stanley, Virginia | F/108 | December 30, 1896 | December 30, 1896 |
| Fuston, Josiah | Keeton, Elizabeth | A2/48 | May 19, 1856 | May 19, 1856 |
| Fuston, Josiah | Rigsby, Sally | A2/134 | December 23, 1865 | December 23, 1865 |
| Fuston, Leroy | Hollandsworth, Miss Malissa | B/80 | February 13, 1869 | February 14, 1869 |
| Fuston, Lucinda | Owen, Alford | A2/45 | December 21, 1855 | December 23, 1855 |
| Fuston, Margaret | Milligan, John A. | C/138 | June 21, 1876 | June 21, 1876 |
| Fuston, Margaret Miss | Gasaway, C. H. | A2/47 | April 1, 1856 | No Return |
| Fuston, Melvina | Higgans, William | A2/111 | January 17, 1864 | January 18, 1864 |
| Fuston, S. A. | Kenedy, Estella | C/240 | January 27, 1880 | January 29, 1880 |
| Fuston, Sarah | Hernidon, J. M. | C/28 | May 30, 1872 | May 31, 1872 |
| Fuston, Sarah | Barrutt, Henry | A2/111 | January 1, 1864 | January 1, 1864 |
| Gains, J. A. | Sanders, Casie | C/240 | January 26, 1880 | January 26, 1880 |
| Gains, J. B. | Cooper, Emeline | A2/91 | February 1, 1860 | No Return |
| Gains, Thomas | Winnett, Elizabeth | C/98 | October 13, 1874 | October 13, 1874 |
| Gaithen, Baswell | Burk, Isabella | A2/120 | February 1, 1865 | February 1, 1865 |

| Groom or Bride | Groom or Bride | Book/Page | Date of License | Date of Marriage |
| --- | --- | --- | --- | --- |
| Gaither, Angeline Miss | Knox, Elijah S. | A/124 | August 2, 1849 | August 2, 1849 |
| Gaither, Ann Miss | Phillips, W. C. | C/388 | April 30, 1887 | No Return |
| Gaither, Annie | Richards, J. D. | C/126 | December 13, 1875 | December 13, 1875 |
| Gaither, Bazel | Cox, Miss Mary A. | A/124 | February 14, 1849 | February 14, 1849 |
| Gaither, C. C. | Curlee, Henretta | C/400 | September 3, 1887 | September 4, 1887 |
| Gaither, C. G. F | Cannahan, N. C. | C/192 | June 20, 1878 | June 20, 1878 |
| Gaither, Cynthia Miss | Fagan, Robert L. | A/87 | February 16, 1846 | February 16, 1846 |
| Gaither, E. Miss | Finley, J. C. | B/116 | November 7, 1870 | November 8, 1870 |
| Gaither, E. S. | Mingle, James | C/212 | February 19, 1879 | February 20, 1879 |
| Gaither, Eliza Jane | Sauls, John H. | A/90 | August 27, 1846 | August 27, 1846 |
| Gaither, Elizabeh Miss | Jones, Thomas E. | A/65 | October 26, 1843 | October 26, 1843 |
| Gaither, Elizabeth F. Miss | Curlee, P. B. | A2/77 | October 10, 1855 | October 11, 1855 |
| Gaither, Elizabeth Miss | Fann, J. Q. | B/126 | February 23, 1871 | February 27, 1871 |
| Gaither, Emma | Burk, Samuell | F/18 | September 23, 1893 | September 23, 1893 |
| Gaither, Emma Miss | Thompkins, Robert | E/197 | August 3, 1889 | August 4, 1889 |
| Gaither, I. R. | Francis, L. S. | C/186 | February 4, 1878 | No Return |
| Gaither, Isaac | Bragg, Miss S. E. | B/128 | April 3, 1871 | April ?, 1871 |
| Gaither, Ivory | Brooks, Martha | C/136 | April 11, 1876 | April 11, 1876 |
| Gaither, J. C. | Nichol, Mollie | C/236 | December 24, 1879 | No Return |
| Gaither, J. H. | Mears, Miss Sarah T. | E/132 | February 4, 1889 | February 4, 1889 |
| Gaither, Jackson | Gannon, Joanna R. | C/70 | November 8, 1873 | November 9, 1873 |
| Gaither, James | Fann, Maggie | F/142 | December 25, 1897 | December 26, 1897 |
| Gaither, James E. | McBroom, Miss Mattie | C/378 | December 25, 1886 | December 26, 1886 |
| Gaither, Jennie | Wallace, James | E/127 | January 7, 1889 | January 7, 1889 |
| Gaither, John W. | Curlee, Amanda | A2/143 | August 27, 1866 | August 28, 1866 |
| Gaither, Joseph | Wilson, Sarah E. | C/120 | September 22, 1875 | September 22, 1875 |
| Gaither, Leve | Bowk, J. D. | C/474 | December 31, 1892 | December 31, 1892 |
| Gaither, Lizie | Dunn, Irving | F/74 | November 13, 1895 | November 13, 1895 |
| Gaither, M. E. | Carnahan, Andy | C/198 | September 5, 1878 | September 5, 1878 |
| Gaither, M. E. Miss | Bassham, T. G. | B/116 | November 18, 1870 | No Return |
| Gaither, M. L. C. Miss | Saffle, W. A. | B/60 | January 22, 1868 | January 23, 1868 |
| Gaither, Mahala Miss | Perry, N. O. | B/40 | February 5, 1867 | Solemnized, No Date |
| Gaither, Marener Miss | Finley, Geo. | B/128 | March 14, 1871 | March 14, 1871 |
| Gaither, Martha Miss | Bowen, Abner B. | A/65 | September 12, 1843 | September 12, 1843 |
| Gaither, Mary C. | McDougal, John D. | E/69 | September 6, 1888 | September 6, 1888 |
| Gaither, Mary E. Miss | Morgan, Hubbard | B/80 | April 15, 1869 | April 15, 1869 |
| Gaither, Mary H. Miss | Curlee, P. B. | A2/74 | September 26, 1853 | September 27, 1853 |
| Gaither, Mary Jane Miss | Tenpenny, Daniel Jr. | A/72 | September 12, 1844 | September 12, 1844 |
| Gaither, Matilda | Good, C. L. | F/104 | December 9, 1896 | December 8, 1896 |
| Gaither, Meran L. Miss | Young, Wm. H. | A2/53 | January 13, 1857 | January 13, 1857 |
| Gaither, Nancy A. | Higgins, J. P. | C/320 | December 5, 1884 | December 5, 1884 |
| Gaither, Oplia Miss | Whitfield, Ag | C/388 | May 7, 1887 | No Return |
| Gaither, Pleasant | Sullivan, Miss Elvira | A2/147 | November 8, 1866 | November 8, 1866 |
| Gaither, R. A. | Mears, Jennie | F/52 | December 8, 1894 | December 9, 1894 |
| Gaither, R. F. | Vance, S. C. | C/448 | October 17, 1891 | October 22, 1891 |
| Gaither, R. L. | Brandon, Miss Margaret E. | A2/136 | January 30, 1866 | February 1, 1866 |

| Groom or Bride | Groom or Bride | Book/Page | Date of License | Date of Marriage |
|---|---|---|---|---|
| Gaither, S. C. Miss | Blanks, S. B. | F/88 | June 8, 1896 | June 9, 1896 |
| Gaither, Sallie | Mears, Wm. | C/316 | Novmeber 20, 1884 | November 20, 1884 |
| Gaither, Sallie | McCrary, J. W. | F/78 | December 17, 1895 | December 18, 1895 |
| Gaither, Sallie | Sullens, W. M. | F/130 | September 15, 1897 | September 15, 1897 |
| Gaither, Sarah B. | Wallace, J. E. | C/266 | December 23, 1880 | December 26, 1880 |
| Gaither, Sarah Miss | Millikian, Albert G. | A/87 | February 26, 1846 | February 26, 1846 |
| Gaither, Silas | Bragg, Rebecca J. | A2/131 | November 2, 1865 | November 2, 1865 |
| Gaither, Susie Miss | Hays, T. E. | F/62 | April 22, 1895 | April 23, 1895 |
| Gaither, T. A. | Fagan, Miss M. J. | A2/145 | March 31, 1866 | April 1, 1866 |
| Gaither, Thomas F. | Horn, Miss Mary Elizabeth | A/107 | January 24, 1848 | January 27, 1848 |
| Gaither, Thomas M. | Hollis, Sarah A. | C/180 | December 11, 1877 | December 11, 1877 |
| Gaither, W. F. | Mears, J. D. | C/316 | October 23, 1884 | October 24, 1884 |
| Gaither, W. P. | Caruther, Miss S. A. E. | A2/78 | March 3, 1856 | March 4, 1856 |
| Gaither, Wilson | Tucker, Miss Katharine | A/61 | April 8, 1843 | April 9, 1843 |
| Gaither, Zella | Simmons, S. K. | F/82 | February 8, 1896 | February 9, 1896 |
| Gaither, Zelpha | Ready, Franklin | B/4 | August 26, 1865 | September 3, 1865 |
| Galahare July | Tarlton, James W. | A2/60 | December 9, 1857 | December 10, 1857 |
| Gallaway, Permelia | Richards, J. T. | C/144 | September 4, 1876 | September 7, 1876 |
| Gandy, Mary | McBroom, Dave | C/296 | November 8, 1883 | November 8, 1883` |
| Gandy, Sopha | Owen, Thomas | C/308 | May 17, 1884 | May 18, 1884 |
| Gan, Allaminta Miss | Bucher, Joshua | A2/50 | September 13, 1856 | Return not Executed |
| Gan, Calidonia | Davenport, John F. | A2/110 | December 24, 1863 | December 27, 1863 |
| Gan, Daniel | Gan, Miss Martha | A2/33 | June 13, 1854 | June 13, 1854 |
| Gan, Forest | Smith, Miss Jane | C/390 | June 27, 1887 | No Return |
| Gan, Marry J. | Gan, Wm. H. | A2/23 | January 4, 1853 | January 5, 1853 |
| Gan, Martha Miss | Gan, Daniel | A2/33 | June 13, 1854 | June 13, 1854 |
| Gan, Sarah Miss | Devanport, Joseph | A2/23 | February 16, 1853 | February 16, 1853 |
| Gan, Wm. H. | Gam, Marry? J. | A2/23 | January 4, 1853 | January 5, 1853 |
| Gandy, E. A. Miss | Mitchell, John E. | A2/61 | December 22, 1857 | No Return |
| Gann, Amandy C. | Miller, Thomas | D/2 | | July 24, 1881 |
| Gann, Ann Miss | Ward, Gemriah | C/456 | March 23, 1892 | March 23, 1892 |
| Gann, Britton | Manus, Miss Ann | B/66 | June 10, 1868 | June 10, 1868 |
| Gann, C. J. | Wilson, T. H. | D/21 | | March 21, 1883 |
| Gann, Cinthia Miss | Tittle, Adam | A/88 | May 2, 1846 | May 3, 1846 |
| Gann, Edmond | Hollandworth, Miss Zade A. | A2/47 | April 19, 1856 | April 20, 1856 |
| Gann, Eliza | Bogle, Robert | A/33 | September 22, 1840 | September 22, 1840 |
| Gann, F. C. | Jones, M. E. | D/19 | | December 21, 1882 |
| Gann, H. | Woods, Sarah | E/148 | March 30, 1889 | March 31, 1889 |
| Gann, James | Parker, Millie | F/76 | December 4, 1895 | December 6, 1895 |
| Gann, James A. | Basham, Miss Elizabeth | A2/47 | March 4, 1856 | March 4, 1856 |
| Gann, Jennie | Hibdon, Henry | E/36 | May 5, 1888 | May 6, 1888 |
| Gann, John | Brandon, Miss Lucinda | B/60 | January 9, 1868 | February 8, 1868 |
| Gann, John | Brandon, Miss Crida | B/76 | January 6, 1869 | January 6, 1869 |
| Gann, John | Wilcher, Eliza | F/78 | December 17, 1895 | December 18, 1895 |
| Gann, John | Bryson, Margarett Ann | F/84 | February 10, 1896 | February 14, 1896 |
| Gann, John H | Stanley, Miss Susan C. | B/42 | March 23, 1867 | March 24, 1867 |

| Groom or Bride | Groom or Bride | Book/Page | Date of License | Date of Marriage |
|---|---|---|---|---|
| Gann, John H. | Bennett, Miss Elizabeth M. | A2/41 | September 18, 1855 | September 18, 1855 |
| Gann, Joshua | Mooneham, Sarah | C/368 | October 2, 1886 | October 3, 1886 |
| Gann, Lizzie | Manus, James | D/16 | | October 2, 1882 |
| Gann, Lucinda | Pitman, M. M. | C/216 | June 10, 1879 | June 12, 1879 |
| Gann, M. C. | Collins, Miss Lavina | B/32 | November 17, 1866 | November 18, 1866 |
| Gann, Margaret | Bogle, William | C/460 | June 10, 1892 | No Return |
| Gann, Margaret A. Miss | Gillum, Benjamin L. | A2/137 | February 13, 1866 | February 14, 1866 |
| Gann, Martha P. | Quals, Wm. | C/316 | October 24, 1884 | October 26, 1884 |
| Gann, Mary | Rodgers, Green | C/356 | April 10, 1886 | April 10, 1886 |
| Gann, Mary C. | Fann, Jno. A. | C/70 | October 28, 1873 | October 29, 1873 |
| Gann, Mary J. Miss | Gann, Wm. H. | A2/73 | January 4, 1853 | January 5, 1853 |
| Gann, Mattie | Smith, John Henry | F/138 | November 19, 1897 | November 19, 1897 |
| Gann, May | Fann, Behtel | F/152 | July 27, 1898 | July27, 1898 |
| Gann, Munroe | Walkes, Cath | C/242 | December 8, 1879 | December 10, 1879 |
| Gann, Nathan | Wilson, Miss Jemima | B/64 | March 2, 1868 | March 4, 1868 |
| Gann, Nathaniel | Harris, Miss P. J. | A2/78 | February 28, 1856 | February 28, 1856 |
| Gann, R. L. | Woods, Josie | F/106 | December 19, 1896 | December 20, 1896 |
| Gann, Rebecca | Stolls (Stoley), Thos. | C/156 | February 15, 1877 | February 15, 1877 |
| Gann, Richard | King, Mollie | E/165 | May 25, 1889 | May 26, 1889 |
| Gann, Robert | Stanly, Miss Marth | A/71 | August 20, 1844 | August 21, 1844 |
| Gann, Robert | Lafevers, Sallie | C/54 | February 21, 1873 | February 21, 1873 |
| Gann, Robert | West, Mary E. | C/276 | March 5, 1881 | March 5, 1881 |
| Gann, Robt | Campbell, Nancy J. | C/318 | November 22, 1884 | November 22, 1884 |
| Gann, Robt. | Amus, Sarah | C/40 | September 19, 1872 | No Return |
| Gann, Russel | Ashford, Miss Elizabeth | A2/81 | July 29, 1857 | July 29, 1857 |
| Gann, S. C. | Parker, W. C. | C/306 | April 5, 1884 | No Return |
| Gann, Samuel M. | Herryman, Miss Lockey J. | B/66 | July 22, 1868 | July 23, 1868 |
| Gann, Sarah E. | Willard, Sam | C/210 | January 4, 1879 | No Return |
| Gann, Tennessee Miss | Bethell, Lafayette | A2/91 | November 26, 1859 | No Return |
| Gann, Thomas | Thomas, Della | F/72 | October 1, 1895 | October 21, 1895 |
| Gann, Viney | Barrett, Thos | C/194 | July 17, 1878 | July 17, 1878 |
| Gann, Willis | Walls, Mary | C/272 | January 27, 1881 | No Return |
| Gann, Wm. H. | Gann, Miss Mary J. | A2/73 | January 4, 1853 | January 5, 1853 |
| Gann?, Nathaniel | Fann, Pelina | A2/134 | December 21, 1865 | December 28, 1865 |
| Gannon, Alonso | Herryman, Miss Teba | E/20 | February 18, 1888 | February 19, 1888 |
| Gannon, Bettie | Brandon, John | C/300 | January 16, 1884 | No Return |
| Gannon, Dillard L. | Smith, Miss Elizabeht | A2/7 | November 5, 1850 | No Return |
| Gannon, Ed | Saules, Alta | F/166 | January 7, 1899 | January 8, 1899 |
| Gannon, G. W. | Vance, Miss E. R. | A2/58 | October 1, 1857 | October 1, 1857 |
| Gannon, G. W. | Todd, Vina | E/178 | May 25, 1889 | May 25, 1889 |
| Gannon, George | Pace, Rebecca | A/53 | September 3, 1842 | September 6, 1842 |
| Gannon, George | Bryson, Miss M. O. | C/452 | December 12, 1891 | December 12, 1891 |
| Gannon, Harvy A. | Simpson, Lidey | A2/108 | August 30, 1863 | August 30, 1863 |
| Gannon, Henry | Fann, Miss Jemima | C/412 | December 17, 1887 | December 18, 1887 |
| Gannon, James | Brooks, July | C/250 | July 7, 1880 | July 7, 1880 |
| Gannon, James P. | Brooks, Tennie W. | C/68 | October 11, 1873 | October 12, 1873 |

| Groom or Bride | Groom or Bride | Book/Page | Date of License | Date of Marriage |
|---|---|---|---|---|
| Gannon, Joanna Miss | Sullivan, William A. | B/48 | July 18, 1867 | July 18, 1867 |
| Gannon, Joanna R. | Gaither, Jackson | C/70 | November 8, 1873 | November 9, 1873 |
| Gannon, John | Hays, Miss Manerva | A/130 | December 18, 1849 | December 18, 1849 |
| Gannon, John | Travis, Susan | C/446 | October 1, 1891 | October 1, 1891 |
| Gannon, John P. | Travis, Ridy E. | A2/95 | February 23, 1860 | February 23, 1860 |
| Gannon, Josie | Mears, Arch | F/134 | October 23, 1897 | October 24, 1897 |
| Gannon, L. J. | Hollen, H. H. | D/15 | | September 12, 1882 |
| Gannon, Martha | Hays, David | A/70 | June 19, 1844 | June 20, 1844 |
| Gannon, Martha Ann Miss | McBroom, Nathan | A2/52 | December 11, 1856 | December 11, 1856 |
| Gannon, Mary Ann | Barrett, Eli B. | C/36 | September 7, 1872 | September 7, 1872 |
| Gannon, Mary Ellen | Tenpeny, John D. | C/180 | December 8, 1877 | December 9, 1877 |
| Gannon, Mary Miss | Esque, Charles | A/104 | October 30, 1847 | October 31, 1847 |
| Gannon, Nitha A. Miss | Simpson, Peter | A/108 | February 26, 1848 | February 27, 1848 |
| Gannon, Roxanna Miss | Brandon, John | A/114 | September 7, 1848 | September 7, 1848 |
| Gannon, S. E. | Taylor, Annie | E/328 | December 29, 1898 | |
| Gannon, S. E. | Vandergriff, Dona | F/28 | December 27, 1893 | December 27, 1893 |
| Gannon, S. E. | Taylor, Ann | F/164 | December 29, 1898 | December 29, 1898 |
| Gannon, S. R. | Nichols, I. Z. | C/302 | January 21, 1884 | No Return |
| Gannon, Saml P. | Stacy, Susanah | A/20 | December 12, 1839 | December 13, 1839 |
| Gannon, Samuel | Sapp, Miss Martha E. | A/87 | March 7, 1846 | March 8, 1846 |
| Gannon, Samuel L. | Allen, Jenie | C/310 | July 26, 1884 | No Return |
| Gannon, Sarah | Todd, Dillard | C/70 | October 29, 1873 | October 29, 1873 |
| Gannon, Sarah C. Miss | Ready, James M. | B/46 | June 13, 1867 | June 13, 1867 |
| Gannon, Susen | Barratt, W. H. | C/160 | March 24, 1877 | March 25, 1877 |
| Gannon, Susie | W. R. Pittard | F/80 | December 31, 1895 | December 31, 1895 |
| Gannon, W. J. | Thrower, Syntha | C/406 | November 12, 1887 | November 13, 1887 |
| Gannon, William | Barrett, Sallie | C/420 | October 25, 1890 | October 26, 1890 |
| Gannon, Wm. E. | Hays, Rebecca | A2/112 | March 24, 1864 | March 24, 1864 |
| Gannon, Wm. H. | Keely, Miss Harriett | A2/90 | November 5, 1859 | November 8, 1859 |
| Gannon, Wm. H. | Fortenberry, Mary E. | C/124 | November 27, 1875 | November 28, 1875 |
| Garaway, James R. | Morris, Miss Caroline | A2/64 | March 16, 1858 | March 17, 1858 |
| Gardener, Virginia | Keeton, Wm. | C/370 | October 11, 1886 | October 13, 1886 |
| Gardner, Miss Martha A. | Mitchell, D. W. | C/6 | August 26, 1871 | August 26, 1871 |
| Garity, Betsey | Melton, Jacob | C/266 | December 31, 1880 | Njo Return |
| Garis, W. G. D. | Babbit, Miss S. F | A2/67 | September 27, 1858 | September 27, 1858 |
| Garis, W. G. O. | Babbett, S. F. | A2/72 | February 18, 1859 | February 18, 1859 |
| Garity, Pattrick | Hale, Miss Sarah M. | B/46 | July 15, 1867 | July 20, 1867 |
| Garment, T. M. | Miligan, Miss Elizabeth | A2/33 | June 15, 1854 | June 15, 1854 |
| Garmon, Samuel | Blanton, R. C. | C/180 | December 22, 1877 | No Return |
| Garmon, Thomas | Gilley, Miss Martha | A2/61 | December 28, 1857 | December 28, 1857 |
| Garner, Matilda J. Miss | Bond, James A. | A2/135 | January 15, 1866 | January 17, 1866 |
| Garris, William G. D. | Babet, Miss S. F. | A2/84 | February 18, 1859 | February 18, 1859 |
| Garrison, C. B. | Kennedy, Miss M. A. | B/56 | November 23, 1867 | November 25, 1867 |
| Garven, Sarah | Mairs, John B. | C/276 | March 16, 1881 | March 18, 1881 |
| Gasaway, C. H. | Ferrell, Miss Elizabeth | A2/29 | December 3, 1853 | No Return |
| Gasaway, C. H. | Fuston, Miss Margaret | A2/47 | April 1, 1856 | No Return |

| Groom or Bride | Groom or Bride | Book/Page | Date of License | Date of Marriage |
|---|---|---|---|---|
| Gassaway, Etna | Shirley, Robert | C/426 | December 18, 1890 | December 21, 1890 |
| Gasaway, Helen | Melton, J. B. | D/18 | | December 17, 1882 |
| Gasaway, Laura | Haley, E. T. | D/13 | | April 5, 1882 |
| Gasaway, M. L. Miss | Grizzle, G. W. | A2/78 | March 7, 1856 | March 10, 1856 |
| Gasaway, Nancy | Burks, Richard, (col) | E/350 | December 20, 1898 | |
| Gasaway, Nancy (col.) | Burks, Richard (col.) | F/166 | December 20, 1898 | December 21, 1898 |
| Gasaway, Rufus | Martin, Elizabeth | C/54 | March 14, 1873 | March 16, 1873 |
| Gasay, Hyram | Turney, Cleo | F/8 | April 18, 1893 | April 19, 1893 |
| Gassoway, Georgiana Miss | Marcun, Job | A/121 | March 3, 1849 | No Return |
| Gates, G. W. | Blaire, Olley | B/8 | October 9, 1865 | October 14, 1865 |
| Gather, Bill | Cooper, Tennie | F/48 | November 20, 1894 | No Return |
| Gather, Sarah L. | Jones, John H. | A/2 | April 3, 1838 | April 3, 1838 |
| Gawing, Lavinda | Bowland, William | F/98 | October 12, 1896 | October 18, 1896 |
| Gay, Wm. | Brewer, Sarah R. | A2/21 | December 7, 1852 | December 8, 1852 |
| Genty, Wm. | Campbell, Betsey J. | C/82 | February 16, 1874 | February 18, 1874 |
| Geons, Bluford H. | Dood, Miss Sinthy J. | A2/83 | February 2, 1859 | No Return |
| Georg, Amanda J. Miss | Hailey, James A. | A2/67 | September 1, 1858 | No Return |
| George, Andy | Martin, Jane | C/316 | October 30, 1884 | November 2, 1884 |
| George, Bill | Dixon, Cally | C/354 | March 6, 1886 | March 7, 1886 |
| George, Emma | Lynch, Kenney | C/116 | July 17, 1875 | No Return |
| George, Harrett | McFerrin, Jack | C/96 | October 8, 1874 | October 8, 1874 |
| George, J. L. | Rigsby, F. L. | E/124 | January 3, 1889 | No Return |
| George, Jacob | Grizzle, Helen | F/104 | December 9, 1896 | December 10, 1896 |
| George, James O. | Trott, Marthaann | A/5 | August 21, 1838 | August 21, 1838 |
| George, John | King, Edna | F/128 | September 1, 1897 | September 1, 1897 |
| George, John A. | Alexander, Miss Nancy | A/46 | January 20, 1842 | January 20, 1842 |
| George, Mariah | Covington, William L. | A/18 | October 8, 1839 | October 8, 1839 |
| George, Marry J. Miss | Stephen, R. K. | A2/41 | August 22, 1855 | Return Missing |
| George, Mary S. Miss | Mitchell, James A. | A2/145 | September 19, 1866 | September 20, 1866 |
| George, Miles B. | Tenpenny, Frances | B/4 | August 23, 1865 | September 2, 1865 |
| George, Pleasant | Hardin, Vina | B/16 | August 13, 1860 | August 14, 1869 |
| George, Rachel | Powell, Thomas | C/36 | August 29, 1872 | August 29, 1872 |
| George, Rufus | Vandergriff, Bettie | C/466 | October 11, 1892 | October 11, 1892 |
| George, Tilman | Bogle, Sarah C. | C/242 | February 14, 1880 | February 14, 1880 |
| Gibson, Aubey | Sullivan, Miss Lizzy | F/108 | December 24, 1896 | December 24, 1896 |
| Gibson, David | Herman, Paralee | C/154 | January 24, 1877 | January 24, 1877 |
| Gibson, Elizabeth A. Miss | Busey, William H. | B/106 | July 20, 1870 | July 21, 1870 |
| Gibson, J. | Peydon, Mandy | C/158 | March 8, 1877 | March 8, 1877 |
| Gibson, James | Reed, Miss Esther | A/129 | December 15, 1849 | December 15, 1849 |
| Gibson, Mary E. | Herriman, Steven | A2/123 | May 8, 1865 | May 8, 1865 |
| Gibson, Richard D. | Southern, Miss Jemima | A/62 | April 13, 1843 | April 17, 1863 |
| Gilither, Tennie | Williams, Howell | C/254 | August 26, 1880 | August 26, 1880 |
| Gillam, J. M. | Bryson, Miss Nancy | A2/99 | July 2, 1860 | No Return |
| Gilley, A. S. | Hollandsworth, Miss Sarah C. | B/42 | February 28, 1867 | February 29, 1867 |
| Gilley, Charles | Bell, Miss Jane Ann | A/48 | April 1, 1842 | March 15, 1842 |
| Gilley, Columbus | Wood, Francis | C/182 | December 22, 1877 | No Rteurn |

| Groom or Bride | Groom or Bride | Book/Page | Date of License | Date of Marriage |
|---|---|---|---|---|
| Gilley, Dovie | Turner, W. C. | F/56 | January 15, 1895 | January 16, 1895 |
| Gilley, Ella | Carnahan, A. L. | F/86 | March 11, 1896 | March 11, 1896 |
| Gilley, Emaline | Wilsher, William | A/95 | December 23, 1846 | December 24, 1846 |
| Gilley, Emma | Cawthon, J. B. | C/446 | September 30, 1891 | October 1, 1891 |
| Gilley, Etta | Higgins, Carmmer A. | F/90 | July 15, 1896 | July 15, 1896 |
| Gilley, Ezzy Miss | Melton, Elisha | A2/143 | August 23, 1866 | August 23, 1866 |
| Gilley, George | Boyles, Ater | C/346 | December 21, 1885 | December 21, 1885 |
| Gilley, Harriet C. Miss | Ritchey, George | B/32 | December 10, 1866 | December 12, 1866 |
| Gilley, Isaac G. | Bogle, S. C. | B/108 | August 20, 1870 | No Return |
| Gilley, Izza Miss | Crabtree, Elijah | A2/74 | February 18, 1854 | February 19, 1854 |
| Gilley, J. B. | Braxton, Catherine | E/73 | September 17, 1888 | September 20, 1888 |
| Gilley, J. B. | Mason, Lula | F/116 | April 24, 1897 | April 24, 1897 |
| Gilley, J. C. | Barnes, Lula | C/464 | August 16, 1892 | August 17, 1892 |
| Gilley, J. Caleb | Meeks, Rosa | C/428 | January 2, 1891 | January 2, 1891 |
| Gilley, J. N. | Lewis, Matildy | F/120 | June 7, 1897 | June 10, 1897 |
| Gilley, J. R. Y. | Bush, Sarah | A2/91 | February 8, 1860 | No Return |
| Gilley, James | Phillips, Mary | C/132 | January 24, 1876 | No Return |
| Gilley, James | Brown, Sarah | C/332 | July 15, 1885 | July 16, 1885 |
| Gilley, James | Cawthon, Miss Helen | C/388 | May 4, 1887 | No Return |
| Gilley, James | Vinson, John Ann | F/48 | November 17, 1894 | November 18, 1894 |
| Gilley, Jane Miss | Preston, John Sr. | A2/10 | January 11, 1851 | January 11, 1851 |
| Gilley, Jesse | Byrum, Nancy P. | C/396 | July 22, 1887 | July 24, 1887 |
| Gilley, Jessie | Turner, B. | C/282 | May 30, 1883 | No Return |
| Gilley, Jesse N. | Bynum, Miss Lucinda | B/90 | October 5, 1869 | No Return |
| Gilley, Jessee N. | Williams, Malvina | C/106 | January 19, 1875 | January 21, 1875 |
| Gilley, Joe | Lillar, Susan | E/40 | May 26, 1888 | May 26, 1888 |
| Gilley, Joe (col.) | Dillard, Lizzie | C/420 | October 16, 1890 | October 17, 1890 |
| Gilley, Joe (col.) | Mitchell, Lizzy (col.) | F/118 | May 22, 1897 | May 24, 1897 |
| Gilley, John | Rigby, Miss Elizabeth Ann | A2/74 | January 2, 1854 | January 5, 1854 |
| Gilley, John | Nichol, Lemmie | C/422 | November 23, 1890 | November 23, 1890 |
| Gilley, John | Elkins, Leona | F/54 | January 6, 1895 | January 6, 1895 |
| Gilley, Joseph D. | Bailey, Ruth | C/400 | September 10, 1887 | September 10, 1887 |
| Gilley, Judah F. Miss | Walker, Jeremiah C. | A/71 | August 5, 1844 | August 5, 1844 |
| Gilley, Lucinda | Bailey, J. N. | C/130 | December 31, 1875 | January 2, 1876 |
| Gilley, M. B. | Murfree, Miss Mary E. | B/84 | August 23, 1869 | August 23, 1869 |
| Gilley, M. C. | Cooper, J. M. | C/142 | August 5, 1876 | August 6, 1876 |
| Gilley, M. E. | Winnett, F. M. | C/254 | August 18, 1880 | August 19, 1880 |
| Gilley, M. E. Miss | Sadler, Adam A. | E/45 | July 7, 1888 | July 8, 1888 |
| Gilley, M. J. Miss | Vanhoozer, W. J. | B/100 | February 7, 1870 | February 8, 1870 |
| Gilley, Malinda Miss | Lemmons, W. J. | C/432 | March 3, 1891 | March 3, 1891 |
| Gilley, Malinda Miss | McCrary, J. H. | A2/151 | May 16, 1866 | May 17, 1866 |
| Gilley, Malinda V. | Parker, Wm. | C/108 | February 5, 1875 | February 11, 1875 |
| Gilley, Martha | Smith, Thos. C. | C/120 | August 7, 1875 | August 8, 1875 |
| Gilley, Martha Miss | Garmon, Thomas | A2/61 | December 28, 1857 | December 28, 1857 |
| Gilley, Mary | Simmons, John | E/11 | January 21, 1888 | January 21, 1888 |
| Gilley, Mary E. | Bush, James L. | C/234 | December 26, 1879 | December 25, 1879 |

| Groom or Bride | Groom or Bride | Book/Page | Date of License | Date of Marriage |
|---|---|---|---|---|
| Gilley, Mary E. | Swoap, W. T. | C/328 | March 2, 1885 | March 5, 1885 |
| Gilley, Mary E. Miss | Merritt, W. H. | B/86 | September 13, 1869 | September 14, 1869 |
| Gilley, May M. Miss | Hawkins, John | A/38 | May 8, 1841 | May 8, 1841 |
| Gilley, Michiga | Wood, Sillie | C/184 | January 5, 1878 | January 6, 1878 |
| Gilley, Miss Mary | Cooper, James | F/170 | February 3, 1899 | February 4, 1899 |
| Gilley, Nettie | Blackburn, David | E/255 | December 31, 1880 | December 6, 1889 |
| Gilley, Robt | VanHooser, Hattie | F/148 | April 23, 1898 | April 24, 1898 |
| Gilley, Samuel | Eledge, Miss Martha | B/114 | October 15, 1870 | October 16, 1870 |
| Gilley, Sallie | Stacy, James | C/376 | December 2, 1886 | No Return |
| Gilley, Sarah E. Miss | Campbell, James | A2/89 | September 18, 1859 | No Return |
| Gilley, Sarah L | Tucker, James W. | C/138 | April 22, 1876 | April 23, 1876 |
| Gilley, Susan | Woods, John (col.) | C/420 | October 18, 1890 | October 18, 1890 |
| Gilley, T. F. | Jones, Miss L. J. | B/74 | December 8, 1868 | December 10, 1868 |
| Gilley, Terisian | Campbell, Wm | A2/95 | April 14, 1860 | No Return |
| Gilley, W. P. | Williams, Miss M. A. | C/458 | May 28, 1892 | No Return |
| Gilley, W. T. | Duncan, N. J. R. | C/310 | July 22, 1884 | July 23, 1884 |
| Gilley, W. T. | Lewis, Lucinda | C/426 | December 27, 1890 | December 27, 1890 |
| Gilley, William | Blanton, Hannah | A/2 | April 14, 1838 | April 15, 1838 |
| Gilley, William | Bush, Linnie | C/284 | May 28, 1883 | May 28, 1883 |
| Gilley, Williams | Williams, Mary Ann | F/8 | May 1, 1893 | May 2, 1893 |
| Gilley, Wm. | Stacy, Sallie | F/70 | September 26, 1895 | September 26, 1895 |
| Gilley, Wm. | Prater, Elizabeth | F/88 | May 18, 1896 | May 19, 1896 |
| Gilley, Wm. P. | Lewis, Mary P. | C/352 | February 6, 1886 | February 6, 1886 |
| Gilley, Zelpha | Lewis, W. J. | F/120 | June 30, 1897 | July 1, 1897 |
| Gillum, Elisabeth | Harris, R. C. | C/258 | October 7, 1880 | No Return |
| Gilliam, Bengamin | Helton, Miss Lucinda | B/94 | December 3, 1869 | December 3, 1869 |
| Gillum, Lucy J. | Sullivan, John R. | C/270 | January 12, 1881 | No Return |
| Gilliam, Malissa Miss | Escue, Charles | A2/144 | August 30, 1866 | August 28, 1866 |
| Gillie, Martha | Lewis, Cab | F/12 | July 18, 1893 | July 18, 1893 |
| Gillis, Nancy | Robinson, Jessee | F | August 24, 1893 | |
| Gillum, Benjamin L. | Gann, Miss Margaret A. | A2/137 | February 13, 1866 | February 14, 1866 |
| Gillum, Henry | Harris, Melvina | A2/126 | August 27, 1865 | August 27, 1865 |
| Gillum, S. E. Miss | Hibdon, P. A. | B/112 | October 12, 1870 | October 12, 1870 |
| Gilly, Amos | Tittle, Miss Elizabeth | A2/31 | February 12, 1854 | February 15, 1854 |
| Gilly, Dorcus Miss | Jernigan, Wm. A. | A2/42 | October 11, 1855 | October 16, 1855 |
| Gilly, Isza Miss | Crabtree, Eligah | A2/31 | January 18, 1854 | January 18, 1854 |
| Gilly, Mary A. Miss | Burket, James | A2/46 | January 17, 1856 | January 17, 1856 |
| Gilly, N. I. Miss | Lewis, H. A. | B/110 | September 21, 1870 | September 22, 1870 |
| Gilly, T. F. | Cope, Elizabeth | C/102 | November 28, 1874 | December 2, 1874 |
| Gilson, Robert | Southerland, Miss Polly | A/88 | March 25, 1846 | March 26, 1846 |
| Ginoe, W. Z. | Jamison, Nancy A. | A2/92 | December 20, 1859 | No Return |
| Gipson, Parilee | Pitman, N. M. | D/8 | | December 11, 1881 |
| Givan, Bluford H. | Dodd, Miss Smithy J. | A2/72 | February 2, 1859 | No Return |
| Givan, W. J. | Hume, Sallie | C/446 | September 16, 1891 | September 16, 1891 |
| Given, William C. | Bralley, Miss Nancy | A/58 | December 24, 1842 | December 24, 1842 |
| Givens, Elizabeth C. Miss | Fuller, James | B/46 | July 11, 1867 | July 11, 1867 |

| Groom or Bride | Groom or Bride | Book/Page | Date of License | Date of Marriage |
| --- | --- | --- | --- | --- |
| Givens, Fordy Miss | Devenport, George | B/118 | December 1, 1870 | December 6, 1870 |
| Givens, J. W. | Alexander, Mary M. | C/124 | November 27, 1875 | November 28, 1875 |
| Givens, Marion | Murphy, Margret | D/14 | | August 17, 1882 |
| Givens, Mary F. Miss | Todd, Jesse | A/78 | March 14, 1845 | March 16, 1845 |
| Givens, Mary Miss | Melton, C. D. | A2/147 | November 1, 1866 | November 7, 1866 |
| Givens, S. J. | Melton, Miss S. J. | B/34 | December 22, 1866 | December 23, 1866 |
| Givens, Sallie Miss | Rigsby, Bailam | B/90 | October 2, 1869 | October 3, 1869 |
| Givens, William A. | Nichols, Miss Eliza A. | A/77 | March 3, 1845 | No Return |
| Givens, William J. | Eason, Miss Harriet | A2/10 | January 20, 1851 | January 21, 1851 |
| Givins, America Miss | Murfree, I. N. B. | B/78 | February 6, 18609 | February 7, 1869 |
| Givins, J. D. | Haley, J. M. | C/228 | October 18, 1879 | October 29, 1879 |
| Givins, M. Miss | Lewis, L. L. | A2/72 | February 22, 1859 | No Return |
| Givins, M. Miss | Lewis, L. L. | A2/84 | February 22, 1859 | No Return |
| Gizzel, Roday | McGill, John | C/304 | February 11, 1884 | No Date |
| Glaspler, Ater | Barton, Albert | C/256 | May 22, 1880 | May ??, 1880 |
| Glasper, Lucinda | Fugitt, Wm | C/76 | December 11, 1873 | December 11, 1873 |
| Glazebrooks, James | Philips, Miss Nancy A. | A/82 | July 17, 1845 | July 17, 1845 |
| Glimes, Jack | Blue, Judy | C/362 | August 11, 1886 | No Return |
| Goad, Ellar C. | Grizzle, Wm | C/264 | November 27, 1880 | No Return |
| Goad, G. B. | Todd, Miss Margret | A2/32 | May 6, 1854 | March 5, 1855 |
| Goad, Louisa Miss | Patterson, R. W. | A/97 | February 11, 1847 | February 11, 1847 |
| Goad, William | Bunch, Mrs. Malinda | B/80 | March 31, 1869 | March 31, 1860 |
| Godwin, Benjamin A. | Brandon, Miss Rebecca | A/62 | May 4, 1843 | May 4, 1843 |
| Goff, Dillard | Spurlock, Martha | C/84 | February 27, 1874 | March 1, 1874 |
| Goff, James E. | Simmons, Mary E. | C/212 | February 28, 1879 | March 2, 1879 |
| Goff, L. P. | Melton, Miss Ann C. | B/100 | March 29, 1870 | March 28, 1868 |
| Goff, L. P. | Brim, Sarah | C/72 | November 21, 1873 | November 21, 1873 |
| Goff, Martha Ann Miss | Wimberly, J. E. | B/62 | March 5, 1868 | March 8, 1868 |
| Goings, Roda Miss | Crawford, John | A2/144 | September 12, 1866 | September 13, 1866 |
| Goins, Carter | Scott, Catharine | B/66 | May 23, 1868 | May 28, 1868 |
| Goins, Carter | Goins, S. A. | C/338 | October 2, 1885 | October 3, 1885 |
| Goins, Henry | Goins, Parla | C/356 | March 20, 1886 | No Return |
| Goins, Henry | Powell, Fannie | D/5 | | October 6, 1881 |
| Goins, James | Goins, Vandera | C/360 | July 16, 1886 | July 17, 1886 |
| Goins, Jefferson | Mooneyham, Sallie | C/212 | February 3, 1879 | February 9, 1879 |
| Goins, John B. | Craft, Chatata | A2/45 | December 28, 1855 | December 28, 1855 |
| Goins, Joshua | Goins, Sunlda | C/360 | July 9, 1886 | July ??, 1886 |
| Goins, Lewis | Robinson, Maggie | C/312 | August 9, 1884 | August 10, 1884 |
| Goins, Parla | Goins, Henry | C/356 | March 20, 1886 | No Return |
| Goins, S. A. | Goins, Carter | C/338 | October 2, 1885 | October 3, 1885 |
| Goins, Samuel | Barrett, Armandy | C/462 | July 16, 1892 | July 17, 1892 |
| Goins, Scyntha Miss | Fields, Martin | B/44 | March 28, 1867 | March 28, 1867 |
| Goins, Sunlda | Goins, Joshua | C/360 | July 9, 1886 | July ??, 1886 |
| Goins, Vandera | Goins, James | C/360 | July 16, 1886 | July 17, 1886 |
| Golahah, Robert | Dubirth, Nancy | A/16 | August 2, 1839 | August 2, 1839 |
| Good, Bettie F. | Bottom, L. M. | C/372 | October 30, 1886 | October 31, 1886 |

| Groom or Bride | Groom or Bride | Book/Page | Date of License | Date of Marriage |
| --- | --- | --- | --- | --- |
| Good, C. L. | Bragg, Ellen E. | C/98 | October 13, 1874 | October 14, 1874 |
| Good, C. L. | Gaither, Matilda | F/104 | December 9, 1896 | December 8, 1896 |
| Good, Dora | Cunningham, Pate | F/30 | February 5, 1894 | No Return |
| Good, Exser | Bowman, Elehue | F/96 | September 16, 1896 | September 17, 1896 |
| Good, Harriet C. Miss | Thompson, W. D. T. | B/96 | December 23, 1869 | Return Not Executed |
| Good, J. C. | Grizzell, Martha | C/158 | February 26, 1877 | February 26, 1877 |
| Good, James | Rizzle, Mattie | F/150 | June 11, 1898 | No Return |
| Good, M. E. | Bailey, M. F. | C/232 | December 4, 1879 | December 4, 1879 |
| Good, Mary A. Miss | Thomas, Henry N. | A/115 | October 12, 1848 | October 12, 1848 |
| Good, Mary Ann | Polock, Daniel M. | A2/132 | November 29, 1865 | November 30, 1865 |
| Good, Mary P. | Bottoms, S. H. | C/344 | December 15, 1885 | December 15, 1885 |
| Good, N. C. | Anderson, J. M. | C/34 | August 14, 1872 | No Return |
| Good, Nancy | Haley, William | A2/44 | December 13, 1855 | No Return |
| Good, Nancy R. | Eskhue, G. G. | A2/81 | July 24, 1857 | July 26, 1857 |
| Good, R. C. | Helton, Ann | C/22 | February 13, 1872 | February 13, 1872 |
| Good, R. C. | Grimes, Mollie | C/308 | May 10, 1884 | May 11, 1884 |
| Good, Cyntha A. | Flemmings, Robert L. | C/374 | November 11, 1886 | November 11, 1886 |
| Good, Elisabeth C. | Owen, Fate | C/262 | November 9, 1880 | No Return |
| Good, Elizbeth | Owens, Fate | C/194 | July 16, 1878 | July 7, 1878 |
| Good, M. P. | Phillips, J. C. | C/16 | December 15, 1871 | December 24, 1871 |
| Good, Mary P. | Phillips, Caney | C/174 | October 22, 1877 | October 22, 1877 |
| Good, Stephen | Sneed, Josephine | C/226 | October 1, 1879 | No Retrun |
| Good, Tennie | Holland, Henry | C/180 | December 20, 1877 | No Return |
| Good, W. M. | Vichers, Maggie | E/219 | October 14, 1889 | October 15, 1889 |
| Good, Willie | Winnett, Deller | C/304 | February 24, 1884 | February 28, 1884 |
| Good, Wm | Laseter, Angeline | A2/12 | November 11, 1851 | November 21, 1851 |
| Goode, Della | Underwood, James | C/438 | June 24, 1891 | June 25, 1891 |
| Gooden, William | Brandon, Sabella | A/8 | November 21, 1838 | No Return |
| Gooding, Abraham | Simpson, Miss Olive | A2/81 | September 19, 1857 | September 20, 1857 |
| Gooding, Elisabeth | Gooding, Wm | C/278 | May 7, 1881 | No Return |
| Gooding, Emeline Miss | Cook, J. W. | A2/42 | November 27, 1855 | December 2, 1855 |
| Gooding, J. A. | Sissom, Nancy E. | D/17 | | November 12, 1882 |
| Gooding, James | Todd, Isabella | C/42 | October 17, 1872 | October 17, 1872 |
| Gooding, James | Davis, Sarah | C/126 | December 18, 1875 | No Return |
| Gooding, Lucinda Miss | Stacy, John W. | A/112 | July 12, 1848 | July 12, 1848 |
| Gooding, Martha Miss | Poff, Charles | A/45 | December 16, 1841 | December 16, 1841 |
| Gooding, Martha Miss | McClain, James | A/101 | August 20, 1847 | No Return |
| Gooding, Mary Miss | Elkins, Hampton | A2/32 | March 2, 1854 | No Return |
| Gooding, Radid? | Beaty, A. J. | A/16 | August 3, 1839 | No Return |
| Gooding, Richard | Carrick, Miss Esther C. | B/34 | December 22, 1866 | December 27, 1866 |
| Gooding, Robert | Winily, Caroline | A2/100 | July 21, 1860 | July 26, 1860 |
| Gooding, Sarah Miss | Smoot, Arthur N. | A2/4 | August 23, 1850 | August 25, 1850 |
| Gooding, Sarah Miss | Lemmons, W. T. | B/78 | February 3, 1869 | February 11, 1869 |
| Gooding, Susanah | Beaty, Thomas H. | A/22 | January 14, 1840 | Solemnized, No Date |
| Gooding, William | Holt, Miss Fanny | A/40 | August 4, 1841 | August 6, 1841 |
| Gooding, William | Escue, Miss Nancy | A2/74 | March 28, 1854 | March 30, 1854 |

| Groom or Bride | Groom or Bride | Book/Page | Date of License | Date of Marriage |
|---|---|---|---|---|
| Gooding, William | Stanfield, Miss Parlee | B/92 | November 5, 1869 | November 17, 1869 |
| Gooding, Wm | Gooding, Elisabeth | C/278 | May 7, 1881 | No Return |
| Goodloe, A. M. | Smith, Miss M. E. | A2/49 | June 17, 1856 | June 17, 1856 |
| Goodloe, Allemira M. | Han (Hare), Bryant | A2/36 | October 4, 1854 | October 5, 1854 |
| Goodloe, B. R. | Crocker, Miss Eugenia | B/44 | April 9, 1867 | April 9, 1867 |
| Goodloe, E. A. | McKnight, A. E. | A2/86 | July 7, 1859 | No Return |
| Goodloe, H. N. | Jetten, ---- | D/22 | | January 18, 1883 |
| Goodloe, Jame E. | Jetton, Mary R. | C/186 | February 4, 1878 | February 5, 1878 |
| Goodwar, Rebeca | St. John, S. M. | E/52 | August 3, 1888 | August 5, 1888 |
| Goodwin, R. D. | Simmons, Jane | A2/121 | March 10, 1865 | March 10, 1865 |
| Gorden, George H. | Brandon, Miss Laviwa | A/41 | October 6, 1841 | No Return |
| Gorden, Mary A. | Boren, Calvin | C/284 | June 11, 1883 | June 11, 1883 |
| Gordon, Amanda Miss | Beargin, Thomas | B/50 | August 26, 1867 | August 27, 1867 |
| Gordon, J. H. | Mitchell, Miss Ann E. | B/120 | December 24, 1870 | December 25, 1870 |
| Gordon, J. H. | Wilson, Callie | C/326 | February 18, 1885 | February 19, 1885 |
| Gordon, John | Patton, Miss Harriett | A/103 | October 28, 1847 | October 28, 1847 |
| Gordon, Julian | Martin, Richard | B/16 | January 27, 1869 | January 27, 1969 |
| Gordon, Lewis | Martin, Lucinda | B/12 | June 22, 1867 | June 21, 1867 |
| Gordon, Mollie | Mitchell, Geo. | C/18 | December 28, 1871 | December 28, 1871 |
| Gordon, Robert | Robinson, Miss Vina A. | A/80 | July 9, 1845 | July 9, 1845 |
| Gordon, Robert | Hays, Miss Sarah | A/106 | January 20, 1848 | January 20, 1848 |
| Gordon, Robert | Robinson, Miss Vina A. | A/81 | July 9, 1845 | July 9, 1845 |
| Gordon, W. M. | Hooker, Miss Mary A. | B/118 | December 7, 1870 | December 23, 1870 |
| Gotcher, W. M. | Dickens, Miss Fanny Dickens | A/104 | November 2, 1847 | November 3, 1847 |
| Gothard, W. J. | Odom, Leona | C/374 | November 20, 1886 | November 25, 1886 |
| Gowen, Charity Miss | Gowin, Nathan | A2/39 | March 29, 1855 | Solemnized, No Date |
| Gowen, H. N. | Brown, M. A. E | C/50 | January 7, 1873 | January 7, 1873 |
| Gowen, Jackson | Bolen, Ella | F/70 | September 5, 1895 | September 8, 1895 |
| Gowen, James J. | Moore, Miss Martha E. | A2/23 | February 17, 1853 | July 20, 1853 |
| Gowen, Julia Y. Miss | Tilford, Nichols C. | A/49 | April 25, 1842 | April 26, 1842 |
| Gowen, Laborn | Clark, Ortime | A2/40 | July 18, 1855 | Returns Missing |
| Gowens, Francis, M. | Gownesn, Nelli J. | E/144 | March 20, 1889 | March 21, 1889 |
| Gowens, Sarah | Bowlin, Richard | A2/117 | October 15, 1864 | No Return |
| Gowens, Wm. | Edge, Mollie | C/396 | August 4, 1887 | August 11, 1887 |
| Gower, Bettie Miss | Brewer, W. M. | B/118 | November 24, 1870 | November 24, 1870 |
| Gowin, John | Gowin, Miss Rhoda | A2/40 | March 29, 1855 | Returns Missing |
| Gowin, Nathan | Gowen, Miss Charity | A2/39 | March 29, 1855 | Solemnized, No Date |
| Gowin, Rhoda Miss | Gowin, John | A2/40 | March 29, 1855 | Returns Missing |
| Gowind, Eulia | Moore, S. L. | F/100 | October 16, 1896 | October 18, 1896 |
| Gowins, William | Parker, Mary | C/374 | November 14, 1886 | November 15, 1886 |
| Gownesn, Nelli J. | Gowens, Francis, M. | E/144 | March 20, 1889 | March 21, 1889 |
| Graham, Cornelia A. | Davenport, W. I. | F/28 | December 27, 1893 | December 27, 1783 |
| Graham, D. Miss | Chapman, E. P. | A2/96 | May 5, 1860 | May 5, 1860 |
| Graham, Earle | Bragg, Jennie | F/76 | December 10, 1895 | December 11, 1895 |
| Graham, J. G. | Hart, Lue | C/104 | December 24, 1874 | December 24, 1874 |
| Graham, J. M. Miss | Ramsey, Luthur S. | A2/75 | June 2, 1855 | June 3, 1855 |

| Groom or Bride | Groom or Bride | Book/Page | Date of License | Date of Marriage |
|---|---|---|---|---|
| Graham, M. G. | Isom, J. B. | C/96 | October 1, 1874 | October 1, 1874 |
| Graham, R. M. | Justice, Miss S. C. | A2/78 | February 14, 1856 | February 14, 1856 |
| Graham, Sallie Miss | Lorance, E. J. | B/36 | January 1, 1867 | January 1, 1867 |
| Graham, T. N | Wheeler | B/126 | March 2, 1871 | March 2, 1871 |
| Graham, W. J. | Justice, Miss M. E. | A2/66 | August 19, 1858 | No Return |
| Graham, W. J. | Justice, Miss M. J. | B/106 | August 3, 1870 | August 7, 1870 |
| Gray, Abraham | Freeze, Emaline | A2/134 | January 1, 1866 | January 4, 1866 |
| Gray, Jemima E. | Williams, W. J. | A2/132 | December 1, 1865 | December 2, 1865 |
| Gray, Jummia Jue | Underwood, Thomas | C/414 | April 12, 1890 | April 13, 1890 |
| Gray, Matte | Catcart, Bascomb | F/12 | June 28, 1893 | June 28, 1893 |
| Gray, Mariah | Robinson, Hugh | C/362 | August 5, 1886 | August 12, 1886 |
| Gray, Matilda | Robinson, Jesse | C/326 | February 18, 1885 | February 19, 1884 |
| Gray, N. E. | McKnab, R. T. | A2/130 | October 7, 1864 | October 19, 1865 |
| Gray, Nancy E. | Williams, Thomas H. | A/8 | October 13, 1838 | October 18, 1838 |
| Gray, Rachel Caroline | McCollough, Thomas | A/6 | September 18, 1838 | September 19, 1838 |
| Gray, Samuel W. | Sagely, Nancy Eleanor | A/60 | February 18, 1843 | February 19, 1843 |
| Gray, Silas M. | Hollis, Miss Martha E. | A2/75 | August 15, 1854 | August 17, 1854 |
| Gray, W. W. | Prater, Mattie A. | C/68 | September 27, 1873 | September 28, 1873 |
| Gray, W. W. | Summar, S. V. | C/136 | March 1, 1876 | March 2, 1876 |
| Gray, W. W. | Miller, Ella | C/210 | January 28, 1879 | January 30, 1879 |
| Gray, William | Webber, Miss Elizabeth | A/52 | August 4, 1842 | August 5, 1842 |
| Gray, Wm. P. | Brown, Tempa Caroline | A2/31 | December 27, 1853 | December 27, 1853 |
| Grear, David | Harris, Sally | A/17 | September 7, 1839 | September 11, 1839 |
| Grear, David | Jones, Miss Edith | A/62 | May 1, 1843 | May 2, 1843 |
| Grear, Elizabeth | Perry, Moses | A2/124 | July 19, 1865 | No Return |
| Grear, Mary Miss | Crouch, J. B. | C/458 | April 28, 1892 | No Return |
| Greear, Polly Ann Miss | Beaty, Philip D. | A/44 | December 4, 1841 | December 5, 1841 |
| Green, Catherine | Williams W. M | F/126 | August 26, 1897 | August 26, 1897 |
| Green, E. H. | York, S. E. | C/228 | October 25, 1875 | October 25, 1879 |
| Green, George | Dunlap, Delor?? | C/414 | July 19, 1890 | July 20, 1890 |
| Green, James C. | Lane, Olive | A/1 | March 8, 1838 | March 9, 1838 |
| Green, Jno | Summars, Catherine | C/122 | November 3, 1875 | November 4, 1875 |
| Green, Mary E. Miss | French, John M. | B/60 | January 7, 1868 | January 8, 1868 |
| Green, Mary Estie Lou | Patterson, R. J. | F/92 | August 19, 1896 | August 20, 1896 |
| Green, Thomas L. | Southerland, Miss Rachael | A/50 | June 4, 1842 | June 5, 1842 |
| Greer, J. H. | Smith, B. D. | D/6 | | November 6, 1881 |
| Greer, John C. | Burk, Miss Jane C. | A2/17 | January 7, 1852 | January 11, 1852 |
| Gribble, Cling | Dillon, Miss Fannie | F/32 | February 1, 1894 | February 1, 1894 |
| Gribble, Girtrude | Odom, C. C. | C/198 | September 18, 1878 | September 22, 1878 |
| Gribble, John | Bradley, Louisa | C/128 | December 23, 1875 | December 23, 1875 |
| Griffa, Elvina | Bearding, H. | C/118 | August 27, 1875 | August 29, 1875 |
| Griffin, Caroline E. | Martin, Wm. | A2/44 | December 17, 1855 | December 20, 1855 |
| Griffin, Floura | Moore, Jacob | C/268 | December 18, 1880 | December 18, 1880 |
| Griggs, Michael | Pitts, Miss Lucinda | A2/87 | July 7, 1859 | July 27, 1859 |
| Grimes, Better Miss | Rollins, Andrew | C/408 | November 15, 1887 | November 15, 1887 |
| Grimes, Billy | Hollis, Miss Kate | F/82 | February 1, 1896 | January 3, 1896 |

| Groom or Bride | Groom or Bride | Book/Page | Date of License | Date of Marriage |
|---|---|---|---|---|
| Grimes, Britton | Hays, Miss Elizabeth | A/64 | August 10, 1843 | August 10, 1843 |
| Grimes, David | Branden, Beckey J. | C/210 | January 18, 1879 | January 20, 1879 |
| Grimes, G. G. C. | Smith, Miss Sarrah J. | A2/22 | January 13, 1853 | January 13, 1853 |
| Grimes, Gerinnia (?) | Rawlings, Andrew | C/26 | March 30, 1872 | March 31, 1872 |
| Grimes, J. B. | McKinney, Nancy | C/362 | July 24, 1886 | No Return |
| Grimes, Mollie | Good, R. C. | C/308 | May 10, 1884 | May 11, 1884 |
| Grimes, Nancy | Lamlet, James | C/284 | June 7, 1883 | June 7, 1883 |
| Grimes, Susan | Bowen, A. S. | C/284 | June 21, 1883 | June 21, 1883 |
| Grimett, Patsey | Sneed, Mose | C/26 | March 14, 1872 | March 14, 1872 |
| Grindstaff, J. H. | Odom, Jennie | C/364 | August 25, 1886 | August 26, 1886 |
| Grindstaff, James | Ritch, Elizabeth | B/18 | May 26, 1870 | May 26, 1870 |
| Grizzel, Francis | Patterson, Perry | C/80 | January 25, 1874 | January 25, 1874 |
| Grizzel, Jno R. | Spurlock, Susanna | C/116 | July 29, 1875 | No Return |
| Grizzel, Martha N. Miss | Dennis, John N. | B/92 | November 11, 1869 | November 14, 1869 |
| Grizzel, Sarah E. | Tassie, E. W. | C/50 | January 2, 1873 | January 2, 1873 |
| Grizzel, Susan | Molley, Robert | A2/32 | April 17, 1854 | May 4, 1854 |
| Grizzel, William | Campbell, Mrs. Dovey | B/106 | August 15, 1870 | August 17, 1870 |
| Grizzel, Wm. | Melton, Eliza | C/96 | September 30, 1874 | September 30, 1874 |
| Grizzell, Calline | Hammons, C. C. | C/150 | November 21, 1876 | November 29, 1876 |
| Grizzell, Izzan | Arnett, Jas. E. | A2/102 | September 11, 1860 | No Return |
| Grizzell, John | Hammons, Elizabeth | C/34 | August 16, 1872 | August 18, 1872 |
| Grizzell, Josie | Vandergriff, N. | C/94 | September 18, 1874 | September 18, 1874 |
| Grizzell, Martha | Good, J. C. | C/158 | February 26, 1877 | February 26, 1877 |
| Grizzell, Martha | Bluer, Munroe | E/202 | August 24, 1889 | No Return |
| Grizzell, Sarah A. Miss | Hailey, James | B/108 | August 23, 1870 | August 28, 1870 |
| Grizzle, Alice Miss | Mahaffy, R. J. | F/176 | May 18, 1899 | May 18, 1899 |
| Grizzle, Babe (col.) | Roberts, Lewis (col.) | F/166 | January 15, 1899 | January 15, 1899 |
| Grizzle, Birtha | McKnight, Ike | F/124 | August 2, 1897 | August 2, 1897 |
| Grizzle, Daniel | Wood, Miss Margarett | A/127 | September 26, 1849 | September 27, 1849 |
| Grizzle, E. A | Campbell, A. J. | C/224 | September 6, 1879 | September 7, 1879 |
| Grizzle, Elisabeth | Crouch, J. B. | C/256 | October 4, 1880 | October 17, 1880 |
| Grizzle, Elze | Cathcart, Ada | C/270 | January 24, 1881 | January 26, 1881 |
| Grizzle, G. S. | Hennessee, Lela | E/334 | December 27, 1898 | |
| Grizzle, G. S. | Hennessee, Lela | F/164 | December 27, 1898 | December 28, 1898 |
| Grizzle, G. W. | Gasaway, Miss M. L. | A2/78 | March 7, 1856 | March 10, 1856 |
| Grizzle, Helen | George, Jacob | F/104 | December 9, 1896 | December 10, 1896 |
| Grizzle, Isaac | Jones, Miss Elizabeth | A2/103 | October 14, 1867 | October 20, 1847 |
| Grizzle, J. W. | Hancock, Leanthe | C/404 | October 18, 1887 | October 19, 1887 |
| Grizzle, James | Melton, Miss Martha | A2/5 | September 14, 1850 | September 16, 1850 |
| Grizzle, Jno R. | Hawkins, Susie | F/168 | January 21, 1899 | January 25, 1899 |
| Grizzle, Mary E. | Hubbard, D. A. | C/262 | November 24, 1880 | November 25, 1880 |
| Grizzle, Paump | Martin, Rody | C/10 | September 27, 1871 | September 27, 1871 |
| Grizzle, Polk | Mathais, Miss Parlee | A2/143 | August 7, 1866 | August 9, 1866 |
| Grizzle, Richard | Burger, Miss Pelina J. | B/42 | February 27, 1867 | February 19, 1867 |
| Grizzle, S. C. | Yeargain, F. J. | C/212 | February 17, 1879 | February 20, 1879 |
| Grizzle, William | Melton, Polly | A/32 | August 15, 1840 | August 16, 1840 |

| Groom or Bride | Groom or Bride | Book/Page | Date of License | Date of Marriage |
|---|---|---|---|---|
| Grizzle, Wm | Goad, Ellar C. | C/264 | November 27, 1880 | No Return |
| Grizzle, Wm. | Foster, Francis | C/270 | January 19, 1881 | January 19, 1881 |
| Grizzle, Wm. | Markum, Delia | D/4 | | August 16, 1881 |
| Grizzle, Wm. | McDougle, Lidia | F/124 | August 4, 1897 | August 4, 1897 |
| Groom, A. E. | Owens, A. G. | C/54 | February 25, 1873 | February 27, 1873 |
| Groom, Beoda Miss | Fite, F. M. | C/458 | April 4, 1892 | No Return |
| Grooms, Allice | King, W. L. | C/298 | December 1, 1883 | December 2, 1884 |
| Groom, Frances Miss | McAdoo, H. E. | B/120 | December 21, 1870 | December 22, 1870 |
| Grooms, Amanda | Bryson, Bethell | F/18 | October 14, 1893 | October 14, 1893 |
| Grooms, E. C. | Thomas, T. A. | C/206 | November 20, 1878 | November 22, 1878 |
| Grooms, Ras | Higgins, Florance | C/318 | November 10, 1884 | November 13, 1884 |
| Grooms, Ras | Higgin, Florance | C/318 | November 10, 1884 | No Return |
| Grooms, Tennie | Warren, Sam | C/206 | November 27, 1878 | November 28, 1878 |
| Gross, Harrison | Brown, Mary | A2/53 | June 2, 1866 | June 3, 1866 |
| Gross, Mary | Barton, Dave | C/94 | August 22, 1874 | August 27, 1874 |
| Guimore, Porter | Walker, Edna | C/466 | September 27, 1892 | September 28, 1892 |
| Gullett, Samuel | Clements, Miss Martha Jane | A/64 | July 25, 1843 | July 25, 1843 |
| Gullette, Mary | Keele, Andesen | F/20 | October 28, 1893 | October 28, 1893 |
| Gunter, A. Miss | Bowren, Zeb | B/116 | November 12, 1870 | November 13, 1870 |
| Gunter, A. J. Miss | Prime, John C. | A2/27 | August 25, 1853 | No Return |
| Gunter, Adaline Miss | Burger, Isaac | B/38 | January 26, 1867 | No Return |
| Gunter, Annie | Sullens, Burley | F/130 | September 18, 1897 | September 19, 1897 |
| Gunter, B. E. | Jones, R. E. | F/50 | November 24, 1894 | December 9, 1894 |
| Gunter, C. C. | Moore, Miss C. Nancy | A2/25 | April 19, 1853 | No Return |
| Gunter, C. D. | Inglis, Mary | C/74 | November 29, 1873 | November 27, 1873 |
| Gunter, C. Y. | Cook, Mary | C/60 | June 28, 1873 | June 29, 1873 |
| Gunter, Campbell | Evans, Miss Sarrah | A2/38 | March 7, 1855 | March 9, 1855 |
| Gunter, Clabe | Melton, Miss Francis | C/384 | February 28, 1887 | February 28, 1887 |
| Gunter, Claiborne Y. | Kersey, Miss Virginia | A/91 | September 27, 1846 | September 28, 1846 |
| Gunter, Ella | King, W. B. | F/52 | December 11, 1894 | No Return |
| Gunter, Evie | Tate, J. B. | F/126 | August 22, 1897 | August 22, 1897 |
| Gunter, Fannie Miss | Evans, Jno. C. | C/454 | February 2, 1892 | February 2, 1892 |
| Gunter, H. K. | Underhill, A. O. | F/50 | November 24, 1894 | December 5, 1894 |
| Gunter, Hatie | Hunt, John | C/328 | March 3, 1885 | March 3, 1885 |
| Gunter, Isaac | Lawrence, Miss Mary | A2/29 | November 8, 1853 | November 8, 1853 |
| Gunter, James M. | Pitman, Miss Disa | A/86 | February 8, 1846 | February 8, 1846 |
| Gunter, Jesse | Elkins, Tennie | D/12 | | March 19, 1882 |
| Gunter, Jno | Patterson, Sarah | C/194 | August 10, 1878 | August 11, 1878 |
| Gunter, John | Mongomery, Laura | C/472 | December 26, 1892 | December 28, 1892 |
| Gunter, Josie Miss | Bailey, C. J. | F/82 | January 9, 1896 | January 9, 1896 |
| Gunter, John L. | Barrett, Miss Lisby | B/62 | January 13, 1868 | January 14, 1868 |
| Gunter, Josephine Miss | Melton, Francis | B/44 | April 10, 1867 | April 11, 1867 |
| Gunter, Margarett Miss | Lasiter, J. B. | B/68 | July 25, 1868 | July 29, 1868 |
| Gunter, Martha Miss | Marcum, Micajah | A/131 | January 30, 1850 | January 30, 1850 |
| Gunter, Mary Miss | Lance, James P. K. | B/54 | October 5, 1867 | October 6, 1867 |

| Groom or Bride | Groom or Bride | Book/Page | Date of License | Date of Marriage |
|---|---|---|---|---|
| Gunter, Mattie | Cantrell, Watson | F/152 | July 16, 1898 | July 17, 1898 |
| Gunter, Mattie Miss | Burger, R. J. | C/454 | February 8, 1892 | February 11, 1892 |
| Gunter, Noley | Lafevers, John | C/250 | July 10, 1880 | July 11, 1880 |
| Gunter, Robt | Richie, Molley | F/136 | October 30, 1897 | October 31, 1897 |
| Gunter, Sam | Melton, Sarah | C/200 | October 4, 1878 | October 6, 1878 |
| Gunter, Sarah | Patterson, Robt | C/352 | February 16, 1886 | March 6, 1886 |
| Gunter, Sarah Miss | McDougald, John D. | A/58 | January 2, 1843 | January 5, 1843 |
| Gunter, W. J. | Hipp, Miss Rebecca J. | B/122 | December 24, 1870 | December 25, 1870 |
| Gunter, William | Kersey, Sarryan | A2/30 | December 10, 1853 | No Return |
| Gunter, William W. | Ramsey, Miss Elizabeth | A/80 | July 12, 1845 | July 13, 1845 |
| Gunter, William W. | Ramsey, Miss Elizabeth | A/81 | July 12, 1845 | July 13, 1845 |
| Gunter, Wm. | Pasby (Pasly) , Sarah | C/106 | December 30, 1874 | December 30, 1874 |
| Gunter, Wm. | Masey, Lockey | C/426 | December 20, 1890 | December 21, 1890 |
| Gunthe, Sarah Miss | Ford, Harry E. | A2/34 | July 27, 1854 | July 17, 1854 |
| Gurty, Mary E. Miss | McCabe, A. J. | A2/25 | May 20, 1853 | No Return |
| Guy, A. J. | Kerby, Sarah A. | C/48 | December 27, 1872 | No Return |
| Guy, James | Pucket, Narcissa | A2/123 | June 1, 1865 | June 1, 1865 |
| Guy, Thomas | Byrum, Fannie | E/242 | December 19, 1889 | December 19, 1889 |
| Hadley, Melissa | Pope, Mark A. | A/24 | February 24, 1840 | February 26, 1840 |
| Hadley, Nancy | Heriman, Westley | A/10 | January 23, 1839 | January 23, 1839 |
| Hagwood, H. B. | Carter, Sarah E. | C/78 | December 24, 1873 | December 25, 1873 |
| Hail, Mary, F. | Williamsm J. H. | C/318 | November 29, 1884 | December 1, 1885 |
| Hailey, Caphus C. | Burk, Miss Sara | A2/45 | January 5, 1856 | January 5, 1856 |
| Hailey, Clementine Miss | Waters, Henry | B/42 | February 27, 1867 | Solemnized, No Date |
| Hailey, Elizabeth | Reed, David | A/6 | September 12, 1838 | September 12, 1838 |
| Hailey, Elizabeth Miss | Mears, Mark | B/46 | July 1, 1867 | July 3, 1867 |
| Hailey, Fannie | Smithson, W. V. | C/370 | October 9, 1886 | No Return |
| Hailey, J. A. | Lynn, Miss L. A. | C/8 | August 30, 1871 | August 31, 1871 |
| Hailey, J. M. | King, M. S. | C/82 | February 6, 1874 | February 11, 1874 |
| Hailey, James | Grizzell, Miss Sarah A. | B/108 | August 23, 1870 | August 28, 1870 |
| Hailey, James A. | Georg, Miss Amanda J. | A2/67 | September 1, 1858 | No Return |
| Hailey, P. J. | Hollis, W. B. | F/102 | November 20, 1896 | November 22, 1896 |
| Hailey, S. A. Miss | Burk, N. J. | A2/67 | September 2, 1858 | Handed in No Return |
| Hailey, Tildey | Muncey, McCaslin | A2/76 | August 4, 1855 | August 5, 1855 |
| Hailey, W. B. | Ring, Miss M. E. | B/92 | November 24, 1869 | November 25, 1869 |
| Haily, Ann E. | Campbell, J. D. | A2/115 | July 19, 1864 | No Return |
| Hainey, John | Marchbanks, Mariah | A/25 | February 26, 1840 | February 25, 1840 |
| Haithcock, James | Cawthan, Sarah | D/5 | | October 9, 1881 |
| Haithcock, James H. | Finly, Elizabeth | A/68 | February 23, 1844 | February 25, 1844 |
| Haithcock, Polly Miss | Stacy, Samuel H. | B/32 | November 18, 1866 | November 18, 1866 |
| Halcomb, J. C. | Moore, Sallie J. | C/304 | February 2, 1884 | February 3, 1884 |
| Hale, Creed W. | Ashford, Miss Nancy Jane | A/122 | May 8, 1849 | May 8, 1849 |
| Hale, Elvira F. Miss | Ritch, James O. | B/56 | December 4, 1867 | December 8, 1867 |
| Hale, George | Smith, Julia | C/220 | August 5, 1879 | August 6, 1879 |
| Hale, George | Worley, Miss Sarah | C/434 | April 24, 1891 | April 24, 1891 |
| Hale, H. G. | Sellars, Helen | C/152 | January 11, 1877 | January 11, 1877 |

| Groom or Bride | Groom or Bride | Book/Page | Date of License | Date of Marriage |
|---|---|---|---|---|
| Hale, Heder Miss | Hall, W. B. | E/223 | October 16, 1889 | October 16, 1889 |
| Hale, Idar | Hancock, J. T. | C/354 | February 25, 1886 | March 2, 1886 |
| Hale, J. P. | Knight, Magnola | F/8 | April 18, 1893 | April 19, 1893 |
| Hale, J. T. | Morris, M. L. | C/358 | June 16, 1886 | June 16, 1886 |
| Hale, James | Watson, Annie | C/116 | July 29, 1875 | August 1, 1875 |
| Hale, James L. | Smithson, Susie B. | C/114 | July 2, 1875 | July 4, 1875 |
| Hale, L. Miss | Warren, J. W. | A2/46 | February 9, 1856 | February 10, 1856 |
| Hale, Mary | Patton, David | A2/95 | March 13, 1860 | March 13, 1860 |
| Hale, Mary D. Miss | Botten, George J. | A2/88 | September 3, 1859 | No Return |
| Hale, Nancy C. Miss | Adamson, Presley A. | B/38 | January 25, 1867 | January 31, 1867 |
| Hale, Nancy E. Miss | Bryant, Ira J. | A2/27 | September 1, 1853 | No Return |
| Hale, Sarah M. Miss | Garity, Pattrick | B/46 | July 15, 1867 | July 20, 1867 |
| Hale, Susan A. T. | Hancock, M. A. D. | C/136 | March 1, 1876 | No Return |
| Hale, Thomas | Keeton, Mary Malissa | A2/111 | January 19, 1864 | January 21, 1864 |
| Hale, Thomas | Dood, Miss Mary E. | B/92 | November 22, 1869 | November 23, 1869 |
| Hale, Vance | Mullenax, Miss H. J. | C/456 | February 26, 1892 | August 4, 1892 |
| Haley, Allen | Young, Miss Martha | A/99 | April 10, 1847 | April 10, 1847 |
| Haley, B. | Janson, J. H. | A2/99 | July 12, 1860 | July 12, 1860 |
| Haley, B. F. | Mean (Mears), Elizabeth A. | C/158 | March 8, 1877 | March 8, 1877 |
| Haley, Barney | Patton, Mary | F/34 | March 17, 1894 | March 17, 1894 |
| Haley, Betty | Thomas, Ben | F/128 | September 1, 1896 | September 1, 1897 |
| Haley, Cynthia | Taylor, S. M. | C/462 | August 1, 1892 | August 2, 1892 |
| Haley, David | Duke, Miss Sarah Ann | A/106 | January 11, 1848 | January 11, 1848 |
| Haley, E. T. | Gasaway, Laura | D/13 | | April 5, 1882 |
| Haley, Eli | Coarcy, Elizabeth | F/96 | September 18, 1896 | September 29, 1896 |
| Haley, Francis C. | Hays, E. | C/268 | December 4, 1880 | December 5, 1880 |
| Haley, George | Rhea, Miss Abagail | A/114 | September 23, 1848 | September 28, 1848 |
| Haley, George | Bowen, Miss Mary | A2/54 | February 20, 1857 | No Return |
| Haley, George | Mears, Elizabeth | D/13 | | July 30, 1882 |
| Haley, Isaac | Pendleton, Betty | C/222 | September 15, 1879 | September 14, 1879 |
| Haley, Isaac | Brandon, Dollie | E/382 | October 29, 1898 | |
| Haley, Isaac | McGowen, Etta | F/128 | August 26, 1897 | August 29, 1897 |
| Haley, Isaac | Brandon, Dollie | F/158 | October 29, 1898 | October 30, 1898 |
| Haley, J. M. | Givins, J. D. | C/228 | October 18, 1879 | October 29, 1879 |
| Haley, J. N. | Stacy, Allace E. | C/300 | January 17, 1884 | January 17, 1884 |
| Haley, James | Dickens, Elizabeth | A/33 | September 19, 1840 | September 20, 1840 |
| Haley, Janie | Duke, I. N. | D/20 | | January 26, 1883 |
| Haley, John | Course, Tennie | D/22 | | April 22, 1883 |
| Haley, John | Course, Tennie | C/282 | April 16, 1883 | No Return |
| Haley, John W. | Williams, Jerusha | A/30 | June 12, 1840 | June 14, 1840 |
| Haley, Joshua | Haynes, Miss Eleanor | A/86 | January 3, 1846 | February 26, 1846 |
| Haley, M. C. | King, W. J. | C/200 | September 26, 1878 | September 26, 1878 |
| Haley, M. E. | McMahan, S. W. | C/300 | January 16, 1884 | January 17, 1884 |
| Haley, Mary A. Miss | Pendleton, H. | A2/65 | June 1, 1858 | June 2, 1858 |
| Haley, Mary J. | Shirley, Geo T. | C/184 | January 5, 1878 | January 20, 1878 |
| Haley, N. J. | Bushs, N. L. | C/342 | December 5, 1885 | December 5, 1885 |

| Groom or Bride | Groom or Bride | Book/Page | Date of License | Date of Marriage |
|---|---|---|---|---|
| Haley, Nance E. Miss | Hancock, A. L. | A2/72 | March 1, 1859 | No Return |
| Haley, Nance E. Miss | Hancock, A. L. | A2/84 | March 1, 1859 | March 1, 1859 |
| Haley, Nancy | Summars, J. J. | C/252 | August 12, 1880 | August 12, 1880 |
| Haley, Nancy J. | McMahan, S. W. | C/404 | October 26, 1887 | October 26, 1887 |
| Haley, S. J. | Keaton, J. M. | C/194 | July 25, 1878 | July 25, 1878 |
| Haley, Sarah | Swan, Wm. | C/114 | May 29, 1875 | June 3, 1875 |
| Haley, Salley | Brandon, J. T. | C/322 | January 5, 1885 | No Return |
| Haley, T. J. | Ridener, M. P. | C/166 | August 4, 1877 | August 5, 1877 |
| Haley, Tennie | Prater, Josephus | D/2 | | August 11, 1881 |
| Haley, Venturian | Duke, N. R. J. | A2/103 | October 24, 1860 | No Return |
| Haley, Vicy C. | Duke, John A. | A2/20 | October 15, 1852 | October 16, 1852 |
| Haley, W. H. | Elkins, Dona | F/98 | October 3, 1896 | October 4, 1896 |
| Haley, W. V. | Duke, S. C. | C/162 | May 30, 1877 | May 30, 1877 |
| Haley, William | Good, Nancy | A2/44 | December 13, 1855 | No Return |
| Hall, A. B. | Morgan, Emma | C/282 | May 7, 1883 | May 7, 1883 |
| Hall, Albert E. | Spry, Miss Nancy C. | B/64 | March 3, 1868 | March 3, 1868 |
| Hall, C. H. | Morris, Miss Sarah | B/78 | February 1, 1869 | February 1, 1869 |
| Hall, Etta Miss | Matthew, Henry | C/450 | November 30, 1891 | December 2, 1891 |
| Hall, Fleming W. | Petty, Miss Eliza A. | A/69 | May 15, 1844 | May 16, 1844 |
| Hall, H. B. | Wale, Miss Celisa Jane | A/109 | February 28, 1848 | February 29, 1848 |
| Hall, H. N. | Walkup, Bettie | C/192 | May 29, 1878 | May 30, 1878 |
| Hall, J. P. | Elkins, Mollie | F/22 | November 16, 1893 | November 16, 1893 |
| Hall, J. W. | Williams, M. D. | C/162 | May 31, 1877 | May 31, 1877 |
| Hall, James | Burket, Miss Mary | A2/57 | August 1, 1857 | August 3, 1857 |
| Hall, James | Owen, Sarah | C/444 | August 21, 1891 | August 23, 1891 |
| Hall, John W. | Lawing, Miss Mary Ann | A2/6 | August 31, 1850 | September 1, 1850 |
| Hall, Jonathan | Wharrey, Miss Louisa Lavina | A/44 | December 9, 1841 | December 9, 1841 |
| Hall, M. A. | St. Clair, Benjamin | A2/126 | August 30, 1865 | August 31, 1865 |
| Hall, Margarett Miss | Miles, Robert S. | A2/25 | May 20, 1853 | May 24, 1853 |
| Hall, Mary E. Miss | Brown, W. M. | A2/158 | June 18, 1866 | No Return |
| Hall, Mary Miss | Brewer, Thomas J. | A/120 | February 14, 1849 | February 15, 1849 |
| Hall, Preston | Wherry, Miss Margarett | A/127 | September 25, 1849 | |
| Hall, R. | Willson, Miss Elizabeth | A2/29 | December 2, 1853 | December 4, 1853 |
| Hall, R. J. | Pearson, Asalin | C/404 | October 8, 1887 | October 9, 1887 |
| Hall, R. S. | Owen, Beckey | F/18 | October 2, 1893 | October 8, 1893 |
| Hall, Sarah W. | Rich, Joseph A. | D/20 | | February 11, 1883 |
| Hall, W. B. | Hale, Miss Heder | E/223 | October 16, 1889 | October 16, 1889 |
| Hall, Walter | Pelham, Nancy | C/198 | September 11, 1878 | September 11, 1878 |
| Hall, William J. | Trollinger, Matilda | A/67 | February 5, 1844 | No Return |
| Hall, William J. | Young, Miss Elizabeth | A/90 | August 19, 1846 | August 20, 1846 |
| Halle, J. C. | Ownby, Mollie | F/144 | January 31, 1898 | No Return |
| Halleyburton, O. G. | McFerren, Bittie | C/40 | September 26, 1872 | September 26, 1872 |
| Halpayne, Martha B. Miss | Roughton, James | A/107 | January 24, 1848 | January 24, 1848 |
| Haltiman, Eliza | Vandergriff, Wm | D/4 | | September 18, 1881 |
| Ham, Bradley | Finley, Miss Sarah Jane | B/34 | December 24, 1866 | December 25, 1866 |
| Hamilton, A. J. | Vandagrift, Delie | F/168 | January 28, 1899 | January 29, 1899 |

| Groom or Bride | Groom or Bride | Book/Page | Date of License | Date of Marriage |
|---|---|---|---|---|
| Hamilton, Harvey | Reed, Peney | A2/111 | January 8, 1864 | No Return |
| Hamilton, Lockey | Mont, Albert | C/396 | August 6, 1887 | August 7, 1887 |
| Hamilton, Mary Miss | Holston, Richard J. | A/127 | September 20, 1849 | September 20, 1849 |
| Hamilton, Mollie | Muncy, Halton | F/136 | November 17, 1897 | November 18, 1897 |
| Hamlet, Nancy Miss | Williams, Isaac | A2/13 | December 18, 1851 | No Return |
| Hammen, Malinda | Morgan, Wesley A. | A2/118 | November 26, 1864 | November 27, 1864 |
| Hammer, J. N. | Whitlock, Catherine | F/82 | January 8, 1896 | No Return |
| Hammer, L. C. | Petty, J. H. | E/150 | October 12, 1888 | October 12, 1888 |
| Hammers, Ann | Thomas, Whity | C/352 | February 13, 1886 | February 14, 1886 |
| Hammon, John | Young, Miss Jane | A/43 | November 1, 1841 | No Return |
| Hammon, Larkin | Sapp, Miss Polly | A/43 | October 30, 1841 | October 30, 1841 |
| Hammond, Mary | Hendrickson, Wm. | A/130 | October 18, 1849 | October 18, 1849 |
| Hammonds, Joice V. Miss | Barrett, Ward Jr. | A/116 | November 9, 1848 | November 9, 1848 |
| Hammons, C. C. | Grizzell, Calline | C/150 | November 21, 1876 | November 29, 1876 |
| Hammons, C. C. | Mason, Mary | F/150 | June 11, 1898 | No Return |
| Hammons, Elizabeth | Grizzell, John | C/34 | August 16, 1872 | August 18, 1872 |
| Hammons, I. I. | Odom, Margaret N. | A2/122 | April 1, 1865 | ?? ?, 1865 |
| Hammons, Jasper | Keaton, Elizabeth | A2/112 | March 17, 1864 | March 18, 1864 |
| Hammons, John J. | Young, Nancy T. | A2/124 | July 29, 1865 | July 30, 1865 |
| Hammons, Reese | Starr, Miss Ruthy | B/32 | December 4, 1866 | December 5, 1866 |
| Hammons, Sally | Moody, John | A2/131 | November 11, 1865 | November 5, 1865 |
| Hammons, Sarah P. Miss | Ashford, George | B/64 | December 31, 1867 | December 31, 1867 |
| Hamons, Tide | Mason, J. G. | F/94 | August 25, 1896 | No Return |
| Han (Hare), Bryant | Goodloe, Allemira M. | A2/36 | October 4, 1854 | October 5, 1854 |
| Hancock, ??? Miss | Ford, Thomas | A2/8 | December 23, 1850 | No Return |
| Hancock, A. J. | Rich, May | F/156 | September 6, 1898 | September 11, 1898 |
| Hancock, A. L. | Haley, Miss Nance E. | A2/72 | March 1, 1859 | No Return |
| Hancock, A. L. | Haley, Miss Nance E. | A2/84 | March 1, 1859 | March 1, 1859 |
| Hancock, A. L. | Vandergriff, M. J. | C/26 | April 1, 1872 | April 1, 1872 |
| Hancock, A. T. | Allen, John M. | A2/39 | February 14, 1855 | No Return |
| Hancock, A. U. | Blair, Parealee | F/46 | October 20, 1894 | October 21, 1894 |
| Hancock, Alace | Martin, Bob | C/346 | December 24, 1885 | December 27, 1885 |
| Hancock, Alaminta Miss | Jewel, N. T. | B/88 | September 23, 1869 | September 25, 1869 |
| Hancock, Alice | Turney, Geo | C/100 | November 4, 1874 | No Return |
| Hancock, America | Vandergriff, Joe | C/402 | September 17, 1887 | September 18, 1887 |
| Hancock, Analiza | Dodd, Joseph Y. | D/7 | | November 20, 1881 |
| Hancock, And Miss | Dodd, J. W. | F/64 | July 6, 1895 | No Return |
| Hancock, B. C. | Odom, Catherine | C/148 | November 22, 1876 | No Return |
| Hancock, Ben | Milligan, Mary | C/278 | April 9, 1881 | April 10, 1881 |
| Hancock, Caroline | King, J. A. | A2/95 | February 20, 1860 | No Return |
| Hancock, Charles | Hubbard, Miss Nancy | B/54 | November 9, 1867 | November 10, 1867 |
| Hancock, Cinda | Odom, John (col) | C/56 | April 12, 1873 | No Return |
| Hancock, Darthuly | Davis, George | C/362 | July 26, 1886 | July 28, 1886 |
| Hancock, Delie | Mount, Simon | D/13 | | May 5, 1882 |
| Hancock, E. C. | Ramsey, R. M. | A2/93 | January 18, 1860 | No Return |
| Hancock, Eliza A. Miss | Turney, Peter S. | B/94 | December 11, 1869 | December 12, 1869 |

| Groom or Bride | Groom or Bride | Book/Page | Date of License | Date of Marriage |
|---|---|---|---|---|
| Hancock, Elizabeth | Chambers, Sam | C/42 | October 16, 1872 | October 17, 1872 |
| Hancock, Elizabeth | Lyon, Alford | C/212 | February 12, 1879 | February 13, 1879 |
| Hancock, Frances | Hancock, Lewis | A2/21 | December 2, 1852 | No Return |
| Hancock, G. F. | Melton, Mollie | C/270 | January 12, 1881 | January 16, 1881 |
| Hancock, Irene | Odom, A. L. | C/314 | September 17, 1884 | September 18, 1884 |
| Hancock, J. T. | Hale, Idar | C/354 | February 25, 1886 | March 2, 1886 |
| Hancock, James | Adams, Tempy | B/8 | September 30, 1865 | September 30, 1865 |
| Hancock, Jane | Martin, Simon | E/86 | October 6, 188 | October 6, 1888 |
| Hancock, Jerry | McKnight, Eliza | C/54 | March ??, 1873 | April 3, 1873 |
| Hancock, John | Sellard, Malissa | B/70 | September 15, 1865 | September 16, 1865 |
| Hancock, Joseph | Adams, Mary | B/10 | October 6, 1866 | October 7, 1866 |
| Hancock, Josie | Hicks, George | C/368 | September 18, 1886 | September 23, 1886 |
| Hancock, Leanthe | Grizzle, J. W. | C/404 | October 18, 1887 | October 19, 1887 |
| Hancock, Lewis | Hancock, Frances | A2/21 | December 2, 1852 | No Return |
| Hancock, Lillian | Odom, B. F. | C/290 | September 3, 1883 | September 6, 1883 |
| Hancock, Lucetta | Hollingsworth, Jos. O. | A2/112 | March 24, 1864 | March 24, 1864 |
| Hancock, M. A. D. | Hale, Susan A. T. | C/136 | March 1, 1876 | No Return |
| Hancock, M. P. Miss | Turner, J. R. | A2/63 | February 22, 1858 | No Return |
| Hancock, Mary | Chambers, Jakes | C/144 | September 28, 1876 | September 29, 1876 |
| Hancock, Mary Miss | Duggam, Prestley | A/70 | June 18, 1844 | June 18, 1844 |
| Hancock, Mollie Miss | Odom, J. D. | C/424 | December 17, 1890 | December 18, 1890 |
| Hancock, Mon. A. | Allen, John M. | A2/39 | February 14, 1855 | No Date |
| Hancock, R. M. | Hancock, Miss S. E. | A2/80 | February 3, 1857 | February 3, 1857 |
| Hancock, R. T. | Francis, Miss E. P. | B/86 | September 9, 1869 | September 9, 1869 |
| Hancock, R. T. | Bratton, Nancy | E/211 | September 10, 1889 | September 10, 1889 |
| Hancock, Rebecca | Morris, G. D. | C/118 | August 20, 1875 | September 1, 1875 |
| Hancock, Rebecca F. | Chambly, David | A2/120 | January 23, 1865 | January 24, 1865 |
| Hancock, Richard | Warren, Miss Martha | A2/34 | August 5, 1854 | August 6, 1854 |
| Hancock, S. E. Miss | Hancock, R. M. | A2/80 | February 3, 1857 | February 3, 1857 |
| Hancock, S. F. | Dodd, H. L. W. | E/212 | September 12, 1889 | September 12, 1889 |
| Hancock, Sallie Miss | Martin, Jack | B/110 | September 24, 1870 | September 27, 1870 |
| Hancock, Sarah | Neal, Wm | C/244 | March 6, 1880 | March 6, 1880 |
| Hancock, Walter | Brown, Claudia | E/352 | December 14, 1898 | |
| Hancock, Walter | Brown, Miss Claudia | F/162 | December 14, 1898 | December 14, 1898 |
| Hancock, Wm. | Milligin, Hallie | F/106 | December 22, 1896 | December 27, 1896 |
| Hancok, Hattie | Bryan, T. M. | C/422 | November 1, 1890 | November 2, 1890 |
| Hanes (Davis), Joseph T. | Elrod, Martha T. | A2/13 | December 20, 1851 | December 23, 1851 |
| Haney, Mary Ann Miss | Manous, Benjamine E. | B/50 | August 21, 1867 | August 22, 1867 |
| Haney, Polly Miss | Ring, John | A/46 | December 25, 1841 | December 25, 1841 |
| Haney, Sarah Miss | Worley, Clark D. | B/104 | June 18, 1870 | June 19, 1870 |
| Hankins, Robert | Powel, Sarah | A2/110 | July 21, 1863 | No Return |
| Hanons, Elizabeth Miss | Cantrell, James | A2/13 | December 31, 1851 | December 31, 1851 |
| Haras, Munro | Summars, Burten | C/214 | March 14, 1879 | March 15, 1879 |
| Hardcastle, L. C. | Byrn, L. C. | C/258 | October 14, 1880 | October 14, 1880 |
| Hardin, Vina | George, Pleasant | B/16 | August 13, 1860 | August 14, 1869 |
| Hare, Bettie H. Miss | Barton, James S. | A2/44 | December 6, 1855 | December 6, 1855 |

| Groom or Bride | Groom or Bride | Book/Page | Date of License | Date of Marriage |
|---|---|---|---|---|
| Hare, Fannie D. | Wright, William | D/7 | | November 27, 1881 |
| Hare, I. L. | McBroom, Jennie | D/8 | | December 21, 1881 |
| Hare, J. H. | McBroom, Eller | C/240 | January 28, 1880 | January 28, 1880 |
| Hare, J. W. Miss | Ferrill, E. W. | A2/63 | February 10, 1858 | February 10, 1858 |
| Hare, John P. | Thompson, Miss Mattie Z. | B/60 | December 25, 1867 | December 25, 1867 |
| Hare, Lucinda D. Miss | McKnight, Samuel P. | A/121 | February 12, 1849 | No Return |
| Hare, M. L. Miss | McKnight, A. D. | A2/23 | February 1, 1853 | February 3, 1853 |
| Hare, Mattie P. Miss | Holmes, John B. | B/36 | January 2, 1867 | January 3, 1867 |
| Hare, Myrtle | North, C. A. | C/234 | December 23, 1879 | December 24, 1879 |
| Hare, Nannie Miss | Jones, G. H. | B/94 | December 11, 1869 | December 15, 1869 |
| Hare, Sallie | Holmes, D. E. | C/102 | December 16, 1874 | December 17, 1874 |
| Hare, Washington | Fugett, Susan | B/10 | January 31, 1867 | January 31, 1867 |
| Hargis, Lidia | Cobert, Valentine | A/14 | June 1, 1839 | June 1, 1839 |
| Hargus, Jerusha Miss | Anderson, John | A/63 | July 13, 1843 | July 14, 1843 |
| Harmon, M. C. Mrs. | Martin, Wm. R. | B/108 | July 28, 1870 | No Return |
| Harney, A. M. | Moore, M. E. | C/246 | March 20, 1880 | March 20, 1880 |
| Harp, Rachael Miss | Watkins, Emanuel | A/64 | August 17, 1843 | August 17, 1843 |
| Harp, Thornton | Moody, Mary Malinda | A/60 | February 16, 1843 | February 16, 1843 |
| Harper, Hunt | Stephens, Laura | C/294 | October 13, 1883 | October 14, 1883 |
| Harper, Hunter | Rideout, Ella | C/76 | December 10, 1873 | December 10, 1873 |
| Harper, Joseph P. | Todd, Nancy P. | A/13 | April 18, 1839 | No Return |
| Harrald, Mary | Ferrell, Young | F/104 | December 1, 1896 | December 6, 1896 |
| Harrell, D. M. | Harrell, Miss Francis | C/456 | March 2, 1892 | March 2, 1892 |
| Harrell, Francis Miss | Harrell, D. M. | C/456 | March 2, 1892 | March 2, 1892 |
| Harrell, H. L. | McMahan, Miss Rebecca Ann | B/60 | January 13, 1868 | January 16, 1868 |
| Harrell, Jessey | Heatherly, Amby | F/60 | February 21, 1895 | February 24, 1895 |
| Harriman, J. A. | Campbell, Jas. A. | F/70 | September 29, 1895 | September 29, 1895 |
| Harris, Amanda | Brandon, Hiram | A/11 | February 26, 1839 | February 26, 1839 |
| Harris, Ambrose | Rideout, Evaline | B/12 | November 25, 1867 | November 28, 1867 |
| Harris, B. C. | Cooper, N. C. | C/320 | December 17, 1884 | No Return |
| Harris, B. D. | Carter, Bettie | F/28 | January 4, 1894 | January 4, 1894 |
| Harris, Billey | Duggin, Delie | F/124 | August 4, 1897 | August 5, 1897 |
| Harris, Caldonia | Phillips, C. E. | C/126 | December 11, 1875 | December 23, 1875 |
| Harris, D. P. | Preston, Miss Rebecca L. | A2/135 | January 16, 1866 | January 16, 1866 |
| Harris, Dorcas Miss | Boxley, Westley | A/118 | November 30, 1848 | December 1, 1848 |
| Harris, Elisabeth J. | McClain, Thomas | C/248 | March 1, 1880 | March 1, 1880 |
| Harris, Emily | West, A. W. | A2/109 | October 7, 1863 | October 7, 1863 |
| Harris, Frances | Petty, James A. | A2/129 | September 18, 1865 | September 21, 1865 |
| Harris, G. W. | Sauls, Miss Ruth | A2/5 | September 14, 1850 | No Return |
| Harris, G. W. | Davenport, L. N. | C/304 | February 9, 1884 | No Return |
| Harris, J. D. | Tenpenny, A. H. | C/338 | October 10, 1885 | October 11, 1885 |
| Harris, J. J. | Pedon, Miss E. A. | C/4 | July 29, 1871 | July 30, 1871 |
| Harris, J. J. | Morgan, Rebecca | C/142 | August 15, 1876 | August 15, 1876 |
| Harris, J. L. | Reed, Rebecca | C/120 | September 16, 1875 | September 16, 1875 |
| Harris, James N. L. | Moore, Miss Jance C. | A2/46 | January 9, 1856 | January 9, 1856 |
| Harris, John L. | Bryson, Miss Sarah | A/82 | August 5, 1845 | August 5, 1845 |

| Groom or Bride | Groom or Bride | Book/Page | Date of License | Date of Marriage |
|---|---|---|---|---|
| Harris, Lizie | Bragg, W. M. | F/70 | September 25, 1895 | September 25, 1895 |
| Harris, M. B. | Fann, Grundy | A2/99 | July 12, 1860 | No Return |
| Harris, Martha A. | Fan, Alexander | A2/113 | April 21, 1864 | April 21, 1864 |
| Harris, Martha J. | Peay, Rufus D. | A2/115 | August 2, 1864 | August 3, 1864 |
| Harris, Mary | Williams, W. C. | C/20 | January 10, 1872 | January 10, 1872 |
| Harris, Mary Ann Miss | Hollis, John | A/46 | January 13, 1842 | January 13, 1842 |
| Harris, Mary J. Miss | Summar, T. D. | A2/142 | August 8, 1866 | September 2, 1866 |
| Harris, Mary Miss | Walls, Will | C/458 | May 15, 1892 | May 15, 1892 |
| Harris, Mary Miss | Medford, Henry | A/70 | June 26, 1844 | June 26, 1844 |
| Harris, Melvina | Gillum, Henry | A2/126 | August 27, 1865 | August 27, 1865 |
| Harris, P. J. Miss | Gann, Nathaniel | A2/78 | February 28, 1856 | February 28, 1856 |
| Harris, Philip | Pettey, Miss Caroline | A/78 | April 17, 1845 | April 17, 1845 |
| Harris, Philmon | Bogle, Miss Media | C/386 | March 17, 1887 | No Return |
| Harris, R. C. | Gillum, Elisabeth | C/258 | October 7, 1880 | No Return |
| Harris, R. H. | Bragg, Susa | F/132 | September 21, 1897 | September 22, 1897 |
| Harris, Ransom P. | Tucker, Sara | A/60 | March 23, 1843 | March 23, 1843 |
| Harris, S. H. | Morgan, Miss M. J. | C/4 | July 29, 1871 | No Return |
| Harris, Sallie | Duggin, J. W. | F/132 | September 28, 1897 | September 30, 1897 |
| Harris, Sally | Grear, David | A/17 | September 7, 1839 | September 11, 1839 |
| Harris, Sarah E. | Wetherspoon, Louis F. W. | A/31 | August 4, 1840 | No Return |
| Harris, Sarah J. Miss | Fann, James | B/84 | September 1, 1869 | September 2, 1869 |
| Harris, Tennie | Bucy, Josh | F/124 | August 4, 1897 | August 8, 1897 |
| Harris, Virginia | Alexander, James | F/154 | August 20, 1898 | August 21, 1898 |
| Harris, William J. | Richardson, Miss Emily M. | A/120 | February 21, 1849 | February 21, 1849 |
| Harris, Zephaniah | Brandon, Elizabeth | A/34 | October 27, 1840 | No Return |
| Harrison, Jane | Higgins, J. P. | C/122 | November 4, 1875 | November 4, 1875 |
| Harrison, Joseph | Davenport, Authy | C/442 | August 1, 1891 | August 2, 1891 |
| Harrison, William H. | Lawrence, Miss Martha Jane | B/48 | July 25, 1867 | July 25, 1867 |
| Harrod, John A. | Martin, Miss Fannie B. | B/126 | January 30, 1871 | February 2, 1871 |
| Harrris, Tixie | Campbell, Jesse | F/12 | July 7, 1893 | July 9, 1893 |
| Hart, David Massan | Lance, Miss Lockey Jane | A2/77 | January 15, 1856 | January 17, 1856 |
| Hart, Em | Ferrell, Eliza P. | C/76 | December 10, 1873 | December 11, 1873 |
| Hart, James M. | Laner, Nancy S. | A2/45 | December 12, 1855 | December 13, 1855 |
| Hart, L. N. | Parton, John | C/22 | February 2, 1872 | February 4, 1872 |
| Hart, Lucinda | Farler, Henry | A/36 | February 12, 1841 | February 14, 1841 |
| Hart, Lue | Graham, J. G. | C/104 | December 24, 1874 | December 24, 1874 |
| Hart, William | Fowler, Laura A. | A2/117 | November 5, 1864 | November 8, 1864 |
| Hart, William T. | Woods, Miss Martha J. | B/104 | June 9, 1870 | June 9, 1870 |
| Harvell, W. L | Winnett, M. C. | C/428 | January 15, 1891 | January 15, 1891 |
| Harvey, Francis M. | Coleman, Barbary | A2/132 | November 27, 1865 | November 29, 1865 |
| Hase, Anthony | Wright, Calline | C/118 | August 27, 1875 | No Return |
| Haskers, Telitha | Rusel, J. R. | D/4 | | July 28, 1881 |
| Hast, Willie B. | Bogle, Leand | C/464 | September 24, 1892 | September 25, 1892 |
| Hatchett, V. S. | Travis, Lillie E. | F/26 | December 23, 1893 | No Return |
| Hatchins, Josephine | Moore, George W. | B/70 | September 24, 1868 | September 24, 1868 |
| Hate, P. J. | Sullens, Miss T. C. | C/400 | September 1, 1887 | September 2, 1887 |

| Groom or Bride | Groom or Bride | Book/Page | Date of License | Date of Marriage |
|---|---|---|---|---|
| Hatfield, Delitha | Spicer, Solomon | A/24 | February 6, 1840 | February 6, 1840 |
| Hatfield, J. W. | Byford, Miss Mary J. | A/103 | October 14, 1847 | No Return |
| Hatfield, Margrett | Lamb, John K | C/140 | July 1, 1876 | July 2, 1876 |
| Hatfield, Mary Miss | Cooper, Peyton L. | A/110 | April 5, 1848 | April 5, 1848 |
| Hatfield, Robert | Mongomery, Miss Sarah Jane | A/108 | February 2, 1848 | February 7, 1848 |
| Hatfield, Sarah E | Owenby, Ruben | C/136 | April 22, 1876 | April 24, 1876 |
| Hatfield, William C. | Spradlin, Miss Elmira C. | A/86 | March 3, 1846 | March 4, 1846 |
| Hatherly, J. R. | Know, S. E. | D/2 | | August 2, 1881 |
| Hatley, Robt | Mathis, Della | F/126 | August 11, 1897 | August 19, 1897 |
| Hawkins | Pittard, Isaac | C/464 | September 21, 1892 | September 21, 892 |
| Hawkins, Angie | Stone, J. P. | E/247 | December 23, 1889 | December 24, 1889 |
| Hawkins, Cornelus J. | McFarlin, Henry | C/324 | January 12, 1885 | January 13, 1885 |
| Hawkins, H. P. Miss | Long, R. F. | A2/62 | January 9, 1858 | January 11, 1858 |
| Hawkins, H. W. | Higgins, Hettie | F/102 | November 17, 1896 | November 19, 1896 |
| Hawkins, J. I. | Burger, F. E. | C/102 | December 15, 1875 | December 16, 1874 |
| Hawkins, J. M. | Petty, Mary F. | C/118 | August 21, 1875 | August 21, 1875 |
| Hawkins, Jacob B. | Martin, Miss Susan | A/126 | September 6, 1849 | September 6, 1849 |
| Hawkins, Jesse | Long, M. H. | C/296 | November 15, 1883 | November 15, 1883 |
| Hawkins, Jo B. | Melton, Mary E. | C/66 | September 20, 1873 | September 21, 1873 |
| Hawkins, John | Gilley, Miss May M. | A/38 | May 8, 1841 | May 8, 1841 |
| Hawkins, John | Jones, Miss M. E. | A2/26 | July 19, 1853 | July 21, 1853 |
| Hawkins, John | Melton, Mary | C/48 | December 28, 1872 | January 5, 1873 |
| Hawkins, John | Lawrence, Eliza | C/472 | December 20, 1892 | December 21, 1892 |
| Hawkins, Malinda | Duke, Marcel | C/204 | November 5, 1878 | November 7, 1878 |
| Hawkins, Martha P. | Lowry, W. B. | C/10 | September 18, 1871 | September 19, 1871 |
| Hawkins, Mary | Bass, A. M. | C/326 | February 18, 1885 | February 19, 1885 |
| Hawkins, Mary Miss | Osment, Joseph L. | A2/161 | June 27, 1866 | June 28, 1866 |
| Hawkins, Meda | Moore, C. N. | F/52 | December 11, 1894 | December 11, 1894 |
| Hawkins, Nancy | Enas, Hayes | C/316 | October 25, 1884 | October 26, 1884 |
| Hawkins, Nora | Higgins, A. S. | F/54 | December 26, 1894 | December 27, 1894 |
| Hawkins, Parelee | Jones, S. E. | C/22 | February 8, 1872 | No Return |
| Hawkins, Pay A. | Parker, Rebecca A. | F/110 | January 12, 1897 | February 7, 1896 |
| Hawkins, Roman Treser | Bryant, Lizzie | C/336 | September 19, 1885 | September 20, 1885 |
| Hawkins, Sam E. | Couch, Alie | F/140 | December 15, 1897 | December 19, 1897 |
| Hawkins, Susie | Grizzle, Jno R. | F/168 | January 21, 1899 | January 25, 1899 |
| Hawkins, Tina | Melton, J. H. | C/472 | December 19, 1892 | December 21, 1892 |
| Hawkins, Wm. B. | Wimberly, Miss P. A. | A2/66 | August 18, 1858 | August 18, 1858 |
| Hay, Miss Anliza | Alexander, James A. | A2/93 | January 1, 1860 | January 3, 1860 |
| Hayes, A. | Odom, July | C/294 | September 26, 1883 | September 27, 1883 |
| Hayes, Adam | Fann, Geriah F. | E/229 | November 2, 1889 | No Return |
| Hayes, Albert | Finley, Fannie | C/362 | July 31, 1886 | August 1, 1886 |
| Hayes, Alexander | Helton, Miss Ibia | B/36 | January 10, 1867 | January 10, 1867 |
| Hayes, B. F. | Finley, Sarah A. | C/150 | November 29, 1876 | November 29, 1876 |
| Hayes, Bud | Womack, Fannie | F/116 | April 5, 1897 | April 7, 1897 |
| Hayes, Cedy | Dennis, M. K. | C/190 | April 20, 1878 | No Return |
| Hayes, Della | Todd, Wiley | E/238 | December 4, 1889 | December 5, 1889 |

| Groom or Bride | Groom or Bride | Book/Page | Date of License | Date of Marriage |
|---|---|---|---|---|
| Hayes, Elias | Hipp, Miss Martha | B/76 | December 28, 1868 | December 29, 1868 |
| Hayes, J. A | Knight, Veer | F | February 9, 1893 | |
| Hayes, J. L. | Blair, Dell F. | E/123 | January 2, 1889 | January 2, 1889 |
| Hayes, Joce (col.) | Clar, Emma | E/118 | December 24, 1888 | December 24, 1888 |
| Hayes, John | Tatum, Emma | C/314 | October 12, 1884 | October 12, 1884 |
| Hayes, Louisa F. | Whittemic, Simon | A2/94 | February 2, 1860 | No Return |
| Hayes, Mary F. | Morgan, Robert A. | C/88 | April 25, 1874 | April 26, 1874 |
| Hayes, Mary M. Miss | Clifford, John H. | B/52 | September 8, 1867 | September 13, 1867 |
| Hayes, Mary R. | Alexander, Francis M. | C/130 | December 30, 1875 | December 30, 1875 |
| Hayes, Nerve | Travis, S. B. | C/290 | August 16, 1883 | August 16, 1883 |
| Hayes, P. | Wilson, M. G. | C/346 | December 23, 1885 | December 23, 1885 |
| Hayes, Peyton H. | Oglesby, Miss Adaline | B/74 | December 21, 1868 | December 22, 1868 |
| Hayes, Pink | Alman, Mollie | C/298 | December 27, 1883 | No Return |
| Hayes, Robert L. | Ruckey, Jennett | F/34 | March 31, 1894 | No Return |
| Hayes, Robert Rush | Fisher, Miss Tina Mai | C/460 | June 1, 1891 | June 1, 1892 |
| Hayes, Susie | Hoover, I. N. | F/152 | July 13, 1898 | No Return |
| Hayes, T. E. | Tatum, M. E. | C/76 | December 10, 1873 | December 10, 1873 |
| Hayes, T. K. | Moody, Hanney | E/112 | December 22, 1888 | December 22, 1888 |
| Hayes, W. M. | Clifford, Miss L. S. | B/46 | June 5, 1867 | June 6, 1867 |
| Hayes, W. T. | McFerrin, Miss Emagene | C/394 | July 3, 1887 | July 31, 1887 |
| Haynes, Eleanor Miss | Haley, Joshua | A/86 | January 3, 1846 | February 26, 1846 |
| Haynes, N. A. | Peay, Roxanna | C/104 | December 23, 1874 | December 23, 1874 |
| Hays, A. P. | Rhyne, Fannie | E/35 | May 3, 1888 | May 3, 1888 |
| Hays, Anne | Lowe, J. A. | C/318 | November 12, 1884 | November 18, 1884 |
| Hays, B. | Burk, Miss Nancy Ann | A2/30 | December 21, 1853 | December 22, 1853 |
| Hays, B. F. | Owens, Margrett | D/1 | | July 28, 1881 |
| Hays, Benjamin J. | Smith, Mary | A/60 | March 7, 1843 | March 7, 1843 |
| Hays, David | Gannon, Martha | A/70 | June 19, 1844 | June 20, 1844 |
| Hays, E. | Haley, Francis C. | C/268 | December 4, 1880 | December 5, 1880 |
| Hays, Elizabeth Miss | Grimes, Britton | A/64 | August 10, 1843 | August 10, 1843 |
| Hays, Fanny Miss | McBroom, Abel | A/37 | April 5, 1841 | No Return |
| Hays, France Miss | Tenpenny, Alfred | A/115 | October 18, 1848 | October 18, 1848 |
| Hays, J. C. | Travis, Miss Mary J. | A2/55 | February 25, 1857 | No Return |
| Hays, J. T. | Wood, Mattie | F/78 | December 17, 1895 | December 18, 1895 |
| Hays, James | Ford, Ellen | C/242 | February 17, 1880 | February 17, 1880 |
| Hays, Jim | Barret, Exie | F/132 | September 22, 1897 | September 23, 1897 |
| Hays, John | Pitard, Miss Roxann | A/45 | December 23, 1841 | December 23, 1841 |
| Hays, John | Pitard, Elizabeth | A2/48 | May 19, 1856 | May 25, 1856 |
| Hays, John Henry | Redder, Rhoda | C/428 | January 10, 189 | January 11, 1891 |
| Hays, Julie A. | Mullins, S. D. | C/48 | December 24, 1872 | December 25, 1872 |
| Hays, Lizzy Miss | McFerrin, Author | F/134 | October 6, 1897 | October 7, 1897 |
| Hays, Luisa Miss | Keel, J. W. | F/50 | November 28, 1894 | November 28, 1894 |
| Hays, Luther E. | Daniel, Sallie | F/96 | September 14, 1896 | No Return |
| Hays, Malisa | Wilson, James | C/218 | July 10, 1879 | No Return |
| Hays, Manerva Miss | Gannon, John | A/130 | December 18, 1849 | December 18, 1849 |
| Hays, Maranda M. Miss | Banks, Dennis | A2/49 | August 11, 1856 | August 12, 1856 |

| Groom or Bride | Groom or Bride | Book/Page | Date of License | Date of Marriage |
|---|---|---|---|---|
| Hays, Margrett | Tenpenny, Mumphard | D/15 | | August 31, 1882 |
| Hays, Mary J. | Wilson, Ben. | C/222 | August 11, 1879 | August 13, 1879 |
| Hays, Mary Miss | McBroom, Robert C. | A/86 | January 8, 1846 | No Return |
| Hays, Nancy Miss | Duboys, James M. | A2/53 | January 1, 1857 | January 15, 1857 |
| Hays, Rachel Miss | McBroom, James | A/131 | January 3, 1850 | January 3, 1850 |
| Hays, Rebecca | Gannon, Wm. E. | A2/112 | March 24, 1864 | March 24, 1864 |
| Hays, S. E | Williams, G. W. | C/206 | November 28, 1878 | December 1, 1878 |
| Hays, S. F. | Armstrong, Miss N. | A2/61 | December 24, 1857 | December 24, 1857 |
| Hays, Sarah Ann | Mullins, William | A/51 | July 7, 1842 | July 8, 1842 |
| Hays, Sarah Miss | Gordon, Robert | A/106 | January 20, 1848 | January 20, 1848 |
| Hays, T. E. | Gaither, Miss Susie | F/62 | April 22, 1895 | April 23, 1895 |
| Hays, Tennie | McBroom, Wm | C/236 | January 7, 1880 | January ??, 1880 |
| Hays, William B. | Dethcart, Miss Rebecca | A/101 | August 9, 1847 | August 9, 1847 |
| Hays, Wm. B. | Bragg, Margart | A2/20 | November 15, 1852 | November 16, 1852 |
| Haywood, John F. | Carter, Mattie J. | C/324 | January 14, 1885 | January 14, 1885 |
| Hazlewood, Cyrene C. | Statom, Henry V. | A2/127 | September 7, 1865 | September 7, 1865 |
| Heam, Henry | Sanford, Bettie V. | C/94 | September 15, 1874 | September 15, 1874 |
| Hearn, H. M | Wharten, Lida | D/22 | | February 1, 1883 |
| Hearne, Mitcheal | Painter, Heneretta | E/83 | September 26, 1888 | September 27, 1888 |
| Heart, Ambie | Woods, Robt Lee | F/150 | May 14, 1898 | May 15, 1898 |
| Heathcock, Anna | Sissom, Isah | A2/117 | November 22, 1864 | December 1, 1864 |
| Heathcock, John | Hollis, Miss Martha | A/116 | October 25, 1848 | October 26, 1848 |
| Heatherly, Amby | Harrell, Jessey | F/60 | February 21, 1895 | February 24, 1895 |
| Heatherly, Geo. | Bevins, Cynthia A. | C/50 | February 1, 1873 | February 4, 1873 |
| Heelton, Calvin | Keath, Miss Etter | B/126 | February 13, 1871 | February 13, 1871 |
| Helms, Creed | Pace, Elizabeth A. | A/28 | April 7, 1840 | April 7, 1840 |
| Helton, Ibia Miss | Hayes, Alexander | B/36 | January 10, 1867 | January 10, 1867 |
| Helton, James | Dubois, Miss Martha | A/125 | July 19, 1849 | July 19, 1849 |
| Helton, Lucinda Miss | Gilliam, Bengamin | B/94 | December 3, 1869 | December 3, 1869 |
| Helton, Nancy | Craft, Johathan | C/256 | July 31, 1880 | July 31, 1880 |
| Helton, Nancy | Craft, Johathan | C/274 | July 31, 1880 | No Return |
| Helton, Nancy F. | Brandon, Abraham | A/128 | November 20, 1849 | November 20, 1849 |
| Hemman, Margaret | Ready, Aaron | A2/121 | February 24, 1865 | February 24, 1865 |
| Henderson, Dan | Moore, Ada | F/78 | December 24, 1895 | No Return |
| Henderson, J. T. | Covington, Miss Frances | A2/123 | April 9, 1865 | April 9, 1865 |
| Henderson, James T. | Seawell, Miss Susan C. | A/78 | May 20, 1845 | May 20, 1845 |
| Henderson, James Y. | Hubbard, Miss Nora | C/394 | July 12, 1887 | July 12, 1887 |
| Henderson, Jo. | Lowe, Frances E. | C/110 | March 17, 1875 | March 21, 1875 |
| Henderson, Julia Ann Miss | Tittle, Adam Jr. | A2/9 | January 4, 1851 | January 5, 1851 |
| Henderson, M. G. | Barrett, Miss S. A. | B/52 | September 24, 1867 | No Return |
| Henderson, Margarett Miss | Prim, Thomas N. | A2/44 | December 6, 1855 | December 6, 1855 |
| Henderson, Mary | Todd, J. L. | D/4 | | September 21, 1881 |
| Henderson, Mary Miss | Taylor, Nathaniel M. | A/40 | August 25, 1841 | August 26, 1841 |
| Henderson, Nat | Brown, Nellie | F/138 | November 20I 1897 | No Return |
| Henderson, Nathaniel | Todd, Mary | C/86 | March 28, 1874 | March 29, 1874 |
| Henderson, Pleasant T. | Furman, Miss Ann E. | A/79 | May 26, 1845 | May 28, 1845 |

| Groom or Bride | Groom or Bride | Book/Page | Date of License | Date of Marriage |
|---|---|---|---|---|
| Hendrick, John R. | Woods, Miss Elizabeth | A2/65 | June 14, 1858 | June ??, 1858 |
| Hendricks, N. M. | Johnson, Miss Sarah | A2/33 | July 12, 1854 | No Return |
| Hendrickson, Elizabeth Miss | Comer, James M. | A2/4 | August 10, 1850 | August 15, 1850 |
| Hendrickson, J. R. | Merritt, Miss Merry Ann | A2/16 | April 17, 1852 | April 18, 1854 |
| Hendrickson, John | Bullard, Elizabeth | A2/96 | April 27, 1860 | April 27, 1860 |
| Hendrickson, John | Hutchins, Mintee | A2/105 | October 13, 1862 | No Return |
| Hendrickson, Mary Miss | Melton, William J. | A/67 | January 4, 1843 | No Return |
| Hendrickson, Nathan | Johnson, Miss Sarah | A2/79 | July 12, 1854 | July 13, 1854 |
| Hendrickson, Wm. | Hammond, Miss Mary | A/130 | October 18, 1849 | October 18, 1849 |
| Hendrix, Sarah | Arnet, James | A2/122 | March 20, 1865 | No Return |
| Hendrix, William M. | Crane, Mary E. | A/121 | March 15, 1849 | March 15, 1849 |
| Hendrixson, John | McDougal, Elizabeth | A2/108 | July 25, 1863 | November 26, 1863 |
| Hearndon, M. J. | Rigsby, Nelson | C/50 | January 2, 1873 | January 2, 1873 |
| Heigdon, Malisa T | Mason, Richard, B. | C/178 | November 23, 1877 | November 23, 1877 |
| Helton, Ann | Good, R. C. | C/22 | February 13, 1872 | February 13, 1872 |
| Helton, Etta | Lyon, G. B | C/154 | January 15, 1877 | January 17, 1877 |
| Henderson, Mry A. | Howell, T. E. | C/368 | August 19, 1886 | August 22, 1886 |
| Henderson, Rachal | West, John | C/340 | November 2, 1885 | No Return |
| Henegar | Fingers, C. M. | D/16 | | October 12, 1882 |
| Heneger, Frank | Miller, Ann | C/86 | April 18, 1874 | April 18, 1874 |
| Heneger, Z. V. | Wood, L. P. | C/80 | January 28, 1874 | January 28, 1874 |
| Henne, Mattie | Finley, Foster | C/128 | December 23, 1875 | December 23, 1875 |
| Hennessee, Lela | Grizzle, G. S. | E/334 | December 27, 1898 | |
| Hennessee, Lela | Grizzle, G. S. | F/164 | December 27, 1898 | December 28, 1898 |
| Herald, Jenetta Miss | Arnold, Howey (Harvey) | A2/13 | December 26, 1851 | December 28, 1851 |
| Herald, Susan A. | Espy, Charles | C/30 | July 11, 1872 | July 12, 1872 |
| Herell, Perry | Newby, Margharet | F/112 | February 13, 1897 | February 14, 1897 |
| Herenden, Joseph B. | Keeton, D. Jan | C/344 | December 8, 1885 | December 10, 1885 |
| Heriman, John | Williams, Susan | A/15 | July ??, 1839 | July or August 1839 |
| Heriman, Josiah | Capshaw, Truly | A/13 | April 12, 1838 | April 12, 1838 |
| Heriman, Nancy | Morgan, Jackson | A/16 | July 24, 1839 | July 25, 1839 |
| Heriman, Westley | Hadley, Nancy | A/10 | January 23, 1839 | January 23, 1839 |
| Herman, Paralee | Gibson, David | C/154 | January 24, 1877 | January 24, 1877 |
| Hernden, M. F. | Bogle, Miss Eliza E. | A2/69 | October 23, 1858 | October 24, 1858 |
| Herndon, J. M. | Tittle, Miss Sarah A. | A2/54 | February 14, 1857 | February 15, 1857 |
| Herndon, James M. | Woodall, Miss Sarah T. | A/96 | January 8, 1847 | January 8, 1847 |
| Herndon, M. M. Miss | Lakew, J. G. | B/34 | December 17, 1866 | December 19, 1866 |
| Herndon, W. J. | McAdow, Miss Margaret J. | B/38 | January 12, 1867 | January 20, 1867 |
| Hernidon, J. M. | Fuston, Sarah | C/28 | May 30, 1872 | May 31, 1872 |
| Herod, D. T. | Martin, Miss Sophia E. | A2/98 | June 30, 1860 | July 4, 1860 |
| Herold, Issabella Miss | Arnold, America | A/122 | January 12, 1849 | January 13, 1849 |
| Heron, Margaret Miss | Cuper, Thomas | C/460 | July 7, 1892 | No Return |
| Herral, Mary | Underwood, Thomas | A2/31 | December 27, 1853 | December 28, 1853 |
| Herrald, J. R | Walker, Miss Annie | E/18 | February 11, 1888 | February 12, 1888 |
| Herrald, Rebeca | Todd, J. T. | C/396 | August 5, 1887 | August 7, 1887 |
| Herrald, Sarah J. Miss | Warren, W. H. | A2/54 | February 4, 1857 | February 5, 1857 |

| Groom or Bride | Groom or Bride | Book/Page | Date of License | Date of Marriage |
| --- | --- | --- | --- | --- |
| Herrall, Joseph | Lambert, Miss Linda | C/464 | September 3, 1892 | September 4, 1892 |
| Herrall, Legrand | Finley, Miss Cristeney C. | A2/136 | January 22, 1866 | January 25, 1866 |
| Herrell, Ann E. Miss | Thompson, Hugh L. | A/68 | April 13, 1844 | April 14, 1844 |
| Herrell, E. F. | Cawthen, Sarah | C/254 | August 18, 1880 | August 18, 1880 |
| Herrell, E. P. | Hollis, Martha | A2/120 | February 7, 1865 | February 7, 1865 |
| Herrell, George | Daniel, Tenne | E/142 | February 28, 1889 | February 28, 1889 |
| Herrell, H. G. | Bell, N. A. | C/224 | September 11, 1879 | September 11, 1879 |
| Herrell, Sallie Miss | Robinson, Jonas | E/201 | August 21, 1889 | No Return |
| Herrell, Tennie | Summars, James | C/228 | October 15, 1879 | October 15, 1879 |
| Herrich, F. M | Shanklin, W. T. | C/230 | November 15, 1879 | November 16, 1879 |
| Herriman, Amanda | Orrand, Anthony | B/8 | December 21, 1865 | Return Not Endorsed |
| Herriman, Analiza | Maxwell, Joseph H. | F/92 | August 14, 1896 | August 16, 1896 |
| Herriman, Bettie | Wilson, J. W. | C/290 | August 15, 1883 | August 15, 1883 |
| Herriman, Columbus | Mears, Fanny | C/432 | March 26, 1891 | March 26, 1891 |
| Herriman, Elizabeth | Pitts, David | C/310 | July 3, 1884 | July 3, 1884 |
| Herriman, George | Barrett, Ella | F/90 | July 8, 1896 | July 10, 1896 |
| Herriman, George M. | Tucker, Savana | E/49 | August 2, 1888 | August 5, 1888 |
| Herriman, J. R. | Tucker, Evaline | F/146 | March 18, 1898 | March 22, 1898 |
| Herriman, John | Reeves Mary Ann | A/58 | January 2, 1843 | January 2, 1843 |
| Herriman, John | Johnson, Miss Rebecca | B/78 | March 6, 1869 | March 6, 1869 |
| Herriman, John | Todd, Eliza | C/286 | July 12, 1883 | No Return |
| Herriman, Mary Miss | Tucker, Pinkney | B/102 | May 23, 1870 | May 26, 1870 |
| Herriman, Nancy | Spurlock, W. C. | A/28 | April 23, 1840 | April 23, 1840 |
| Herriman, Nancy A. | Barratt, James N. | C/154 | February 3, 1877 | February 3, 1877 |
| Herriman, Sterling B. | Spurlock, Miss Elizabeth | A2/2 | April 27, 1850 | April 28, 1850 |
| Herriman, Steven | Gibson, Mary E | A2/123 | May 8, 1865 | May 8, 1865 |
| Herriman, Susan | Barret, Wm. | C/278 | April 16, 1881 | April 17, 1881 |
| Herriman, Tiney | Rigsby, James | C/292 | September 11, 1883 | September 11, 1883 |
| Herriman, Wesley | Jones, Miss Mary | C/4 | July 20, 1871 | July 21, 1871 |
| Herrimon, John | Ready, Shophia | A2/112 | March 22, 1864 | March 24, 1864 |
| Herrimon, Senate | Rigsby, Lilly | C/188 | March 7, 1878 | March 7, 1878 |
| Herrin, Sally Miss | Brashears, William | A/84 | November 1, 1845 | November 3, 1845 |
| Herrod, Dora | Young, James | F/8 | April 28, 1893 | May 1, 1893 |
| Herrod, Rebecca | Lee, John | C/166 | August 11, 1877 | August 12, 1877 |
| Herryman, John S. | St. John, Miss Emaline | B/80 | May 4, 1869 | May 5, 1869 |
| Herryman, Lockey J. Miss | Gann, Samuel M. | B/66 | July 22, 1868 | July 23, 1868 |
| Herryman, Mary E. Miss | Sullivan, Zachariah | B/38 | January 24, 1867 | January 24, 1867 |
| Herryman, Teba Miss | Gannon, Alonso | E/20 | February 18, 1888 | February 19, 1888 |
| Herter?, A. | McKnight, Miss M. E | A2/94 | February 13, 1861 | No Return |
| Hetherly, Luella | Burks, Roeevans | C/448 | October 7, 1891 | No Return |
| Hettson, Mary Miss | Dabbs, John T. | A2/62 | January 12, 1858 | January 12, 1858 |
| Hibden, Malissie | Smith, M. P. | C/292 | September 16, 1883 | September 16, 1883 |
| Hibdon, A. J. | Besheas, Mary E. | C/308 | April 15, 1884 | April 15, 1884 |
| Hibdon, C. C. Miss | Thomas, Joel | A2/89 | October 19, 1859 | No Return |
| Hibdon, Henry | Melton, Josie | C/398 | August 22, 1887 | August 22, 1887 |
| Hibdon, Henry | Gann, Jennie | E/36 | May 5, 1888 | May 6, 1888 |

| Groom or Bride | Groom or Bride | Book/Page | Date of License | Date of Marriage |
|---|---|---|---|---|
| Hibdon, Isaac F. | Sissom, Malvinia | C/188 | December 20, 1877 | December 27, 1877 |
| Hibdon, J. F. | Evans, Nancy | C/356 | April 8, 1886 | April 11, 1886 |
| Hibdon, J. H. | Parker, S. B. | E/258 | January 8, 1890 | No Return |
| Hibdon, John | Sullivn, Miss Tildy | A2/61 | December 21, 1857 | December 21, 1857 |
| Hibdon, Josie | Parton, J. B. | E/264 | January 28, 1890 | No Return |
| Hibdon, M. S. Miss | Fann, Alford | A2/15 | February 28, 1852 | February 28, 1852 |
| Hibdon, P. A. | Gillum, Miss S. E. | B/112 | October 12, 1870 | October 12, 1870 |
| Hibdon, R. B. | Parker, Annie E. | C/314 | September 24, 1884 | September 25, 1885 |
| Hibdon, Susan | Davenport, Wm. A. | A2/115 | July 28, 1864 | August 2, 1864 |
| Hibdon, William C. | Barrett, Charity M. | A2/79 | September 19, 1856 | September 19, 1856 |
| Hickenbotham, Thomas | Vernan, Edy | C/360 | July 6, 1886 | No Return |
| Hickenbottom, Elizabeth Miss | Sullens, Alexander | A2/73 | October 25, 1852 | October 25, 1852 |
| Hickey, Ben | Davenport, M. | C/296 | November 3, 1883 | November 3, 1883 |
| Hicks, Elizabeth M. | Knight, Jessemin | A2/43 | October 28, 1855 | October ??, 1855 |
| Hicks, Elizabeth Miss | Jones, Robert M. | A/52 | August 25, 1842 | |
| Hicks, G. D. | Sherley | A2/132 | November 22, 1865 | November 22, 1865 |
| Hicks, George | Hancock, Josie | C/368 | September 18, 1886 | September 23, 1886 |
| Hicks, Ruth Miss | Ragland, William J. | A/102 | September 29, 1847 | September 26, 1847 |
| Hicks, W. R. | Airs, Paralee | C/154 | February 3, 1877 | February 4, 1877 |
| Hiff, M. H. | Maxey, J. C. | C/286 | July 9, 1883 | No Return |
| Higdon, Malvina | Morris, G. D. | C/404 | October 14, 1887 | October 14, 1887 |
| Higdon, Miss Allie | Bailey, Robert | C/464 | September 8, 1892 | September 8, 1892 |
| Hiet, Mary | Basham, John | A/57 | December 7, 1842 | December 13, 1842 |
| Hiff, J. P. | McMahan, July A. | D/15 | | September 10, 1882 |
| Hiff, S. E. | Moore, J. T. | D/10 | | December 29, 1881 |
| Higdon, Allice | Davis, Wm. | C/356 | April 22, 1886 | April 22, 1886 |
| Higdon, Allie Miss | Bailey, Robert | C/464 | September 8, 1892 | September 8, 1892 |
| Higdon, Edna | Bryson, B. M. | C/382 | January 22, 1887 | January 23, 1887 |
| Higdon, G. A. | Woods, Levada | F/98 | October 1, 1896 | October 1, 1896 |
| Higdon, Hettie | Vinson, Colewall | F/54 | January 3, 1895 | January 9, 1895 |
| Higdon, James | St. John, Willie G. | F/54 | January 7, 1895 | January 8, 1895 |
| Higdon, Lucy | Rigsby, John K. | E/5 | January 18, 1888 | January 13, 1888 |
| Higdon, Maggie | Bailey, Mack | E/236 | December 31, 1898 | |
| Higdon, Maggie | Bailey, Wade | F/164 | December 31, 1898 | January 1, 1899 |
| Higdon, Mollie | Markum, Will | F/66 | August 24, 1895 | August 22, 1895 |
| Higdon, Salatha J. | Robertson, S. W. | A2/33 | July 4, 1854 | July 5, 1854 |
| Higdon, Sarah E. Miss | Neeley, Eligah | B/36 | January 10, 1867 | January 10, 1867 |
| Higgans, John | Patrick, Miss Locky J. | A2/5 | September 21, 1850 | September 22, 1850 |
| Higgans, July Ann Miss | Hutchins, David | A/111 | May 11, 1848 | May 11, 1848 |
| Higgans, Nancy Miss | Marcum, Isaac | A2/11 | February 11, 1851 | February 14, 1851 |
| Higgans, Robert W. | Sullens, Miss Susan | A/125 | August 9, 1849 | August 9, 1849 |
| Higgans, William | Fuston, Melvina | A2/111 | January 17, 1864 | January 18, 1864 |
| Higgenbottom, James | Cousley, Marinda A. | A2/62 | January 21, 1858 | January 25, 1858 |
| Higgin, Fill | Ready, Miss Emeline | C/384 | February 27, 1887 | February 27, 1887 |
| Higgin, Florance | Grooms, Ras | C/318 | November 10, 1884 | No Return |
| Higgin, Sarah A | Milligan, Abner A. | C/178 | November 29, 1877 | November 29, 1877 |

| Groom or Bride | Groom or Bride | Book/Page | Date of License | Date of Marriage |
| --- | --- | --- | --- | --- |
| Higgins, A. S. | Hawkins, Nora | F/54 | December 26, 1894 | December 27, 1894 |
| Higgins, Alex (col.) | Cantrell, Sarah (col.) | F/142 | January 1, 1898 | January 3, 1898 |
| Higgins, Alexander | Spurlock, Liza | C/278 | April 2, 1881 | April 3, 1881 |
| Higgins, Alta | Betherl, C. D. | D/20 | | May 14, 1882 |
| Higgins, Amanda S. Miss | Stephens, J. W. | B/76 | January 12, 1869 | January 20, 1869 |
| Higgins, Angeline | Willson, J. | C/88 | July 18, 1874 | July 19, 1874 |
| Higgins, Angeline | Wilson, Joe | C/90 | July 18, 1874 | No Return |
| Higgins, Anthony | Scott, Babe | E/23 | February 29, 1888 | February 29, 1888 |
| Higgins, C. J. | Mingle, J. R. | C/102 | December 11, 1874 | December 13, 1874 |
| Higgins, Carmmer A. | Gilley, Etta | F/90 | July 15, 1896 | July 15, 1896 |
| Higgins, Clara | Milligan, James (col.) | C/298 | December 27, 1883 | No Return |
| Higgins, Cleo | Vance, J. D. | C/432 | March 17, 1891 | March 19, 1891 |
| Higgins, E. C. | Wilson, P. A. | C/140 | July 29, 1876 | July 30, 1876 |
| Higgins, Eligah | Kelly, Miss Sary Ann | A2/25 | May 28, 1853 | May 28, 1853 |
| Higgins, Elijah C. | Womack, Miss Amanda J. | B/106 | August 15, 1870 | August 18, 1870 |
| Higgins, Eliza | Nichols, B. F. | C/278 | April 8, 1881 | No Return |
| Higgins, Eliza | Perry, James P. | A/25 | March 12, 1840 | March 12, 1840 |
| Higgins, Eliza Ann | Elkins, H. R. | B/62 | February 4, 1868 | February 4, 1868 |
| Higgins, Emma | Markum, Mike | F/64 | May 15, 1895 | May 15, 1895 |
| Higgins, Eula | Tenpenny, J. E. | F/116 | April 30, 1897 | May 24, 1897 |
| Higgins, Florance | Grooms, Ras | C/318 | November 10, 1884 | November 13, 1884 |
| Higgins, Francis | Milligan, Johnie | C/340 | November 2, 1885 | November 2, 1885 |
| Higgins, George Ann | Martin, Ed | F/30 | January 27, 1894 | January 27, 1894 |
| Higgins, H. H | Williams, Sarah | E/1 | January 7, 1888 | January 8,1888 |
| Higgins, Hargis | Mullinax, Effie | F/102 | November 23, 1896 | No Return |
| Higgins, Hettie | Hawkins, H. W. | F/102 | November 17, 1896 | November 19, 1896 |
| Higgins, Howard | Summers, Jenny | C/440 | July 4, 1891 | July 5, 1891 |
| Higgins, Isaac | Tittle, Miss Barbary Ann | B/38 | January 17, 1867 | January 17, 1867 |
| Higgins, J. | Starr, Bettie | C/208 | December 20, 1878 | Not Satisfied |
| Higgins, J. H. | King, Maggie | C/338 | October 4, 1885 | October 6, 1885 |
| Higgins, J. H. | Barrett, Fanny B. | C/436 | May 2, 1891 | May 3, 1891 |
| Higgins, J. L. | Walker, Kizzie | C/282 | April 12, 1883 | No Return |
| Higgins, J. L. | Walker, ---- | D/21 | | April 12, 1883 |
| Higgins, J. P. | Harrison, Jane | C/122 | November 4, 1875 | November 4, 1875 |
| Higgins, J. P. | Gaither, Nancy A. | C/320 | December 5, 1884 | December 5, 1884 |
| Higgins, J. W. | Higgins, Meeks | C/438 | June 19, 1891 | June 19, 1891 |
| Higgins, James | Duggan, Susan | A/10 | January 22, 1839 | January 24, 1839 |
| Higgins, James | Mettar, Emaline | A/36 | January 18, 1841 | January 28, 1841 |
| Higgins, James | York, Elizabeth | B/18 | January 9, 1870 | January 9, 1870 |
| Higgins, Jane Miss | Mason, Joseph F. | B/72 | November 20, 1868 | November 27, 1868 |
| Higgins, Jennie | Stone, Elija | F/24 | December 13, 1893 | December 14, 1893 |
| Higgins, Jesse | Melton, Bettie | C/218 | July 26, 1879 | July 27, 1879 |
| Higgins, John | Wilcher, Melissa | C/438 | June 22, 1891 | June 22, 1891 |
| Higgins, John G. | Melton, Clem | C/130 | January 6, 1876 | No Return |
| Higgins, Josie | Thomas, Nathan (col.) | C/426 | December 24, 1890 | December 24, 1890 |
| Higgins, Julian Miss | Davis, Robert | B/102 | May 28, 1870 | May 29, 1870 |

| Groom or Bride | Groom or Bride | Book/Page | Date of License | Date of Marriage |
|---|---|---|---|---|
| Higgins, Lockey J. | Mayo, B. F. | D/6 | | October 23, 1881 |
| Higgins, Locky Jane Miss | Tittle, Samuel | A2/56 | June 15, 1857 | June 21, 1857 |
| Higgins, Lucy | Milligan, George W. | B/16 | March 4, 1869 | March 4, 1869 |
| Higgins, Lucy Miss | Brown, Calvin | B/122 | January 6, 1871 | January 8, 1871 |
| Higgins, Margaret Miss | Nokes, John | B/106 | July 29, 1870 | July 31, 1870 |
| Higgins, Margarett Miss | Walkup, C. N. | A2/22 | December 27, 1852 | December 25, 1852 |
| Higgins, Martha E. | Mays, A. H. | C/322 | January 9, 1885 | January 11, 1885 |
| Higgins, Mary | Pendleton, Benjamin | A/26 | March 14, 1840 | March 15, 1840 |
| Higgins, Mary | Oconner, Jeremiah | A/117 | November 29, 1848 | November 29, 1848 |
| Higgins, Mary E. | Webb, Alsa | C/40 | September 25, 1872 | September 29, 1872 |
| Higgins, Meeks | Higgins, J. W. | C/438 | June 19, 1891 | June 19, 1891 |
| Higgins, Mollie | Jones, J. A. | E/169 | April 13, 1889 | April 15, 1889 |
| Higgins, Murph | Milliganin, Susie | F/140 | December 21, 1897 | December 21, 1897 |
| Higgins, Nancy E. | Wilson, Saml. B. | C/94 | September 10, 1874 | September 10, 1874 |
| Higgins, Nettie | Dobbs, Elija | F/176 | May 11, 1899 | May 14, 1899 |
| Higgins, Noah | Smithson, Mollie | F/154 | August 10, 1898 | August 10, 1898 |
| Higgins, Peggy | Dennis, William | A/13 | May 8, 1839 | May 15, 1839 |
| Higgins, Pleas (col.) | Bounds, Lissie? | C/420 | October 16, 1890 | October 16, 1890 |
| Higgins, Polly Miss | Hutchins, John | A/32 | August 28, 1840 | August 30, 1840 |
| Higgins, Presley | Mullenax, Mary | A2/119 | January 18, 1865 | No Return |
| Higgins, R. L. | Rigsby, Miss Mary E. | B/96 | December 20, 1869 | December 22, 1869 |
| Higgins, Rance | Martin, Miss Paralee | B/130 | April 14, 1871 | April 14, 1871 |
| Higgins, Sabrina | Hollinsworth, Josiah | A/56 | November 23, 1842 | November 25, 1842 |
| Higgins, Sandy | Thomas, Allice | C/146 | October 21, 1876 | October 22, 1076 |
| Higgins, Sarah S. | Preston, J. A. | C/284 | June 30, 1883 | July 1, 1883 |
| Higgins, Susan J. | Johnson, Isaac | C/222 | September 19, 1879 | September 19, 1879 |
| Higgins, W. F. | Smith, Maggie | C/222 | August 23, 1879 | August 24, 1879 |
| Higgins, Zora | Mayes, H. L. | F/22 | November 4, 1893 | November 9, 1893 |
| High, C. J. | Brewer, Hattie E. | F/48 | November 13, 1894 | November 15, 1894 |
| Hill, Gilbert | Chambers, Manerva | B/18 | July 11, 1870 | July 11, 1870 |
| Hill, Agnis | Ashley, D. J. | C/122 | October 23, 1875 | October 24, 1875 |
| Hill, C. G. | Miller, Miss Fannie | F/170 | February 6, 1899 | February 6, 1899 |
| Hill, Darny | Laswell, Miss Elizabeth | A2/28 | October 17, 1853 | October 18, 1853 |
| Hill, Eli | Richardson, Lucy | B/94 | December 6, 1869 | December 6, 1869 |
| Hill, Eliza | Carrick, Thomas | C/42 | October 19, 1872 | October 20, 1872 |
| Hill, G. W. | Bryant, Matildy | F/152 | July 22, 1898 | July 17, 1898 |
| Hill, J. R. | Rains, Elizabeth | C/86 | April 6, 1874 | April 6, 1874 |
| Hill, J. W. | Byrum, Fannie | E/237 | December 3, 1889 | No Return |
| Hill, James | Petty, Miss Mary | A/114 | September 20, 1848 | September 21, 1848 |
| Hill, James | Carrick, Florence | F/158 | September 30, 1898 | October 2, 1898 |
| Hill, John N. | Summers, Miss Amanda J. | B/56 | November 19, 1867 | November 20, 1867 |
| Hill, Lucinda Miss | Smith, Joseph | A/124 | February 20, 1849 | February 22, 1849 |
| Hill, Mary E. | Simon, Jacob | C/132 | February 2, 1876 | February 3, 1876 |
| Hill, Rebecca Elizabeth Miss | Johnson, Nathan S. | A/118 | December ??, 1848 | December 16, 1848 |
| Hill, William R. | Moore, Miss Nancy Eleanore | A/111 | March 6, 1848 | March 7, 1848 |
| Hill, William T. | Walls, Rebecca E. | C/26 | May 11, 1872 | May 11, 1872 |

| Groom or Bride | Groom or Bride | Book/Page | Date of License | Date of Marriage |
|---|---|---|---|---|
| Hill, Wm. | Sessin, C. I. | A2/38 | January 6, 1855 | No Return |
| Hill, Wm. G. | Frazier, Margaret C. | C/222 | August 20, 1879 | August 20, 1879 |
| Hillis, Daniel | Bush, Arnettie | F/60 | February 12, 1895 | February 12, 1895 |
| Hillis, Elizabeth Jane Miss | Cannon, Rayford | A/64 | August 17, 1843 | August 19, 1843 |
| Hipp, A. R. | Bailey, Miss L. A. | B/34 | December 26, 1866 | December 26, 1866 |
| Hipp, E. C. | Anderson, W. C. | C/192 | June 22, 1878 | June 23, 1878 |
| Hipp, Emeline | Lynn, John H. | C/32 | July 22, 1872 | August 1, 1872 |
| Hipp, Etta Miss | Maxey, William | C/390 | June 25, 1887 | No Return |
| Hipp, Etta Miss | Maxey, William | C/392 | June 25, 1887 | No Return |
| Hipp, J. D. | Summars, Bettie | C/344 | December 16, 1885 | December 16, 1885 |
| Hipp, James D. | Moore, Miss Eliza | C/412 | December 20, 1887 | December 21, 1887 |
| Hipp, Jennie | Campbell, Charles T. | E/78 | September 18, 1888 | September 19, 1888 |
| Hipp, Margaret | McGee, J. S. | C/166 | August 8, 1877 | August 12, 1877 |
| Hipp, Martha Miss | Hayes, Elias | B/76 | December 28, 1868 | December 29, 1868 |
| Hipp, Mary | Ferrell, Polk | C/94 | September 25, 1874 | September 27, 1874 |
| Hipp, N. J. Miss | McMahan, J. T. | A2/146 | October 17, 1866 | October 18, 1866 |
| Hipp, Rebecca J. Miss | Gunter, W. J. | B/122 | December 24, 1870 | December 25, 1870 |
| Hipp, Sallie B. | Barrett, A. B. | C/30 | July 17, 1872 | No Return |
| Hitson, William | Cooper, Nealie | F/98 | October 3, 1896 | October 4, 1896 |
| Hitt, Mary Ann | Meddows, Vincent | A/9 | December 24, 1838 | No Return |
| Hobbs, James | Smithson, Annie | C/322 | December 27, 1884 | No Return |
| Hobbs, James | Smithson, Miss Gavena | C/390 | June 30, 1887 | No Return |
| Hobbs, James | Smithson, Miss Levina | C/392 | June 28, 1887 | June 30, 1887 |
| Hobbs, James | Smithson, Annie | D/23 | | December 27, 1884 |
| Hodge, James L. | Burger, Miss Josephine | B/52 | September 12, 1867 | September 12, 1867 |
| Hodges, Sarah E. Miss | Ward, M. S. | A2/87 | August 17, 1859 | August 17, 1859 |
| Hogwood, D. I. | Dement, Mattie E. | D/9 | | December 22, 1881 |
| Hogwood, James R. | Carter, Miss Amanda J. | B/70 | September 23, 1868 | September 24, 1868 |
| Hogwood, Lizzie | Smith, Fred | F/72 | October 3, 1895 | October 10, 1895 |
| Hogwood, Mattie A. Miss | Freeze, John | B/54 | October 19, 1867 | October 20, 1867 |
| Hogwood, Roxanna | Spangler, John M. | C/176 | November 3, 1877 | November 4, 1877 |
| Holandsworth, Ira | Wood, Miss Sarah | B/106 | June 26, 1870 | June 26, 1870 |
| Hold, Clavin | Perry, Eliza | F/138 | December 1, 1897 | December 5, 1897 |
| Holder, B. H. | Warren, Miss Mary | B/44 | April 15, 1867 | April 15, 1867 |
| Holemane, L. | Travis, Miss J. C. | A2/44 | December 11, 1855 | No Return |
| Holland, Amandy A. | Burch, J. M. | C/60 | July 5, 1873 | No Return |
| Holland, Elizabeth | Spicer, Joseph A. | A2/106 | January 13, 1863 | No Return |
| Holland, Ella | Barrett, James | F/100 | November 7, 1896 | November 9, 1896 |
| Holland, Geo | Blades, Huldy | C/90 | June 2, 1874 | June 3, 1877 |
| Holland, Henry | Good, Tennie | C/180 | December 20, 1877 | No Return |
| Holland, Jas | Summar, Sarah | C/174 | October 25, 1877 | No Return |
| Holland, John | Kirk, Miss Sarah B. | A2/135 | January 3, 1866 | January 18, 1866 |
| Holland, Mary K. | Mares, Wm. | A2/106 | November 23, 1862 | November 23, 1862 |
| Holland, Mattie | Manus, William | C/440 | July 20, 1891 | July 20, 1891 |
| Holland, Sarah S. | Philips, Wm. C. | A2/36 | November 13, 1854 | November 17, 1854 |
| Holland, Speaker | Stewart, Miss Elizabeth | B/128 | March 23, 1871 | March 23, 1871 |

| Groom or Bride | Groom or Bride | Book/Page | Date of License | Date of Marriage |
|---|---|---|---|---|
| Hollandsworth, A. | Jetton, Malisa | C/186 | February 21, 1878 | February 21, 1878 |
| Hollandsworth, Cole | Bogle, Hattie | C/260 | November 4, 1880 | No Return |
| Hollandsworth, Florence Miss | Mears, Mark | C/454 | January 12, 1892 | January 18, 1892 |
| Hollandsworth, Francis | Melton, Miss Nancy J. | B/98 | December 25, 1869 | December 27, 1869 |
| Hollandsworth, H. | Neeley, Nancy E. | C/36 | September 3, 1872 | September 3, 1872 |
| Hollandsworth, J. F. | Beshears, Margrett A | C/178 | November 20, 1877 | November 20, 1877 |
| Hollandsworth, J. M. | Smith, Mary | D/8 | | December 25, 1881 |
| Hollandsworth, James F. | Butcher, Miss Ruthy | A2/139 | March 13, 1866 | March 15, 1866 |
| Hollandsworth, Jennie | Pattrick, Hugh | F/172 | March 18, 1899 | March 19, 1899 |
| Hollandsworth, John | Crabtree, Miss Eliza J. | B/68 | July 23, 1868 | July 23, 1868 |
| Hollandsworth, John | Vinson, Miss Bettie | B/106 | August 3, 1870 | August 3, 1870 |
| Hollandsworth, John | Watson, Elisabeth | C/260 | October 20, 1880 | October 21, 1880 |
| Hollandsworth, John | Nokes, Delie | C/356 | March 26, 1886 | March 27, 1886 |
| Hollandsworth, Johnson | Scott, Sarah A. | C/116 | July 5, 1875 | July 5, 1875 |
| Hollandsworth, Lizzie | Vinson, D. B. | C/28 | June 13, 1872 | June 13, 1872 |
| Hollandsworth, Malissa Miss | Fuston, Leroy | B/80 | February 13, 1869 | February 14, 1869 |
| Hollandsworth, Mary | Barrett, Thos. | C/30 | June 25, 1872 | June 26, 1872 |
| Hollandsworth, Mary E. | Davenport, Sam | F/18 | September 14, 1893 | September 14, 1893 |
| Hollandsworth, N. | Barrett, Mary | C/56 | April 22, 1873 | April 23, 1873 |
| Hollandsworth, N. J. Miss | Youngblood, James T. | A2/92 | December 27, 1859 | No Return |
| Hollandsworth, Nancy A. | Melton, George G. | C/396 | July 18, 1887 | July 18, 1887 |
| Hollandsworth, Nova | Alexander, Martin | E/365 | January 15, 1920 | |
| Hollandsworth, Robert | Crabtree, Malisa | C/96 | October 10, 1874 | October 13, 1874 |
| Hollandsworth, Sarah | McKnight, W. W. | C/266 | December 31, 1880 | January 2, 1881 |
| Hollandsworth, Sarah C. Miss | Gilley, A. S. | B/42 | February 28, 1867 | February 29, 1867 |
| Hollandsworth, Tilford | Dennis, Luarel | C/442 | August 4, 1891 | August 6, 1891 |
| Hollandswoth, Susan | Barrett, Wm. | C/28 | May 23, 1872 | May 24, 1872 |
| Hollandworth, Cahal | Morris, C. | A2/130 | October 9, 1865 | October 19, 1865 |
| Hollandworth, Elizabeth | Markum, A. | A2/99 | July 6, 1860 | July 15, 1860 |
| Hollandworth, Gailen | M. J. Hutchins | C/10 | October 3, 1871 | October 3, 1871 |
| Hollandworth, James M. | Stone, Patience | E/99 | November 7, 1888 | November 7, 1888 |
| Hollandworth, Jas. O. | Smith, Logie | F/56 | January 18, 1895 | January 20, 1895 |
| Hollandworth, Wm. | Nancey Jetton | C/10 | September 18, 1871 | September 20, 1871 |
| Hollandworth, Zade A. Miss | Gann, Edmond | A2/47 | April 19, 1856 | April 20, 1856 |
| Hollansworth, J. B. | Tassey, Mollie | F/102 | November 20, 1896 | November 22, 1896 |
| Hollansworth, Miss Hettie | Stewart, W. T. | F/170 | February 16, 1899 | February 19, 1899 |
| Hollen, H. H. | Gannon, L. J. | D/15 | | September 12, 1882 |
| Hollensworth, D. A. | Foster, Mary J. | C/200 | October 5, 1878 | October 6, 1878 |
| Hollenworth, V. B. | Stewart, S. H. | F/84 | February 25, 1896 | February 25, 1896 |
| Hollingsworth, Ira | Neely, Sarah A. | A2/119 | January 4, 1865 | January 5, 1865 |
| Hollingsworth, Jos. O. | Hancock, Lucetta | A2/112 | March 24, 1864 | March 24, 1864 |
| Hollingsworth, Nancy A. | Murphy, J. D. | A2/118 | December 17, 1864 | December 21, 1864 |
| Hollinsworth, Aden | Murfrep, Miss Lucretia | A/78 | May 8, 1845 | May 8, 1845 |
| Hollinsworth, Charles W. | Vandagriffe, Miss Mary | A/126 | August 17, 1849 | August 19, 1849 |
| Hollinsworth, Ira | Milligan, Elizabeth | A/29 | June 4, 1840 | June 4, 1840 |
| Hollinsworth, John | Dennis, Charlotte | A/31 | July 10, 1840 | July 10, 1840 |

| Groom or Bride | Groom or Bride | Book/Page | Date of License | Date of Marriage |
|---|---|---|---|---|
| Hollinsworth, Josiah | Higgins, Sabrina | A/56 | November 23, 1842 | November 25, 1842 |
| Hollis A. L. | Vance, Sallie | F/2 | February 2, 1893 | No Return |
| Hollis, A. E. | James, Thos. E. | A2/80 | January 5, 1857 | January 7, 1857 |
| Hollis, Anne | Peay, John | F/12 | July 20, 1893 | July 20, 1893 |
| Hollis, Celurten | Lowe, A. G. | C/232 | December 11, 1879 | December 11, 1879 |
| Hollis, D. A. | Tolbert, Mary | C/370 | October 16, 1886 | No Return |
| Hollis, D. C. | Nichol, J. Y. | A2/118 | December 6, 1864 | December 6, 1864 |
| Hollis, Dennie | Curlee, Fannie | C/294 | October 5, 1883 | October 7, 1883 |
| Hollis, E. Matilda | Neely, Joseph H. | A2/95 | February 21, 1860 | February 22, 1860 |
| Hollis, Elizabeth | Bond, Lewis W. | A/15 | July ??, 1839 | July 29, 1839 |
| Hollis, Ella | Shelton, J. W. | E/217 | October 5, 1889 | October 6, 1889 |
| Hollis, Elsie | Carric, Thomas A. | F/150 | June 11, 1898 | No Return |
| Hollis, F. | Mitchell, Mattie | C/266 | December 25, 1880 | No Date |
| Hollis, Francis | Elkins, Wm. | C/192 | May 11, 1878 | May 12, 18878 |
| Hollis, George W. | Edwards, Elizabeth | A/16 | August 1, 1839 | No Return |
| Hollis, Harriet | Davis, James | B/14 | August 23, 1868 | No Return |
| Hollis, J. B. | Creson, Miss Mary | A2/137 | February 17, 1866 | February 18, 1866 |
| Hollis, J. B. | Lasiter, N. B. | F/4 | July 18, 1893 | February 19, 1893 |
| Hollis, J. E. | Cates, Caroline | A2/117 | November 14, 1864 | November 14, 1864 |
| Hollis, J. E. | Smart, D. C. | D/23 | | January 23, 1883 |
| Hollis, J. H. | Tenpenny, Jane | A2/101 | August 14, 1860 | No Return |
| Hollis, J. L. | Todd, Alice E. | A2/138 | February 28, 1866 | March 1, 1866 |
| Hollis, J. W. D. | Orand, Miss E. M. | A2/51 | November 26, 1856 | No Return |
| Hollis, James E. | Saffle, M. E. | F/22 | November 15, 1893 | November 15, 1893 |
| Hollis, John | Harris, Miss Mary Ann | A/46 | January 13, 1842 | January 13, 1842 |
| Hollis, John | Todd, Elizabeth | A/128 | November 19, 1849 | No Return |
| Hollis, John H. | Simpson, Miss Joanah F. | B/86 | September 9, 1869 | September 9, 1869 |
| Hollis, Kate Miss | Grimes, Billy | F/82 | February 1, 1896 | January 3, 1896 |
| Hollis, Lamira L. Miss | Lasater, Luke | A/116 | November 7, 1848 | November 7, 1848 |
| Hollis, Lena | Moss, Robt. | E/170 | April 18, 1889 | April 18, 1889 |
| Hollis, Lewis J. | Edwards, Susannah | A/15 | July 9, 1839 | July 11, 1839 |
| Hollis, Louisa Caroline Miss | Dozier, Jonathan | A/101 | August 12, 1847 | August 12, 1847 |
| Hollis, Lucy M. Miss | Stacey, William D. | A/39 | July 7, 1841 | July 13, 1841 |
| Hollis, M. L. Miss | Youree, W. H. | A2/94 | February 13, 1860 | February 14, 1860 |
| Hollis, Mandy Miss | McKnight, Morge | C/6 | August 5, 1871 | August 6, 1871 |
| Hollis, Margaret Miss | Nugan, John S. | A2/145 | September 20, 1866 | September 20, 1866 |
| Hollis, Martha | Herrell, E. P. | A2/120 | February 7, 1865 | February 7, 1865 |
| Hollis, Martha E. Miss | Gray, Silas M. | A2/75 | August 15, 1854 | August 17, 1854 |
| Hollis, Martha Miss | Heathcock, John | A/116 | October 25, 1848 | October 26, 1848 |
| Hollis, Mary Ann | Walkup, Willia J. | A/6 | September 8, 1838 | September 9, 1838 |
| Hollis, Mary E. Miss | Williams, Harvey T. | A/117 | November 14, 1849 | November 15, 1849 |
| Hollis, Mayn Miss | Snipes, C. W. | A2/13 | December 25, 1851 | December 25, 1851 |
| Hollis, Mollie | Fowler, Thomas | C/400 | September 8, 1887 | September 8, 1887 |
| Hollis, N. C. | Brandon, C. A. | F/28 | January 17, 1894 | January 11, 1894 |
| Hollis, Paulina Miss | Thompson, William | A/82 | July 31, 1845 | July 31, 1845 |
| Hollis, R. M. | McRead, W. | A2/99 | July 14, 1860 | No Return |

| Groom or Bride | Groom or Bride | Book/Page | Date of License | Date of Marriage |
|---|---|---|---|---|
| Hollis, Sarah A. | Gaither, Thomas M. | C/180 | December 11, 1877 | December 11, 1877 |
| Hollis, Susan | Rollins, Simeon | F/30 | January 17, 1894 | January 17, 1894 |
| Hollis, Susan Jane Miss | Duboise, John Irvin | A/68 | March 8, 1844 | March 14, 1844 |
| Hollis, W. B. | Hailey, P. J. | F/102 | November 20, 1896 | November 22, 1896 |
| Hollis, W. J | Lambert, Martha B. | E/354 | December 10, 1898 | |
| Hollis, W. J. | Lambert, Martha B | F/162 | December 10, 1898 | December 11, 1898 |
| Hollis, William C. | DeLoach, Miss Martha | A/39 | June 28, 1841 | June 28, 1841 |
| Hollowman, Oley | Neeley, Franklin | A2/30 | October 10, 1865 | October 11, 1865 |
| Holmes, D. E. | Hare, Sallie | C/102 | December 16, 1874 | December 17, 1874 |
| Holmes, John B. | Hare, Miss Mattie P. | B/36 | January 2, 1867 | January 3, 1867 |
| Holms, Mary R. Miss | Nichol, J. W. | B/34 | December 19, 1866 | December 20, 1866 |
| Holston, Richard J. | Hamilton, Miss Mary | A/127 | September 20, 1849 | September 20, 1849 |
| Holt, B. A. | Parker, Milley | C/270 | January 6, 1881 | January 6, 1881 |
| Holt, Blackburn | Stacy, Miss Emaline | B/74 | December 9, 1868 | December 13, 1868 |
| Holt, Clem | Bryant, J. T. | C/290 | August 13, 1883 | August 14, 1883 |
| Holt, Coleman | Reed, Mary C. | C/242 | February 20, 1880 | February 20, 1880 |
| Holt, Dovey J. | Summars, W. A. | C/296 | November 23, 1883 | November 25, 1883 |
| Holt, Fanny Miss | Gooding, William | A/40 | August 4, 1841 | August 6, 1841 |
| Holt, Fielding | Reed, L. E. | C/116 | July 30, 1875 | August 1, 1876 |
| Holt, H. N. | Williams, Miss Martha C. | B/78 | February 9, 1869 | February 28, 1869 |
| Holt, Hord | Reed, Amendy | C/178 | November 22, 1877 | No Return |
| Holt, Isabella A. Miss | Stacy, Abram H. | B/88 | September 24, 1869 | October 3, 1869 |
| Holt, John | Thompson, Ella | F/126 | August 20, 1897 | August 22, 1897 |
| Holt, Lee | Burgett, Jane | F/62 | April 9, 1895 | April 11, 1895 |
| Holt, Malisa | Ashley, Wm. S. | C/132 | January 22, 1876 | January 23, 1876 |
| Holt, Margaret | Pumphrey, Matthew T. | A/4 | August 1, 1838 | August 2, 1838 |
| Holt, Milly | Hoover, Martin S. | A/14 | June 20, 1839 | No Return |
| Holt, Minnerva | Travis, Johnson | A/22 | January 16, 1840 | January 16, 1840 |
| Holt, Newman | Wood, Clem | C/254 | August 21, 1880 | August 22, 1880 |
| Holt, Norman | Maxey, Clercy | C/288 | August 8, 1883 | August 8, 1883 |
| Holt, Robert | Wood, Lue | C/248 | June 19, 1880 | June 20, 1880 |
| Holt, Roxey | Simmons, J. A. | D/18 | | December 7, 1882 |
| Holt, Sallie | Simmons, H. P. | D/101 | | February 2, 1882 |
| Holt, T. A. | Robinson, J. P. | F/144 | January 14, 1898 | January 15, 1898 |
| Holt, Thomas | Ring, Miss Elizabeth | A/54 | October 6, 1842 | October 6, 1842 |
| Holt, Whiteman | Spry, Sarah | C/196 | August 30, 1878 | September 1, 1878 |
| Holt, William | Bryant, Miss Elizabeth | B/50 | August 17, 1867 | August 17, 1867 |
| Holtermand, John | Melton, Rhody | A2/107 | February 8, 1863 | February 8, 1863 |
| Holy, Tildy | Muny, McCaslen | A2/40 | August 3, 1855 | Returns Missing |
| Holyfield, Sally Miss | Spicer, Henry | A/39 | June 10, 1841 | June 10, 1841 |
| Hoobs, John | Smithson, Ellen | F/108 | January 9, 1897 | January 12, 1897 |
| Hoodenpyle, W. W. | Mitchell, Mollie E. | C/470 | December 7, 1892 | December 7, 1892 |
| Hooker, Elizabeth Miss | Bush, H. L. | B/58 | December 18, 1867 | December 19, 1867 |
| Hooker, Mary A. Miss | Gordon, W. M. | B/118 | December 7, 1870 | December 23, 1870 |
| Hooper, David | Worley, Eliza | D/1 | | May 29, 1881 |
| Hooper, James | Youngblood, Miss Polly | A/89 | July 25, 1846 | July 26, 1846 |

| Groom or Bride | Groom or Bride | Book/Page | Date of License | Date of Marriage |
| --- | --- | --- | --- | --- |
| Hooper, Nancy E. Miss | Youngblood, Archelaus | A/91 | October 5, 1846 | October 6, 1846 |
| Hooper, Walter Edger | McKnight, Miss Daisy Dean | F/166 | January 3, 1899 | January 4, 1899 |
| Hoover, Gay | Jamerson, W. L. | F/110 | February 3, 1897 | February 3, 1897 |
| Hoover, Beatrice | Downing, W. R. | F/18 | September 16, 1893 | September 16, 1893 |
| Hoover, Bengamin | Todd, Miss Mary J. | B/86 | September 23, 1869 | September 23, 1869 |
| Hoover, C. C. | Curlee, E. M. | C/276 | March 17, 1881 | March 17, 1881 |
| Hoover, Eliza | Stafford, R. F. | C/148 | November 21, 1876 | November 21, 1876 |
| Hoover, Elizabeth | Brynum, John | A/9 | December 6, 1838 | December 6, 1838 |
| Hoover, Etta | Stroud, B. B. | F/70 | September 12, 1895 | September 13, 1895 |
| Hoover, G. W. | Mitchell, Sarah D. | A2/91 | December 9,1859 | No Return |
| Hoover, Henry | Stroud, Gay | C/442 | August 4, 1891 | August 5, 1891 |
| Hoover, Henry W. | Knox, Miss Mary Jane E. | A/106 | January 3, 1848 | January 6, 1848 |
| Hoover, I. N. | Hayes, Susie | F/152 | July 13, 1898 | No Return |
| Hoover, Isaac | Todd, Miss Jane | B/40 | February 6, 1867 | February 7, 1867 |
| Hoover, J. I. | Downing, July | C/302 | January 22, 1884 | January 22, 1884 |
| Hoover, J. L. | Bailey, Ida | C/470 | December 17, 1892 | December 18, 1892 |
| Hoover, J. M. | Stroud, Barcelona | C/26 | March 28, 1872 | March 28, 1872 |
| Hoover, J. P. | Downing, Jennie | F/150 | June 4, 1898 | June 5, 1898 |
| Hoover, Jasper | McBroom, Tennie | F/136 | November 13, 1897 | November ??, 1897 |
| Hoover, Marlin S. | Robinson, Suffrona | A/4 | June 14, 1838 | June 14, 1838 |
| Hoover, Martin S. | Holt, Milly | A/14 | June 20, 1839 | No Return |
| Hoover, Mary | McBroom, Alexander | C/18 | December 21, 1871 | December 21, 1871 |
| Hoover, Mary | McCartin, W. C. | C/106 | January 20, 1875 | January 20, 1875 |
| Hoover, Mary | McKee, William | A2/133 | December 11, 1865 | December 12, 1865 |
| Hoover, Mary | Downing, George R. | C/322 | December 27, 1884 | December 28, 1884 |
| Hoover, Mary F. | Miller, F. J. | D/15 | | September 14, 1882 |
| Hoover, Millia | Hoover, Thomas J. | A2/133 | December 11, 1865 | December 12, 1865 |
| Hoover, Newton | Mason, Miss Mary | C/6 | August 9, 1871 | August 10, 1871 |
| Hoover, O. A. | Tenpenny, Orrila | F/138 | November 17, 1897 | November 17, 1897 |
| Hoover, Susan | West, Henry | C/232 | November 20, 1879 | November 20, 1879 |
| Hoover, Thomas J. | Hoover, Millia | A2/133 | December 11, 1865 | December 12, 1865 |
| Hoover, Thos. J. | Mitchel, Miss Susan | | December 9, 1858 | December 9, 1858 |
| Hoover, Wm. | Carnahan, Jane R. | C/32 | July 22, 1872 | July 22, 1872 |
| Hope, F. M. | Rains, N. E. | A2/131 | November 7, 1865 | November 7, 1865 |
| Hopkins, Elijah | Price, Miss Nancy | A/71 | August 21, 1844 | August 23, 1844 |
| Hopkins, Harmon H. | Ennie, Miss Isabella | A/48 | February 19, 1842 | February 20, 1842 |
| Hopkins, Joel | Petty, Miss Easther | A/62 | May 13, 1843 | No Return |
| Hopkins, Joseph W. | Edwards, Miss Mary | A/117 | November 24, 1848 | November 21, 1848 |
| Hopkins, Lucy Ann Miss | Cummins, L. L. C. | B/72 | October 17, 1868 | October 18, 1868 |
| Hopkins, Samuel A. | Seales, Miss Martha E. | A2/52 | December 16, 1856 | No Return |
| Hopp, Fannie | Ferrell, Jesse | F/6 | March 13, 1893 | March 15, 1893 |
| Hoppins, Annie | Ewing, Rufus (col) | C/416 | September 7, 1890 | September 7, 1890 |
| Horn, John | Usselton, Miss Elizabeth | A2/138 | February 26, 1866 | No Return |
| Horn, Mary Elizabeth Miss | Gaither, Thomas F. | A/107 | January 24, 1848 | January 27, 1848 |
| Horn, Thomas W. | Patton, Miss Nancy Eleanor | A/125 | December 20, 1848 | No Return |
| Horral, Sarah M. Miss | Night, John | A2/15 | February 26, 1852 | February 26, 1852 |

| Groom or Bride | Groom or Bride | Book/Page | Date of License | Date of Marriage |
|---|---|---|---|---|
| House, Bell D. | Walker, J. W. | C/170 | September 17, 1877 | September 18, 1877 |
| House, E. J. Miss | Melton, W. S. | A2/139 | March 6, 1866 | March 6, 1866 |
| House, Elizabeth | Sullivan, Caswell | A/76 | January 8, 1845 | January 9, 1845 |
| House, Hartwell | Fagan, Miss Mollie E. | B/48 | July 23, 1867 | July 25, 1867 |
| House, Sally Ann Miss | Perry, Henry R. | A/47 | February 2, 1842 | February 6, 1842 |
| House, W. D. | Phillipps, Miss Janie | B/120 | December 22, 1870 | December 22, 1870 |
| House, William | Sullivan, Jane | A2/14 | January 13, 1852 | January 13, 1852 |
| Howard, Elmira Miss | Spurlock, Josiah Jr. | A/89 | May 28, 1846 | May 28, 1846 |
| Howel, E. J. | Wharton, Jennie C. | C/150 | December 17, 1876 | December 17, 1876 |
| Howell, T. E. | Henderson, Mry A. | C/368 | August 19, 1886 | August 22, 1886 |
| Howeth, James A. | Mingle, Miss Nancy J. | A/102 | September 13, 1847 | September 14, 1847 |
| Howeth, Nancy | Finley, Wiley | F/52 | December 22, 1894 | December 23, 1894 |
| Howeth, Nancy J. Mrs. | McBroom, Isaac | B/84 | August 19, 1869 | August 19, 1869 |
| Howeth, R. B. | McBroom, L. A. | C/108 | February 6, 1875 | No Return |
| Howeton, Jas A. | Lassiter, Miss Lou | C/458 | May 25, 1892 | May 22, 1892 |
| Hubbard, D. A. | Grizzle, Mary E. | C/262 | November 24, 1880 | November 25, 1880 |
| Hubbard, F. M. | Summar, Sopha | C/320 | December 10, 1884 | December 10, 1884 |
| Hubbard, M. A. F. Miss | Mathews, W. H. | B/94 | November 30, 1869 | December 2, 1869 |
| Hubbard, Nancy | Bryson, Daniel | A2/105 | October 18, 1862 | October 21, 1862 |
| Hubbard, Nancy Miss | Hancock, Charles | B/54 | November 9, 1867 | November 10, 1867 |
| Hubbard, Nora Miss | Henderson, James Y. | C/394 | July 12, 1887 | July 12, 1887 |
| Hudeston, Marshal | Alexander, Addi | F/8 | May 1, 1893 | May 2, 1893 |
| Huff, Etta | Maxey, William | E/51 | June 25, 1888 | June 26, 1888 |
| Hughs, Adaline Miss | McCaslin | A2/91 | December 15, 1859 | No Return |
| Hughs, Jos | Johnson, M. J. | F/146 | February 26, 1898 | February 27, 1898 |
| Hughs, L. | Carrell | A2/20 | November 4, 1852 | November 4, 1852 |
| Hulehens, William | Starr, Jane | A2/37 | December 28, 1854 | December 28, 1854 |
| Hulet, Sallie | Nokes, Thomas | C/272 | February 14, 1881 | February 14, 1881 |
| Humble, L. D. | Justice, Sophia | C/222 | August 10, 1879 | August 10, 1879 |
| Hume, Sallie | Givan, W. J. | C/446 | September 16, 1891 | September 16, 1891 |
| Hunt, John | Gunter, Hatie | C/328 | March 3, 1885 | March 3, 1885 |
| Hunt, John T. | Milstead, Nannie B. | E/122 | January 1, 1889 | January 1, 1889 |
| Hunt, T. J. | Lorance, Miss M. A. | A2/85 | March 31, 1859 | March 31, 1859 |
| Hunt, T. J. | Millsted, M. A. | C/50 | December 28, 1872 | December 29, 1872 |
| Hunt, Mollie | Tubs, James | C/294 | September 28, 1883 | No Return |
| Hunter, Mary A. | Blue, John | A2/82 | August 28, 1858 | August 30, 1858 |
| Hurst, H. H. | Byford, E. B. | E/268 | July 4, 1904 | No Return |
| Hutcheans, David | Denis, Miss Emerline | A2/85 | April 13, 1859 | May 2, 1859 |
| Hutchens, Frances L. | Moore, Jessee | A2/126 | September 2, 1865 | No Return |
| Hutchens, Ruth S. | Bynum, Red | C/240 | January 30, 1880 | January 30, 1880 |
| Hutchens, Vina C. | Brashears, Alexr. | A2/112 | March 20, 1864 | March 20, 1864 |
| Hutchenson, M. H. | Long, Isul | C/76 | December 13, 1873 | December 14, 1873 |
| Hutcherson, Nancy | Underhill, A. E. | A2/126 | August 24, 1865 | August 27, 1864 |
| Hutcheson, J. F. | Bragg, M. E | C/208 | December 27, 1878 | January 1, 1879 |
| Hutchin, Salley | King, James | D/101 | | January 22, 1882 |
| Hutchins, Aaron | Star, Miss Sarah | A/38 | May 15, 1841 | No Return |

| Groom or Bride | Groom or Bride | Book/Page | Date of License | Date of Marriage |
|---|---|---|---|---|
| Hutchins, David | Higgans, Miss July Ann | A/111 | May 11, 1848 | May 11, 1848 |
| Hutchins, John | Higgins, Miss Polly | A/32 | August 28, 1840 | August 30, 1840 |
| Hutchins, Lavina C. Miss | Moore, Zachariah T. | B/102 | May 14, 1870 | May 15, 1870 |
| Hutchins, M. J. | Hollandworth, Gailen | C/10 | October 3, 1871 | October 3, 1871 |
| Hutchins, Mintee | Hendrickson, John | A2/105 | October 13, 1862 | No Return |
| Hutchins, Patsy | Smithson, James | A/29 | June 3, 1840 | June 4, 1840 |
| Hutchins, Sarah Ann Miss | Lance, Joseph | A/99 | May 3, 1847 | May 3, 1847 |
| Hyse, Mary | Sowell, Wm. | C/182 | December 29, 1877 | December 29, 1877 |
| Ingles, Dianitia Catharine | Parker, Franklin | A/27 | April 2, 1840 | April 6, 1840 |
| Inglis, Evan A. | Byford, Miss Elizabeth | A/72 | September 14, 1844 | September 17, 1844 |
| Inglis, M. E. Miss | Prator, T. E. | B/50 | August 12, 1867 | No Return |
| Inglis, Mary | Gunter, C. D. | C/74 | November 29, 1873 | November 27, 1873 |
| Inglis, Uriah F. | Marberry, Miss Sarah | A/93 | November 18, 1846 | November 19, 1846 |
| Inglish, Alex | Eledge, Miss Clannatin | C/402 | September 145, 1887 | September 15, 1887 |
| Inglish, Emma | McCasline, J. P. | F/134 | October 1, 1897 | October 3, 1897 |
| Inglish, Nancy E. | Shelton, B. F | C/274 | February 28, 1881 | March 2, 1881 |
| Inglish, Sallie | Elam, N. B. | C/256 | September 16, 1880 | No Return |
| Inglish, W. B. | Todd, Nancy | C/226 | October 29, 1879 | October 30, 1879 |
| Irvin, Daisey | Melton, Wiley | F/154 | August 6, 1898 | August 7, 1898 |
| Irvin, H. A. | Brandon, Miss M. J. | B/62 | February 10, 1868 | February 18, 1868 |
| Irvin, J. H. | Patton, M. E. | C/264 | December 22, 1880 | December 23, 1880 |
| Irvin, Myrtle | Knox, S. A. | E/204 | September 3, 1889 | September 3, 1889 |
| Irvin, Sarah E. | Vasser, J. B. | D/21 | | January 30, 1883 |
| Irvin, T. N. | Todd, M. F. | C/332 | July 25, 1885 | July 26, 1885 |
| Irvine, Myrtle, S. C. | Tenpenny, T. B. | E/206 | September 3, 1889 | September 3, 1889 |
| Isam, R. C. | Underwood, Joseph | A2/101 | August 27, 1860 | August 29, 1860 |
| Isom, J. B. | Graham, M. G. | C/96 | October 1, 1874 | October 1, 1874 |
| Ivey, Philip | Dickens, Deley A. | B/6 | September 1, 1865 | No Return |
| Ivie, Ellar | Brandon, George | C/220 | July 22, 1879 | July 24, 1879 |
| Ivie, Nettie | Martin, Frank (col.) | C/442 | August 6, 1891 | August 6, 1891 |
| Ivie, T. B. | McGill, R. E. | C/84 | March 23, 1874 | March 24, 1874 |
| Ivory, Sarah E. | Miller, Henry | C/176 | November 14, 1877 | November 15, 1877 |
| Ivy, Amanda Miss | Chapin, Lawyer | C/386 | April 2, 1887 | April 3, 1887 |
| Ivy, Bill (col.) | Pinkerton, Lizzie | F/78 | December 19, 1895 | December 21, 1894 |
| Ivy, Bud (col.) | Thompson, Fanny | C/444 | August 27, 1891 | August 30, 1891 |
| Jaco, E. J. | James, Druclia | C/148 | November 6, 1876 | November 6, 1876 |
| Jaco, E. J. | Percell, Nancy P. | C/14 | November 27, 1871 | December 9, 1871 |
| Jaco, Mary C. | Barrett, Levi | C/30 | July 12, 1872 | July 14, 1872 |
| Jaco, Samanther M. J. | Bogle, Jas | C/134 | March 1, 1876 | March 2, 1876 |
| Jaco, T. J. | Young, James A. | C/262 | November 22, 1880 | November 20, 1880 |
| Jacobs, Arminda | Pemelton, Thos. | A2/108 | July 9, 1863 | No Return |
| Jacobs, Elizabeth | Low, Calvin | A2/109 | September 14, 1863 | No Return |
| Jacobs, Malvina Miss | Parker, D. F. | A2/26 | June 14, 1853 | No Return |
| Jacobs, W. H. | Tuples, Martha | D/3 | | August 24, 1881 |
| Jacobs, W. J. | Jernigan, C. L. | C/164 | July 5, 1877 | July 5, 1877 |
| Jamerson, John | Orand, Miss Maggie | F/86 | April 22, 1896 | April 22, 1896 |

| Groom or Bride | Groom or Bride | Book/Page | Date of License | Date of Marriage |
|---|---|---|---|---|
| Jamerson, W. L. | Hoov er, Gay | F/110 | February 3, 1897 | February 3, 1897 |
| James A. F. | Miss Mandy Odom | A2/71 | January 11, 1859 | January 11, 1859 |
| James A. F. | Miss Mandy Odom | A2/83 | January 11, 1859 | January 11, 1859 |
| James, Daniel | Mears, Miss Nancy Manerva | A/37 | April 1, 1841 | April 1, 1841 |
| James, Druclia | Jaco, E. J | C/148 | November 6, 1876 | November 6, 1876 |
| James, E. M. | Maddex, E. | C/374 | November 20, 1886 | November 21, 1886 |
| James, F. M. | Devenport, Miss Eliza | A2/71 | January 5, 1859 | No Return |
| James, George | Johnson, Mega | C/416 | September 6, 1890 | No Date |
| James, Nancy C. | Ridinger, J. B. | C/256 | September 30, 1880 | September 30, 1880 |
| James, Robert G. | Freemon, Elizabeth | A/23 | January 20, 1840 | January 20, 1840 |
| James, Samuel R. | Bates, Mrs. Lucy | A2/5 | August 10, 1850 | August 11, 1850 |
| James, Thos. E. | Hollis, A. E. | A2/80 | January 5, 1857 | January 7, 1857 |
| James, Wm. | Todd, Tennie | C/202 | October 26, 1878 | October 27, 1878 |
| Jameson, John A. | Ford, Miss Nancy E. | B/52 | September 23, 1867 | October 3, 1867 |
| Jamison, Nancy A. | Ginoe, W. Z. | A2/92 | December 20, 1859 | No Return |
| Jamison, Robert | Espy, Narcissa | A2/40 | July 12, 1855 | July 12, 1855 |
| Jamison, T. G. | Smith, S. J. | A2/59 | November 16, 1857 | November 19, 1857 |
| Jamison, William | Bell, Emaline | A/30 | June 18, 1840 | No Return |
| Jamison, William | Mitchell, Octavia | C/398 | August 19, 1887 | August 19, 1887 |
| Jamison, William A. | Webber, Miss Jane Adaline | B/50 | August 12, 1867 | August 18, 1867 |
| Janson, J. H. | Haley, B. | A2/99 | July 12, 1860 | July 12, 1860 |
| Jarnagin, Cary | Whitfield, Haly | A/9 | November 29, 1838 | No Return |
| Jarnagin, Nedham | Nivens, Sarah | A/55 | November 9, 1842 | November 9, 1842 |
| Jarnegin, Wm. A. | Couthen, Miss Martha J. | A2/64 | May 5, 1858 | No Return |
| Jarratt, Mary C. | Mitchell, J. T. | C/28 | May 31, 1872 | June 2, 1872 |
| Jarrett, Isaac L. | Caruthers, May E. | A2/33 | June 21, 1854 | June 22, 1854 |
| Jarrett, July | Perriman, John M. | C/342 | November 21, 1885 | November 22, 1885 |
| Jemson, J. R. | Mitchell, Delila | C/340 | November 19, 1885 | November 29, 1885 |
| Jennings, Esther | Thompson, Andrew | E/171 | April 18, 1889 | April 18, 1889 |
| Jennings, J. W. | Barrett, Sylvia | 3/137 | February 8, 1889 | February 10, 1889 |
| Jennings, Jim | Carr, Ann | C/248 | July 1, 1880 | July 1, 1880 |
| Jennings, L. L. | Rodgers, Nannie | F/96 | September 18, 1896 | September 18, 1896 |
| Jennings, Leander | Overall, America C. | B/12 | December 12, 1867 | December 12, 1867 |
| Jennings, Nelson | Talley, Tennessee | C/198 | September 4, 1878 | Setember 8, 1878 |
| Jennings, Ollie | Maddux, Miss Hassie | F/174 | April 3, 1899 | April 6, 1899 |
| Jennings, Wesley | Dickens, Sis | C/256 | September 8, 1880 | September 8, 1880 |
| Jernigan, A. M. | Tolbert, Matilda | E/32 | April 25, 1888 | April 26, 1888 |
| Jernigan, Andrew J. | Todd, Miss Rebecca Jane | A2/85 | April 2, 1859 | ?? 6, 1859 |
| Jernigan, Ann | Bynum, F. G. | D/4 | | September 1, 1881 |
| Jernigan, C. L. | Jacobs, W. J. | C/164 | July 5, 1877 | July 5, 1877 |
| Jernigan, Carline | Jernigan, John | F/46 | October 22, 1894 | No Return |
| Jernigan, E. | Moore, Sarah M. | D/19 | | December 17, 1882 |
| Jernigan, Ella | Merriman, Jas M. | C/354 | March 12, 1886 | March 12, 1886 |
| Jernigan, Henry | Nichols, Sarah | C/168 | August 29, 1877 | August 30, 1877 |
| Jernigan, J. C. | Sissom, Mrs. Rebecca | B/74 | December 24, 1868 | December 24, 1868 |
| Jernigan, Jasper | Stricklin, Josie | F/94 | September 3, 1896 | September 6, 1896 |

| Groom or Bride | Groom or Bride | Book/Page | Date of License | Date of Marriage |
|---|---|---|---|---|
| Jernigan, Jim | Reed, Nettie | F/156 | September 20, 1898 | September 21, 1898 |
| Jernigan, John | Jernigan, Carline | F/46 | October 22, 1894 | No Return |
| Jernigan, L. W. | Whitfield, Mary J. | A2/134 | December 27, 1865 | December 27, 1865 |
| Jernigan, M. L. | Landan, J. A. C. | D/10 | | December 29, 1881 |
| Jernigan, Mary A. | Lemmons, J. K. P. | C/226 | October 13, 1879 | October 13, 1879 |
| Jernigan, Mattie | Pinkerton, J. F. | C/376 | December 22, 1886 | December 23, 1886 |
| Jernigan, N. | Northcutt, N. J. | C/140 | July 14, 1876 | July 18, 1876 |
| Jernigan, Nancy | Phillips, J. H. | D/12 | | February 5, 1882 |
| Jernigan, Newton | Brnum, Amandy | D/7 | | December 8, 1881 |
| Jernigan, R. B | Fox, C. R. | E/65 | August 29, 1888 | August 29, 1888 |
| Jernigan, Richard | Sissom, Sarah | C/58 | April 25, 1873 | April 27, 1873 |
| Jernigan, W. H. | Cawthorn, Miss C. R. | C/412 | July 25, 1889 | July 25, 1889 |
| Jernigan, W. H. | Cawthon, C. R. | E/193 | July 25, 1889 | No Return |
| Jernigan, W. H. | Byran, Bettie | E/342 | December, 22, 1898 | |
| Jernigan, W. H. | Bynuim, Gettie | F/164 | December 22, 1898 | December 22, 1898 |
| Jernigan, Willie E. | Whitlock, J. H. | F/78 | December 16, 1895 | December 16, 1895 |
| Jernigan, Wm. A. | Gilly, Miss Dorcus | A2/42 | October 11, 1855 | October 16, 1855 |
| Jernison, S. J. | Miller, Laura | D/17 | | November 30, 1882 |
| Jerrett, Wesley (col.) | Alexander, Adre (col.) | F/102 | November 30, 1896 | November 30, 1896 |
| Jetten, ---- | Goodloe, H. N. | D/22 | | January 18, 1883 |
| Jetten, Betsey A. | Merrett, James | C/262 | November 16, 1880 | November 17, 1880 |
| Jetten, Robert | Frigiter | E/157 | December 25, 1888 | December 25, 1888 |
| Jetton, Alexander | Milligan, Miss Elizabeth | A2/58 | October 20, 1857 | October 20, 1857 |
| Jetton, Bettie | Stone, Robert | C/368 | September 27, 1886 | No Return |
| Jetton, Daniel | Melton, Miss Sarah A. | A2/90 | November 1, 1859 | No Return |
| Jetton, Edna | Mason, Charles | E/6 | January 19, 1888 | January 19, 1888 |
| Jetton, Elbert | Pinkerton, Lillie | E/119 | December 25, 1888 | December 25, 1888 |
| Jetton, Eller | Rideout, Johnson | B/16 | December 28, 1868 | December 29, 1869 |
| Jetton, Francis | Mitchell, J. A. | C/358 | June 23, 1886 | July 1, 1886 |
| Jetton, Granville | Corn, Mrs. Sarah E. | A2/14 | January 29, 1852 | January 29, 1852 |
| Jetton, Granville | Chapell, Miss T. A. | A2/38 | December 30, 1854 | January 4, 1855 |
| Jetton, James | Petty, Sophy | C/16 | December 7, 1871 | No Return |
| Jetton, Jamie R. | Barton, Miss Mary C. | C/430 | February 24, 2891 | February 25, 1891 |
| Jetton, Jim | Milligan, Maggie | F/108 | December 30, 1896 | December 30, 1896 |
| Jetton, John B. | Stewart, Isabell Jane | A/27 | April 2, 1840 | No Return |
| Jetton, Julia | Weedon, John | B/10 | March 26, 1867 | No Return |
| Jetton, Julia | Weedon, John | B/14 | October 8, 1868 | November 22, 1868 |
| Jetton, L. M. | Stephen, Viola | C/220 | June 28, 1879 | June 29, 1879 |
| Jetton, Malisa | Hollandsworth, A. | C/186 | February 21, 1878 | February 21, 1878 |
| Jetton, Martha Miss | Ledbetter, Thomas | B/68 | August 3, 1868 | August ?, 1868 |
| Jetton, Mary | Smith, John | E/257 | January 4, 1890 | No Return |
| Jetton, Mary E. Miss | McKnight, James T. | A/93 | November 25, 1846 | 1846 |
| Jetton, Mary Miss | Melton, Dillard | A2/43 | December 7, 1855 | December 8, 1855 |
| Jetton, Mary R. | Goodloe, Jame E. | C/186 | February 4, 1878 | February 5, 1878 |
| Jetton, Myrtle | Lyons, Wm (col.) | C/428 | January 14, 1891 | January 14, 1891 |
| Jetton, Nancy | Hollandworth, Wm. | C/10 | September 18, 1871 | September 20, 1871 |

| Groom or Bride | Groom or Bride | Book/Page | Date of License | Date of Marriage |
|---|---|---|---|---|
| Jetton, Robert | Daughtery, Mary | C/378 | December 25, 1886 | December 26, 1886 |
| Jetton, Rolley | Robinson, Miss Alis | C/388 | April 23, 1887 | April 24, 1887 |
| Jetton, Sarah E. | Stone, John W. | A/84 | November 6, 1845 | November 6, 1845 |
| Jetton, Sarah Miss | Young, Samuel | B/62 | January 13, 1868 | January 14, 1868 |
| Jetton, Sarah R. Miss | McKnight, Amzi B. | B/72 | November 3, 1868 | November 3, 1868 |
| Jetton, Sophia | Robinson, J. | C/130 | January 6, 1876 | January 6, 1876 |
| Jetton, T. J. | Burger, Miss S. P. | A2/34 | July 31, 1854 | July 31, 1854 |
| Jetton, William | Markum, Miss Mary | B/82 | May 28, 1869 | May 28, 1869 |
| Jetton, William | Lamberson, Chris | C/448 | October 24, 1891 | October 25, 1891 |
| Jetton, Wm | McGee, L. R. | C/72 | November 20, 1873 | November 20, 1873 |
| Jewel, N. T. | Hancock, Miss Alaminta | B/88 | September 23, 1869 | September 25, 1869 |
| Jewell, Jacob W. | Shelton, Margret W. | A/23 | February 1, 1840 | February 2, 1840 |
| Jewell, N. W. | Vaught, J. M. | C/310 | July 12, 1884 | July 13, 1884 |
| Jewell, S. T. | Bryant, M. E. | C/140 | July 21, 1876 | No Return |
| Jimerson, E. Miss | Caric, T. J. | A2/57 | August 6, 1857 | August 6, 1857 |
| Jimerson, Narcissa Miss | Rickets, Robert S. | A2/91 | November 2, 1859 | No Return |
| Jimmerson, R. C. Miss | Ford, Larkin | B/118 | November 24, 1870 | November 24, 1870 |
| Johns, Thomas | Ashford, Elizabeth | C/308 | June 14, 1884 | June 14, 1884 |
| Johnson, Alice | Lewis, A. D | C/188 | March 2, 1878 | March 3, 1878 |
| Johnson, Callie | Womack, J. B. | F/90 | July 14, 1896 | July 16, 1896 |
| Johnson, Charles | Johnson, Miss Sarah Jane | B/46 | June 19, 1867 | No Return |
| Johnson, David | Couch, Lizzie | F/54 | January 5, 1895 | January 6, 1895 |
| Johnson, Elizabeth M. Miss | Colvert, William A. | A/80 | July 10, 1845 | July 10, 1845 |
| Johnson, Elizabeth M. Miss | Colvert, William A. | A/81 | July 10, 1845 | July 10, 1845 |
| Johnson, F. H. | Couch, Tennessee | C/382 | January 19, 1887 | January 20, 1887 |
| Johnson, Isaac | Higgins, Susan J. | C/222 | September 19, 1879 | September 19, 1879 |
| Johnson, Isaac N. | Marchall, Sarah Ann | A/109 | March 13, 1848 | March 14, 1848 |
| Johnson, Issac N. | Thomas, Sarah M. | A2/3 | July 26, 1850 | July 30, 1850 |
| Johnson, Jake | Rushing, Ellen | C/162 | June 16, 1877 | No Return |
| Johnson, Jake | Fugitt, Emley | C/264 | August 5, 1880 | August 5, 1880 |
| Johnson, James N. | Reed, Miss Mary E. | B/66 | May 23, 1868 | May 22, 1868 |
| Johnson, John | Barton, Susan | C/244 | March 19, 1880 | March 19, 1880 |
| Johnson, John B. | Thomas, Ema M. | A2/78 | January 26, 1856 | January 26, 1856 |
| Johnson, John C. | Bynum, Mary | C/206 | December 18, 1878 | December 22, 1878 |
| Johnson, John H. | Pitts, Celina | D/18 | | December 31, 1882 |
| Johnson, John T. | Phillips, Miss Elizabeth | B/96 | December 24, 1869 | December 25, 1869 |
| Johnson, Libe | Teeples, | A2/109 | October 8, 1863 | No Return |
| Johnson, Lula | Tucker, Solomaon | E/366 | November 26, 1898 | |
| Johnson, M. J. | Hughs, Jos | F/146 | February 26, 1898 | February 27, 1898 |
| Johnson, M. L. | Lawson, Charity | C/326 | February 15, 1885 | February 16, 1885 |
| Johnson, Mattie | McDougle, Wm. | F/146 | February 22, 1898 | February 23, 1898 |
| Johnson, Mattie | Sessom, Albert | C/398 | August 18, 1887 | August 18, 1887 |
| Johnson, Mega | James, George | C/416 | September 6, 1890 | No Date |
| Johnson, Miariah Miss | Bush, Uriah | A/78 | May 6, 1845 | May 6, 1845 |
| Johnson, Nathan S. | Hill, Miss Rebecca Elizabeth | A/118 | December ??, 1848 | December 16, 1848 |
| Johnson, Nelson | Patrick, Miss Mary A. | A2/11 | March 23, 1851 | March 23, 1851 |

| Groom or Bride | Groom or Bride | Book/Page | Date of License | Date of Marriage |
|---|---|---|---|---|
| Johnson, P. P. | Francis, Miss Lucinda | A/73 | October 1, 1844 | October 2, 1844 |
| Johnson, Rebecca Miss | Herriman, John | B/78 | March 6, 1869 | March 6, 1869 |
| Johnson, Richard P. | Webber, Elizabeth E. | A/2 | April 14, 1838 | April 20, 1838 |
| Johnson, Sarah Jane Miss | Johnson, Charles | B/46 | June 19, 1867 | No Return |
| Johnson, Sarah Miss | Hendricks, N. M. | A2/33 | July 12, 1854 | No Return |
| Johnson, Sarah Miss | Hendrickson, Nathan | A2/79 | July 12, 1854 | July 13, 1854 |
| Johnson, Sarah P. | Martin, John W. | C/332 | July 11, 1885 | July 12, 1885 |
| Johnson, Stella | Wood, J. H. | F/126 | August 7, 1897 | August 8, 1897 |
| Johnson, William (col.) | Martin, Fanny | C/438 | June 27, 1891 | No Return |
| Johnson, William (col.) | Smith, Minnie (col.) | F/124 | August 3, 1897 | August 3, 1897 |
| Johnson, Wm. | Brown, Josey | C/264 | December 23, 1880 | December 23, 1880 |
| Jones, Ada | Wilson, Isham | C/340 | November 13, 1885 | November 15, 1885 |
| Jones, A. A. B. | Crabtree, Sarah E. | C/144 | September 1, 1876 | September 3, 1876 |
| Jones, A. D. | Skirlock, John | C/220 | July 26, 1879 | No Return |
| Jones, A. F. | Adams, Miss Nancy | A2/15 | February 13, 1852 | February ??, 1852 |
| Jones, A. V. | McCabe, Mary | C/68 | October 16, 1873 | October 19, 1873 |
| Jones, Aaron F. | Carter, Mahaly | A2/18 | August 5, 1852 | August 5, 1852 |
| Jones, Alabama Miss | Jones, John E. | A/132 | February 19, 1850 | No Return |
| Jones, AnEliza | Davenport, J. A. | E/200 | August 17, 1889 | August 18, 1889 |
| Jones, Anne F. Miss | Smith, Joseph F. | A/93 | November 13, 1846 | November 13, 1846 |
| Jones, Ans (col.) | Ovie, Laura | C/462 | August 2, 1892 | No Return |
| Jones, B. F. | Cos, Mary M. | A2/114 | July 25, 1864 | August 4, 1864 |
| Jones, B. M. | Devenport, Miss Eliza | A2/83 | January 5, 1859 | January 6, 1859 |
| Jones, Ba--- | Rigsby, Robert | A2/102 | September 15, 1860 | September 15, 1860 |
| Jones, Beckey | Milligan, Alex | C/224 | September 6, 1879 | September 7, 1879 |
| Jones, Bill H. | Mitchell, Charlot | C/360 | July 5, 1886 | No Return |
| Jones, C. B. | Alexander, M. E. | C/460 | July 14, 1892 | July 17, 1892 |
| Jones, Celia Mrs. | Jones, Marion | B/88 | September 27, 1869 | September 27, 1869 |
| Jones, Christeney Miss | Brandon, S. S. | B/40 | February 15, 1867 | February 17, 1867 |
| Jones, Claudie | Burroughs, J. S. | D/19 | | December 14, 1882 |
| Jones, D. A. | Kirk, Miss Lucinda | B/80 | April 8, 1869 | April 9, 1869 |
| Jones, Dock | Winnett, Malissie | F/92 | August 7, 1896 | August 9, 1896 |
| Jones, E. J. Miss | Jones, J. J. | B/78 | January 30, 1869 | January 31, 1869 |
| Jones, Edith Miss | Grear, David | A/62 | May 1, 1843 | May 2, 1843 |
| Jones, Elizabeth C. | Youngblood, James H. | A/66 | December 21, 1843 | No Date |
| Jones, Elizabeth Miss | Grizzle, Isaac | A2/103 | October 14, 1867 | October 20, 1847 |
| Jones, Enoch | Burger, Mary | A2/31 | February 8, 1854 | February 8, 1854 |
| Jones, Eunice | Duggin, Thos. | C/74 | November 26, 1873 | November 27, 1863 |
| Jones, G. H. | Hare, Miss Nannie | B/94 | December 11, 1869 | December 15, 1869 |
| Jones, G. W. | Markins, A. E | C/402 | September 17, 1887 | September 18, 1887 |
| Jones, H. J. | Burger, W. O. | A2/94 | January 30, 1860 | No Return |
| Jones, Hannah J. | Freeman, Jake | C/66 | September 16, 1873 | September 22, 1873 |
| Jones, Harriett C. Miss | Stotts, Wm. | A2/47 | May 9, 1856 | No Return |
| Jones, Henry | Richardson, Roxanah | A2/145 | September 29, 1866 | September 30, 1866 |
| Jones, Ida | St. John, Lonnie | C/466 | October 13, 1892 | October 13, 1892 |
| Jones, J. | Youngblood, Amandy | C/170 | September 12, 1877 | September 15, 1877 |

| Groom or Bride | Groom or Bride | Book/Page | Date of License | Date of Marriage |
|---|---|---|---|---|
| Jones, J. A. | Higgins, Mollie | E/169 | April 13, 1889 | April 15, 1889 |
| Jones, J. F. | Davenport, A. L. | C/378 | December 25, 1886 | December 26, 1886 |
| Jones, J. F. | Jones, Mollie | F/24 | December 2, 1893 | No Return |
| Jones, J. J. | Jones, Miss E. J. | B/78 | January 30, 1869 | January 31, 1869 |
| Jones, J. L. | Knight, Betty | C/438 | July 3, 1891 | July 4, 1891 |
| Jones, James | Milligan, Geneva | C/422 | November 2, 1890 | November 2, 1890 |
| Jones, James | Mazy, Miss Harriett | A2/34 | August 31, 1854 | September 7, 1854 |
| Jones, James A. | Cox, Miss Celia | A2/135 | January 13, 1866 | January 13, 1866 |
| Jones, Jessie Herbert | Wright, Billie Calvin | E/41 | May 29, 1888 | May 29, 1888 |
| Jones, John | Martin, Elizabeth | A/67 | January 10, 1844 | January 12, 1844 |
| Jones, John | Cook, Miss Manerva | A/132 | January 19, 1850 | January 19, 1850 |
| Jones, John | Brown, Mary | C/396 | July 23, 1887 | July 24, 1887 |
| Jones, John E. | Jones, Miss Alabama | A/132 | February 19, 1850 | No Return |
| Jones, John H. | Gather, Sarah L. | A/2 | April 3, 1838 | April 3, 1838 |
| Jones, John M | McCow, Miss Martha | A/128 | November 9, 1849 | No Return |
| Jones, John M. | Spears, Elizabeth | D/5 | | October 6, 1881 |
| Jones, Josphene Miss | Lasiter, Richard | C/4 | August 2, 1871 | August 3, 1871 |
| Jones, July A. Miss | Bogle, Layfayette | A2/12 | October 1, 1851 | October 9, 1851 |
| Jones, Katharine Miss | Carter, James | A/91 | September 11, 1846 | September 11, 1846 |
| Jones, Kit (col.) | Thompson, Mary | C/308 | June 19, 1884 | No Return |
| Jones, L. C. | Smithson, Ida | C/470 | December 14, 1892 | December 15, 1892 |
| Jones, L. J. Miss | Gilley, T. F. | B/74 | December 8, 1868 | December 10, 1868 |
| Jones, Lafayette | Ellison, Miss Martha | B/104 | June 24, 1870 | June 26, 1870 |
| Jones, Laurah E. | Stone, James | D/3 | | September 7, 188 |
| Jones, Lizzie | Fisher, R. E. | E/152 | December 17, 1888 | December 17, 1888 |
| Jones, Lizzie Miss | Elkins, J. T. | E/12 | January 21, 1888 | ?? |
| Jones, M. E. | Gann, F. C. | D/19 | | December 21, 1882 |
| Jones, M. E. Miss | Hawkins, John | A2/26 | July 19, 1853 | July 21, 1853 |
| Jones, M. E. Miss | Laster, J. H. | B/128 | March 6, 1871 | No Return |
| Jones, M. J. | Ross, W. S. | C/118 | August 20, 1875 | August 22, 1875 |
| Jones, M. M. | Vandergriff, J. B. | F/24 | December 12, 1893 | December 17, 1893 |
| Jones, M. T. Miss | Bogle, L. F. | A2/38 | March 3, 1855 | No Return |
| Jones, Malinda | Peerce, James | A2/107 | February 26, 1863 | No Return |
| Jones, Margret | Martin, W. T. | B/116 | November 21, 1870 | November 23, 1870 |
| Jones, Marion | Jones, Mrs. Celia | B/88 | September 27, 1869 | September 27, 1869 |
| Jones, Martha Ann Miss | Wade, Wm. | A2/38 | February 5, 1855 | June 5, 1855 |
| Jones, Martha Jane Miss | Byrum, Redmon | A/35 | November 18, 1840 | November 23, 1840 |
| Jones, Martha R. | Powel, John H. | C/246 | March 26, 1880 | March 28, 1880 |
| Jones, Mary | Ellidge, Paompey | C/24 | February 29, 1872 | February 29, 1872 |
| Jones, Mary | Theirs, Isaac | A2/27 | August 4, 1853 | No Return |
| Jones, Mary | Elrod, S. H. | A2/104 | October 24, 1860 | No Return |
| Jones, Mary E. | Patrick, John J. | C/368 | September 28, 1886 | No Return |
| Jones, Mary E. Miss | Davenport, Thomas W. | A2/4 | August 20, 1850 | August 20, 1850 |
| Jones, Mary F. | Woods, B. F. | E/9 | January 21, 1888 | January 21, 1888 |
| Jones, Mary Miss | Martin, Richard B. | A2/5 | September 9, 1850 | September 9, 1850 |
| Jones, Mary Miss | Covington, W. C. | C/378 | December 22, 1886 | December 22, 1886 |

| Groom or Bride | Groom or Bride | Book/Page | Date of License | Date of Marriage |
|---|---|---|---|---|
| Jones, Mary Miss | Herriman, Wesley | C/4 | July 20, 1871 | July 21, 1871 |
| Jones, Mattie L. | Bennet, J. D. | C/14 | November 16, 1871 | November 16, 1871 |
| Jones, Melton | Markum, Bettie Dean | F/86 | March 3, 1896 | March 3, 1896 |
| Jones, Mennie | Davenport, Susan | F/2 | January 14, 1893 | No Return |
| Jones, Mollie | Jones, J. F. | F/24 | December 2, 1893 | No Return |
| Jones, Nancy | McKenny, Mike T. | C/306 | April 12, 1884 | April 12, 1884 |
| Jones, Nancy Ann | Wilcher, W. B. | C/448 | October 14, 1891 | October 15, 1891 |
| Jones, Nancy Miss | Nichols, W. B. | C/424 | December 17, 1890 | December 18, 1890 |
| Jones, Nancy C. Miss | King, R. A. | B/46 | June 26, 1867 | June 16, 1867 |
| Jones, Nancy P. Miss | Barrett, James P. | A2/145 | September 18, 1866 | September 18, 1866 |
| Jones, Pattie | Preston, Gent | C/274 | February 26, 1881 | No Return |
| Jones, Pinking | Vandergriph, Lucinda | A/21 | January 7, 1840 | No Return |
| Jones, R. B. | Davenport, S. L | C/462 | July 26, 1892 | July 26, 1892 |
| Jones, R. B. | McMahan, Dollie | F/48 | November 10, 1894 | November 11, 1894 |
| Jones, R. E. | Gunter, B. E. | F/50 | November 24, 1894 | December 9, 1894 |
| Jones, Robert M. | Hicks, Miss Elizabeth | A/52 | August 25, 1842 | |
| Jones, Roxanah | Worley, Isaac C. | B/82 | December 31, 1869 | December 31, 1869 |
| Jones, Rutha | Martin, Robert | C/136 | March 4, 1876 | March 5, 1876 |
| Jones, S. E. | Hawkins, Parelee | C/22 | February 8, 1872 | No Return |
| Jones, Samuel | Orand, Miss Margrett | A2/48 | May 13, 1856 | Handed in no return |
| Jones, Sarah | Smithson, David | C/150 | December 27, 1876 | December 28, 1876 |
| Jones, Sarah | Freeze, Hiram | A/75 | December 26, 1844 | December 26, 1844 |
| Jones, Sarah T. | Wimberly, Wm. A. | D/21 | | January 4, 1883 |
| Jones, Sarrah M. Miss | Bryson, James H. | A2/57 | September 7, 1857 | No Return |
| Jones, Serena | Webb, J. B. | F/140 | December 16, 1897 | December 17, 1897 |
| Jones, Susan | Davenport, John C. | A2/101 | September 1, 1860 | No Return |
| Jones, T. B. | Todd, Martha C. | C/60 | July 7, 1873 | No Return |
| Jones, Thomas E. | Gaither, Miss Elizabeht | A/65 | October 26, 1843 | October 26, 1843 |
| Jones, W. C. | Mingle, Miss Christeny | A2/66 | August 4, 1858 | August 4, 1858 |
| Jones, W. H. | Lorance, L. C. | F/128 | August 25, 1897 | August 25, 1897 |
| Jones, W. J. | Womack, Etta | C/418 | September 23, 1890 | September 28,1890 |
| Jones, Wm. F. | Summar, Miss Lula | F/56 | January 22, 1894 | No Return |
| Jonran, Lucinda Miss | Vosser, Wm | A2/16 | May 3, 1852 | May 4, 1852 |
| Jonsen, Margarett Miss | Barrett, Harm | A2/45 | December 22, 1855 | December 23, 1855 |
| Jordan, Barton (col.) | Lyons, Snow | F/158 | October 11, 1898 | October 11, 1898 |
| Jordan, E. L. Jr. | Barton, Lizzie | C/358 | May 5, 1886 | No Return |
| Jourdan, John | Thrower, Miss Fanny | A/64 | July 25, 1843 | No Return |
| Jurnigan, Edmund | Manous, Margaret | A2/131 | November 11, 1865 | November 12, 1865 |
| Justice, Alice | Watson, F. E. | C/78 | December 30, 1873 | December 30, 1873 |
| Justice, Andrew | Stroud, Mary D. | C/100 | November 12, 1874 | November 12, 1874 |
| Justice, Elen | Swindle, W. P. | C/308 | April 22, 1884 | April 22, 1884 |
| Justice, Fannie | Lance, E. P. | C/310 | August 2, 1884 | August 2, 1884 |
| Justice, H. A. | Daniel, Miss E. A. | A2/69 | November 4, 1858 | November 4, 1858 |
| Justice, J. M. | Pryor, Sinnie | C/302 | January 26, 1884 | No Return |
| Justice, J. W. | Wilson, Sarah | F/168 | January 21, 1899 | January 22, 1899 |

| Groom or Bride | Groom or Bride | Book/Page | Date of License | Date of Marriage |
|---|---|---|---|---|
| Justice, John B. | Warren, Miss Margarette Ann | A/113 | August 26, 1848 | September 5, 1848 |
| Justice, Kate | Kerr, Wm | C/186 | February 9, 1878 | February 10, 1878 |
| Justice, Laura Miss | Patton, Robert | E/85 | October 6, 1888 | October 8, 1888 |
| Justice, M. E. Miss | Graham, W. J. | A2/66 | August 19, 1858 | No Return |
| Justice, M. J. Miss | Graham, W. J. | B/106 | August 3, 1870 | August 7, 1870 |
| Justice, Robert N. | Rucker, Miss Elizabeth C. | A2/135 | January 16, 1866 | January 16, 1866 |
| Justice, S. C. Miss | Graham, R. M. | A2/78 | February 14, 1856 | February 14, 1856 |
| Justice, Sophia | Humble, L. D. | C/222 | August 10, 1879 | August 10, 1879 |
| Justice, Susan Miss | Elrod, A. T. | B/124 | January 12, 1871 | January 12, 1871 |
| Justice, W. E. | Elrod, Miss I. J. | A2/61 | December 23, 1857 | No Return |
| Justice, William J. | Preston, Mattie | E/182 | June 12, 1889 | June 12, 1889 |
| Keath, Etter Miss | Heelton, Calvin | B/126 | February 13, 1871 | February 13, 1871 |
| Keath, L. | Bowlin, Z. | C/62 | July 17, 1873 | July 20, 1873 |
| Keath, Sarah E. Miss | Beshers, Elijah | C/2 | May 24, 1871 | May 25, 1871 |
| Keaton, Alonzo | Dobbs, Clotie | F/122 | July 28, 1897 | No Return |
| Keaton, Catherine | Fuston, G. N | C/102 | December 12, 1874 | December 13, 1874 |
| Keaton, Charlotte Miss | Bogle, John | A/118 | December 21, 1848 | December 22, 1848 |
| Keaton, Elizabeth | Hammons, Jasper | A2/112 | March 17, 1864 | March 18, 1864 |
| Keaton, Gabriel | King, Mary A. | A2/120 | February 7, 1865 | February 7, 1865 |
| Keaton, H. L. | Davis, Miss Annie | B/124 | January 2?, 1871 | January 29, 1871 |
| Keaton, Henry | Distin, Miss Clarissa | A/91 | September 17, 1846 | September 20, 1846 |
| Keaton, Henry | McDarnell, Mallice | C/416 | September 15, 1890 | September 15, 1890 |
| Keaton, J. M. | Haley, S. J. | C/194 | July 25, 1878 | July 25, 1878 |
| Keaton, John | Fouston, Miss Ann | A/51 | July 12, 1842 | July 14, 1842 |
| Keaton, John | Turney, Nancy E. | C/56 | March 19, 1873 | March 20, 1873 |
| Keaton, Lee | Anderson, Martha | F/76 | November 23, 1895 | November 27, 1895 |
| Keaton, Mary P. | Collins, Jeremiah | A2/125 | August 6, 1865 | August 6, 1865 |
| Keaton, Peter N. J. | McGee, Miss Nancy T. A. | B/90 | October 4, 1869 | October 10, 1869 |
| Keaton, Saml | King, S. M. A. | C/96 | October 1, 1874 | October 1, 1874 |
| Keaton, T. B. Miss | King, Jacob K. | B/38 | January 12, 1867 | January 13, 1867 |
| Keaton, Tennessee A. | King, S. A. | C/120 | September 16, 1875 | September 16, 1875 |
| Keaton, Tom | Rogers, Susan | F/130 | September 13, 1897 | September 14, 1897 |
| Keaton, W. A. | Rigsby, Miss Fanny | C/424 | December 12, 1890 | December 14, 1890 |
| Keaton, W. T. | Ready, M. E. | C/20 | January 1, 1872 | January 4, 1872 |
| Keaton, William | King, Lillie | F/122 | July 30, 1897 | August 1, 1897 |
| Keel, J. W. | Hays, Miss Luisa | F/50 | November 28, 1894 | November 28, 1894 |
| Keel, Louisa Miss | Sherley, Luke | A2/84 | February 24, 1859 | February 24, 1859 |
| Keel, T. M. | Alexander, Miss E. | A2/51 | December 4, 1856 | No Return |
| Keele, Anderson | Mitchell, Mariah | B/10 | January 4, 1866? | January 4, 1867 |
| Keele, Andesen | Gullette, Mary | F/20 | October 28, 1893 | October 28, 1893 |
| Keele, C. W. | Travis, Mary | C/336 | September 16, 1885 | September 16, 1885 |
| Keele, Emma | Francis, Dalton | F/136 | November 17, 1897 | November 17, 1897 |
| Keele, Fanny | Thrower, Wm. T. | E/195 | July 27, 1889 | July 28, 1889 |
| Keele, James A. | Travis, Miss Sarah M. | A2/67 | September 16, 1858 | September 16, 1858 |
| Keele, James M. | Barnes, Laura | C/190 | April 3, 1874 | April 4, 1878 |

| Groom or Bride | Groom or Bride | Book/Page | Date of License | Date of Marriage |
|---|---|---|---|---|
| Keele, Joe (col.) | Dearley, Martha (col.) | F/90 | July 13, 1896 | July 14, 1896 |
| Keele, Margaret J. Miss | Mullin, John H. | A2/146 | October 15, 1866 | October 15, 1866 |
| Keele, Mary E. | Bragg, Thomas | C/350 | January 19, 1886 | January 19, 1886 |
| Keele, Sarah J. | Fugitt, Nath | D/22 | | January 18, 1883 |
| Keele, Sarah Miss | Nichol, Joseph | A/106 | December 21, 1847 | December 22, 1847 |
| Keele, Thomas | Kuykenday | A2/131 | November 14, 1865 | November 16, 1865 |
| Keele, Thomas | Barnes, Rachal | C/190 | April 3, 1878 | April 4, 1878 |
| Keely, Harriett Miss | Gannon, Wm. H. | A2/90 | November 5, 1859 | November 8, 1859 |
| Keeny, James | Cummings, Miss Cyrena | A/63 | July 18, 1843 | July 20, 1843 |
| Keeny, R. A. | Bogle, Miss Sarah A. | A2/59 | November 4, 1857 | November 4, 1857 |
| Kees, Erasmus S. | Macey, Miss Elizabeth | A/66 | December 13, 1843 | Not Executed |
| Keetan, William | Fuston, Miss Elizabeth | A2/76 | March 17, 1855 | March 20, 1855 |
| Keeton, D. Jan | Herenden, Joseph B. | C/344 | December 8, 1885 | December 10, 1885 |
| Keeton, Eliza A. | Bogle, W. M. | D/14 | | August 10, 1882 |
| Keeton, Elizabeth | Fuston, Josiah | A2/48 | May 19, 1856 | May 19, 1856 |
| Keeton, H. A. | King, A. C. | C/362 | August 13, 1886 | No Return |
| Keith, Mary | Wade, Enoch | C/416 | September 3, 1890 | September 2, 1890 |
| Keeton, James | Sryson, Susan | E/199 | August 14, 1889 | August 15, 1889 |
| Keeton, L. J. | Keeton, S. M. | E/224 | October 22, 1889 | October 24, 1889 |
| Keeton, M. E. | Bogle, F. P. | C/326 | February 26, 1885 | March 1, 1885 |
| Keeton, Mary Malissa | Hale, Thomas | A2/111 | January 19, 1864 | January 21, 1864 |
| Keeton, Nancy A. | Oneal, W. J. | D/21 | | January 15, 1883 |
| Keeton, Robert | Keith, Miss Luiza | A2/19 | August 30, 1852 | August 30, 1852 |
| Keeton, S. M. | Keeton, L. J. | E/224 | October 22, 1889 | October 24, 1889 |
| Keeton, Sam | King, N. E. J. | F/108 | January 1, 197 | January 3, 1897 |
| Keeton, Sarah J. Miss | King, A. | A2/14 | February 2, 1852 | February 6, 1852 |
| Keeton, Wm. | Gardener, Virginia | C/370 | October 11, 1886 | October 13, 1886 |
| Keile, Samm | Brewer, Fannie | C/318 | November 2, 1884 | November 2, 1884 |
| Keith, John | Alexander, Sissie | E/88 | October 17, 1888 | October 18, 1888 |
| Keith, Luiza Miss | Keeton, Robert | A2/19 | August 30, 1852 | August 30, 1852 |
| Keith, Nancy | Mathews, Nathan | A/26 | March 26, 1840 | March 31, 1840 |
| Kell, Louisa Miss | Shirley, Luk | A2/72 | February 21, 1859 | February 24, 1859 |
| Kell, Rebeca C. | Bell, W. W. | A2/34 | August 16, 1854 | August 16, 1854 |
| Kelley, Minty | Summar, J. J. | C/322 | January 24, 1885 | January 25, 1885 |
| Kelley, Mota | Rich, Marcus | F/130 | September 2, 1897 | September 5, 1897 |
| Kelly, B. A. | Ward, S. J. | C/194 | July 25, 1878 | July 28, 1878 |
| Kelly, Jacob A. | Patrick, Laura Ann | A/54 | September 20, 1842 | September 26, 1842 |
| Kelly, Reepes P. | Odom, Miss N. M. | A2/8 | December 23, 1850 | No Return |
| Kelly, Sary Ann Miss | Higgins, Eligah | A2/25 | May 28, 1853 | May 28, 1853 |
| Kelly, William B. | King, Miss Lucinda | A/96 | January 13, 1847 | January 14, 1847 |
| Kelton, Sarah M. E. Miss | Lorance, Michael | B/96 | December 20, 1869 | December 21, 1869 |
| Kenedy, Annie | Flower, Willie | C/366 | September 18, 1886 | No Return |
| Kenedy, Estella | Fuston, S. A. | C/240 | January 27, 1880 | January 29, 1880 |
| Kenedy, H. H. | Byrn, Susan | C/228 | October 1, 1879 | October 1, 1879 |
| Kenedy, J. H. | Bogle, Miss Lela | F/174 | April 3, 1899 | No Return |
| Kenedy, John M. | Patterson, Nettie | C/428 | January 6, 1891 | January 11, 1891 |

| Groom or Bride | Groom or Bride | Book/Page | Date of License | Date of Marriage |
|---|---|---|---|---|
| Kennady, Frances M. Miss | Spidle, R. S. | A2/48 | June 15, 1856 | June 16, 1856 |
| Kennedy, B. L. Miss | Wharton, W. T. H. | A2/53 | January 24, 1857 | No Return |
| Kennedy, J. W. | Bethell, Miss Lydia H. | B/76 | January 12, 1869 | January 14, 1869 |
| Kennedy, Josie Miss | Ritch, Rufus | B/126 | February 21, 1871 | February 23, 1871 |
| Kennedy, L. K. | Stephens, J. W. | C/110 | March 24, 1875 | March 28, 1875 |
| Kennedy, M. A. | Tolbert, Miss Elizabeth B. | A/126 | September 7, 1849 | No Return |
| Kennedy, M. A. Miss | Garrison, C. B. | B/56 | November 23, 1867 | November 25, 1867 |
| Kennedy, W. C. | Thomas, Julie | D/13 | | April 25, 1882 |
| Kennedy, Zula | Odom, Bogine | C/420 | October 24, 1890 | No Return |
| Kenser, Rebecca Ann | Barret, James P. | A2/123 | May 5, 1865 | May 7, 1865 |
| Kep, Charley | Ferbush, Lizzie | C/464 | September 1, 1892 | September 1, 1892 |
| Kerby, Elizabeth | Tucker, Jack | C/40 | September 26, 1872 | September 26, 1872 |
| Kerby, Mitita | Meanis, John | A/3 | May 14, 1838 | June 10, 1838 |
| Kerby, Sarah A. | Guy, A. J. | C/48 | December 27, 1872 | No Return |
| Kerby, R. S. | Young, Sarah D. | C/330 | March 28, 1885 | No Return |
| Kerklin, E. J. Miss | Williams, John B. | A2/60 | November 23, 1857 | November 23, 1857 |
| Kerklin, Isaac | Daraberry, Miss Cindy R. | A2/24 | September 27, 1852 | November 27, 1852 |
| Kerr, Wm | Justice, Kate | C/186 | February 9, 1878 | February 10, 1878 |
| Kersey, Elizabeth Miss | Tate, Jacob B. | A2/13 | December 30, 1851 | January 3, 1852 |
| Kersey, Luan Miss | Smithson, William C. | A/131 | December 21, 1849 | December 23, 1849 |
| Kersey, Mary J. | Conley, John | A2/129 | September 21, 1865 | September 21, 1865 |
| Kersey, Sarryan | Gunter, William | A2/30 | December 10, 1853 | No Return |
| Kersey, Thaney Miss | Patterson, Enoch | A/82 | July 26, 1845 | July 27, 1845 |
| Kersey, Virginia Miss | Gunter, Claiborne Y. | A/91 | September 27, 1846 | September 28, 1846 |
| Kersy, Eathcindy | Mason, John | A2/103 | October 22, 1860 | No Return |
| Kertz, Katharine Miss | Prator, J. C. | A2/51 | December 3, 1856 | No Return |
| Keter, Issabella Elizbeth Ann Miss | Fagan, Albert T. | A/48 | March 19, 1842 | March 19, 1842 |
| Keth, Nervie A. | Wade, Wm | D/101 | | January 30, 1882 |
| Keyton, George H. | Lanier, Rebeca E. | A2/11 | October 8, 1851 | October 9, 1851 |
| Kincaid, Nancy | Bradberry, Cullen | A/12 | March 23, 1839 | March 24, 1839 |
| Kincaid, Thomas | Cummins, Miss Elizabeth | A2/6 | September 5, 1850 | September 6, 1850 |
| King, N. E. J. | Keeton, Sam | F/108 | January 1, 197 | January 3, 1897 |
| King, A. | Keeton, Miss Sarah J. | A2/14 | February 2, 1852 | February 6, 1852 |
| King, A. C. | Keeton, H. A. | C/362 | August 13, 1886 | No Return |
| King, A. J. Miss | Scoot, J. M. | F/78 | December 30, 1895 | December 30, 1895 |
| King, Alamenta | Vandergriff, Alexander | A/1 | March 20, 1838 | March 27, 1838 |
| King, Annie | Campbell, John D. | F/130 | September 16, 1897 | September 19, 1897 |
| King, Anthen | Reed, Wm. | C/286 | July 24, 1883 | July 24, 1883 |
| King, B. A. | Patton, Mattie J. | C/62 | July 14, 1873 | July 16, 1873 |
| King, Betsy | Duke, Gideon | A/24 | February 12, 1840 | February 13, 1840 |
| King, Della | Dennis, R. A. | F/28 | January 15, 1894 | January 18, 1894 |
| King, Edna | George, John | F/128 | September 1, 1897 | September 1, 1897 |
| King, Edney B | Moss, W. H. | C/314 | September 17, 1884 | September 17, 1884 |
| King, Emeline | Campbell, J. D. | C/416 | September 13, 1890 | September 14, 1890 |
| King, George | Pealer, Miss Katharine | A/102 | August 21, 1847 | August 24, 1847 |

| Groom or Bride | Groom or Bride | Book/Page | Date of License | Date of Marriage |
|---|---|---|---|---|
| King, Hence (col.) | Wiley, Ida (col.) | D/9 | | December 25, 1881 |
| King, Ida | Murry, Frank | E/38 | May 19, 1888 | May 19, 1888 |
| King, J. A. | Hancock, Caroline | A2/95 | February 20, 1860 | No Return |
| King, J. D. | Raikes, Mary | C/444 | August 20, 1891 | Augus 22, 1891 |
| King, J. J. | King, Miss M. A. | B/40 | February 19, 1867 | February 21, 1867 |
| King, Jacob A. | Williams, Miss Luraney | A2/92 | October 21, 1867 | October 21, 1867 |
| King, Jacob K. | Keaton, Miss T. B. | B/38 | January 12, 1867 | January 1ᴗ 1867 |
| King, James | Hutchin, Salley | D/101 | | January 22, 1882 |
| King, James H. H. | Mathis, Ibby Elizabeth | A2/102 | September 12, 1860 | No Return |
| King, Jno. E. | Stroud, Mariah | C/64 | August 2, 1873 | August 3, 1873 |
| King, John M. | Barratt, Lucy | C/146 | September 30, 1876 | October 1, 1876 |
| King, Lidy P. | Knight, Joel A. | C/20 | December 28, 1871 | December 28, 1871 |
| King, Lillie | Keaton, William | F/122 | July 30, 1897 | August 1, 1897 |
| King, Lucinda Miss | Kelly, William B. | A/96 | January 13, 1847 | January 14, 1847 |
| King, Lyda Miss | Knight, W. J. | A2/79 | July 7, 1856 | July 10, 1856 |
| King, M. A. Miss | King, J. J. | B/40 | February 19, 1867 | February 21, 1867 |
| King, M. E. | Bogle, N. S. | C/68 | October 11, 1873 | October 19, 1873 |
| King, M. S. | Hailey, J. M. | C/82 | February 6, 1874 | February 11, 1874 |
| King, Maggie | Higgins, J. H. | C/338 | October 4, 1885 | October 6, 1885 |
| King, Margaret E. Miss | Cooper, J. A. | B/84 | August 27, 1869 | August 27, 1869 |
| King, Martin | Williams, Miss Sarah | A/108 | February 25, 1848 | February 25, 1848 |
| King, Martha A. | Womack, James M. | C/210 | January 25, 1879 | January 26, 1879 |
| King, Mary A. | Keaton, Gabriel | A2/120 | February 7, 1865 | February 7, 1865 |
| King, Mary F. | Bynum, John | D/2 | | July 31, 1881 |
| King, Mollie | Gann, Richard | E/165 | May 25, 1889 | May 26, 1889 |
| King, Nancy | Carrick, James | D/7 | | December 8, 1881 |
| King, Nancy C. | Watson, Joseph T. | C/214 | March 5, 1879 | March 5, 1879 |
| King, Nancy E. Miss | McGee, Jesse | A/115 | October 19, 1848 | October 19, 1848 |
| King, Nancy E. Miss | Dodd, James H. | A2/24 | January 5, 1853 | January 5, 1853 |
| King, Nora | Stanley, B. M. | C/436 | May 29, 1891 | May 30, 1891 |
| King, R. A. | Jones, Miss Nancy C. | B/46 | June 26, 1867 | June 16, 1867 |
| King, R. P. Miss | Young, P. A. | C/412 | December 13, 1887 | December 15, 1887 |
| King, S. A. | Keaton, Tennessee A. | C/120 | September 16, 1875 | September 16, 1875 |
| King, S. M. A. | Keaton, Saml | C/96 | October 1, 1874 | October 1, 1874 |
| King, Sampson J. | Parton, Nancy A. | A2/124 | July 21, 1865 | July 21, 1865 |
| King, W. B. | Gunter, Ella | F/52 | December 11, 1894 | No Return |
| King, W. J. | Mason, Anthon | C/172 | September 27, 1877 | September 30, 1877 |
| King, W. J. | Haley, M. C. | C/200 | September 26, 1878 | September 26, 1878 |
| King, W. L. | Grooms, Allice | C/298 | December 1, 1883 | December 2, 1884 |
| King, William | Pealer, Miss Sally | A/129 | December 12, 1849 | December 12, 1849 |
| King, William J. | Bogle, Miss Martha E. | A2/147 | November 1, 1866 | November 1, 1866 |
| King, Wm | Barrett, E. L. | E/102 | November 20, 1888 | November 20, 1888 |
| King, Wm. | Moon, Miss Nancy | A2/45 | December 17, 1855 | December 17, 1855 |
| King, Wm. M. | Markum, Nancy L. | C/76 | December 13, 1873 | December 14, 1873 |
| Kinnamon, Nelly Miss | Enos, Henry | A/115 | October 12, 1848 | October 12, 1848 |
| Kipp, G. B. | Dickens, Miss Nancy M. A. | A2/61 | January 5, 1857 | No Return |

| Groom or Bride | Groom or Bride | Book/Page | Date of License | Date of Marriage |
|---|---|---|---|---|
| Kirby, Ada | Bethel, J. L. | C/100 | November 18, 1874 | November 19, 1874 |
| Kirby, Bud | Stone, Jose | C/114 | June 19, 1875 | June 20, 1875 |
| Kirby, Ellen | Wilson, John A | C/440 | July 22, 1891 | July 23, 1891 |
| Kirby, J. R. | Rich, N. N. | F/64 | June 26, 1895 | June 27, 1895 |
| Kirby, James | Campbell, Mattie | E/67 | September 28, 1888 | September 30, 1888 |
| Kirby, James | Campbell, Mattie | E/84 | September 28, 1888 | September 28, 1888 |
| Kirby, Julena Miss | Sutten, Lavender | A2/47 | March 15, 1856 | March 16, 1856 |
| Kirby, R. Miss | St. John, George | A2/43 | November 27, 1855 | November 27, 1855 |
| Kirby, R. S. | Elam, Jackline | C/226 | October 9, 1879 | October 9, 1879 |
| Kirby, Robt. S. | Smithson, Sarah J. | C/12 | October 4, 1871 | No Return |
| Kirby, Thos. | Powell | A2/116 | October 12, 1864 | October 12, 1864 |
| Kirk, E. Miss | St. John, John | A2/88 | August 31, 1859 | No Return |
| Kirk, Lucinda Miss | Jones, D. A. | B/80 | April 8, 1869 | April 9, 1869 |
| Kirk, Sarah B. Miss | Holland, John | A2/135 | January 3, 1866 | January 18, 1866 |
| Kirkland, J. H. | Davenport, Nancy | C/336 | September 1, 1885 | September 1, 1885 |
| Kirsey, Ethalinda Miss | Evans, Lemuel D. | A2/4 | August 27, 1850 | August 27, 1850 |
| Kirsey, Frances Miss | Braton, Wm | A2/35 | September 13, 1854 | September 13, 1854 |
| Kittrell, Elen | Bragg, George | F/144 | January 12, 1898 | January 12, 1898 |
| Kittrell, George | Stewart, Miss Caroline | B/56 | December 4, 1867 | December 5, 1867 |
| Kittrell, J. J. | Bragg, Miss M. E. | F/48 | November 7, 1894 | November 7, 1894 |
| Kittrell, Prudie Miss | Rushing, H. B. | B/100 | March 2, 1870 | March 2, 1870 |
| Knapper, John | Cawthers, Mahaley | C/214 | March 1, 1879 | March 2, 1879 |
| Knight, Betty | Jones, J. L. | C/438 | July 3, 1891 | July 4, 1891 |
| Knight, Druzila | Peden, John R. | C/258 | October 10, 1880 | October 10, 1880 |
| Knight, Francis | Stoner, Burr | F/20 | October 19, 1893 | October 22, 1893 |
| Knight, James | Ase, Miss Sarah Ann | A2/63 | March 4, 1858 | March 4, 1858 |
| Knight, James M. | Thomas, Miss Sarah | A/119 | January 22, 1849 | No Return |
| Knight, Jessemin | Hicks, Elizabeth M. | A2/43 | October 28, 1855 | October ??, 1855 |
| Knight, Joel A. | King, Lidy P. | C/20 | December 28, 1871 | December 28, 1871 |
| Knight, John | Barkley, Lidia | C/376 | November 23, 1886 | November 24, 1886 |
| Knight, Liddie | Bryson, Daniel | C/90 | May 26, 1874 | No Return |
| Knight, Lou Miss | Dodd, J. J. | C/458 | April 26, 1892 | April 28, 1892 |
| Knight, Magnola | Hale, J. P. | F/8 | April 18, 1893 | April 19, 1893 |
| Knight, Mary F. | Derting, S. L. | C/246 | March 26,1880 | March 28, 1880 |
| Knight, Veer | Hayes, J. A. | F | February 9, 1893 | |
| Knight, W. J. | King, Miss Lyda | A2/79 | July 7, 1856 | July 10, 1856 |
| Knott, R. F. | McBroom, Miss Fannie | C/2 | June 3, 1871 | June 4, 1871 |
| Know, Jeff | Reed, Mary M. | F/2 | February 4, 1893 | No Return |
| Know, Martha P. Miss | Fox, James M. | A2/136 | January 19, 1866 | January 23, 1866 |
| Know, Mary Miss | Cramner, Robert | B/8 | November ??, 1870 | No Return |
| Know, Mell | Tompkins, Ella | F/24 | December 9, 1893 | December 9, 1893 |
| Know, N. A. Miss | Reed, G. L. | E/236 | November 30, 1889 | December 1, 1889 |
| Know, P. Miss | Ford, Orvell H. | A2/127 | September 14, 1865 | September 21, 1865 |
| Know, S. E. | Hatherly, J. R. | D/2 | | August 2, 1881 |
| Knox, Ada | Conley, Thoomas | F/104 | December 1, 1896 | December 2, 1896 |
| Knox, Elijah S. | Gaither, Miss Angeline | A/124 | August 2, 1849 | August 2, 1849 |

| Groom or Bride | Groom or Bride | Book/Page | Date of License | Date of Marriage |
|---|---|---|---|---|
| Knox, Emeline | Elkins, W. J. | D/8 | | December 16, 1881 |
| Knox, Emma | Elroy, A. B. | C/418 | September 29, 1890 | No Return |
| Knox, Issabell Ann R. | Lyon, Nathan J. | A/56 | December 7, 1842 | December 8, 1842 |
| Knox, J. B. | Carnahan, Loe | C/376 | December 20, 1886 | December 22, 1886 |
| Knox, J. F. | Thomason, A. J. | F/144 | January 26, 1898 | January 30, 1898 |
| Knox, J. R. | Peay, Miss R. A. | A2/135 | January 14, 1866 | January 15, 1866 |
| Knox, James B. | Cox, Miss Salina Jane | A/132 | January 5, 1850 | January 16, 1850 |
| Knox, Jennie Miss | Whitfield, A. J. | F/176 | May 13, 1899 | No Return |
| Knox, Joe | Reed, Mollie | F/134 | October 6, 1897 | October 6, 1897 |
| Knox, Joe A. | Morgan, Elizabeth | A2/113 | April 22, 1864 | April 24, 1864 |
| Knox, John G. | Smith, Miss Elizabeth | B/64 | March 19, 1868 | March 22, 1868 |
| Knox, L. G. | McMiller, Martha J. | C/162 | May 12, 1877 | May 13, 1877 |
| Knox, Leroy | Lasiter, Bettie | C/266 | December 4, 1880 | No Return |
| Knox, M. A. | Todd, L. C. | C/238 | January 13, 1880 | January 14, 1880 |
| Knox, Margrett | McMillan, John | C/172 | October 9, 1 877 | October 10, 1877 |
| Knox, Marinda M. M. | Laseter, Luke | A/9 | December 19, 1838 | December 19, 1838 |
| Knox, Mary Jane E. Miss | Hoover, Henry W. | A/106 | January 3, 1848 | January 6, 1848 |
| Knox, Mollie Miss | St. John, J. M. | C/378 | December 23, 1886 | December 23, 1886 |
| Knox, Nancy C. Miss | Dunn, Wm. J. | A/108 | February 14, 1848 | February 17, 1848 |
| Knox, R. P. | McGil, M. J. | C/368 | September 23, 1886 | September 26, 1886 |
| Knox, S. A. | Irvin, Myrtle | E/204 | September 3, 1889 | September 3, 1889 |
| Knox, S. J. Miss | Moon, C. T. | A2/78 | March 3, 1856 | March 4, 1856 |
| Knox, S. W. | MeDow, Miss Nancy E. | A2/48 | May 15, 1856 | No Return |
| Knox, Sophiz E. Miss | McCrary, Arthur | A/71 | August 16, 1844 | August 19, 1844 |
| Knox, Syntha E. Miss | Ownby, E. D. | B/60 | January 9, 1868 | January 9, 1868 |
| Knox, Thomas | Luster, Disey | B/10 | June 21, 1867 | June 21, 1867 |
| Knox, William | Cooper, Miss Mary C. | A2/50 | August 30, 1856 | No Return |
| Knox, William A. | Todd, Miss Nancy J. | A/127 | September 15, 1849 | September ?, 1849 |
| Kurkendall, Cyntha L. Miss | Kurkendall, Simon | A2/43 | October 18, 1855 | October 19, 1855 |
| Kurkendall, Simon | Kurkendall, Miss Cyntha L. | A2/43 | October 18, 1855 | October 19, 1855 |
| Kuykendall, Easter J. Miss | Curtis, Silas R. | A/94 | December 22, 1846 | December 22, 1846 |
| Kuykendall, Jacob | Fowler, Miss Nancy | A2/33 | June 6, 1854 | No Return |
| Kuykendall, Norris | Beaty, Mary | A/75 | December 3, 1844 | December 3, 1844 |
| Kuykendall, Telitha F. Miss | Williams, John | A2/138 | February 21, 1866 | February 23, 1866 |
| Kuykenday | Keele, Thomas | A2/131 | November 14, 1865 | November 16, 1865 |
| Lackey, Sarah | Moore, Joseph | A/18 | October 8, 1839 | October 8, 1839 |
| Lackey, William R. | Nancy M. McKnight | A/18 | October 19, 1839 | October 24, 1839 |
| Lafever, Wm. | Cummins, Bettie | D/1 | | July 14, 1881 |
| Lafevers, Bettie Miss | Todd, Wm. F. | E/89 | October 17, 1888 | October 17, 1888 |
| Lafevers, John | Gunter, Noley | C/250 | July 10, 1880 | July 11, 1880 |
| Lafevers, M. A. | Tenpeny, J. H. | F/30 | January 18, 1894 | No Return |
| Lafevers, Laura | Smithson, C. C. | C/430 | February 19, 1891 | February 19, 1891 |
| Lafevers, Mamie | Campbell, W. T. | F/142 | December 26, 1897 | December 26, 1897 |
| Lafevers, Maud | West, Thomas | F/6 | March 29, 1893 | April 2, 1983 |
| Lafevers, R. S. | Sullivan, Marthy A. | A2/55 | May 28, 1857 | May 28, 1857 |
| Lafevers, Sallie | Gann, Robert | C/54 | February 21, 1873 | February 21, 1873 |

| Groom or Bride | Groom or Bride | Book/Page | Date of License | Date of Marriage |
|---|---|---|---|---|
| Lafevers, Sary Miss | Bowers, Francis | A2/73 | March 8, 1859 | No Return |
| Lafevers, Sary Miss | Bowers, Francis | A2/84 | March 8, 1859 | March 10, 1859 |
| Lafevers, Wm. J. | McCabe, Miss Marry J. | A2/25 | April 12, 1853 | No Return |
| Lakew, J. G. | Herndon, Miss M. M. | B/34 | December 17, 1866 | December 19, 1866 |
| Lamb, John K. | Hatfield, Margrett | C/140 | July 1, 1876 | July 2, 1876 |
| Lamberson, Chris | Jetton, William | C/448 | October 24, 1891 | October 25, 1891 |
| Lambert, A. J. | Daughtry, H. B. | C/174 | October 23, 1877 | October 26, 1877 |
| Lambert, David | Laseter, Purity | A/17 | September 4, 1839 | September 4, 1839 |
| Lambert, David | Underwood, Mary | A2/110 | July 18, 1863 | No Return |
| Lambert, Elizabeth Miss | Reed, John | A/132 | February 14, 1850 | February 14, 1850 |
| Lambert, J. E. | Burgett, Miss Martha A. | A2/46 | March ?, 1856 | March 2, 1856 |
| Lambert, Linda Miss | Herrall, Joseph | C/464 | September 3, 1892 | September 4, 1892 |
| Lambert, Martha B | Hollis, W. J. | F/162 | December 10, 1898 | December 11, 1898 |
| Lambert, Martha B. | Hollis, W. J. | E/354 | December 10, 1898 | |
| Lambert, Robert | Bush, Barbery | C/124 | December 6, 1875 | December 12, 1876 |
| Lamberth, Anderson | Bush, Rebecca Anne | A/32 | August 26, 1840 | August 27, 1840 |
| Lamberth, David | Wron, Elizabeth | A/30 | June 17, 1840 | June 18, 1840 |
| Lamberth, Harrison H. | Lamberth, Miss Ney | A/98 | February 17, 1847 | February 18, 1847 |
| Lamberth, James | Patton, Margaret F. | A/4 | July 31, 1838 | July 31, 1838 |
| Lamberth, Ney Miss | Lamberth, Harrison H. | A/98 | February 17, 1847 | February 18, 1847 |
| Lambirth, Mary Ann | Bush, Uriah | A/15 | July 22, 1839 | July 22, 1839 |
| Lambuth, Mary Ann Miss | Reed, Hugh | A/111 | May 15, 1848 | May 17, 1848 |
| Lamlet, James | Grimes, Nancy | C/284 | June 7, 1883 | June 7, 1883 |
| Lance, Catharine Miss | Milligan, John | B/102 | June 2, 1870 | June 8, 1870 |
| Lance, E. | Perry, Miss Lillie | F/170 | February 21, 1899 | February 22, 1899 |
| Lance, E. P. | Justice, Fannie | C/310 | August 2, 1884 | August 2, 1884 |
| Lance, Frances E. | Fowler, James M. | B/74 | December 7, 1868 | December 7, 1868 |
| Lance, J. A. | Miller, J. J. | D/14 | | August 27, 1882 |
| Lance, J. L. | Thompson, Miss M. J. | A2/69 | November 10, 1858 | November 11, 1858 |
| Lance, J. M. | Webb, Anni | C/374 | November 10, 1886 | November 11, 1886 |
| Lance, James | Thomas, Nancy | D/101 | | February 12, 1882 |
| Lance, James P. K. | Gunter, Miss Mary | B/54 | October 5, 1867 | October 6, 1867 |
| Lance, Jas. R. | Melton, Martha M. | C/66 | September 1, 1873 | September 2, 1873 |
| Lance, John | Litrell, Miss Sarah | A/42 | October 13, 1841 | October 15, 1841 |
| Lance, Joseph | Hutchins, Miss Sarah Ann | A/99 | May 3, 1847 | May 3, 1847 |
| Lance, Lockey Jane Miss | Hart, David Massan | A2/77 | January 15, 1856 | January 17, 1856 |
| Lance, Manerva Miss | Barrett, John W. | A2/1 | March 14, 1850 | March 14, 1850 |
| Lance, Mary Jane | Owen, J. J. | F/134 | October 6, 1897 | October 7, 1897 |
| Lance, N. L. J. | Merritt, B. M. | C/134 | February 26, 1876 | February 28, 1876 |
| Lance, Paralee | Phillips, J. H. | C/108 | February 10, 1875 | February 11, 1875 |
| Lance, Polly Miss | Elam, Reuben | A/66 | December 24, 1843 | December 27, 1843 |
| Lance, R. L. | Ervin, Wm. | C/94 | September 16, 1874 | September 19, 1874 |
| Lance, S. H. | Winnett, Miss Jennie | F/88 | May 8, 1896 | May 10, 1896 |
| Lance, Sarah | Tittle, S. C. | C/140 | July 29, 1876 | July 30, 1876 |
| Lance, Sarah L. | Wallace W. H. | C/342 | December 5, 1885 | December 6, 1885 |
| Lance, Wm. H. | Millar, Miss Sarrah M. | A2/58 | October 3, 1857 | October 7, 1857 |

| Groom or Bride | Groom or Bride | Book/Page | Date of License | Date of Marriage |
|---|---|---|---|---|
| Land, Lular | Cummings, John M. | C/298 | December 28, 1883 | December 28, 1883 |
| Landan, J. A. C. | Jernigan, M. L. | D/10 | | December 29, 1881 |
| Landsden, John | Mickey, Mary | B/12 | September 13, 1867 | September 14, 1867 |
| Lane, Miss Sibie | Parker, Jarrett | F/82 | February 1, 1896 | February 2, 1896 |
| Lane, Olive | Green, James C. | A/1 | March 8, 1838 | March 9, 1838 |
| Lane, Will | Parker, Nannie | F/80 | January 3, 1896 | January 5, 1896 |
| Laner, Lee | Campbell, Hallie | C/466 | October 17, 1892 | October 17, 1892 |
| Laner, Nancy S. | Hart, James M. | A2/45 | December 12, 1855 | December 13, 1855 |
| Lang, Margarett | Barrett, James | A2/81 | March 1, 1858 | March 1, 1858 |
| Lanier, Charles B. | Melton, Miss Eliza | A2/35 | September 20, 1854 | September 21, 1854 |
| Lanier, James H. | Edwards, Miss Nancy | A2/68 | October 21, 1858 | October 21, 1858 |
| Lanier, Rebeca E. | Keyton, George H. | A2/11 | October 8, 1851 | October 9, 1851 |
| Lanier, Wm. J. | Cooper, Miss Rutha | A2/68 | October 14, 1858 | No Return |
| Lansden, Sarah P. Miss | Donnelle, William C. | A/97 | February 8, 1847 | February 23, 1847 |
| Lansden, Susan C. | Smith, Zachariah | A/74 | November 9, 1844 | No Return |
| Lansley, Issabella Miss | Mitchel, Nile A. | A2/4 | August 8, 1850 | August 8, 1850 |
| Larance, Sarah J. | Travis, S. D. | A2/93 | December 29, 1859 | No Return |
| Larrence, Allie | Mason, J. T. | C/416 | September 6, 1890 | September 7, 1890 |
| Larx, L. J. | Owen, F. J. | E/218 | October 9, 1889 | October 10, 1889 |
| Lasater, Cinderella Miss | Derryberry, Jacob | A/114 | September 29, 1848 | October 1, 1848 |
| Lasater, Luke | Hollis, Miss Lamira L. | A/116 | November 7, 1848 | November 7, 1848 |
| Lasater, Mary Elizabeth Miss | Stacy, James F. | A/88 | March 30, 1846 | March 30, 1846 |
| Lasater, Nancy Ann | Tabour, Nathan C. (Talor) | A/77 | February 26, 1845 | February 26, 1845 |
| Lasater, Purity Miss | Simmons, William | A/47 | January 24, 1842 | January 25, 1842 |
| Laseter, Angeline | Good, Wm | A2/12 | November 11, 1851 | November 21, 1851 |
| Laseter, Hardy | Clemments, Sarah | A/7 | October 3, 1838 | October 3, 1838 |
| Laseter, J. H. | Saffle, Miss M. A. | B/78 | March 10, 1869 | March 11, 1869 |
| Laseter, Luke | Knox, Marinda M. M. | A/9 | December 19, 1838 | December 19, 1838 |
| Laseter, Mariah Miss | York, Jonathan | B/62 | February 12, 1868 | February 16, 1868 |
| Laseter, Mary | Bivens, Alford | C/12 | October 5, 1871 | No Return |
| Laseter, Mary E. | McBroom, Henry | C/160 | April 17, 1877 | April 17, 1877 |
| Laseter, Mary Miss | Reed, James | B/88 | February 17, 1869 | May 18, 1869 |
| Laseter, Nancy E. | Youree, G. C. | A2/94 | February 1, 1860 | No Return |
| Laseter, Peyton | Bowen, Miss Mary Frances | A2/143 | August 16, 1866 | August 17, 1866 |
| Laseter, Purity | Lambert, David | A/17 | September 4, 1839 | September 4, 1839 |
| Lasiter, Ann | Todd, J. D. | F/106 | December 17, 1896 | December 23, 1896 |
| Lasiter, Bettie | Knox, Leroy | C/266 | December 4, 1880 | No Return |
| Lasiter, F. E. Miss | Youree, G. C. | C/456 | March 1, 1892 | No Return |
| Lasiter, J. B. | Gunter, Miss Margarett | B/68 | July 25, 1868 | July 29, 1868 |
| Lasiter, J. B. | Merritt, Miss Sarah | B/100 | March 18, 1870 | No Return |
| Lasiter, J. L. | Allman, Polema | F/128 | August 25, 1897 | August 29, 1897 |
| Lassiter, Lou | MissHoweton, Jas A. | C/458 | May 25, 1892 | May 22, 1892 |
| Lasiter, Maggie | Bottom, Andrew | C/402 | September 22, 1887 | September 22, 1887 |
| Lasiter, Minnie | Reed, James | F/176 | May 9, 1899 | May 10, 1899 |
| Lasiter, N. B. | Hollis, J. B. | F/4 | July 18, 1893 | February 19, 1893 |
| Lasiter, Peyton | Bowen, Miss Mary Frances | A2/142 | August 16, 1866 | August 17, 1866 |

| Groom or Bride | Groom or Bride | Book/Page | Date of License | Date of Marriage |
|---|---|---|---|---|
| Lasiter, Richard | Jones, Miss Josphene | C/4 | August 2, 1871 | August 3, 1871 |
| Lasiter, Sinia E. | Spatton, Nathan | B/14 | September 4, 1868 | September 4, 1868 |
| Laster, J. H. | Jones, Miss M. E. | B/128 | March 6, 1871 | No Return |
| Laswell, Elizabeth Miss | Hill, Darny | A2/28 | October 17, 1853 | October 18, 1853 |
| Latemore, Huldy | Fann, Hardy | C/240 | February 2, 1880 | February 3, 1880 |
| Lattimer, Eliza Miss | Parker, Isaiah | E/3 | January 11, 1888 | January 12, 1888 |
| Latymoore, George | Bogle, Sarah | C/200 | October 5, 1878 | October 6, 1878 |
| Latymore, Elizabeth | Fann, Levie | C/290 | August 18, 1883 | August 19, 1883 |
| Laugthery, J. N. | Bether, Susan | C/238 | January 19, 1880 | January 22, 1880 |
| Law, Jane Miss | Bynum, S. W. | A2/80 | October 17, 1857 | October 17, 1857 |
| Lawing, Mary Ann Miss | Hall, John W. | A2/6 | August 31, 1850 | September 1, 1850 |
| Lawrance, Dora Miss | Raines, J. | C/452 | December 13, 1891 | December 15, 1891 |
| Lawrence, Eliza | Hawkins, John | C/472 | December 20, 1892 | December 21, 1892 |
| Lawrance, M. W. | Todd, S. E. | A2/103 | September 19, 1860 | No Return |
| Lawrence, Hiram (col.) | Farris, Birdie (col.) | F/110 | January 30, 1897 | January 31, 1897 |
| Lawrence, J. B. | Mason, Franchie | F/140 | December 21, 1897 | December 22, 1897 |
| Lawrence, J. H. | Powell, Eliza | C/84 | February 28, 1874 | February 29, 1874 |
| Lawrence, James T. | Cummins, Miss Lucy E. | B/90 | October 6, 1869 | October 7, 1869 |
| Lawrence, James T. | Bailey, Mollie | E/116 | December 29, 1888 | No Return |
| Lawrence, Jim B. | Merrett, Vioa | F/140 | December 12, 1897 | December 12, 1897 |
| Lawrence, Martha Jane Miss | Harrison, William H. | B/48 | July 25, 1867 | July 25, 1867 |
| Lawrence, Mary Miss | Gunter, Isaac | A2/29 | November 8, 1853 | November 8, 1853 |
| Lawrence, Robert | Bailey, Aline | C/426 | December 20, 1890 | December 21, 1890 |
| Lawrence, Sallie | Throwe, W. R. | F/24 | December 4, 1893 | December 8, 1893 |
| Lawson, Charity | Johnson, M. L. | C/326 | February 15, 1885 | February 16, 1885 |
| Lawson, Mary | Southerland, Archibald | A/55 | November 1, 1842 | November 1, 1842 |
| Layman, Nancy Miss | Cooper, H. J. | A2/41 | September 18, 1855 | September 18, 1855 |
| Lea, Mat | Cook, John W. | A2/104 | November 17, 1860 | November 17, 1860 |
| Leach, Nancy | Meadow, Wm. L. | A/24 | February 13, 1840 | |
| Leak, Georg P. | Simmons, Mary E. | E/356 | December 10, 1898 | |
| Leak, George P. | Simmons, Mary E. | F/162 | December 10, 1898 | No Return |
| Leal, L. A. Miss | Mason, K. M. | B/96 | December 29, 1869 | December 30, 1869 |
| Ledbetter, Alford | Powell, Zanie A. | C/58 | May 10, 1873 | May 10, 1873 |
| Ledbetter, Bettie | Bogle, Isaac | C/330 | July 4, 1885 | July 4, 1885 |
| Ledbetter, Bettie | Markum, Hall | F/4 | February 18,1893 | February 20, 1893 |
| Ledbetter, Caroline | Smith, Wm | C/134 | February 12, 1876 | February 15, 18786 |
| Ledbetter, Eli | Ashford, Polly | A/2 | April 25, 1838 | |
| Ledbetter, James | Reeves, Miss Salina | A/122 | May ?, 1849 | May 11, 1849 |
| Ledbetter, Mattie Miss | Markum, Samuel | C/412 | December 27, 1887 | January 1, 1888 |
| Ledbetter, Nancy | McDougald, Alexander | A/96 | January 11, 1847 | January 18, 1847 |
| Ledbetter, Sarah | Northcutt, D. A. | F/96 | September 26, 1896 | September 30, 1896 |
| Ledbetter, Thomas | Jetton, Miss Martha | B/68 | August 3, 1868 | August ?, 1868 |
| Ledbetter, Tiff | Bratton, Delia | C/422 | November 20, 1890 | November 20, 1890 |
| Ledbetter, William | Sullens, Miss Susan | A/49 | April 25, 1842 | April 26, 1842 |
| Ledbetter, William | Murphy, Martha | C/84 | March 14, 1874 | March 15, 1874 |
| Ledford, Mary M. | Warnack, D. D. | A2/133 | December 12, 1865 | December 13, 1865 |

| Groom or Bride | Groom or Bride | Book/Page | Date of License | Date of Marriage |
|---|---|---|---|---|
| Lee, Annie | McGee, James | F/34 | September 28, 1894 | September 30, 1894 |
| Lee, Charles | Womberly, Martha J. | A2/132 | November 16, 1865 | No Return |
| Lee, John | Herrod, Rebecca | C/166 | August 11, 1877 | August 12, 1877 |
| Lee, Ozburn | Stacey, Mary | A/11 | March 2, 1839 | March 4, 1839 |
| Leech, A. L. | Duggin, S. A. | C/126 | December 23, 1875 | December 23, 1875 |
| Leech, Caldonia | Duggin, James C. | C/132 | January 27, 1876 | January 27, 1876 |
| Leech, John C. | Blanks, Miss Julia Ann | A/86 | December 28, 1845 | January 12, 1846 |
| Leech, M. J. | Davenport, Robert | A2/114 | July 13, 1864 | July 14, 1864 |
| Leech, W. N. | Davenport, F. J. | C/110 | March 8, 1875 | No return |
| Leech, William C. | Thomas, Miss Amanda E. | A/114 | September 12, 1848 | September 12, 1848 |
| Lefever, Martha Miss | Pitman, Thos. M. | A2/18 | August 21, 1852 | August 22, 1852 |
| Lefevers, Isah | Ratliff, ? ? | F/50 | December 7, 1894 | December 9, 1894 |
| Lefevers, Mollie | Smithson, E. W. | F/102 | November 29, 1896 | November 29, 1896 |
| Lehmay, Martha A. | Wilson, Walter | E/358 | December 3, 1898 | |
| Leigh, Elizabeth W. Miss | Creson, Joshua | A/94 | December 17, 1846 | December 17, 1846 |
| Leigh, John | Shores, Jane | A2/80 | December 21, 1856 | January 1, 1857 |
| Leigh, Manerva J. Miss | Finley, Alexander | A2/1 | March 7, 1850 | March 7, 1850 |
| Leigh, Marry L. | Epsey, James R. | A2/34 | July 27, 1854 | July 29, 1854 |
| Leigh, Mary Miss | Wilson, John | A/132 | February 23, 1850 | February 24, 1850 |
| Leigh, Nancy C. Miss | Roberts, Thomas J. | B/92 | November 22, 1869 | November 25, 1869 |
| Leigh, Ware | Creson, Miss Sarah | A/92 | October 22, 1846 | October 22, 1846 |
| Leigh, William J. | Cummings, Miss Rebecca J. | B/76 | December 25, 1868 | January 7, 1869 |
| Lemay, J. A. | Wilson, M. J. | F/164 | December 28, 1898 | No Return |
| Lemay, Martha A. | Wilson, Walter | F/162 | December 3, 1898 | December 4, 1898 |
| Lemay, P. W. | Wilson, Margret C. | C/204 | December 4, 1878 | December ??, 1878 |
| Lemay, S. E. Miss | Manus, S. | A2/26 | July 9, 1853 | July 9, 1853 |
| Lemay, S. E. Miss | Manus, S. | A2/73 | July 9, 1853 | July 9, 1853 |
| Lemay, T. P. | Barrett, Miss M. | A2/26 | July 9, 1853 | No Return |
| Lemmon, Sarah L. | Bush, Wm. H. | D/8 | | December 14, 1881 |
| Lemmons, Alice | Saddler, Ransom | F/132 | September 22, 1897 | October 2, 1897 |
| Lemmons, H. B. | Cawthon, Parlee | C/354 | March 6, 1886 | No Return |
| Lemmons, Issac N. | Todd, Martha J. | C/34 | August 14, 1872 | August 15, 1872 |
| Lemmons, J. B. | Duke, Tilda E. | C/160 | March 21, 1877 | March 22, 1877 |
| Lemmons, J. K. P. | Jernigan, Mary A. | C/226 | October 13, 1879 | October 13, 1879 |
| Lemmons, John W. | Cawthen, Sarah | C/258 | October 12, 1880 | October 14, 1880 |
| Lemmons, Mahaley | West, John | C/300 | January 21, 1884 | January 21, 1884 |
| Lemmons, Mary | Tunnell, Milton R. | C/466 | October 8, 1892 | October 8, 1892 |
| Lemmons, Mary | Bush, J. W. | C/168 | August 20, 1877 | September 16, 1877 |
| Lemmons, Sarah E. | Tenpenny, Samuel A. | C/14 | November 23, 1871 | November 23, 1871 |
| Lemmons, W. A. | Anderson, Sarah | C/204 | November 12, 1878 | November 17, 1878 |
| Lemmons, W. J. | Gilley, Miss Malinda | C/432 | March 3, 1891 | March 3, 1891 |
| Lemmons, W. T | Gooding, Miss Sarah | B/78 | February 3, 1869 | February 11, 1869 |
| Lemons, Isaac | Duncan, Miss Manerva | A/84 | October 25, 1845 | Executed--No Date |
| Lemons, Jacob M. | Pelham, Miss Elizabeth C. | B/58 | December 19, 1867 | December 19, 1867 |
| Lemons, Sam | Smithson, Ida | F/34 | October 6, 1894 | October 7, 1894 |
| Lening, N. J. | Baley, Miss S. F. | B/122 | December 28, 1870 | December 28, 1870 |

| Groom or Bride | Groom or Bride | Book/Page | Date of License | Date of Marriage |
|---|---|---|---|---|
| Lenox, Nancy K. | Byford, Thomas | A/12 | April 13, 1839 | No Return |
| Leonard, Cyrena A. Miss | Williams, Berry | A/105 | November 18, 1847 | November 18, 1847 |
| Lett, Permiana Ann Miss | Mays, Sherod | A/48 | April 7, 1842 | April 7, 1842 |
| Lewellen, Ellen | Smith, Copen | A2/130 | October 30, 1865 | October 30, 1865 |
| Lewin, Jane Miss | Edwards, Alford | A2/60 | December 19, 1857 | No Return |
| Lewis, A. D | Johnson, Alice | C/188 | March 2, 1878 | March 3, 1878 |
| Lewis, A. D. | Lewis, M. L. | C/260 | October 18, 1880 | October 21, 1880 |
| Lewis, Bell | Williams, J. W. | F/2 | February 6, 1893 | February 7, 1893 |
| Lewis, Cab | Gillie, Martha | F/12 | July 18, 1893 | July 18, 1893 |
| Lewis, Ella | Estep, Edward | E/174 | April 30, 1889 | April 30, 1889 |
| Lewis, Geo W. | Bryant, Amandy J. | C/142 | August 19, 1876 | August 20, 1876 |
| Lewis, H. A. | Gilly, Miss N. I. | B/110 | September 21, 1870 | September 22, 1870 |
| Lewis, J. M | Williams, Nance E. | F | August 21, 1893 | No Return |
| Lewis, J. O. | Williams, Mattie | F/92 | August 3, 1896 | August 9, 1896 |
| Lewis, J. W. | West, Miss Nancy E. | A2/91 | November 29, 1859 | No Return |
| Lewis, James | Reed, Fannie | F/18 | September 25, 1893 | October 3, 1893 |
| Lewis, Jane Miss | Elkins, James | A2/86 | July 4, 1859 | No Return |
| Lewis, Janie | Bush, Pate | C/422 | November 8, 1890 | November 9, 1890 |
| Lewis, Jesse G. | Duke, Miss Sarah P. | B/90 | October 5, 1869 | October 10, 1869 |
| Lewis, John W. | Saddler, Mary L. | C/258 | October 13, 1880 | October 13, 1880 |
| Lewis, John W. | Sadler, Mary C. | E/160 | February 17, 1889 | February 18, 1889 |
| Lewis, L. L. | Givins, Miss M. | A2/72 | February 22, 1859 | No Return |
| Lewis, L. L. | Givins, Miss M. | A2/84 | February 22, 1859 | No Return |
| Lewis, Lucinda | Simmons, J. | A2/117 | October 30, 1864 | October 31, 1864 |
| Lewis, Lucinda | Gilley, W. T. | C/426 | December 27, 1890 | December 27, 1890 |
| Lewis, M. L. | Lewis, A. D. | C/260 | October 18, 1880 | October 21, 1880 |
| Lewis, Margaret | Brown, James W. | A2/125 | August 4, 1865 | August 6, 1865 |
| Lewis, Martha E. Miss | Summers, James | A2/37 | December 4, 1854 | December 7, 1854 |
| Lewis, Mary P. | Gilley, Wm. P. | C/352 | February 6, 1886 | February 6, 1886 |
| Lewis, Mary P. | Wood, James | F/26 | December 26, 1893 | No Return |
| Lewis, Matildy | Gilley, J. N. | F/120 | June 7, 1897 | June 10, 1897 |
| Lewis, Minervie J. | Finley, Henry M. | E/194 | July 25, 1889 | No Return |
| Lewis, Minnie | Bryant, Thomas | F/110 | February 8, 1897 | February 28, 1897 |
| Lewis, Peter J. | Finley, Manerva J. | B/74 | December 12, 1868 | December 12, 1868 |
| Lewis, S. H. | Cooper, S. L. | C/72 | November 18, 1873 | November 19, 1873 |
| Lewis, S. P. | Williams, N. C. | E/209 | September 7, 1889 | September 8, 1889 |
| Lewis, S. T. | Mathis, Malisa P. | C/18 | December 27, 1871 | December 28, 1871 |
| Lewis, W. C. | Tucker, Sarah | C/328 | March 5, 1885 | March 5, 1885 |
| Lewis, W. J. | Gilley, Zelpha | F/120 | June 30, 1897 | July 1, 1897 |
| Lewis, William C. | Deraberry, Miss Pelina A. | B/100 | April 2, 1870 | April 2, 1870 |
| Lillar, Susan | Gilley, Joe | E/40 | May 26, 1888 | May 26, 1888 |
| Lillard, Brist | Woods, Mary | C/74 | November 23, 1873 | November 25, 1873 |
| Lillard, Jim (col.) | Pinkerton, Mary (col.) | F/176 | May 11, 1899 | May 14, 1899 |
| Lince, Francis | Petty, Nathan | C/298 | December 1, 1883 | December 2, 1883 |
| Linch, L. B. Miss | Brailer, J. A. | A2/90 | November 8, 1859 | No Return |
| Linder, J. N. | Stone, Lizzie | C/322 | December 24, 1884 | December 24, 1884 |

| Groom or Bride | Groom or Bride | Book/Page | Date of License | Date of Marriage |
|---|---|---|---|---|
| Litle, W. M. | Qualls, Miss Juliann | A2/66 | August 4, 1858 | August ?, 1858 |
| Litrell, Jane Miss | Young, William | A/42 | October 9, 1841 | October 10, 1841 |
| Litrell, Sarah Miss | Lance, John | A/42 | October 13, 1841 | October 15, 1841 |
| Litrell, Wilford | Melton, Miss Polly | A/44 | November 23, 1841 | November 27, 1841 |
| Litter, George | Barrett, Cressy | C/218 | July 14, 1879 | July 14, 1879 |
| Litteral, Saunder | Boyd, Elizabeth | A/6 | September 14, 1838 | September 14, 1838 |
| Little, Camelee | Milligan, J. P. | A2/121 | February 25, 1865 | No Return |
| Little, Sarah Miss | Rigsby, J. A. | A2/66 | August 7, 1858 | August 8, 1858 |
| Loftton, R. Y. | Williams, Mary | F/24 | December 12, 1893 | December 13, 1893 |
| Logan, Bettie | Parris, J. R. | A2/142 | July 25, 1866 | July 25, 1866 |
| Logan, Eugene | Nichol, Miss Nova M. | E/68 | September 1, 1888 | September 2, 1888 |
| Logan, G. W. | Warren, Mary | C/254 | August 19, 1880 | August 19, 1880 |
| Logan, J. M. | Fowler, Sarah | C/348 | January 4, 1886 | No Return |
| Logan, M. Miss | Wooton, J. M. | B/32 | December 16, 1866 | December 16, 1866 |
| Logan, Roy | Smithson, Millie | F/160 | October 29, 1898 | October 30, 1898 |
| Login, Own | Proter, Porter | F/54 | January 2, 1895 | No Return |
| Logue, Andrew | Moffitt, Miss May | A/99 | April 12, 1847 | April 12, 1847 |
| Lollin, Margarett Miss | Cooper, Phillip | A2/17 | May 6, 1852 | May 6, 1852 |
| Long, Hanah P. Miss | Clark, Joseph M. | B/44 | April 6, 1867 | April 7, 1867 |
| Long, Isul | Hutchenson, M. H. | C/76 | December 13, 1873 | December 14, 1873 |
| Long, M. H. | Hawkins, Jesse | C/296 | November 15, 1883 | November 15, 1883 |
| Long, Miss H. J. | Davenport, R. B. F. | F/58 | January 26, 1895 | January 27, 1895 |
| Long, Nancy J. | Cabbage, J. F. | C/112 | April 23, 1875 | April 25, 1875 |
| Long, R. F. | Hawkins, Miss H. P. | A2/62 | January 9, 1858 | January 11, 1858 |
| Lorance, A. C. | Winnett, Nannie | F/148 | April 18, 1898 | April 21, 1898 |
| Lorance, B. B. | West, Barbey | C/244 | February 26, 1880 | February 26, 1880 |
| Lorance, E. J. | Graham, Miss Sallie | B/36 | January 1, 1867 | January 1, 1867 |
| Lorance, F. J. | Elrod, Nannie A. | A2/120 | February 8, 1865 | February 8, 1865 |
| Lorance, G. M. | Prior, Nannie B. | C/148 | November 21, 1876 | November 21, 1876 |
| Lorance, G. R. | Wimberly, Miss Julian | B/88 | September 28, 1869 | September 28, 1869 |
| Lorance, J. M. | Todd, M. T. | C/24 | February 22, 1872 | No Return |
| Lorance, Josie | Dyer, Charlie | C/300 | January 12, 1884 | January 12, 1884 |
| Lorance, L. C. | Jones, W. H. | F/128 | August 25, 1897 | August 25, 1897 |
| Lorance, M. A. | Winnett, Norman | C/192 | May 18, 1878 | May 19, 1878 |
| Lorance, M. A. Miss | Hunt, T. J. | A2/85 | March 31, 1859 | March 31, 1859 |
| Lorance, M. W. | Cosbey, Mary E. | C/64 | August 23, 1873 | August 24, 1873 |
| Lorance, Manerva | Stone, Henry D. | A2/121 | March 6, 1865 | March 8, 1865 |
| Lorance, Martha A. | Allen, John D. | C/172 | September 27, 1877 | September 27, 1877 |
| Lorance, Michael | Kelton, Miss Sarah M. E. | B/96 | December 20, 1869 | December 21, 1869 |
| Lorance, N. E. Miss | Winnett, W. S. | F/56 | January 1, 1895 | No Return |
| Lorance, R. C. | Akeres, Miss T. P. | B/100 | February 23, 1870 | February 24, 1870 |
| Lorance, W. B. | St. John, M. T. | F/122 | July 31, 1897 | July 31, 1897 |
| Lorance, Wm. W. | Winnett, Miss R. J. | B/82 | December 31, 1868 | December 31, 1868 |
| Lorancer, Malissa | Foster, Richard | E/246 | December 23, 1889 | December 24, 1889 |
| Lord, Mitchel | Clemmets, Miss Permelia Ann | A/34 | October 15, 1840 | October 15, 1840 |
| Lorrance, Bettie Miss | Bailey, Isaac | C/412 | December 21, 1887 | December 21, 1887 |

| Groom or Bride | Groom or Bride | Book/Page | Date of License | Date of Marriage |
|---|---|---|---|---|
| Low, A. | St. John W. F. | D/101 | | January 8, 1882 |
| Low, Calvin | Jacobs, Elizabeth | A2/109 | September 14, 1863 | No Return |
| Low, Charly | Moon, Sarah | A2/49 | July 12, 1856 | July 12, 1856 |
| Low, Joe | Paschal, Miss Atha | F/48 | November 20, 1894 | November 24, 1894 |
| Low, Martha | Ruller, Robt | C/298 | December 5, 1883 | No Return |
| Low, Mary | Dixon, Wash | F/46 | October 20, 1894 | October 21, 1894 |
| Low, Sam | Sissom, Mattie | F/60 | March 4, 1895 | March 4, 1895 |
| Low, Thos. N. | Summer, Sarah E. | A2/115 | August 9, 1864 | August 9, 1864 |
| Lowe, A. G. | Hollis, Celurten | C/232 | December 11, 1879 | December 11, 1879 |
| Lowe, Bettie | Sissom, Fred | F/8 | May 1, 1893 | May 3, 1893 |
| Lowe, C. T. | Moore, R. J. | C/58 | May 1, 1873 | May 14, 1873 |
| Lowe, Elizabeth Miss | Miller, Elihu J. | A/83 | October 17, 1845 | October 19, 1845 |
| Lowe, Frances E. | Smith, J. B. | C/56 | April 26, 1873 | April 27, 1873 |
| Lowe, Frances E. | Henderson, Jo. | C/110 | March 17, 1875 | March 21, 1875 |
| Lowe, Frances M. | Patton, Robert H. | A/75 | November 20, 1844 | November 21, 1844 |
| Lowe, Harriet Miss | Brandon, Jonathan J. | A2/9 | January 3, 1851 | No Return |
| Lowe, J. A. | Hays, Anne | C/318 | November 12, 1884 | November 18, 1884 |
| Lowe, John | Burnett, Jimmie | C/164 | June 30, 1877 | July 1, 1877 |
| Lowe, John | Wallace, Dovie Matilla | E/216 | October 5, 1889 | October 6, 1889 |
| Lowe, Sarah | Bolt, C. R. | F/96 | September 26, 1896 | September 27, 1896 |
| Lowe, Simion | St. John, Alantic | C/252 | August 5, 1880 | August 5, 1880 |
| Lowe, T. J. | Brandon, B. B. | F/94 | August 29, 1896 | August 30, 1896 |
| Lowe, T. W. | Moore, Mollie | F/50 | December 4, 1894 | December 5, 1894 |
| Lowe, Tobe | Wilson, Martha | F/130 | September 6, 1897 | September 6, 1897 |
| Lowing, Jane | Elrod, Adam | A/5 | August 2, 1838 | August 2, 1838 |
| Lowis, Wm. C. | Retton, Miss E. | A2/68 | October 5, 1858 | October 5, 1858 |
| Lowrance, M. N. | Allen, G. R. | C/52 | February 13, 1873 | February 13, 1873 |
| Lowrance, Mandy | Elkins, John | C/54 | February 27, 1873 | February 30, 1873 |
| Lowry, W. B. | Hawkins, Martha P. | C/10 | September 18, 1871 | September 19, 1871 |
| Ludsdon, Mary | Odom, Harry | B/2 | August 21, 1865 | No Return |
| Luster, Disey | Knox, Thomas | B/10 | June 21, 1867 | June 21, 1867 |
| Luster, Katharine | Couch, Wm. H. | A/36 | February 8, 1841 | February 10, 1841 |
| Luster, Letheia Miss | Perry, Nathaniel | A/39 | June 14, 1841 | June 14, 1841 |
| Luster, Sally | Preston, Joseph | A/4 | July 2, 1838 | July 3, 1838 |
| Lvaner, Sarah | Meton, Anul | A2/16 | July 21, 1851 | July 24, 1851 |
| Lynch, Kenney | George, Emma | C/116 | July 17, 1875 | No Return |
| Lynch, L. J. | Evans, R. D. | F/66 | July 27, 1895 | July 28, 1895 |
| Lynn, D. B. | Cooper, Mary J. | C/170 | September 19, 1877 | September 20, 1877 |
| Lynn, George | Baltimore, Ader | F/12 | July 7, 1893 | July 11, 1893 |
| Lynn, J. B. | Freeze, Mary E. | C/170 | September 19, 1877 | September 20, 1877 |
| Lynn, John H. | Hipp, Emeline | C/32 | July 22, 1872 | August 1, 1872 |
| Lynn, L. A. Miss | Hailey, J. A. | C/8 | August 30, 1871 | August 31, 1871 |
| Lynn, Lavisa J. Miss | Warrick, J. W. | B/106 | August 20, 1870 | No Return |
| Lynn, Martha J. | Finley, Geo. W. | C/64 | August 4, 1873 | August 7, 1873 |
| Lynn, Mary E. Miss | Pendleton, John L. | B/52 | September 26, 1867 | No Return |
| Lynn, Rachal | Duke, J. M. | A2/133 | December 6, 1865 | December 7, 1865 |

| Groom or Bride | Groom or Bride | Book/Page | Date of License | Date of Marriage |
|---|---|---|---|---|
| Lynn, Richard | Baltimore, Roxie | F/34 | March 28, 1894 | April 14, 1894 |
| Lynn, Sarah Miss | Duke, Monroe | B/50 | August 31, 1867 | September 1, 1867 |
| Lyon, Alford | Hancoch, Elisabeth | C/212 | February 12, 1879 | February 13, 1879 |
| Lyon, D. S. (col.) | Clark, A. E. (col.) | D/17 | | October 23, 1882 |
| Lyon, G. B. | Helton, Etta | C/154 | January 15, 1877 | January 17, 1877 |
| Lyon, George W. | McKnight, Miss Mary A. | A2/9 | December 23, 1850 | December 24, 1850 |
| Lyon, M. D. | McCaslin, Mattie J. | C/220 | August 13, 1879 | August 13, 1879 |
| Lyon, Miss Sallie | Tolber, L. G. | E/42 | June 22, 1888 | June 22, 1888 |
| Lyon, N. J. S. | Sissom, Miss Emaline | B/32 | November 17, 1866 | November 18, 1866 |
| Lyon, Nathan J. | Knox, Issabell Ann R. | A/56 | December 7, 1842 | December 8, 1842 |
| Lyon, Snow | Barton, Jordan | E/390 | October 11, 1898 | |
| Lyon, Stephen (col.) | Bivens, Lizzy (col.) | F/172 | March 15, 1899 | No Return |
| Lyon, Toney | Wilson, Nancy | C/340 | October 17, 1885 | October 18, 1885 |
| Lyon, Yander | Taylor, David | E/62 | August 18, 1888 | August 19, 1888 |
| Lyons, Bettie | McGill, A. T. | E/156 | December 22, 1888 | December 25, 1888 |
| Lyons, Catherine Miss | Rushing, Al | B/114 | October 15, 1870 | October 15, 1870 |
| Lyons, Ed | Miller, Miss Lany | B/124 | January 12, 1871 | January 12, 1871 |
| Lyons, Frank | Todd, Mollie | C/38 | September 8, 1872 | September 8, 1872 |
| Lyons, Frank | Blue, Tenne | C/336 | September 18, 1885 | September 18, 1885 |
| Lyons, Snow | Jordan, Barton (col.) | F/158 | October 11, 1898 | October 11, 1898 |
| Lyons, T. M. | Puketon, Sallie | C/206 | December 18, 1879 | No Return |
| Lyons, Wm (col.) | Jetton, Myrtle | C/428 | January 14, 1891 | January 14, 1891 |
| Mabry, Abe | McKnight, Abigale | B/12 | December 3, 1867 | December 5, 1867 |
| Macey, Elizabeth Miss | Kees, Erasmus S. | A/66 | December 13, 1843 | Not Executed |
| Macey, Mary | Brandon, Jesse | D/23 | | October 26, 1884 |
| Maclan, Harriet Miss | Thomas, J. F. | A2/73 | March 10, 1859 | No Return |
| Maclin, Harriet | Thomas, J. F. | A2/84 | March 10, 1859 | No Return |
| Macon, James | Tayler, Phebe | F/14 | August 5, 1893 | August 27, 1893 |
| Maddex, E. | James, E. M. | C/374 | November 20, 1886 | November 21, 1886 |
| Maddox, Florence | Wilson, James A. | E/63 | August 20, 188 | August 23, 1888 |
| Maddox, William | Martin, Miss Eliza | C/406 | November 2, 1887 | November 2, 1887 |
| Maddux, Margrett | Phillips, Jessie | F/30 | January 25, 1894 | January 25, 1894 |
| Maddux, Hassie Miss | Jennings, Ollie | F/174 | April 3, 1899 | April 6, 1899 |
| MaGlocklin, Sarah Jane Miss | Vasser, James | A/128 | October 17, 1849 | No Return |
| Magon, Jackson | Moore, Nancy | A2/12 | November 18, 1851 | November 2, 1851 |
| Mahaffa, E. D. | Wood, Mary A. | C/142 | August 16, 1876 | August 17, 1876 |
| Mahaffa, Susan J. | Bullard, J. T. | C/166 | August 15, 1877 | August 16, 1877 |
| Mahaffa, Wm. | Stanley, Sarah E. | C/88 | May 16, 1874 | May 5, 1876 |
| Mahaffy, M. C. | Parker, W. S. | C/402 | September 16, 1887 | September 17, 1887 |
| Mahaffy, R. J. | Grizzle, Miss Alice | F/176 | May 18, 1899 | May 18, 1899 |
| Mahather, James | Allen, Isabeller | C/310 | July 16, 1884 | July 16, 1884 |
| Maines, Arrmanda Miss | Moonyham, John | A2/82 | December 11, 1858 | December 12, 1858 |
| Mairs, Dillard | Summars, Malissie | C/364 | August 28, 1886 | August 29, 1886 |
| Mairs, James | Wheeler, Elizabeth | D/3 | | June 29, 1881 |
| Mairs, John B. | Garven, Sarah | C/276 | March 16, 1881 | March 18, 1881 |
| Mairs, Rose E. | Youngblood, Allen | C/292 | September 19, 1883 | September 19, 1883 |

| Groom or Bride | Groom or Bride | Book/Page | Date of License | Date of Marriage |
|---|---|---|---|---|
| Major, Allice | Spurlock, John | F/24 | December 2, 1893 | December 2, 1893 |
| Major, Hannah A. Miss | Trott, Henry | A/47 | February 15, 1842 | February 15, 1842 |
| Makum, P. D. Miss | Ford, D. S. | A2/90 | October 31, 1859 | November 9, 1859 |
| Malard, Eugene | Barrett, E. A. | D/12 | | March 23, 1882 |
| Malard, W. A. | Tucker, H. E. | C/246 | April 10, 1880 | April 11, 1880 |
| Malone, Erskine | McEwin, Miss Eliza | A/90 | September 1, 1846 | September 1, 1846 |
| Malone, John J. | Beashears, Rebecca | A/51 | July 13, 1842 | No Return |
| Maness, George W. | Capps, Ruthy | A2/15 | February 8, 1852 | February 8, 1852 |
| Maney, H. J. | Dougherty, Miss Martha A. | B/80 | March 15, 1869 | March 16, 1869 |
| Maney, M. E. | Byrn, Wm. | C/370 | October 18, 1886 | October 18, 1886 |
| Maney, Polly Miss | Whitter, Sammie | B/94 | December 13, 1869 | December 13, 1869 |
| Maney, Priscilla Miss | Bright, James R. | A/104 | November 2, 1847 | No Return |
| Maney, Virginia Miss | Donoho, Edward | A/112 | June 27, 1848 | June 27, 1848 |
| Maney, William L. | Elkins, Miss Jennie | C/390 | June 2, 1887 | June 2, 1887 |
| Manfres, George | Milligan, Mariah | B/16 | June 21, 1869 | June 22, 1869 |
| Mangrum, J. S. | Moore, M. D. | E/100 | November 10, 1888 | November 11, 1888 |
| Mangrum, Wm. S. | Spurlock, Mary E. | C/230 | November 8, 1879 | November 9, 1879 |
| Mangum, M. E. | Sims, J. P. | C/326 | February 9, 1885 | February 9, 1885 |
| Manis, E. D. | Teples, Malvira | A2/113 | March 27, 1864 | March 27, 1864 |
| Manius, M. A. | Moonaham, Robert | A2/60 | December 20, 1857 | December 20, 1857 |
| Manking, Isabella Miss | Ford, Gorley T. S. | A2/88 | September 13, 1859 | No Return |
| Manns, Lee | Thomas, Minnie | F/134 | October 29, 1897 | October 29, 1897 |
| Manns, Mary E. | Manns, Tilman | C/216 | May 1, 1879 | May ??, 1879 |
| Manns, Tilman | Manns, Mary E. | C/216 | May 1, 1879 | May ??, 1879 |
| Manns, Wm. M. | Murphy, Martha E. | C/216 | June 21, 1879 | June 22, 1879 |
| Manous, Bengamine E. | Haney, Miss Mary Ann | B/50 | August 21, 1867 | August 22, 1867 |
| Manous, Margaret | Jurnigan, Edmund | A2/131 | November 11, 1865 | November 12, 1865 |
| Manus, Ann Miss | Gann, Britton | B/66 | June 10, 1868 | June 10, 1868 |
| Manus, D. E. | Barrett, Miss A. | A2/70 | December 16, 1858 | December 17, 1858 |
| Manus, Daniel | Elkins, Susannah | A/29 | June 11, 1840 | June 11, 1840 |
| Manus, Elijah | Patrick, Mary Ann | A/76 | February 14, 1845 | February 13, 1845 |
| Manus, James | Gann, Lizzie | D/16 | | October 2, 1882 |
| Manus, M. H. | Muncy, Emley | C/72 | November 20, 1873 | November 20, 1873 |
| Manus, Malisa | Prater, Wm. | C/82 | February 12, 1874 | February 15, 1874 |
| Manus, Malissa Miss | Taylor, J. R. | B/108 | September 1, 1870 | September 1, 1870 |
| Manus, Margrett | West, T. F. | E/235 | November 28, 1889 | November 28, 1889 |
| Manus, Marian Miss | Manus, William | A/37 | February 26, 1841 | February 27, 1841 |
| Manus, N. | Manus, V. E. | A2/101 | August 3, 1860 | No Return |
| Manus, Nancy | Stanley, Charley | C/370 | October 14, 1886 | October 14, 1886 |
| Manus, Nathan | Steeples, Miss Nancy A. | A2/29 | November 11, 1853 | No Return |
| Manus, S. | Lemay, Miss S. E. | A2/26 | July 9, 1853 | July 9, 1853 |
| Manus, S. | Lemay, Miss S. E. | A2/73 | July 9, 1853 | July 9, 1853 |
| Manus, Thomas | Thomas, Miss Jane | A/102 | September 25, 1847 | No Return |
| Manus, Thomas E. | Thomas, Josie | E/56 | August 4, 1888 | August 5, 1888 |
| Manus, V. E. | Manus, N. | A2/101 | August 3, 1860 | No Return |
| Manus, W. J. | Mars, Dovey | C/86 | April 6, 1874 | April 6, 1874 |

| Groom or Bride | Groom or Bride | Book/Page | Date of License | Date of Marriage |
|---|---|---|---|---|
| Manus, William | Manus, Miss Marian | A/37 | February 26, 1841 | February 27, 1841 |
| Manus, William | Holland, Mattie | C/440 | July 20, 1891 | July 20, 1891 |
| Marberry, Sarah Miss | Inglis, Uriah F. | A/93 | November 18, 1846 | November 19, 1846 |
| Marchall, Sarah Ann | Johnson, Isaac N. | A/109 | March 13, 1848 | March 14, 1848 |
| Marchbanks, James | Brown, Elizabeth H. | A/19 | November 1, 1839 | November 2, 1839 |
| Marchbanks, Mariah | Hainey, John | A/25 | February 26, 1840 | February 25, 1840 |
| Marcuis, Jacob | Thomas, Miss Margarett | A2/17 | June 10, 1852 | June 10, 1852 |
| Marcum, Charles | Blair, Miss Sarah C. | A2/48 | May 15, 1856 | No Return |
| Marcum, Charles | Blue, Miss Sarah C. | A2/79 | May 15, 1856 | May 15, 1856 |
| Marcum, Isaac | Higgans, Miss Nancy | A2/11 | February 11, 1851 | February 14, 1851 |
| Marcum, John | Owen, Miss Nancy | A2/28 | September 9, 1853 | September 12, 1853 |
| Marcum, Melvina J. Miss | Baly, John S. | A2/91 | November 25, 1859 | No Return |
| Marcum, Micajah | Gunter, Miss Martha | A/131 | January 30, 1850 | January 30, 1850 |
| Marcum, Miss Eliza | Bethel, Green W. | A2/11 | March 22, 1851 | No Return |
| Marcum, Paulina Miss | Burkett, John | A/121 | March 10, 1849 | March 11, 1849 |
| Marcun, Job | Gassoway, Miss Georgiana | A/121 | March 3, 1849 | No Return |
| Mare, M. N. | Williams, Mrs. M. E. | A2/100 | July 18, 1860 | No Return |
| Mares, Elizabeth | Morgan, Jackson | A/54 | October 7, 1842 | October 7, 1842 |
| Mares, Fanny | Herriman, Columbus | C/432 | March 26, 1891 | March 26, 1891 |
| Mares, William | Curis, Miss Ann | A/48 | April 11, 1842 | April 11, 1842 |
| Mares, Wm. | Holland, Mary K. | A2/106 | November 23, 1862 | November 23, 1862 |
| Marker, H. B. | Seals, Martha A. | A2/110 | December 2, 1863 | December 3, 1863 |
| Markin, T. T. | Bogle, Leanthe | C/402 | September 17, 1887 | September 18, 1887 |
| Markins, A. E | Jones, G. W. | C/402 | September 17, 1887 | September 18, 1887 |
| Markum, A. | Hollandworth, Elizabeth | A2/99 | July 6, 1860 | July 15, 1860 |
| Markum, Alfred | Dennis, Miss Mary | B/92 | November 11, 1869 | November 14, 1869 |
| Markum, Anthon A. | McGee, Robt. | C/38 | September 12, 1872 | September 12, 1872 |
| Markum, Arch | Owen, A. H. | A2/114 | May 4, 1864 | May 8, 1864 |
| Markum, Berry | Burkett, Miss Matilda | A/64 | August 26, 1843 | August 26, 1843 |
| Markum, Bettie Dean | Jones, Melton | F/86 | March 3, 1896 | March 3, 1896 |
| Markum, Cajor | Sullens, Sarah E. | C/138 | May 24, 1876 | No Return |
| Markum, Calafornia Miss | Bailey, Jacob | B/108 | August 25, 1870 | August 24?, 1870 |
| Markum, Charles | Winnett, Bettie | C/374 | November 16, 1886 | November 17, 1886 |
| Markum, D. | Summar, Mattie | E/215 | September 30, 1889 | September 30, 1889 |
| Markum, Delia | Grizzle, Wm. | D/4 | | August 16, 1881 |
| Markum, Eliza | Stone, John B. | F/1 | January 4, 1893 | January 4, 1893 |
| Markum, Ella | Ritchey, J. P. | C/440 | July 25, 1891 | July 25, 1891 |
| Markum, Frances | Vinson, James | C/38 | September 19, 1872 | September 19, 1872 |
| Markum, G. H. | Readman, Y. F. | C/250 | July 15, 1880 | July 15, 1880 |
| Markum, Hall | Ledbetter, Bettie | F/4 | February 18,1893 | February 20, 1893 |
| Markum, Healen | Evans, E. L. | C/98 | October 31, 1874 | November 1, 1874 |
| Markum, Helen | Melton, Johna | F/24 | December 12, 1893 | December 13, 1893 |
| Markum, Helen | Brown, Robt. | F/118 | May 29, 1897 | No Return |
| Markum, Isaac | Mitchell, Addie | C/350 | December 31, 1885 | December 31, 1885 |
| Markum, John | Sullins, Sug | C/300 | January 17, 1884 | January 17, 1884 |
| Markum, John B. | Vinson, Dela | D/19 | | December 25, 1882 |

| Groom or Bride | Groom or Bride | Book/Page | Date of License | Date of Marriage |
|---|---|---|---|---|
| Markum, Lizzie | Brown, Brit | F/130 | September 17, 1897 | September 18, 1897 |
| Markum, M. A. Miss | Foster, J. D. | A2/87 | August 27, 1859 | No Return |
| Markum, Martha | Cummins, W. B. | C/224 | September 6, 1879 | No Return |
| Markum, Martha A. | York, J. N. | A2/118 | December 17, 1864 | No Return |
| Markum, Mary E. | Bailey, Jim B. | C/206 | November 30, 1878 | November 31, 1878 |
| Markum, Mary Miss | Jetton, William | B/82 | May 28, 1869 | May 28, 1869 |
| Markum, Mike | Higgins, Emma | F/64 | May 15, 1895 | May 15, 1895 |
| Markum, Nancy L. | King, Wm. M. | C/76 | December 13, 1873 | December 14, 1873 |
| Markum, Rebeccer P. | Vinson, Theopolis | C/154 | February 2, 1877 | February 2, 1877 |
| Markum, Sam T. | Parker, Elizabeth | C/330 | July 3, 1885 | November 5, 1885 |
| Markum, Samuel | Ledbetter, Miss Mattie | C/412 | December 27, 1887 | January 1, 1888 |
| Markum, Sifie | Wilson, Stephen H. | F/34 | September 6, 1894 | September 7, 1894 |
| Markum, Will | Higdon, Mollie | F/66 | August 24, 1895 | August 22, 1895 |
| Markum, Wm | Elkins, N. A. | C/22 | January 24, 1872 | January 25, 1872 |
| Markum, Wm | Byfor, Prilee | D/19 | | December 24, 1882 |
| Markum, Wm. | Spurlock, Francis | C/348 | January 9, 1886 | January 9, 1886 |
| Marler, M. M. | Womack, M. P. | C/242 | December 27, 1879 | December 27, 1879 |
| Marlin, Merry Jane | Woodroff, Wm | A2/12 | November 22, 1851 | No Return |
| Maroony, A. D. | Smith S. F. | E/24 | March 1, 1888 | March 1, 1888 |
| Marris, Samuel B. | Yarbro, Florence | F/12 | June 28, 1893 | June 28, 1893 |
| Marrs, M. A. | Evans, J. W. | C/350 | January 15, 1886 | January 17, 1886 |
| Mars, Dovey | Manus, W. J. | C/86 | April 6, 1874 | April 6, 1874 |
| Mars, May Miss | Whitt, Em. M. | A2/93 | July 6, 1859 | No Return |
| Marshall, Eliza Jane | Cox, Thomas | A2/7 | November 16, 1850 | November 16, 1850 |
| Marshall, Martha C. Miss | Smith, William J. | A2/3 | July 26, 1850 | No Return |
| Marthis, Geo L. | Spurlock, Ruth | C/138 | June 21, 1876 | June 21, 1876 |
| Martin, Anthony | Moore, Jose | C/60 | July 12, 1873 | July 12, 1873 |
| Martin, Anzie | McKnight, Miss Isaberlla E. | A/37 | March 12, 1841 | March 25, 1841 |
| Martin, Bill | Wiley, Fanie | C/334 | August 29, 1885 | August 29, 1885 |
| Martin, Bob | Hancock, Alace | C/346 | December 24, 1885 | December 27, 1885 |
| Martin, Bob (col.) | Dunn, Annie (col.) | F/148 | April 3, 1898 | April 3, 1898 |
| Martin, Burton | Odom, Caroline | C/106 | January 18, 1875 | January 21, 1875 |
| Martin, Charles | Covington, Miss Hattie | B/16 | December 28, 1868 | December 30, 1868 |
| Martin, Daisey (col.) | Martin, Wayman (col.) | F/174 | April 1, 1899 | April 1, 1899 |
| Martin, Ed | Higgins, George Ann | F/30 | January 27, 1894 | January 27, 1894 |
| Martin, Eliza Miss | Maddox, William | C/406 | November 2, 1887 | November 2, 1887 |
| Martin, Elizabeth | Jones, John | A/67 | January 10, 1844 | January 12, 1844 |
| Martin, Elizabeth | Gasaway, Rufus | C/54 | March 14, 1873 | March 16, 1873 |
| Martin, Fanny | Johnson, William (col.) | C/438 | June 27, 1891 | No Return |
| Martin, Fannie B. Miss | Harrod, John A. | B/126 | January 30, 1871 | February 2, 1871 |
| Martin, Frank (col.) | Ivie, Nettie | C/442 | August 6, 1891 | August 6, 1891 |
| Martin, George | McKnight, Allie | C/472 | December 20, 1892 | December 21, 1892 |
| Martin, Grand | Peak, Sallie | D/5 | | October 6, 1881 |
| Martin, Jack | Hancock, Miss Sallie | B/110 | September 24, 1870 | September 27, 1870 |
| Martin, Jackson | Moore, Josephine | B/16 | February 25, 1869 | February 25, 1869 |
| Martin, Jane | George, Andy | C/316 | October 30, 1884 | November 2, 1884 |

| Groom or Bride | Groom or Bride | Book/Page | Date of License | Date of Marriage |
|---|---|---|---|---|
| Martin, John (col.) | Vance, Irene (col.) | F/88 | May 7, 1896 | May 10, 1896 |
| Martin, John W. | Johnson, Sarah P. | C/332 | July 11, 1885 | July 12, 1885 |
| Martin, Josie | Barnes, Stephens | C/110 | March 15, 1875 | March 15, 1875 |
| Martin, L. B. | Wilcher F. C. | C/218 | July 19, 1879 | July 20, 1879 |
| Martin, Lewis G. | Conn, Alley | A/11 | March 4, 1839 | March 4, 1839 |
| Martin, Linnie | Wood, W. J. | C/86 | April 25, 1874 | April 26, 1874 |
| Martin, Lucinda | Gordon, Lewis | B/12 | June 22, 1867 | June 21, 1867 |
| Martin, Malisa | Thompson, Jim | C/46 | December 18, 1872 | December 18, 1872 |
| Martin, Martha | Office, James | B/18 | February 1, 1870 | February 2, 1870 |
| Martin, Martha | Finetta, John | F/140 | December 8, 1897 | December 9, 1897 |
| Martin, Martha J. | McGill, B. J. | C/156 | February 17, 1877 | February 22, 1877 |
| Martin, Mary | Talley, Martin | E/117 | December 24, 1888 | December 24, 1888 |
| Martin, Mary J. | English, John D. | A2/14 | January 10, 1852 | January 12, 1852 |
| Martin, Mat | Woodward, Lucy | C/382 | January 19, 1887 | No Return |
| Martin, Mat | Bevins, Lizzie | C/408 | November 26, 1887 | November 26, 1887 |
| Martin, Matie | Runels, Harris | C/216 | June 24, 1879 | June 26, 1879 |
| Martin, Nancy | Barton, Exeakie | F/56 | December 27, 1895 | December 30, 1895 |
| Martin, Nannie | Davis, Charles | E/95 | October 31, 1888 | October 31, 1888 |
| Martin, Paralee | Dickens, John | C/58 | June 13, 1873 | June 15, 1873 |
| Martin, Paralee Miss | Higgins, Rance | B/130 | April 14, 1871 | April 14, 1871 |
| Martin, Richard | Gordon, Julian | B/16 | January 27, 1869 | January 27, 1969 |
| Martin, Richard B. | Jones, Miss Mary | A2/5 | September 9, 1850 | September 9, 1850 |
| Martin, Robert | Jones, Rutha | C/136 | March 4, 1876 | March 5, 1876 |
| Martin, Rody | Grizzle, Paump | C/10 | September 27, 1871 | September 27, 1871 |
| Martin, Roslin L. | Douglass, James I. | A2/121 | February 21, 1865 | February 22, 1865 |
| Martin, Sarah | Right, Alford | C/250 | July 22, 1880 | July 22, 1880 |
| Martin, Selina | McBroom, Geo. | C/28 | June 6, 1872 | June 6, 1872 |
| Martin, Simon | Hancock, Jane | E/86 | October 6, 188 | October 6, 1888 |
| Martin, Sophia E. Miss | Herod, D. T. | A2/98 | June 30, 1860 | July 4, 1860 |
| Martin, Susan J. Miss | Wright, William B. | A2/1 | March 1, 1850 | March 3, 1850 |
| Martin, Susan Miss | Hawkins, Jacob B. | A/126 | September 6, 1849 | September 6, 1849 |
| Martin, Thomas | Mitchell, Mattie | C/436 | April 25, 1891 | April 25, 1891 |
| Martin, Thomas S. | Bowen, Miss Emaliza | A/74 | October 24, 1844 | October 24, 1844 |
| Martin, W. A. | English, Sarah | C/34 | August 19, 1872 | August 21, 1872 |
| Martin, W. T. | Jones, Miss Margret | B/116 | November 21, 1870 | November 23, 1870 |
| Martin, Wayman (col.) | Martin, Daisey (col.) | F/174 | April 1, 1899 | April 1, 1899 |
| Martin, Wm. | Griffin, Caroline E. | A2/44 | December 17, 1855 | December 20, 1855 |
| Martin, Wm. | Bullen, Miss Sarah Ann | B/130 | April 1, 1871 | April 1, 1871 |
| Martin, Wm. R. | Harmon, Mrs. M. C. | B/108 | July 28, 1870 | No Return |
| Martin, Zinas A. | McKnight, Eliza E. | A/29 | May 13, 1840 | May 20, 1840 |
| Masey, J. R. | Cooper, M. P. | F/28 | January 8, 1894 | January 8, 1894 |
| Masey, James | Wilson, Lillie | C/444 | August 8, 1891 | August 9, 1891 |
| Masey, James | Bailey, Helen | C/446 | October 3, 1891 | October 3, 1891 |
| Masey, Lockey | Gunter, Wm. | C/426 | December 20, 1890 | December 21, 1890 |
| Masey, Margarett | Purser, John | F/100 | November 20, 1896 | November 20, 1896 |
| Masey, R. L. | Wilson, Jenny | C/438 | July 3, 1891 | July 5, 1891 |

| Groom or Bride | Groom or Bride | Book/Page | Date of License | Date of Marriage |
|---|---|---|---|---|
| Mason, Amanda | Mitchell, W. N. | F/26 | December 23, 1893 | December 25, 1893 |
| Mason, Angie | Evans, W. J. | E/263 | January 15, 1890 | No Return |
| Mason, Ann Miss | Elkins, J. W. | C/450 | December 7, 1891 | December 8, 1891 |
| Mason, Anthon | King, W. J. | C/172 | September 27, 1877 | September 30, 1877 |
| Mason, Charles | Jetton, Edna | E/6 | January 19, 1888 | January 19, 1888 |
| Mason, Charley | Melton, E. A. | C/474 | December 31, 1892 | December 31, 1892 |
| Mason, Daisie | Farrell, W. H. | E/344 | December 21, 1898 | |
| Mason, Daisie | Ferrell, W. H. | F/164 | December 21, 1898 | December 22, 1898 |
| Mason, Franchie | Lawrence, J. B. | F/140 | December 21, 1897 | December 22, 1897 |
| Mason, J. G. | Hammons, Tide | F/94 | August 25, 1896 | No Return |
| Mason, J. T. | Vance, Miss Eliza J. | B/56 | November 27, 1867 | November 28, 1867 |
| Mason, J. T. | Larrence, Allie | C/416 | September 6, 1890 | September 7, 1890 |
| Mason, J. W. | Curry, Amand | E/80 | September 20, 1888 | September 20, 1888 |
| Mason, James G. | Smith, Cassinda | A/8 | November 15, 1838 | November 18, 1838 |
| Mason, John | Kersy, Eathcindy | A2/104 | October 22, 1860 | No Return |
| Mason, Joseph F. | Higgins, Miss Jane | B/72 | November 20, 1868 | November 27, 1868 |
| Mason, K. M. | Leal, Miss L. A. | B/96 | December 29, 1869 | December 30, 1869 |
| Mason, Lestia | Melton, James B. | C/444 | August 27, 1891 | August 27, 1891 |
| Mason, Lillie | Cummins, Dallas | D/13 | | June 30, 1882 |
| Mason, Lula | Gilley, J. B. | F/116 | April 24, 1897 | April 24, 1897 |
| Mason, Mary | Campbell, J. D. | C/166 | August 1, 1877 | August 2, 1877 |
| Mason, Mary | Hammons, C. C. | F/150 | June 11, 1898 | No Return |
| Mason, Mary Miss | Hoover, Newton | C/6 | August 9, 1871 | August 10, 1871 |
| Mason, May | Bell, J. H. | F/140 | December 18, 1897 | December 20, 1897 |
| Mason, N. F. | Bell, S. J. | A2/100 | July 18, 1860 | July 19, 1860 |
| Mason, Pearl | Stephens, Joe | F/122 | July 31, 1897 | August 1, 1897 |
| Mason, Plina | Stone, Wm. | C/332 | July 30, 1885 | July 30, 1885 |
| Mason, R. L. | Walkup, Miss Hassie | F/86 | March 10, 1896 | March 17, 1896 |
| Mason, Regneer H. | Stone, Flora M. | A/129 | December 4, 1849 | December 8, 1849 |
| Mason, Rena | Burch, J. G. | E/191 | July 13, 1889 | July 14, 1889 |
| Mason, Richard, B. | Heigdon, Malisa T. | C/178 | November 23, 1877 | November 23, 1877 |
| Mason, Sarah E. | Neel, T. M. | A2/34 | August 24, 1854 | August 24, 1854 |
| Mason, T. B. | Preston, Mary E. | C/174 | October 12, 1877 | October 14, 1877 |
| Mason, T. P. | Clark, Eliza J. | C/108 | February 19, 1875 | February 21, 1875 |
| Mason, Taylor | Corner, Isabella | C/430 | February 5, 1891 | February 5, 1891 |
| Mason, William C. | Spurlock, Miss S. A. | B/84 | September 1, 1869 | September 2, 1869 |
| Massey, Martha | Nelson, Samuel | B/10 | December 22, 1866 | December 27, 1866 |
| Massie, W. M. | Dillon, Miss Eliza | B/96 | December 14, 1869 | December 14, 1869 |
| Mathais, Parlee Miss | Grizzle, Polk | A2/143 | August 7, 1866 | August 9, 1866 |
| Mathews, Cephas | Eagleton, Elvira | F/144 | January 20, 1898 | January 20, 1898 |
| Mathews, J. W. | Williams, Miss Annie | B/118 | December 7, 1870 | December 7, 1870 |
| Mathews, John W. | Dodd, Miss Mary | A/46 | January 19, 1842 | January 20, 1842 |
| Mathews, John W. | Davis, Miss Mary E. | A2/79 | May 3, 1856 | May 26, 1870 |
| Mathews, Mary E. Miss | McKnight, A. B. | A2/12 | October 22, 1851 | No Return |
| Mathews, Miss Johanna E. | Colvert, James L. | A/88 | April 1, 1846 | April 1, 1846 |
| Mathews, Nancy | Orr, John M. | A/19 | November 4, 1839 | No Return |

| Groom or Bride | Groom or Bride | Book/Page | Date of License | Date of Marriage |
|---|---|---|---|---|
| Mathews, Nathan | Keith, Nancy | A/26 | March 26, 1840 | March 31, 1840 |
| Mathews, Paulina J. P. | Weedon, A. M. | A/61 | March 27, 1843 | March 30, 1843 |
| Mathews, Robert | Turpen, Nettie | C/436 | May 13, 1891 | May 13, 1891 |
| Mathews, Samuel | Summar, Miss Milley | A/100 | July 22, 1847 | July 22, 1847 |
| Mathews, Sarah C. Miss | Bond, R. J. | A2/8 | November 18, 1850 | November 19, 1850 |
| Mathews, Sarah Miss | Davenport, Reuben | A/99 | May 4, 1847 | May 4, 1847 |
| Mathews, W. H. | Hubbard, Miss M. A. F. | B/94 | November 30, 1869 | December 2, 1869 |
| Mathews, Walter | Ashford, Miss Antaliza | A/51 | July 21, 1842 | April 20, 1842 |
| Mathis, Clarinda Miss | Williams, R. H. | A2/144 | September 8, 1866 | September 11, 1866 |
| Mathis, Dan | Parton, Elizabeth | C/160 | April 24, 1877 | April 24, 1877 |
| Mathis, Della | Pitman, Isaack | F/10 | May 24, 1893 | May 25, 1893 |
| Mathis, Della | Hatley, Robt | F/126 | August 11, 1897 | August 19, 1897 |
| Mathis, Donnie | Rule, Miss Batie | F/62 | April 16, 1895 | April 17, 1895 |
| Mathis, Elisabeth | Turpin, Daniel | C/220 | May 22, 1879 | May 22, 1879 |
| Mathis, Ibby Elizabeth | King, James H. H. | A2/102 | September 12, 1860 | No Return |
| Mathis, J. H. | Arnett, M. J. | C/432 | March 26, 1891 | March 29, 1891 |
| Mathis, Malisa P. | Lewis, S. T. | C/18 | December 27, 1871 | December 28, 1871 |
| Mathis, Nancy F. | Morris, Levi | C/50 | January 24, 1873 | January 29, 1873 |
| Mathis, Thomas | Williams, Miss Delila A. | C/390 | June 9, 1887 | June 13, 1887 |
| Mathis, Willie | Elkins, Miss Minnie | F/176 | May 20, 1899 | No Return |
| Matthew, Henry | Hall, Miss Etta | C/450 | November 30, 1891 | December 2, 1891 |
| Matthews, Charlotte Miss | Dodd, William | A/48 | March 12, 1842 | March 18, 1842 |
| Maxey, Clercy | Holt, Norman | C/288 | August 8, 1883 | August 8, 1883 |
| Maxey, Daniel | McDougal, Anna C. | A2/119 | December 28, 1864 | No Return |
| Maxey, Emeline | Talley, Martin | C/248 | May 13, 1880 | May 13, 1880 |
| Maxey, J. C. | Hiff, M. H. | C/286 | July 9, 1883 | No Return |
| Maxey, J. J. | Cunningham, F. P. | C/80 | January 5, 1874 | No Return |
| Maxey, Lewis | Philips, Miss Sarah | B/72 | October 21, 1868 | October 22, 1868 |
| Maxey, Mary | Brandon, Jesse | C/316 | October 22, 1884 | No Return |
| Maxey, Nancy | Prater, David M. | A2/133 | December 6, 1865 | December 7, 1965 |
| Maxey, P. P. | Baly, Martha H. | A2/111 | January 6, 1864 | January 7, 1864 |
| Maxey, Peggy Jane Miss | Stacy, Benjamin L. | A/89 | July 4, 1846 | July 5, 1846 |
| Maxey, Richard | Batson, Elizabeth M. | A/18 | October 26, 1839 | October 29, 1839 |
| Maxey, William | Hipp, Miss Etta | C/390 | June 25, 1887 | No Return |
| Maxey, William | Hipp, Miss Etta | C/392 | June 25, 1887 | No Return |
| Maxey, William | Huff, Etta | E/51 | June 25, 1888 | June 26, 1888 |
| Maxwell, Joseph H. | Herriman, Analiza | F/92 | August 14, 1896 | August 16, 1896 |
| Maxwell, Matilda | Cronk, G. W. | C/134 | February 15, 1876 | February 15, 1876 |
| Mayes, H. L. | Higgins, Zora | F/22 | November 4, 1893 | November 9, 1893 |
| Mayes, Susan A. | Meants, James | A2/14 | November 10, 1851 | December 1, 1851 |
| Mayfield, Edny S. | Elledge, James B. | C/66 | September 20, 1873 | September 21, 1873 |
| Mayfield, Irene | Vance, J. J. | C/446 | September 10, 1891 | September 10, 1891 |
| Mayfield, Queen | Crouch, S. B. | C/148 | November 24, 1876 | November 24, 1876 |
| Mayo, B. F. | Higgins, Lockey J. | D/6 | | October 23, 1881 |
| Mayo, Bengamin F. | Melton, Miss Stacy | B/104 | July 21, 1870 | No Return |
| Mayo, Ester A. | Moore, Z. H. | C/306 | April 7, 1884 | April 10, 1884 |

| Groom or Bride | Groom or Bride | Book/Page | Date of License | Date of Marriage |
|---|---|---|---|---|
| Mayo, W. M. | Stanley, Nora | F/52 | December 11, 1894 | December 11, 1894 |
| Mays, A. H. | Higgins, Martha E. | C/322 | January 9, 1885 | January 11, 1885 |
| Mays, Sherod | Lett, Miss Permiana Ann | A/48 | April 7, 1842 | April 7, 1842 |
| Mazey, W. W. | Young, Miss Margarett J. | B/36 | December 26, 1866 | January 3, 1867 |
| Mazo, B. F. | Witty, M. G. | C/392 | July 1, 1887 | July 3, 1887 |
| Mazy, Harriett Miss | Jones, James | A2/34 | August 31, 1854 | September 7, 1854 |
| Mazy, Louisa A. Miss | Young, E. J. | B/90 | October 20, 1869 | No Return |
| McAdams, A. Miss | Moore, Abner | A2/85 | May 27, 1859 | Execution Not Clear |
| McAdoe, J. N. | Francis, Miss C. J. | B/34 | December 24, 1866 | December 25, 1866 |
| McAdoo, Angie Miss | Robinson, S. R. | C/424 | December 17, 1890 | December 18, 1890 |
| McAdoo, Ellen | McClemen, Ed | C/128 | December 30, 1875 | December 30, 1875 |
| McAdoo, H. E. | Groom, Miss Frances | B/120 | December 21, 1870 | December 22, 1870 |
| McAdoo, J. C. | Summar, Miss C. R. | B/90 | October 12, 1869 | October 14, 1869 |
| McAdoo, J. C. | Byrn, Mollie | C/244 | March 10, 1880 | March 10, 1880 |
| McAdoo, Laura | Todd, B. L. | D/20 | | August 10, 1882 |
| McAdoo, Lizie | Bryan, Manson | C/398 | August 29, 1887 | August 29, 1887 |
| McAdoo, Mary Jane | Ewing, John L. | A/20 | December 9, 1839 | December 19, 1839 |
| McAdoo, N. C. | Alexander, Geo. | C/48 | December 31, 1872 | December 31, 1872 |
| McAdoo, R. F. | Donel, M. M. | C/208 | December 2, 1878 | December 23, 1878 |
| McAdoo, Richard | Trimble, Milley | C/310 | July 24, 1884 | No Return |
| McAdoo, Richard | Blay, Mary | E/94 | October 25, 1888 | October 28, 1888 |
| McAdoo, Tennie | Franklin, Ed | E/181 | June 11, 1889 | No Return |
| McAdoo, V. P. | Francis, A. F. | C/74 | December 3, 1873 | December 4, 1873 |
| McAdow, Aelisa Miss | Pendleton, Benjamin | A/107 | January 26, 1848 | January 26, 1848 |
| McAdow, Azaline Miss | Cooper, John D. | B/98 | January 7, 1870 | January 12, 1870 |
| McAdow, Eliza Miss | Tatum, A. C. | A2/9 | December 30, 1850 | December 30, 1850 |
| McAdow, Hanah | Odom, Abrahm | B/10 | May 31, 1867 | No Return |
| McAdow, L. F. Miss | Witherspoon, D. | A2/29 | October 18, 1853 | October 18, 1853 |
| McAdow, Margaret J. Miss | Herndon, W. J. | B/38 | January 12, 1867 | January 20, 1867 |
| McAdow, Margaret J. Miss | Simms, M. T. | B/38 | January 14, 1867 | No Return |
| McAdow, P. A. Miss | Moore, Wm. A. T. | A2/92 | December 3, 1859 | Executed--No Date |
| McAffry, S. L. | Brewis, Tammie | C/380 | December 28, 1886 | January 2, 1886 |
| McAffy, M. F. | McBroom, M. J. | C/264 | November 25, 1880 | November 25, 1880 |
| McAlexander, J. | Sullivan, Mahama | C/44 | November 18, 1872 | November 21, 1872 |
| McAlexander, Rebecca Miss | Watson, James N. | A/107 | February 3, 1848 | February 9, 1848 |
| McBorren, Isaac | Tenpenny, Maryann | A2/15 | February 17, 1852 | February 17, 1852 |
| McBride, Janus | Richardson, Fannie | E/198 | August 10, 1889 | No Return |
| McBride, Martha | Cawthan, David | C/332 | July 11, 1885 | July 11, 1885 |
| McBride, O. J. | Northcut, Mattie J. | C/142 | August 19, 1876 | August 20, 1876 |
| McBride, Polly | Underwood, Jacob | A/29 | June 8, 1840 | June 8, 1840 |
| McBride, S. J. | Sissom, W. J. | F/124 | August 6, 1897 | August 12, 1897 |
| McBroom, Abel | Hays, Miss Fanny | A/37 | April 5, 1841 | No Return |
| McBroom, Alexander | Hoover, Mary | C/18 | December 21, 1871 | December 21, 1871 |
| McBroom, Alexander D. | Tenpenny, Miss Charleny | A2/49 | August 12, 1856 | No Return |
| McBroom, Anelyn | Curlee, James P. | C/232 | December 4, 1879 | December 4, 1879 |
| McBroom, Ann | Owen, P. L. | D/3 | | September 7, 1881 |

| Groom or Bride | Groom or Bride | Book/Page | Date of License | Date of Marriage |
|---|---|---|---|---|
| McBroom, B. H. | Sullivan, Bettie | C/102 | December 2, 1874 | December 2, 1874 |
| McBroom, B. T. | McBroom, Miss Kissia J. | B/88 | September 23, 1869 | September 23, 1869 |
| McBroom, Benjamine | Willard, S. E. | C/472 | December 23, 1892 | December 28, 1892 |
| McBroom, Bettie | McKnight, S. O. | C/76 | December 18, 1873 | No Return |
| McBroom, Bettie Miss | Carter, James R. | B/52 | September 12, 1867 | September 12, 1867 |
| McBroom, D. T. | Alexander, Nancy A. | D/9 | | December 29, 1881 |
| McBroom, Dave | Gandy, Mary | C/296 | November 8, 1883 | November 8, 1883 |
| McBroom, E. J. | Mingle, W. T. | C/62 | July 26, 1873 | July 27, 1873 |
| McBroom, Eller | Hare, J. H. | C/240 | January 28, 1880 | January 28, 1880 |
| McBroom, Elizabeth Miss | Bragg, S. E. | B/72 | November 11, 1868 | November 12, 1868 |
| McBroom, Eppie | Drennen, J. C. | F/140 | December 22, 1897 | December 22, 1897 |
| McBroom, Fannie Miss | Knott, R. F. | C/2 | June 3, 1871 | June 4, 1871 |
| McBroom, Flora | McBroom, Sampson | B/8 | November 17, 1865 | November 19, 1965 |
| McBroom, Geo. | Martin, Selina | C/28 | June 6, 1872 | June 6, 1872 |
| McBroom, Henry | Laseter, Mary E. | C/160 | April 17, 1877 | April 17, 1877 |
| McBroom, Isaac | Howeth, Mrs. Nancy J. | B/84 | August 19, 1869 | August 19, 1869 |
| McBroom, J. G. | Odom, Lena | F/46 | November 8, 1894 | November 8, 1894 |
| McBroom, J. W. | Fagan, Miss I. N. | B/128 | April 4, 1871 | April 5, 1871 |
| McBroom, James | Hays, Miss Rachel | A/131 | January 3, 1850 | January 3, 1850 |
| McBroom, Jennie | Hare, I. L. | D/8 | | December 21, 1881 |
| McBroom, Jessee | Mullins, Frances E. | C/70 | November 4, 1873 | November 4, 1873 |
| McBroom, John | Alexander, Miss Roxanna | A/117 | November 15, 1848 | November 16, 1848 |
| McBroom, John | Ferrel, Margaret | A2/109 | October 5, 1863 | October 5, 1863 |
| McBroom, John | Wilson, E. C. | C/158 | February 24, 1877 | February 25, 1877 |
| McBroom, Kissia J. Miss | McBroom, B. T. | B/88 | September 23, 1869 | September 23, 1869 |
| McBroom, L. A. | Howeth, R. B. | C/108 | February 6, 1875 | No Return |
| McBroom, Linner | Barton, Dan | E/250 | December 26, 1889 | December 26, 1889 |
| McBroom, Lizzie Miss | McKnight, B. R. | E/13 | January 23, 1888 | January 23, 1888 |
| McBroom, M. J. | McAffy, M. F. | C/264 | November 25, 1880 | November 25, 1880 |
| McBroom, M. H. | Womack, A. J. | D/20 | | July 16, 1882 |
| McBroom, Mahala | Wheeler, Forest | C/406 | October 9, 1887 | October 10, 1887 |
| McBroom, Manerva | Taylor, John M. | A2/124 | July 18, 1865 | July 18, 1865 |
| McBroom, Mary | Sellars, Robt | C/160 | April 18, 1877 | April 19, 1877 |
| McBroom, Mary F. | Alexander, Geo H. | C/134 | February 4, 1876 | February 4, 1876 |
| McBroom, Mattie Miss | Gaither, James E. | C/378 | December 25, 1886 | December 26, 1886 |
| McBroom, Minnia | Robinson, E. B. | C/366 | September 13, 1886 | September 15, 1886 |
| McBroom, Minnie | Davis, Simeon | E/82 | September 22, 1888 | September 23, 1888 |
| McBroom, Minnie | Summar, T. H. | F/156 | September 17, 1898 | September 18, 1898 |
| McBroom, Nancy | Stephens, John | B/8 | September 22, 1865 | November 19, 1865 |
| McBroom, Nancy E. Miss | Sullivan, James T. | B/124 | January 18, 1871 | January 19, 1871 |
| McBroom, Nathan | Gannon, Miss Martha Ann | A2/52 | December 11, 1856 | December 11, 1856 |
| McBroom, Narissie | Wales, J. M. | C/306 | February 29, 1884 | March 2, 1884 |
| McBroom, Rachel | Barton, Daniel | B/10 | December 24, 1866 | March 4, 1867 |
| McBroom, Robert | Mitchell, Etter | D/17 | | October 8, 1882 |
| McBroom, Robert C. | Hays, Miss Mary | A/86 | January 8, 1846 | No Return |
| McBroom, Sampson | McBroom, Flora | B/8 | November 17, 1865 | November 19, 1965 |

| Groom or Bride | Groom or Bride | Book/Page | Date of License | Date of Marriage |
|---|---|---|---|---|
| McBroom, Sarah J. | Barton, William Jr. | A/8 | November 1, 1838 | November 1, 1838 |
| McBroom, Stella Miss | Odom, B. B. | F/176 | May 18, 1899 | May 18, 1899 |
| McBroom, Sopha (col.) | Officer, Andy (col.) | F/88 | May 15, 1896 | May 15, 1896 |
| McBroom, Tennie | Hoover, Jasper | F/136 | November 13, 1897 | November ??, 1897 |
| McBroom, Thomas | Carnes, E. M. | C/142 | August 10, 1876 | August 10, 1876 |
| McBroom, Thomas L. | Summar, Miss Ella | F/168 | January 31, 1899 | February 1, 1899 |
| McBroom, W. B. | Curlee, Maggie | F/14 | August 19, 1893 | September 11, 1893 |
| McBroom, W. H. | McGill, Miss E. A. | B/110 | September 15, 1870 | September 15, 1870 |
| McBroom, Wm | Hays, Tennie | C/236 | January 7, 1880 | January ??, 1880 |
| McBroon, R. L. | Basham, Mollie | E/97 | November 3, 1888 | November 4, 1888 |
| McBrum, M. A. | Carter, J. T. | C/108 | February 10, 1875 | February 11, 1875 |
| McCabe, A. J. | Gurty, Miss Mary E. | A2/25 | May 20, 1853 | No Return |
| McCabe, Cornelia A. Miss | Todd, James H. | A2/146 | November 1, 1866 | November 1, 1866 |
| McCabe, Houston | Elkins, Mary C. | A2/93 | January 23, 1860 | No Return |
| McCabe, J. B. | St. John , Jennie | C/346 | December 26, 1885 | December 26, 1885 |
| McCabe, James A. | Todd, Sarah | C/30 | July 12, 1872 | July 14, 1872 |
| McCabe, James M. | Todd, Ann L. | C/216 | June 13, 1879 | June 23, 1879 |
| McCabe, Jeff | St. John, Miss Helen | C/384 | February 20, 1887 | February 20, 1887 |
| McCabe, John C. | Merit, Miss Elizabeth | A/79 | June 18, 1845 | June 18, 1845 |
| McCabe, Marry J. Miss | Lafevers, Wm. J. | A2/25 | April 12, 1853 | No Return |
| McCabe, Mary | Jones, A. V. | C/68 | October 16, 1873 | October 19, 1873 |
| McCabe, Mary C. Miss | Thomas, William | B/108 | August 25, 1870 | No Return |
| McCabe, Mary J. Miss | Todd, W. L. | B/86 | September 9, 1869 | September 9, 1869 |
| McCabe, Sarah | Wood, B. F. L | C/260 | November 8, 1880 | November 9, 1880 |
| McCabe, Tina | Cummings, A. J. | E/378 | October 29, 1898 | |
| McCabe, Tina | Cummings, O. J. | F/160 | October 29, 1898 | October 30, 1898 |
| McCabe, Wm. B. | Adcock, Miss America Ann | A2/26 | June 7, 1853 | June 9, 1853 |
| McCaffrey, Malissa Miss | Neval, John | B/42 | March 1, 1867 | March 1, 1867 |
| McCarlin, Elisabeth | Stacy, J. H. | C/230 | November 12, 1879 | No Return |
| McCarlin, Susan | Nesbett, J. A. | C/232 | December 16, 1879 | No Return |
| McCartin, W. C. | Hoover, Mary | C/106 | January 20, 1875 | January 20, 1875 |
| McCaslin | Hughs, Miss Adaline | A2/91 | December 15, 1859 | No Return |
| McCaslin, Bell | Shelton, Jno A. | C/188 | February 21, 1878 | February 21, 1878 |
| McCaslin, C. E. | Bynum, Lucinda | C/62 | July 30, 1873 | July 31, 1873 |
| McCaslin, Elisabeth | Stacy, J. H | C/242 | November 12, 1879 | November 13, 1879 |
| McCaslin, Emaline Miss | McGill, James P. | A/53 | September 8, 1842 | September 13, 1842 |
| McCaslin, Logan | Cooper, Betty | A2/102 | September 12, 1860 | September ?, 1860 |
| McCaslin, Margarett E. Miss | Soape, William C. | A/124 | August 31, 1848 | August 31, 1848 |
| McCaslin, Mattie J. | Lyon, M. D. | C/220 | August 13, 1879 | August 13, 1879 |
| McCaslin, R. E. | Shelton, B. M. | C/114 | June 17, 1875 | June 17, 1875 |
| McCasline, Roxannah | Donnell, Jas. W. | C/152 | January 17, 1877 | January 19, 1877 |
| McCaster, Logan | Stacy, Malindy | E/75 | September 18, 1888 | September 18, 1888 |
| McClain, James | Gooding, Miss Martha | A/101 | August 20, 1847 | No Return |
| McClain, James P. | Petty, Miss Martha | A2/131 | November 12, 1865 | November 12, 1865 |
| McClain, Jane Miss | Rodgers, John | A2/64 | April 8, 1858 | April 8, 1858 |
| McClain, M. J. | Reed, J. I. | C/56 | March 22, 1873 | March 23, 1873 |

| Groom or Bride | Groom or Bride | Book/Page | Date of License | Date of Marriage |
|---|---|---|---|---|
| McClain, Mary | Elladge, Wm. C. | A/94 | December 23, 1846 | December 24, 1846 |
| McClain, Thomas | Harris, Elisabeth J. | C/248 | March 1, 1880 | March 1, 1880 |
| McClain, W. H. | Oliver, Miss Tennie | F/100 | November 3, 1896 | November 4, 1896 |
| McClemen, Ed | McAdoo, Ellen | C/128 | December 30, 1875 | December 30, 1875 |
| McClennen, Fannie | Callico, Jack | C/152 | January 17, 1877 | No Return |
| McCollough, Angeline | Bryant, Spence | C/296 | November 24, 1883 | November 25, 1883 |
| McCollough, Thomas | Gray, Rachel Caroline | A/6 | September 18, 1838 | September 19, 1838 |
| McCow, Martha Miss | Jones, John M. | A/128 | November 9, 1849 | No Return |
| McCoy, Catherine | Anderson, William | E/261 | January 10, 1890 | No Return |
| McCrary, Abram | Smith, Mary | B/18 | December 16, 1869 | December 16, 1869 |
| McCrary, Arthur | Knox, Miss Sophiz E. | A/71 | August 16, 1844 | August 19, 1844 |
| McCrary, Hattie (col) | Barton, Edman (col) | E/370 | November 21, 1898 | |
| McCrary, J. H. | Gilley, Miss Malinda | A2/151 | May 16, 1866 | May 17, 1866 |
| McCrary, J. W. | Gaither, Sallie | F/78 | December 17, 1895 | December 18, 1895 |
| McCray, Hattie (col) | Barton, Jordan (col.) | F/160 | November 21, 1898 | November 22, 1898 |
| McCray, Nancy | Brandon, John E. | A/13 | May 16, 1839 | May 16, 1839 |
| McCullar, Samuel | Cawthon, Miss Mary | B/112 | October 7, 1870 | October 18, 1870 |
| McCuller, R. S. Miss | Baltimore, P. J. | B/112 | September 28, 1870 | September 29, 1870 |
| McCulloch, Martin | Roberts, Miss Melberry | A2/137 | February 13, 1866 | February 18, 1866 |
| McCullough, Alexander | Stacy, Miss Rebecca | A/42 | October 14, 1841 | October 20, 1841 |
| McCullough, Angeline | William, W. L. | E/46 | July 11, 1888 | July 16, 1888 |
| McCullough, Elvira | Espey, Geo. W. | C/162 | June 3, 1877 | June 3, 1877 |
| McCullough, Huldah | Stacy, Jim | F/112 | February 10, 1897 | February 10, 1897 |
| McCullough, John | West, Miss Ester | C/412 | December 16, 1887 | December 18, 1887 |
| McCullough, John A. | McDaniel, Elvira | A/60 | March 14, 1843 | March 15, 1843 |
| McCullough, Mary A. Miss | Elliott, A. C. | C/6 | August 29, 1871 | August 30, 1871 |
| McCullough, Millie W. | Messick, Elijah | C/130 | January 12, 1876 | January 12, 1876 |
| McCullough, R. J. | Taylor, J. L. | C/14 | November 9, 1871 | November 12, 1871 |
| McCullough, Rada S. | Williams, Benjamin | A2/126 | September 4, 1865 | September 7, 1865 |
| McCullough, Sarah A. Miss | Fight, Obediah | B/100 | February 9, 1870 | February 16, 1870 |
| McCullough, William W. | Wharry, Malvina Ann | A/59 | January 11, 1843 | January 12, 1843 |
| McDanel, Roda A. Miss | Crane, A. W. | A2/152 | May 23, 1866 | May 23, 1866 |
| McDaniel, David | Reynolds, Miss Adaline D. | A/51 | July 16, 1842 | July 18, 1842 |
| McDaniel, Elvira | McCullough, John A. | A/60 | March 14, 1843 | March 15, 1843 |
| McDaniel, James | Reynods, Nancy | A/20 | December 10, 1839 | December 10, 1839 |
| McDarnell, Mallice | Keaton, Henry | C/416 | September 15, 1890 | September 15, 1890 |
| McDengal, J. D. | Vandygrift, Lucinda | C/218 | July 19, 1879 | July 20, 1879 |
| McDougal, Anna C. | Maxey, Daniel | A2/119 | December 28, 1864 | No Return |
| McDougle, Eliza | Spicer, Wm | C/48 | December 20, 1872 | December 22, 1872 |
| McDougal, Elizabeth | Hendrixson, John | A2/108 | July 25, 1863 | November 26, 1863 |
| McDougal, John D. | Gaither, Mary C. | E/69 | September 6, 1888 | September 6, 1888 |
| McDougal, John W. | St. John, Miss Margaret J. | A2/144 | September 3, 1866 | Executed No Date |
| McDougal, John W. | Todd, Miss Eliza J. | B/102 | April 7, 1870 | April 7, 1870 |
| McDougal, Malisa | Barns, Asbery | C/232 | December 9, 1879 | December 9, 1879 |
| McDougal, Mary | Campbell, Henry V. | D/5 | | October 9, 1881 |
| McDougald, Alexander | Ledbetter, Nancy | A/96 | January 11, 1847 | January 18, 1847 |

| Groom or Bride | Groom or Bride | Book/Page | Date of License | Date of Marriage |
|---|---|---|---|---|
| McDougald, John D. | Gunter, Miss Sarah | A/58 | January 2, 1843 | January 5, 1843 |
| McDougle, Gunter | St. John, Miss Malisa | B/124 | January 2, 1871 | No Return |
| McDougle, John | St. John, Miss Betty | A2/103 | October 2, 1860 | No Return |
| McDougle, Lidia | Grizzle, Wm. | F/124 | August 4, 1897 | August 4, 1897 |
| McDougle, Margarett | Taylor, R. | C/160 | April 7, 1877 | April 8, 1877 |
| McDougle, T. B | Ferrell, Laura | C/174 | October 24, 1877 | October 24, 1877 |
| McDougle, Wm. | Johnson, Mattie | F/146 | February 22, 1898 | February 23, 1898 |
| McDow, Nancy E. Miss | Knox, S. W. | A2/48 | May 15, 1856 | No Return |
| McDowell, Eliza | Murphy, John | D/1 | | July 9, 1881 |
| McElroy, B. N. | McKnight, E. S. | C/364 | August 11, 1886 | August 11, 1886 |
| McElroy, E. P. | McKnight, Sallie | C/180 | December 18, 1877 | December 18, 1877 |
| McElroy, James | Patton, Margaret | A2/126 | September 4, 1865 | December 5, 1865 |
| McElroy, John James | Patton, Miss Mary Ann | A/87 | February 25, 1846 | March 2, 1846 |
| McElroy, S. N. | Porterfield, M. M. | C/14 | November 16, 1871 | November 16, 1871 |
| McElroy, W. H. | McKnight, M. E. | F/26 | December 13, 1893 | December 14, 1893 |
| McEwen, John Dixson | Tate, Miss Hannah Emaline | A/111 | May 25, 1848 | May 25, 1848 |
| McEwin, Eliza Miss | Malone, Erskine | A/90 | September 1, 1846 | September 1, 1846 |
| McEwin, Joseph | Thomas, Emaliza | A/12 | April 6, 1839 | April 7, 1839 |
| McEwin, Sarah Miss | Ready, Elias Alexander | A/113 | August 7, 1848 | August 7, 1848 |
| McFaddan, Miss Ann M. | Fagan, Granville | A2/75 | September 18, 1854 | September 18, 1854 |
| McFarland, Benjamin P. | McKnight, Miss Ervina C. | A/101 | August 9, 1847 | August 12, 1847 |
| McFarland, D. J. | Boren, M. J. | F/112 | February 10, 1897 | February 14, 1897 |
| McFarland, H. R. | Swanger, Mary Ann | C/88 | July 20, 1874 | July 23, 1874 |
| McFarland, W. R. | Swanger, Mary Ann | C/92 | July 20, 1874 | No Return |
| McFarlin, Henry | Hawkins, Cornelus J. | C/324 | January 12, 1885 | January 13, 1885 |
| McFerin, L. B. | Webb, Mary E. | A2/120 | February 7, 1865 | February 7, 1865 |
| McFerin, Mary J. | Reagan, R. A. | A2/118 | November 28, 1864 | November 29, 1864 |
| McFerin, Wm | Fisher, Marian E. | A2/108 | August 17, 1863 | No Return |
| McFerren, Fannie F. Miss | Page, John W. | A2/143 | August 21, 1866 | August 23, 1866 |
| McFerren, Bittie | Halleyburton, O. G. | C/40 | September 26, 1872 | September 26, 1872 |
| McFerrin, Alford | Cummins, Rebecca A. | C/44 | November 16, 1872 | November 17, 1872 |
| McFerrin, Alfred | Eason, Emily | B/2 | August 23, 1865 | August 25, 1865 |
| McFerrin, Annie Miss | Rayburn, Adam | F/66 | July 10, 1895 | July 10, 1895 |
| McFerrin, Author | Hays, Miss Lizzy | F/134 | October 6, 1897 | October 7, 1897 |
| McFerrin, Burton L. | Young, Miss Martha | A/62 | June 1, 1843 | June 1, 1843 |
| McFerrin, E. C. Miss | Oliver, J. R. | A2/92 | December 21, 1859 | No Return |
| McFerrin, Edmund | Duncan, Jane | B/4 | August 24, 1865 | No Return |
| McFerrin, Emagene Miss | Hayes, W. T. | C/394 | July 3, 1887 | July 31, 1887 |
| McFerrin, Fannie | Raburn, Eugene | F/60 | March 18, 1895 | March 19, 1895 |
| McFerrin, J. A. | Wood, Miss Tennie | B/122 | January 1, 1871 | January 1, 1871 |
| McFerrin, Jack | George, Harrett | C/96 | October 8, 1874 | October 8, 1874 |
| McFerrin, Jack | Rushing, Jennie | C/130 | January 13, 1876 | January 13, 1876 |
| McFerrin, James (col.) | Taylor, Laura (col.) | D/2 | | August 23, 1881 |
| McFerrin, Joe | Taylor, Aggie | C/224 | September 10, 1879 | September 10, 1879 |
| McFerrin, Joe | Fugette, Jane | F/6 | March 18, 1893 | March 18, 1893 |
| McFerrin, Louisa | Wright, Joseph | B/4 | August 23, 1865 | September 3, 1865 |

| Groom or Bride | Groom or Bride | Book/Page | Date of License | Date of Marriage |
|---|---|---|---|---|
| McFerrin, Mary E. | Oliver, John H. | A2/125 | August 22, 1865 | August 22, 1865 |
| McFerrin, Mattie | Taylor, Davill | C/380 | December 29, 1886 | December 30, 1886 |
| McFerrin, S. J. | Robertson, J. G. | C/192 | May 4, 1878 | May 5, 1878 |
| McFerrin, Sallie | Norman, G. R. | C/300 | January 19, 1884 | No Return |
| McFerrin, Sophia | Officer, Anderson | C/100 | October 31, 1874 | October 31, 1874 |
| McFerrin, William H. | Mitchell, Miss Sarah J. | A2/147 | November 8, 1866 | November 8, 1866 |
| McFerrin, Zeke | Barnes, Lutisia | C/66 | September 20, 1873 | September 22, 1873 |
| McGee, J. S. | Hipp, Margaret | C/166 | August 8, 1877 | August 12, 1877 |
| McGee, J. S. | Wilcher, Eliza J. | D/23 | | February 7, 1883 |
| McGee, James | Lee, Annie | F/34 | September 28, 1894 | September 30, 1894 |
| McGee, Jane Miss | Vandagriff, John | A2/32 | April 28, 1854 | No Return |
| McGee, Jesse | King, Miss Nancy E. | A/115 | October 19, 1848 | October 19, 1848 |
| McGee, L. R. | Jetton, Wm | C/72 | November 20, 1873 | November 20, 1873 |
| McGee, Mary | Scott, Mark | D/18 | | December 3, 1882 |
| McGee, Nancy T. A. Miss | Keaton, Peter N. J. | B/90 | October 4, 1869 | October 10, 1869 |
| McGee, Robt. | Markum, Anthon A. | C/38 | September 12, 1872 | September 12, 1872 |
| McGee, Sarah | Patterson, John Meth | F/100 | October 23, 1896 | October 25, 1896 |
| McGee, William | Cox, Miss Lavina Ann Sophia | A/40 | July 28, 1841 | July 29, 1841 |
| McGill, A. T. | Lyons, Bettie | E/156 | December 22, 1888 | December 25, 1888 |
| McGill, Andy | Prutherbin, Rebeckey | C/234 | December 21, 1879 | December 25, 1879 |
| McGill, B. J. | Martin, Martha J. | C/156 | February 17, 1877 | February 22, 1877 |
| McGill, Bettie | Creson, James | F/156 | September 2, 1898 | No Return |
| McGill, Dora | McMahan, John F. | C/258 | October 14, 1880 | October 14, 1880 |
| McGill, E. A. Miss | McBroom, W. H. | B/110 | September 15, 1870 | September 15, 1870 |
| McGill, James P. | McCaslin, Miss Emaline | A/53 | September 8, 1842 | September 13, 1842 |
| McGill, Jane Miss | Patton, David M. | A/123 | July 20, 1848 | July 20, 1848 |
| McGill, Jane Miss | Patton, David M. | A/125 | July 20, 1848 | |
| McGill, John | Gizzel, Roday | C/304 | February 11, 1884 | No Date |
| McGill, Lillie | Willas, Wiley | C/358 | May 27, 1886 | May 30, 1886 |
| McGill, M. J. | Knox, R. P. | C/368 | September 23, 1886 | September 26, 1886 |
| McGill, Martha Miss | Anderson, J. G. | A2/143 | August 22, 1866 | August 26, 1866 |
| McGill, Mary A. | Carson, Green | C/132 | February 1, 1876 | March 19, 1876 |
| McGill, P. T. | Allmon, E. H. | A2/115 | July 13, 1864 | July 13, 1864 |
| McGill, R. E. | Ivie, T. B. | C/84 | March 23, 1874 | March 24, 1874 |
| McGill, Sarah E. Miss | Summers, J. A. | B/56 | December 3, 1867 | December 3, 1867 |
| McGill, William | Fagan, Miss Eliza | A/83 | August 15, 1845 | August ?, 1845 |
| McGlocklin, Eleanor | Mitchell, Daniel W. | A/30 | June 18, 1840 | June 18, 1840 |
| McGlothin, W. C. | Young, Miss Matilda J. | A2/71 | December 21, 1858 | December 22, 1858 |
| McGowen, Etta | Haley, Isaac | F/128 | August 26, 1897 | August 29, 1897 |
| McGregar, Isaac | Brim, Cyntha | C/244 | March 15, 1880 | March 15, 1880 |
| McGregger, S. J. Miss | McGregger, Wm. B. | A2/51 | November 15, 1856 | No Return |
| McGregger, Wm. B. | McGregger, Miss S. J. | A2/51 | November 15, 1856 | No Return |
| McGregor, Dent | Merryman, Jennie | E/33 | April 13, 1888 | April 14, 1888 |
| McGregor, Denton | Webb, Eliza J. | C/194 | July 30, 1878 | July 30, 1878 |
| McGuire, Thos. G. | Simpson, Miss Martha J. | A/127 | September 8, 1849 | September 9, 1849 |
| McIntire, Arren | Tenpenny, S. J. | C/288 | August 13, 1883 | August 13, 1883 |

| Groom or Bride | Groom or Bride | Book/Page | Date of License | Date of Marriage |
|---|---|---|---|---|
| McKee, William | Hoover, Mary | A2/133 | December 11, 1865 | December 12, 1865 |
| McKenny, Mike T. | Jones, Nancy | C/306 | April 12, 1884 | April 12, 1884 |
| McKinney, Nancy | Grimes, J. B. | C/362 | July 24, 1886 | No Return |
| McKnab, R. T. | Gray, N. E. | A2/130 | October 7, 1864 | October 19, 1865 |
| McKnabb, J. F. | Todd, Miss L. J. | A2/136 | January 20, 1866 | January 31, 1866 |
| McKnight, A. B. | Mathews, Miss Mary E. | A2/12 | October 22, 1851 | No Return |
| McKnight, A. D. | Hare, Miss M. L. | A2/23 | February 1, 1853 | February 3, 1853 |
| McKnight, A. E. | Goodloe, E. A. | A2/86 | July 7, 1859 | No Return |
| McKnight, A. G. | Fare, Miss D. L. | A2/59 | November 3, 1857 | November 3, 1857 |
| McKnight, Abigale | Mabry, Abe | B/12 | December 3, 1867 | December 5, 1867 |
| McKnight, Abner | Fuller, Susan | B/14 | December 28, 1867 | December 28, 1867 |
| McKnight, Aimey | Barkley, Franklin | B/2 | August 21, 1865 | August 26, 1865 |
| McKnight, Allie | Martin, George | C/472 | December 20, 1892 | December 21, 1892 |
| McKnight, Amzi B. | Jetton, Miss Sarah R. | B/72 | November 3, 1868 | November 3, 1868 |
| McKnight, Ann | Nrizar, Neely | D/17 | | October 13, 1882 |
| McKnight, Annie | Dement, W. M. | F/78 | December 17, 1895 | December 18, 1895 |
| McKnight, B. R | McBroom, Miss Lizzie | E/13 | January 23, 1888 | January 23, 1888 |
| McKnight, Bella J. | Barkley, Charley H. | D/9 | | December 22, 1881 |
| McKnight, C. R. | Baxter, R. F. | C/80 | January 17, 1874 | January 29, 1874 |
| McKnight, Charles | McKnight, Harriet | B/2 | August 21, 1865 | August 26, 1865 |
| McKnight, Daisy Dean Miss | Hooper, Walter Edger | F/166 | January 3, 1899 | January 4, 1899 |
| McKnight, David | Odom, Charity | C/82 | February 4, 1874 | February 4, 1874 |
| McKnight, David | Sauls, Better | E/203 | August 31, 1889 | August 31, 1889 |
| McKnight, E. A. | Carter, M. L. | C/264 | December 23, 1880 | December 23, 1880 |
| McKnight, E. S. | McElroy, B. N. | C/364 | August 11, 1886 | August 11, 1886 |
| McKnight, Eliza | Hancock, Jerry | C/54 | March ??, 1873 | April 3, 1873 |
| McKnight, Easter S. Miss | Rodgers, Ramzel H. | A/69 | May 2, 1844 | No Return |
| McKnight, Ed | Barrett, Babe | C/46 | December 14, 1872 | December 15, 1872 |
| McKnight, Elim | Collins, M. M. | A2/33 | May 18, 1854 | May 18, 1854 |
| McKnight, Eliza E. | Martin, Zinas A. | A/29 | May 13, 1840 | May 20, 1840 |
| McKnight, Elizabeth | Smith, Albert | B/2 | August 21, 1865 | August 26, 1865 |
| McKnight, Ella | Tucker, J. D. | F/52 | December 11, 1894 | December 13, 1894 |
| McKnight, Eller | Weeden, George (col.) | F/70 | September 11, 1895 | September 12, 1895 |
| McKnight, Ervina C. Miss | McFarland, Benjamin P. | A/101 | August 9, 1847 | August 12, 1847 |
| McKnight, G. D. A. | Andrews, Miss Eleanor F. | A/126 | September 5, 1849 | No Return |
| McKnight, Harriet | McKnight, Charles | B/2 | August 21, 1865 | August 26, 1865 |
| McKnight, Hattie (col.) | Daniel, Boregard (col.) | D/14 | | July 2, 1882 |
| McKnight, Henry | Mason, Alice | C/56 | March 9, 1873 | March 20, 1873 |
| McKnight, Henry | Palmer, Mary | C/374 | November 16, 1886 | November 16, 1886 |
| McKnight, Ike | Grizzle, Birtha | F/124 | August 2, 1897 | August 2, 1897 |
| McKnight, Isaberlla E. Miss | Martin, Anzie | A/37 | March 12, 1841 | March 25, 1841 |
| McKnight, Issabella A. | Ralston, David N. | A/53 | September 10, 1842 | September 15, 1842 |
| McKnight, James | Barton, Florance | D/7 | | November 24, 1881 |
| McKnight, James L. | McKnight, Miss Margarett Jane | A/84 | November 5, 1845 | November 6, 1845 |
| McKnight, James T. | Jetton, Miss Mary E. | A/93 | November 25, 1846 | |
| McKnight, Joe D. | Webb, Mary L. | C/106 | February 1, 1875 | February 4, 1875 |

| Groom or Bride | Groom or Bride | Book/Page | Date of License | Date of Marriage |
|---|---|---|---|---|
| McKnight, John (col.) | Thompson, Sarah (ol.) | F/104 | December 15, 1896 | December 17, 1896 |
| McKnight, John N. | Moon, Miss Charlota | A2/88 | September 1, 1859 | No Return |
| McKnight, Joseph D. | Stepehens, Miss Artalia P. | B/64 | March 20, 1868 | March 22, 1868 |
| McKnight, Laura | Alexander, Madison | C/324 | January 28, 1885 | January 28, 1885 |
| McKnight, Lue | Davenport, B. L. | F/120 | July 3, 1897 | July 4, 1897 |
| McKnight, M. E. | McElroy, W. H. | F/26 | December 13, 1893 | December 14, 1893 |
| McKnight, M. E. Miss | Herter?, A. | A2/94 | February 13, 1861 | No Return |
| McKnight, M. H. | Carter, D. R. | C/302 | January 22, 1884 | January 23, 1884 |
| McKnight, Margarett E. Miss | Smith, William H. | A/94 | December 23, 1846 | December 25, 1846 |
| McKnight, Margarett Jane Miss | McKnight, James L. | A/84 | November 5, 1845 | November 6, 1845 |
| McKnight, Mary A. Miss | Lyon, George W. | A2/9 | December 23, 1850 | December 24, 1850 |
| McKnight, Mary Ann | Trimble, Aaron | B/8 | February 17, 1866 | February 18, 1866 |
| McKnight, Mary J. | Duggin, W. P. | C/64 | July 31, 1873 | July 31, 1873 |
| McKnight, Mat | Summers, Ell | E/249 | December 24, 1889 | December 25, 1889 |
| McKnight, Mattie Miss | Davenport, Jessie | C/452 | December 26, 1891 | December 27, 1891 |
| McKnight, Merry | Writh, Wingo (col.) | C/412 | December 30, 1887 | December 30, 1887 |
| McKnight, Morge | Hollis, Miss Mandy | C/6 | August 5, 1871 | August 6, 1871 |
| McKnight, Moses W. | Fare, Mary A. | A2/41 | September 24, 1855 | Returns Missing |
| McKnight, Nancy | Weatherly, Jesse | B/12 | November 9, 1867 | November 14, 1867 |
| McKnight, Nancy M. | Lackey, William R | A/18 | October 19, 1839 | October 24, 1839 |
| McKnight, Nannie A. Miss | Carter, D. R | B/70 | September 16, 1868 | September 16, 1868 |
| McKnight, Ruben | Rucker, Miss L. | B/114 | October 14, 1870 | No Return |
| McKnight, S. H. A. | Andrew, Miss Mary F. | A/104 | November 9, 1847 | November 11, 1847 |
| McKnight, S. O. | McBroom, Bettie | C/76 | December 18, 1873 | No Return |
| McKnight, Sallie | Williams, D. C. | C/148 | November 19, 1876 | November 19, 1876 |
| McKnight, Sallie | McElroy, E. P. | C/180 | December 18, 1877 | December 18, 1877 |
| McKnight, Samuel P. | Hare, Miss Lucinda D. | A/121 | February 12, 1849 | No Return |
| McKnight, Sarah E. | Byrne, James H. | A/76 | February 16, 1845 | February 20, 1845 |
| McKnight, Sarah E. | Milligan, Joel | F/94 | September 8, 1896 | September 9, 1896 |
| McKnight, Sarah E. Miss | Duggan, Henry S. | A/105 | December 20, 1847 | December 21, 1847 |
| McKnight, Sarah J. Miss | Andrews, J. M. | A/93 | October 31, 1846 | November 24, 1846 |
| McKnight, Sarah M. Miss | Bryson, Samuel H. | B/104 | July 7, 1870 | July 7, 1870 |
| McKnight, Susan | Talley, Abe | C/276 | March 8, 1881 | No Return |
| McKnight, Sylva | Brantley, Franklin | B/2 | August 21, 1865 | August 26, 1865 |
| McKnight, Tennessee | McNairy, Malone | B/10 | January 10, 1867 | January 10, 1867 |
| McKnight, W. A. | Walkup, Hanar | C/202 | October 16, 1878 | October 16, 1878 |
| McKnight, W. M. | Bethell, T. N. | B/74 | December 23, 1868 | December 25, 1868 |
| McKnight, W. W. | Hollandsworth, Sarah | C/266 | December 31, 1880 | January 2, 1881 |
| McKnight, Wanda (col.) | Smith, Buck (col.) | F/62 | March 26, 1895 | No Return |
| McKnight, William W. | Sutton, Miss Elizabeth | A/123 | July 5, 1849 | No Return |
| Mclain, E. J. Miss | Petty, John | A2/29 | November 19, 1853 | November 20, 1853 |
| McLea?, Margarette | Ferrell, E. E. | E/256 | January 1, 1890 | No Return |
| McLin, Allice M. Miss | Rucker, J. E. | B/98 | December 7, 1869 | December 8, 1869 |
| McMahan | Fleming, S. H. | D/16 | | September 14, 1882 |
| McMahan, Brownlow | Allison, Jane | C/202 | October 30, 1878 | October 30 1878 |
| McMahan, Dollie | Jones, R. B. | F/48 | November 10, 1894 | November 11, 1894 |

| Groom or Bride | Groom or Bride | Book/Page | Date of License | Date of Marriage |
|---|---|---|---|---|
| McMahan, Frances | Tolbert, Silas | E/115 | December 22, 1888 | December 23, 1888 |
| McMahan, J. T. | Hipp, Miss N. J. | A2/146 | October 17, 1866 | October 18, 1866 |
| McMahan, J. T. | Elkins, Angeline | C/96 | October 1, 1874 | October 1, 1874 |
| McMahan, J. T. | Thomas, Margrett | C/98 | October 23, 1874 | October 24, 1874 |
| McMahan, John F. | McGill, Dora | C/258 | October 14, 1880 | October 14, 1880 |
| McMahan, John S. | Thomas, Miss Luda | F/168 | January 24, 1899 | No Return |
| McMahan, July A. | Hiff, J. P. | D/15 | | September 10, 1882 |
| McMahan, L. J. | Parker, A. W. | C/16 | December 18, 1871 | December 24, 1871 |
| McMahan, Lillie | Thomas, W. C. | F/152 | July 4, 1898 | July 5, 1898 |
| McMahan, M. J. | Fuston, H. T. | C/138 | May 30, 1876 | May 30, 1876 |
| McMahan, Maggie | Moody, Jessie | F/34 | March 7, 1894 | No Return |
| McMahan, Mattie L. | Parker, H. C. | C/342 | November 27, 1885 | No Return |
| McMahan, Minnie | Simpson, H. E. | F/1 | January 14, 1893 | January 15, 1893 |
| McMahan, Rebecca Ann Miss | Harrell, H. L. | B/60 | January 13, 1868 | January 16, 1868 |
| McMahan, Rebecca J. | Duke, C. J. | C/144 | September 15, 1876 | September 17, 1876 |
| McMahan, Rosa | Stacy, W. H. E. | F/32 | February 22, 1894 | February 28, 1894 |
| McMahan, S. W. | Haley, M. E. | C/300 | January 16, 1884 | January 17, 1884 |
| McMahan, S. W. | Haley, Nancy J. | C/404 | October 26, 1887 | October 26, 1887 |
| McMahan, Sarah J. | Elam, J. M. | C/92 | August 18, 1874 | August 20, 1874 |
| McMahan, T. V. | Cates, Mollie | F/102 | November 24, 1896 | November 25, 1896 |
| McMickley, William | Ford, Nancy | A/6 | September 4, 1838 | September 4, 1838 |
| McMillan, John | Knox, Margrett | C/172 | October 9, 1 877 | October 10, 1877 |
| McMillen, Eliza | Prater, Pat | C/262 | November 19, 1880 | November 26, 1880 |
| McMillen, Wm. | Peay, Lena | E/105 | November 29, 1888 | November 30, 1888 |
| McMiller, Martha J. | Knox, L. G. | C/162 | May 12, 1877 | May 13, 1877 |
| McMillon, Wason | Willard, Eag. | F/92 | August 3, 1896 | August 23, 1896 |
| McMurry, Miss Hattie E. | Moore, R. A. | C/44 | November 13, 1872 | November 14, 1872 |
| McNabb, Dilelah | Odom, J. S. | C/12 | October 12, 1871 | October 16, 1871 |
| McNabb, G. R. | Francis, N. H. | C/122 | September 29, 1875 | September 30, 1875 |
| McNairy, Malone | McKnight, Tennessee | B/10 | January 10, 1867 | January 10, 1867 |
| McNeely, Mary Ann | Davis, Andy | F/88 | June 13, 1896 | June 13, 1896 |
| McNelly, Rubin R. | Stanley, Nancy F. | C/342 | November 28, 1885 | November 28, 1885 |
| McNelly, Yonan | Bly, William | C/394 | July 16, 1887 | July 17, 1887 |
| McNelly, Yonan | Bly, William | C/394 | July 16, 1887 | July 17, 1887 |
| McNight, Mary F. Miss | Carter, W. P. | B/128 | March 16, 1871 | March 16, 1871 |
| McPhearson, Margarett E. Miss | Ashford, Compton | A/44 | November 24, 1841 | November 25, 1841 |
| McRead, W. | Hollis, R. M. | A2/99 | July 14, 1860 | No Return |
| McWhearter, L. H. | Wale, J. H. | C/46 | November 23, 1872 | November 24, 1872 |
| McWhirter, S. A. | Youngblood, Mary E. | C/198 | September 14, 1878 | September 15, 1878 |
| Meadow, Wm. L. | Leach, Nancy | A/24 | February 13, 1840 | |
| Meadows, M. M. | Rigsby, Catherine | C/88 | May 2, 1874 | No Return |
| Mean (Mears), Elizabeth A. | Haley, B. F. | C/158 | March 8, 1877 | March 8, 1877 |
| Meanis, John | Kerby, Mitita | A/3 | May 14, 1838 | June 10, 1838 |
| Meants, James | Mayes, Susan A. | A2/14 | November 10, 1851 | December 1, 1851 |
| Meares, Alta | Alexander, Bob | F/156 | September 27, 1898 | September 27, 1898 |
| Meares, Myrtle | Davis, Tom | F/176 | May 5, 1899 | May 7, 1899 |

| Groom or Bride | Groom or Bride | Book/Page | Date of License | Date of Marriage |
|---|---|---|---|---|
| Meares, T. J. | Turney, Mai | E/384 | October 15, 1898 | |
| Meares, T. J. | Turney, Miss Mai | F/158 | October 15, 1898 | October 23, 1898 |
| Meares, Willey | Saules, Miss Haulie | F/166 | January 9, 1899 | January 19, 1899 |
| Mears, Amandy A. | Mullenix, J. P. | C/200 | September 28, 1878 | No Return |
| Mears, Arch | Gannon, Josie | F/134 | October 23, 1897 | October 24, 1897 |
| Mears, Elijah | Bailey, Nancy | A/28 | April 22, 1840 | April 24, 1840 |
| Mears, Eliza J. | Thomas, George W. | E/228 | November 2, 1889 | November 2, 1889 |
| Mears, Elizabeth | Haley, George | D/13 | | July 30, 1882 |
| Mears, Francis | Miller, Frank | C/156 | February 18, 1877 | February 18, 1877 |
| Mears, J. D. | Gaither, W. F. | C/316 | October 23, 1884 | October 24, 1884 |
| Mears, Hallie | Seals, Radege | F/124 | August 4, 1897 | August 5, 1897 |
| Mears, James | Elkins, Nancy | A/50 | July 2, 1842 | July 3, 1842 |
| Mears, James | Tedder, Mrs. Mary C. | A/117 | November 14, 1848 | November 14, 1848 |
| Mears, James H. | Petty, Mary | C/352 | February 16, 1886 | February 17, 1886 |
| Mears, Jennie | Gaither, R. A. | F/52 | December 8, 1894 | December 9, 1894 |
| Mears, John C. | Wherry, Miss Frances E. | B/34 | December 20, 1866 | December 20, 1866 |
| Mears, M. | Tarwater, Thomas | A2/28 | October 13, 1853 | October 14, 1853 |
| Mears, Marcus | Youngblood, M. J. | C/84 | March 19, 1874 | No Return |
| Mears, Mark | Hailey, Miss Elizabeth | B/46 | July 1, 1867 | July 3, 1867 |
| Mears, Mark | Hollandsworth, Miss Florence | C/454 | January 12, 1892 | January 18, 1892 |
| Mears, Melvina | Cummings, P. D. | A2/131 | November 9, 1865 | November 12, 1865 |
| Mears, Nancy Manerva Miss | James, Daniel | A/37 | April 1, 1841 | April 1, 1841 |
| Mears, Rebecca | Thomas, Joel | C/54 | February 26, 1873 | February 26, 1873 |
| Mears, Robert R. | Watter, R. J. | A2/117 | November 2, 1864 | November 3, 1864 |
| Mears, Robt. F. | Thomas, Nancy | C/316 | November 14, 1884 | November 14, 1884 |
| Mears, Sarah Miss | Bucy, George W. | A2/10 | January 11, 1851 | January 12, 1851 |
| Mears, Sarah T. Miss | Gaither, J. H. | E/132 | February 4, 1889 | February 4, 1889 |
| Mears, T. B. | Elledge, Sarah F. | C/136 | April 9, 1876 | April 9, 1876 |
| Mears, Thomas J. | Alexander, Miss Elixabeth | A2/75 | December 30, 1854 | December 30, 1854 |
| Mears, W. S. | Cooper, L. M. F. | C/434 | April 10, 1891 | April 12, 1891 |
| Mears, W. T. | Bryson, Emley F. | C/16 | December 2, 1871 | December 3, 1871 |
| Mears, William | Morgan, Liddia | A/3 | June 7, 1838 | June 7, 1838 |
| Mears, William | Wood, Miss Mary S. | B/114 | October ??, 1870 | October 20, 1870 |
| Mears, Wm. | Gaither, Sallie | C/316 | November 20, 1884 | November 20, 1884 |
| Measel, N. C. | Patton, A. D. | C/60 | July 12, 1873 | No Return |
| McClelland, Andrew | Wright, Jennie | F/4 | February 16, 1893 | February 16, 1893 |
| Meddows, Vincent | Hitt, Mary Ann | A/9 | December 24, 1838 | No Return |
| Medford, Henry | Harris, Miss Mary | A/70 | June 26, 1844 | June 26, 1844 |
| Medford, Henry | _____, Miss Malinda | A2/47 | March 22, 1856 | March 22, 1856 |
| Medlock, Thomas | Fletcher, Hariett | C/18 | December 27, 1871 | December 28, 1871 |
| Meeks, Isaac | Burk, Sarah F. | C/324 | January 21, 1885 | January 21, 1885 |
| Meeks, J. W. | Burnett, Matilda | C/60 | July 5, 1873 | No Return |
| Meeks, Rosa | Gilley, J. Caleb | C/428 | January 2, 1891 | January 2, 1891 |
| Meers, Gabriel | Bolen, Miss Martha | A2/142 | August 2, 1866 | Executed No Date |
| Mellon, Thomas J. | Turner, Sarah Katharine | A2/27 | August 3, 1853 | August 3, 1853 |
| Melton, A. | Smithson, Lona | F/10 | June 17, 1893 | June 18, 1893 |

| Groom or Bride | Groom or Bride | Book/Page | Date of License | Date of Marriage |
|---|---|---|---|---|
| Melton, Ailcy C. Miss | Melton, Greefield | A/119 | January 8, 1849 | January 8, 1849 |
| Melton, Ann C. Miss | Goff, L. P. | B/100 | March 29, 1870 | March 28, 1868 |
| Melton, Anne | Cummins, John | A/28 | May 5, 1840 | No Return |
| Melton, Bemjaman | Neely, Bettie | C/346 | December 25, 1885 | December 30, 1885 |
| Melton, Benjamin | Elkins, Miss Malissa Caroline | A/86 | January 28, 1846 | January 28, 1846 |
| Melton, Bettie | Higgins, Jesse | C/218 | July 26, 1879 | July 27, 1879 |
| Melton, C. D. | Givens, Miss Mary | A2/147 | November 1, 1866 | November 7, 1866 |
| Melton, Clem | Higgins, John G. | C/130 | January 6, 1876 | No Return |
| Melton, Cythian Miss | Campbell, Henry | A2/57 | August 29, 1857 | Return not Exectued |
| Melton, Dallas | Rigsby, Miss Myrtle | C/456 | March 11, 1892 | March 13, 1892 |
| Melton, David | Vandegriff, Sarah P. | C/88 | July 14, 1874 | July 14, 1874 |
| Melton, David | Vandegriff, Sarah P | C/90 | July 13, 1874 | No Return |
| Melton, Dillard | Jetton, Miss Mary | A2/43 | December 7, 1855 | December 8, 1855 |
| Melton, E. A. | Mason, Charley | C/474 | December 31, 1892 | December 31, 1892 |
| Melton, E. J. Miss | Sherley, Charles | A2/14 | January 30, 1852 | February 2, 1852 |
| Melton, E. R. | Smith, Rachel A. | A2/100 | July 25, 1860 | July 25, 1860 |
| Melton, E. R. | Campbell, Miss Sarah | B/48 | July 31, 1867 | August 1, 1867 |
| Melton, E. T. | Fite, Nannie | F/76 | December 13, 1895 | December 22, 1895 |
| Melton, Edny | Powell, James T. | C/80 | January 10, 1874 | January 11, 1874 |
| Melton, Elias R. | Bailey, Miss R. A. | A2/70 | November 18, 1858 | No Return |
| Melton, Elias R. | Bailey, Miss Rutha A. | A2/82 | November 18, 1858 | November 18, 1858 |
| Melton, Elisha | Gilley, Miss Ezzy | A2/143 | August 23, 1866 | August 23, 1866 |
| Melton, Eliza | Grizzel, Wm. | C/96 | September 30, 1874 | September 30, 1874 |
| Melton, Eliza Jane Miss | Stone, Jonathan G. | A/116 | October 26, 1848 | October 26, 1848 |
| Melton, Eliza Miss | Evans, David | A/110 | April 20, 1848 | No Return |
| Melton, Eliza Miss | Lanier, Charles B. | A2/35 | September 20, 1854 | September 21, 1854 |
| Melton, Elizabeth Miss | Melton, J. M. | A2/80 | March 7, 1857 | March 8, 1857 |
| Melton, Elizabeth Miss | Tittle, H. Y. | B/106 | August 19, 1870 | August 21, 1870 |
| Melton, Emeline | Montley, J. R. | C/136 | March 4, 1875 | No Return |
| Melton, Francis | Gunter, Miss Josephine | B/44 | April 10, 1867 | April 11, 1867 |
| Melton, Francis Miss | Gunter, Clabe | C/384 | February 28, 1887 | February 28, 1887 |
| Melton, George G. | Walkup, Miss Martha E. | A2/74 | January 16, 1854 | January 17, 1854 |
| Melton, George G. | Hollandsworth, Nancy A. | C/396 | July 18, 1887 | July 18, 1887 |
| Melton, Greefield | Melton, Miss Ailcy C. | A/119 | January 8, 1849 | January 8, 1849 |
| Melton, Greenfield | Vandergriff, Nancy A. | C/136 | March 22, 1876 | No Return |
| Melton, H. P. | Cummins, Miss Margaret | B/36 | May 9, 1867 | May 14, 1867 |
| Melton, Helen | Estes, W. R. | C/434 | April 16, 1891 | April 16, 1891 |
| Melton, Henderson | Vinson, Fannie | C/160 | March 24, 1877 | March 27, 1877 |
| Melton, Higdon | Nokes, Miss M. | B/44 | May 10, 1867 | May 14, 1867 |
| Melton, Hugh | Blair, Miss Bobillo | C/452 | December 16, 1891 | December 24, 1891 |
| Melton, Ida | Bailey, E. J. | C/472 | December 27, 1892 | December 27, 1892 |
| Melton, Isaac | Sullins, Coril A. | C/206 | November 28, 1878 | December 1, 1878 |
| Melton, Isabell | Ferrell, Enoch | E/145 | March 20, 1889 | March 20, 1889 |
| Melton, J. A. | Cummins, Miss M. | A2/90 | October 28, 1859 | No Return |
| Melton, J. B. | Gasaway, Helen | D/18 | | December 17, 1882 |
| Melton, J. D. | Neugent, Miss Martha | A2/22 | January 7, 1853 | January 7, 1853 |

| Groom or Bride | Groom or Bride | Book/Page | Date of License | Date of Marriage |
|---|---|---|---|---|
| Melton, J. H. | Sullins, Miss S. E. | A2/94 | February 13, 1860 | No Return |
| Melton, J. H. | Hawkins, Tina | C/472 | December 19, 1892 | December 21, 1892 |
| Melton, J. M. | Melton, Miss Elizabeth | A2/80 | March 7, 1857 | March 8, 1857 |
| Melton, Jacob | Garity, Betsey | C/266 | December 31, 1880 | No Return |
| Melton, Jacob | Spurlock, Nancy | D/2 | | August 10, 1881 |
| Melton, James | Patterson, Sarah | C/400 | September 2, 1887 | September 4, 1887 |
| Melton, James B. | Mason, Lestia | C/444 | August 27, 1891 | August 27, 1891 |
| Melton, James M. | Pendleton, Mary | A/80 | July 8, 1845 | July 10, 1845 |
| Melton, James M. | Pendleton, Mary | A/81 | July 8, 1845 | July 10, 1845 |
| Melton, Jane Caroline | Blair, James | A/56 | November 25, 1842 | No Return |
| Melton, Janie | Arnett, Joe E. | F/162 | December 24, 1898 | August 11, 1898 |
| Melton, Jennie | Bailey, Wiley | F/102 | November 17, 1896 | November 19, 1896 |
| Melton, Jo Miss | Sherley, Benj. | B/124 | January 12, 1871 | January 12, 1871 |
| Melton, Joel D. | Walkup, Miss Mary J. | A2/1 | March 4, 1850 | March 5, 1850 |
| Melton, Joel D. | Neely, Miss Elisabeth | A2/96 | April 21, 1860 | April 21, 1860 |
| Melton, Joh | Motley, Elisabeth | D/2 | | August 14, 1881 |
| Melton, John | Warren, Miss Sarahfine | B/44 | March 28, 1867 | March 28, 1867 |
| Melton, John | Deberry, Molley | E/39 | May 19, 1888 | May 19, 1888 |
| Melton, John M. | Turner, Miss Hanah D. | B/102 | May 14, 1870 | May 15, 1870 |
| Melton, John W. | Burger, Rutha | A2/16 | March 11, 1852 | March 11, 1852 |
| Melton, John | Markum, Helen | F/24 | December 12, 1893 | December 13, 1893 |
| Melton, Jonnathan | Moore, Sarah J. | C/56 | March 29, 1873 | March 30, 1873 |
| Melton, Joseph | Smith, Miss Biddy | A/41 | October 2, 1841 | October 5, 1841 |
| Melton, Josh | Ashford, Handsom | F/98 | October 18, 1896 | October 18, 1096 |
| Melton, Josie | Hibdon, Henry | C/398 | August 22, 1887 | August 22, 1887 |
| Melton, Llza | Ferrell, J. A. | C/352 | February 1, 1886 | February 7, 1886 |
| Melton, Lucy J. | Foard, Harris | C/222 | August 21, 1879 | August 19, 1879 |
| Melton, Lue | Walker, W. A. | F/120 | July 10, 1897 | July 11, 1897 |
| Melton, Luke | Powell, Miss Parlee | B/76 | December 25, 1868 | December 27, 1868 |
| Melton, M. J. Miss | Shirley, Tolbert F. | A2/73 | September 21, 1852 | September 22, 1852 |
| Melton, Martha | Spurlock, Elija | D/5 | | September 29, 1881 |
| Melton, Martha E. Miss | Bailey, Wm. | A2/89 | September 20, 1859 | No Return |
| Melton, Martha M. | Lance, Jas. R. | C/66 | September 1, 1873 | September 2, 1873 |
| Melton, Martha Miss | Grizzle, James | A2/5 | September 14, 1850 | September 16, 1850 |
| Melton, Mary | Hawkins, John | C/48 | December 28, 1872 | January 5, 1873 |
| Melton, Mary E. | Hawkins, Jo B. | C/66 | September 20, 1873 | September 21, 1873 |
| Melton, Mary H. | Preston, W. H. | D/6 | | November 13, 1881 |
| Melton, Mary Miss | Cummings, A. H. | A2/24 | March 30, 1853 | March 20, 1853 |
| Melton, Matilda J. | Sherly, Tolbert | A2/21 | September 21, 1852 | September 22, 1852 |
| Melton, Menerva Miss | Purtan, Man P. | A2/80 | March 26, 1857 | March 26, 1857 |
| Melton, Mollie | Hancock, G. F. | C/270 | January 12, 1881 | January 16, 1881 |
| Melton, Mollie | Spurlock, W. F. | F/128 | August 25, 1897 | August 29, 1897 |
| Melton, Nancy J. Miss | Hollandsworth, Francis | B/98 | December 25, 1869 | December 27, 1869 |
| Melton, Nancy Miss | Pitman, William | A/69 | May 11, 1844 | May 12, 1844 |
| Melton, Noah | Patterson Opha | F/130 | September 3, 1897 | September 5, 1897 |
| Melton, Oakly | Bailey, Sallie | F/106 | December 16, 1896 | December 20, 1896 |

| Groom or Bride | Groom or Bride | Book/Page | Date of License | Date of Marriage |
|---|---|---|---|---|
| Melton, Ochasy | Parton, Louis | C/206 | November 9, 1878 | November 10, 1878 |
| Melton, Ochey K. | Arnett, Elijah D. | C/336 | September 7, 1885 | September 10, 1885 |
| Melton, Polly | Grizzle, William | A/32 | August 15, 1840 | August 16, 1840 |
| Melton, Polly Miss | Litrell, Wilford | A/44 | November 23, 1841 | November 27, 1841 |
| Melton, Polly Miss | Parten, Abraham | A/122 | May 3, 1849 | May 3, 1849 |
| Melton, R. C. | Arnett, J. E. | C/242 | February 21, 1880 | No Return |
| Melton, Rhody | Holtermand, John | A2/107 | February 8, 1863 | February 8, 1863 |
| Melton, Richard | Ashford, Mallisa | A/39 | July 24, 1841 | July 25, 1841 |
| Melton, Robert | Patterson, Miss F. M. | F/84 | January 30, 1896 | February 5, 1896 |
| Melton, S. J. | Moore, J. T. | C/24 | February 21, 1872 | February 22, 1872 |
| Melton, S. J. Miss | Givens, S. J. | B/34 | December 22, 1866 | December 23, 1866 |
| Melton, Sallie | Sullins, Buck | C/224 | September 2, 1879 | No Return |
| Melton, Sallie | Stephens, J. W. | C/238 | January 11, 1880 | January 11, 1880 |
| Melton, Sallie Miss | Witty, W. W. | C/452 | December 11, 1891 | December 12, 1891 |
| Melton, Samuel | Motley, Sarah | C/138 | June 10, 1876 | No Return |
| Melton, Sandy (col.) | Webb, Vivan (col.) | F/104 | December 12, 1896 | December 12, 1896 |
| Melton, Sarah | Powell, H. N. | A2/52 | December 16, 1856 | December 18, 1856 |
| Melton, Sarah | Gunter, Sam | C/200 | October 4, 1878 | October 6, 1878 |
| Melton, Sarah A. Miss | Jetton, Daniel | A2/90 | November 1, 1859 | No Return |
| Melton, Sarah F. Miss | Turner, Pleasant R. | B/88 | September 27, 1869 | September 28, 1869 |
| Melton, Sarah Jane Miss | Cummins, Benjamin | A/49 | April 28, 1842 | April 23, 1842 |
| Melton, Selina | Parsley, Bethel | C/18 | December 26, 1871 | December 28, 1871 |
| Melton, Stacy Miss | Mayo, Bengamin F. | B/104 | July 21, 1870 | No Return |
| Melton, Susan | York, Sam | C/254 | August 14, 1880 | August 15, 1880 |
| Melton, Susan Miss | Powell, William | A/90 | September 5, 1846 | September 6, 1846 |
| Melton, Vicky | Mitchell, John A. | F/134 | October 22, 1897 | October 24, 1897 |
| Melton, W. E. | Moore, Lusey | C/218 | July 19, 1879 | July 20, 1879 |
| Melton, W. L. | Estragre, Mary F. | E/16 | January 30, 1888 | January 30, 1888 |
| Melton, W. S. | House, Miss E. J. | A2/139 | March 6, 1866 | March 6, 1866 |
| Melton, Wiley | Irvin, Daisey | F/154 | August 6, 1898 | August 7, 1898 |
| Melton, William J. | Hendrickson, Miss Mary | A/67 | January 4, 1843 | No Return |
| Melton, Willie | Elkins, Ann | E/177 | May 10, 1889 | May 10, 1889 |
| Melton, Wm. | Vinson, Miss Dollie | C/456 | March 16, 1892 | March 17, 1892 |
| Melton, Zanie | Arnett, Joe | E/360 | December 2, 1898 | |
| Melton, Zeruna (?) | Campbell, John D. | C/10 | September 30, 1871 | October 1, 1871 |
| Merit, Elizabeth Miss | McCabe, John C. | A/79 | June 18, 1845 | June 18, 1845 |
| Meritt, Madison | Wilmoth, Miss Easter | A/41 | September 8, 1841 | September 9, 1841 |
| Merphey, V. S. | Philips, John | A2/38 | March 8, 1855 | March 8, 1855 |
| Merratt, Josiah | Smith, Miss Mary Y. | A/66 | December 6, 1843 | No Return |
| Merrett, James | Jetten, Betsey A. | C/262 | November 16, 1880 | November 17, 1880 |
| Merrett, John | Whitt, Miss Sarah Jane | A2/23 | January 15, 1853 | January 16, 1853 |
| Merrett, Nancy Miss | Devenport, J. B | A2/73 | October 13, 1852 | October 15, 1852 |
| Merrett, Presley | Wimberly, Elizabeth | A2/129 | September 16, 1865 | September 17, 1865 |
| Merrett, Vioa | Lawrence, Jim B. | F/140 | December 12, 1897 | December 12, 1897 |
| Merrett, Wm | Woods, M. E. | C/216 | May 16, 1879 | May 18, 1879 |
| Merrick, Flora | Merritt, John | F/142 | December 31, 1897 | January 2, 1898 |

| Groom or Bride | Groom or Bride | Book/Page | Date of License | Date of Marriage |
|---|---|---|---|---|
| Merriman, Alek | Collins, Edna | F/46 | October 20, 1894 | October 21, 1894 |
| Merriman, Ella | Millinax, Henry | F | August 26, 1893 | |
| Merriman, Ewin | Spurlock, Miss Nancy | A2/47 | April 23, 1856 | April 23, 1856 |
| Merriman, Ezekiel | Capps, Elizabeth | A/12 | March 23, 1839 | March 24, 1839 |
| Merriman, Filia Ann Miss | Spurlock, Monroe | A2/52 | November 23, 1856 | November 24 1856 |
| Merriman, Jas M. | Jernigan, Ella | C/354 | March 12, 1886 | March 12, 1886 |
| Merriman, Jefferson | Prater, Mary A. | D/13 | | May 17, 1882 |
| Merriman, Matilda Miss | Sullivan, William | A/101 | August 13, 1847 | August 18, 1847 |
| Merriman, Roda | Webber, Henry | D/20 | | March 19, 1883 |
| Merriman, Sarah | Pitts, Josiah | A/65 | September 13, 1843 | September 13, 1843 |
| Merriman, Sarah J. | Allen, Wm | C/210 | January 10, 1879 | January 10, 1879 |
| Merriman, Thomas | Farler, Mahala | A/68 | February 5, 1844 | No Return |
| Merriman, Wesley | Elkins, Miss Bettie | C/464 | August 29, 1892 | No Return |
| Merriman, Wm. F. | Brim, Surmantha | C/186 | February 5, 1878 | February 5, 1878 |
| Merrimon, Thomas | Cantrell, Roda | B/88 | September 29, 1869 | September 29, 1869 |
| Merriter, C. C. | Pennington, E. B. | E/149 | November 3, 1888 | November 3, 1888 |
| Merritt, B. M. | Lance, N. L. J. | C/134 | February 26, 1876 | February 28, 1876 |
| Merritt, Catharine Miss | Vaughn, Thomas | B/74 | December 2, 1868 | December 2, 1868 |
| Merritt, Harman | Smithson, Miss Nancy | A/120 | February 21, 1849 | February 21, 1849 |
| Merritt, Jackson | Wimberly, Miss Marry | A2/26 | July 2, 1853 | No Return |
| Merritt, James M. | Turner, Miss Mary A | A/130 | December 27, 1849 | January 9, 1850 |
| Merritt, Jane | Wood, Miss Elizabeth | B/50 | August 29, 1867 | August 29, 1867 |
| Merritt, John | Merrick, Flora | F/142 | December 31, 1897 | January 2, 1898 |
| Merritt, Laura | Adams, Minnor | C/396 | August 6, 1887 | August 7, 1887 |
| Merritt, Mary A. Miss | Smith, Joel | A2/144 | September 4, 1866 | September 4, 1866 |
| Merritt, Merry Ann Miss | Hendrickson, J. R. | A2/16 | April 17, 1852 | April 18, 1854 |
| Merritt, Nancy | Edding, Plesant | A2/19 | September 25, 1852 | No Return |
| Merritt, Nancy Miss | Davenport, J. B. | A2/42 | October 13, 1855 | No Return |
| Merritt, Sarah Miss | Lasiter, J. B. | B/100 | March 18, 1870 | No Return |
| Merritt, Thomas | Elkins, Mrs. Mary C. | C/2 | May 2, 1871 | May 3, 1871 |
| Merritt, W. H. | Gilley, Miss Mary E. | B/86 | September 13, 1869 | September 14, 1869 |
| Merritt, William | Shitt, Miss Servella | A2/145 | September 22, 1866 | September 23, 1866 |
| Merryman, Jennie | McGregor, Dent | E/33 | April 13, 1888 | April 14, 1888 |
| Messick, Elijah | McCullough, Millie W. | C/130 | January 12, 1876 | January 12, 1876 |
| Messick, Sarah Miss | Williams, Washington | A/112 | June 10, 1848 | June 11, 1848 |
| Meton, Anul | Lvaner, Sarah | A2/16 | July 21, 1851 | July 24, 1851 |
| Mettar, Emaline | Higgins, James | A/36 | January 18, 1841 | January 28, 1841 |
| Metton, J. D. | Neugent, Miss Martha T. | A2/26 | June 7, 1853 | June 9, 1853 |
| Mickey, Mary | Landsden, John | B/12 | September 13, 1867 | September 14, 1867 |
| Mickey, Moses | Summar, Miss Cyntha | B/48 | July 27, 1867 | July 30, 1867 |
| Middleton, Patience | Carmon, Samue | A/26 | March 28, 1840 | March 28, 1840 |
| Miles, Mahala A. Miss | Smithson, James A. | A/97 | February 11, 1847 | February 11, 1847 |
| Miles, Robert S. | Hall, Miss Margarett | A2/25 | May 20, 1853 | May 24, 1853 |
| Miligan, Elizabeth Miss | Garment, T. M. | A2/33 | June 15, 1854 | June 15, 1854 |
| Miligan, G. L. | Tapley, Mattie | F/146 | March 10, 1898 | March 10, 1898 |
| Millar, Sarrah M. Miss | Lance, Wm. H. | A2/58 | October 3, 1857 | October 7, 1857 |

| Groom or Bride | Groom or Bride | Book/Page | Date of License | Date of Marriage |
|---|---|---|---|---|
| Miller, Amandy C. | Wallace, James A. | D/13 | | April 16, 1882 |
| Miller, Ann | Heneger, Frank | C/86 | April 18, 1874 | April 18, 1874 |
| Miller, Annica | Chaffen, Geo | C/134 | February 25, 1876 | No Return |
| Miller, Bethany Miss | Womack, Bery | A2/9 | December 26, 1850 | January 19, 1851 |
| Miller, Caroline Miss | Pelham, Wm. | A2/22 | January 8, 1853 | January 9, 1853 |
| Miller, Carisanda | Youngblood, Johnson | C/398 | August 25, 1887 | August 25, 1887 |
| Miller, Charlie | Fugitte, Dora | C/158 | March 8, 1877 | March 8, 1877 |
| Miller, Elihu J. | Lowe, Miss Elizabeth | A/83 | October 17, 1845 | October 19, 1845 |
| Miller, Eliza | Beaty, J. A. | C/156 | February 12, 1877 | February 15, 1877 |
| Miller, Ella | Gray, W. W. | C/210 | January 28, 1879 | January 30, 1879 |
| Miller, F. J. | Hoover, Mary F. | D/15 | | September 14, 1882 |
| Miller, Flora C. | Coleman, N. M. | D/9 | | December 22, 1881 |
| Miller, Fannie Miss | Hill, C. G. | F/170 | February 6, 1899 | February 6, 1899 |
| Miller, Frank | Mears, Francis | C/156 | February 18, 1877 | February 18, 1877 |
| Miller, George | Moore, Eliza | E/336 | December 24, 1898 | |
| Miller, George | Murphy, Maggie | D/3 | | August 25, 1881 |
| Miller, George | Carr, Allice | F/126 | August 22, 1897 | August 22, 1897 |
| Miller, George | Moore, Eliza | F/164 | December 24, 1898 | January 25, 1899 |
| Miller, Henry | Ivory, Sarah E. | C/176 | November 14, 1877 | November 15, 1877 |
| Miller, J. | Wilson, Miss Emma | F/80 | December 30, 1895 | December 31, 1895 |
| Miller, J. E. | New, Tennie | C/98 | October 29, 1874 | October 29, 1874 |
| Miller, J. J. | Lance, J. A. | D/14 | | August 27, 1882 |
| Miller, James | Moore, July A. | C/218 | July 22, 1879 | July 23, 1879 |
| Miller, James | Eatherly, Elizabeth | C/302 | January 30, 1884 | January 30, 1884 |
| Miller, Jennie | Spurlock, John W. | C/282 | May 10, 1883 | May 10, 1883 |
| Miller, John | Can, Maggie | F/140 | December 22, 1897 | December 23, 1897 |
| Miller, Joseph | Bragg, Miss Susan | A2/77 | January 19, 1856 | Executed--No Date |
| Miller, July A. | Young, E. L. | C/234 | December 18, 1879 | December 18, 1879 |
| Miller, L. D. | Brown, Ann | C/322 | December 25, 1884 | December 26, 1884 |
| Miller, Lany Miss | Lyons, Ed | B/124 | January 12, 1871 | January 12, 1871 |
| Miller, Laura | Jernison, S. J. | D/17 | | November 30, 1882 |
| Miller, M. H. | Ward, W. M. | E/251 | December 27, 1889 | December 29, 1889 |
| Miller, Martha | Moore, Peter | C/144 | August 23, 1876 | August 24, 1876 |
| Miller, Rachel | Carrick, Thomas A. | F/154 | August 16, 1898 | August 18, 1898 |
| Miller, Rebecca J. | Byrn (?), W. B | C/168 | August 14, 1877 | No Return |
| Miller, Richard | Denton, Miss Margaret | A2/77 | January 12, 1856 | January 13, 1856 |
| Miller, Richard | Todd, Margaret | C/150 | December 4, 1876 | December 5, 1876 |
| Miller, Richard | Summars, Mattie | D/5 | | October 2, 1881 |
| Miller, Rosa | Moody, Bob | F/154 | August 31, 1898 | August 31, 1898 |
| Miller, Ruby | Bell, J. T. | E/340 | December 22, 1888 | |
| Miller, Ruby | Bell, J. T. | F/164 | December 22, 1898 | December 22, 1898 |
| Miller, S. T. | Ferrell, J. H. | E/252 | December 27, 1889 | December 29, 1889 |
| Miller, T. J. | Pendleton, Martha | E/254 | December 30, 1889 | January 1, 1890 |
| Miller, Thomas | Gann, Amandy C. | D/2 | | July 24, 1881 |
| Miller, Visey A. | Allen, A. G. | C/302 | January 18, 1884 | January 20, 1884 |
| Miller, William C. | Seawell, Miss Elmira L. | A/41 | September 25, 1841 | September 26, 1841 |

| Groom or Bride | Groom or Bride | Book/Page | Date of License | Date of Marriage |
|---|---|---|---|---|
| Miller, William C. | Brewer, Miss Martha | A2/18 | July 25, 1852 | July 25, 1852 |
| Miller, Wm. H. | Carmichael, Miss Anna E. | B/98 | February 3, 1870 | February 3, 1870 |
| Milligan, Abner A. | Higgin, Sarah A. | C/178 | November 29, 1877 | November 29, 1877 |
| Milligan, Alex | Jones, Beckey | C/224 | September 6, 1879 | September 7, 1879 |
| Milligan, Alneeda | Womach, W. J. | E/245 | December 23, 1889 | December 24, 1889 |
| Milligan, Asezeline | Cooper, W. D. | F/1 | January 11, 1893 | No Return |
| Milligan, B. B. | Fox, Mollie | F/116 | April 29, 1897 | April 29, 1897 |
| Milligan, David T. | Thompson, Elizabeth | A/13 | April 13, 1839 | May 9, 1839 |
| Milligan, Elizabeth Miss | Jetton, Alexander | A2/58 | October 20, 1857 | October 20, 1857 |
| Milligan, Elizabeth | Hollinsworth, Ira | A/29 | June 4, 1840 | June 4, 1840 |
| Milligan, Elizabeth | Morgan, James A. | A2/129 | October 2, 1865 | October 2, 1865 |
| Milligan, G. A. | Wamack, C. B. | C/214 | March 12, 1879 | No Return |
| Milligan, Geneva | Jones, James | C/422 | November 2, 1890 | November 2, 1890 |
| Milligan, George W. | Higgins, Lucy | B/16 | March 4, 1869 | March 4, 1869 |
| Milligan, Hattie | Bogle, John | F/46 | October 11, 1894 | October 11, 1894 |
| Milligan, Hattie | Bogle, John | F/52 | October 11, 1894 | October 11, 1894 |
| Milligan, Henry | Davenport, G. L. | E/92 | October 25, 1888 | October 25, 1888 |
| Milligan, J. P. | Little, Camelee | A2/121 | February 25, 1865 | No Return |
| Milligan, James (col.) | Higgins, Clara | C/298 | December 27, 1883 | No Return |
| Milligan, James C. | Vasser, Miss Cyntha | A/35 | December 19, 1840 | December 25, 1840 |
| Milligan, Joel | Pedigo, Penney | A/4 | June 18, 1838 | June 20, 1838 |
| Milligan, Joel | Tittle, Susan | A/77 | February 26, 1845 | February 26 1845 |
| Milligan, Joel | Bogle, Charlotta | C/90 | July 25, 1874 | July 26, 1874 |
| Milligan, Joel | Carroll, Martha | C/192 | June 17, 1878 | June 17, 1878 |
| Milligan, Joel | McKnight, Sarah E. | F/94 | September 8, 1896 | September 9, 1896 |
| Milligan, John | Crabtree, Dorcas | A/12 | April 5, 1839 | April 21, 1839 |
| Milligan, John | Lance, Miss Catharine | B/102 | June 2, 1870 | June 8, 1870 |
| Milligan, John | Odom, Martha A | C/2 | July 5, 1871 | No Return |
| Milligan, John A. | Fuston, Margrett | C/138 | June 21, 1876 | June 21, 1876 |
| Milligan, John P. | Bryson, Mary J. | C/56 | March 22, 1873 | March 23, 1873 |
| Milligan, Johnie | Higgins, Francis | C/340 | November 2, 1885 | November 2, 1885 |
| Milligan, Julie A. | Collins, William | C/16 | December 15, 1871 | December 17, 1871 |
| Milligan, Liza A. | Womack, John S. | C/304 | February 3, 1884 | February 3, 1884 |
| Milligan, Lotty | Davenport, R. | C/168 | September 1, 1877 | September 2, 1877 |
| Milligan, M. B. | Powell, Frances | C/24 | February 17, 1872 | February 18, 1872 |
| Milligan, Maggie | Jetton, Jim | F/108 | December 30, 1896 | December 30, 1896 |
| Milligan, Mariah | Manfres, George | B/16 | June 21, 1869 | June 22, 1869 |
| Milligan, Mary | Hancock, Ben | C/278 | April 9, 1881 | April 10, 1881 |
| Milligan, Nancy Miss | Patrick, Jesse | A/118 | December 25, 1848 | December 28, 1848 |
| Milligan, Paralee | Odom, J. S. | C/48 | December 26, 1872 | December 26, 1872 |
| Milligan, R. L. | Preston, S. E. | C/184 | February 1, 1878 | February 3, 1878 |
| Milligan, R. R. | Oneal, N. A. | E/208 | September 6, 1889 | September 7, 1889 |
| Milligan, Rance | Stone, Nancy A. | C/262 | November 11, 1880 | November 11, 1880 |
| Milligan, Ruth J. | Wilcher, J. B. | C/86 | April 8, 1874 | April 9, 1874 |
| Milligan, Ruthy Miss | Ashford, Richard | A2/85 | May 5, 1859 | No Return |
| Milligan, Sam D. | Shirley, Mary J. | C/256 | September 11, 1880 | September 11, 1880 |

| Groom or Bride | Groom or Bride | Book/Page | Date of License | Date of Marriage |
|---|---|---|---|---|
| Milligan, Susan | Sellars, Jack | C/154 | January 22, 1877 | No Return |
| Milligan, W. H. | Summar, Miss Alsena E. | A2/142 | July 26, 1866 | August 2, 1866 |
| Milligan, W. P. | Mingle, L. J. | F/26 | December 26, 1893 | December 26, 1893 |
| Milliganin, Susie | Higgins, Murph | F/140 | December 21, 1897 | December 21, 1897 |
| Milligin, Annie Miss | Elrod, B. F. | C/8 | September 6, 1871 | September 6, 1871 |
| Milligin, Hallie | Hancock, Wm. | F/106 | December 22, 1896 | December 27, 1896 |
| Milligin, Mathew | Willard, Ann | F/108 | December 30, 1896 | December 30, 1896 |
| Millikeen, Virginia | Byford, James | C/154 | January 20, 1877 | January 21, 1877 |
| Millikian, Albert G. | Gaither, Miss Sarah | A/87 | February 26, 1846 | February 26, 1846 |
| Millikin, A. G. | Byford, Miss L. E. | A2/160 | June 21, 1866 | June 21, 1866 |
| Millikin, Albert G. | Tenerson, Miss Mary J. | A2/75 | August 31, 1854 | August 31, 1854 |
| Millikin, John | Byford, Miss Partheny O. | A2/74 | January 2, 1854 | January 3, 1854 |
| Millikin, Parlee Miss | Bess, A. M. | B/94 | November 13, 1869 | November 13, 1869 |
| Millikin, Parthana | Faulkam, James | A2/81 | February 7, 1858 | February 7, 1858 |
| Millikin, Parthena Miss | Burchett, Thomas | A2/62 | January 7, 1858 | No Return |
| Millinax, Henry | Merriman, Ella | F | August 26, 1893 | |
| Mills, Mollie | Brown, Joseph M. | F/138 | December 3, 1897 | December 4, 1897 |
| Millstead, James | Sullins, Louisa | A2/31 | February 8, 1854 | February 8, 1854 |
| Millsted, M. A. | Hunt, T. J. | C/50 | December 28, 1872 | December 29, 1872 |
| Milstead, Nannie B. | Hunt, John T. | E/122 | January 1, 1889 | January 1, 1889 |
| Milton, James | Patterson, Harriet | C/394 | July 9, 1887 | No Return |
| Milton, John | Preston, L. | C/312 | August 9, 1884 | August 10, 1884 |
| Milton, Lizzie | Powell, Henry | F/146 | February 12, 1898 | February 13, 1898 |
| Milton, Sandy | Barton, Miss Sopha | B/118 | December 7, 1870 | December 15, 1870 |
| Mingle, Better Miss | Alexander, William T. | C/386 | March 23, 1887 | March 23, 1887 |
| Mingle, Christeny Miss | Jones, W. C. | A2/66 | August 4, 1858 | August 4, 1858 |
| Mingle, Elizabeth | Travis, James | C/344 | December 20, 1885 | December 21, 1885 |
| Mingle, George | Travis, Miss Polly | A/105 | November 26, 1847 | November 26, 1847 |
| Mingle, Georgie | Mors, Monroe | F/146 | March 3, 1898 | March 3, 1898 |
| Mingle, H. L. | Willard, Patsy | F/168 | January 25, 1899 | January 29, 1899 |
| Mingle, J. D. | Flowers, Cora | C/174 | October 23, 1877 | October 24, 1877 |
| Mingle, J. R. | Higgins, C. J. | C/102 | December 11, 1874 | December 13, 1874 |
| Mingle, James | Gaither, E. S. | C/212 | February 19, 1879 | February 20, 1879 |
| Mingle, L. J. | Milligan, W. P. | F/26 | December 26, 1893 | December 26, 1893 |
| Mingle, L. K. | Barrett, Sallie | F/30 | January 30, 1894 | No Return |
| Mingle, Nancy J. Miss | Howeth, James A. | A/102 | September 13, 1847 | September 14, 1847 |
| Mingle, S. E. | Robertson, R. S. | C/174 | October 23, 1877 | October 24, 1877 |
| Mingle, Sarah J. | Devenport, Henry W. | C/16 | December 13, 1871 | December 13, 1871 |
| Mingle, Taylor | Cooper, D. T. | C/430 | January 31, 1891 | February 1, 1891 |
| Mingle, W. F. | Bryson, M. A. | C/250 | July 23, 1880 | July 23, 1880 |
| Mingle, W. T. | McBroom, E. J. | C/62 | July 26, 1873 | July 27, 1873 |
| Mingle, William J. | Cathey, Miss Alice | A2/11 | February 10, 1851 | February 10, 1851 |
| Mingles, G. W. | Davenport, Davey | D/20 | | January 10, 1883 |
| Mingles, S. H. | Bryson, Laura | C/328 | March 5, 1885 | March 5, 1885 |
| Minten, J. G. | Travis, Miss Martha Jane | A2/71 | December 14, 1858 | December 14, 1858 |
| Mitchel, E. H. | Young, Miss Martha A. | A2/89 | October 24, 1859 | No Return |

| Groom or Bride | Groom or Bride | Book/Page | Date of License | Date of Marriage |
|---|---|---|---|---|
| Mitchel, G. W. P. | Barrett, Miss E. C. | A2/42 | October 2, 1855 | October 4, 1855 |
| Mitchel, James H. | Elrod, Miss Elizabeth | A/105 | November 20, 1847 | November 20, 1847 |
| Mitchel, Jane | Childress, Stephen | A/56 | November 16, 1842 | November 17, 1842 |
| Mitchel, N. A. Miss | Rains, G. P. | A2/68 | September 30, 1858 | October ?, 1858 |
| Mitchel, Nile A. | Lansley, Miss Issabella | A2/4 | August 8, 1850 | August 8, 1850 |
| Mitchel, Susan Miss | Hoover, Thos. J. | | December 9, 1858 | December 9, 1858 |
| Mitchel, Syntha | Brandon, E. T. | A2/110 | November 14, 1863 | November 15, 1863 |
| Mitchel, W. E. | Wallace, Mollie | C/270 | January 22, 1881 | January 23, 1881 |
| Mitchell, A. L. | Carrack, T. F. | A2/122 | March 11, 1865 | No Return |
| Mitchell, Addie | Markum, Isaac | C/350 | December 31, 1885 | December 31, 1885 |
| Mitchell, Alexander | Tollier, Tennie | C/402 | September 24, 1887 | No Return |
| Mitchell, Amandy | Wooderd, Henry | F/26 | December 233, 1893 | December 23, 1893 |
| Mitchell, Andy | Ferrell, Mary | C/52 | February 18, 1873 | February 18, 1873 |
| Mitchell, Andy | Ferrell, Mary | C/172 | October 4, 1877 | October 7, 1877 |
| Mitchell, Ann E. Miss | Gordon, J. H. | B/120 | December 24, 1870 | December 25, 1870 |
| Mitchell, Callie Miss | Bragg, W. M. | C/16 | December 2, 1871 | December 2, 1871 |
| Mitchell, Charlot | Jones, Bill H. | C/360 | July 5, 1886 | No Return |
| Mitchell, Coleman | Thompson, Sophia | C/128 | December 23, 1875 | December 23, 1875 |
| Mitchell, D. W. | Gardner, Miss Martha A. | C/6 | August 26, 1871 | August 26, 1871 |
| Mitchell, Daniel W. | McGlocklin, Eleanor | A/30 | June 18, 1840 | June 18, 1840 |
| Mitchell, Delila | Jemson, J. R. | C/340 | November 19, 1885 | November 29, 1885 |
| Mitchell, Elizabeth J. Miss | Stroud, George S. | A2/60 | November 12, 1857 | November 12, 1857 |
| Mitchell, Etter | McBroom, Robert | D/17 | | October 8, 1882 |
| Mitchell, Geo. | Gordon, Mollie | C/18 | December 28, 1871 | December 28, 1871 |
| Mitchell, Green | Wright, Alice | C/126 | December 11, 1875 | December 12, 1875 |
| Mitchell, Henry | Talley, Locky (col) | E/26 | March 18, 1888 | March 18, 1888 |
| Mitchell, Hessie Miss | Phillips, Jack | C/394 | July 9, 1887 | July 10, 1887 |
| Mitchell, Isaac S. | Cook, Miss Elizabeth S. | A2/61 | December 31, 1857 | December 31, 1857 |
| Mitchell, J. A. | Jetton, Francis | C/358 | June 23, 1886 | July 1, 1886 |
| Mitchell, J. T. | Jarratt, Mary C. | C/28 | May 31, 1872 | June 2, 1872 |
| Mitchell, Jackson | Fugitte, Addie | C/146 | September 28, 1876 | September 28, 1876 |
| Mitchell, James A. | George, Miss Mary S. | A2/145 | September 19, 1866 | September 20, 1866 |
| Mitchell, James A. | Turner, Elisabeth | C/246 | May 8, 1880 | May 9, 1880 |
| Mitchell, John A. | Melton, Vicky | F/134 | October 22, 1897 | October 24, 1897 |
| Mitchell, John E. | Gandy, Miss E. A. | A2/61 | December 22, 1857 | No Return |
| Mitchell, John F. | Wamack, Miss Bethena | A2/75 | November 17, 1855 | November 17, 1855 |
| Mitchell, John N. | Rigsby, Mary | C/18 | December 22, 1871 | December 22, 1871 |
| Mitchell, Lizzy (col.) | Gilley, Joe (col.) | F/118 | May 22, 1897 | May 24, 1897 |
| Mitchell, Mariah | Keele, Anderson | B/10 | January 4, 1866 | January 4, 1867 |
| Mitchell, Mary | Summars, Wm. | C/288 | July 26, 1883 | July 26, 1883 |
| Mitchell, Mary | Smith, Dave | C/320 | December 18, 1884 | No Return |
| Mitchell, Mary J. | Smith, George W. | A2/116 | September 20, 1864 | No Return |
| Mitchell, Mattie | Thompson, Samuel | B/14 | July 30, 1868 | July 30, 1868 |
| Mitchell, Mattie | Hollis, F. | C/266 | December 25, 1880 | No Date |
| Mitchell, Mattie . | Martin, Thomas | C/436 | April 25, 1891 | April 25, 1891 |
| Mitchell, Mira A. Miss | Smith, Robert G. | B/58 | December 11, 1867 | December 12, 1867 |

| Groom or Bride | Groom or Bride | Book/Page | Date of License | Date of Marriage |
|---|---|---|---|---|
| Mitchell, Missey | Mullenix, Benj. | C/174 | October 25, 1877 | October 25, 1877 |
| Mitchell, Mollie | Ellison, Joseph M. | B/16 | December 24, 1868 | December 25, 1868 |
| Mitchell, Mollie E. | Hoodenpyle, W. W. | C/470 | December 7, 1892 | December 7, 1892 |
| Mitchell, Nancy A. Miss | Yearwood, D. B. | B/82 | July 24, 1869 | July 27, 1869 |
| Mitchell, Octavia | Jamison, William | C/398 | August 19, 1887 | August 19, 1887 |
| Mitchell, Robt | Patton, Dora | C/176 | November 10, 1877 | November 11, 1877 |
| Mitchell, Robty | Craye, Jennie | D/16 |  | September 21, 1881 |
| Mitchell, Roxey | Downing, A. L. | C/320 | December 10, 1884 | December 10, 1884 |
| Mitchell, Salley | Rucker, Wm. | D/9 |  | December 28, 1881 |
| Mitchell, Sallie | Boren, Calvin | C/462 | July 28, 1892 | July 30, 1892 |
| Mitchell, Sarah D. | Hoover, G. W. | A2/91 | December 9,1859 | No Return |
| Mitchell, Sarah J. Miss | McFerrin, William H. | A2/147 | November 8, 1866 | November 8, 1866 |
| Mitchell, Sarah Miss | Patton, John | E/168 | April 6, 1889 | April 7, 1889 |
| Mitchell, Sopha | Danning?, George | C/236 | January 1, 1880 | January 1, 1880 |
| Mitchell, W. N. | Mason, Amanda | F/26 | December 23, 1893 | December 25, 1893 |
| Mithcel, Thos. P. | Teague, Miss M. J. | A2/80 | July 15, 1857 | July 21, 1857 |
| Mitty, Allis | Shirley, Ewing | C/334 | August 6, 1885 | No Return |
| Moffitt, May Miss | Logue, Andrew | A/99 | April 12, 1847 | April 12, 1847 |
| Mollen, J. C. Miss | Poston, James C. | A2/18 | June 16, 1852 | June 18, 1852 |
| Molley, Robert | Grizzel, Susan | A2/32 | April 17, 1854 | May 4, 1854 |
| Mongomery, Laura | Gunter, John | C/472 | December 26, 1892 | December 28, 1892 |
| Mongomery, Sarah Jane Miss | Hatfield, Robert | A/108 | February 2, 1848 | February 7, 1848 |
| Mont, Albert | Hamilton, Lockey | C/396 | August 6, 1887 | August 7, 1887 |
| Montley, J. R. | Melton, Emeline | C/136 | March 4, 1875 | No Return |
| Moody, Allis | Patten, E. W. | F/76 | December 7, 1895 | December 10, 1895 |
| Moody, Bob | Miller, Rosa | F/154 | August 31, 1898 | August 31, 1898 |
| Moody, Charles | Morgan, Miss Malinda | B/104 | July 16, 1870 | July 17, 1870 |
| Moody, Hanney | Hayes, T. K. | E/112 | December 22, 1888 | December 22, 1888 |
| Moody, James | Walker, Mattie | E/131 | January 31, 1889 | January 31, 1889 |
| Moody, Jessie | McMahan, Maggie | F/34 | March 7, 1894 | No Return |
| Moody, Jno. | Richerson, Melvina | C/64 | August 14, 1873 | August 14, 1873 |
| Moody, John | Hammons, Sally | A2/131 | November 11, 1865 | November 5, 1865 |
| Moody, M. E. Miss | Perryman, G. W. | A2/91 | November 29, 1859 | No Return |
| Moody, Margarett H. Miss | Smith, William | A2/98 | January 19, 1860 | January 19, 1860 |
| Moody, Martha | Reed, J. F. | D/2 |  | August 3, 1881 |
| Moody, Mary Malinda | Harp, Thornton | A/60 | February 16, 1843 | February 16, 1843 |
| Moody, S. E. | Travis, Thomas J. | F/10 | May 27, 1893 | May 28, 1893 |
| Moody, S. L | Barrett, J. H. | C/360 | July 15, 1886 | July 15, 1886 |
| Moody, Sue | Barratt, Samuel | C/190 | March 27, 1878 | March 27, 1878 |
| Moody, William | Barrett, Elender | A2/36 | October 4, 1854 | October 4, 1854 |
| Mooer, Iby | Parris, John | F/150 | May 26, 1898 | No Return |
| Moon, Alexander | Stroud, Miss S. | A2/82 | July 24, 1858 | July 26, 1858 |
| Moon, Benjaman | Sapp, Miss Nancy Ann | A2/77 | January 12, 1856 | January 13, 1856 |
| Moon, C. T. | Knox, Miss S. J. | A2/78 | March 3, 1856 | March 4, 1856 |
| Moon, Charlota Miss | McKnight, John N. | A2/88 | September 1, 1859 | No Return |
| Moon, Charlotte Miss | Davis, Jacob | A/70 | July 10, 1844 | July 11, 1844 |

| Groom or Bride | Groom or Bride | Book/Page | Date of License | Date of Marriage |
| --- | --- | --- | --- | --- |
| Moon, Fannie | Tenpenny, John W. | C/248 | April 1, 1880 | April 2, 1880 |
| Moon, Isabella Miss | Barratt, Eli B. | A/73 | September 23, 1844 | September 23, 1844 |
| Moon, Jennie | Bearder, Andrew | E/185 | June 22, 1889 | June 22, 1889 |
| Moon, John | Edwards, Miss Charity | A2/43 | October 22, 1855 | October 29, 1855 |
| Moon, John | Edwards, Martha E. | C/52 | February 1, 1873 | February 2, 1873 |
| Moon, John | Peeler, Martha J. | C/432 | February 26, 1891 | March 1, 1891 |
| Moon, Josie | Ferrell, J. B. | C/300 | January 3, 1884 | January 3, 1884 |
| Moon, Julie | Youree, T. W. | C/400 | September 6, 1887 | September 7, 1887 |
| Moon, Margaret | Davis, Samuel A. | A2/134 | December 30, 1865 | December 31, 1865 |
| Moon, Martha C. Miss | Wilson, Hiram | A/40 | August 10, 1841 | August 15, 1841 |
| Moon, Mary F. | Smith, M. S. | C/52 | February 7, 1873 | February 8, 1873 |
| Moon, Nancy Miss | Rogers, John | A/50 | June 11, 1842 | June 12, 1842 |
| Moon, Nancy Miss | King, Wm. | A2/45 | December 17, 1855 | December 17, 1855 |
| Moon, Nancy Mrs. | Campbell, Thomas | A2/8 | December 19, 1850 | December 20, 1850 |
| Moon, Nancy J. | Moore, F. P. | C/112 | April 3, 1875 | April 4, 1875 |
| Moon, Pierce | Smithson, Mary | C/158 | February 24, 1877 | February 25, 1877 |
| Moon, Sarah | Low, Charly | A2/49 | July 12, 1856 | July 12, 1856 |
| Mooneham, Axy | Thomas, Catherine | F/6 | March 1, 1893 | March 2, 1893 |
| Mooneham, Dovie Miss | Tatum, James | C/388 | May 17, 1887 | No Return |
| Moonaham, Robert | Manius, M. A. | A2/60 | December 20, 1857 | December 20, 1857 |
| Mooneham, Sarah | Gann, Joshua | C/368 | October 2, 1886 | October 3, 1886 |
| Mooneham, Tennessee | Somers, William | C/378 | December 24, 1886 | December 26, 1886 |
| Mooneyham, Dora | Mooneyham, J. C. | C/284 | June 27, 1883 | No Return |
| Mooneyham, J. C. | Mooneyham, Dora | C/284 | June 27, 1883 | No Return |
| Mooneyham, John | Bates, Emma | C/290 | August 25, 1883 | No Return |
| Mooneyham, Mandy | Barrett, Frank | C/334 | August 27, 1885 | No Return |
| Mooneyham, Robert | Bates, Carril | C/436 | April 25, 1891 | April 26, 1891 |
| Mooneyham, Sallie | Goins, Jefferson | C/212 | February 3, 1879 | February 9, 1879 |
| Mooneyhen, M. J. | Wheelr, B. F. | C/340 | November 7, 1885 | No Return |
| Moonyham, John | Morris, Sarah E. | A2/105 | January 8, 1862 | October 21, 1862 |
| Moore ? | Toddd, Adeline | C/416 | September 12, 1890 | September 14, 1890 |
| Moore, Abner | McAdams, Miss A. | A2/85 | May 27, 1859 | Execution Not Clear |
| Moore, Ada Miss | Patton, John M. | C/404 | October 10, 1887 | October 12, 1887 |
| Moore, Ada | Henderson, Dan | F/78 | December 24, 1895 | No Return |
| Moore, Ada Lee | Williams, Charlie | F/174 | April 29, 1899 | April 29, 1899 |
| Moore, B. H. | Bogle, N. C. | C/74 | December 4, 1873 | December 5, 1873 |
| Moore, C. N. | Hawkins, Meda | F/52 | December 11, 1894 | December 11, 1894 |
| Moore, C. Nancy Miss | Gunter, C. C. | A2/25 | April 19, 1853 | No Return |
| Moore, Delila Miss | Ferrell, James W. | B/102 | May 13, 1870 | May 15, 1870 |
| Moore, E. B. Miss | Todd, R. R. | C/398 | August 13, 1887 | No Return |
| Moore, E. C. Miss | Taylor, A. B. | B/54 | October 28, 1867 | October 29, 1967 |
| Moore, Eliza | Miller, George | E/336 | December 24, 1898 | |
| Moore, Eliza | Miller, George | F/164 | December 24, 1898 | January 25, 1899 |
| Moore, Eliza Miss | Hipp, James D. | C/412 | December 20, 1887 | December 21, 1887 |
| Moore, Elizabeth J. Miss | Swoape, Samuel A. | A2/123 | April 20, 1865 | April 20, 1865 |
| Moore, Ella Miss | Sullivan, J. V. | C/452 | Decmeber 30, 1891 | December 31, 1891 |

| Groom or Bride | Groom or Bride | Book/Page | Date of License | Date of Marriage |
|---|---|---|---|---|
| Moore, Elvira | Tobbert, J. J. | A2/114 | May 16, 1864 | No Return |
| Moore, F. P. | Moon, Nancy J. | C/112 | April 3, 1875 | April 4, 1875 |
| Moore, Florence | Barton, Alf | C/54 | March 13, 1873 | March 13, 1873 |
| Moore, Frana | Moore, J. M. | F/114 | March 22, 1897 | No Return |
| Moore, Frances C. Miss | Sparks, Alexander | B/70 | September 18, 1868 | September 18, 1868 |
| Moore, George W. | Hatchins, Josephine | B/70 | September 24, 1868 | September 24, 1868 |
| Moore, H. E. | Cummings, Sarah | D/18 | | December 24, 1882 |
| Moore, Idella | Atnip, J. H. | C/474 | December 29, 1892 | December 29, 1892 |
| Moore, J. A. | Campbell, H. U. | C/122 | October 16, 1875 | October 21, 1875 |
| Moore, J. B. | Odom, S. M. | D/4 | | September 1, 1881 |
| Moore, J. B. | Smith, Miss Lucy | F/68 | August 30, 1895 | August 31, 1895 |
| Moore, J. G. | Travis, Miss Martha M. | A2/52 | January 20, 1857 | January 20, 1857 |
| Moore, J. G. | Taylor, Miss Bettie | B/120 | December 15, 1870 | December 15, 1870 |
| Moore, J. M. | Moore, Frana | F/114 | March 22, 1897 | No Return |
| Moore, J. T. | Melton, S. J. | C/24 | February 21, 1872 | February 22, 1872 |
| Moore, J. T. | Hiff, S. E. | D/10 | | December 29, 1881 |
| Moore, Jacob | Soape, Miss Lucy F. | A/47 | February 3, 1842 | February 3, 1842 |
| Moore, Jacob | Akers, N. J. | C/38 | September 17, 1872 | September 19, 1872 |
| Moore, Jacob | Griffin, Floura | C/268 | December 18, 1880 | December 18, 1880 |
| Moore, Jance C. Miss | Harris, James N. L. | A2/46 | January 9, 1856 | January 9, 1856 |
| Moore, Jane | Walker, Isaac | C/80 | January 17, 1874 | January 18, 1874 |
| Moore, Jennie Miss | Stewart, W. D. | F/76 | November 28, 1895 | November 28, 1895 |
| Moore, Jessee | Hutchens, Frances L. | A2/126 | September 2, 1865 | No Return |
| Moore, Jessee G. | Taylor, Virginia P. | A2/121 | February 27, 1865 | February 28, 1865 |
| Moore, Jose | Martin, Anthony | C/60 | July 12, 1873 | July 12, 1873 |
| Moore, Joseph | Lackey, Sarah | A/18 | October 8, 1839 | October 8, 1839 |
| Moore, Josephine | Martin, Jackson | B/16 | February 25, 1869 | February 25, 1869 |
| Moore, July A | Miller, James | C/218 | July 22, 1879 | July 23, 1879 |
| Moore, L. B. | Odom, Miss Elizabeth | A/63 | July 5, 1843 | July 5, 1843 |
| Moore, Liza | Burnett, James | C/128 | December 23, 1875 | December 23, 1875 |
| Moore, Lizzie | Dixon, Joseph | F/6 | March 11, 1893 | March 12, 1893 |
| Moore, Lotty | Davis, David | C/66 | September 11, 1873 | September 11, 1873 |
| Moore, Lusey | Melton, W. E. | C/218 | July 19, 1879 | July 20, 1879 |
| Moore, M. A. Miss | Stephens, S. H. | B/60 | December 21, 1867 | December 22, 1867 |
| Moore, M. D | Mangrum, J. S. | E/100 | November 10, 1888 | November 11, 1888 |
| Moore, M. E. | Harney, A. M. | C/246 | March 20, 1880 | March 20, 1880 |
| Moore, M. L. Miss | Bryson, Wm. B. | A2/30 | December 10, 1853 | December 11, 1853 |
| Moore, M. P. | Dodd, S. A. | D/6 | | November 3, 1881 |
| Moore, Margaret | Davanport, J. B. | A2/112 | March 3, 1864 | No Return |
| Moore, Marshack | Bounds, Ellen | E/113 | December 22, 1888 | December 23, 1888 |
| Moore, Martha E. Miss | Gowen, James J. | A2/23 | February 17, 1853 | July 20, 1853 |
| Moore, Mary D. | Rigsby, John | C/254 | August 14, 1880 | August 15, 1880 |
| Moore, Mary J. Miss | Stacy, William C. | B/84 | August 17, 1869 | August 17, 1869 |
| Moore, Mollie | Lowe, T. W. | F/50 | December 4, 1894 | December 5, 1894 |
| Moore, Nancy | Bell, James | A/16 | August 27, 1839 | August 29, 1839 |
| Moore, Nancy | Spry, G. W. | F/20 | November 2, 1893 | November 2, 1893 |

| Groom or Bride | Groom or Bride | Book/Page | Date of License | Date of Marriage |
|---|---|---|---|---|
| Moore, Nancy | Magon, Jackson | A2/12 | November 18, 1851 | November 2, 1851 |
| Moore, Nancy E. Miss | Smith, Benjamin | A/109 | March 6, 1848 | No Return |
| Moore, Nancy Eleanore Miss | Hill, William R. | A/111 | March 6, 1848 | March 7, 1848 |
| Moore, Nancy Miss | Bryson, J. A. | A2/88 | August 30, 1859 | No Return |
| Moore, Nute | Stacy, Willie | F/72 | October 12, 1895 | October 13, 1895 |
| Moore, Permela Miss | Eads, Samuel | A2/17 | March 2, 1852 | No Return |
| Moore, Peter | Miller, Martha | C/144 | August 23, 1876 | August 24, 1876 |
| Moore, R. A. | McMurry, Miss Hattie E. | C/44 | November 13, 1872 | November 14, 1872 |
| Moore, R. L. | Page, Edith E. | E/72 | September 13, 1888 | September 13, 1888 |
| Moore, R. J. | Lowe, C. T. | C/58 | May 1, 1873 | May 14, 1873 |
| Moore, Robert D. | Alexander, Miss Helan | B/78 | February 1, 1869 | February 4, 1869 |
| Moore, Ruth | Smith, Nimrod | A2/94 | February 6, 1860 | No Return |
| Moore, S. E. | Peeler, Jessee | C/104 | November 21, 1874 | November 26, 1874 |
| Moore, S. L. | Gowind, Eulia | F/100 | October 16, 1896 | October 18, 1896 |
| Moore, Sallie J. | Halcomb, J. C. | C/304 | February 2, 1884 | February 3, 1884 |
| Moore, Sarah J. | Melton, Jonnathan | C/56 | March 29, 1873 | March 30, 1873 |
| Moore, Samuel | Smith, Frances Ann | A/69 | May 15, 1844 | May 18, 1844 |
| Moore, Samuel A. | Berks, Miss Mary | A/108 | February 14, 1848 | February 14, 1848 |
| Moore, Samuel Jr. | Brashears, Miss Ruth | A/79 | June 2, 1845 | June 5, 1845 |
| Moore, Sarah M. | Jernigan, E. | D/19 | | December 17, 1882 |
| Moore, Sarah Miss | Vance, Isham | A2/156 | May 29, 1866 | May 29, 1866 |
| Moore, T. C. | Sullins, Zona | F/146 | February 24, 1898 | No Return |
| Moore, Tennie | Taylor, Adam | F/68 | September 14, 1895 | September 16, 1895 |
| Moore, Thomas C. | Wimberly, Mary | D/16 | | June 2, 1882 |
| Moore, V. H. | Duncan, J. H. | E/230 | November 4, 1889 | No Return |
| Moore, William | Noakes, Mary | E/167 | April 3, 1889 | April 6, 1889 |
| Moore, Wm. A. T. | McAdow, Miss P. A. | A2/92 | December 3, 1859 | Executed--No Date |
| Moore, Wm. N. | Brown, Miss Lucinda | A2/59 | November 3, 1857 | November 5, 1857 |
| Moore, Wm. W. | Walkup, Nora | F/12 | July 19, 1893 | July 20, 1893 |
| Moore, Z. H. | Mayo, Ester A. | C/306 | April 7, 1884 | April 10, 1884 |
| Moore, Zachariah T. | Hutchins, Miss Lavina C. | B/102 | May 14, 1870 | May 15, 1870 |
| Moran, Jane | Stone, J. B. | C/190 | April 22, 1878 | April 22, 1878 |
| More, Fannie | Carrick, Smith | F/28 | December 28, 1893 | December 28, 1893 |
| More, Howel | Wommacs, Miss Matilda | A2/16 | March 11, 1852 | March 11, 1852 |
| Morgan, Alexander | Rodgers, Katharine | A/11 | March 2, 1839 | No Return |
| Morgan, Alexander | Pitts, Miss Sarah Jane | B/92 | November 4, 1869 | November 4, 1869 |
| Morgan, Anderson | Alford, Malinda | A2/133 | December 15, 1865 | December 15, 1865 |
| Morgan, Caroline Miss | Tenpenny, Wm. | A2/65 | July 27, 1858 | July 27, 1858 |
| Morgan, Catharine | Barratt, A. B. | A2/102 | September 15, 1860 | No Return |
| Morgan, Cynthia | Duke, William | A/1 | March 19, 1838 | March 22, 1838 |
| Morgan, Delila C. Miss | Smith, James G. | A2/136 | January 17, 1866 | January 18, 1866 |
| Morgan, Delina | Spears, Samuel | C/116 | July 12, 1875 | No Return |
| Morgan, Ed | Brnum, Callie | E/187 | July 6, 1889 | No Return |
| Morgan, Elizabeth | Knox, Joe A. | A2/113 | April 22, 1864 | April 24, 1864 |
| Morgan, Elizabeth C. Miss | Whitt, Felix | A/90 | August 20, 1846 | August 27, 1846 |
| Morgan, Emma | Hall, A. B. | C/282 | May 7, 1883 | May 7, 1883 |

| Groom or Bride | Groom or Bride | Book/Page | Date of License | Date of Marriage |
|---|---|---|---|---|
| Morgan, Fani | West, Frank | F/160 | November 5, 1898 | No Return |
| Morgan, Gordon | Elkins, Arta M. | A/6 | September 7, 1838 | September 10, 1838 |
| Morgan, Hubbard | Gaither, Miss Mary E. | B/80 | April 15, 1869 | April 15, 1869 |
| Morgan, J. I. | Womack, A. C. | D/6 | | November 10, 1881 |
| Morgan, J. S. | Cox, Miss D. F. | A2/87 | August 19, 1859 | No Return |
| Morgan, Jackson | Heriman, Nancy | A/16 | July 24, 1839 | July 25, 1839 |
| Morgan, Jackson | Mares, Elizabeth | A/54 | October 7, 1842 | October 7, 1842 |
| Morgan, Jackson | Morgan, Miss Nancy | A/74 | October 26, 1844 | October 27, 1844 |
| Morgan, James | Barnes, Mary C. | F/86 | March 23, 1896 | No Return |
| Morgan, James A. | Milligan, Elizabeth | A2/129 | October 2, 1865 | October 2, 1865 |
| Morgan, James A. | Reed, Miss Sarah E. | B/106 | July 27, 1870 | July 27, 1870 |
| Morgan, Larena | Campbell, Amos | B/72 | October 21, 1868 | October 22, 1868 |
| Morgan, Liddia | Mears, William | A/3 | June 7, 1838 | June 7, 1838 |
| Morgan, Lidy E. Miss | Young, W. E. | B/120 | December 21, 1870 | No Return |
| Morgan, Liza E. | Vance, David | A2/115 | August 4, 1864 | August 4, 1864 |
| Morgan, M. J. Miss | Harris, S. H. | C/4 | July 29, 1871 | No Return |
| Morgan, Malinda Miss | Moody, Charles | B/104 | July 16, 1870 | July 17, 1870 |
| Morgan, Nancy Miss | Morgan, Jackson | A/74 | October 26, 1844 | October 27, 1844 |
| Morgan, Rebecca | Harris, J. J. | C/142 | August 15, 1876 | August 15, 1876 |
| Morgan, Robert A. | Hayes, Mary F. | C/88 | April 25, 1874 | April 26, 1874 |
| Morgan, Roxanah Miss | Todd, John H. | B/66 | May 15, 1868 | May 17, 1868 |
| Morgan, S. F. | Patterson, S. A. | C/126 | December 21, 1875 | December 22, 1875 |
| Morgan, Sarah G. | Walker, J. R. | A2/126 | September 1, 1865 | September 3, 1865 |
| Morgan, Serecia E. Miss | Campbell, J. W. | B/40 | January 30, 1867 | January 31, 1867 |
| Morgan, Staly | Barratt, George | C/214 | March 12, 1879 | No Return |
| Morgan, Wesley A. | Hammen, Malinda | A2/118 | November 26, 1864 | November 27, 1864 |
| Morgan, William | Barrett, Annis | A2/129 | September 23, 1865 | September 24, 1865 |
| Morris, Annie | Turner, Lee | C/468 | November 19, 1892 | November 20, 1892 |
| Morris, C. | Hollandworth, Cahal | A2/130 | October 9, 1865 | October 19, 1865 |
| Morris, Caroline Miss | Garaway, James R. | A2/64 | March 16, 1858 | March 17, 1858 |
| Morris, Elizabeth Miss | Mullenix, C. D. | C/8 | September 4, 1871 | September 4, 1871 |
| Morris, G. D. | Hancock, Rebecca | C/118 | August 20, 1875 | September 1, 1875 |
| Morris, G. D. | Higdon, Malvina | C/404 | October 14, 1887 | October 14, 1887 |
| Morris, Levi | Mathis, Nancy F. | C/50 | January 24, 1873 | January 29, 1873 |
| Morris, M. L. | Hale, J. T. | C/358 | June 16, 1886 | June 16, 1886 |
| Morris, Mary | Dixon, Armsted | F/34 | October 6, 1894 | No Return |
| Morris, Mary P. Miss | Mullinix, Bluford J. | B/40 | February 1, 1867 | February 3, 1867 |
| Morris, Mary W. Miss | Travis, Daniel | B/126 | February 10, 1871 | February 10, 1871 |
| Morris, Sarah E. | Moonyham, John | A2/105 | January 8, 1862 | October 21, 1862 |
| Morris, Sarah Miss | Hall, C. H. | B/78 | February 1, 1869 | February 1, 1869 |
| Morris, William | Thompson, Talitha | A/99 | May 29, 1847 | May 29, 1847 |
| Mors, Monroe | Mingle, Georgie | F/146 | March 3, 1898 | March 3, 1898 |
| Moses, R. R. | Berrett, Miss E. M. | A2/55 | April 20, 1857 | No Return |
| Mosey, Doretha Miss | Blue, N. J. | A2/69 | October 28, 1858 | October 28, 1858 |
| Moss, Charles D. | Cunningham, Miss Jane | A2/85 | April 3, 1859 | April 3, 1859 |
| Moss, Robt. | Hollis, Lena | E/170 | April 18, 1889 | April 18, 1889 |

| Groom or Bride | Groom or Bride | Book/Page | Date of License | Date of Marriage |
|---|---|---|---|---|
| Moss, Sallie | Elrod, Thomas | C/328 | February 10, 1885 | February 12, 1885 |
| Moss, Thomas | Berryhill, P. I. | C/312 | August 4, 1884 | August 4, 1884 |
| Moss, W. D. | Alford, Mary | A2/93 | January 24, 1860 | No Return |
| Moss, W. H. | King, Edney B | C/314 | September 17, 1884 | September 17, 1884 |
| Moss, Willie | Shirley, Martha | D/10 | | January 3, 1881 |
| Moten, Margarett Miss | Bankston, John | A2/24 | March 26, 1853 | March 27, 1853 |
| Motley, Ann | Arnett, James | C/400 | September 3, 1887 | September 4, 1887 |
| Motley, Elisabeth | Melton, Johm | D/2 | | August 14, 1881 |
| Motley, Saphrona | Blair, H. T. | C/398 | August 20, 1887 | August 21, 1887 |
| Motley, Sarah | Melton, Samuel | C/138 | June 10, 1876 | No Return |
| Motone, Mariah | Fugett, Wat | C/214 | March 1, 1879 | March 2, 1879 |
| Mount, America O. | Wood, Isaac | C/412 | November 28, 1887 | November 28, 1887 |
| Mount, Mollie | Tubs, James | D/21 | | September 29, 1883 |
| Mount, Simon | Hancock, Delie | D/13 | | May 5, 1882 |
| Mullen, Nancy | Ashford, George | A2/16 | February 3, 1852 | February 3, 1852 |
| Mullenax, H. J. Miss | Hale, Vance | C/456 | February 26, 1892 | August 4, 1892 |
| Mullenax, Mary | Higgins, Presley | A2/119 | January 18, 1865 | No Return |
| Mullenix, Benj. | Mitchell, Missey | C/174 | October 25, 1877 | October 25, 1877 |
| Mullenix, C. D. | Morris, Miss Elizabeth | C/8 | September 4, 1871 | September 4, 1871 |
| Mullenix, J. P. | Mears, Amandy A, | C/200 | September 28, 1878 | No Return |
| Mullenix, Mariah | Tally, David | C/98 | October 24, 1874 | October 24, 1874 |
| Mullennix, Veny | Rushing, A. | C/220 | June 28, 1879 | No Return |
| Mullens, Joseph | Ashford, Nancy˙ | A/5 | August 14, 1838 | August 16, 1838 |
| Mullican, Antney | Preston, Miss Josephine | B/52 | September 23, 1867 | September 25, 1867 |
| Mullican, Josie | Bailey, Francis | C/340 | October 24, 1885 | October 25, 1885 |
| Mullican, Mary Ann | Cummings, Thomas | F/88 | June 17, 1896 | June 21, 1896 |
| Mullin, John H. | Keele, Miss Margaret J. | A2/146 | October 15, 1866 | October 15, 1866 |
| Mullinax, Effie | Higgins, Hargis | F/102 | November 23, 1896 | No Return |
| Mullinax, Harriet | Woods, Frank | C/156 | February 4, 1877 | February 4, 1877 |
| Mullinax, James S. | Powell, Miss Elizabeth E. | A/131 | January 19, 1850 | January 23, 1850 |
| Mullinex, John A. | Cummings, John | C/312 | August 22, 1884 | August 24, 1884 |
| Mullinax, Odie | Spurlock, J. D. | C/422 | November 13, 1890 | November 16, 1890 |
| Mullingax, Sarah E. Miss | Bogle, G. W. | A2/54 | February 2, 1857 | No Return |
| Mullinix, Bluford J. | Morris, Miss Mary P. | B/40 | February 1, 1867 | February 3, 1867 |
| Mullinix, W. G. | Tittle, Sarah A. | C/128 | December 25, 1875 | December 26, 1875 |
| Mullins, Daniel C. | Jane Mullins | A/15 | July 20, 1829 | July 25, 1839 |
| Mullins, David | Covington, Leath | A/29 | May 20, 1840 | June 4, 1840 |
| Mullins, Dosune | Cathey, Mary | A/25 | February 26, 1840 | February 16, 1840 |
| Mullins, Dozier | Sutton, Miss Adaline | A/69 | April 26, 1844 | April 26, 1844 |
| Mullins, Frances E. | McBroom, Jessee | C/70 | November 4, 1873 | November 4, 1873 |
| Mullins, Henry B. | Cantrell, Miss Janette | A/97 | February 16, 1847 | February 16, 1847 |
| Mullins, J. B. | Young, R. E. | A2/99 | July 13, 1860 | Executed--No Date |
| Mullins, J. H. | Phillips, N. J. | C/42 | October 11, 1872 | October 13, 1872 |
| Mullins, James B. | Young, Miss Martha E. | A2/145 | September 24, 1866 | September 24, 1866 |
| Mullins, James R. | Rigsby, Martha T. | C/122 | October 16, 1875 | October 17, 1875 |
| Mullins, Jane | Mullins, Daniel C. | A/15 | July 20, 1829 | July 25, 1839 |

| Groom or Bride | Groom or Bride | Book/Page | Date of License | Date of Marriage |
|---|---|---|---|---|
| Mullins, Jane Mrs. | Young, John | B/104 | June 23, 1870 | June 23, 1870 |
| Mullins, John A. | Beeson, Miss Margarett J. | A/104 | October 17, 1847 | October 18, 1847 |
| Mullins, John W. | Sapp, Miss Hannah C. | A/79 | June 15, 1845 | June 20, 1845 |
| Mullins, Joseph | Ritchey, Harritt | C/100 | November 28, 1874 | November 29, 1874 |
| Mullins, Julia Ann Miss | Williams, John A. | A/130 | December 13, 1849 | December 13, 1849 |
| Mullins, Julia Miss | Evans, James M. | A2/131 | November 9, 1865 | November 9, 1865 |
| Mullins, Louisa | Cox, Henry | A2/107 | February, 9, 1863 | February 15, 1863 |
| Mullins, Lucinda Miss | Cantrell, Stephen | A/87 | March 19, 1846 | March 19, 1846 |
| Mullins, Mahala Miss | Vaughn, Thomas | A/49 | April 28, 1842 | April 28, 1842 |
| Mullins, Maggie Miss | Fann, W. T. | C/454 | January 4, 1892 | January 4, 1892 |
| Mullins, Margret | Denton, William | A/23 | February 4, 1840 | February 4, 1840 |
| Mullins, Martha | Arvin, William | A2/125 | August 3, 1865 | August 10, 1865 |
| Mullins, Rebecca Miss | Thompson, T. J. | A2/137 | February15, 1866 | February 18, 1866 |
| Mullins, S. D. | Hays, Julie A. | C/48 | December 24, 1872 | December 25, 1872 |
| Mullins, Sallie | Brown, D. S. | D/13 |  | May 25, 1882 |
| Mullins, Sarah | Young, Samuel | A2/115 | July 22, 1864 | No Return |
| Mullins, Sarah | Webb, J. C. | E/248 | December 23, 1889 | December 24, 1889 |
| Mullins, Vina Jane Miss | Spears, Samuel | A/31 | July 11, 1840 | July 13, 1840 |
| Mullins, W. H. | Owens, Miss Nancy E. | C/6 | August 26, 1871 | August 27, 1871 |
| Mullins, William | Hays, Sarah Ann | A/51 | July 7, 1842 | July 8, 1842 |
| Mullins, William S. | Cantrell, Miss Elizabeth | A/118 | December 7, 1848 | December 7, 1848 |
| Mullins, Wm. | Fann, Amanda | C/368 | September 25, 1886 | September 26, 1886 |
| Muncey, Amanda C. | Murphy, Timothy P. | C/168 | August 22, 1877 | August 22, 1877 |
| Muncey, McCaslin | Hailey, Tildey | A2/76 | August 4, 1855 | August 5, 1855 |
| Muncy, Elizabeth | Eddings, Wm. R. | A2/21 | December 8, 1852 | December 8, 1852 |
| Muncy, Elizabeth Miss | Orrick, James A. | A2/144 | August 30, 1866 | August 30, 1866 |
| Muncy, Emley | Manus, M. H. | C/72 | November 20, 1873 | November 20, 1873 |
| Muncy, H. | Story, Mary M. | C/128 | December 30, 1875 | December 30, 1876 |
| Muncy, Halton | Hamilton, Mollie | F/136 | November 17, 1897 | November 18, 1897 |
| Muncy, Hester Miss | Smithson, Riston | B/114 | November 4, 1870 | November 6, 1870 |
| Muncy, L. J. | Campbell, M. E. | C/322 | January 10, 1884 | January 11, 1885 |
| Muncy, Sarah Miss | Wilson, L. D. H. | B/92 | November 19, 1869 | November 21, 1869 |
| Muny, McCaslen | Holy, Tildy | A2/40 | August 3, 1855 | Return Missing |
| Muny, Sarah Miss | Pendleton, Wm. G. | A2/40 | June 9, 1855 | June 10, 1855 |
| Murfree, I. N. B. | Givins, Miss America | B/78 | February 6, 18609 | February 7, 1869 |
| Murfee, Mary Miss | Spicer, Henry | C/384 | February 26, 1886 | No Return |
| Murfree, Mary E. Miss | Gilley, M. B. | B/84 | August 23, 1869 | August 23, 1869 |
| Murfrep, Lucretia Miss | Hollinsworth, Aden | A/78 | May 8, 1845 | May 8, 1845 |
| Murfrey, B. F. | Dennis, Miss Eliza | A/124 | August 2, 1849 | August 2, 1849 |
| Murfrey, Robert S. | Farrell, Miss Sarah Jane | A/83 | October 3, 1845 | No Return |
| Murfrey, Sally Ann Miss | Vasser, Joshua | A/100 | June 3, 1847 | No Return |
| Murphey, J. K. | Campbell, Della | E/374 | October 5, 1898 |  |
| Murphrey, W. G. | Spurlock, Miss Prudy | A2/138 | February 28, 1866 | March 2, 1866 |
| Murphy, Emma | Ferrell, John | F/132 | September 28, 1897 | September 30, 1897 |
| Murphy, J. D. | Hollingsworth, Nancy A. | A2/118 | December 17, 1864 | December 21, 1864 |
| Murphy, James | Campbell, Della | F/160 | November 5, 1898 | November 6, 1898 |

| Groom or Bride | Groom or Bride | Book/Page | Date of License | Date of Marriage |
|---|---|---|---|---|
| Murphy, James A. | Barrett, Tennie | C/324 | January 19, 1885 | No Return |
| Murphy, John | Arnett, Susan | C/228 | October 1, 1079 | October 5, 1879 |
| Murphy, John | McDowell, Eliza | D/1 | | July 9, 1881 |
| Murphy, John A. | Sullins, Cardin | F/22 | November 13, 1893 | November 16, 1893 |
| Murphy, Maggie | Miller, George | D/3 | | August 25, 1881 |
| Murphy, Margret | Givens, Marion | D/14 | | August 17, 1882 |
| Murphy, Martha | Ledbetter, William | C/84 | March 14, 1874 | March 15, 1874 |
| Murphy, Martha E. | Manns, Wm. M | C/216 | June 21, 1879 | June 22, 1879 |
| Murphy, Mary A. | Powel, Thos. | C/86 | April 2, 1874 | April 2, 1874 |
| Murphy, Robt | Cantrell, Mary J. | D/20 | | January 14, 1883 |
| Murphy, Robt. | Smith, Miss Candis | A2/40 | April 12, 1855 | Return Missing |
| Murphy, Robt. T. | Driver, Aldona | C/62 | July 30, 1873 | July 30, 1873 |
| Murphy, Sarah Jane Miss | Young, Samuel | A2/88 | September 10, 1859 | No Return |
| Murphy, Timothy P. | Muncey, Amanda C. | C/168 | August 22, 1877 | August 22, 1877 |
| Murry, Alice | Barnes, James | C/286 | July 17, 1883 | July 17, 1883 |
| Murry, Clera M. | Williams, Joshua | C/132 | February 3, 1876 | February 3, 1876 |
| Murry, Davis B. | Pinkerton, Miss Sarah A. | A2/139 | March 28, 1866 | March 29, 1866 |
| Murry, Frank | King, Ida | E/38 | May 19, 1888 | May 19, 1888 |
| Murry, Samuel | Officer, Mattie | C/344 | December 18, 1885 | December 18, 1885 |
| Murry, Samuel | Barkley, Hattie | D/4 | | August 9, 1881 |
| Muse, J. L. | Bairns, Euhley | C/224 | September 25, 1879 | September 25, 1879 |
| Naper, John | Smith, Carline | A2/97 | No Dates | |
| Napper, Caroline | Webber, Albert | C/248 | May 11, 1880 | May 17, 1880 |
| Neal, Alex | Sims, Laura | C/236 | December 31, 1879 | December 31, 1879 |
| Neal, Jim | Blair, Alley | C/230 | November 8, 1879 | November 9, 1879 |
| Neal, Lou G. | Cothran, W. P. | C/76 | December 18, 1873 | December 24, 1873 |
| Neal, Tom (col) | Adams, Mary, (col) | E/386 | October 14, 1898 | |
| Neal, Wm | Hancock, Sarah | C/244 | March 6, 1880 | March 6, 1880 |
| Nealey, Medford C. | Smith, Mary Frances | A2/127 | September 14, 1865 | September 17, 1865 |
| Nealy, Callie | Vinson, J. B. | C/370 | October 9, 1886 | No Return |
| Nealy, Mary Ann Miss | Rogers, Wm. J. | A2/56 | May 27, 1857 | No Return |
| Neel, T. M. | Mason, Sarah E. | A2/34 | August 24, 1854 | August 24, 1854 |
| Neeley, Eligah | Higdon, Miss Sarah E. | B/36 | January 10, 1867 | January 10, 1867 |
| Neeley, Frank | Vinson, George | C/264 | November 26, 1880 | November 28, 1880 |
| Neeley, Franklin | Hollowman, Oley | A2/30 | October 10, 1865 | October 11, 1865 |
| Neeley, J. G. | Young, J. B. | C/324 | January 20, 1885 | January 22, 1885 |
| Neeley, Jennie | Preston, J. B. | E/207 | September 9, 1889 | September 15, 1889 |
| Neeley, Mary Miss | Barker, Donalson | A2/138 | February 27, 1866 | March 1, 1866 |
| Neeley, Nancy E. | Hollandsworth, H. | C/36 | September 3, 1872 | September 3, 1872 |
| Neely, Bettie | Melton, Bemjaman | C/346 | December 25, 1885 | December 30, 1885 |
| Neely, Caroline Miss | Baily, Robert | A2/56 | June 5, 1857 | June 7, 1857 |
| Neely, Elisabeth Miss | Melton, Joel D. | A2/96 | April 21, 1860 | April 21, 1860 |
| Neely, Elizabeth Miss | Bailey, William M. | A2/1 | March 22, 1850 | No Date |
| Neely, Harriet Delila Miss | Rankhorn, C. M. | B/42 | February 25, 1867 | February 25, 1867 |
| Neely, Isaacah | Capps, Miss Ann | A/69 | April 20, 1844 | April 24, 1844 |
| Neely, Isaah | Evon, Miss Elizabeth | A2/14 | January 12, 1852 | January 12, 1852 |

| Groom or Bride | Groom or Bride | Book/Page | Date of License | Date of Marriage |
|---|---|---|---|---|
| Neely, Joseph H. | Hollis, E. Matilda | A2/95 | February 21, 1860 | February 22, 1860 |
| Neely, L. A. Miss | Neely, R. W. | A2/87 | August 25, 1859 | No Return |
| Neely, N. L. | Elkins, Miss Hariett | A2/30 | March 30, 1854 | March 30, 1854 |
| Neely, Nanie | Carnes, J. E. | C/352 | February 8, 1886 | April 26, 1886 |
| Neely, R. E. Miss | Elkins, H. R. | A2/86 | July 9, 1859 | July 10, 1859 |
| Neely, R. W. | Neely, Miss L. A. | A2/87 | August 25, 1859 | No Return |
| Neely, Sarah A. | Hollingsworth, Ira | A2/119 | January 4, 1865 | January 5, 1865 |
| Neely, Sarah Miss | Vinson, Benjamin | A2/32 | March 15, 1854 | March 15, 1854 |
| Neely, Sarah Miss | Vinson, Benjamin | A2/75 | March 15, 1854 | March 15, 1854 |
| Neely, Susan | Warren, W. M. | C/396 | August 4, 1887 | No Return |
| Neely, W. R. | Cummins, Sarah | C/152 | January 13, 1877 | January 14, 1877 |
| Nelson, J. S. | Dodd, Mollie | C/110 | March 11, 1875 | March 11, 1875 |
| Nelson, Martha | Anderson, Geol | C/148 | November 15, 1876 | November 24, 1876 |
| Nelson, Mary | Erving, Charles | C/320 | December 23, 1884 | December 24, 1884 |
| Nelson, Samuel | Massey, Martha | B/10 | December 22, 1866 | December 27, 1866 |
| Nesbett, J. A. | McCarlin, Susan | C/232 | December 16, 1879 | No Return |
| Nesbitt, S. V. | Ring, Sarah J. | C/130 | January 11, 1876 | January 11, 1876 |
| Neugent, Martha Miss | Melton, J. D. | A2/22 | January 7, 1853 | January 7, 1853 |
| Neugent, Martha T. Miss | Metton, J. D. | A2/26 | June 7, 1853 | June 9, 1853 |
| Neval, John | McCaffrey, Miss Malissa | B/42 | March 1, 1867 | March 1, 1867 |
| New, Allen | New, Hannah | B/4 | August 24, 1865 | August 27, 1865 |
| New, C. B. | Patrick, Callie | C/146 | November 1, 1876 | November 1, 1876 |
| New, Fanny Miss | Franks, L. B. | A2/159 | June 18, 1866 | June 21, 1866 |
| New, Hannah | New, Allen | B/4 | August 24, 1865 | August 27, 1865 |
| New, John C. | Orron, Mary E. | A2/124 | July 20, 1865 | July 20, 1865 |
| New, Maria | Taylor, James | B/6 | September 1, 1865 | July 1, 1865? |
| New, Pollie Miss | Roach, George T. | C/412 | December 17, 1887 | December 18, 1887 |
| New, Tennie | Miller, J. E. | C/98 | October 29, 1874 | October 29, 1874 |
| New, W. R. | Eagleton, Adell | E/259 | January 8, 1890 | No Return |
| Newby, George | Wood, Fanny | B/14 | January 16, 1868 | January 16, 1868 |
| Newby, William | Pitman, Elizabeth | A2/109 | October 7, 1863 | No Return |
| Newgent, Judah Mrs. | Smith, John J. | A/111 | May 10, 1848 | May 11, 1848 |
| Nichol, J. J. | Bowen, Amandy | C/254 | August ??, 1880 | No Return |
| Nichol, J. W. | Holms, Miss Mary R. | B/34 | December 19, 1866 | December 20, 1866 |
| Nichol, J. Y. | Hollis, D. C. | A2/118 | December 6, 1864 | December 6, 1864 |
| Nichol, J. Y. | Bowen, Amandy | C/274 | August 20, 1880 | No Return |
| Nichol, J. Y. | Richards, M. E. | E/139 | February 19, 1889 | February 20, 1889 |
| Nichol, Joseph | Keele, Miss Sarah | A/106 | December 21, 1847 | December 22, 1847 |
| Nichol, Lemmie | Gilley, John | C/422 | November 23, 1890 | November 23, 1890 |
| Nichol, Lucy | Paty, C. E. | C/374 | November 22, 1886 | November 23, 1886 |
| Nichol, Mollie | Gaither, J. C. | C/236 | December 24, 1879 | No Return |
| Nichol, Nova M. Miss | Logan, Eugene | E/68 | September 1, 1888 | September 2, 1888 |
| Nichol, Synthia C. Miss | Reed, Jackson | A2/7 | December 12, 1850 | December 12, 1850 |
| Nichols, B. F. | Higgins, Eliza | C/278 | April 8, 1881 | No Return |
| Nichols, Daniel A. | Vinson, Miss Sarah M. | A2/55 | March 17, 1857 | No Return |
| Nichols, Eliza A. Miss | Givens, William A. | A/77 | March 3, 1845 | No Return |

| Groom or Bride | Groom or Bride | Book/Page | Date of License | Date of Marriage |
|---|---|---|---|---|
| Nichols, I. Z | Gannon, S. R. | C/302 | January 21, 1884 | No Return |
| Nichols, Inthy Adaline Miss | Walkup, Wm. J. | A2/27 | August 23, 1853 | August 24, 1853 |
| Nichols, Margarett Jane Miss | Parker, John Westley | A/100 | June 24, 1847 | June 24, 1847 |
| Nichols, Pheba J. Miss | Berrett, Samuel | A2/56 | April 29, 1857 | April 30, 1857 |
| Nichols, Sarah | Jernigan, Henry | C/168 | August 29, 1877 | August 30, 1877 |
| Nichols, W. B. | Jones, Miss Nancy | C/424 | December 17, 1890 | December 18, 1890 |
| Nickels, Sarah Miss | Rogers, Henry | A2/24 | March 10, 1853 | March 13, 1853 |
| Night, Calvin | Bogle, Miss Margarett | A2/54 | February 16, 1857 | February 18, 1857 |
| Night, John | Horral, Miss Sarah M. | A2/15 | February 26, 1852 | February 26, 1852 |
| Nivens, Sarah | Jarnagin, Nedham | A/55 | November 9, 1842 | November 9, 1842 |
| Noakes, Mary | Moore, William | E/167 | April 3, 1889 | April 6, 1889 |
| Nobles, A. J. | Williams, N. E. | C/434 | April 1, 1891 | April 4, 1891 |
| Nokes, Delie | Hollandsworth, John | C/356 | March 26, 1886 | March 27, 1886 |
| Nokes, John | Higgins, Miss Margaret | B/106 | July 29, 1870 | July 31, 1870 |
| Nokes, M. Miss | Melton, Higdon | B/44 | May 10, 1867 | May 14, 1867 |
| Nokes, Mary Ann Miss | Thompson, T. J. | A2/38 | February 2, 1855 | February 2, 1854? |
| Nokes, Mollie | Dobbs, James | C/88 | May 15, 1874 | May 16, 1874 |
| Nokes, Nancy | Brasheares, William | A/57 | December 10, 1842 | December 13, 1842 |
| Nokes, Nancy W. | Spurlock, Wm. | C/64 | July 31, 1873 | August 1, 1873 |
| Nokes, Nelson | Elam, Miss Flora | A/63 | June 3, 1843 | June 4, 1843 |
| Nokes, O. B. | Tittle, Juia Ann | C/420 | October 15, 1890 | October 16, 1890 |
| Nokes, Sam | Davis, Parlee | C/272 | February 14, 1881 | February 15, 1881 |
| Nokes, Thomas | Hulet, Sallie | C/272 | February 14, 1881 | February 14, 1881 |
| Nokes, W. B. | Sullins, Susan F. | C/82 | February 4, 1874 | February 5, 1874 |
| Nokes, William B. | Stone, Mary | A/19 | November 16, 1839 | November 21, 1839 |
| Norman, Alice | Warley, Jasper | C/266 | December 25, 1880 | No Return |
| Norman, G. R. | McFerrin, Sallie | C/300 | January 19, 1884 | No Return |
| North, C. A. | Hare, Myrtle | C/234 | December 23, 1879 | December 24, 1879 |
| Northcott, U. N. | Perry, Josephine | C/426 | December 23, 1890 | December 26, 1890 |
| Northcut, H. J. | Downing, W. A. | C/342 | December 3, 1885 | December 13, 1885 |
| Northcut, James M. | Elrodd, Miss Luda | C/408 | November 14, 1887 | November 14, 1887 |
| Northcut, Lockey | Anderson, John | C/356 | April 9, 1886 | April 11, 1886 |
| Northcut, Mandy | Parten, Wm. B. | C/238 | January 17, 1880 | January 18, 1880 |
| Northcut, Mattie J. | McBride, O. J. | C/142 | August 19, 1876 | August 20, 1876 |
| Northcut, Snne? | Powell, George | C/350 | January 21, 1886 | January 24, 1886 |
| Northcutt, N. J. | Jernigan, N. | C/140 | July 14, 1876 | July 18, 1876 |
| Northcut, Visa E. | Boners, Giles S. | A2/111 | December 31, 1863 | December 31, 1863 |
| Northcutt, George E. | Scott, Miss Nancy | B/58 | December 21, 1867 | No Return |
| Northcutt, J. M. | Alexander, N. M. | C/228 | October 1, 1874 | October 1, 1879 |
| Northcutt, William | Todd, Caroline | C/78 | December 25, 1873 | December 25, 1873 |
| Nuckley, Mary Miss | Reed, Daniel | A/52 | August 9, 1842 | August 14, 1842 |
| Nugan, John S. | Hollis, Miss Margaret | A2/145 | September 20, 1866 | September 20, 1866 |
| Oconner, Caroline | Chumbey, Pleasant | A2/82 | March 1, 1859 | March 3, 1858 |
| Oconner, Jeremiah | Higgins, Mary | A/117 | November 29, 1848 | November 29, 1848 |
| Odem, S. F. Miss | Owen, R. L. | A2/14 | January 28, 1852 | January 29, 1852 |
| Oden, Ophelia | Simpson, W. C. | E/50 | June 2, 1888 | June 2, 1888 |

| Groom or Bride | Groom or Bride | Book/Page | Date of License | Date of Marriage |
|---|---|---|---|---|
| Odom, A. L. | Hancock, Irene | C/314 | September 17, 1884 | September 18, 1884 |
| Odom, A. L. Miss | Dill, W. C. | B/32 | November 27, 1866 | November 28, 1866 |
| Odom, A. R. | Turner, Bettie | C/218 | June 28, 1879 | June 29, 1879 |
| Odom, Abrahm | McAdow, Hanah | B/10 | May 31, 1867 | No Return |
| Odom, Andrew | Terry, Drew | C/86 | April 2, 1874 | April 2, 1874 |
| Odom, Ann Eliza Miss | Orand, James W. | A/122 | April 25, 1849 | No Return |
| Odom, Armsted J. | Bogle, Eliza J. | A/103 | October 14, 1847 | October 15, 1847 |
| Odom, B. F. | Hancock, Lillian | C/290 | September 3, 1883 | September 6, 1883 |
| Odom, Bogine | Kennedy, Zula | C/420 | October 24, 1890 | No Return |
| Odom, C. | Brown, E. W. | C/316 | November 17, 1884 | November 17, 1884 |
| Odom, C. C. | Owen, Lucy | A2/42 | October 13, 1855 | No Return |
| Odom, C. C. | Gribble, Girtrude | C/198 | September 18, 1878 | September 22, 1878 |
| Odom, C. C. | Adamson, Francis | C/282 | May 27, 1883 | April 29, 1883 |
| Odom, Cantrell B. | Owen, Miss Elizabeth | A/101 | August 19, 1847 | August 19, 1847 |
| Odom, Caroline | Martin, Burton | C/106 | January 18, 1875 | January 21, 1875 |
| Odom, Catherine | Hancock, B. C. | C/148 | November 22, 1876 | No Return |
| Odom, Charity | McKnight, David | C/82 | February 4, 1874 | February 4, 1874 |
| Odom, D. F. | Tenpenny, Emma | C/90 | July 20, 1874 | July 20, 1874 |
| Odom, D. F. | Tenpenny, Emma | C/92 | July 30, 1874 | No Return |
| Odom, D. T. | Willard, M. W. | C/14 | November 16, 1871 | November 19, 1871 |
| Odom, Donnie Miss | Simpson, William C. | C/390 | June 2, 1887 | No Return |
| Odom, E. H. | Couch, Miss Florence | C/400 | August 30, 1887 | September 2, 1887 |
| Odom, Edney | Paty, J. H. | C/268 | December 22, 1880 | December 23, 1880 |
| Odom, Edney A. | Bryson, L. C. | C/286 | July 16, 1883 | July 19, 1883 |
| Odom, Ednie A. | Duggins, J. T. | C/230 | November 10, 1879 | November 12, 1879 |
| Odom, Elizabeth G. Miss | Ramsey, James A. | A/85 | December 27, 1845 | December 28, 1845 |
| Odom, Elizabeth Miss | Moore, L. B. | A/63 | July 5, 1843 | July 5, 1843 |
| Odom, Etter | Delong, Wm. | C/364 | August 17, 1886 | September 30, 1886 |
| Odom, F. E. | Vaughan, H. C. | A2/111 | January 30, 1864 | No Return |
| Odom, Fanny | Dillon, Charles | B/10 | July 19, 1866 | July 20, 1866 |
| Odom, Fanny | Dillon, Charles | B/10 | July 19, 1866 | July 20, 1866 |
| Odom, Hanah J. Miss | Willard, J. A. | A2/59 | November 5, 1857 | No Return |
| Odom, Hanah Miss | Tembleton, William | B/48 | July 24, 1867 | July 24, 1867 |
| Odom, Harry | Ludsdon, Mary | B/2 | August 21, 1865 | No Return |
| Odom, Ida | Floyd, R. F. | C/100 | November 4, 1874 | November 5, 1874 |
| Odom, J. D. | Hancock, Miss Mollie | C/424 | December 17, 1890 | December 18, 1890 |
| Odom, J. H. | Brewies, A. E. | C/44 | October 23, 1872 | October 25, 1872 |
| Odom, J. M. A. | Stephens, L. H. | C/182 | December 22, 1877 | No Return |
| Odom, J. S. | McNabb, Dilelah | C/12 | October 12, 1871 | October 16, 1871 |
| Odom, J. S. | Milligan, Paralee | C/48 | December 26, 1872 | December 26, 1872 |
| Odom, J. S. | Smith, P. A. | C/286 | July 23, 1883 | July 23, 1883 |
| Odom, James W. | Owen, Miss Eliza L. | B/32 | November 11, 1866 | November 11, 1866 |
| Odom, James W. | Owen, Miss Eliza L. | B/32 | November 11, 1866 | November 11, 1866 |
| Odom, Jennie | Grindstaff, J. H. | C/364 | August 25, 1886 | August 26, 1886 |
| Odom, Jetter | Cooper, A. H. | E/166 | April 1, 1889 | No Return |
| Odom, John | Byrn, Eliza | C/222 | August 14, 1879 | August 14, 1879 |

| Groom or Bride | Groom or Bride | Book/Page | Date of License | Date of Marriage |
|---|---|---|---|---|
| Odom, John (col) | Hancock, Cinda | C/56 | April 12, 1873 | No Return |
| Odom, John S. | Odom, Miss Julian | A2/147 | November 10, 1866 | November 28, 1866 |
| Odom, Juda Ann | Dillon, Charles | B/8 | January 27, 1866 | No Return |
| Odom, Judea Ann | Sneed, Moses | B/12 | December 28, 1867 | December 28, 1867 |
| Odom, Julian Miss | Odom, John S. | A2/147 | November 10, 1866 | November 28, 1866 |
| Odom, July | Hayes, A. | C/294 | September 26, 1883 | September 27, 1883 |
| Odom, L. A. | Willard, Wm. P. | A2/112 | February 12, 1865 | February 17, 1864 |
| Odom, L. C. | Baxter, R. M. | C/422 | November 22, 1890 | No Return |
| Odom, L. C. | Baxter, R. M. | C/422 | November 22, 1890 | No Return |
| Odom, Leona | Gothard, W. J. | C/374 | November 20, 1886 | November 25, 1886 |
| Odom, Louise | Summar, Berton | B/2 | August 21, 1865 | No Return |
| Odom, M. M. | Floyd, Miss S. E. | C/8 | August 30, 1871 | August 31, 1871 |
| Odom, Mandy Miss | James A. F. | A2/71 | January 11, 1859 | January 11, 1859 |
| Odom, Mandy Miss | James A. F. | A2/83 | January 11, 1859 | January 11, 1859 |
| Odom, Margaret N. | Hammons, I. I. | A2/122 | April 1, 1865 | ?? ?, 1865 |
| Odom, Martha A | Milligan, John | C/2 | July 5, 1871 | No Return |
| Odom, Mattie | Rich, Willie | C/262 | November 18, 1880 | November 18, 1880 |
| Odom, Mary | Wilson, M. V. | A2/107 | May 13, 1863 | May 13, 1863 |
| Odom, Mary Miss | Patrick, William C. | A/70 | June 13, 1844 | June 13, 1844 |
| Odom, Mary E. Miss | Sparks, W. B. | A2/62 | January 6, 1858 | January 7, 1858 |
| Odom, Mary L. | Owen, R. L. | A2/116 | September 13, 1864 | September 14, 1864 |
| Odom, N. C. | Peden, J. D | C/272 | February 2, 1881 | February 10, 1881 |
| Odom, N. M. Miss | Kelly, Reepes P. | A2/8 | December 23, 1850 | No Return |
| Odom, Nancy | Willard, John A. | A2/110 | November 21, 1863 | November 22, 1863 |
| Odom, Nannie Miss | Stone, John R. | A2/147 | November 14, 1866 | November 14, 1866 |
| Odom, R. E. | Wilson, J. W. | C/186 | February 11, 1878 | No Return |
| Odom, R. H. | Stephens, Miss Minnie | E/180 | June 11, 1889 | June 12, 1889 |
| Odom, R. L. | Brewin, Miss L. J. | C/6 | August 5, 1871 | August 6, 1871 |
| Odom, Robt | Smith, Mary F. | C/138 | May 26, 1876 | No Return |
| Odom, S. M. Miss | Couch, J. M. | B/100 | February 24, 1870 | February, 24, 1870 |
| Odom, Sallie | Summers, Rufus | C/418 | October 11, 1890 | No Return |
| Odom, Samuel C. | Bogle, Josephine | C/40 | September 21, 1872 | September 22, 1872 |
| Odom, Sarah L. Miss | Fite, J. C. | C/6 | August 28, 1871 | September 3, 1871 |
| Office, James | Martin, Martha | B/18 | February 1, 1870 | February 2, 1870 |
| Officer, Ann | Thompson, Jessee | C/12 | October 17, 1871 | October 19, 1871 |
| Officer, Anderson | McFerrin, Sophia | C/100 | October 31, 1874 | October 31, 1874 |
| Officer, Ed | Tally, Amandy | C/118 | August 26, 1875 | No Return |
| Officer, Martin | York, Sallie | C/358 | June 27, 1886 | June 27, 1886 |
| Officer, Mattie | Murry, Samuel | C/344 | December 18, 1885 | December 18, 1885 |
| Officer, Millie | Stephens, Andrew (col.) | C/460 | June 25, 1892 | No Return |
| Officer, Sophia | Taylor, Chas | C/172 | October 11, 1877 | October 11, 1877 |
| Ogelsy, Margarett H. | Painter, Geo. B. | C/188 | March 14, 1878 | March 15, 1878 |
| Oglesby, Adaline Miss | Hayes, Peyton H. | B/74 | December 21, 1868 | December 22, 1868 |
| Oglesby, J. H. | Caruthers, Miss R. J. | B/78 | February 24, 1869 | February 25, 1869 |
| Oglesby, S. H. | Smith, Miss Margrett | C/2 | June 7, 1871 | June 29, 1871 |
| Olford, Margrett | Rodgers, J. T. | C/16 | December 6, 1871 | December 6, 1871 |

| Groom or Bride | Groom or Bride | Book/Page | Date of License | Date of Marriage |
|---|---|---|---|---|
| Olivar, Thomas | Ford, Mary | A/76 | February 19, 1845 | February 19, 1845 |
| Oliver, Delia Miss | Woodall, William C. | A/108 | February 21, 1848 | February 21, 1848 |
| Oliver, Laura | Talley, Wm. (col) | C/228 | October 16, 1879 | October 16, 1879 |
| Oliver, J. R. | McFerrin, Miss E. C. | A2/92 | December 21, 1859 | No Return |
| Oliver, John H. | McFerrin, Mary E. | A2/125 | August 22, 1865 | August 22, 1865 |
| Ollivar, Hixie | White, George J. | E/17 | January 30, 1888 | January 31, 1888 |
| Oneal, E. G. | Tinsly, Miss Maud America | A2/93 | January 2, 1860 | No Return |
| Oneal, N. A. | Milligan, R. R. | E/208 | September 6, 1889 | September 7, 1889 |
| O'Neal, Wade | Smithson, Wm. | C/98 | October 12, 1875 | October 17, 1874 |
| ONeel, Sarah Jane Miss | Simmons, Isham | A/68 | April 10, 1844 | April 10, 1844 |
| Orand, E. M. Miss | Hollis, J. W. D. | A2/51 | November 26, 1856 | No Return |
| Orand, Elizabeth Miss | Elder, Edward | A2/38 | January 9, 1855 | January 9, 1855 |
| Orand, J. M. | Tribble, Elizabeth | A2/107 | February 19, 1863 | No Return |
| Orand, James W. | Odom, Miss Ann Eliza | A/122 | April 25, 1849 | No Return |
| Orand, Margrett Miss | Jones, Samuel | A2/48 | May 13, 1856 | Handed in no return |
| Orr, D. T. | Robets, Miss Bell | C/412 | December 14, 1887 | December 14, 1887 |
| Orr, Linda | Williams, Schudder | C/468 | October 18, 1892 | October 18, 1892 |
| Orr, Malinda | Parten, Wm | C/348 | December 28, 1885 | December 29, 1885 |
| Orr, John M. | Mathews, Nancy | A/19 | November 4, 1839 | No Return |
| Orrand, Anthony | Herriman, Amanda | B/8 | December 21, 1865 | Return Not Endorsed |
| Orrand, Joannah Miss | Brandon, Jonathan | A2/153 | May 24, 1866 | May 24, 1866 |
| Orrand, Thomas A. | Davenport, Miss Nancy M. | B/54 | October 19, 1867 | October 20, 1867 |
| Orrick, James A. | Muncy, Miss Elizabeth | A2/144 | August 30, 1866 | August 30, 1866 |
| Orron, Mary E. | New, John C. | A2/124 | July 20, 1865 | July 20, 1865 |
| Osbon, Harvey | Travis, N. L. | A2/117 | October 31, 1864 | November 2, 1864 |
| Osburn, Jane | Tittle, Sam | C/238 | January 10, 1880 | January 10, 1880 |
| Osborn, H. M. | Vaughn, G. W. | A2/96 | May 5, 1860 | May 9, 1860 |
| Osburn, Nancy J. | Robertson, Hugh | C/90 | June 25, 1874 | June 25, 1874 |
| Osburn, Poley A. | Pack, John | C/238 | January 10, 1880 | January 10, 1880 |
| Osment, H. S. | Sullins, Francis | E/213 | September 19, 1889 | No Return |
| Osment, Joseph L. | Hawkins, Miss Mary | A2/161 | June 27, 1866 | June 28, 1866 |
| Osment, Lucinda C. Miss | Parker, Edmund | B/70 | September 23, 1868 | September 24, 1868 |
| Osment, Martha I. | Eddington, Hugh | A2/106 | October 21, 1862 | October 22, 1862 |
| Osment, T. A. | Stone, M. V. | C/114 | July 5, 1875 | July 6, 1875 |
| Overall, America C. | Jennings, Leander | B/12 | December 12, 1867 | December 12, 1867 |
| Overall, Horace A. | Owen, Miss Caroline | A2/2 | April 9, 1850 | No Return |
| Ovie, Laura | Jones, Ans (col.) | C/462 | August 2, 1892 | No Return |
| Owen, A. H. | Markum, Arch | A2/114 | May 4, 1864 | May 8, 1864 |
| Owen, Abraham | Bailey, Miss Malissa | B/60 | December 26, 1867 | December 26, 1867 |
| Owen, Alford | Fuston, Lucinda | A2/45 | December 21, 1855 | December 23, 1855 |
| Owen, B. A. | Dodd, W. A. | C/418 | October 11, 1890 | October 12, 1890 |
| Owen, Bettie | Watson, J. M. | C/312 | August 14, 1884 | August 14, 1884 |
| Owen, Caroline Miss | Overall, Horace A. | A2/2 | April 9, 1850 | No Return |
| Owen, Drucilla Miss | Cooper, William B. | A/98 | March 11, 1847 | No Return |
| Owen, Elbert | Parker, Miss Mary | A/73 | September 23, 1844 | September 24, 1844 |
| Owen, Eliza L. Miss | Odom, James W. | B/32 | November 11, 1866 | November 11, 1866 |

| Groom or Bride | Groom or Bride | Book/Page | Date of License | Date of Marriage |
|---|---|---|---|---|
| Owen, Eliza L. Miss | Odom, James W. | B/32 | November 11, 1866 | November 11, 1866 |
| Owen, Elizabeth Miss | Odom, Cantrell B. | A/101 | August 19, 1847 | August 19, 1847 |
| Owen, F. J. | Larx, L. J. | E/218 | October 9, 1889 | October 10, 1889 |
| Owen, Fate | Good, Elisabeth C. | C/262 | November 9, 1880 | No Return |
| Owen, Geo | Cooper, Melia J. | C/114 | June 5, 1875 | June 6, 1875 |
| Owen, H. D. Miss | Basham, Wm. | A2/66 | August 15, 1858 | August 15, 1858 |
| Owen, J. S. | Campbell, Noley | C/354 | February 23, 1886 | February 24, 1886 |
| Owen, James | Watson, M. H. | C/260 | October 30, 1880 | October 30, 1880 |
| Owen, Jeremiah J. | Finley, Miss Aleathy | A2/10 | November 21, 1850 | November 21, 1850 |
| Owen, Jos. D. | Francis, Mary Ann | A2/112 | March 10, 1864 | March 15, 1864 |
| Owen, Kansas | Thompson, John R. | E/128 | January 7, 1889 | January 8, 1889 |
| Owen, Lena Miss | Tenpenny, Tobias | E/133 | February 6, 1889 | February 7, 1889 |
| Owen, Lucy | Odom, C. C. | A2/42 | October 13, 1855 | No Return |
| Owen, Mary E. | Saules, Andy A. | C/332 | July 22, 1885 | July 22, 1885 |
| Owen, Mary Miss | Reed, Ezekeil | C/2 | May 20, 1871 | May 21, 1871 |
| Owen, Mary | Rickets, Peter | A2/106 | November 4, 1862 | No Return |
| Owen, Nancy Miss | Marcum, John | A2/28 | September 9, 1853 | September 12, 1853 |
| Owen, R. L. | Odem, Miss S. F. | A2/14 | January 28, 1852 | January 29, 1852 |
| Owen, R. L. | Odom, Mary L. | A2/116 | September 13, 1864 | September 14, 1864 |
| Owen, S. E. H. | Adamson, Malissa | B/86 | September 18, 1860 | September 19, 1869 |
| Owen, Sarah | Hall, James | C/444 | August 21, 1891 | August 23, 1891 |
| Owen, Thomas | Blancet, Miss Eliza | A2/32 | February 2, 1854 | February 2, 1854 |
| Owen, Thomas | Gandy, Sopha | C/308 | May 17, 1884 | May 18, 1884 |
| Owen, Thomas | Smithson, Dover | E/111 | December 19, 1888 | December 20, 1888 |
| Owen, Thos J. | Brooks, Mattie | C/210 | January 16, 1879 | January 18, 1870 |
| Owen, William B. | Cathy, E. W. | A/27 | April 5,1840 | April 5,1840 |
| Owenby, E. C. | Turner, Madora | C/106 | January 15, 1875 | No return |
| Owenby, L. M. | Smith, Miss K. J. | B/58 | December 24, 1867 | No Return |
| Owenby, M. E. | Spangler, J. H. | C/258 | October 13, 1880 | October 17, 1880 |
| Owenby, Ruben | Hatfield, Sarah E. | C/136 | April 22, 1876 | April 24, 1876 |
| Owens, A. G. | Groom, A. E. | C/54 | February 25, 1873 | February 27, 1873 |
| Owens, Alford | Burger, Susan | C/106 | January 14, 1875 | January 14, 1875 |
| Owens, Claiborne | Blanks, Miss Mary Ann | A/58 | December 31, 1842 | January 1, 1843 |
| Owens, Fate | Good, Elizbeth | C/194 | July 16, 1878 | July 7, 1878 |
| Owens, Ira | Rich, Elizabeth | C/104 | January 14, 1875 | January 14, 1875 |
| Owens, Jeremiah J. | Teague, Emaly | A/50 | July 5, 1842 | July 5, 1842 |
| Owens, Jessie | Summers, Martiller | C/82 | February 5, 1874 | February 5, 1875 |
| Owens, Nancy E. Miss | Mullins, W. H. | C/6 | August 26, 1871 | August 27, 1871 |
| Owensby, Lizzie N. | Taylor, J. L. | C/68 | October 14, 1873 | October 16, 1873 |
| Owens, W. B. Jr. | Finley, E. E. | C/150 | December 22, 1876 | December 22, 1876 |
| Owin, Susan M. Miss | Dom (Odom), James H. | A2/35 | September 12, 1854 | September 12, 1854 |
| Ownby, E. D. | Knox, Miss Syntha E. | B/60 | January 9, 1868 | January 9, 1868 |
| Ownby, Eli | Peay, Eliza | C/442 | August 5, 1891 | August 5, 1891 |
| Pace, Elizabeth A. | Helms, Creed | A/28 | April 7, 1840 | April 7, 1840 |
| Pace, Leathey | Philips, Robert | A/20 | December 10, 1839 | December 10, 1839 |
| Pace, Rebecca | Gannon, George | A/53 | September 3, 1842 | September 6, 1842 |

| Groom or Bride | Groom or Bride | Book/Page | Date of License | Date of Marriage |
|---|---|---|---|---|
| Pack, John | Osburn, Poley A. | C/238 | January 10, 1880 | January 10, 1880 |
| Pack, M. | Stacy, Susannah | C/166 | August 10, 1877 | August 14, 1877 |
| Pack, N. M. | Aushus, J. H. | C/234 | December 24, 1879 | December 25, 1879 |
| Page, Edith E. | Moore, R. L. | E/72 | September 13, 1888 | September 13, 1888 |
| Page, John W. | McFerren, Miss Fannie F. | A2/143 | August 21, 1866 | August 23, 1866 |
| Painter, Geo. B. | Ogelsy, Margarett H. | C/188 | March 14, 1878 | March 15, 1878 |
| Painter, Heneretta | Hearne, Mitcheal | E/83 | September 26, 1888 | September 27, 1888 |
| Paits, Mary E. | Young, Isaac | C/208 | January 2, 1879 | January 2, 1879 |
| Pallett, Elizabeth Miss | Acres, Meredith | A/45 | December 25, 1841 | December 25, 1841 |
| Pallett, G. W. D. | Ervin, Miss Nancy E. | A/130 | October 25, 1849 | October 25, 1849 |
| Palmer, Mary | McKnight, Henry | C/374 | November 16, 1886 | November 16, 1886 |
| Paris, D | Webb R. | C/230 | November 15, 1879 | November 16, 1879 |
| Paris, F. M. (col.) | Wood, Marie | C/456 | March 12, 1892 | March 13, 1892 |
| Paris, John | Robtson, Vina (col) | E/27 | March 18, 1888 | March 18, 1888 |
| Parker, A. W. | McMahan, L. J. | C/16 | December 18, 1871 | December 24, 1871 |
| Parker, Adam | Adcock, Katharine | A/32 | September 9, 1840 | September 9, 1840 |
| Parker, Angeline Miss | Cothran, Plesant | A2/22 | January 12, 1853 | January 18, 1853 |
| Parker, Annie E. | Hibdon, R. B. | C/314 | September 24, 1884 | September 25, 1885 |
| Parker, Betsy Ann Miss | Stasy, Gidan | B/110 | September 17, 1870 | September 18, 1870 |
| Parker, Bettie | Davis, James | C/124 | November 12, 1875 | November 14, 1875 |
| Parker, Caroline Miss | Spry, Allen | A2/62 | January 21, 1858 | No Return |
| Parker, Cornelius | Sauls, Miss Charity | A/93 | October 28, 1846 | October 29, 1846 |
| Parker, D. F. | Jacobs, Miss Malvina | A2/26 | June 14, 1853 | No Return |
| Parker, D. I. | Simmons, Mattie J. | E/175 | May 2, 1889 | May 2, 1889 |
| Parker, Edmund | Osment, Miss Lucinda C. | B/70 | September 23, 1868 | September 24, 1868 |
| Parker, Elizabeth | Markum, Sam T. | C/330 | July 3, 1885 | November 5, 1885 |
| Parker, Franklin | Ingles, Dianitia Catharine | A/27 | April 2, 1840 | April 6, 1840 |
| Parker, George | Finley, Mary A. | A2/125 | August 9, 1865 | August 9, 1865 |
| Parker, H. C. | McMahan, Mattie L. | C/342 | November 27, 1885 | No Return |
| Parker, Isabella Miss | Stacy, John J. | A/42 | October 19, 1841 | October 20, 1841 |
| Parker, Isaiah | Lattimer, Miss Eliza | E/3 | January 11, 1888 | January 12, 1888 |
| Parker, J. A. | Freeman, Marthie | E/243 | December 20, 1889 | December 10, 1889 |
| Parker, J. E. | Rains, Miss Mary J. R. | B/100 | February 15, 1870 | February 17, 1870 |
| Parker, J. E. | Creson, Elizabeth | C/132 | February 2, 1876 | February 2, 1876 |
| Parker, J. L. | Burkes, Belle | C/440 | July 18, 1891 | July 18, 1891 |
| Parker, J. W. | Bearden, Mary E. | C/214 | March 23, 1879 | March 30, 1879 |
| Parker, Jessee | Finley, Rebecca | C/188 | March 19, 1878 | March 29, 1878 |
| Parker, John | Cherry, Miss Martha | A/36 | February 25, 1841 | February 25, 1841 |
| Parker, John | Banks, Arrenea | A2/36 | November 9, 1854 | November 9, 1854 |
| Parker, John A. | Finly, Miss Catharine Jane | A2/50 | September 13, 1856 | September 14, 1856 |
| Parker, John M. | Duke, Martha A. | C/350 | January 29, 1886 | January 31, 1886 |
| Parker, John Westley | Nichols, Miss Margarett Jane | A/100 | June 24, 1847 | June 24, 1847 |
| Parker, July Ann Miss | Womack, James Jasper | A2/4 | August 15, 1850 | August 15, 1850 |
| Parker, Lewis | Rigsby, Miss M. A. | A2/72 | February 3, 1859 | No Return |
| Parker, Lewis | Rigsby, Miss M. A. | A2/83 | February 3, 1859 | No Return |
| Parker, Lorenzo D. | Webber, Miss Jane | A/35 | November 5, 1840 | No Return |

| Groom or Bride | Groom or Bride | Book/Page | Date of License | Date of Marriage |
|---|---|---|---|---|
| Parker, Lucy J. | Parker, Robt. A. | E/368 | November 21, 1898 | |
| Parker, Mahala | Dukes, Calvin | C/144 | August 26, 1876 | September 17, 1876 |
| Parker, Margrett | Duncan, W. J. | C/296 | November 24, 1883 | November 25, 1883 |
| Parker, Mary | Braxton, J. M. | C/78 | December 20, 1873 | January 1, 1874 |
| Parker, Mary | Gowins, William | C/374 | November 14, 1886 | November 15, 1886 |
| Parker, Mary Ann Miss | Estes, Edward | A/112 | December 8, 1847 | December 8, 1847 |
| Parker, Mary J. | Ersry, Wm. L. | A2/21 | November 19, 1852 | November 22, 1852 |
| Parker, Mary Miss | Owen, Elbert | A/73 | September 23, 1844 | September 24, 1844 |
| Parker, Milley | Holt, B. A. | C/270 | January 6, 1881 | January 6, 1881 |
| Parker, Nancy Miss | Duke, John | B/44 | April 17, 1867 | April 18, 1867 |
| Parker, Nathaniel | Tucker, Miss Malissa | B/70 | September 3, 1868 | September 3, 1868 |
| Parker, Omy M. | Duke, James | C/124 | December 6, 1875 | December 5, 1875 |
| Parker, R. S. | Cates, Florence | E/205 | September 3, 1889 | September 4, 1889 |
| Parker, Rachal | Reed, W. H. | C/344 | December 12, 1885 | December 13, 1885 |
| Parker, Rebecca | Spry, George | A2/127 | September 14, 1865 | September 15, 1865 |
| Parker, Robt. A | Parker, Lucy J. | E/368 | November 21, 1898 | |
| Parker, S. B. | Hibdon, J. H. | E/258 | January 8, 1890 | No Return |
| Parker, Samuel F. | Peyton, Miss Margaret | A2/147 | April 24, 1866 | April 25, 1866 |
| Parker, Sarah C | Parker, W. C. | C/362 | July 24, 1886 | No Return |
| Parker, Sarah C. | Wilson, T. A. | C/420 | October 14, 1890 | October 15, 1890 |
| Parker, Sarah Elizabeth | Spry, William | A2/2 | March 23, 1850 | March 31, 1850 |
| Parker, Sarah L. A. Miss | Ready, Thomas | A/132 | February 16, 1850 | No Return |
| Parker, Silas | Brown, Miss Fannie | B/44 | April 9, 1867 | April 11, 1867 |
| Parker, T. | Spry, Miss Mary E. | C/458 | April 4, 1892 | No Return |
| Parker, Thomas | Cantrell, Miss Easter | A/119 | January 4, 1849 | January 4, 1849 |
| Parker, Thomas | Williams, Sarah | A2/20 | November 19, 1852 | November 23, 1852 |
| Parker, Thomas | Freeze, Sarah | C/272 | January 28, 1881 | January 29, 1881 |
| Parker, Violet Miss | Wiser, William | A/65 | November 27, 1843 | November 30, 1843 |
| Parker, W. C. | Gann, S. C. | C/306 | April 5, 1884 | No Return |
| Parker, W. C. | Barrett, Canzade | C/344 | December 17, 1885 | No Return |
| Parker, W. C. | Parker, Sarah C | C/362 | July 24, 1886 | No Return |
| Parker, W. F. | Dunlap, E. F. | C/334 | August 8, 1885 | August 9, 1885 |
| Parker, W. S. | Mahaffy, M. C. | C/402 | September 16, 1887 | September 17, 1887 |
| Parker, William L. | Rains, Elizabeth | A2/139 | October 4, 1865 | October 8, 1865 |
| Parker, Wm. | Gilley, Malinda V. | C/108 | February 5, 1875 | February 11, 1875 |
| Parkerson, J. F. | Patterson, Miss S. A. | B/108 | August 27, 1870 | August 29, 1870 |
| Parrett, Hyram | Bowen, Miss D. C. | B/110 | September 9, 1870 | September 11, 1870 |
| Parris, Harriett Miss | Elkins, J. P. | A2/71 | January 6, 1859 | January 6, 1859 |
| Parris, Harriett Miss | Elkins, J. P. | A2/83 | January 6, 1859 | January 6, 1859 |
| Parris, J. B. | Elkins, Miss M. J. | A2/87 | August 13, 1859 | No Return |
| Parris, J. B. Jr. | Bogle, Caroline | C/30 | July 22, 1872 | July 22, 1872 |
| Parris, J. R. | Logan, Bettie | A2/142 | July 25, 1866 | July 25, 1866 |
| Parsley, Bethel | Melton, Selina | C/18 | December 26, 1871 | December 28, 1871 |
| Parsley, Brice | Daniel, Nancy | A/5 | August 16, 1838 | August 16, 1838 |
| Parsley, James | Davis Manervia | A/1 | March 1, 1838 | March 1, 1838 |
| Parsley, James | Blair, Miss Rilda | C/384 | February 27, 1887 | February 27, 1887 |

| Groom or Bride | Groom or Bride | Book/Page | Date of License | Date of Marriage |
|---|---|---|---|---|
| Parten, Abraham | Melton, Miss Polly | A/122 | May 3, 1849 | May 3, 1849 |
| Parten, Henry | Davenport, Miss Nancy | A2/95 | April 3, 1860 | April 3, 1860 |
| Parten, John L. | Starr, Miss Susan | A/120 | February 15, 1849 | February 15, 1849 |
| Parten, William H. | Young, Miss Ruth | A/97 | January 26, 1847 | January 27, 1847 |
| Parten, Wm | Orr, Malinda | C/348 | December 28, 1885 | December 29, 1885 |
| Parten, Wm. B. | Northcut, Mandy | C/238 | January 17, 1880 | January 18, 1880 |
| Partin, Eliza | Anos, Henry | A/35 | January 1, 1841 | January 7, 1841 |
| Parton, Charlotte Miss | Tubb, John | B/40 | January 31, 1867 | January 31, 1867 |
| Parton, Elizabeth | Richardson, John L. | A2/130 | October 26, 1865 | October 27, 1865 |
| Parton, Elizabeth | Mathis, Dan | C/160 | April 24, 1877 | April 24, 1877 |
| Parton, Henry | Walls, Elizabeth | A2/113 | May 3, 1864 | May 3, 1864 |
| Parton, Isaac | Davenport, Jennie | C/444 | August 15, 1891 | August 16, 1891 |
| Parton, Isaac | Furbus, Callie | E/161 | March 2, 1889 | March 4, 1889 |
| Parton, J. B. | Hibdon, Josie | E/264 | January 28, 1890 | No Return |
| Parton, John | Hart, L. N. | C/22 | February 2, 1872 | February 4, 1872 |
| Parton, Louis | Melton, Ochasy | C/206 | November 9, 1878 | November 10, 1878 |
| Parton, Nancy A. | King, Sampson J. | A2/124 | July 21, 1865 | July 21, 1865 |
| Parton, Salinda | Young, Wm. | C/36 | August 31, 1872 | September 1, 1872 |
| Parton, Thomas | Davis, Nancy D. | C/244 | February 27, 1880 | No Return |
| Parton, Wiley | Smith, Amand | E/146 | March 23, 1889 | March 24, 1889 |
| Parton, Wm. | Partrick, Locky J. | C/108 | March 3, 1875 | No return |
| Partrick, Annie L. | Fite, Moses G. | C/130 | January 17, 1876 | No Return |
| Partrick, Isaac | Bogle, Ednie F. | C/112 | March 27, 1875 | March 28, 1875 |
| Partrick, Locky J. | Parton, Wm. | C/108 | March 3, 1875 | No return |
| Pascal, Thomas | Porterfield, Miss Malisa | A2/25 | May 3, 1853 | May 3, 1853 |
| Paschal, J. F. | Francis, A. L. | E/90 | October 18, 1888 | October 18, 1888 |
| Paschal, N. T. | Carnahan, Sallie E. | C/58 | May 14, 1873 | No Return |
| Paschall, S. J. | Travis, L. E. | E/227 | October 31, 1889 | October 31, 1889 |
| Pasby (Pasly), Sarah | Gunter, Wm. | C/106 | December 30, 1874 | December 30, 1874 |
| Paterson, Emily K. | Foster, W. L. | A2/124 | July 24, 1865 | July 26, 1865 |
| Paterson, Fannie | Dennis, Thos | C/140 | July 31, 1876 | No Return |
| Patrick, Callie | New, C. B. | C/146 | November 1, 1876 | November 1, 1876 |
| Patrick, Jesse | Milligan, Miss Nancy | A/118 | December 25, 1848 | December 28, 1848 |
| Patrick, Jessee | Cox, Miss J. S. H. | A2/70 | November 27, 1858 | November 30, 1858 |
| Patrick, John J. | Jones, Mary E. | C/368 | September 28, 1886 | No Return |
| Patrick, Laura Ann | Kelly, Jacob A. | A/54 | September 20, 1842 | September 26, 1842 |
| Patrick, Locky J. Miss | Higgans, John | A2/5 | September 21, 1850 | September 22, 1850 |
| Patrick, M. D. | Robinson, E. J. | C/266 | December 4, 1880 | December 5, 1880 |
| Patrick, Mary A. Miss | Johnson, Nelson | A2/11 | March 23, 1851 | March 23, 1851 |
| Patrick, Mary Ann | Manus, Elijah | A/76 | February 14, 1845 | February 13, 1845 |
| Patrick, Robert | Vasser, Cynthia | A/50 | July 4, 1842 | July 14, 1842 |
| Patrick, William C. | Odom, Miss Mary | A/70 | June 13, 1844 | June 13, 1844 |
| Patten, J. A. | Roberts, Miss M. C. | A2/131 | November 9, 1865 | November 9, 1865 |
| Patterson, A. B. | York, Susan | C/392 | July 1, 1886 | July 3, 1887 |
| Patterson, Ann | Denby, William | A/79 | June 28, 1845 | No Return |
| Patterson, Bettie Miss | Ferrell, W. M. | C/392 | June 18, 1887 | June 19, 1887 |

| Groom or Bride | Groom or Bride | Book/Page | Date of License | Date of Marriage |
|---|---|---|---|---|
| Patterson, Enoch | Kersey, Miss Thaney | A/82 | July 26, 1845 | July 27, 1845 |
| Patterson, Emma | Pearcey, Drewery | C/14 | November 8, 1871 | No Return |
| Patterson, Harriet | Milton, James | C/394 | July 9, 1887 | No Return |
| Patterson, Frances Miss | Blanton, William | B/66 | May 15, 1868 | May 18, 1868 |
| Patterson, J. C. | Cope, Miss Mary | B/120 | December 21, 1870 | December 22, 1870 |
| Patterson, J. M. | Ramsey, Nancy M. | C/24 | March 13, 1872 | March 14, 1872 |
| Patterson, John | Sellars, Susan | A/41 | September 1, 1841 | September 2, 1841 |
| Patterson, Joseph | Simpson, Emma | E/138 | February 13, 1889 | February 14, 1889 |
| Patterson, L. J. | Summar, H. C. | C/276 | March 30, 1881 | March 31, 1881 |
| Patterson, Lee | Burkett, Mary | C/260 | October 27, 1880 | No Return |
| Patterson, M. E. | Stephens, J. W. | C/174 | October 13, 1877 | October 13, 1877 |
| Patterson, Marey C. | Russell, Wm. H. | A2/113 | April 30, 1864 | April 30, 1864 |
| Patterson, Martha Miss | Porter, Alexander | B/36 | December 26, 1866 | December 26, 1866 |
| Patterson, Mary | Denley, John | C/272 | January 25, 1881 | January 30, 1881 |
| Patterson, Nancy | Ward, Milton | A/9 | December 24, 1838 | No Return |
| Patterson, Nettie | Kenedy, John M. | C/428 | January 6, 1891 | January 11, 1891 |
| Patterson, O. E. | Cantrell, P. P. | C/80 | January 26, 1874 | January 26, 1874 |
| Patterson, Perry | Grizzel, Francis | C/80 | January 25, 1874 | January 25, 1874 |
| Patterson, R. W. | Goad, Miss Louisa | A/97 | February 11, 1847 | February 11, 1847 |
| Patterson, Robert | Binges, Miss Caroline | A/38 | May 12, 1841 | May 13, 1841 |
| Patterson, Robt | Gunter, Sarah | C/352 | February 16, 1886 | March 6, 1886 |
| Patterson, S. A. | Morgan, S. F. | C/126 | December 21, 1875 | December 22, 1875 |
| Patterson, S. A. Miss | Parkerson, J. F. | B/108 | August 27, 1870 | August 29, 1870 |
| Patterson, Sarah | Gunter, Jno | C/194 | August 10, 1878 | August 11, 1878 |
| Patterson, Sarah | Melton, James | C/400 | September 2, 1887 | September 4, 1887 |
| Patterson, Susan Miss | Campbell, Wm | A2/30 | December 24, 1853 | No Return |
| Patterson, T. E. | Burger, Sara | C/312 | September 7, 1884 | September 9, 1884 |
| Patterson, Thomas | Sullin, Melissa | C/436 | May 25, 1891 | May 26, 1891 |
| Patton, A. D. | Measel, N. C. | C/60 | July 12, 1873 | No Return |
| Patton, Addie L. | Curlee, James P. | E/232 | November 13, 1889 | November 13, 1889 |
| Patton, Callie | Smithson, Thos. G. | C/176 | October 27, 1877 | October 28, 1877 |
| Patton, Caroline M. Miss | Spangler, Asa | A/63 | July 15, 1843 | July 16, 1843 |
| Patton, D. F. | Phillips, Alice | C/94 | August 22, 1874 | August 23, 1874 |
| Patton, David | Hale, Mary | A2/95 | March 13, 1860 | March 13, 1860 |
| Patton, David M. | McGill, Miss Jane | A/123 | July 20, 1848 | July 20, 1848 |
| Patton, David M. | McGill, Miss Jane | A/125 | July 20, 1848 | |
| Patton, Dillard | Young, Hattie | C/382 | January 25, 1887 | January 26, 1887 |
| Patton, Dora | Mitchell, Robt | C/176 | November 10, 1877 | November 11, 1877 |
| Patton, Elizabeth Miss | Brandon, David G. | A/74 | November 18, 1844 | November 19, 1844 |
| Patton, Harriett Miss | Gordon, John | A/103 | October 28, 1847 | October 28, 1847 |
| Patton, J. A. | Byron, Sallie | E/103 | November 28, 1888 | November 28, 1888 |
| Patton, James | Youree, J. A. | C/276 | December 20, 1880 | December 23, 1880 |
| Patton, James R. | French, Lona | C/468 | October 22, 1892 | October 23, 1892 |
| Patton, John | Wimberley, Polly | A/128 | October 15, 1849 | October 17, 1849 |
| Patton, John | Mitchell, Miss Sarah | E/168 | April 6, 1889 | April 7, 1889 |
| Patton, John M. | Moore, Miss Ada | C/404 | October 10, 1887 | October 12, 1887 |

| Groom or Bride | Groom or Bride | Book/Page | Date of License | Date of Marriage |
|---|---|---|---|---|
| Patton, Katharine | Bradford, James | A/10 | February 20, 1839 | February 20, 1839 |
| Patton, M. E. | Irvin, J. H. | C/264 | December 22, 1880 | December 23, 1880 |
| Patton, Margaret | McElroy, James | A2/126 | September 4, 1865 | December 5, 1865 |
| Patton, Margaret F. | Lamberth, James | A/4 | July 31, 1838 | July 31, 1838 |
| Patton, Mary | Watson, James | A/7 | September 25, 1838 | September 26, 1838 |
| Patton, Mary Ann Miss | McElroy, John James | A/87 | February 25, 1846 | March 2, 1846 |
| Patton, Mary H. | Bush, L. P. | C/314 | October 9, 1884 | No Return |
| Patton, Mary S. Miss | Reed, James H. | B/50 | August 30, 1867 | September 1, 1867 |
| Patton, Mattie J. | King, B. A. | C/62 | July 14, 1873 | July 16, 1873 |
| Patton, Nancy Eleanor Miss | Horn, Thomas W. | A/125 | December 20, 1848 | No Return |
| Patton, Ophie | Williams, W. P. | E/43 | June 26, 1888 | June 26, 1888 |
| Patton, Robert | Justice, Miss Laura | E/85 | October 6, 1888 | October 8, 1888 |
| Patton, Robert H. | Lowe, Frances M. | A/75 | November 20, 1844 | November 21, 1844 |
| Patton, Sarah | Phillips, M. L. | C/296 | November 17, 1883 | November 18, 1883 |
| Patton, Tempa Miss | Templeton, Samuel | A2/17 | March 16, 1852 | March 16, 1852 |
| Pattrick, Isaac | Bogle, Delia | C/422 | November 3, 1890 | November 3, 1890 |
| Pattrick, Mary E. Miss | Ferrell, E. G. | B/88 | September 23, 1869 | September 23, 1860 |
| Pattrick, Piney Miss | Summar, J. D. | B/54 | October 15, 1867 | October 15, 1867 |
| Paty, C. E. | Nichol, Lucy | C/374 | November 22, 1886 | November 23, 1886 |
| Paty, H. A. Miss | Fite, John A. | B/126 | February 7, 1871 | February 9, 1871 |
| Paty, J. H. | Odom, Edney | C/268 | December 22, 1880 | December 23, 1880 |
| Patz, Addie H. | Avert, Albert | E/66 | August 31, 1888 | September 4, 1888 |
| Paul, Clendenen | Espey, Sarah L. | C/10 | September 18, 1871 | September 21, 1871 |
| Payne, Eliza | Edwards, William | A/54 | September 27, 1842 | September 27, 1842 |
| Payton, Callie | Davenport, Jas. H. | C/96 | September 26, 1874 | September 28, 1874 |
| Payton, Margarett | Davenport, J. B. | C/196 | August 14, 1878 | August 14, 1878 |
| Pealer, Katharine Miss | King, George | A/102 | August 21, 1847 | August 24, 1847 |
| Pealer, King | Anderson, Mary | A/25 | February 25, 1840 | February 25, 1840 |
| Pealer, Leny | Anderson, Miss Martha | A/77 | March 8, 1845 | March 9, 1845 |
| Pealer, Page | Cherry, Miss Milley | A/90 | July 28, 1846 | July 30, 1846 |
| Pealer, Sally Miss | King, William | A/129 | December 12, 1849 | December 12, 1849 |
| Pearce, Malinda J. Miss | Bogle, H. M. | B/64 | February 6, 1868 | February 9, 1868 |
| Pearcey, Drewery | Patterson, Emma | C/14 | November 8, 1871 | No Return |
| Pearson, Asalin | Hall, R. J. | C/404 | October 8, 1887 | October 9, 1887 |
| Pearson, R. C. | Simman, Miss C. N. | B/116 | November 16, 1870 | November 16, 1870 |
| Pearson, Richard | Brown, Jane | A2/108 | July 9, 1863 | No Return |
| Pearson, Thomas | White, Miss Malinda T. | A/53 | August 31, 1842 | August 31, 1842 |
| Peay, Eliza | Ownby, Eli | C/442 | August 5, 1891 | August 5, 1891 |
| Peay, Roxanna | Haynes, N. A. | C/104 | December 23, 1874 | December 23, 1874 |
| Peay, Lena | McMillen, Wm. | E/105 | November 29, 1888 | November 30, 1888 |
| Peay, R. A. Miss | Knox, J. R. | A2/135 | January 14, 1866 | January 15, 1866 |
| Peay, Rufus D. | Harris, Martha J. | A2/115 | August 2, 1864 | August 3, 1864 |
| Peay, Tiendolphus | Walkup, Miss J. R. | B/38 | January 16, 1867 | January 16, 1867 |
| Peden, J. D | Odom, N. C. | C/272 | February 2, 1881 | February 10, 1881 |
| Peden, James | Whiteley, Miss Sarah | A/85 | December 27, 1845 | December 27, 1845 |
| Peden, John R. | Knight, Druzila | C/258 | October 10, 1880 | October 10, 1880 |

| Groom or Bride | Groom or Bride | Book/Page | Date of License | Date of Marriage |
|---|---|---|---|---|
| Peden, Monford | Bragg, Miss Nancy J. | A2/4 | August 17, 1850 | August 18, 1850 |
| Pedigo, Penney | Milligan, Joel | A/4 | June 18, 1838 | June 20, 1838 |
| Pedigo, Sarah | Davenport, Henry | A/7 | October 3, 1838 | October 5, 1838 |
| Pedon, Amanda | Campbell, J. C. | C/38 | September 13, 1872 | September 13, 1872 |
| Pedon, E. A. Miss | Harris, J. J. | C/4 | July 29, 1871 | July 30, 1871 |
| Pedon, Isaac | Sneed, Paralee | C/134 | February 13, 1876 | February 13, 1876 |
| Pedon, M. J. Miss | Devenport, H. G. | C/8 | September 7, 1871 | September 7, 1871 |
| Pedon, Mary J. | Richards, Jessee | C/74 | December 1, 1873 | December 1, 1873 |
| Pedon, Sarah Miss | Burke, Daniel | A2/49 | August 2, 1856 | August 2, 1856 |
| Peedon, Elisar | Vance, Richard | A2/106 | January 6, 1863 | January 6, 1863 |
| Peeler, Jessee | Moore, S. E. | C/104 | November 21, 1874 | November 26, 1874 |
| Peeler, John | Porutes (?), Nancy | C/128 | December 30, 1875 | December 30, 1876 |
| Peeler, K. S. | Craft, Mary | C/112 | May 4, 1875 | May 5, 1875 |
| Peeler, Martha J. | Moon, John | C/432 | February 26, 1891 | March 1, 1891 |
| Peeler, Mary A. | Rodgers, Wilburn | C/260 | October 20, 1880 | October 20, 1880 |
| Peeler, Mary A. | Clark, W. J. | C/66 | September 20, 1873 | September 21, 1873 |
| Peerce, James | Jones, Malinda | A2/107 | February 26, 1863 | No Return |
| Pelham, Elizabeth C. Miss | Lemons, Jacob M. | B/58 | December 19, 1867 | December 19, 1867 |
| Pelham, John | Conoley, George E. | E/8 | January 21, 1888 | January 22, 1888 |
| Pelham, Levi | Daniel, Miss Martha | A/97 | January 25, 1847 | February 3, 1847 |
| Pelham, Mary J. | Wilson, H. W. | C/38 | September 12, 1872 | September 12, 1872 |
| Pelham, Nancy | Hall, Walter | C/198 | September 11, 1878 | September 11, 1878 |
| Pelham, Thomas | Wilson, Eliza J. | C/130 | January 18, 1876 | January 18, 1876 |
| Pelham, W. H. | Pendleton, M. E. | C/360 | July 5, 1886 | July 11, 1886 |
| Pelham, Wm. | Miller, Miss Caroline | A2/22 | January 8, 1853 | January 9, 1853 |
| Pemelton, Thos. | Jacobs, Arminda | A2/108 | July 9, 1863 | No Return |
| Pendergrass, Mary Miss | Ratley, Alexander | A2/143 | August 14, 1866 | August 15, 1866 |
| Pendleton, Benjamin | Higgins, Mary | A/26 | March 14, 1840 | March 15, 1840 |
| Pendleton, Benjamin | McAdow, Miss Aelisa | A/107 | January 26, 1848 | January 26, 1848 |
| Pendleton, Betty | Haley, Isaac | C/222 | September 15, 1879 | September 14, 1879 |
| Pendleton, E. G. | Pendleton, Wm | C/362 | August 14, 1886 | August 14, 1886 |
| Pendleton, Elizabeth | Elam, Henry | A/34 | October 22, 1840 | October 24, 1840 |
| Pendleton, Elizabeth Miss | Sparks, William | A2/149 | May 11, 1866 | No Return |
| Pendleton, H. | Haley, Miss Mary A. | A2/65 | June 1, 1858 | June 2, 1858 |
| Pendleton, J. W. | Brown, Matilda E. | C/88 | April 27, 1874 | April 27, 1874 |
| Pendleton, John Jr. | West, Miss Lucinda | A/101 | August 9, 1847 | August 9, 1847 |
| Pendleton, John L. | Lynn, Miss Mary E. | B/52 | September 26, 1867 | No Return |
| Pendleton, M. E. | Pelham, W. H. | C/360 | July 5, 1886 | July 11, 1886 |
| Pendleton, Martha | Miller, T. J. | E/254 | December 30, 1889 | January 1, 1890 |
| Pendleton, Mary | Melton, James M. | A/80 | July 8, 1845 | July 10, 1845 |
| Pendleton, Mary | Melton, James M. | A/81 | July 8, 1845 | July 10, 1845 |
| Pendleton, Mary Ann Miss | Perry, John W. | A/46 | January 19, 1842 | January 19, 1842 |
| Pendleton, Melinda Miss | West, Charles | A/115 | October 7, 1848 | October 7, 1848 |
| Pendleton, Rachel Miss | Bowers, H. S. | B/72 | November 27, 1868 | No Return |
| Pendleton, Samuel | Thomas, Mary | A/57 | December 21, 1842 | December 21, 1842 |
| Pendleton, Samuel | Brnum, Caroline | C/188 | December 19, 1877 | December 20, 1877 |

| Groom or Bride | Groom or Bride | Book/Page | Date of License | Date of Marriage |
|---|---|---|---|---|
| Pendleton, Sarah | Bowers, Francis | A2/104 | November 14, 1860 | No Return |
| Pendleton, Sarah Miss | Prator, J. H. | B/78 | February 22, 1869 | February 25, 1869 |
| Pendleton, Stacy C. Miss | Stone, Benjamin A. | A/80 | July 16, 1845 | July 17, 1845 |
| Pendleton, Stacy C. Miss | Stone, Benjamin A. | A/81 | July 16, 1845 | July 17, 1845 |
| Pendleton, Thomas D. | Shepherd, Miss Elizabeth | A/124 | August 3, 1849 | August 4, 1849 |
| Pendleton, W. G. | Duncan, L. G. | C/12 | October 10, 1871 | No Return |
| Pendleton, William T. | Ferrell, Miss Mary Elizabeth | B/50 | August 8, 1867 | August 11, 1867 |
| Pendleton, Wm | Pendleton, E. G. | C/362 | August 14, 1886 | August 14, 1886 |
| Pendleton, Wm. G. | Muny, Miss Sarah | A2/40 | June 9, 1855 | June 10, 1855 |
| Pennington, E. B. | Merriter, C. C. | E/149 | November 3, 1888 | November 3, 1888 |
| People, Jennie Miss | Daniel, Sam | C/8 | September 7, 1871 | September 7, 1871 |
| People, Martha | Wright, J. D. | C/42 | October 2, 1872 | October 2, 1872 |
| Peoples, Jack | Reeves, Fanny | B/14 | August 18, 1868 | August 18, 1868 |
| Peoples, John | Vaughn, Miss Judie | B/124 | January 7, 1871 | January 12, 1871 |
| Peoples, Parthena | Smith, Joe | C/284 | June 20, 1883 | July 1, 1883 |
| Peoples, Sallie Miss | Tippet, Thomas | C/372 | November 9, 1886 | November 10, 1886 |
| Percell, Nancy P. | Jaco, E. J. | C/14 | November 27, 1871 | December 9, 1871 |
| Perriman, John M. | Jarrett, July | C/342 | November 21, 1885 | November 22, 1885 |
| Perry, Albert | Sullivan, Miss Louisa | A/36 | February 3, 1841 | February 4, 1841 |
| Perry, Catharine Miss | St. John, Joseph | A2/135 | January 11, 1866 | January 11, 1866 |
| Perry, E. | Bush, Sarah | C/252 | July 31, 1880 | August 1, 1880 |
| Perry, Ed | Creson, H. J. | C/20 | January 11, 1872 | January 11, 8172 |
| Perry, Edmond | Collins, Miss Mary | A2/62 | January 31, 1858 | January 31, 1858 |
| Perry, Henry R. | House, Miss Sally Ann | A/47 | February 2, 1842 | February 6, 1842 |
| Perry, J. B. | Creson, Miss Martha | C/380 | January 1, 1887 | January 3, 1887 |
| Perry, J. H. | Walkup, Miss Rocinda | C/8 | September 7, 1871 | September 7, 1871 |
| Perry, James P. | Higgins, Eliza | A/25 | March 12, 1840 | March 12, 1840 |
| Perry, Jennie Miss | Campbell, Thos | B/112 | October 1, 1870 | October 2, 1870 |
| Perry, John L. | Bush, Amanda J. | C/168 | August 25, 1877 | August 28, 1877 |
| Perry, John W. | Pendleton, Miss Mary Ann | A/46 | January 19, 1842 | January 19, 1842 |
| Perry, John W. | Stone, Nancy | A2/12 | October 25, 1851 | October 26, 1851 |
| Perry, Josephine | Northcott, U. N. | C/426 | December 23, 1890 | December 26, 1890 |
| Perry, Malisa Miss | Crain, Henry | A2/39 | March 20, 1855 | March 20, 1855 |
| Perry, Martha E. | Sissom, John | A2/107 | February 3, 1863 | February 11, 1863 |
| Perry, Mary | Elam, Fate | C/260 | November 4, 1880 | November 4, 1880 |
| Perry, Moses | Grear, Elizabeth | A2/124 | July 19, 1865 | No Return |
| Perry, N. O. | Gaither, Miss Mahala | B/40 | February 5, 1867 | Solemnized, No Date |
| Perry, Nanny | Todd, Willie | C/424 | December 18, 1890 | December 18, 1890 |
| Perry, Nathaniel | Luster, Miss Letheia | A/39 | June 14, 1841 | June 14, 1841 |
| Perry, Sarah J. | Bush, Jess. H. | C/178 | November 29, 1877 | No Return |
| Perryman, G. W. | Moody, Miss M. E. | A2/91 | November 29, 1859 | No Return |
| Petrill, Martha Miss | Copland, Arnold | A2/28 | September 6, 1853 | No Return |
| Pettley, Caroline Miss | Harris, Philip | A/78 | April 17, 1845 | April 17, 1845 |
| Pettus, J. A. | Roberts, Miss M. A. | B/58 | December 9, 1867 | December 12, 1867 |
| Petty, Ambrose | Bell, Susan | C/232 | August 6, 1879 | August 7, 1879 |
| Petty, Ambus | Bell, Susan | C/220 | August 6, 1879 | No Return |

| Groom or Bride | Groom or Bride | Book/Page | Date of License | Date of Marriage |
|---|---|---|---|---|
| Petty, Aseah Miss | Craft, J. J. | B/104 | June 5, 1870 | June 5, 1870 |
| Petty, Easther Miss | Hopkins, Joel | A/62 | May 13, 1843 | No Return |
| Petty, Eliza A. Miss | Hall, Fleming W. | A/69 | May 15, 1844 | May 16, 1844 |
| Petty, Elizabeth Ann | Williams, James | A/76 | January 30, 1845 | No Return |
| Petty, G. A. | Smith, Miss Mary | A2/77 | January 14, 1856 | February 3, 1856 |
| Petty, J. H. | Hammer, L. C. | E/150 | October 12, 1888 | October 12, 1888 |
| Petty, James | Peyton, Miss Annis | A/78 | April 19, 1845 | April 20, 1845 |
| Petty, James A. | Harris, Frances | A2/129 | September 18, 1865 | September 21, 1865 |
| Petty, James A. | Brandon, Margaret E. | A2/133 | December 2, 1865 | December 3, 1865 |
| Petty, John | Mclain, Miss E. J. | A2/29 | November 19, 1853 | November 20, 1853 |
| Petty, Mariar F. | Davis, Wm. H. | A2/121 | March 1, 1865 | March 25, 1865 |
| Petty, Martha Miss | McClain, James P. | A2/131 | November 12, 1865 | November 12, 1865 |
| Petty, Mary Miss | Hill, James | A/114 | September 20, 1848 | September 21, 1848 |
| Petty, Mary | Mears, James H. | C/352 | February 16, 1886 | February 17, 1886 |
| Petty, Mary F. | Hawkins, J. M. | C/118 | August 21, 1875 | August 21, 1875 |
| Petty, Micagah | Cunningham, Mary | A2/76 | September 28, 1855 | September 29, 1855 |
| Petty, Mollie | Prater, W. P. | C/224 | September 8, 1879 | September 9, 1879 |
| Petty, Nancy | Stewart, Buch | C/212 | February 8, 1879 | February 15, 1879 |
| Petty, Nancy Ann Miss | Philips, Wm. | A2/29 | December 7, 1853 | December 8, 1853 |
| Petty, Nannie D. Miss | Davis, T. Y. | B/76 | December 26, 1868 | No Return |
| Petty, Nathan | Lince, Francis | C/298 | December 1, 1883 | December 2, 1883 |
| Petty, Sophy | Jetton, James | C/16 | December 7, 1871 | No Return |
| Petty, William E. | Rhea, Miss Ruth | A/104 | November 10, 1847 | November 11, 1847 |
| Petty, William E. | Craft, Miss Hessie Ann | A2/143 | August 14, 1866 | August 15, 1866 |
| Petty, Willie | Allen, Maud | E/364 | November 26, 1898 | |
| Peydan, Nancy | Burk, John | A2/20 | November 18, 1852 | November 18, 1852 |
| Peyden, Barbara A. Miss | Davenport, W. S. | A2/27 | August 12, 1853 | August 12, 1853 |
| Peydon, Joseph | Richards, Susan A. | A2/35 | September 22, 1854 | September 22, 1854 |
| Peydon, Mandy | Gibson, J. | C/158 | March 8, 1877 | March 8, 1877 |
| Peyton, Annis Miss | Petty, James | A/78 | April 19, 1845 | April 20, 1845 |
| Peyton, Margaret Miss | Parker, Samuel F. | A2/147 | April 24, 1866 | April 25, 1866 |
| Phalon, E. H. | Dillon, Miss Frances E. | A2/127 | September 11, 1865 | September 12, 1865 |
| Philips, Benjamin H. F. | Church, Elizabeth | A/54 | September 24, 1842 | September 24, 1842 |
| Philips, David H. | Bralley, Margarett | A/53 | September 10, 1843 | September 11, 1842 |
| Philips, Haney Miss | Farler, Patton | A/67 | January 30, 1844 | February 2, 1844 |
| Philips, Hugh B. | Prator, Miss Mary L. E. | B/48 | August 3, 1867 | August 6, 1867 |
| Philips, James | Turne, Elizabeth | A/128 | November 27, 1849 | November 27, 1849 |
| Philips, John | Merphey, V. S. | A2/38 | March 8, 1855 | March 8, 1855 |
| Philips, Martha | Woods, Benjamin F. | A2/41 | August 22, 1855 | ? ? |
| Philips, Mary | Todd, David | A2/124 | July 1, 1865 | July 8, 1865 |
| Philips, Mary Ann Miss | Sumner, Wm. G. | A2/64 | April 22, 1858 | April 22, 1858 |
| Philips, Nancy A. Miss | Glazebrooks, James | A/82 | July 17, 1845 | July 17, 1845 |
| Philips, Robert | Pace, Leathey | A/20 | December 10, 1839 | December 10, 1839 |
| Philips, Samuel R. | Bralley, Sarah A. | A/59 | February 3, 1843 | February 5, 1843 |
| Philips, Sarah Miss | Maxey, Lewis | B/72 | October 21, 1868 | October 22, 1868 |
| Philips, Seth | Shipes, Miss Martha | A2/39 | March 19, 1855 | No Return |

| Groom or Bride | Groom or Bride | Book/Page | Date of License | Date of Marriage |
|---|---|---|---|---|
| Philips, Wm. | Petty, Miss Nancy Ann | A2/29 | December 7, 1853 | December 8, 1853 |
| Philips, Wm. C. | Holland, Sarah S. | A2/36 | November 13, 1854 | November 17, 1854 |
| Philips, Wm. C. | Edward, Nancy | A2/85 | May 23, 1859 | Execution not Clear |
| Phillips, Alice | Patton, D. F. | C/94 | August 22, 1874 | August 23, 1874 |
| Phillips, C. E. | Williams, M. G. | C/112 | May 23, 1875 | ?? |
| Phillips, C. E. | Harris, Caldonia | C/126 | December 11, 1875 | December 23, 1875 |
| Phillips, Caney | Good, Mary P. | C/174 | October 22, 1877 | October 22, 1877 |
| Phillips, Caroline | Wood, N. C. C. | C/32 | August 10, 1872 | August 10, 1872 |
| Phillips, E. M. | Blanton, M. J. | C/22 | January 26, 1872 | January 28, 1872 |
| Phillips, Elizabeth | Barrat, Richard | A/45 | December 18, 1841 | December 19, 1841 |
| Phillips, Elizabeth Miss | Johnson, John T. | B/96 | December 24, 1869 | December 25, 1869 |
| Phillips, Elizabeth Miss | St. John, George | B/98 | January 8, 1870 | No Return |
| Phillips, H. B. | Fowler, Mary B. | C/114 | June 9, 1875 | June 10, 1875 |
| Phillips, J. C. | Good, M. P. | C/16 | December 15, 1871 | December 24, 1871 |
| Phillips, J. H. | Lance, Paralee | C/108 | February 10, 1875 | February 11, 1875 |
| Phillips, J. L. | Womack, A. J. | C/336 | September 17, 1885 | September 17, 1885 |
| Phillips, Jack | Mitchell, Miss Hessie | C/394 | July 9, 1887 | July 10, 1887 |
| Phillipps, Janie Miss | House, W. D. | B/120 | December 22, 1870 | December 22, 1870 |
| Phillips, Jennie | Smithson, N. B. | C/360 | July 3, 1886 | July 4, 1886 |
| Phillips, John | Prater, Lucinda A. | C/160 | March 24, 1877 | March 25, 1877 |
| Phillips, John | Sumars, Miss Maggie | C/372 | November 4, 1886 | No Return |
| Phillips, Laura | Barratt, Samuel | C/162 | June 15, 1877 | June 15, 1877 |
| Phillips, M. L. | Patton, Sarah | C/296 | November 17, 1883 | November 18, 1883 |
| Phillips, M. T | Woods, B. F. L | C/140 | July 22, 1876 | July 23, 1876 |
| Phillips, Margarett Miss | Woods, Nathan T. | A2/58 | October 15, 1857 | October 15, 1857 |
| Phillips, Mary | Gilley, James | C/132 | January 24, 1876 | No Return |
| Phillips, N. J. | Mullins, J. H. | C/42 | October 11, 1872 | October 13, 1872 |
| Phillips, Samuel | Tabour, Miss Unice E. | A/125 | July 17, 1849 | No Return |
| Phillips, Tennie | Fuller, Landers | C/308 | April 26, 1884 | April 27, 1884 |
| Phillips, Tinnie J. | Todd, Wm. M. | C/186 | February 19, 1878 | February 22, 1878 |
| Phillips, W. C. | Gaither, Miss Ann | C/388 | April 30, 1887 | No Return |
| Phillips, William | Warren, M. V. | A2/82 | April 13, 1858 | April 13, 1858 |
| Phins, Wm. M. | Auston, Miss Sarah | A2/58 | October 9, 1857 | October 10, 1857 |
| Pilotte, S. M. J. | Sadler, A. J. | E/222 | October 15, 1889 | October 15, 1889 |
| Pinkerton | Daniel, George | B/4 | August 22, 1865 | August 27, 1865 |
| Pinketon, Mary | Thomas, Oscar (col.) | C/354 | March 6, 1886 | March 8, 1886 |
| Pinkerton, Ada | Bryson, Beth (col.) | C/444 | August 26, 1891 | August 27, 1891 |
| Pinkerton, J. F. | Jernigan, Mattie | C/376 | December 22, 1886 | December 23, 1886 |
| Pinkerton, Jesse | Wright, Peal | C/470 | November 27, 1892 | November 22, 1892 |
| Pinkerton, Lillie | Jetton, Elbert | E/119 | December 25, 1888 | December 25, 1888 |
| Pinkerton, Mary F. | Denton, Smith J. | E/37 | May 14, 1888 | May 14, 1888 |
| Pinkerton, Richard | Barton, Joannah | C/162 | May 31, 1877 | May 31, 1877 |
| Pinkerton, Richard | Alexander | E/184 | June 22, 1889 | June ??, 1889 |
| Pinkerton, Sallie | Barnes, Alex (col.) | C/458 | March 25, 1892 | March 25, 1892 |
| Pinkerton, Sarah A. Miss | Murry, Davis B. | A2/139 | March 28, 1866 | March 29, 1866 |
| Pitar, Sarah Jane Miss | Bragg, D. F. | A2/55 | February 24, 1857 | No Return |

| Groom or Bride | Groom or Bride | Book/Page | Date of License | Date of Marriage |
|---|---|---|---|---|
| Pitard, Elizabeth | Hays, John | A2/48 | May 19, 1856 | May 25, 1856 |
| Pitard, Roxann Miss | Hays, John | A/45 | December 23, 1841 | December 23, 1841 |
| Pitman, Amandy | West, T. F. | C/28 | June 10, 1872 | June 10, 1872 |
| Pitman, Disa Miss | Gunter, James M. | A/86 | February 8, 1846 | February 8, 1846 |
| Pitman, Elizabeth | Newby, William | A2/109 | October 7, 1863 | No Return |
| Pitman, J. N. M. | Wilson, G. M. | C/38 | September 9, 1872 | September 11, 1872 |
| Pitman, Lee | Woodside, Sallie | C/382 | January 8, 1887 | January 8, 1887 |
| Pitman, M. M. | Gann, Lucinda | C/216 | June 10, 1879 | June 12, 1879 |
| Pitman, Sarah Ann | Campbell, Vincent | A2/109 | September 26, 1863 | Solemnized, No date |
| Pitman, Stanford | Elkins, Lucy Ann | B/34 | December 25, 1866 | December 25, 1866 |
| Pitman, Thos. M. | Lefever, Miss Martha | A2/18 | August 21, 1852 | August 22, 1852 |
| Pitman, William | Melton, Miss Nancy | A/69 | May 11, 1844 | May 12, 1844 |
| Pitman, William | Ford, Miss Easter L. | A/123 | June 27, 1849 | June 27, 1849 |
| Pitman, Vicy J. | Elkins, J. D. | C/110 | March 3, 1875 | March 7, 1875 |
| Pitts, Elizabeth | Underwood, Benj. | C/164 | June 22, 1877 | June 22, 1877 |
| Pitt, Reuben | Byford, Miss Mary A. | A2/43 | November 26, 1855 | November 27, 1855 |
| Pittard, Isaac | Hawkins | C/464 | September 21, 1892 | September 21, 892 |
| Pittard, Jas. L. | Tenpenny, B. F. | A2/101 | July 28, 1860 | July 29, 1860 |
| Pittard, Mary L. Miss | Tenpenny, Joseph W. | A2/87 | August 16, 1859 | No Return |
| Pittard, W. R. | Gannon, Susie | F/80 | December 31, 1895 | December 31, 1895 |
| Pittered, P. H. | Weatherford, Miss S. M. | B/52 | September 4, 1867 | September 4, 1867 |
| Pittman, Elizabeth Miss | St. John, George | A/52 | August 2, 1842 | August 4, 1842 |
| Pitts, David | Herriman, Elizabeth | C/310 | July 3, 1884 | July 3, 1884 |
| Pitts, James | Spurlock, Emaline | A2/105 | October 17, 1862 | No Return |
| Pitts, James | Brown, Matilda | E/108 | December 15, 1888 | December 16, 1888 |
| Pitts, Jno. A. | Birmet. <oss :pi | C/452 | December 26, 1891 | December 27, 1891 |
| Pitts, Josiah | Merriman, Sarah | A/65 | September 13, 1843 | September 13, 1843 |
| Pitts, Julia A. E. | Allen, John | C/184 | January 3, 1878 | January 3, 1878 |
| Pitts, Lucinda Miss | Griggs, Michael | A2/87 | July 7, 1859 | July 27, 1859 |
| Pitts, Mandy M. Miss | Bowen, Samuel | A2/37 | December 7, 1854 | December 7, 1854 |
| Pitts, Sarah Jane Miss | Morgan, Alexander | B/92 | November 4, 1869 | November 4, 1869 |
| Pitts, Thomas | Allen, Babe | E/126 | January 4, 1889 | January 13, 1889 |
| Pitts, Wiley | Tetters, Fanny | C/442 | August 5, 1891 | August 6, 1891 |
| Pitts, William | Yancey, Laura | E/231 | November 9, 1889 | November 15, 1889 |
| Pitz, Mattie | Brim, Columbus | C/382 | January 26, 1887 | No Return |
| Poff, Charles | Gooding, Miss Martha | A/45 | December 16, 1841 | December 16, 1841 |
| Poff, Mary Ann | Reed, James | A/21 | January 6, 1840 | January 19, 1840 |
| Polock, Daniel M. | Good, Mary Ann | A2/132 | November 29, 1865 | November 30, 1865 |
| Polock, Elizabeth Ann Miss | Bryant, James W. | A/94 | December 3, 1846 | No Return |
| Pond, Miss Sarah | Travis, John | A2/68 | October 14, 1858 | October 14, 1858 |
| Pope, Mark A. | Hadley, Melissa | A/24 | February 24, 1840 | February 26, 1840 |
| Porter, Alexander | Patterson, Miss Martha | B/36 | December 26, 1866 | December 26, 1866 |
| Porter, Solom | Burkett, Margrett | C/28 | May 17, 1872 | May 17, 1872 |
| Porterfield, Leonades F. | Witherspoon, Miss Septima F. | A/66 | November 29, 1843 | November 30, 1843 |
| Porterfield, M. M. | McElroy, S. N. | C/14 | November 16, 1871 | November 16, 1871 |
| Porterfield, Malisa Miss | Pascal, Thomas | A2/25 | May 3, 1853 | May 3, 1853 |

| Groom or Bride | Groom or Bride | Book/Page | Date of License | Date of Marriage |
|---|---|---|---|---|
| Porterfield, Margaret | Reed, Lemuel A. | A/28 | April 16, 1840 | April 16, 1840 |
| Porterfield, Mariah E. Miss | Fisher, John | A/74 | November 20, 1844 | November 21, 1844 |
| Porterfield, Mary Miss | Travis, Daniel | A2/52 | December 30, 1856 | December 30, 1856 |
| Porterfield, P. C. Miss | Watts, Milton E. | A/52 | August 31, 1842 | September 1, 1842 |
| Porterfield, Samuel G. | Summar, Miss Mary | A/109 | March 7, 1848 | March 9, 1848 |
| Porutes (?), Nancy | Peeler, John | C/128 | December 30, 1875 | December 30, 1876 |
| Poston, James C. | Mollen, Miss J. C. | A2/18 | June 16, 1852 | June 18, 1852 |
| Poterfield, M. J. | Spain, W. M. | C/126 | December 14, 1875 | No Return |
| Poterfield, Mary E. | Sullivan, William | A2/124 | July 27, 1865 | July 28, 1865 |
| Poterfield, W. F. | Davenport, L. M. | C/116 | July 28, 1875 | July 29, 1875 |
| Powel, John | Fanen, Rebecca | A2/113 | March 26, 1864 | March 25, 1864 |
| Powel, John H. | Jones, Martha R. | C/246 | March 26, 1880 | March 28, 1880 |
| Powel, Peyton | Wood, Miss Parlee | A2/164 | July 18, 1866 | July 18, 1866 |
| Powel, Sarah | Hankins, Robert | A2/110 | July 21, 1863 | No Return |
| Powel, Thos. | Murphy, Mary A. | C/86 | April 2, 1874 | April 2, 1874 |
| Powell | Kirby, Thos. | A2/116 | October 12, 1864 | October 12, 1864 |
| Powell, Eliza | Lawrence, J. H. | C/84 | February 28, 1874 | February 29, 1874 |
| Powell, Elizabeth E. Miss | Mullinax, James S. | A/131 | January 19, 1850 | January 23, 1850 |
| Powell, Frances | Milligan, M. B. | C/24 | February 17, 1872 | February 18, 1872 |
| Powell, Francis Miss | Bogle, J. W. | C/414 | October 16, 1887 | October 18, 1887 |
| Powell, George | Northcut, Snne? | C/350 | January 21, 1886 | January 24, 1886 |
| Powell, H. N. | Melton, Sarah | A2/52 | December 16, 1856 | December 18, 1856 |
| Powell, Hervey | Shirley, M. J. | C/286 | July 12, 1883 | July 15, 1883 |
| Powell, James | Reeves, Miss Lucy | A2/5 | September 5, 1850 | September 8, 1850 |
| Powell, James T. | Melton, Edny | C/80 | January 10, 1874 | January 11, 1874 |
| Powell, Parlee Miss | Melton, Luke | B/76 | December 25, 1868 | December 27, 1868 |
| Powell, Rhoda Miss | Smithsen, Wm. C. | A2/53 | January 24, 1857 | No Return |
| Powell, Thomas | George, Rachel | C/36 | August 29, 1872 | August 29, 1872 |
| Powell, William | Melton, Miss Susan | A/90 | September 5, 1846 | September 6, 1846 |
| Powell, Wm. | Bragg, Lizzie | C/58 | June 11, 1873 | June 12, 1873 |
| Powell, Zanie A. | Ledbetter, Alford | C/58 | May 10, 1873 | May 10, 1873 |
| Prater, A. M. | Woods, S. E. | C/112 | May 15, 1875 | May 15, 1875 |
| Prater, Adam | Tenpenny, Saphrona | E/153 | December 14, 1888 | December 14, 1888 |
| Prater, Arch | Sanders, Paralee | C/56 | April 7, 1873 | April 7, 1873 |
| Prater, C. L. | Elkins, Lucinda | C/62 | July 17, 1873 | No Return |
| Prater, David M. | Maxey, Nancy | A2/133 | December 6, 1865 | December 7, 1965 |
| Prater, Dona Miss | Collins, F. M. | C/382 | January 15, 1887 | January 16, 1887 |
| Prater, Eliza B. | Allen, J. G. | C/170 | September 5, 1877 | September 6, 1877 |
| Prater, J. D. | Tittle, M. D. | C/320 | December 13, 1884 | December 15, 1884 |
| Prater, J. H. | Wallace, Martha A. | C/84 | February 25, 1874 | February 25, 1874 |
| Prater, J. H. | Tenpenny, B. A. | C/470 | November 28, 1892 | November 29, 1892 |
| Prater, J. H. | Tenpenny, Lizzie | E/70 | September 6, 1888 | September 6, 1888 |
| Prater, James | Elkins, Miss Margarett E. | A/132 | February 18, 1850 | February 18, 1850 |
| Prater, John | Darbery, Miss Eliza | B/126 | March 4, 1871 | March 5, 1871 |
| Prater, Kessiah Miss | Woods, Nathan | A/74 | November 19, 1844 | November 19, 1844 |

| Groom or Bride | Groom or Bride | Book/Page | Date of License | Date of Marriage |
|---|---|---|---|---|
| Prater, Logan | Stroud, Jane C. | C/176 | November 3, 1877 | November 4, 1877 |
| Prater, M. M. | Ekens, Miss Liza Jane | A2/51 | December 1, 1856 | No Return |
| Prater, Martha C. Miss | Farly, Charles | A2/75 | January 4, 1855 | January 5, 1855 |
| Prater, Mary Eliz. Miss | Prater, Thos. | A2/91 | November 17, 1859 | No Return |
| Prater, Mary Elizabeth Miss | Prater, Thos. Dillard | A2/71 | November 1, 1859 | No Return |
| Prater, Moses | Collins, Miss Tennessee | C/384 | February 12, 1887 | February 13, 1887 |
| Prater, P. T. | Clark, Marcy C. | C/434 | April 6, 1891 | April 7, 1891 |
| Prater, Pat | McMillen, Eliza | C/262 | November 19, 1880 | November 26, 1880 |
| Prater, T. G. | Summers, Miss Rilda | C/390 | June 14, 1887 | June 15, 1887 |
| Prater, T. J. | Youngblood, Martha A. | C/248 | June 11, 1880 | June 16, 1880 |
| Prater, Thomas M. | Farley, Miss Letty | A/92 | October 26, 1846 | October 26, 1846 |
| Prater, Thos. Dillard | Prater, Miss Mary Elizabeth | A2/91 | November 17, 1859 | No Return |
| Prater, Thos. Dillard | Prater, Miss Mary Elizabeth | A2/71 | November 1, 1859 | No Return |
| Prater, W. C. | Edge, Mary C. | C/406 | November 9, 1887 | November 9, 1887 |
| Prater, W. P. | Petty, Mollie | C/224 | September 8, 1879 | September 9, 1879 |
| Prater, William C. | Stanfield, Delila | A/60 | February 17, 1843 | February 17, 1843 |
| Prater, Wm. | Manus, Malisa | C/82 | February 12, 1874 | February 15, 1874 |
| Prater, Wm. | Simmons, Barbarey | E/183 | June 13, 1889 | No Return |
| Prator, Benjamin P. | Warren, Elizabeth A. | A/11 | March 9, 1839 | March 10, 1839 |
| Prator, Clayton | Sullivan, Miss K. J. | A2/163 | July 7, 1866 | Executed No Date |
| Prator, Eliza J. Miss | Woods, Andrew J. | B/52 | September 25, 1867 | September 26, 1867 |
| Prator, G. D. | Woods, Miss M. F. | B/82 | June 2, 1869 | June 6, 1869 |
| Prator, J. C. | Kertz, Miss Katharine | A2/51 | December 3, 1856 | No Return |
| Prater, J. H. | Pendleton, Miss Sarah | B/78 | February 22, 1869 | February 25, 1869 |
| Prater, Lucinda A. | Phillips, John | C/160 | March 24, 1877 | March 25, 1877 |
| Prator, M. E. Miss | Bashham, William | A2/65 | June 24, 1858 | Handed in no Return |
| Prator, M. J. Miss | Dukin, J. F. | A2/69 | October 27, 1858 | October 28, 1858 |
| Prator, Marcus | Durrett, Miss Rhamy | A2/75 | January 3, 1855 | January 4, 1855 |
| Prater, Mary L. E. Miss | Philips, Hugh B. | B/48 | August 3, 1867 | August 6, 1867 |
| Prater, Mattie A. | Gray, W. W. | C/68 | September 27, 1873 | September 28, 1873 |
| Prater, Nancy E. Miss | Fowler, Patton | A2/40 | June 13, 1855 | June 13, 1855 |
| Prater, Octavia | St. John, Jordon | C/394 | July 18, 1887 | July 19, 1887 |
| Prator, Stacy A. | Fuller, J. N. Jr. | C/116 | July 27, 1875 | July 27, 1875 |
| Prator, T. E. | Inglis, Miss M. E. | B/50 | August 12, 1867 | No Return |
| Prator, W. R. J. | Farley, Miss Tebipha | A2/76 | January 22, 1855 | January 22, 1855 |
| Preston, Ann | Dillon, Henry | C/378 | December 25, 1886 | December 26, 1886 |
| Preston, E. C. | Tenpenny, Misss Elizabeth | A2/52 | December 16, 1856 | No Return |
| Preston, Eli | Walls, Miss Polly | A/43 | November 12, 1841 | November 14, 1841 |
| Preston, Elizabeth Miss | Barratt, Ward, Jr. | A/73 | September 18, 1844 | September 18, 1844 |
| Preston, Frances C. Miss | Cummins, W. B. | B/86 | September 8, 1869 | September 9, 1869 |
| Preston, Gent | Jones, Pattie | C/274 | February 26, 1881 | No Return |
| Preston, H. L. | Doak, T. C. | A2/127 | September 7, 1865 | September 7, 1865 |
| Preston, Helen | Adams, A. T. | E/214 | September 20, 1889 | September 20, 1889 |
| Preston, J. A. | Higgins, Sarah S. | C/284 | June 30, 1883 | July 1, 1883 |
| Preston, J. B. | Neeley, Jennie | E/207 | September 9, 1889 | September 15, 1889 |
| Preston, James | Young, Mary | A2/125 | August 2, 1865 | August 2, 1865 |

| Groom or Bride | Groom or Bride | Book/Page | Date of License | Date of Marriage |
|---|---|---|---|---|
| Preston, James | Young, Elizabeth | A2/127 | September 11, 1865 | September 11, 1865 |
| Preston, Jane | Byres, F. B. | E/265 | January 30, 1890 | No Return |
| Preston, John | Rigsby, Malisa | C/48 | December 26, 1872 | December 27, 1872 |
| Preston, John F. | Stone, Miss Parlee | A/106 | December 22, 1847 | December 22, 1847 |
| Preston, John Sr. | Gilley, Miss Jane | A2/10 | January 11, 1851 | January 11, 1851 |
| Preston, Joseph | Luster, Sally | A/4 | July 2, 1838 | July 3, 1838 |
| Preston, Josephine Miss | Mullican, Antney | B/52 | September 23, 1867 | September 25, 1867 |
| Preston, Josie | Davis, Wm. P. | C/12 | October 6, 1871 | October 11, 1871 |
| Preston, L. | Milton, John | C/312 | August 9, 1884 | August 10, 1884 |
| Preston, Lucinda Miss | Teasley, William | A/45 | December 23, 1841 | December 23, 1841 |
| Preston, M. J. | Bogle, G. W. | C/108 | February 18, 1875 | February 18, 1875 |
| Preston, M. J. | Doak, R. D. | C/120 | September 15, 1875 | September 16, 1875 |
| Preston, Martha E. Miss | Young, James H. | B/50 | August 10, 1867 | August 11, 1867 |
| Preston, Martha J. | Davenport, Sam B. | C/70 | November 1, 1873 | November 2, 1873 |
| Preston, Mary | Davenport, J. B. | C/172 | October 3, 1877 | October 4, 1877 |
| Preston, Mary | Adams, Wm | E/210 | September 9, 1889 | September 9, 1889 |
| Preston, Mary E. | Mason, T. B. | C/174 | October 12, 1877 | October 14, 1877 |
| Preston, Mary L. | Davenport, R. B. F. | C/112 | May 15, 1875 | No Return |
| Preston, Mattie | Justin, William J. | E/182 | June 12, 1889 | June 12, 1889 |
| Preston, Nancy E. | Young, Wm. H. | A2/111 | January 5, 1864 | January 7, 1864 |
| Preston, Rebecca | Davenport, Geo. | C/68 | October 3, 1873 | November 2, 1873 |
| Preston, Rebecca L. Miss | Harris, D. P. | A2/135 | January 16, 1866 | January 16, 1866 |
| Preston, Rebecca Miss | Teasly, Thomas | A/38 | April 12, 1841 | April 18, 1841 |
| Preston, Ruth | Cumins, N. B. | C/292 | September 15, 1883 | September 16, 1883 |
| Preston, S. E. | Milligan, R. L. | C/184 | February 1, 1878 | February 3, 1878 |
| Preston, Sallie Miss | Bailey, Joseph | B/56 | November 25, 1867 | December 8, 1867 |
| Preston, Samuel | Foster, Sarah Jane | A2/2 | May 27, 1850 | June 8, 1850 |
| Preston, Sara E. | Scott, J. F. | A2/134 | December 30, 1865 | December 31, 1865 |
| Preston, Sarah Miss | Walls, Henry M. T. | A/110 | April 6, 1848 | April 6, 1848 |
| Preston, Thomas | Rigsby, Miss Eliza | A/76 | January 22, 1845 | January 23, 1845 |
| Preston, William Jr. | Rigsby, Miss Jane | A2/3 | June 29, 1850 | June 30, 1850 |
| Preston, Wm | Sullins, Betsy | C/230 | November 15, 1879 | No Return |
| Preston, Wm. L. | Fitspatrick, Susan | C/12 | October 17, 1871 | October 18, 1871 |
| Price, J. D. | Bryan, Fannie | C/324 | January 15, 1885 | January 15, 1885 |
| Price, James M. | Smith, Miss Mary Ann | A/96 | January 5, 1847 | January 5, 1847 |
| Price, Nancy Miss | Hopkins, Elijah | A/71 | August 21, 1844 | August 23, 1844 |
| Price, Peter | Essary, Miss Martha F. | A/131 | January 12, 1850 | January 12, 1850 |
| Price, William | Clements, Miss Elizagbeth | A/75 | November 19, 1844 | November 19, 1844 |
| Prim, Thomas N. | Henderson, Miss Margarett | A2/44 | December 6, 1855 | December 6, 1855 |
| Prime, John C. | Gunter, Miss A. J. | A2/27 | August 25, 1853 | No Return |
| Prior, Nannie B. | Lorance, G. M. | C/148 | November 21, 1876 | November 21, 1876 |
| Prior, Sarah | Baker, John W. | A2/12 | November 11, 1851 | November 13, 1851 |
| Prutherbin, Rebeckey | McGill, Andy | C/234 | December 21, 1879 | December 25, 1879 |
| Pryor, Sinnie | Justice, J. M. | C/302 | January 26, 1884 | No Return |
| Pucket, Narcissa | Guy, James | A2/123 | June 1, 1865 | June 1, 1865 |
| Puckett, C. S. | Sand, Miss M. Cleair | A2/27 | August 30, 1853 | August 30, 1853 |

| Groom or Bride | Groom or Bride | Book/Page | Date of License | Date of Marriage |
|---|---|---|---|---|
| Puketon, Sallie | Lyons, T. M. | C/206 | December 18, 1879 | No Return |
| Pulliam, B. H. | Bell, Mary J. | C/180 | December 13, 1877 | December 13, 1877 |
| Pullium, Dolly | Summers, Susan | C/152 | January 17, 1877 | January 18, 1877 |
| Pumphrey, Matthew T. | Holt, Margaret | A/4 | August 1, 1838 | August 2, 1838 |
| Purtan, Man P. | Melton, Miss Menerva | A2/80 | March 26, 1857 | March 26, 1857 |
| Qualls, Juliann Miss | Litle, W. M. | A2/66 | August 4, 1858 | August ?, 1858 |
| Quals, Wm. | Gann, Martha P. | C/316 | October 24, 1884 | October 26, 1884 |
| Quarles, J. T. | Bethel, Miss Idie | C/46 | November 25, 1872 | No Return |
| Quarles, Wm. | Stanley, Darkus J. | C/52 | February 18, 1873 | No Return |
| Quarls, W. C. | Paty, Ula H. | F/54 | December 26, 1894 | December 27, 1894 |
| Raburn, Eugene | McFerrin, Fannie | F/60 | March 18, 1895 | March 19, 1895 |
| Rackley, Mary | Wilson, Riley | C/164 | July 17, 1877 | July 17, 1877 |
| Rackley, Wiley | Bush, Eliza | C/168 | August 14, 1877 | No Return |
| Rackley, Wiley | Whittemore, Jane | C/240 | January 21, 1880 | No Return |
| Ragland, William J. | Hicks, Miss Ruth | A/102 | September 29, 1847 | September 26, 1847 |
| Raikes, Mary | King, J. D. | C/444 | August 20, 1891 | August 22, 1891 |
| Raines, J. | Lawrance, Miss Dora | C/452 | December 13, 1891 | December 15, 1891 |
| Rains, Delphia | Cummings, William | A/2 | March 27, 1838 | March 27, 1838 |
| Rains, E. L. | Wood, Annie | F/24 | December 11, 1893 | December 17, 1893 |
| Rains, Elizabeth | Hill, J. R. | C/86 | April 6, 1874 | April 6, 1874 |
| Rains, Elizabeth | Parker, William L. | A2/139 | October 4, 1865 | October 8, 1865 |
| Rains, G. P. | Mitchel, Miss N. A. | A2/68 | September 30, 1858 | October ?, 1858 |
| Rains, I. W. | Duke, Bettie | C/436 | May 4, 1891 | May 7, 1891 |
| Rains, J. B. | Bailey, Malessie | C/338 | October 8, 1885 | October 8, 1885 |
| Rains, James B. | Stans, Miss S. J. | A2/19 | September 30, 1852 | October 9, 1852 |
| Rains, John | Webber, Miss Mary | A2/5 | September 12, 1850 | September 22, 1850 |
| Rains, M. E. | Schott, H. A. | F/100 | October 28, 1896 | October 29, 1896 |
| Rains, Mary J. R. Miss | Parker, J. E. | B/100 | February 15, 1870 | February 17, 1870 |
| Rains, N. E. | Hope, F. M. | A2/131 | November 7, 1865 | November 7, 1865 |
| Rains, R. D. Miss | Duncan, W. B. D. | A2/32 | March 18, 1854 | January 17, 1854 |
| Rains, Rhoda Miss | Bailey, Robert | A/129 | December 14, 1849 | December 19, 1849 |
| Raker, Miss Ella | Cooper, Branchford | F/66 | August 12, 1895 | No Return |
| Ralston, David N. | McKnight, Issabella A. | A/53 | September 10, 1842 | September 15, 1842 |
| Ramsey, Caroline Miss | Armstrong, John | B/74 | December 5, 1868 | December 6, 1868 |
| Ramsey, E. J. | Bryson, W. K. | C/268 | January 5, 1881 | No Return |
| Ramsey, Elizabeth Miss | Gunter, William W. | A/80 | July 12, 1845 | July 13, 1845 |
| Ramsey, Elizabeth Miss | Gunter, William W. | A/81 | July 12, 1845 | July 13, 1845 |
| Ramsey, J. C. | Carter, W. A. | C/164 | July 24, 1877 | July 24, 1877 |
| Ramsey, James A. | Odom, Miss Elizabeth G. | A/85 | December 27, 1845 | December 28, 1845 |
| Ramsey, Luthur S. | Graham, Miss J. M. | A2/75 | June 2, 1855 | June 3, 1855 |
| Ramsey, Nancy M. | Patterson, J. M. | C/24 | March 13, 1872 | March 14, 1872 |
| Ramsey, R. M. | Hancock, E. C. | A2/93 | January 18, 1860 | No Return |
| Raney, Eliza J. Miss | Ford, Thomas | A2/35 | December 21, 1854 | December 21, 1854 |
| Rankhorn, C. M. | Neely, Miss Harriet Delila | B/42 | February 25, 1867 | February 25, 1867 |
| Rankin, Duglass | Thompson, Ellen | C/86 | April 9, 1874 | April 9, 1874 |
| Ranson, S. H. | Collins, G. W. | D/22 | | January 4, 1883 |

| Groom or Bride | Groom or Bride | Book/Page | Date of License | Date of Marriage |
|---|---|---|---|---|
| Ratley, Alexander | Pendergrass, Miss Mary | A2/143 | August 14, 1866 | August 15, 1866 |
| Ratliff, | Lefevers, Isah | F/50 | December 7, 1894 | December 9, 1894 |
| Ratly, Miss Malisa | Underwood, James | A2/28 | October 1, 1853 | October 2, 1853 |
| Rawlings, Andrew | Grimes, Gerinnia (?) | C/26 | March 30, 1872 | March 31, 1872 |
| Rawlings, Manervy | Brawley, Wm | C/22 | February 13, 1872 | February 13, 1872 |
| Rawlins, Mary | Coughanour, J. A. | A2/110 | December 25, 1863 | December 29, 1863 |
| Ray, Miss Bula F. | Northdutt, J. D. | F/62 | April 11, 1895 | April 11, 1895 |
| Rayburn, Adam | McFerrin, Miss Annie | F/66 | July 10, 1895 | July 10, 1895 |
| Read, James | Richards, Miss Rutha | A2/12 | October 4, 1851 | October ?, 1851 |
| Readman, Y. F. | Markum, G. H. | C/250 | July 15, 1880 | July 15, 1880 |
| Ready, Aaron | Hemman, Margaret | A2/121 | February 24, 1865 | February 24, 1865 |
| Ready, C. C. | Alexander, Miss Mary A. | C/6 | August 14, 1871 | August 15, 1871 |
| Ready, C. H. | Campbell, G. L. | F/70 | September 10, 1895 | September 11, 1895 |
| Ready, Callie | Elledge, Charles | B/122 | December 28, 1870 | December 30, 1870 |
| Ready, Elias Alexander | McEwin, Miss Sarah | A/113 | August 7, 1848 | August 7, 1848 |
| Ready, Emeline Miss | Higgin, Fill | C/384 | February 27, 1887 | February 27, 1887 |
| Ready, Emeline Miss | Reed, J. F. | A2/82 | July 22, 1858 | No Return |
| Ready, F. M. | Carter, Nettie | C/442 | August 5, 1891 | August 5, 1891 |
| Ready, Franklin | Gaither, Zelpha | B/4 | August 26, 1865 | September 3, 1865 |
| Ready, J. F. | Barrett, L. J. | C/144 | September 21, 1876 | September 21, 1876 |
| Ready, J. H. | Bedden, Magie | C/200 | October 5, 1878 | October 6, 1878 |
| Ready, J. S. | Davenport, Fannie | F/66 | July 15, 1895 | July 16, 1895 |
| Ready, James M. | Gannon, Miss Sarah C. | B/46 | June 13, 1867 | June 13, 1867 |
| Ready, John S. | Bryson, Miss Mahaly T. | C/4 | July 27, 1871 | July 27, 1871 |
| Ready, M. E. | Keaton, W. T. | C/20 | January 1, 1872 | January 4, 1872 |
| Redder, Rhoda | Hays, John Henry | C/428 | January 10, 189 | January 11, 1891 |
| Ready, M. J. | Bogle, R. B. | C/158 | February 24, 1877 | March 1, 1877 |
| Ready, Shophia | Herrimon, John | A2/112 | March 22, 1864 | March 24, 1864 |
| Ready, T. B | Young, Laura | D/15 | | September 14, 1882 |
| Ready, Thomas | Parker, Miss Sarah L. A. | A/132 | February 16, 1850 | No Return |
| Ready, William | Willard, Martha Elizabeth | A/115 | October 12, 1848 | October 12, 1848 |
| Reagan, R. A. | McFerin, Mary J. | A2/118 | November 28, 1864 | November 29, 1864 |
| Reaves, A. H. | Burger, Miss M. J. | A2/23 | January 1, 1853 | January 4, 1853 |
| Reddy, Ben | Thompson, Eliza | C/206 | December 18, 1878 | December 19, 1878 |
| Reddy, Miram | Byrn, John | B/10 | June 20, 1867 | June 21, 1867 |
| Redener, Annie | Petty, W. J. | F/20 | October 25, 1893 | No Return |
| Reed, A. J. | Robertson, S. F. | C/176 | October 31, 1877 | November 15, 1879 |
| Reed, Allen | Perkins, Hallie | F/46 | October 24, 1894 | October 28, 1894 |
| Reed, Amanda Miss | Blancett, Jordan | A2/96 | April 23, 1860 | April 26, 1860 |
| Reed, Amandy | Denton, J. S. | A2/32 | July 30, 1856 | August 1, 1872 |
| Reed, Amandy | Denton, J. E. | C/32 | July 30, 1872 | August 1, 1872 |
| Reed, Amendy | Holt, Hord | C/178 | November 22, 1877 | No Return |
| Reed, C. P. | Ferrell, Sue | F/148 | April 23, 1898 | April 24, 1898 |
| Reed, D. B. | Fann, Miss Malissa | A/105 | November 29, 1847 | November 30, 1847 |
| Reed, Daniel | Nuckley, Miss Mary | A/52 | August 9, 1842 | August 14, 1842 |
| Reed, David | Hailey, Elizabeth | A/6 | September 12, 1838 | September 12, 1838 |

| Groom or Bride | Groom or Bride | Book/Page | Date of License | Date of Marriage |
|---|---|---|---|---|
| Reed, David | Fann, Jane | C/78 | January 5, 1874 | January 11, 1874 |
| Reed, Ed | Travis, Mary | E/60 | August 15, 1888 | August 15, 1888 |
| Reed, Eleazon? | Beaty, Sissy | A/34 | October 17, 1840 | October 17, 1840 |
| Reed, Esther Miss | Gibson, James | A/129 | December 15, 1849 | December 15, 1849 |
| Reed, Ezekeil | Owen, Miss Mary | C/2 | May 20, 1871 | May 21, 1871 |
| Reed, Ezekiel | Couch, Tennie | F/122 | July 29, 1897 | July 29, 1897 |
| Reed, Fannie | Lewis, James | F/18 | September 25, 1893 | October 3, 1893 |
| Reed, G. L. | Know, Miss N. A. | E/236 | November 30, 1889 | December 1, 1889 |
| Reed, G. P. | Davenport, S. A. | C/210 | January 21, 1870 | January 23, 1870 |
| Reed, G. W. | Preston, Sarah | D/8 | | December 15, 1881 |
| Reed, George | Soape, Miss Sarah | A/112 | June 16, 1848 | June 17, 1847 |
| Reed, H. B. | Saffle, Miss Malissa J. | B/52 | September 25, 1867 | September 26, 1871 |
| Reed, Hugh | Lambuth, Miss Mary Ann | A/111 | May 15, 1848 | May 17, 1848 |
| Reed, Isie | Campbell, J. D. | F/104 | December 9, 1896 | December 10, 1896 |
| Reed, J. B. | Cawthon, E. M. J. | C/84 | March 17, 1874 | March 17, 1874 |
| Reed, J. F. | Ready, Miss Emeline | A2/82 | July 22, 1858 | No Return |
| Reed, J. F. | Moody, Martha | D/2 | | August 3, 1881 |
| Reed, J. I. | McClain, M. J. | C/56 | March 22, 1873 | March 23, 1873 |
| Reed, J. R. | Williams, Nancy E. | C/70 | October 20, 1873 | October 21, 1873 |
| Reed, Jackson | Nichol, Miss Synthia C. | A2/7 | December 12, 1850 | December 12, 1850 |
| Reed, James | Poff, Mary Ann | A/21 | January 6, 1840 | January 19, 1840 |
| Reed, James | Laseter, Miss Mary | B/88 | February 17, 1869 | May 18, 1869 |
| Reed, James | Patton, Tennie | D/6 | | November 7, 1881 |
| Reed, James | Lasiter, Minnie | F/176 | May 9, 1899 | May 10, 1899 |
| Reed, James | Davis, Sarah J. | F | August 22, 1893 | No Return |
| Reed, James H. | Patton, Miss Mary S. | B/50 | August 30, 1867 | September 1, 1867 |
| Reed, Jane | Davis, Ross | C/434 | April 9, 1891 | April 9, 1891 |
| Reed, Jane Miss | Thomas, E. K. | A2/2 | April 13, 1850 | No Return |
| Reed, Jane Miss | Caruthers, John | B/54 | November 16, 1867 | November 19, 1867 |
| Reed, John | Lambert, Miss Elizabeth | A/132 | February 14, 1850 | February 14, 1850 |
| Reed, John H. | Edwards, Miss Nancy A. | A2/86 | June 25, 1859 | No Return |
| Reed, L. E. | Holt, Fielding | C/116 | July 30, 1875 | August 1, 1876 |
| Reed, Lemuel A. | Porterfield, Margaret | A/28 | April 16, 1840 | April 16, 1840 |
| Reed, Lucy | Tolbert, W. C. | A2/108 | May 8, 1863 | No Return |
| Reed, Luke | Saffle, Eliza M. | C/34 | August 22, 1872 | August 22, 1872 |
| Reed, Lydia A. | Wammack, Thomas | A2/124 | July 10, 1865 | July 12, 1865 |
| Reed, M. F. | Summar, J. F. | C/156 | February 8, 1877 | February 8, 1877 |
| Reed, Malissa C. Miss | Busey, Thomas J. | B/36 | January 7, 1867 | January 8, 1867 |
| Reed, Marah (col.) | Stewart, John (col.) | D/3 | | September 1, 1881 |
| Reed, Martha Miss | Vance, Daniel | A2/60 | December 3, 1857 | December 3, 1857 |
| Reed, Mary | Davenport, J. M. | C/146 | September 30, 1876 | October 1, 1876 |
| Reed, Mary | Vasser, Alf | C/336 | September 22, 1885 | September 22, 1885 |
| Reed, Mary C. | Holt, Coleman | C/242 | February 20, 1880 | February 20, 1880 |
| Reed, Mary E. Miss | Johnson, James N. | B/66 | May 23, 1868 | May 22?, 1868 |
| Reed, Mary M. | Know, Jeff | F/2 | February 4, 1893 | No Return |
| Reed, Mollie | Knox, Joe | F/134 | October 6, 1897 | October 6, 1897 |

| Groom or Bride | Groom or Bride | Book/Page | Date of License | Date of Marriage |
|---|---|---|---|---|
| Reed, Nettie | Jernigan, Jim | F/156 | September 20, 1898 | September 21, 1898 |
| Reed, Peney | Hamilton, Harvey | A2/111 | January 8, 1864 | No Return |
| Reed, Rebecca | Harris, J. L | C/120 | September 16, 1875 | September 16, 1875 |
| Reed, Sarah | Spry, Thos. A. G. | C/306 | March 4, 1884 | March 9, 1884 |
| Reed, Sarah | Brandon, Jonnathan | C/12 | October 28, 1871 | October 30, 1871 |
| Reed, Sarah E. Miss | Morgan, James A. | B/106 | July 27, 1870 | July 27, 1870 |
| Reed, W. A | Barrett, Martha C. | C/180 | December 6, 1877 | December 6, 1877 |
| Reed, W. H. | Parker, Rachal | C/344 | December 12, 1885 | December 13, 1885 |
| Reed, William | Fann, Jemima | A/7 | October 4, 1838 | October 4, 1838 |
| Reed, William | Walker, Bettie | D/5 | | October 6, 1881 |
| Reed, William M. | Stacy, Miss Mary Jane | B/54 | November 2, 1867 | November 3, 1867 |
| Reed, Wm. | King, Anthen | C/286 | July 24, 1883 | July 24, 1883 |
| Reeves, Mary Ann | Herriman, John | A/58 | January 2, 1843 | January 2, 1843 |
| Reeves, Fanny | Peoples, Jack | B/14 | August 18, 1868 | August 18, 1868 |
| Reeves, Lucy Miss | Powell, James | A2/5 | September 5, 1850 | September 8, 1850 |
| Reeves, Salena | Dennis, Mathew | A/67 | February 8, 1844 | February 8, 1844 |
| Reeves, Salina Miss | Ledbetter, James | A/122 | May ?, 1849 | May 11, 1849 |
| Reid, Alford | Young, Miss Marry J. | A2/35 | September 28, 1854 | September 28, 1854 |
| Retton, E. Miss | Lowis, Wm. C. | A2/68 | October 5, 1858 | October 5, 1858 |
| Rewed, Miss M. J. | Campbell, J. E. | F/160 | October 1, 1898 | October 2, 1898 |
| Reynods, Nancy | McDaniel, James | A/20 | December 10, 1839 | December 10, 1839 |
| Reynolds, Adaline D. Miss | McDaniel, David | A/51 | July 16, 1842 | July 18, 1842 |
| Reynolds, John | Weatherspoon, Mary Eliza | A/21 | December 23, 1839 | December 24, 1839 |
| Reynolds, John A. | Wilkerson, Miss Martha M. | A2/16 | April 15, 1852 | April 15, 1852 |
| Reynolds, Margarett | Bonds, William | A/17 | September 18, 1839 | No Return |
| Reynolds, William | Witherspoon, Miss Mary S. | A/85 | December 23, 1845 | December 24, 1845 |
| Rhea, Abagail Miss | Haley, George | A/114 | September 23, 1848 | September 28, 1848 |
| Rhea, Betsy Miss | Spangler, David | A/108 | February 24, 1848 | No Return |
| Rhea, Eleanor Miss | Duke, Mordecai M. | A/98 | March 17, 1847 | March 17, 1847 |
| Rhea, Ruth Miss | Petty, William E. | A/104 | November 10, 1847 | November 11, 1847 |
| Rhyne, Fannie | Hays, A. P. | E/35 | May 3, 1888 | May 3, 1888 |
| Rich, Alice E. | Woodsides, Shela L. | C/462 | July 23, 1892 | July 24, 1892 |
| Rich, Elizabeth | Owens, Ira | C/104 | January 14, 1875 | January 14, 1875 |
| Rich, Joseph A. | Hall, Sarah W. | D/20 | | February 11, 1883 |
| Rich, Julia A. | Bryson, John | C/380 | December 27, 1886 | December 28, 1886 |
| Rich, Marcus | Kelley, Mota | F/130 | September 2, 1897 | September 5, 1897 |
| Rich, May | Hancock, A. J. | F/156 | September 6, 1898 | September 11, 1898 |
| Rich, N. N. | Kirby, J. R. | F/64 | June 26, 1895 | June 27, 1895 |
| Rich, William | Cox, Eleanor | A/77 | February 26, 1845 | February 27, 1845 |
| Rich, Willie | Odom, Mattie | C/262 | November 18, 1880 | November 18, 1880 |
| Rich, Wm. | Stone, Palme | F/134 | October 19, 1897 | October 19, 1897 |
| Richards, F. C. | Brown, Jesse | E/221 | October 15, 1889 | October 16, 1889 |
| Richards, I. G. | Campbell, Miss Bettie | C/424 | December 17, 1890 | December 17, 1890 |
| Richards, J. A. | Walkup, M. E. | C/90 | June 22, 1874 | June 22, 1874 |
| Richards, J. D. | Gaither, Annie | C/126 | December 13, 1875 | December 13, 1875 |
| Richards, J. T. | Gallaway, Permelia | C/144 | September 4, 1876 | September 7, 1876 |

| Groom or Bride | Groom or Bride | Book/Page | Date of License | Date of Marriage |
|---|---|---|---|---|
| Richards, Jas T. | Travis, Malisa | C/178 | November 24, 1877 | No Return |
| Richards, Jesse | Vance, Miss Katharine | A/102 | September 16, 1847 | September 16, 1847 |
| Richards, Jessee | Bucy, Mrs. Sarah J. | B/124 | January 17, 1871 | January 17, 1871 |
| Richards, Jessee | Pedon, Mary J. | C/74 | December 1, 1873 | December 1, 1873 |
| Richards, M. E. | Nichol, J. Y. | E/139 | February 19, 1889 | February 20, 1889 |
| Richards, Mandy | Bowen, Wm. | C/64 | August 20, 1873 | August 21, 1873 |
| Richards, Miss Ida | Davenport, Sam | F/152 | July 2, 1898 | July 3, 1898 |
| Richards, N. J. | Vance, J. R. | E/136 | February 8, 1889 | February 8, 1889 |
| Richards, Nancy A. Miss | Burkett, Job | B/86 | September 16, 1869 | September 16, 1869 |
| Richards, Rebecca Miss | Tenpenny, James | A/71 | July 27, 1844 | July 27, 1844 |
| Richards, Rutha Miss | Read, James | A2/12 | October 4, 1851 | October ?, 1851 |
| Richards, Susan A. | Peydon, Joseph | A2/35 | September 22, 1854 | September 22, 1854 |
| Richardson, Agness Miss | Bowlin, John B. | A/131 | January 30, 1850 | January 30, 1850 |
| Richardson, B. W. | Wadkins, S. Y. | D/17 | | October 29, 1882 |
| Richardson, Brice M. | Fann, Emaline | A/28 | April 15, 1840 | April 15, 1840 |
| Richardson, C. D. | Wilson, Miss Sarah F. | C/396 | August 8, 1887 | August 8, 1887 |
| Richardson, Emily M. Miss | Harris, William J. | A/120 | February 21, 1849 | February 21, 1849 |
| Richardson, Fannie | McBride, Janus | E/198 | August 10, 1889 | No Return |
| Richardson, John L. | Parton, Elizabeth | A2/130 | October 26, 1865 | October 27, 1865 |
| Richardson, Lucy | Hill, Eli | B/94 | December 6, 1869 | December 6, 1869 |
| Richardson, Matilda | Underwood, Thomas | E/48 | July 28, 1888 | July 28, 1888 |
| Richardson, May | Smith, Miss Martha A. | A2/142 | August 6, 1866 | August 6, 1866 |
| Richardson, Roxanah | Jones, Henry | A2/145 | September 29, 1866 | September 30, 1866 |
| Richardson, Susan Miss | Summar, Wm. | B/124 | January 14, 1871 | January 15, 1871 |
| Richardson, Willis | Alexander, Dora | D/12 | | March 12, 1882 |
| Richerson, Drew | Underwood, Miss Reniah | A2/66 | August 21, 1858 | August 22, 1858 |
| Richerson, Franklin | Burk, Miss C. | A2/86 | June 11, 1859 | No Return |
| Richerson, Melvina | Moody, Jno. | C/64 | August 14, 1873 | August 14, 1873 |
| Richerson, Serge D. | Underwood, Miss E. D. | A2/65 | May 12, 1858 | May 13, 1858 |
| Richerson, Wm. G. | Suthern, Miss Nancy L. | A2/42 | September 27, 1855 | September 27, 1855 |
| Richetts, John | Young, Etta | C/316 | November 20, 1884 | November 20, 1884 |
| Richie, Molley | Gunter, Robt | F/136 | October 30, 1897 | October 31, 1897 |
| Rickets, Peter | Owen, Mary | A2/106 | November 4, 1862 | No Return |
| Rickets, Robert S. | Jimerson, Miss Narcissa | A2/91 | November 2, 1859 | No Return |
| Ridener, L. W. | Watson, Miss P. E. | C/4 | July 28, 1871 | July 28, 1871 |
| Ridener, M. P. | Haley, T. J. | C/166 | August 4, 1877 | August 5, 1877 |
| Rideout, Ella | Harper, Hunter | C/76 | December 10, 1873 | December 10, 1873 |
| Rideout, Evaline | Harris, Ambrose | B/12 | November 25, 1867 | November 28, 1867 |
| Rideout, Johnson | Jetton, Eller | B/16 | December 28, 1868 | December 29, 1869 |
| Rideout, Manca | Ferrell, William | C/68 | October 3, 1873 | October 4, 1873 |
| Ridinger, J. B. | James, Nancy C. | C/256 | September 30, 1880 | September 30, 1880 |
| Ridner, Tennie | Perkins, L. T. | F/60 | February 26, 1895 | March 8, 1895 |
| Rigby, Elizabeth Ann Miss | Gilley, John | A2/74 | January 2, 1854 | January 5, 1854 |
| Riggby, Almand | Sullivan, Miss R. J. | A2/33 | July 12, 1854 | July 16, 1854 |
| Right, Alford | Martin, Sarah | C/250 | July 22, 1880 | July 22, 1880 |
| Right, Jesie | Cope, G. P. | C/306 | March 3, 1884 | March 6, 1885 |

| Groom or Bride | Groom or Bride | Book/Page | Date of License | Date of Marriage |
|---|---|---|---|---|
| Right, Jnda | Rucker, George | D/3 | | July 18, 1881 |
| Rigsby, B. A. | Young, I. L | F/74 | November 2, 1895 | November 3, 1895 |
| Rigsby, Catherine | Meadows, M. M. | C/88 | May 2, 1874 | No Return |
| Rigsby, Bailam | Givens, Miss Sallie | B/90 | October 2, 1869 | October 3, 1869 |
| Rigsby, Caroline | Burkett, J. M. | C/34 | August 22, 1872 | August 22, 1872 |
| Rigsby, Deley | Womack, D. M. | D/6 | | November 3, 1881 |
| Rigsby, Eliza Miss | Preston, Thomas | A/76 | January 22, 1845 | January 23, 1845 |
| Rigsby, F. L | George, J. L. | E/124 | January 3, 1889 | No Return |
| Rigsby, Fances A. | Ferrell, J. B. | C/36 | August 31, 1872 | September 1, 1872 |
| Rigsby, Fanny Miss | Keaton, W. A. | C/424 | December 12, 1890 | December 14, 1890 |
| Rigsby, Florance | Armstrong, Knox | C/202 | October 16, 1878 | October 17, 1878 |
| Rigsby, G. A. | Wooton, Miss Allie | F/62 | April 20, 1895 | April 21, 1895 |
| Rigsby, Helen | Taylor, John | C/356 | April 5, 1886 | April 5, 1886 |
| Rigsby, J. A. | Little, Miss Sarah | A2/66 | August 7, 1858 | August 8, 1858 |
| Rigsby, J. M. | Bogle, Lamartha | C/208 | December 28, 1878 | December 29, 1878 |
| Rigsby, James | Herriman, Tiney | C/292 | September 11, 1883 | September 11, 1883 |
| Rigsby, Jane Miss | Preston, William Jr. | A2/3 | June 29, 1850 | June 30, 1850 |
| Rigsby, Jane Miss | Ashford, Baxel | A2/67 | September 17, 1858 | September 27, 1858 |
| Rigsby, John | Moore, Mary D. | C/254 | August 14, 1880 | August 15, 1880 |
| Rigsby, John K. | Davis, Sarah | A/75 | December 25, 1844 | December 26, 1844 |
| Rigsby, John K. | Higdon, Lucy | E/5 | January 18, 1888 | January 13, 1888 |
| Rigsby, L. L. L. | Underhill, G. W. | C/54 | February 22, 1873 | February 26, 1873 |
| Rigsby, Lilly | Herrimon, Senate | C/188 | March 7, 1878 | March 7, 1878 |
| Rigsby, M. A. Miss | Parker, Lewis | A2/72 | February 3, 1859 | No Return |
| Rigsby, M. A. Miss | Parker, Lewis | A2/83 | February 3, 1859 | No Return |
| Rigsby, M. J. | Vinson, Thomas | C/22 | January 21, 1872 | January 21, 1872 |
| Rigsby, Malinda C. Miss | Capshaw, J. J. C. | B/104 | July 12, 1870 | |
| Rigsby, Malisa | Preston, John | C/48 | December 26, 1872 | December 27, 1872 |
| Rigsby, Martha | Wilcher, C. M. | D/21 | | April 4, 1883 |
| Rigsby, Martha J. Miss | Vinson, Thomas J. | B/90 | October 16, 1869 | No Return |
| Rigsby, Martha Miss | Blanton, Vinson | A/88 | April 4, 1846 | April 26, 1846 |
| Rigsby, Martha T. | Mullins, James R. | C/122 | October 16, 1875 | October 17, 1875 |
| Rigsby, Mary | Mitchell, John N. | C/18 | December 22, 1871 | December 22, 1871 |
| Rigsby, Mary E. | Ford, D. S. | C/16 | December 16, 1871 | December 17, 1871 |
| Rigsby, Mary E. Miss | Higgins, R. L. | B/96 | December 20, 1869 | December 22, 1869 |
| Rigsby, Mary L. | Debery, Bill | C/326 | February 21, 1885 | February 22, 1885 |
| Rigsby, Myrtle Miss | Melton, Dallas | C/456 | March 11, 1892 | March 13, 1892 |
| Rigsby, Nelson | Hearndon, M. J. | C/50 | January 2, 1873 | January 2, 1873 |
| Rigsby, Robert | Jones, Ba--- | A2/102 | September 15, 1860 | September 15, 1860 |
| Rigsby, Ruthey Miss | Davis, John | A2/64 | March 25, 1858 | No Return |
| Rigsby, Sally | Fuston, Josiah | A2/134 | December 23, 1865 | December 23, 1865 |
| Rigsby, Thomas | Young, Margaret | A2/20 | October 9, 1852 | October 10, 1852 |
| Rigsby, Thomas | Young, Miss Jane | A2/76 | January 12, 1855 | January 14, 1855 |
| Rigsby, William | Woods, Sarah B. | C/376 | December 18, 1886 | December 18, 1886 |
| Rigsby, William T. | Tuttle, Miss Martha | A/129 | November 29, 1849 | November 29, 1849 |
| Rigsby, Willie | Womach, L. N. | C/260 | October 21, 1880 | October 21, 1880 |

| Groom or Bride | Groom or Bride | Book/Page | Date of License | Date of Marriage |
|---|---|---|---|---|
| Rigsby, Wm. | Young, Sarah A. | C/26 | April 18, 1872 | April 18, 1872 |
| Ring, Elizabeth Miss | Holt, Thomas | A/54 | October 6, 1842 | October 6, 1842 |
| Ring, Francis | Vasor, William | C/404 | October 9, 1887 | October 9, 1887 |
| Ring, John | Haney, Miss Polly | A/46 | December 25, 1841 | December 25, 1841 |
| Ring, L. A. | Sissom, Wm | C/150 | December 8, 1876 | October 15, 1877 |
| Ring, Layfayett | Campell, Miss Emla | A2/22 | December 22, 1852 | December 23, 1852 |
| Ring, M. E. Miss | Hailey, W. B. | B/92 | November 24, 1869 | November 25, 1869 |
| Ring, Nancy Anne Miss | Saine, Noah | A/32 | September 8, 1840 | September 9, 1840 |
| Ring, Sarah J. | Nesbitt, S. V. | C/130 | January 11, 1876 | January 11, 1876 |
| Ring, William | Espy, Miss Nancy | A/90 | September 4, 1846 | September 6, 1846 |
| Ring, Wm. | Whitefield, Miss M. C. | A2/35 | September 20, 1854 | September 21, 1854 |
| Ritch, Elizabeth | Grindstaff, James | B/18 | May 26, 1870 | May 26, 1870 |
| Ritch, James O. | Hale, Miss Elvira F. | B/56 | December 4, 1867 | December 8, 1867 |
| Ritch, Rufus | Kennedy, Miss Josie | B/126 | February 21, 1871 | February 23, 1871 |
| Ritchey, George | Gilley, Miss Harriet C. | B/32 | December 10, 1866 | December 12, 1866 |
| Ritchey, Harritt | Mullins, Joseph | C/100 | November 28, 1874 | November 29, 1874 |
| Ritchey, J. P. | Markum, Ella | C/440 | July 25, 1891 | July 25, 1891 |
| Rizzle, Mattie | Good, James | F/150 | June 11, 1898 | No Return |
| Roach, George T. | New, Miss Pollie | C/412 | December 17, 1887 | December 18, 1887 |
| Roach, J. L. | Brown, Elvira | C/102 | December 12, 1874 | December 14, 1874 |
| Roberson, Elizabeth | Stone, James | C/116 | August 14, 1875 | No Return |
| Roberson, Foster M. | Davenport, Miss Martha | B/96 | December 22, 1869 | December 26, 1869 |
| Roberson, Jane | Wood, Russ | C/114 | June 24, 1875 | June 24, 1875 |
| Roberson, Josephine Miss | Brandon, K. T. | B/64 | March 28, 1868 | March 29, 1868 |
| Roberson, Lahama E. | Bragg, James | B/104 | July 20, 1870 | July 21, 1870 |
| Roberson, Mary P. Miss | Bragg, Thomas D. | B/42 | February 27, 1867 | February 28, 1867 |
| Roberson, Robert | Woods, Susan | B/16 | January 2, 1869 | January 3, 1869 |
| Roberson, Samuel | Ewing, Tennie | C/30 | July 17, 1872 | No Return |
| Roberson, W. M. | Summer, Miss Sarah | A2/88 | August 28, 1859 | No Return |
| Roberson, Wm. | Duke, Mary J. | F/60 | March 9, 1895 | March 10, 1895 |
| Robert, Milton | Patterson, F. M. | F/80 | January 3, 1896 | January 5, 1896 |
| Roberts, Amandy | Blue, Lewis (col.) | C/298 | December 6, 1883 | No Retrun |
| Roberts, E. Miss | Tittle, James | A2/35 | September 29, 1854 | No Return |
| Roberts, Elizabeth | Taylor, George | B/6 | August 28, 1865 | August 28, 1865 |
| Roberts, J. B. | Cantrell, Bertha | F/32 | February 20, 1894 | February 25, 1894 |
| Roberts, Joe (col.) | Blue, Rachel (col.) | F/90 | July 8, 1896 | July 8, 1896 |
| Roberts, Lewis (col.) | Grizzle, Babe (col.) | F/166 | January 15, 1899 | January 15, 1899 |
| Roberts, Lize | Wamack, John | C/128 | December 29, 1875 | December 29, 1875 |
| Roberts, M. A. Miss | Pettus, J. A. | B/58 | December 9, 1867 | December 12, 1867 |
| Roberts, M. C. Miss | Patten, J. A. | A2/131 | November 9, 1865 | November 9, 1865 |
| Roberts, Manervia | Bush, Peterson | C/104 | December 26, 1874 | December 27, 1874 |
| Roberts, Melberry Miss | McCulloch, Martin | A2/137 | February 13, 1866 | February 18, 1866 |
| Roberts, Sarrah Jane | Wade, William | A2/40 | July 14, 1855 | Returns Missing |
| Roberts, Thomas | Spry, Miss Nancy C. | A2/148 | May 4, 1866 | No Return |
| Roberts, Thomas J. | Leigh, Miss Nancy C. | B/92 | November 22, 1869 | November 25, 1869 |
| Robertson, Aubry | Vance, Jennie | F/118 | May 29, 1897 | May 29, 1897 |

| Groom or Bride | Groom or Bride | Book/Page | Date of License | Date of Marriage |
|---|---|---|---|---|
| Robertson, Bill (col.) | French, Susie (col.) | F/118 | May 28, 1897 | May 29, 1897 |
| Robertson, Charloote | Stewart, John (col) | C/462 | July 28, 1892 | July 30, 1892 |
| Robertson, Fannie | Dass, Shelby | F/34 | September 18, 1894 | September 18, 1894 |
| Robertson, Hugh | Osburn, Nancy J. | C/90 | June 25, 1874 | June 25, 1874 |
| Robertson, J. G. | McFerrin, S. J. | C/192 | May 4, 1878 | May 5, 1878 |
| Robertson, Phessy | Sadler, George W. | A/19 | November 20, 1839 | November 20, 1839 |
| Robertson, R. S. | Mingle, S. E. | C/174 | October 23, 1877 | October 24, 1877 |
| Robertson, S. F. | Reed, A. J. | C/176 | October 31, 1877 | November 15, 1879 |
| Robertson, S. W. | Higdon, Salatha J. | A2/33 | July 4, 1854 | July 5, 1854 |
| Robertson, Sarah A. | Womack, Jo B. | C/182 | January 3, 1878 | January 3, 1878 |
| Robertson, Sophia | Thompson, Jessee | C/176 | November 1, 1877 | November 1, 1877 |
| Robets, Bell Miss | Orr, D. T. | C/412 | December 14, 1887 | December 14, 1887 |
| Robinson, A. W. | Todd, Margarett M. | C/156 | February 14, 1877 | February 15, 1877 |
| Robinson, Alis Miss | Jetton, Rolley | C/388 | April 23, 1887 | April 24, 1887 |
| Robinson, Amanda Miss | Witherspoon, Lewis E. W. | A2/7 | October 29, 1850 | October 29, 1850 |
| Robinson, C. F. | Watson, Beulah | F/72 | October 3, 1895 | October 4, 1895 |
| Robinson, Charity | Woods, Isaac | D/21 | | January 16, 1883 |
| Robinson, E. B. | McBroom, Minnia | C/366 | September 13, 1886 | September 15, 1886 |
| Robinson, E. J. | Patrick M. D. | C/266 | December 4, 1880 | December 5, 1880 |
| Robinson, Hugh | Gray, Mariah | C/362 | August 5, 1886 | August 12, 1886 |
| Robinson, J. | Jetton, Sophia | C/130 | January 6, 1876 | January 6, 1876 |
| Robinson, J. P. | Holt, T. A. | F/144 | January 14, 1898 | January 15, 1898 |
| Robinson, Jacob | Wimbley, Elizabeth | A2/45 | December 29, 1855 | No Return |
| Robinson, Jesse | Mason, Ada | C/314 | October 19, 1884 | October 20, 1884 |
| Robinson, Jesse | Gray, Matilda | C/326 | February 18, 1885 | February 19, 1884 |
| Robinson, Jessee | Gillis, Nancy | F | August 24, 1893 | |
| Robinson, Jonas | Herrell, Miss Sallie | E/201 | August 21, 1889 | No Return |
| Robinson, Jones (col.) | Odom, Lillie | F/74 | November 1, 1895 | November 3, 1895 |
| Robinson, Joseph | Bogle, R. M. | A2/37 | November 4, 1854 | November 5, 1854 |
| Robinson, Joseph W. | Boyle, Reia M. | A2/36 | November 4, 1854 | November 5, 1854 |
| Robinson, Maggie | Goins, Lewis | C/312 | August 9, 1884 | August 10, 1884 |
| Robinson, R. S. | St. John, Miss Mary | A2/46 | January 10, 1856 | January 10, 1856 |
| Robinson, Robert | Willard, Miss Mattie | C/450 | December 7, 1891 | No Return |
| Robinson, Rose Ann | Earles, G. A. | C/448 | October 5, 1891 | October 12, 1891 |
| Robinson, S. R. | McAdoo, Miss Angie | C/424 | December 17, 1890 | December 18, 1890 |
| Robinson, Sallie | Skurlock, John | E/98 | November 6, 1888 | November 6, 1888 |
| Robinson, Sam | Stacy, Fannie | F/108 | January 4, 1897 | January 4, 1897 |
| Robinson, Sarah E. | Walkup, J. A. | C/268 | December 15, 1880 | December 16, 1880 |
| Robinson, Suffrona | Hoover, Marlin S. | A/4 | June 14, 1838 | June 14, 1838 |
| Robinson, Vina A. Miss | Gordon, Robert | A/80 | July 9, 1845 | July 9, 1845 |
| Robinson, Vina A. Miss | Gordon, Robert | A/81 | July 9, 1845 | July 9, 1845 |
| Robinson, William M. | Summers, Miss Iza Evaline | A2/2 | May 27, 1850 | No Return |
| Robinson, Wm. | Young, Nancy A. | C/328 | March 10, 1885 | March 12, 1885 |
| Robison, John | Brooks, Elracy | C/372 | October 26, 1886 | No Return |
| Robtson, Vina (col) | Paris, John | E/27 | March 18, 1888 | March 18, 1888 |
| Rodger, Maggie | Rodgers, James | E/31 | April 23, 1888 | April 23, 1888 |

| Groom or Bride | Groom or Bride | Book/Page | Date of License | Date of Marriage |
|---|---|---|---|---|
| Rodgers, Green | Gann, Mary | C/356 | April 10, 1886 | April 10, 1886 |
| Rodgers, J. T. | Olford, Margrett | C/16 | December 6, 1871 | December 6, 1871 |
| Rodgers, James | Rodger, Maggie | E/31 | April 23, 1888 | April 23, 1888 |
| Rodgers, John | McClain, Miss Jane | A2/64 | April 8, 1858 | April 8, 1858 |
| Rodgers, John B. | Simmons, Elisa | C/274 | March 3, 1881 | No Return |
| Rodgers, Katharine | Morgan, Alexander | A/11 | March 2, 1839 | No Return |
| Rodgers, Nannie | Jennings, L. L. | F/96 | September 18, 1896 | September 18, 1896 |
| Rodgers, Ramzel H. | McKnight, Miss Easter S. | A/69 | May 2, 1844 | No Return |
| Rodgers, W. B. | Brandon, Nitha Jane | C/446 | September 9, 1891 | September 10, 1891 |
| Rodgers, Wilburn | Peeler, Mary A. | C/260 | October 20, 1880 | October 20, 1880 |
| Rodgers, William | Bush, Miss Emily Mariah | B/58 | December 16, 1867 | December 17, 1867 |
| Rodgers, Willie | Dixon, Mattie L. | C/318 | November 3, 1884 | No Return |
| Rodgers, Zion | Russell, Stacy J. | A2/108 | September 6, 1863 | No Return |
| Roemines, Eleanor Miss | Womack, William | A/98 | April 9, 1847 | April 11, 1847 |
| Roger, Polk | Bush, Daisy | F/120 | June 9, 1897 | June 13, 1897 |
| Rogers, Ary Ursula | Bowen, John | A/55 | October 28, 1842 | October 28, 1842 |
| Rogers, Elizabeth Miss | Cuningham, J. | A2/14 | February 2, 1852 | February 2, 1852 |
| Rogers, Henry | Nickels, Miss Sarah | A2/24 | March 10, 1853 | March 13, 1853 |
| Rogers, J. H. | Brown, Martha A. | C/114 | June 4, 1875 | June 4, 1875 |
| Rogers, James | Alford, Miss Elizabeth | A2/49 | August 11, 1856 | August 12, 1856 |
| Rogers, John | Moon, Miss Nancy | A/50 | June 11, 1842 | June 12, 1842 |
| Rogers, John Jr. | Davis, Miss Cintha | A/79 | June 6, 1845 | June 6, 1845 |
| Rogers, John Jr. | Bulling, Miss Polly | A/89 | June 17, 1846 | June 17, 1846 |
| Rogers, L. F. | Stiles, Josie | E/173 | April 27, 1889 | No Return |
| Rogers, L. R. | Wilson, M. A. | C/122 | October 1, 1875 | October 1, 1875 |
| Rogers, Leanah Mrs. | Conner, William O. | A/112 | July 27, 1848 | July 27, 1848 |
| Rogers, Lucinda | Bullard, Nathan | C/246 | April 10, 1880 | April 10, 1880 |
| Rogers, Miss Sarah | Parker, W. J. | F/74 | October 16, 1895 | October 16, 1895 |
| Rogers, Susa | Keaton, Tom | F/130 | September 13,1897 | September 14, 1897 |
| Rogers, Wilbern | Bullen, Miss Mahulda | A/95 | January 4, 1847 | January 10, 1847 |
| Rogers, Wilburn | Allen, Clemmsy | C/92 | August 19, 1874 | August 30, 1874 |
| Rogers, Will | Brandon, Linda | F/98 | October 7, 1896 | October 14, 1896 |
| Rogers, Wm. J. | Nealy, Miss Mary Ann | A2/56 | May 27, 1857 | No Return |
| Rogers, Zilpha Miss | Davis, Lewis | A/109 | March 14, 1848 | March 14, 1848 |
| Rollens, Dave | Tolbert, Mollie | F/76 | December 7, 1895 | December 7, 1895 |
| Rollins, Andrew | Grimes, Miss Better | C/408 | November 15, 1887 | November 15, 1887 |
| Rollins, Ben | Shirley, Mary | C/330 | April 15, 1885 | April 16, 1885 |
| Rollins, Maggie | Broyles, J. H. | C/390 | September 5, 1883 | No Return |
| Rollins, Maggie T. | Broyles, J. H. | C/292 | September 5, 1883 | No Return |
| Rollins, Simeon | Hollis, Susan | F/30 | January 17, 1894 | January 17, 1894 |
| Romine, James | Davis, Elizabeth | C/164 | July 14, 1877 | July 15, 1877 |
| Romine, Jeremiah | Emery, Miss Elizabeth Selah | A/113 | August 4, 1848 | August 8, 1848 |
| Rood, C. C. | Smith, Miss Polly | A/105 | December 6, 1847 | December 6, 1847 |
| Roper, Walter | Duggin, N. E. | F/50 | November 22, 1894 | November 25, 1894 |
| Ross, James | Spangler, Miss Disa | A/110 | April 10, 1848 | April 11, 1848 |
| Ross, James | Whittamore, Miss Abagale | A2/139 | March 5, 1866 | March 15, 1866 |

| Groom or Bride | Groom or Bride | Book/Page | Date of License | Date of Marriage |
|---|---|---|---|---|
| Ross, Malinda Miss | Whittamore, Newton | A2/138 | February 23, 1866 | February 25, 1866 |
| Ross, W. S. | Jones, M. J. | C/118 | August 20, 1875 | August 22, 1875 |
| Ross, William S. | Bush, Miss Mary E. | B/54 | October 30, 1867 | October 30, 1867 |
| Rotty, Jackson | Whitfield, Miss Marry Ann | A2/25 | May 21, 1853 | May 22, 1853 |
| Roughton, James | Halpayne, Miss Martha B. | A/107 | January 24, 1848 | January 24, 1848 |
| Rucker, Amanda M. | Stewart, John H. | A2/133 | December 7, 1865 | December 7, 1865 |
| Rucker, Angie | Crank, James A. | C/288 | July 22, 1883 | July 22, 1883 |
| Rucker, Casie | Alexander, Marshal | C/302 | January 23, 1884 | No Return |
| Rucker, Elizabeth C. Miss | Justice, Robert N. | A2/135 | January 16, 1866 | January 16, 1866 |
| Rucker, George | Right, Juda | D/3 | | July 18, 1881 |
| Rucker, Goodloe | Rushing, Henry | B/4 | August 24, 1865 | August 27, 1865 |
| Rucker, J. E. | McLin, Miss Allice M. | B/98 | December 7, 1869 | December 8, 1869 |
| Rucker, James | Rucker, Jane | B/12 | November 29, 1867 | December 30, 1867 |
| Rucker, Jane | Rucker, James | B/12 | November 29, 1867 | December 30, 1867 |
| Rucker, John E. | Stewart, Miss Lucinda A. | A2/146 | November 1, 1866 | November 1, 1866 |
| Rucker, July | Weatherly, Jesse | C/268 | December 8, 1880 | December 9, 1880 |
| Rucker, L. Miss | McKnight, Ruben | B/114 | October 14, 1870 | No Return |
| Rucker, Mandy | Daniel, James | D/12 | | March 16, 1882 |
| Rucker, Mariah S. | Weedon, Daniel F. | A/14 | June 6, 1839 | No Return |
| Rucker, Wiley | Elkins, Bezie | F/108 | December 27, 1896 | December 27, 1896 |
| Rucker, Wm. | Tatum, Julia | C/314 | September 21, 1884 | September 21, 1884 |
| Rucker, Wm. | Mitchell, Salley | D/9 | | December 28, 1881 |
| Ruckey, Jennett | Hayes, Robert L. | F/34 | March 31, 1894 | No Return |
| Ruckley, Alexander | Smith, Sarah E. | C/120 | September 24, 1875 | September 26, 1875 |
| Ruckley, Wiley | Todd, Mary | C/84 | February 24, 1874 | February 28, 1874 |
| Rudy, Wm. | Carter, Miss Nannie | F/150 | June 12, 1898 | June 12, 1898 |
| Rule, Miss Batie | Mathis, Donnie | F/62 | April 16, 1895 | April 17, 1895 |
| Ruller, Robt | Low, Martha | C/298 | December 5, 1883 | No Return |
| Runels, Harris | Martin, Matie | C/216 | June 24, 1879 | June 26, 1879 |
| Rusel, J. R. | Haskers, Telitha | D/4 | | July 28, 1881 |
| Rushing, A. | Mullennix, Veny | C/220 | June 28, 1879 | No Return |
| Rushing, Al | Lyons, Miss Catherine | B/114 | October 15, 1870 | October 15, 1870 |
| Rushing, Allice | Turner, Harras | C/208 | December 31, 1878 | December 31, 1878 |
| Rushing, Ellen | York, Si | C/26 | May 16, 1872 | May 16, 1872 |
| Rushing, Ellen | Johnson, Jake | C/162 | June 16, 1877 | No Return |
| Rushing, Emily | Barnes, Henry | B/14 | August 15, 1868 | August 18, 1868 |
| Rushing, Frank | Barnes, Miss Dosia | B/128 | March 10, 1871 | March 10, 1871 |
| Rushing, H. B. | Kittrell, Miss Prudie | B/100 | March 2, 1870 | March 2, 1870 |
| Rushing, Henry | Rucker, Goodloe | B/4 | August 24, 1865 | August 27, 1865 |
| Rushing, Jennie | McFerrin, Jack | C/130 | January 13, 1876 | January 13, 1876 |
| Rushing, John R. | Bethell, Miss Tennie L. | A2/136 | January 31, 1866 | January 31, 1866 |
| Rushing, Martha | Williams, L. W. | C/30 | June 15, 1872 | June 15, 1872 |
| Rushing, Martha Miss | Cathcart, W. A. | B/124 | January 11, 1871 | No Return |
| Rushing, Stephen | Rushing, Venie | D/20 | | March 24, 1883 |
| Rushing, Venie | Rushing, Stephen | D/20 | | March 24, 1883 |
| Russel, M. W. | Boren, Barthena J. | A2/111 | January 28, 1864 | January 31, 1864 |

| Groom or Bride | Groom or Bride | Book/Page | Date of License | Date of Marriage |
|---|---|---|---|---|
| Russell, Stacy J. | Rodgers, Zion | A2/108 | September 6, 1863 | No Return |
| Russell, Wm. H. | Patterson, Marey C. | A2/113 | April 30, 1864 | April 30, 1864 |
| Saddler, J. H. | Williams, Sarah A. | C/288 | August 11, 1883 | August 12, 1883 |
| Saddler, J. W. | Walker, Miss Oallie | F/170 | February 4, 1899 | February 5, 1899 |
| Saddler, Ransom | Lemmons, Alice | F/132 | September 22, 1897 | October 2, 1897 |
| Saddler, Sarah M. N. | Duncan, M. R. | C/302 | January 25, 1884 | January 27, 1884 |
| Sadler, A. J. | Duncan, P. J. | C/308 | June 2, 1884 | June 8, 1884 |
| Sadler, A. J. | Pilotte, S. M. J. | E/222 | October 15, 1889 | October 15, 1889 |
| Sadler, Adam A. | Gilley, Miss M. E. | E/45 | July 7, 1888 | July 8, 1888 |
| Sadler, George W. | Robertson, Phessy | A/19 | November 20, 1839 | November 20, 1839 |
| Sadler, Mary C. | Lewis, John W. | E/160 | February 17, 1889 | February 18, 1889 |
| Saddler, Mary L. | Lewis, John W. | C/258 | October 13, 1880 | October 13, 1880 |
| Saffal, Emeline | Thomas, Zack | C/298 | November 26, 1883 | November 27, 1883 |
| Saffle, Eliza M. | Reed, Luke | C/34 | August 22, 1872 | August 22, 1872 |
| Saffle, M. A. Miss | Laseter, J. H. | B/78 | March 10, 1869 | March 11, 1869 |
| Saffle, M. E. | Hollis, James E. | F/22 | November 15, 1893 | November 15, 1893 |
| Saffle, Malissa J. Miss | Reed, H. B. | B/52 | September 25, 1867 | September 26, 1871 |
| Saffle, Margrett C. | Barrett, Thos. J. | C/82 | February 18, 1874 | February 19, 1874 |
| Saffle, Mary Miss | Thomas, William | C/466 | September 20, 1892 | September 21, 1892 |
| Saffle, W. A. | Gaither, Miss M. L. C. | B/60 | January 22, 1868 | January 23, 1868 |
| Saffley, Jerry | Biles, Ellen | F/94 | September 23, 1896 | September 13, 1896 |
| Sagely, B. L. | Todd, Nancy | C/48 | December 21, 1872 | December 29, 1872 |
| Sagely, Mariah Elvina Miss | Arnold, William Jefferson | A/106 | December 25, 1847 | December 25, 1847 |
| Sagely, Mary Ann Miss | Bynum, William | A/95 | December 30, 1846 | December 31, 1846 |
| Sagely, Nancy Eleanor | Gray, Samuel W. | A/60 | February 18, 1843 | February 19, 1843 |
| Sain, G. J. | Stroud, N. A. | C/418 | October 4, 1890 | October 4, 1890 |
| Saine, Noah | Ring, Miss Nancy Anne | A/32 | September 8, 1840 | September 9, 1840 |
| Salers, J. D. | Bryson, Sarah J. | C/202 | October 16, 1878 | October 16, 1878 |
| Sand, M. Cleair Miss | Puckett, C. S. | A2/27 | August 30, 1853 | August 30, 1853 |
| Sand?, Martha Frances Miss | Alexander, A. O. | A/102 | October 5, 1847 | October 5, 1847 |
| Sander, Charlotte | Thomas, Anlzo | F/8 | April 29, 1893 | April 29, 1893 |
| Sanders, Casie | Gains, J. A. | C/240 | January 26, 1880 | January 26, 1880 |
| Sanders, Paralee | Prater, Arch | C/56 | April 7, 1873 | April 7, 1873 |
| Sanders, Sarah T. Miss | Wood, John A. | A2/78 | February 21, 1856 | February 22, 1856 |
| Sanders, Sarrah A. Miss | Todd, Wm. T. | A2/37 | December 21, 1854 | December 21, 1854 |
| Sands, Nancy Miss | Alexander, Abner D. | A/49 | May 25, 1842 | May 25, 1842 |
| Sanford, Bettie V. | Heam, Henry | C/94 | September 15, 1874 | September 15, 1874 |
| Sanford, Thomas B. | Taylor, Mrs. Elizabeth R. | A/119 | February 14, 1849 | February 15, 1848? |
| Sapp, E. S. Miss | Crane, A. M. | A2/56 | June 6, 1857 | June 7, 1857 |
| Sapp, Hannah C. Miss | Mullins, John W. | A/79 | June 15, 1845 | June 20, 1845 |
| Sapp, Jane | Barrett, John | A/16 | August 20, 1839 | August 11, 1839 |
| Sapp, Martha E. Miss | Gannon, Samuel | A/87 | March 7, 1846 | March 8, 1846 |
| Sapp, Nancy Ann Miss | Moon, Benjamin | A2/77 | January 12, 1856 | January 13, 1856 |
| Sapp, Polly Miss | Hammon, Larkin | A/43 | October 30, 1841 | October 30, 1841 |
| Satine, Laura | Webb, J. W. | A2/13 | December 25, 1851 | December 25, 1851 |
| Saules, Alta | Gannon, Ed | F/166 | January 7, 1899 | January 8, 1899 |

| Groom or Bride | Groom or Bride | Book/Page | Date of License | Date of Marriage |
|---|---|---|---|---|
| Saules, Andy A. | Owen, Mary E. | C/332 | July 22, 1885 | July 22, 1885 |
| Saules, Miss Haulie | Meares, Willey | F/166 | January 9, 1899 | January 19, 1899 |
| Sauls, Better | McKnight, David | E/203 | August 31, 1889 | August 31, 1889 |
| Sauls, Caroline Miss | Fann, Grundy | A/68 | March 5, 1844 | March 10, 1844 |
| Sauls, Charity E. Miss | Bogle, James | A2/146 | October 18, 1866 | October 18, 1866 |
| Sauls, Charity Miss | Parker, Cornelius | A/93 | October 28, 1846 | October 29, 1846 |
| Sauls, David | Duggin, Miss Juliann | A2/84 | March 21, 1859 | No Return |
| Sauls, Henry | Cooper, Martha L. | B/90 | October 6, 1869 | October 10, 1869 |
| Sauls, Jerush | Bowe, W. M. | D/13 | | July 15, 1882 |
| Sauls, John H. | Gaither, Eliza Jane | A/90 | August 27, 1846 | August 27, 1846 |
| Sauls, Mary | Smith, Neal H. | C/354 | February 20, 1886 | February 21, 1886 |
| Sauls, Rhoda Miss | Tedder, Thomas | A/88 | March 26, 1846 | March 26, 1846 |
| Sauls, Ruth Miss | Harris, G. W. | A2/5 | September 14, 1850 | No Return |
| Sauls, William | Bogle, Martha | A/57 | December 8, 1842 | December 8, 1842 |
| Sawles, Allice | Duggin, Henry | F/156 | September 9, 1898 | September 9, 1898 |
| Sawles, J. D. | Beadon, Miss S. E. | B/114 | November 5, 1870 | November 7, 1870 |
| Sawyers, Elvira | Wood, Larry | C/170 | September 7, 1877 | No Return |
| Sayley, W. W. | Paschal, Sallie | D/8 | | December 11, 1881 |
| Schobt, Jane | Young, J. E. | F/106 | December 19, 1896 | December 20, 1896 |
| Schott, H. A. | Rains, M. E. | F/100 | October 28, 1896 | October 29, 1896 |
| Scissam, Milley E. Miss | Spry, G. W. | A2/75 | December 21, 1854 | December 21, 1854 |
| Scoot, J. M. | King, Miss A. J. | F/78 | December 30, 1895 | December 30, 1895 |
| Scot, James | Deberry, Mry | C/368 | September 28, 1886 | No Return |
| Scott, Babe | Higgins, Anthony | E/23 | February 29, 1888 | February 29, 1888 |
| Scott, Catharine | Goins, Carter | B/66 | May 23, 1868 | May 28, 1868 |
| Scott, Eliza Miss | Womack, J. J. | C/430 | February 24, 1891 | March 13, 1891 |
| Scott, H. A. | Shelton, Nannie | C/34 | August 14, 1872 | August 14, 1872 |
| Scott, Henry | Wilson, Miss Mary | A/91 | October 3, 1846 | October 3, 1846 |
| Scott, J. F. | Preston, Sara E. | A2/134 | December 30, 1865 | December 31, 1865 |
| Scott, John S. | Campbell, Dealy | C/350 | January 16, 1886 | January 17, 1886 |
| Scott, July Ann D. | Womack, John N. | A2/2 | April 6, 1850 | April 7, 1850 |
| Scott, Mark | McGee, Mary | D/18 | | December 3, 1882 |
| Scott, Marry Ann Miss | Todd, Granvill | A2/21 | December 15, 1852 | December 15, 1852 |
| Scott, Martin | Deberry, Angeline | C/420 | October 18, 1890 | October 19, 1890 |
| Scott, Mary Ann Miss | Wilson, Benjamin | A/52 | August 6, 1842 | August 7, 1842 |
| Scott, Mary Drue | Smith, James | E/188 | July 5, 1889 | July 5, 1889 |
| Scott, Mary E. Miss | Duncan, L. T. | B/44 | April 9, 1867 | No Return |
| Scott, Nancy Miss | Northcutt, George E. | B/58 | December 21, 1867 | No Return |
| Scott, Rachel | Bassham, Adam | F/34 | September 20, 1894 | September 20, 1894 |
| Scott, Sam | Bogle, Miss Nancy | B/122 | December 26, 1870 | December 26, 1870 |
| Scott, Sarah A. | Hollandsworth, Johnson | C/116 | July 5, 1875 | July 5, 1875 |
| Scruggs, Fannie | Thompson, Dan (col.) | F/68 | September 21, 1895 | September 21, 1895 |
| Scrugs, Ed | Floyd, Fan | C/304 | December 8, 1884 | December 8, 1884 |
| Scurlock, America | Brashers, J. L. | A2/46 | February 5, 1856 | February 6, 1856 |
| Scurlock, H. N. | Carrick, Eliza | C/430 | January 26, 1891 | January 19, 1891 |
| Sea, Abb | Talley, Ada | C/376 | November 25, 1886 | November 25, 1886 |

| Groom or Bride | Groom or Bride | Book/Page | Date of License | Date of Marriage |
|---|---|---|---|---|
| Seal, John | Woodside, Miss Mary | B/62 | February 13, 1868 | February 13, 1868 |
| Seal, Sarh Jane | Shearly, Newton | A2/41 | September 26, 1855 | Returns Missing |
| Seal, Thursey A. Miss | Wilson, Benjamin Jr. | B/38 | January 19, 1867 | January 22, 1867 |
| Seales, Martha E. Miss | Hopkins, Samuel A. | A2/52 | December 16, 1856 | No Return |
| Seals, B. F. | Campbell, Miss Hattie | C/454 | February 10, 1892 | February 11, 1892 |
| Seals, James | Baley, Miss Martha A. | B/130 | April 12, 1871 | April 12, 1871 |
| Seals, Martha A. | Marker, H. B. | A2/110 | December 2, 1863 | December 3, 1863 |
| Seals, Radege | Mears, Hallie | F/124 | August 4, 1897 | August 5, 1897 |
| Seat, Nancy M. Miss | Wamach, Robert | A2/23 | February 10, 1853 | February 10, 1853 |
| Seates, Alisold | Cox, William H. | A/26 | March 4, 1840 | No Return |
| Seawell, Elmira L. Miss | Miller, William C. | A/41 | September 25, 1841 | September 26, 1841 |
| Seawell, Frances M. | Bates, Miss Abagail | A/58 | January 5, 1842 | January 5, 1842 |
| Seawell, Susan C. Miss | Henderson, James T. | A/78 | May 20, 1845 | May 20, 1845 |
| Seay, Wm | Flaners, Mary | C/364 | August 19, 1886 | August 19, 1886 |
| See, Andrew | Bogle, Nancy M. | A2/115 | July 21, 1864 | No Return |
| Sellard, Malissa | Hancock, John | B/70 | September 15, 1865 | September 16, 1865 |
| Sellars, Helen | Hale, H. G. | C/152 | January 11, 1877 | January 11, 1877 |
| Sellars, Jack | Milligan, Susan | C/154 | January 22, 1877 | No Return |
| Sellars, Jordan B. | Crulee, Eliza | A/30 | June 26, 1840 | June 28, 1840 |
| Sellars, Robt | McBroom, Mary | C/160 | April 18, 1877 | April 19, 1877 |
| Sellars, Salina Miss | Brown, Martin | A/120 | February, 13, 1849 | February 13, 1849 |
| Sellars, Susan | Patterson, John | A/41 | September 1, 1841 | September 2, 1841 |
| Sessin, C. I. | Hill, Wm. | A2/38 | January 6, 1855 | No Return |
| Sessom, Albert | Johnson, Mattie | C/398 | August 18, 1887 | August 18, 1887 |
| Sessoms, T. A. | Fuston, Hatty A. | C/406 | October 29, 1887 | October 29, 1887 |
| Sewell, Burt | Franks, Hettie | C/350 | January 14, 1886 | January 14, 1886 |
| Sewell, Emerson | Wamack, Miss Patsey | B/50 | August 3, 1867 | August 4, 1867 |
| Shachelford, Fannie | Cummins, W. G. | F/114 | March 6, 1897 | March 8, 1897 |
| Shacklett, John L. | Bates, Miss Lou | B/32 | December 13, 1866 | December 14, 1866 |
| Shackley, Lenora | Parke, W. I. | F/82 | January 6, 1896 | January 8, 1896 |
| Shanklin, W. T. | Herrich, F. M. | C/230 | November 15, 1879 | November 16, 1879 |
| Shannon McKnight | Withersproon, Thurza Einaline | A/91 | September 28, 1846 | No Return |
| Shaver, J. N. | Alman, Armenta | C/78 | January 3, 1874 | January 4, 1874 |
| Shearly, Newton | Seal, Sarah Jane | A2/41 | September 26, 1855 | Returns Missing |
| Shelby, Deaderna Miss | Smith, John C. | A/35 | January 12, 1841 | January 14, 1841 |
| Shelton, B. F | Inglish, Nancy E. | C/274 | February 28, 1881 | March 2, 1881 |
| Shelton, B. F. | Finley, Sarah E. | C/364 | August 28, 1886 | August 29, 1886 |
| Shelton, B. M. | McCaslin, R. E. | C/114 | June 17, 1875 | June 17, 1875 |
| Shelton, Charles | Crouch, Miss C. G. | C/458 | May 28, 1892 | May 29, 1892 |
| Shelton, Everitt | Underwood, Emma | C/440 | July 25, 1891 | July 26, 1891 |
| Shelton, Henry | Smith, Tabitha | C/34 | August 22, 1872 | August 22, 1872 |
| Shelton, J. B. | Alexander, Dellar | F/106 | December 19, 1896 | Decmeber 20, 1896 |
| Shelton, J. W. | Hollis, Ella | E/217 | October 5, 1889 | October 6, 1889 |
| Shelton, Jno A. | McCaslin, Bell | C/188 | February 21, 1878 | February 21, 1878 |
| Shelton, L. E. D. | Woods, B. F. L. | F/74 | November 6, 1895 | November 7, 1895 |
| Shelton, Margret W. | Jewell, Jacob W. | A/23 | February 1, 1840 | February 2, 1840 |

| Groom or Bride | Groom or Bride | Book/Page | Date of License | Date of Marriage |
|---|---|---|---|---|
| Shelton, Nannie | Scott, H. A. | C/34 | August 14, 1872 | August 14, 1872 |
| Shelton, R. A. | Elam, J. B. | C/270 | January 20, 1881 | January 20, 1881 |
| Shelton, Thomas | Young, Nancy J. | F/74 | November 20, 1895 | November 20, 1895 |
| Shelton, Thomas W. | Bynum, Miss Louisa J. | B/96 | December 21, 1869 | December 21, 1869 |
| Shelton, Zettie | Brandon, Monroe | F/116 | April 29, 1897 | April 29, 1897 |
| Shepherd, Elizabeth Miss | Pendleton, Thomas D. | A/124 | August 3, 1849 | August 4, 1849 |
| Shepherd, F. H. | Wade, Laura | C/224 | September 20, 1879 | September 21, 1879 |
| Sheres, Jane Miss | Brandon, Wm. | A2/38 | February 27, 1855 | No Return |
| Sheriden, John | Williams, Lucy J. | C/464 | September 8, 1892 | September 8, 1892 |
| Sherley | Hicks, G. D. | A2/132 | November 22, 1865 | November 22, 1865 |
| Sherley, Benj. | Melton, Miss Jo | B/124 | January 12, 1871 | January 12, 1871 |
| Sherley, Charles | Melton, Miss E. J. | A2/14 | January 30, 1852 | February 2, 1852 |
| Sherley, Emily Miss | Delang, David | A2/80 | March 14, 1857 | March 15, 1857 |
| Sherley, Luke | Keel, Miss Louisa | A2/84 | February 24, 1859 | February 24, 1859 |
| Sherley, M. J. | Witty, W. W. | C/58 | April 22, 1873 | April 22, 1873 |
| Sherly, Tolbert | Melton, Matilda J. | A2/21 | September 21, 1852 | September 22, 1852 |
| Sherrril, John A. | Cherry, Miss Emaline | A2/76 | September 20, 1855 | September 20, 1855 |
| Shipes, Martha Miss | Philips, Seth | A2/39 | March 19, 1855 | No Return |
| Shipp, Margrett E. | Brewer, Joel | C/322 | January 24, 1885 | January 25, 1885 |
| Shirley, Alfred | Bailey, Miss Sarah N. | A2/136 | January 30, 1866 | January 30, 1866 |
| Shirley, Angeline | Braxton, Patrick | C/162 | June 4, 1877 | No Return |
| Shirley, Calvin C. | Neely, Mary | D/14 | | July 23, 1882 |
| Shirley, Ewing | Mitty, Allis | C/334 | August 6, 1885 | No Return |
| Shirley, Geo T. | Haley, Mary J. | C/184 | January 5, 1878 | January 20, 1878 |
| Shirley, John W. | Baily, Miss Margaret E. | A2/93 | December 28, 1859 | No Return |
| Shirley, Luke | Kell, Miss Louisa | A2/72 | February 21, 1859 | February 24, 1859 |
| Shirley, M. J. | Powell, Hervey | C/286 | July 12, 1883 | July 15, 1883 |
| Shirley, Manervey | Carick, Thomas A. | C/290 | September 1, 1883 | September 4, 1883 |
| Shirley, Martha | Moss, Willie | D/10 | | January 3, 1881 |
| Shirley, Mary | Rollins, Ben | C/330 | April 15, 1885 | April 16, 1885 |
| Shirley, Mary J. | Milligan, Sam D. | C/256 | September 11, 1880 | September 11, 1880 |
| Shirley, R. L. | Bogle, Peny | F/144 | January 19, 1898 | January 19, 1898 |
| Shirley, Robert | Gassaway, Etna | C/426 | December 18, 1890 | December 21, 1890 |
| Shirley, Sarah | Dodson, Carrol | C/278 | May 12, 1881 | No Return |
| Shirley, Tolbert F. | Melton, Miss M. J. | A2/73 | September 21, 1852 | September 22, 1852 |
| Shitt, Servella Miss | Merritt, William | A2/145 | September 22, 1866 | September 23, 1866 |
| Shoelford, Mary E. Miss | Wily, H. A. | A2/41 | August 14, 1855 | Returns Missing |
| Shoemate, Salenda Miss | Star, John | A/63 | June 26, 1843 | June 28, 1843 |
| Shores, Jane | Leigh, John | A2/80 | December 21, 1856 | January 1, 1857 |
| Silvertooth, Elizabeth Miss | Covington, Edmond | A2/13 | December 15, 1851 | December 19, 1851 |
| Simman, C. N. Miss | Pearson, R. C. | B/116 | November 16, 1870 | November 16, 1870 |
| Simmon, Mattie | Zuarles, Alex | F/156 | September 12, 1898 | September 14, 1898 |
| Simmons, A. B. | Teel, Miss M. E. | F/50 | November 27, 1894 | November 28, 1894 |
| Simmons, A. N | Bryant, D. J. | E/2 | January 10, 1888 | January 15, 1888 |
| Simmons, Adam | Cawthorn, Amanda | F/86 | March 4, 1896 | March 5, 1896 |
| Simmons, Andrew | Williams, Josie | F/142 | December 29, 1897 | December 29, 1897 |

| Groom or Bride | Groom or Bride | Book/Page | Date of License | Date of Marriage |
|---|---|---|---|---|
| Simmons, Barbarey | Prater, Wm. | E/183 | June 13, 1889 | No Return |
| Simmons, Barbary Miss | Stanfield, Jefferson | A/47 | February 15, 1842 | February 15, 1842 |
| Simmons, Bettie | Cummins, Wm (col.) | C/370 | October 22, 1886 | No Return |
| Simmons, Elisa | Rodgers, John B. | C/274 | March 3, 1881 | No Return |
| Simmons, H. P. | Holt, Sallie | D/101 | | February 2, 1882 |
| Simmons, Isham | ONeel, Miss Sarah Jane | A/68 | April 10, 1844 | April 10, 1844 |
| Simmons, Isham | Tolivar, Miss Katharine | A/119 | January 5, 1849 | January 5, 1849 |
| Simmons, J. | Lewis, Lucinda | A2/117 | October 30, 1864 | October 31, 1864 |
| Simmons, J. A. | Holt, Roxey | D/18 | | December 7, 1882 |
| Simmons, J. C. | Smith, Sallie | F/46 | October 24, 1894 | October 25, 1894 |
| Simmons, James | Byford, Miss Matilda J. | B/70 | September 11, 1868 | September 12, 1868 |
| Simmons, Jane | Goodwin, R. D. | A2/121 | March 10, 1865 | March 10, 1865 |
| Simmons, Jese | Duncan, Eliza A. | A2/134 | December 22, 1865 | December 24, 1865 |
| Simmons, John | Gilley, Mary | E/11 | January 21, 1888 | January 21, 1888 |
| Simmons, Jothason | Phillips, Annie | F/108 | December 24, 1896 | December 24, 1896 |
| Simmons, Mary E. | Leak, George P. | E/356 | December 10, 1898 | |
| Simmons, Mary E. | Leak, George P. | F/162 | December 10, 1898 | No Return |
| Simmons, Mary E. | Goff, James E. | C/212 | February 28, 1879 | March 2, 1879 |
| Simmons, Mary E. Miss | Byford, Leander | B/60 | December 28, 1867 | December 31, 1867 |
| Simmons, Mattie J. | Parker, D. I. | E/175 | May 2, 1889 | May 2, 1889 |
| Simmons, Prudie | Smith, Thomas | F/84 | February 24, 1896 | February 25, 1896 |
| Simmons, S. K. | Gaither, Zella | F/82 | February 8, 1896 | February 9, 1896 |
| Simmons, Sallie | Duke, C. P. | D/8 | | December 25, 1881 |
| Simmons, W. M. | Bearden, M. J. | C/184 | January 23, 1878 | January 23, 1878 |
| Simmons, W. T. | Williams, Laura | F/56 | January 17, 1895 | January 24, 1895 |
| Simmons, Willey | Catherine, Miss Annie | F/58 | February 3, 1895 | February 3, 1895 |
| Simmons, William | Lasater, Miss Purity | A/47 | January 24, 1842 | January 25, 1842 |
| Simms, M. T. | McAdow, Miss Margaret J. | B/38 | January 14, 1867 | No Return |
| Simon, Jacob | Hill, Mary E. | C/132 | February 2, 1876 | February 3, 1876 |
| Simons, Emiline | Creson, J. F. | C/132 | February 2, 1876 | February 2, 1876 |
| Simons, Joseph | Crockett, Kitty | C/120 | September 27, 1875 | September 28, 1875 |
| Simpson, Andrew S. | Finly, Miss Elenor | A2/53 | January 1, 1857 | No Return |
| Simpson, Cinthy | Webber, John | A2/20 | October 28, 1852 | Return Crossed out |
| Simpson, David | Tolbert, L. N. | C/18 | December 23, 1871 | December 24, 1871 |
| Simpson, Davis E. | Stacy, Mary E. | A2/73 | May 13, 1853 | May 13, 1853 |
| Simpson, E. A. | Summers, Nola | E/244 | December 21, 1889 | December 24, 1889 |
| Simpson, Emma | Patterson, Joseph | E/138 | February 13, 1889 | February 14, 1889 |
| Simpson, G. W. | Todd, L. M. | C/118 | September 11, 1875 | September 12, 1875 |
| Simpson, H. E. | McMahan, Minnie | F/1 | January 14, 1893 | January 15, 1893 |
| Simpson, Isaac T. | Stephens, Miss Melinda C. | A/115 | October 10, 1848 | October10, 1848 |
| Simpson, James | Trollinger, Miss Elizabeth M. | A/97 | February 4, 1847 | February 4, 1847 |
| Simpson, Jane Miss | Baltimore, Joseph | A2/30 | December 19, 1853 | December 20, 1853 |
| Simpson, Joanah F. Miss | Hollis, John H. | B/86 | September 9, 1869 | September 9, 1869 |
| Simpson, John A. | Cherry, Miss Margaret | A/83 | September 11, 1845 | September 12, 1845 |
| Simpson, Lidey | Gannon, Harvy A. | A2/108 | August 30, 1863 | August 30, 1863 |
| Simpson, Louisa Jane Miss | Tinley, Josephus | A/107 | January 19, 1848 | January 19, 1848 |

| Groom or Bride | Groom or Bride | Book/Page | Date of License | Date of Marriage |
|---|---|---|---|---|
| Simpson, Martha A. Miss | Brandon, Jesse B. | A/94 | December 2, 1846 | December 2, 1846 |
| Simpson, Martha J. Miss | McGuire, Thos. G. | A/127 | September 8, 1849 | September 9, 1849 |
| Simpson, Mary Elizabeth Miss | Baltimore, Philip J. | A/116 | November 7, 1848 | November 7, 1848 |
| Simpson, Nancy | Bowenen, Rich | F/64 | July 22, 1895 | July 22, 1895 |
| Simpson, Nova | Summar, Thomas | F/120 | July 23, 1897 | July 24, 1897 |
| Simpson, Olive Miss | Gooding, Abraham | A2/81 | September 19, 1857 | September 20, 1857 |
| Simpson, P. M. | Williams, Mary T. | C/36 | September 4, 1872 | No Return |
| Simpson, Peter | Gannon, Miss Nitha A. | A/108 | February 26, 1848 | February 27, 1848 |
| Simpson, R. Miss | Brandon, A. T. | B/110 | September 6, 1870 | September 6, 1870 |
| Simpson, Rocindy | Alexander, Donnie | F/108 | January 9, 1897 | January 10, 1897 |
| Simpson, Thomas | Aronheart, Nancy Ann | F/48 | November 16, 1894 | November 18, 1874 |
| Simpson, W. C. | Oden, Ophelia | E/50 | June 2, 1888 | June 2, 1888 |
| Simpson, William C. | Odom, Miss Donnie | C/390 | June 2, 1887 | No Return |
| Sims, J. P. | Mangum, M. E. | C/326 | February 9, 1885 | February 9, 1885 |
| Sims, James (col.) | Davis, Drew (col.) | D/4 | | October 9, 1881 |
| Sims, Laura | Neal, Alex | C/236 | December 31, 1879 | December 31, 1879 |
| Sims, Sarah L. (col.) | Wright, Allen (col.) | D/18 | | December 24, 1882 |
| Singleton, H. D. | Warren, Miss S. J. | B/70 | September 2, 1868 | September 2, 1868 |
| Sisom, Josie | Anderson, T. A. | E/107 | December 7, 1888 | December 9, 1888 |
| Sison, J. D. | West, Sarah M. | E/58 | August 10, 1888 | August 11, 1888 |
| Sissam, Lisa A. | Duncan, Peter B. | A2/78 | March 3, 1856 | March 4, 1856 |
| Sissom, Bettie | Cawthone, A. J. | D/19 | | December 28, 1882 |
| Sissom, Calvin | Todd, Miss Martha | B/114 | October 14, 1870 | October 20, 1870 |
| Sissom, Delila C. Miss | Cooper, Isaiah | B/42 | March 14, 1867 | March 14, 1867 |
| Sissom, Emaline Miss | Lyon, N. J. S. | B/32 | November 17, 1866 | November 18, 1866 |
| Sissom, Fred | Lowe, Bettie | F/8 | May 1, 1893 | May 3, 1893 |
| Sissom, H. A. | Cooper, Sara E. | C/36 | September 6, 1872 | September 13, 1872 |
| Sissom, Isah | Heathcock, Anna | A2/117 | November 22, 1864 | December 1, 1864 |
| Sissom, J. H. | Williams, Senna J. | C/118 | August 26, 1875 | August 26, 1875 |
| Sissom, J. L. | Taylor, L. B. | F/4 | February 18, 1893 | February 26, 1893 |
| Sissom, J. M. | Stacy, Emeline | C/274 | December 20, 1880 | December 24, 1880 |
| Sissom, J. T. | Tindell, Sallie A. | D/14 | | August 2, 1882 |
| Sissom, Jesse | Angles, Melinda Jane | A/7 | October 13, 1838 | No Return |
| Sissom, Jesse | Cooper, Mary | C/202 | October 12, 1878 | October 13, 1878 |
| Sissom, John | Perry, Martha E. | A2/107 | February 3, 1863 | February 11, 1863 |
| Sissom, Joseph H. | Ford, Miss Luanna J. | B/114 | October 15, 1870 | October 16, 1870 |
| Sissom, Lillie | Finley, Thomas | F/142 | December 31, 897 | January 2, 1898 |
| Sissom, M. C. | Burchett, A. J. | C/434 | April 4, 1891 | April 5, 1891 |
| Sissom, Malvinia | Hibdon, Isaac F. | C/188 | December 20, 1877 | December 27, 1877 |
| Sissom, Mary C. | Campbell, J. H. | C/442 | July 28, 1891 | July 29, 1891 |
| Sissom, Mattie | Low, Sam | F/60 | March 4, 1895 | March 4, 1895 |
| Sissom, Miss Sarah | Creson, Benjamin F. | A/86 | January 3, 1846 | January 3, 1846 |
| Sissom, Nancy E. | Gooding, J. A. | D/17 | | November 12, 1882 |
| Sissom, Rebecca Mrs. | Jernigan, J. C. | B/74 | December 24, 1868 | December 24, 1868 |
| Sissom, Sarah | Jernigan, Richard | C/58 | April 25, 1873 | April 27, 1873 |
| Sissom, Sarah E. Miss | Cooper, Thomas J. | B/40 | February 20, 1867 | February 21, 1867 |

| Groom or Bride | Groom or Bride | Book/Page | Date of License | Date of Marriage |
|---|---|---|---|---|
| Sissom, Thomas | Webber, Rebecca | A/117 | November 14, 1848 | November 14, 1848 |
| Sissom, Thomas | Carrick, Sarah A. | C/80 | January 19, 1874 | January 25, 1874 |
| Sissom, Thomas | Spry, Miss Callie | E/125 | January 4, 1889 | January 6, 1889 |
| Sissom, W. F. | Bearden, P. A. | C/268 | December 11, 1880 | December 12, 1880 |
| Sissom, W. J. | Tindel, E. A. | C/18 | December 27, 1871 | December 27, 1871 |
| Sissom, W. J. | McBride, S. J. | F/124 | August 6, 1897 | August 12, 1897 |
| Sissom, William | Webber, Miss Sarah | A/69 | June 5, 1844 | June 6, 1844 |
| Sissom, Wm | Ring, L. A. | C/150 | December 8, 1876 | October 15, 1877 |
| Sissom, Wm. J. | Tobert, Miss Permeline J. | B/96 | December 14, 1869 | No Retrun |
| Sissom, Wm. T. | Elledge, Eliza J. | C/168 | August 21, 1877 | August 23, 1877 |
| Sissome, James | Sissome, Miss Nancy | A2/70 | November 17, 1858 | November 17, 1858 |
| Sissome, Nancy Miss | Sissome, James | A2/70 | November 17, 1858 | November 17, 1858 |
| Sissoms, Mary A. C. Miss | Cooper?, James W. | B/116 | November 20, 1870 | November 20, 1870 |
| Sisson, J. D. | West, Sarah M. | E/77 | August 10, 1888 | August 12, 1888 |
| Skirlock, John | Jones, A. D. | C/220 | July 26, 1879 | No Return |
| Skirlock, M. C. | Womack, H. B. | C/182 | December 24, 1877 | December 25, 1877 |
| Skirlock, Sallie | St.John, Thomas G. | E/110 | December 19, 1888 | December 20, 1888 |
| Skurlock, John | Robinson, Sallie | E/98 | November 6, 1888 | November 6, 1888 |
| Skurlock, Lucinda Miss | Brashears, Alexander | A/112 | July 26, 1848 | July 26, 1848 |
| Slendly, Sarah Miss | Cooper, M. D. L. | A2/63 | February 3, 1858 | February 3, 1858 |
| Sloan, W. A. | Davenport, Fanny | C/198 | September 21, 1878 | No Return |
| Slone, Ruth | Smith, Nimrod | A2/91 | February 6, 1860 | No Return |
| Smart, D. C. | Hollis, J. E. | D/23 | | January 23, 1883 |
| Smith Miss Biddy | Melton, Joseph | A/41 | October 2, 1841 | October 5, 1841 |
| Smith S. F. | Maroony, A. D. | E/24 | March 1, 1888 | March 1, 1888 |
| Smith, A. A. | Alexander, Ella | F/172 | March 13, 1899 | March 15, 1899 |
| Smith, A. B. | Stone, M. E. | C/14 | November 9, 1871 | November 9, 1871 |
| Smith, A. M. | Bryson, S. S. | C/72 | November 18, 1873 | No Return |
| Smith, Adaline | Willard, Beverly | A2/107 | April 15, 1863 | No Return |
| Smith, Albert | McKnight, Elizabeth | B/2 | August 21, 1865 | August 26, 1865 |
| Smith, Amanda | Parton, Wiley | E/146 | March 23, 1889 | March 24, 1889 |
| Smith, Andrew | St. John, Miss Katharine | A/126 | September 5, 1849 | September 5, 1849 |
| Smith, Ann F. Miss | Davenport, Warren | B/66 | July 9, 1868 | July 9, 1868 |
| Smith, B. D. | Greer, J. H. | D/6 | | November 6, 1881 |
| Smith, Bell | Stacey, Gideon | C/418 | September 24, 1890 | September 25, 1890 |
| Smith, Benjamin | Moore, Miss Nancy E. | A/109 | March 6, 1848 | No Return |
| Smith, Brown (col.) | Bowlin, Mattie | C/440 | July 11, 1891 | No Return |
| Smith, Buck (col.) | McKnight, Wanda (col.) | F/62 | March 26, 1895 | No Return |
| Smith, C. G. O. | Andrews, Elizabeth | A2/9 | January 7, 1851 | No Return |
| Smith, Candis Miss | Murphy, Robt. | A2/40 | April 12, 1855 | Return Missing |
| Smith, Carline | Naper, John | A2/97 | No Dates | |
| Smith, Caroline Miss | Woods, James H. | A2/19 | August 30, 1852 | September 2, 1852 |
| Smith, Cassinda | Mason, James G. | A/8 | November 15, 1838 | November 18, 1838 |
| Smith, Copen | Lewellen, Ellen | A2/130 | October 30, 1865 | October 30, 1865 |
| Smith, Corddie | Davenport, Wm. | E/79 | September 20, 1888 | September 20, 1888 |
| Smith, Dave | Mitchell, Mary | C/320 | December 18, 1884 | No Return |

| Groom or Bride | Groom or Bride | Book/Page | Date of License | Date of Marriage |
|---|---|---|---|---|
| Smith, E. N. Miss | Adams, Wm. J. | A2/32 | March 2, 1854 | March 2, 1854 |
| Smith, Elbert M. | Pendleton, Salley A. | F/120 | July 17, 1897 | July 18, 1897 |
| Smith, Eliza | Daniel, Geo. | C/26 | April 24, 1872 | April 25, 1872 |
| Smith, Eliza | Todd, Ive | F/34 | September 13, 1894 | September 13, 1894 |
| Smith, Eliza J. | Burger, W. O. | C/468 | November 22, 1892 | November 24, 1892 |
| Smith, Elizabeth Miss | Gannon, Dillard L. | A2/7 | November 5, 1850 | No Return |
| Smith, Elizabeth Miss | Knox, John G. | B/64 | March 19, 1868 | March 22, 1868 |
| Smith, Emeline | Allen, James | C/46 | December 13, 1872 | December 13, 1872 |
| Smith, Feriba Miss | Brown, John | B/34 | December 19, 1866 | December 20, 1866 |
| Smith, Frances Ann | Moore, Samuel | A/69 | May 15, 1844 | May 18, 1844 |
| Smith, Francis | Williams, John | C/200 | October 12, 1878 | October 13, 1878 |
| Smith, Fred | Hogwood, Lizzie | F/72 | October 3, 1895 | October 10, 1895 |
| Smith, George W. | Mitchell, Mary J. | A2/116 | September 20, 1864 | No Return |
| Smith, Greenberry | Barratt, Miss Polly | A/114 | September 26, 1848 | October 5, 1848 |
| Smith, Harvey | Winnett, Tabitha | C/146 | October 14, 1876 | October 15, 1876 |
| Smith, Henry | Sullivan, Miss Manerva | A/51 | July 26, 1842 | July 26, 1842 |
| Smith, Isaac | Elkins, Calidonia | A2/114 | May 18, 1864 | May 18, 1864 |
| Smith, Isabela Miss | Williams, John | A2/70 | December 1, 1858 | December 1, 1858 |
| Smith, J. B. | Lowe, Frances E. | C/56 | April 26, 1873 | April 27, 1873 |
| Smith, J. B. | West, Anna | C/236 | December 28, 1879 | No Return |
| Smith, J. B. | Finley, M. C. | C/306 | March 15, 1884 | March 16, 1884 |
| Smith, J. C. | Fagan, Miss Elizabeth A. | A/119 | January 26, 1849 | January 28, 1849 |
| Smith, James | Scott, Mary Drue | E/188 | July 5, 1889 | July 5, 1889 |
| Smith, James G. | Morgan, Miss Delila C. | A2/136 | January 17, 1866 | January 18, 1866 |
| Smith, Jane | Ashworth, Thomas C. | A/55 | November 4, 1842 | November 4, 1842 |
| Smith, Jane Miss | Gan, Forest | C/390 | June 27, 1887 | No Return |
| Smith, Jas. I. | St. John, M. J. | A2/91 | December 10, 1859 | December 10, 1859 |
| Smith, Jennie Miss | Bush, W. H. | C/392 | June 30, 1887 | No Return |
| Smith, Jennie Miss | Bush, W. H. | C/392 | June 30, 1887 | June 30, 1887 |
| Smith, Jesse | Fann, Miss Melissa | A/100 | July 13, 1847 | Return Not Executed |
| Smith, Joe | Peoples, Parthena | C/284 | June 20, 1883 | July 1, 1883 |
| Smith, Joel | Merritt, Miss Mary A. | A2/144 | September 4, 1866 | September 4, 1866 |
| Smith, John | Thompson, Miss Barbary | A/80 | July 10, 1845 | July 10, 1845 |
| Smith, John | Thompson, Miss Barbary | A/81 | July 10, 1845 | July 10, 1845 |
| Smith, John | Sullins, Miss Polly | A2/3 | July 13, 1850 | July 13, 1850 |
| Smith, John | Jetton, Mary | E/257 | January 4, 1890 | No Return |
| Smith, John | Curlee, D. E. | F/32 | February 15, 1894 | No Return |
| Smith, John C. | Shelby, Miss Deaderna | A/35 | January 12, 1841 | January 14, 1841 |
| Smith, John Henry | Gann, Mattie | F/138 | November 19, 1897 | November 19, 1897 |
| Smith, John J. | Newgent, Mrs. Judah | A/111 | May 10, 1848 | May 11, 1848 |
| Smith, John R. | Derryberry, Miss Barbary | A2/7 | November 6, 1850 | Return Not Endorsed |
| Smith, Joseph | Hill, Miss Lucinda | A/124 | February 20, 1849 | February 22, 1849 |
| Smith, Joseph F. | Jones, Miss Anne F. | A/93 | November 13, 1846 | November 13, 1846 |
| Smith, Josephine A. | Spicer, Solomon | A2/125 | August 19, 1865 | August 19, 1865 |
| Smith, Julia | Hale, George | C/220 | August 5, 1879 | August 6, 1879 |
| Smith, K. J. Miss | Owenby, L. M. | B/58 | December 24, 1867 | No Return |

| Groom or Bride | Groom or Bride | Book/Page | Date of License | Date of Marriage |
|---|---|---|---|---|
| Smith, Laura | Barnes, Bill | C/338 | September 27, 1885 | September 27, 1885 |
| Smith, Lizzie | Carter, Thos. | C/68 | October 8, 1873 | October 9, 1873 |
| Smith, Lucy Miss | Moore, J. B. | F/68 | August 30, 1895 | August 31, 1895 |
| Smith, Logie | Hollandworth, Jas. O. | F/56 | January 18, 1895 | January 20, 1895 |
| Smith, Lorenzo D. | Crow, Miss Martha Jane | A/87 | February 26, 1846 | February 26, 1846 |
| Smith, Lou | Bryson, Nathan | C/90 | August 6, 1874 | August 6, 1874 |
| Smith, Lou | Bryson, Nathan | C/92 | August 6, 1874 | No Return |
| Smith, Lucy Miss | Moore, J. B. | F/68 | August 30, 1895 | August 31, 1895 |
| Smith, M. A. | Foster, W. R. | C/100 | November 28, 1874 | December 3, 1874 |
| Smith, M. D. | Weedon, Miss Sallie M. | B/80 | March 24, 1869 | March 25, 1869 |
| Smith, M. E. Miss | Goodloe, A. M. | A2/49 | June 17, 1856 | June 17, 1856 |
| Smith, M. P. | Hibden, Malissie | C/292 | September 16, 1883 | September 16, 1883 |
| Smith, M. S. | Moon, Mary F. | C/52 | February 7, 1873 | February 8, 1873 |
| Smith, Maggie | Higgins, W. F | C/222 | August 23, 1879 | August 24, 1879 |
| Smith, Maggie E. | Youree, J. P. | C/142 | August 7, 1876 | No Return |
| Smith, Margrett Miss | Oglesby, S. H. | C/2 | June 7, 1871 | June 29, 1871 |
| Smith, Martha A. Miss | Richardson, May | A2/142 | August 6, 1866 | August 6, 1866 |
| Smith, Mary | Hays, Benjamin J. | A/60 | March 7, 1843 | March 7, 1843 |
| Smith, Mary | McCrary, Abram | B/18 | December 16, 1869 | December 16, 1869 |
| Smith, Mary | Hollandsworth, J. M. | D/8 | | December 25, 1881 |
| Smith, Mary Ann Miss | Price, James M. | A/96 | January 5, 1847 | January 5, 1847 |
| Smith, Mary F. | Odom, Robt | C/138 | May 26, 1876 | No Return |
| Smith, Mary L. | Wallace, Wm. (Wilburn H.) | C/40 | October 2, 1872 | October 3, 1872 |
| Smith, Mary Frances | Nealey, Medford C. | A2/127 | September 14, 1865 | September 17, 1865 |
| Smith, Mary Miss | Petty, G. A. | A2/77 | January 14, 1856 | February 3, 1856 |
| Smith, Mary Y. Miss | Merratt, Josiah | A/66 | December 6, 1843 | No Return |
| Smith, Mat | Francis, M. C. | C/348 | January 9, 1886 | January 10, 1886 |
| Smith, Mattie | Pinkerton, George | F/66 | July 12, 1895 | July 12, 1895 |
| Smith, Minnie | Brevard, W. F. | D/9 | | December 29, 1881 |
| Smith, Minnie (col.) | Johnson, William (col.) | F/124 | August 3, 1897 | August 3, 1897 |
| Smith, Mollie | Patterson, J. H. | F/96 | September 27, 1896 | September 27, 1896 |
| Smith, Moses A. | Smith, Miss Nancy | A/92 | October 8, 1846 | October 8, 1846 |
| Smith, Nancy Miss | Smith, Moses A. | A/92 | October 8, 1846 | October 8, 1846 |
| Smith, Nancy M. | Davenport, Kerry | C/354 | March 7, 1886 | March 11, 1886 |
| Smith, Nancy Miss | Smith, William | A/82 | July 25, 1845 | July 27, 1845 |
| Smith, Nannie | Northcutt, Ans | F/152 | July 14, 1898 | July 15, 1898 |
| Smith, Neal H. | Sauls, Mary | C/354 | February 20, 1886 | February 21, 1886 |
| Smith, Neil H. | Davenport, Miss Fanny E. | A/106 | December 21, 1847 | December 22, 1847 |
| Smith, Nellie | Barrett, George | F/4 | February 23, 1893 | February 24, 1893 |
| Smith, Nimrod | Slone, Ruth | A2/91 | February 6, 1860 | No Return |
| Smith, Nimrod | Moore, Ruth | A2/94 | February 6, 1860 | No Return |
| Smith, O. J. Miss | Brandon, J. M. | C/2 | July 5, 1871 | July 13, 1871 |
| Smith, P. A. | Odom, J. S. | C/286 | July 23, 1883 | July 23, 1883 |
| Smith, Polly Ann Miss | Bogle, Daniel | A/37 | February 27, 1841 | February 28, 1841 |
| Smith, Polly Miss | Rood, C. C. | A/105 | December 6, 1847 | December 6, 1847 |
| Smith, Rachel A. | Melton, E. R. | A2/100 | July 25, 1860 | July 25, 1860 |

| Groom or Bride | Groom or Bride | Book/Page | Date of License | Date of Marriage |
|---|---|---|---|---|
| Smith, Robert G. | Mitchell, Miss Mira A. | B/58 | December 11, 1867 | December 12, 1867 |
| Smith, S. C. Mrs. | Bethell, C. F. | B/70 | October 2, 1868 | October 2, 1868 |
| Smith, S. J. | Jamison, T. G. | A2/59 | November 16, 1857 | November 19, 1857 |
| Smith, Sallie | Simmons, J. C. | F/46 | October 24, 1894 | October 25, 1894 |
| Smith, Sarah | Adams, W. F. | C/60 | July 8, 1873 | July 9, 1873 |
| Smith, Sarah Miss | Davenport, John | B/116 | November 10, 1870 | November 10, 1870 |
| Smith, Sarah E. | Ruckley, Alexander | C/120 | September 24, 1875 | September 26, 1875 |
| Smith, Sarrah J. Miss | Grimes, G. G. C. | A2/22 | January 13, 1853 | January 13, 1853 |
| Smith, Sophia Ann Miss | Boyd, John B. | A2/74 | February 2, 1854 | February 2, 1854 |
| Smith, Susan L. Miss | Taylor, James T. | A2/76 | August 16, 1855 | August 16, 1855 |
| Smith, T. B. | Baly, Mary | A2/98 | June 20, 1860 | June 20, 1860 |
| Smith, Tabitha | Shelton, Henry | C/34 | August 22, 1872 | August 22, 1872 |
| Smith, Thomas | Fowler, Josephine | A2/106 | November 12, 1862 | No Return |
| Smith, Thomas | Simmons, Prudie | F/84 | February 24, 1896 | February 25, 1896 |
| Smith, Thos. C. | Gilley, Martha | C/120 | August 7, 1875 | August 8, 1875 |
| Smith, Tinnie | Tittle, Sam | F/148 | March 26, 1898 | March 27, 1898 |
| Smith, Viola (col.) | Vernon, Lewis (col.) | F/122 | July 31, 1897 | July 31, 1897 |
| Smith, W. J. | Finley, Miss Frances | A2/144 | June 30, 1866 | July 1, 1866 |
| Smith, W. R. | Woods, Miss I. M. | F/86 | April 16, 1896 | April 16, 1896 |
| Smith, William | Smith, Miss Nancy | A/82 | July 25, 1845 | July 27, 1845 |
| Smith, William | Moody, Miss Margarett H. | A2/98 | January 19, 1860 | January 19, 1860 |
| Smith, William | Fletcher, Miss Mary | C/378 | December 24, 1886 | December 24, 1886 |
| Smith, William A. | Barrett, Miss Eliza Tennessee Gowen | B/36 | December 28, 1866 | January 2, 1867 |
| Smith, William H. | McKnight, Miss Margarett E. | A/94 | December 23, 1846 | December 25, 1846 |
| Smith, William J. | Marshall, Miss Martha C. | A2/3 | July 26, 1850 | No Return |
| Smith, Wm | Ledbetter, Caroline | C/134 | February 12, 1876 | February 15, 18786 |
| Smith, Wm. | Ford, Mary | A2/114 | May 13, 1864 | May 15, 1864 |
| Smith, Wm. | Fugitt, Elizabeth | C/180 | December 13, 1877 | No Return |
| Smith, Zachariah | Lansden, Susan C. | A/74 | November 9, 1844 | No Return |
| Smithe, Stella | Foster, Sam | F/104 | December 7, 1896 | December 10, 1896 |
| Smithsen, Wm. C. | Powell, Miss Rhoda | A2/53 | January 24, 1857 | No Return |
| Smithson, Albert | Clark, Annie E. | F/18 | September 23, 1893 | September 23, 1893 |
| Smithson, Allen | Smithson, Sarah | F/58 | February 9, 1895 | February 10, 1895 |
| Smithson, Alma C. | Young, P. V. | F/164 | December 24, 1898 | December 25, 1898 |
| Smithson, Annie | Hobbs, James | D/23 | | December 27, 1884 |
| Smithson, Annie | Hobbs, James | C/322 | December 27, 1884 | No Return |
| Smithson, C. C. | Lafevers, Laura | C/430 | February 19, 1891 | February 19, 1891 |
| Smithson, Cledar | Young, R. W. | F/150 | May 19, 1898 | May 22, 1898 |
| Smithson, D. A. | Wilson, Catherine | C/146 | October 28, 1876 | October 29, 1876 |
| Smithson, D. C. | Campbell, Docia | C/106 | January 19, 1875 | January 19, 1875 |
| Smithson, D. S. | Ferrell, Miss Samantha | E/143 | March 13, 1889 | March 15, 1889 |
| Smithson, David | Jones, Sarah | C/150 | December 27, 1876 | December 28, 1876 |
| Smithson, Dessie | Winnett, Willie | C/432 | February 25, 1891 | No Return |
| Smithson, Dover | Owen, Thomas | E/111 | December 19, 1888 | December 20, 1888 |
| Smithson, E. W. | Lefevers, Mollie | F/102 | November 29, 1896 | November 29, 1896 |

| Groom or Bride | Groom or Bride | Book/Page | Date of License | Date of Marriage |
|---|---|---|---|---|
| Smithson, Ellen | Hobbs, John | F/108 | January 9, 1897 | January 12, 1897 |
| Smithson, Eliza | Stone, Benj. | C/122 | October 23, 1875 | October 24, 1875 |
| Smithson, Emma | Young, Willey | F/80 | January 4, 1896 | January 5, 1896 |
| Smithson, Frasier | Young, Lennie | F/94 | August 29, 1896 | August 30, 1896 |
| Smithson, G. W. B. | Williams, M. J. | C/356 | April 6, 1886 | April 11, 1886 |
| Smithson, Gardner | Duke, Miss Sarah | C/452 | December 30, 1891 | December 31, 1891 |
| Smithson, Gavena Miss | Hobbs, James | C/390 | June 30, 1887 | No Return |
| Smithson, H. | Bragg, Miss Sarah | A2/42 | October 2, 1855 | October 4, 1855 |
| Smithson, Helen A. | Northcut, H. E. | F/30 | January 15, 1894 | No Return |
| Smithson, Ida | Lemons, Sam | F/34 | October 6, 1894 | October 7, 1894 |
| Smithson, Ida | Jones, L. C. | C/470 | December 14, 1892 | December 15, 1892 |
| Smithson, J. A. | Smithson, Sarah | F/58 | February 4, 1895 | No Return |
| Smithson, J. A. | Duke, Nancy | F/112 | February 23, 1897 | February 27, 1897 |
| Smithson, J. F. | Estes, Martha | C/358 | May 10, 1886 | May 10, 1886 |
| Smithson, J. J. | Barrett, M. E. | C/246 | April 26, 1880 | May 5, 1880 |
| Smithson, James | Hutchins, Patsy | A/29 | June 3, 1840 | June 4, 1840 |
| Smithson, James | Tenpenny, Sallie | C/258 | October 6, 1880 | October 6, 1880 |
| Smithson, James A. | Miles, Miss Mahala A. | A/97 | February 11, 1847 | February 11, 1847 |
| Smithson, John M. F. | Boren, Sarah E. | B/72 | October 7, 1868 | October 11, 1868 |
| Smithson, Joshua C. | Bank, Miss Lucy P. | A2/36 | October 17, 1854 | October 17, 1854 |
| Smithson, Lavisa J. Miss | Wilson, A. F. | A2/138 | February 20, 1866 | No Return |
| Smithson, Lee | Woods, Ida | C/470 | December 17, 1892 | December 22, 1892 |
| Smithson, Lennie Miss | Campbell, G. W. | F/82 | February 1, 1896 | February 2, 1896 |
| Smithson, Lona | Melton, A. | F/10 | June 17, 1893 | June 18, 1893 |
| Smithson, Levina Miss | Hobbs, James | C/392 | June 28, 1887 | June 30, 1887 |
| Smithson, Marisu | West, Dallas | C/364 | September 1, 1886 | No Return |
| Smithson, Mary | Moon, Pierce | C/158 | February 24, 1877 | February 25, 1877 |
| Smithson, Milley | Dugan, Roy | E/380 | October 29, 1898 | |
| Smithson, Millie | Logan, Roy | F/160 | October 29, 1898 | October 30, 1898 |
| Smithson, Mollie | Higgins, Noah | F/154 | August 10, 1898 | August 10, 1898 |
| Smithson, N. B. | Phillips, Jennie | C/360 | July 3, 1886 | July 4, 1886 |
| Smithson, Nancy Miss | Merritt, Harman | A/120 | February 21, 1849 | February 21, 1849 |
| Smithson, Olivia C. | Young, P. V. | E/338 | December 24, 1898 | |
| Smithson, Riston | Muncy, Miss Hester | B/114 | November 4, 1870 | November 6, 1870 |
| Smithson, S. V. | Dixon, A. J. | F/176 | May 4, 1899 | May 7, 1899 |
| Smithson, Sarah | Smithson, J. A. | F/58 | February 4, 1895 | No Return |
| Smithson, Sarah | Smithson, Allen | F/58 | Febraruy 9, 1895 | February 10, 1895 |
| Smithson, Sarah J. | Kirby, Robt. S. | C/12 | October 4, 1871 | No Return |
| Smithson, Susan | Fuller, Robert | C/198 | September 19, 1878 | September 22, 1878 |
| Smithson, Susie B. | Hale, James L. | C/114 | July 2, 1875 | July 4, 1875 |
| Smithson, Thos. G. | Patton, Callie | C/176 | October 27, 1877 | October 28, 1877 |
| Smithson, W. L. | O'Neal, Dora | F/150 | May 2, 1898 | May 3, 1898 |
| Smithson, W. V. | Hailey, Fannie | C/370 | October 9, 1886 | No Return |
| Smithson, William C. | Kersey, Miss Luan | A/131 | December 21, 1849 | December 23, 1849 |
| Smithson, Wm. | O'Neal, Wade | C/98 | October 12, 1875 | October 17, 1874 |
| Smoot, Arthur N. | Gooding, Miss Sarah | A2/4 | August 23, 1850 | August 25, 1850 |

| Groom or Bride | Groom or Bride | Book/Page | Date of License | Date of Marriage |
|---|---|---|---|---|
| Sneed, Josephine | Good, Stephen | C/226 | October 1, 1879 | No Retrun |
| Sneed, Mose | Grimett, Patsey | C/26 | March 14, 1872 | March 14, 1872 |
| Sneed, Moses | Odom, Judea Ann | B/12 | December 28, 1867 | December 28, 1867 |
| Sneed, Paralee | Pedon, Isaac | C/134 | February 13, 1876 | February 13, 1876 |
| Sneed, T. H. Miss | Fann, G. | A2/57 | September 26, 1857 | September 26, 1857 |
| Snipes, C. W. | Hollis, Miss Mayn | A2/13 | December 25, 1851 | December 25, 1851 |
| Snow, Samuel | Adamson, Alse | B/98 | January 18, 1870 | January 18, 1870 |
| Soap, Gorge, W. | Underwood, Nancy C. | A2/18 | June 3, 1852 | June 3, 1852 |
| Soape, Elizabeth Ann Miss | Byford, James Hardy | A/110 | April 13, 1848 | April 13, 1848 |
| Soape, Lucy F. Miss | Moore, Jacob | A/47 | February 3, 1842 | February 3, 1842 |
| Soape, Sarah Miss | Reed, George | A/112 | June 16, 1848 | June 17, 1847 |
| Soape, William C. | McCaslin, Miss Margarett E. | A/124 | August 31, 1848 | August 31, 1848 |
| Soape, Zenobia F. Miss | Foster, Robert M. | A2/8 | December 5, 1850 | December 5, 1850 |
| Somers, William | Mooneham, Tennessee | C/378 | December 24, 1886 | December 26, 1886 |
| Southerland, Archibald | Lawson, Mary | A/55 | November 1, 1842 | November 1, 1842 |
| Southerland, Polly Miss | Gilson, Robert | A/88 | March 25, 1846 | March 26, 1846 |
| Southerland, Rachael Miss | Green, Thomas L. | A/50 | June 4, 1842 | June 5, 1842 |
| Southern, Jemima Miss | Gibson, Richard D. | A/62 | April 13, 1843 | April 17, 1863 |
| Sowell, Nettie | Tubb, John | F/20 | October 21, 1893 | October 22, 1893 |
| Sowell, Sarh Jane | Tucker, David | A/68 | February 17, 1844 | February 19, 1844 |
| Sowell, William F. | Elkins, Dosia E. | B/42 | March 20, 1867 | March 20, 1867 |
| Sowell, Wm. | Hyse, Mary | C/182 | December 29, 1877 | December 29, 1877 |
| Sowells, Wm. | Davis, M. A. | F/128 | August 25, 1897 | August 26, 1897 |
| Sowels, M. E. | Woods, W. L. | C/290 | August 13, 1883 | August 22, 1883 |
| Sowels, M. L. | Todd, Richard D. | C/294 | October 7, 1883 | October ??, 1883 |
| Sowls, Allie | Davenport, J. M. | F/58 | February 12, 1895 | No Return |
| Spain, W. M. | Poterfield, M. J. | C/126 | December 14, 1875 | No Return |
| Spangler, Abigail Miss | Whitamore, Jesse G. | A/66 | December 21, 1843 | December 24, 1843 |
| Spangler, Asa | Patton, Miss Caroline M. | A/63 | July 15, 1843 | July 16, 1843 |
| Spangler, David | Rhea, Miss Betsy | A/108 | February 24, 1848 | No Return |
| Spangler, Disa Miss | Ross, James | A/110 | April 10, 1848 | April 11, 1848 |
| Spangler, J. H. | Owenby, M. E. | C/258 | October 13, 1880 | October 17, 1880 |
| Spangler, John M. | Hogwood, Roxanna | C/176 | November 3, 1877 | November 4, 1877 |
| Spangler, M. D. | Elam, M. R. | C/108 | February 18, 1875 | February 19, 1875 |
| Spangler, Mary E. | Brewer, Joel | A2/94 | February 22, 1860 | No Return |
| Spangler, Milly Miss | Swaner, John | A2/16 | March 11, 1852 | March 16, 1852 |
| Spangler, N. D. | St. John, A. H. | C/22 | January 31, 1872 | No Return |
| Spangler, Samuel | Whitsmore, Miss Tabitha | A/42 | October 14, 1841 | October 14, 1841 |
| Spangler, Samuel | Banks, Lethie J. | A2/44 | November 29, 1855 | November 29, 1855 |
| Spangler, Sarah A. | St. John, F. A. | A2/118 | December 21. 1964 | No Return |
| Sparkman, P. M. | Davis, Martha A. E. | D/17 | | November 2, 1882 |
| Sparks, Alexander | Moore, Miss Frances C. | B/70 | September 18, 1868 | September 18, 1868 |
| Sparks, Better Miss | Etherly, John | C/384 | February 26, 1887 | No Return |
| Sparks, Mariah C. | Amos, W. A. | C/372 | October 23, 1886 | No Return |
| Sparks, Mary F. Miss | Douglas, James T. | C/4 | August 5, 1871 | August 6, 1871 |
| Sparks, Mary T. | Tenpenny, Lish (Elijah) | C/238 | January 9, 1880 | January 10, 1880 |

| Groom or Bride | Groom or Bride | Book/Page | Date of License | Date of Marriage |
|---|---|---|---|---|
| Sparks, W. B. | Odom, Miss Mary E. | A2/62 | January 6, 1858 | January 7, 1858 |
| Sparks, William | Pendleton, Miss Elizabeth | A2/149 | May 11, 1866 | No Return |
| Spatton, Nathan | Lasiter, Sinia E. | B/14 | September 4, 1868 | September 4, 1868 |
| Spears, Elizabeth | Jones, John M. | D/5 | | October 6, 1881 |
| Spears, Geo. M. | Wood, Mary E. | C/76 | December 22, 1873 | December 22, 1873 |
| Spears, Samuel | Mullins, Miss Vina Jane | A/31 | July 11, 1840 | July 13, 1840 |
| Spears, Samuel | Morgan, Delina | C/116 | July 12, 1875 | No Return |
| Spiceer, Henry | Pendleton, Sarah | D/22 | | March 7, 1883 |
| Spicer, Emma | Todd, J. W. | A2/132 | November 25, 1865 | November 25, 1865 |
| Spicer, Henry | Holyfield, Miss Sally | A/39 | June 10, 1841 | June 10, 1841 |
| Spicer, Henry | Murfee, Miss Mary | C/384 | February 26, 1886 | No Return |
| Spicer, Henry | Wilson, Jennie | F/172 | March 16, 1899 | March 16, 1899 |
| Spicer, James H. | Todd, Martha A. | D/101 | | February 7, 1882 |
| Spicer, Joseph A. | Holland, Elizabeth | A2/106 | January 13, 1863 | No Return |
| Spicer, Sarah | Fowler, F. L. | D/19 | | December 27, 1882 |
| Spicer, Solomon | Hatfield, Delitha | A/24 | February 6, 1840 | February 6, 1840 |
| Spicer, Solomon | Smith, Josephine A. | A2/125 | August 19, 1865 | August 19, 1865 |
| Spicer, Vester | Elkins, S. W. | F/46 | October 20, 1894 | October 21, 1894 |
| Spicer, William | Nancy Anne Youngblood | A/30 | June 18, 1840 | June 18, 1840 |
| Spicer, William | Cantrell, Nora Bell | C/416 | September 10, 1890 | No Date |
| Spicer, Wm | McDougle, Eliza | C/48 | December 20, 1872 | December 22, 1872 |
| Spicer, Wm | West, Vesta | F/32 | February 28, 1894 | February 28, 1894 |
| Spidell, R. S. | Turner, Jennie | F/32 | February 24, 1894 | February 25, 1894 |
| Spidle, R. S. | Kennady, Miss Frances M. | A2/48 | June 15, 1856 | June 16, 1856 |
| Spradley, Fannie | Vinson, F. Buck | F/64 | July 25, 1895 | July 4,1895 |
| Spradley, Minnie Miss | Taylor, J. A. | C/450 | November 14, 1891 | November 15, 1891 |
| Spradley, W. T. | Womack, Margarette | E/266 | January 31, 1890 | No Return |
| Spradlin, Elmira C. Miss | Hatfield, William C. | A/86 | March 3, 1846 | March 4, 1846 |
| Spray, J. M. | Burt, Miss Sarah | A2/19 | August 23, 1852 | No Return |
| Spry, Allen | Parker, Miss Caroline | A2/62 | January 21, 1858 | No Return |
| Spry, Callie Miss | Sissom, Thomas | E/125 | January 4, 1889 | January 6, 1889 |
| Spry, Elizabeth | Tabour, Charles O. | A2/25 | July 18, 1853 | July 19, 1853 |
| Spry, G. W. | Scissam, Miss Milley E. | A2/75 | December 21, 1854 | December 21, 1854 |
| Spry, G. W. | Moore, Nancy | F/20 | November 2, 1893 | November 2, 1893 |
| Spry, George | Parker, Rebecca | A2/127 | September 14, 1865 | September 15, 1865 |
| Spry, H. A. | Williams, Dennis | C/72 | November 19, 1873 | November 20, 1873 |
| Spry, Harriett | Batimore, J. W. | C/186 | February 19, 1878 | February 21, 1878 |
| Spry, J. H. | Bagett, Rosanar H. | C/218 | July 23, 1879 | July 24, 1879 |
| Spry, J. W. | Stacy, Mary | F/34 | October 3, 1894 | October 4, 1894 |
| Spry, Isabella | Williams, Thos. | C/42 | October 15, 1872 | October 29, 1872 |
| Spry, Mary E. Miss | Parker, T. | C/458 | April 4, 1892 | No Return |
| Spry, Mary M. Miss | Ashly, William C. | A2/1 | March 9, 1850 | March 9, 1850 |
| Spry, May | Byford, C. A. | C/366 | September 16, 1886 | September 19, 1886 |
| Spry, Nancy | Bush, John H. | C/366 | July 23, 1886 | July 25, 1886 |
| Spry, Nancy C. Miss | Roberts, Thomas | A2/148 | May 4, 1866 | No Return |
| Spry, Nancy C. Miss | Hall, Albert E. | B/64 | March 3, 1868 | March 3, 1868 |

| Groom or Bride | Groom or Bride | Book/Page | Date of License | Date of Marriage |
|---|---|---|---|---|
| Spry, Sarah | Holt, Whiteman | C/196 | August 30, 1878 | September 1, 1878 |
| Spry, Thos. A. G. | Reed, Sarah | C/306 | March 4, 1884 | March 9, 1884 |
| Spry, William | Parker, Sarah Elizabeth | A2/2 | March 23, 1850 | March 31, 1850 |
| Spurlock E. J. | Watson, Nancy | D/12 | | March 5, 1882 |
| Spurlock, A. T. Miss | Bogle, T. L. | B/118 | December 7, 1870 | December 7, 1870 |
| Spurlock, B. A. | Spurlock, Nancy A. | C/268 | December 22, 1880 | December 23, 1880 |
| Spurlock, Bettie | Worley, Vann | C/324 | January 13, 1885 | January 14, 1885 |
| Spurlock, Bettie | Worley, Vann | C/324 | January 13, 1885 | January 14, 1885 |
| Spurlock, C. J. F. Miss | Bramer, C. P. | A2/53 | January 8, 1857 | No Return |
| Spurlock, Elija | Melton, Martha | D/5 | | September 29, 1881 |
| Spurlock, Elizabeth Miss | Herriman, Sterling B. | A2/2 | April 27, 1850 | April 28, 1850 |
| Spurlock, Elizabeth Miss | Campbell, G. R. | A2/19 | September 14, 1852 | September 14, 1852 |
| Spurlock, Emaline | Pitts, James | A2/105 | October 17, 1862 | No Return |
| Spurlock, Francis | Markum, Wm. | C/348 | January 9, 1886 | January 9, 1886 |
| Spurlock, Fannie | Brown, Newton | C/320 | December 24, 1884 | December 24, 1884 |
| Spurlock, J. B. | Sullens, Miss Angeline | A2/58 | October 19, 1857 | October 19, 1857 |
| Spurlock, J. D. | Mullinax, Odie | C/422 | November 13, 1890 | November 16, 1890 |
| Spurlock, John | Woods, Mollie | C/124 | November 19, 1875 | November 20, 1875 |
| Spurlock, John | Major, Allice | F/24 | December 2, 1893 | December 2, 1893 |
| Spurlock, John A. | Ferrell, Miss Mary | A/130 | December 27, 1849 | No Return |
| Spurlock, John W. | Miller, Jennie | C/282 | May 10, 1883 | May 10, 1883 |
| Spurlock, Joseph | Vandagriff, Miss Marry A. | A2/88 | September 14, 1859 | September 14, 1859 |
| Spurlock, Joseph | Carmichael, Malissa J. | A2/123 | May 3, 1865 | May 4, 1865 |
| Spurlock, Joseph | Webb, Miss Ibbia | B/98 | January 18, 1870 | January 18, 1870 |
| Spurlock, Josiah Jr. | Howard, Miss Elmira | A/89 | May 28, 1846 | May 28, 1846 |
| Spurlock, Julian | Brim, Osias D. | B/90 | October 28, 1869 | October 28, 1869 |
| Spurlock, Liza | Higgins, Alexander | C/278 | April 2, 1881 | April 3, 1881 |
| Spurlock, Lottie | Thompson, William (col.) | C/446 | September 21, 1891 | September 21, 1891 |
| Spurlock, Mariah D. Miss | Sullivan, Harbert H. | A/123 | July 25, 1849 | July 25, 1849 |
| Spurlock, Martha | Goff, Dillard | C/84 | February 27, 1874 | March 1, 1874 |
| Spurlock, Mary | Watson, Jeff | C/266 | December 4, 1880 | December 5, 1880 |
| Spurlock, Mary E. | Mangrum, Wm., S. | C/230 | November 8, 1879 | November 9, 1879 |
| Spurlock, Mon | Fugett, Lucindy | C/276 | January 19, 1881 | January 19, 1881 |
| Spurlock, Monroe | Merriman, Miss Filia Ann | A2/52 | November 23, 1856 | November 24 1856 |
| Spurlock, Nancy | Melton, Jacob | D/2 | | August 10, 1881 |
| Spurlock, Nancy A. | Spurlock, B. A. | C/268 | December 22, 1880 | December 23, 1880 |
| Spurlock, Nancy Miss | Merriman, Ewin | A2/47 | April 23, 1856 | April 23, 1856 |
| Spurlock, Parmelia A. | Ford, Daniel S. | A/10 | February 22, 1839 | No Return |
| Spurlock, Prudy Miss | Murphrey, W. G. | A2/138 | February 28, 1866 | March 2, 1866 |
| Spurlock, Ruth | Marthis, Geo L. | C/138 | June 21, 1876 | Juen 21, 1876 |
| Spurlock, S. A. Miss | Mason, William C. | B/84 | September 1, 1869 | September 2, 1869 |
| Spurlock, Sarah | Ferrell, John | A/67 | February 15, 1844 | February 15, 1844 |
| Spurlock, Sarah | Sullins, Andrew | D/5 | | October 6, 1881 |
| Spurlock, Sindy (col.) | Weedon, Jim (col.) | F/162 | December 10, 1898 | January 2, 1899 |
| Spurlock, Susanna | Grizzel, Jno R. | C/116 | July 29, 1875 | No Return |
| Spurlock, W. C. | Herriman, Nancy | A/28 | April 23, 1840 | April 23, 1840 |

| Groom or Bride | Groom or Bride | Book/Page | Date of License | Date of Marriage |
|---|---|---|---|---|
| Spurlock, W. F. | Melton, Mollie | F/128 | August 25, 1897 | August 29, 1897 |
| Spurlock, William | Ferrell, Miss Marinda | A/110 | April 28, 1848 | April 30, 1848 |
| Spurlock, Wm. | Nokes, Nancy W. | C/64 | July 31, 1873 | August 1, 1873 |
| Spurlock, Wm. | Young, Mollie | C/346 | December 23, 1885 | December 24, 1885 |
| Spurlock, Wm. M. | Sullins, Susan A. | C/94 | September 21, 1874 | September 22, 1874 |
| Bryson, Susan | Keeton, James | E/199 | August 14, 1889 | August 15, 1889 |
| St. Clair, Benjamin | Hall, M. A. | A2/126 | August 30, 1865 | August 31, 1865 |
| St. John A. L. | Woods, A. C. | C/142 | August 5, 1876 | August ??, 1876 |
| St. John, A. H. | Spangler, N. D. | C/22 | January 31, 1872 | No Return |
| St. John, Alantic | Lowe, Simion | C/252 | August 5, 1880 | August 5, 1880 |
| St. John, Bettie | Todd, Allie L. | C/182 | December 31. 1877 | January 1, 1878 |
| St. John, Betty Miss | McDougle, John | A2/103 | October 2, 1860 | No Return |
| St. John, Callie | Bowers, A. J. | D/17 | | November 30, 1882 |
| St. John, E. A. | Blackwell, J. G. | C/78 | January 3, 1874 | January 3, 1874 |
| St. John, E. B. | Womack, Malisie | F/74 | November 22, 1895 | November 22, 1895 |
| St. John, E. M. | Stone, Miss Jane | A2/22 | December 29, 1852 | December 29, 1852 |
| St. John, Eliza | Todd, Jno . T. | C/64 | August 8, 1873 | August 8, 1873 |
| St. John, Emaline Miss | Herryman, John S. | B/80 | May 4, 1869 | May 5, 1869 |
| St. John, Etter | Woods, J. V. | E/176 | May 6, 1889 | No Return |
| St. John, F. A. | Spangler, Sarah A. | A2/118 | December 21. 1964 | No Return |
| St. John, Floyd | Cumins, Matilda | A/121 | March 8, 1849 | March 8, 1849 |
| St. John, George | Stanley, Elizqbeth | A/15 | July 13, 1839 | July 13, 1839 |
| St. John, George | Pittman, Miss Elizabeth | A/52 | August 2, 1842 | August 4, 1842 |
| St. John, George | Kirby, Miss R. | A2/43 | November 27, 1855 | November 27, 1855 |
| St. John, George | Phimlips, Miss Elizabeth | B/98 | January 8, 1870 | No Return |
| St. John, H. J. | Stone, Miss Buenavista | B/52 | September 11, 1867 | September 11, 1867 |
| St. John, Harmon | Bates, Miss Martha Jane | A/88 | April 29, 1846 | April 30, 1846 |
| St. John, Helen Miss | McCabe, Jeff | C/384 | February 20, 1887 | February 20, 1887 |
| St. John, J. A. | Woods, Eley | C/382 | January 25, 1887 | January 25, 1887 |
| St. John, J. M. | Knox, Miss Mollie | C/378 | December 23, 1886 | December 23, 1886 |
| St. John, J. W. | Espy, M. J. | C/46 | December 16, 1872 | December 22, 1872 |
| St. John, Jennie Miss | Todd, James H. | E/14 | January 26, 1888 | January 26, 1888 |
| St. John, Jennie | McCabe, J. B. | C/346 | December 26, 1885 | December 26, 1885 |
| St. John, John | Edwards, Uphey | A2/54 | January 29, 1857 | January 29, 1857 |
| St. John, John | Kirk, Miss E. | A2/88 | August 31, 1859 | No Return |
| St. John, Jordon | Prater, Octavia | C/394 | July 18, 1887 | July 19, 1887 |
| St. John, Joseph | Perry, Miss Catharine | A2/135 | January 11, 1866 | January 11, 1866 |
| St. John, Katharine Miss | Smith, Andrew | A/126 | September 5, 1849 | September 5, 1849 |
| St. John, Lidelia | Bailey, John R. | C/170 | September 13, 1877 | September 13, 1877 |
| St. John, Lonnie | Jones, Ida | C/466 | October 13, 1892 | October 13, 1892 |
| St. John, M. C. | Blanton, John | D/2 | | August 18, 188 |
| St. John, M. E. | Wood, Martha H. | A2/106 | October 30, 1862 | October 30, 1862 |
| St. John, M. J. | Smith, Jas. I. | A2/91 | December 10, 1859 | December 10, 1859 |
| St. John, M. T. | Lorance, W. B. | F/122 | July 31, 1897 | July 31, 1897 |
| St. John, Malisa Miss | McDougle, Gunter | B/124 | January 2, 1871 | No Return |
| St. John, Margaret J. Miss | McDougal, John W. | A2/144 | September 3, 1866 | Executed No Date |

| Groom or Bride | Groom or Bride | Book/Page | Date of License | Date of Marriage |
|---|---|---|---|---|
| St. John, Martha | Ferrel, James | A2/127 | September 16, 1865 | September 16, 1865 |
| St. John, Mary L. Miss | Ward, James E. | A/123 | August 2, 1849 | August 2, 1849 |
| St. John, Mary Miss | Robinson, R. S. | A2/46 | January 10, 1856 | January 10, 1856 |
| St. John, S. E. | Woods, T. S. | D/22 | | No Date |
| St. John, S. M. | Goodwar, Rebeca | E/52 | August 3, 1888 | August 5, 1888 |
| St. John, Syntha | Bains, A. D. | C/250 | July 8, 1880 | July 8, 1880 |
| St. John, W. F. | Low, A. | D/101 | | January 8, 1882 |
| St. John, W. T. | Whitfield, Sarah Ann B. | A2/142 | July 28, 1866 | Executed No Date |
| St. John, Willie G. | Higdon, James | F/54 | January 7, 1895 | January 8, 1895 |
| St. Johns, Marry C. Miss | Bates, Alvin | A2/34 | August 14, 1854 | August 14, 1854 |
| St.John, Rosie Miss | Duke, Tom | F/122 | July 27, 1897 | July ??, 1897 |
| St.John, Thomas G. | Skirlock, Sallie | E/110 | December 19, 1888 | December 20, 1888 |
| Stacey, Gideon | Smith, Bell | C/418 | September 24, 1890 | September 25, 1890 |
| Stacey, Mary | Lee, Ozburn | A/11 | March 2, 1839 | March 4, 1839 |
| Stacey, Sarah M. C. | Cooper, John | C/132 | January 27, 1976 | January 27, 1876 |
| Stacey, William D. | Hollis, Miss Lucy M. | A/39 | July 7, 1841 | July 13, 1841 |
| Stacy, Abram H. | Holt, Miss Isabella A. | B/88 | September 24, 1869 | October 3, 1869 |
| Stacy, Adline Miss | Cowthron, Hugh | A2/15 | March 11, 1852 | March 11, 1852 |
| Stacy, Allace E. | Haley, J. N. | C/300 | January 17, 1884 | January 17, 1884 |
| Stacy, Benjamin L. | Maxey, Miss Peggy Jane | A/89 | July 4, 1846 | July 5, 1846 |
| Stacy, Elizabeth | Williams, C. H. | A2/55 | April 18, 1857 | April 17, 1857 |
| Stacy, Elizabeth N. | Wimberley, G. W. | B/94 | November 30, 1869 | December 1, 1869 |
| Stacy, Emeline | Sissom, J. M. | C/274 | December 20, 1880 | December 24, 1880 |
| Stacy, Emaline Miss | Holt, Blackburn | B/74 | December 9, 1868 | December 13, 1868 |
| Stacy, Fannie | Robinson, Sam | F/108 | January 4, 1897 | January 4, 1897 |
| Stacy, G. C. | Bryant, Lizzie | C/440 | July 25, 1891 | July 30, 1891 |
| Stacy, H. B. | Bush, Lillie | F/104 | December 7, 1896 | December 10, 1896 |
| Stacy, Harvy | Bynum, Roxey | C/258 | October 14, 1880 | October 14, 1880 |
| Stacy, J. A. J. | Cawthon, N. E. | C/104 | January 4, 1875 | January 8, 1875 |
| Stacy, J. H. | McCaslin, Elisabeth | C/242 | November 12, 1879 | November 13, 1879 |
| Stacy, J. H. | McCarlin, Elisabeth | C/230 | November 12, 1879 | No Return |
| Stacy, J. M. | Whittemore, T. L. | E/121 | December 27, 1888 | December 20, 1888 |
| Stacy, James | Gilley, Sallie | C/376 | December 2, 1886 | No Return |
| Stacy, James F. | Lasater, Miss Mary Elizabeth | A/88 | March 30, 1846 | March 30, 1846 |
| Stacy, Jim | McCullough, Huldah | F/112 | February 10, 1897 | February 10, 1897 |
| Stacy, John A. | Brynum, Miss Mary Elizabeth Jane | B/66 | April 4, 1868 | April 5, 1868 |
| Stacy, John J. | Parker, Miss Isabella | A/42 | October 19, 1841 | October 20, 1841 |
| Stacy, John P. | Wilson, Nancy | C/212 | February 6, 1879 | February 8, 1779 |
| Stacy, John W. | Gooding, Miss Lucinda | A/112 | July 12, 1848 | July 12, 1848 |
| Stacy, Jonnie | Brant, Melvina | E/196 | July 31, 1889 | July 31, 1889 |
| Stacy, Joseph | -----, Miss E. J. | A2/76 | September 3, 1855 | September 4, 1855 |
| Stacy, Lucinda | Bynum, Wm | A2/117 | November 8, 1864 | November 11, 1864 |
| Stacy, M. J. | Edwards, W. H. | D/1 | | June 9, 1881 |
| Stacy, Malindy | McCaster, Logan | E/75 | September 18, 1888 | September 18, 1888 |
| Stacy, Mary | Spry, J. W. | F/34 | October 3, 1894 | October 4, 1894 |

| Groom or Bride | Groom or Bride | Book/Page | Date of License | Date of Marriage |
|---|---|---|---|---|
| Stacy, Mary A. | Vanhooser, I. W. | F/32 | February 28, 1894 | No Return |
| Stacy, Mary E. | Simpson, Davis E. | A2/73 | May 13, 1853 | May 13, 1853 |
| Stacy, Mary Jane Miss | Reed, William M. | B/54 | November 2, 1867 | November 3, 1867 |
| Stacy, Nancy | Taylor, J. R. | C/232 | November 11, 1879 | November 12, 1879 |
| Stacy, Permlie | Wood, Wiley | C/362 | July 29, 1886 | July 29, 1886 |
| Stacy, Prudence | Freeman, Simeon | C/144 | August 31, 1876 | September 3, 1876 |
| Stacy, Rebecca Miss | McCullough, Alexander | A/42 | October 14, 1841 | October 20, 1841 |
| Stacy, Roxie | Willson, Bill | F/2 | January 15, 1893? | No Return |
| Stacy, Roxie | Wilson, Bill | F/10 | June 15, 1893 | June 19, 1893 |
| Stacy, S. H | Burchett, M. G. L. | C/166 | August 1, 1877 | August 2, 1877 |
| Stacy, S. P. | Farless, Margrett | C/184 | January 17, 1878 | No Return |
| Stacy, Sallie | Gilley, Wm. | F/70 | September 26, 1895 | September 26, 1895 |
| Stacy, Samuel H. | Haithcock, Miss Polly | B/32 | November 18, 1866 | November 18, 1866 |
| Stacy, Sarah Adaline Miss | Brown, John | B/112 | October 7, 1870 | October 9, 1870 |
| Stacy, Sarah E. | Edwards, Wm. H. | A2/114 | May 3, 1864 | No Return |
| Stacy, Stephen | Ferrell, Sallie | C/276 | March 30, 1881 | March 30, 1881 |
| Stacy, Susan A. | Bush, W. J. | A2/134 | January 2, 1866 | No Return |
| Stacy, Susanah | Gannon, Saml P. | A/20 | December 12, 1839 | December 13, 1839 |
| Stacy, Susannah | Pack, M. | C/166 | August 10, 1877 | August 14, 1877 |
| Stacy, Susanna | Bryant, Wm. S. | C/36 | August 23, 1872 | August 25, 1862 |
| Stacy, Susanna | Bryan, Spence | F/84 | February 15, 1896 | February 16, 1896 |
| Stacy, W. H. E. | McMahan, Rosa | F/32 | February 22, 1894 | February 28, 1894 |
| Stacy, W. J. | West, Miss Z. A. | A2/89 | October 20, 1859 | October 20, 1859 |
| Stacy, W. J. | Wilson, Miss Mary J. | C/10 | September 12, 1871 | September 17, 1871 |
| Stacy, William | Duke, Della | F/156 | September 15, 1898 | September 17, 1898 |
| Stacy, William C. | Moore, Miss Mary J. | B/84 | August 17, 1869 | August 17, 1869 |
| Stacy, William J. | Bush, Nancy Jane | C/426 | December 19, 1890 | December 28, 1890 |
| Stacy, Willie | Moore, Nute | F/72 | October 12, 1895 | October 13, 1895 |
| Stafford, Charlotte | Vernon, Elias | B/14 | October 16, 1868 | October 16, 1868 |
| Stafford, Mary A. | Basham, James, M. | A2/86 | June 30, 1859 | No Return |
| Stafford, R. F. | Hoover, Eliza | C/148 | November 21, 1876 | November 21, 1876 |
| Stamper, James | Bell, Rebecca C. | A2/133 | December 2, 1865 | December 3, 1865 |
| Standly, Angaline | Cathey, Robert | A/130 | January 9, 1850 | January 9, 1850 |
| Standly, Elizabeth Miss | Childress, Stephen P. | A/74 | October 17, 1844 | October 17, 1844 |
| Standly, T. | Summer, Miss Jane | A2/73 | December 26, 1853 | December 27, 1865 |
| Stanfield, Delila | Prater, William C. | A/60 | February 17, 1843 | February 17, 1843 |
| Stanfield, Jefferson | Simmons, Miss Barbary | A/47 | February 15, 1842 | February 15, 1842 |
| Stanfield, Parlee Miss | Gooding, William | B/92 | November 5, 1869 | November 17, 1869 |
| Stanley, B. M. | King, Nora | C/436 | May 29, 1891 | May 30, 1891 |
| Stanley, Charley | Manus, Nancy | C/370 | October 14, 1886 | October 14, 1886 |
| Stanley, Darkus J. | Quarles, Wm. | C/52 | February 18, 1873 | No Return |
| Stanley, Eliza | Davenport, Wm. C. | A2/45 | January 1, 1856 | No Return |
| Stanley, Elizabeth | St. John, George | A/15 | July 13, 1839 | July 13, 1839 |
| Stanley, J. C. | Wilcher, Eliza | F/50 | November 28, 1894 | November 28, 1894 |
| Stanley, J. N. | Adams, Annie | F/136 | November 6, 1897 | November 7, 1897 |
| Stanley, Mary | Preston, W. F. | D/8 | | December 8, 1881 |

| Groom or Bride | Groom or Bride | Book/Page | Date of License | Date of Marriage |
|---|---|---|---|---|
| Stanley, Mattie | Bogle, T. A. | C/346 | December 24, 1885 | December 24, 1885 |
| Stanley, Nancy F. | McNelly, Rubin R. | C/342 | November 28, 1885 | November 28, 1885 |
| Stanley, Nora | Mayo, W. M. | F/52 | December 11, 1894 | December 11, 1894 |
| Stanley, Sarah E. | Mahaffa, Wm. | C/88 | May 16, 1874 | May 5, 1876 |
| Stanley, Susan C. Miss | Gann, John H. | B/42 | March 23, 1867 | March 24, 1867 |
| Stanley, Virginia | Fuston, John | F/108 | December 30, 1896 | December 30, 1896 |
| Stanly, Martha Miss | Gann, Robert | A/71 | August 20, 1844 | August 21, 1844 |
| Stanly, Mort | Davis, Rebecca | C/58 | June 24, 1873 | No Return |
| Stanly, Robert M. | Cox, Christena | A2/120 | February 18, 1865 | February 21, 1865 |
| Stanly, Susan C. | Davis Andy | C/52 | February 17, 1873 | No Retrun |
| Stans, S. J. Miss | Rains, James B. | A2/19 | September 30, 1852 | October 9, 1852 |
| Stanton, Rebecca Miss | Baine, Isaiah | A/67 | January 16, 1844 | January 18, 1844 |
| Star, John | Shoemate, Miss Salenda | A/63 | June 26, 1843 | June 28, 1843 |
| Star, Joseph | Barrett, Alsie C. | C/366 | September 8, 1886 | No Return |
| Star, Sarah Miss | Hutchins, Aaron | A/38 | May 15, 1841 | No Return |
| Starr, Bettie | Higgins, J. | C/208 | December 20, 1878 | Not Satisfied |
| Starr, Jane | Hulehens, William | A2/37 | December 28, 1854 | December 28, 1854 |
| Starr, John | Vaughan, Miss Sallie Ann | B/48 | August 2, 1867 | August 3, 1867 |
| Starr, Josephine Miss | Sullins, Robert L. | A2/155 | May 26, 1866 | May 26, 1866 |
| Starr, Nancy Miss | Wildman, William | A/95 | January 1, 1847 | No Return |
| Starr, Ruthy Miss | Hammons, Reese | B/32 | December 4, 1866 | December 5, 1866 |
| Starr, Susan Miss | Parten, John L. | A/120 | February 15, 1849 | February 15, 1849 |
| Stasy, Gidan | Parker, Miss Betsy Ann | B/110 | September 17, 1870 | September 18, 1870 |
| Statom, Henry V. | Hazlewood, Cyrene C. | A2/127 | September 7, 1865 | September 7, 1865 |
| Steeples, Nancy A. Miss | Manus, Nathan | A2/29 | November 11, 1853 | No Return |
| Stepehens, Artalia P. Miss | McKnight, Joseph D. | B/64 | March 20, 1868 | March 22, 1868 |
| Stephen, D. R. | Brewer, Mattie | E/346 | December 21, 1898 | |
| Stephen, D. R. | Brown, Mattie | F/162 | December 21, 1898 | December 21, 1898 |
| Stephen, Mary J. Miss | Tarply, James M. | A2/150 | May 12, 1866 | No Return |
| Stephen, R. K. | George, Miss Marry J. | A2/41 | August 22, 1855 | Returns Missing |
| Stephen, Viola | Jetton, L. M. | C/220 | June 28, 1879 | June 29, 1879 |
| Stephen, Willie | Doak, John | C/264 | May 23, 1880 | May 23, 1880 |
| Stephens, Andrew (col.) | Officer, Millie | C/460 | June 25, 1892 | No Return |
| Stephens, Benj. | Wood, Miss Ann | C/4 | August 3, 1871 | August 3, 1871 |
| Stephens, Benj. | Taylor, Mary | C/74 | November 22, 1873 | November 23, 1873 |
| Stephens, Clem | Wilkenson, Ben | C/352 | February 6, 1`886 | February 7, 1886 |
| Stephens, E. Jr. | Talley, Maggie | C/318 | November 24, 1884 | November 24, 1884 |
| Stephens, H. G. | Byrns, Miss Tennessee | B/94 | December 13, 1869 | December 15, 1869 |
| Stephens, J. F. | Elkins, Allice | C/338 | October 15, 1885 | October 15, 1885 |
| Stephens, J. W. | Higgins, Miss Amanda S. | B/76 | January 12, 1869 | January 20, 1869 |
| Stephens, J. W. | Kennedy, L. K. | C/110 | March 24, 1875 | March 28, 1875 |
| Stephens, J. W. | Patterson, M. E. | C/174 | October 13, 1877 | October 13, 1877 |
| Stephens, J. W. | Melton, Sallie | C/238 | January 11, 1880 | January 11, 1880 |
| Stephens, James H. | Cook, Miss Martha R. | B/98 | January 13, 1870 | January 13, 1870 |
| Stephens, Joe | Mason, Pearl | F/122 | July 31, 1897 | August 1, 1897 |
| Stephens, John | McBroom, Nancy | B/8 | September 22, 1865 | November 19, 1865 |

| Groom or Bride | Groom or Bride | Book/Page | Date of License | Date of Marriage |
|---|---|---|---|---|
| Stephens, L. H. | Odom, J. M. A. | C/182 | December 22, 1877 | No Return |
| Stephens, Laura | Harper, Hunt | C/294 | October 13, 1883 | October 14, 1883 |
| Stephens, M. J. Miss | Dillen, Joseph | A2/127 | September 14, 1865 | September 14, 1865 |
| Stephens, Marry Miss | Crank, G. W. | A2/24 | February 10, 1853 | February 10, 1853 |
| Stephens, Martha F. Miss | Brewer, John L. | B/94 | December 9, 1869 | December 9, 1869 |
| Stephens, Melinda C. Miss | Simpson, Isaac T. | A/115 | October 10, 1848 | October 10, 1848 |
| Stephens, Minnie Miss | Odom, R. H. | E/180 | June 11, 1889 | June 12, 1889 |
| Stephens, Mrs. Allice | Parris, C. C. | F/116 | April 21, 1897 | April 21, 1897 |
| Stephens, S. E. | Webb, W. J. | C/92 | August 13, 1874 | August 16, 1874 |
| Stephens, S. H. | Moore, Miss M. A. | B/60 | December 21, 1867 | December 22, 1867 |
| Stephens, S. J. A. | Stone, John | C/30 | June 30, 1872 | June 30, 1872 |
| Stephens, Simeon D. | Caroll, Miss Charlotte | A/122 | December 7, 1848 | December 7, 1848 |
| Sternly, Josephine | Woods, J. K. P. | C/232 | November 29, 1879 | November 30, 1879 |
| Stewart, Bethany | Baley, J. A. | C/152 | January 3, 1877 | January 4, 1877 |
| Stewart, Bethell (col.) | Vernon, Maggie | C/412 | December 31, 1887 | December 31, 1887 |
| Stewart, Booker | Campbell, Mary | E/30 | April 20, 1888 | April 22, 1888 |
| Stewart, Buch | Petty, Nancy | C/212 | February 8, 1879 | February 15, 1879 |
| Stewart, Caroline Miss | Kittrell, George | B/56 | December 4, 1867 | December 5, 1867 |
| Stewart, Elizabeth Miss | Holland, Speaker | B/128 | March 23, 1871 | March 23, 1871 |
| Stewart, Hoyt | Cummings, Media | E/376 | October 30, 1898 | |
| Stewart, Hoyt | Cummings, Media | F/160 | October 30, 1898 | October 30, 1898 |
| Stewart, Hugh | Ashfor, Nola | F/14 | August 17, 1893 | No Return |
| Stewart, Isabell Jane | Jetton, John B. | A/27 | April 2, 1840 | No Return |
| Stewart, James | Taylor, Miss Frances | A2/69 | October 21, 1858 | October 21, 1858 |
| Stewart, Jane | Fugitt, Irvin | C/272 | February 11, 1881 | February 11, 1881 |
| Stewart, John | Patterson, Mattie | F/22 | November 16, 1893 | November 16, 1893 |
| Stewart, John (col) | Robertson, Charloote | C/462 | July 28, 1892 | July 30, 1892 |
| Stewart, John (col.) | Reed, Marah (col.) | D/3 | | September 1, 1881 |
| Stewart, John H. | Rucker, Amanda M. | A2/133 | December 7, 1865 | December 7, 1865 |
| Stewart, Lucinda A. Miss | Rucker, John E. | A2/146 | November 1, 1866 | November 1, 1866 |
| Stewart, Mandy | Woods, Andy | C/154 | February 2, 1877 | February 3, 1877 |
| Stewart, Mary | Webb, George | C/212 | February 16, 1879 | February 16, 1879 |
| Stewart, Mattie Miss | Throw, J. H. | B/116 | November 17, 1870 | November 17, 1870 |
| Stewart, R. C. | Tatum, Elvia | C/202 | November 2, 1878 | November 3, 1878 |
| Stewart, Robert | Walker, Sarah C. | A/20 | December 10, 1839 | December 12, 1839 |
| Stewart, S. H. | Hollenworth, V. B. | F/84 | February 25, 1896 | February 25, 1896 |
| Stewart, Sarah E. | Blair, John | C/374 | November 10, 1886 | November 11, 1886 |
| Stewart, W. D. | Moore, Miss Jennie | F/76 | November 28, 1895 | November 28, 1895 |
| Stewart, W. T. | Hollansworth, Miss Hettie | F/170 | February 16, 1899 | February 19, 1899 |
| Stile, Sarah | Fowler, Lerd | E/15 | January 28, 1888 | January 18, 1888 |
| Stiles, Josie | Rogers, L. F. | E/173 | April 27, 1889 | No Return |
| Stiles, Wm. H. | Bogle, Mary J. | C/240 | February 4, 1880 | February 5, 1880 |
| Stine, W. G. | Cumins, Miss Julina | A2/91 | December 14, 1859 | No Return |
| Stolls (Stoley), Thos. | Gann, Rebecca | C/156 | February 15, 1877 | February 15, 1877 |
| Stone, Benj. | Smithson, Eliza | C/122 | October 23, 1875 | October 24, 1875 |
| Stone, Benjamin A. | Pendleton, Miss Stacy C. | A/80 | July 16, 1845 | July 17, 1845 |

| Groom or Bride | Groom or Bride | Book/Page | Date of License | Date of Marriage |
| --- | --- | --- | --- | --- |
| Stone, Benjamin A. | Pendleton, Miss Stacy C. | A/81 | July 16, 1845 | July 17, 1845 |
| Stone, Buenavista Miss | St. John, H. J. | B/52 | September 11, 1867 | September 11, 1867 |
| Stone, Burnavista Miss | Wilcher, Wm. B. | B/88 | September 23, 1868 | No Return |
| Stone, Doscha | Duke, Willey | C/204 | November 26, 1878 | November 26, 1878 |
| Stone, Elija | Higgins, Jennie | F/24 | December 13, 1893 | December 14, 1893 |
| Stone, Elizabeth | Evans, James M. | A/57 | December 22, 1842 | December 23, 1842 |
| Stone, Flora M. | Mason, Regneer H. | A/129 | December 4, 1849 | December 8, 1849 |
| Stone, Henry D. | Lorance, Manerva | A2/121 | March 6, 1865 | March 8, 1865 |
| Stone, Issabella Miss | Bailey, Robert | A/63 | July 18, 1843 | July 20, 1843 |
| Stone, J. B. | Moran, Jane | C/190 | April 22, 1878 | April 22, 1878 |
| Stone, J. P. | Hawkins, Angie | E/247 | December 23, 1889 | December 24, 1889 |
| Stone, James | Roberson, Elizabeth | C/116 | August 14, 1875 | No Return |
| Stone, James | Jones, Laurah E. | D/3 | | September 7, 188 |
| Stone, Jane | Summer, James | C/34 | August 14, 1872 | August 18, 1872 |
| Stone, Jane Miss | St. John, E. M. | A2/22 | December 29, 1852 | December 29, 1852 |
| Stone, John | Stephens, S. J. A. | C/30 | June 30, 1872 | June 30, 1872 |
| Stone, John B. | Markum, Eliza | F/1 | January 4, 1893 | January , 1893 |
| Stone, John R. | Odom, Miss Nannie | A2/147 | November 14, 1866 | November 14, 1866 |
| Stone, John W. | Jetton, Sarah E. | A/84 | November 6, 1845 | November 6, 1845 |
| Stone, John W. | Sullivan, Miss Elizabeth | A2/3 | May 28, 1850 | May 28, 1850 |
| Stone, Jonathan G. | Melton, Miss Eliza Jane | A/116 | October 26, 1848 | October 26, 1848 |
| Stone, Josaphine Miss | White, W. J. | A2/10 | January 28, 1851 | No Return |
| Stone, Jose | Kirby, Bud | C/114 | June 19, 1875 | June 20, 1875 |
| Stone, Lizzie | Linder, J. N. | C/322 | December 24, 1884 | December 24, 1884 |
| Stone, M. E. | Smith, A. B. | C/14 | November 9, 1871 | November 9, 1871 |
| Stone, M. V. | Osment, T. A. | C/114 | July 5, 1875 | July 6, 1875 |
| Stone, Margarett A. Miss | Foster, Porter | A/41 | September 9, 1841 | September 9, 1841 |
| Stone, Mary | Baily, John N. | A/3 | May 23, 1838 | June 3, 1838 |
| Stone, Mary | Nokes, William B. | A/19 | November 16, 1839 | November 21, 1839 |
| Stone, Mary V. | Earnhart, Harriman | C/312 | August 22, 1884 | August 22, 1884 |
| Stone, Nancy | Perry, John W. | A2/12 | October 25, 1851 | October 26, 1851 |
| Stone, Nancy Ann | Varton, Edmund | A/22 | January 9, 1840 | January 9, 1840 |
| Stone, Nancy A. | Milligan, Rance | C/262 | November 11, 1880 | November 11, 1880 |
| Stone, Nannie A. Mrs. | Vaughn, G. W. | C/460 | June 21, 1892 | June 21, 1892 |
| Stone, Palme | Rich, Wm. | F/134 | October 19, 1897 | October 19, 1897 |
| Stone, Parlee Miss | Preston, John F. | A/106 | December 22, 1847 | December 22, 1847 |
| Stone, Patience | Hollandworth, James M. | E/99 | November 7, 1888 | November 7, 1888 |
| Stone, Robert | Jetton, Bettie | C/368 | September 27, 1886 | No Return |
| Stone, Ruth A. | Bailey, Dillard | C/20 | January 13, 1872 | January 14, 1872 |
| Stone, Sallie | Walkup, W. H. | C/152 | December 28, 1876 | No Return |
| Stone, Sarah Miss | Weedon, A. M. | A/110 | April 11, 1848 | No Return |
| Stone, Thos. D. | Bogle, Miss Nancy M. | B/126 | February 11, 1871 | February 12, 1871 |
| Stone, William J. | Foster Miss Polly Ann | A/120 | February 15, 1849 | February 15, 1849 |
| Stone, Wm. | Mason, Plina | C/332 | July 30, 1885 | July 30, 1885 |
| Stoner, Burr | Knight, Francis | F/20 | October 19, 1893 | October 22, 1893 |
| Stoner, Norvena Miss | Delony, Watser | A2/55 | February 16, 1859 | No Return |

| Groom or Bride | Groom or Bride | Book/Page | Date of License | Date of Marriage |
|---|---|---|---|---|
| Stor, Mary | Evans, C. C. | C/40 | September 28, 1872 | September 29, 1872 |
| Story, Mary M. | Muncy, H. | C/128 | December 30, 1875 | December 30, 1876 |
| Stotts, Wm. | Jones, Miss Harriett C. | A2/47 | May 9, 1856 | No Return |
| Stricklin, Josie | Jernigan, Jasper | F/94 | September 3, 1896 | September 6, 1896 |
| Strong, Julie | Davenport, Hardy | C/46 | December 5, 1872 | December 5, 1872 |
| Stroud, A. E. | Stroud, Bettie | C/252 | August 11, 1880 | August 19, 1880 |
| Stroud, Aline Miss | Tenpenny, A. A. | F/110 | January 20, 1897 | January 20, 1897 |
| Stroud, Angie Miss | Odom, C. D. | F/58 | November 18, 1894 | No Return |
| Stroud, B. B. | Hoover, Etta | F/70 | September 12, 1895 | September 13, 1895 |
| Stroud, Barcelona | Hoover, J. M. | C/26 | March 28, 1872 | March 28, 1872 |
| Stroud, Bettie | Stroud, A. E. | C/252 | August 11, 1880 | August 19, 1880 |
| Stroud, F. R. | Addams, N. A. | C/270 | January 5, 1881 | No Return |
| Stroud, Gay | Hoover, Henry | C/442 | August 4, 1891 | August 5, 1891 |
| Stroud, George S. | Mitchell, Miss Elizabeth J. | A2/60 | November 12, 1857 | November 12, 1857 |
| Stroud, Jane C. | Prater, Logan | C/176 | November 3, 1877 | November 4, 1877 |
| Stroud, Jessee | Banks, Miss Elizabeht | A2/66 | August 7, 1858 | No Return |
| Stroud, Lavander | Todd, Annie | C/188 | March 23, 1878 | March 23, 1878 |
| Stroud, Mariah | King, Jno. E. | C/64 | August 2, 1873 | August 3, 1873 |
| Stroud, Mary D. | Justice, Andrew | C/100 | November 12, 1874 | November 12, 1874 |
| Stroud, N. A. | Sain, G. J. | C/418 | October 4, 1890 | October 4, 1890 |
| Stroud, N. E. | Finley, Josie | C/288 | July 27, 1883 | July 29, 1883 |
| Stroud, N. E. | Winnett, C. F. | F/140 | December 22, 1897 | December 23, 1897 |
| Stroud, S. Miss | Moon, Alexander | A2/82 | July 24, 1858 | July 26, 1858 |
| Stroud, W. P. | Todd, Mary A. | C/310 | August 4, 1884 | August 4, 1884 |
| Sullen, Balane | Davis, Parisade | C/92 | July 21, 1874 | No Return |
| Sullens, Alexander | Hickenbottom, Miss Elizabeth | A2/73 | October 25, 1852 | October 25, 1852 |
| Sullens, Angeline Miss | Spurlock, J. B. | A2/58 | October 19, 1857 | October 19, 1857 |
| Sullens, Balam | Davis, Parisade | C/88 | July 21, 1874 | July 21, 1874 |
| Sullens, Burley | Gunter, Annie | F/130 | September 18, 1897 | September 19,. 1897 |
| Sullens, J. | Bailey, Ada | E/388 | October 12, 1898 | |
| Sullens, J. D. | Carter, Emma | F/60 | March 14, 1895 | No Return |
| Sullens, James | Barnes, Miss Harrett | A2/18 | July 20, 1852 | July 21, 1852 |
| Sullens, M. Miss | Ferrell, C. | A2/86 | July 16, 1859 | No Return |
| Sullens, Margaret Miss | Cooper, Philip | A2/17 | May 6, 1852 | May 6, 1852 |
| Sullens, Margaret Miss | Cooper, Phillip | A2/18 | May 6, 1852 | May 6, 1852 |
| Sullens, Richmond | Womack, Miss Lucinda | A/127 | September 18, 1849 | September 18, 1849 |
| Sullens, Sarah E. | Markum, Cajor | C/138 | May 24, 1876 | No Return |
| Sullens, Susan Miss | Ledbetter, William | A/49 | April 25, 1842 | April 26, 1842 |
| Sullens, Susan Miss | Higgans, Robert W. | A/125 | August 9, 1849 | August 9, 1849 |
| Sullens, Susie Ann | Anderson, W. H. | F/72 | October 19, 1895 | October 20, 1895 |
| Sullens, T. C. Miss | Hate, P. J. | C/400 | September 1, 1887 | September 2, 1887 |
| Sullens, W. M. | Gaither, Sallie | F/130 | September 15, 1897 | September 15, 1897 |
| Sullens, William | Cummins, Mrs. Dove | A/121 | March 18, 1849 | March 18, 1849 |
| Sullin, Melissa | Patterson, Thomas | C/436 | May 25, 1801 | May 26, 1891 |
| Sullins, A. M. P. Miss | Bogle, Joseph Y. | A2/64 | March 29, 1858 | March 29, 1858 |
| Sullins, Alex | Berryhill, M. J. | C/190 | April 4, 1878 | No Return |

| Groom or Bride | Groom or Bride | Book/Page | Date of License | Date of Marriage |
|---|---|---|---|---|
| Sullins, Andrew | Spurlock, Sarah | D/5 | | October 6, 1881 |
| Sullins, Betsy | Preston, Wm | C/230 | November 15, 1879 | No Return |
| Sullins, Buck | Melton, Sallie | C/224 | September 2, 1879 | No Return |
| Sullins, Cardin | Murphy, John A. | F/22 | November 13, 1893 | November 16, 1893 |
| Sullins, Caroline | Sullins, Eli | C/304 | February 7, 1884 | February 7, 1884 |
| Sullins, Coril A. | Melton, Isaac | C/206 | Novmeber 28, 1878 | December 1, 1878 |
| Sullins, Eli | Sullins, Caroline | C/304 | February 7, 1884 | February 7, 1884 |
| Sullins, Eli | Crane, Elisabeth | D/2 | | August 4, 1881 |
| Sullins, Francis | Osment, H. S. | E/213 | September 19, 1889 | No Return |
| Sullins, J. | Bailey, Ida | F/158 | October 12, 1898 | October 13, 1898 |
| Sullins, James | Cummings, Matilda P. | D/12 | | February 28, 1882 |
| Sullins, John J. | Bunch, Miss Nancy | B/80 | May 1, 1869 | May 1, 1869 |
| Sullins, Joseph D. | Webb, Julina | C/372 | October 30, 1886 | No Return |
| Sullins, Louisa | Millstead, James | A2/31 | February 8, 1854 | February 8, 1854 |
| Sullins, Marietta Miss | Bailey, E. J. | E/10 | January 21, 1888 | ??? |
| Sullins, Matilda | Conley, Isah | A2/108 | September 2, 1863 | No Return |
| Sullins, Polly Miss | Smith, John | A2/3 | July 13, 1850 | July 13, 1850 |
| Sullins, Robert L. | Starr, Miss Josephine | A2/155 | May 26, 1866 | May 26, 1866 |
| Sullins, Ruth | Elkins, Thomas | C/190 | April 18, 1878 | April 18, 1878 |
| Sullins, S. E. Miss | Melton, J. H | A2/94 | February 13, 1860 | No Return |
| Sullins, Sadie | Berryhill, Charlie | C/150 | December 8, 1876 | December 8, 1876 |
| Sullins, Sallie | Bowlin, Polk | C/292 | September 8, 1883 | No Return |
| Sullins, Saml | Davis, Ark | C/124 | November 8, 1875 | November 11, 1875 |
| Sullins, Samuel | Ferrell, Miss Ruth | B/54 | October 1, 1867 | October 3, 1867 |
| Sullins, Samuel | Webb, Jane | E/186 | June 24, 1889 | June 24, 1889 |
| Sullins, Sug | Markum, John | C/300 | January 17, 1884 | January 17, 1884 |
| Sullins, Susan A. | Spurlock, Wm. M. | C/94 | September 21, 1874 | September 22, 1874 |
| Sullins, Susan F. | Nokes, W. B. | C/82 | February 4, 1874 | February 5, 1874 |
| Sullins, Susan F. | Wood, James | C/184 | January 3, 1878 | January 3, 1878 |
| Sullins, Susanah Miss | Ferrell, Enoch | A2/92 | December 20, 1859 | No Return |
| Sullins, V. A. Miss | Conley, N. C. | B/82 | May 21, 1869 | May 21, 1869 |
| Sullins, Wm. | Taylor, Eliza | F/18 | September 12, 1893 | September 14, 1893 |
| Sullins, Zacriah | -----, Miss Margarett | A2/36 | October 26, 1854 | No Return |
| Sullins, Zona | Moore, T. C. | F/146 | February 24, 1898 | No Return |
| Sullivan | Branon, Calvin C. | A/72 | August 29, 1844 | No Return |
| Sullivan | Dodd, Albert | A2/130 | October 5, 1865 | October 5, 1865 |
| Sullivan | Wilson, R. T. | E/114 | December 22, 1888 | December 23, 1888 |
| Sullivan, A. E. | Burke, N. J. | A2/147 | November 10, 1866 | November 10, 1866 |
| Sullivan, Aesen H. | Finley, Mary L. | C/272 | February 19, 1881 | No Return |
| Sullivan, Andrew | Bragg, Frances | A/77 | February 25, 1845 | February 25, 1845 |
| Sullivan, Andy | Foreman, Rachael M. | C/154 | January 30, 1877 | January 30, 1877 |
| Sullivan, Ann E. Miss | Dodd, John A. | B/84 | August 25, 1869 | August 25, 1869 |
| Sullivan, Annie | Woodruff, J. W. | D/9 | | December 29, 1881 |
| Sullivan, Bettie | McBroom, B. H. | C/102 | December 2, 1874 | December 2, 1874 |
| Sullivan, Bettie Miss | Bragg, Henry M. | C/412 | December 31, 1887 | January 1, 1888 |
| Sullivan, Caswell | House, Elizabeth | A/76 | January 8, 1845 | January 9, 1845 |

| Groom or Bride | Groom or Bride | Book/Page | Date of License | Date of Marriage |
| --- | --- | --- | --- | --- |
| Sullivan, Dove | Cummings, Warren | A/11 | March 5, 1839 | March 6, 1839 |
| Sullivan, Drucilla | Alford, John | A2/121 | March 6, 1865 | March 6, 1865 |
| Sullivan, Elizabeth Miss | Stone, John W. | A2/3 | May 28, 1850 | May 28, 1850 |
| Sullivan, Elvira Miss | Gaither, Pleasant | A2/147 | November 8, 1866 | November 8, 1866 |
| Sullivan, Harbert H. | Spurlock, Miss Mariah D. | A/123 | July 25, 1849 | July 25, 1849 |
| Sullivan, J. B. | Alexander, M. A. | A2/105 | October 23, 1862 | October 23, 1862 |
| Sullivan, J. V. | Moore, Miss Ella | C/452 | December 30, 1891 | December 31, 1891 |
| Sullivan, J. V. | Bryant, Sarah | F/66 | August 10, 1895 | August 11, 1895 |
| Sullivan, James T. | McBroom, Miss Nancy E. | B/124 | January 18, 1871 | January 19, 1871 |
| Sullivan, Jane | House, William | A2/14 | January 13, 1852 | January 13, 1852 |
| Sullivan, Jesse | Byron, Miss Minnie | C/404 | October 6, 1887 | No Return |
| Sullivan, John R. | Brown, Mrs. Nancy | A2/1 | March 5, 1850 | March 5, 1850 |
| Sullivan, John R. | Gillum, Lucy J. | C/270 | January 12, 1881 | No Return |
| Sullivan, K. J. Miss | Prator, Clayton | A2/163 | July 7, 1866 | Executed No Date |
| Sullivan, L. C. | Carter, James | A2/116 | October 4, 1864 | October 6, 1864 |
| Sullivan, Laura Ann Miss | Bailey, Andrew J. | A2/11 | April 21, 1852 | No Return |
| Sullivan, Lillie | Campbell, J. A. | F/144 | January 22, 1898 | January 23, 1898 |
| Sullivan, Louisa Miss | Perry, Albert | A/36 | February 3, 1841 | February 4, 1841 |
| Sullivan, M. E. | Finley, A. F. | C/364 | September 4, 1886 | September 5, 1886 |
| Sullivan, M. G. | Brandon, M. C. | C/240 | January 27, 1880 | January 29, 1880 |
| Sullivan, Mahama | McAlexander, J. | C/44 | November 18, 1872 | November 21, 1872 |
| Sullivan, Manerva Miss | Smith, Henry | A/51 | July 26, 1842 | July 26, 1842 |
| Sullivan, Marthy A. | Lafevers, R. S. | A2/55 | May 28, 1857 | May 28, 1857 |
| Sullivan, Mary A. | Tenpenny, David | A2/129 | September 21, 1865 | September 21, 1865 |
| Sullivan, Minty Miss | Walkup, A. O. | A2/42 | October 9, 1855 | October 9, 1855 |
| Sullivan, Miss Lizzy | Gibson, Aubey | F/108 | December 24, 1896 | December 24, 1896 |
| Sullivan, Nancy Ruth Miss | Thurston, George W. | A2/10 | February 2, 1851 | February 2, 1851 |
| Sullivan, Netter | Tosh, Charles A. | E/172 | April 25, 1889 | June 25, 1889 |
| Sullivan, Nettie | Pittard, Thomas | F/34 | September 26, 1894 | September 26, 1894 |
| Sullivan, R. F. | Falkenbery, Miss Isabella | B/32 | November 29, 1866 | November 29, 1866 |
| Sullivan, R. J. Miss | Riggby, Almand | A2/33 | July 12, 1854 | July 16, 1854 |
| Sullivan, Rebeccah | Warren, Arthur | A/17 | September 5, 1839 | No Return |
| Sullivan, Samuel C. | Bailey, Miss Manerva | A/50 | June 30, 1842 | June 30, 1842 |
| Sullivan, T. C. | Finly, E. | A2/103 | September 25, 1860 | No Return |
| Sullivan, T. G. | Barry, Mrs. Matilda B. | B/84 | July 26, 1869 | July 27, 1869 |
| Sullivan, Thomas G. | Bragg, Margarett | A/53 | September 6, 1842 | September 6, 1842 |
| Sullivan, Tildy Miss | Hibdon, John | A2/61 | December 21, 1857 | December 21, 1857 |
| Sullivan, Tomary | Ferrell, W. G. | A2/113 | March 27, 1864 | March 27, 1864 |
| Sullivan, W. H. | Ferrell, M. L. | C/24 | March 7, 1872 | March 7, 1872 |
| Sullivan, William | Merriman, Miss Matilda | A/101 | August 13, 1847 | August 18, 1847 |
| Sullivan, William | Poterfield, Mary E. | A2/124 | July 27, 1865 | July 28, 1865 |
| Sullivan, William A. | Gannon, Miss Joanna | B/48 | July 18, 1867 | July 18, 1867 |
| Sullivan, William L. | Teasley, Miss Matilda | A/43 | October 30, 1841 | October 31, 1841 |
| Sullivan, William L. | Dodd, Miss Demaries E. | A2/136 | January 17, 1866 | January 18, 1866 |
| Sullivan, Wm. H. | Teague, Miss Rachel A. | A2/60 | November 19, 1857 | November 19, 1857 |
| Sullivan, Zachariah | Herryman, Miss Mary E. | B/38 | January 24, 1867 | January 24, 1867 |

| Groom or Bride | Groom or Bride | Book/Page | Date of License | Date of Marriage |
|---|---|---|---|---|
| Sumars, Maggie Miss | Phillips, John | C/372 | November 4, 1886 | No Return |
| Sumer, Cindy L. H. Miss | Bryson, J. J. | A2/41 | August 14, 1855 | Returns Missing |
| Sumers, George | Teel, Elizza | F/34 | September 8, 1894 | September 19, 1894 |
| Sumers, Sarah | Bogle, William | A/19 | November 12, 1839 | November 14, 1839 |
| Summar, ---- | Davenport, ---- | F | August 26, 1893 | |
| Summar, Alsena E. Miss | Milligan, W. H. | A2/142 | July 26, 1866 | August 2, 1866 |
| Summar, Baldy H. | Blair, Miss Polly | A/74 | November 4, 1844 | November 5, 1844 |
| Summar, Berton | Odom, Louise | B/2 | August 21, 1865 | No Return |
| Summar, Berton | Summar, Louisa | B/18 | January 1, 1870 | No Return |
| Summar, Bette Miss | Bryan, J. V. | C/380 | January 3, 1887 | No Return |
| Summar, C. R. Miss | McAdoo, J. C. | B/90 | October 12, 1869 | October 14, 1869 |
| Summar, Cantrell B. | Brandon, Mrs. Mary | A/75 | November 21, 1844 | November 21, 1844 |
| Summar, Cyntha Miss | Mickey, Moses | B/48 | July 27, 1867 | July 30, 1867 |
| Summar, E. A. | Duggin, W. H. | C/102 | December 16, 1874 | December 17, 1874 |
| Summar, Elizabeth | Francis, Armsted | A/34 | October 14, 1840 | No Return |
| Summar, Elizabeth | Willard, M. A. | A2/116 | August 21, 1864 | No Return |
| Summar, Elizabeth Miss | Vance, James | A2/137 | February 8, 1866 | February 8, 1866 |
| Summar, Ella Miss | McBroom, Thomas L. | F/168 | January 31, 1899 | February 1, 1899 |
| Summar, Eunicy | Summer, Elijah | A/73 | October 17, 1844 | October 17, 1844 |
| Summar, Eunicy Miss | Tenpenny, Richard Jr. | A/100 | July 19, 1847 | July 20, 1847 |
| Summar, Florence | Diehl, A. R. | C/432 | March 7, 1891 | March 8, 1891 |
| Summar, Florence | Diehl, A. R. | C/432 | March 7, 1891 | March 8, 1891 |
| Summar, H. C. | Patterson, L. J. | C/276 | March 30, 1881 | March 31, 1881 |
| Summar, Ida M. | Thomas, Robert F. | C/470 | November 27, 1892 | November 17, 1892 |
| Summar, J. C. | Warren, Miss Susan | B/100 | March 18, 1870 | No Return |
| Summar, J. D. | Pattrick, Miss Piney | B/54 | October 15, 1867 | October 15, 1867 |
| Summar, J. F. | Reed, M. F. | C/156 | February 8, 1877 | February 8, 1877 |
| Summar, J. F. | Walker, D. B. | C/342 | November 20, 1885 | November 22, 1885 |
| Summar, J. J. | Kelley, Minty | C/322 | January 24, 1885 | January 25, 1885 |
| Summar, J. N. | Donnell, Miss Sarah E. | B/42 | March 15, 1867 | March 15, 1867 |
| Summar, John P. | Fuston, H. D. | C/266 | December 28, 1880 | December 30, 1880 |
| Summar, Josie | Patterson, Charley | F/156 | September 19, 1898 | September 22, 1898 |
| Summar, L. J. Miss | Francis, M. C. | A2/63 | February 26, 1858 | February 28, 1858 |
| Summar, Lavis Miss | Francis, C. C. | B/62 | March 9, 1868 | March 9, 1868] |
| Summar, Lillian | Bell, John B. | F/22 | November 25, 1893 | November 26, 1893 |
| Summar, Louisa | Summar, Berton | B/18 | January 1, 1870 | No Return |
| Summar, Lula Miss | Jones, Wm. F. | F/56 | January 22, 1894 | No Return |
| Summar, Maggie | Davenport, Henry | F/84 | February 18, 1896 | February 19, 1896 |
| Summar, Martha Miss | Cantrell, James W. | B/58 | December 21, 1867 | December 28, 1867 |
| Summar, Mary Lavisa Miss | Vickers, William | B/84 | July 27, 1869 | No Return |
| Summar, Mary Miss | Porterfield, Samuel G. | A/109 | March 7, 1848 | March 9, 1848 |
| Summar, Mattie | Markum, D. | E/215 | September 30, 1889 | September 30, 1889 |
| Summar, Medie | Bogle, James | C/298 | December 27, 1883 | No Return |
| Summar, Milley Miss | Mathews, Samuel | A/100 | July 22, 1847 | July 22, 1847 |
| Summar, Misa | Williams, Frances | A2/123 | April 3, 1865 | April 6, 1865 |
| Summar, S. M. | Temply, R. D. | C/472 | December 21, 1892 | December 22, 1892 |

| Groom or Bride | Groom or Bride | Book/Page | Date of License | Date of Marriage |
|---|---|---|---|---|
| Summar, S. V. | Gray, W. W. | C/136 | March 1, 1876 | March 2, 1876 |
| Summar, Sally Miss | Vasser, Joshua Jr. | A/73 | October 3, 1844 | September 3, 1844 |
| Summar, Samuel | Barrett, Nancy E. | C/112 | April 29, 1875 | May 2, 1875 |
| Summar, Sarah | Holland, Jas | C/174 | October 25, 1877 | No Return |
| Summar, Sopha | Hubbard, F. M. | C/320 | December 10, 1884 | December 10, 1884 |
| Summar, T. D. | Harris, Miss Mary J. | A2/142 | August 8, 1866 | September 2, 1866 |
| Summar, T. H. | McBroom, Minnie | F/156 | September 17, 1898 | September 18, 1898 |
| Summar, Talitha | Willard, William | A/54 | September 19, 1842 | No Return |
| Summar, Thomas | Simpson, Nova | F/120 | July 23, 1897 | July 24, 1897 |
| Summar, Verin | Bogle, Tolbert | F/104 | December 12, 1896 | December 21, 1896 |
| Summar, Wm. | Richardson, Miss Susan | B/124 | January 14, 1871 | January 15, 1871 |
| Summar, Z. T. | Bryson, Miss Parthena | B/78 | January 28, 1869 | January 28, 1869 |
| Summars, Asaline | Bailey, France | F/88 | June 17, 1896 | June 21, 1896 |
| Summars, Bettie | Hipp, J. D. | C/344 | December 16, 1885 | December 16, 1885 |
| Summars, Burten | Haras, Munro | C/214 | March 14, 1879 | March 15, 1879 |
| Summars, C. B. | Adams, Armenty A. | C/304 | February 13, 1884 | February 13, 1884 |
| Summars, C. T. | Odum, A. H. | F/26 | December 20, 1893 | No Return |
| Summars, Callie | Orrick A. J. | D/1 | | July 10, 1881 |
| Summars, Catherine | Green, Jno | C/122 | November 3, 1875 | November 4, 1875 |
| Summars, Evert | Witherspoon, Mary M. | A/8 | November 22, 1838 | November 22, 1838 |
| Summars, J. J. | Haley, Nancy | C/252 | August 12, 1880 | August 12, 1880 |
| Summars, James | Herrell, Tennie | C/228 | October 15, 1879 | October 15, 1879 |
| Summars, Malissie | Mairs, Dillard | C/364 | August 28, 1886 | August 29, 1886 |
| Summars, Mary | Brandon, Cornelius | A/34 | October 23, 1840 | No Return |
| Summars, Mattie | Miller, Richard | D/5 | | October 2, 1881 |
| Summars, Nannie | Teal, Ed | F/20 | October 17, 1893 | No Return |
| Summars, R. C. | Vicars, Sarah | C/244 | March 6, 1880 | March 8, 1880 |
| Summars, Robert H. | Brandon, Sarah | D/1 | | June 4, 1881 |
| Summars, Rosa Miss | Combs, J. B. | F/174 | April 22, 1899 | April 23, 1899 |
| Summars, T. J. | Warrick, M. E. | C/380 | December 27, 1886 | December 28, 1886 |
| Summars, W. A. | Holt, Dovey J. | C/296 | November 23, 1883 | November 25, 1883 |
| Summars, Wm. | Mitchell, Mary | C/288 | July 26, 1883 | July 26, 1883 |
| Summer, B. D. | Bryson, Miss Elizabeth | A2/60 | November 22, 1857 | November 20?, 1857 |
| Summer, Charley | Willard, Florence | F/4 | February 22, 1893 | February 23, 1893 |
| Summer, Elijah | Summar, Eunicy | A/73 | October 17, 1844 | October 17, 1844 |
| Summer, Jacob L. | Willson, Miss Sarrah J. | A2/57 | September 25, 1857 | No Return |
| Summer, James | Stone, Jane | C/34 | August 14, 1872 | August 18, 1872 |
| Summer, Jane Miss | Standly, T. | A2/73 | December 26, 1853 | December 27, 1865 |
| Summer, P. E. Miss | Francis, J. D. | A2/46 | January 30, 1856 | January 31, 1856 |
| Summer, Pitson Miss | Davenport, W. R. | B/70 | September 19, 1868 | September 20, 1868 |
| Summer, R. H. | Davenport, S. M. | F/72 | October 19, 1895 | October 20, 1895 |
| Summer, Sarah E. | Low, Thos. N. | A2/115 | August 9, 1864 | August 9, 1864 |
| Summer, Sarah Miss | Roberson, W. M. | A2/88 | August 28, 1859 | No Return |
| Summer, W. A. | Blank, William | A2/68 | October 8, 1858 | No Return |
| Summers, Amanda J. | Cooper, P. G. | B/56 | November 25, 1867 | November 26, 1867 |
| Summers, Amanda J. Miss | Hill, John N. | B/56 | November 19, 1867 | November 20, 1867 |

| Groom or Bride | Groom or Bride | Book/Page | Date of License | Date of Marriage |
|---|---|---|---|---|
| Summers, E. G. Miss | Odom, A. M. | F/48 | November 21, 1894 | November 22, 1894 |
| Summers, Ell | McKnight, Mat | E/249 | December 24, 1889 | December 25, 1889 |
| Summers, Emma D. | Carrol, John F. | C/432 | March 26, 1891 | No Return |
| Summers, Iza Evaline Miss | Robinson, William M. | A2/2 | May 27, 1850 | No Return |
| Summers, J. A. | McGill, Miss Sarah E. | B/56 | December 3, 1867 | December 3, 1867 |
| Summers, J. H. | Elrod, Nannie D. | F/50 | December 8, 1894 | No Return |
| Summers, James | Lewis, Miss Martha E. | A2/37 | December 4, 1854 | December 7, 1854 |
| Summers, Jenny | Higgins, Howard | C/440 | July 4, 1891 | July 5, 1891 |
| Summers, M. A. Miss | Brown, T. J. | A2/61 | December 24, 1857 | December 24, 1857 |
| Summers, Manie | Teal, Ed | F/34 | March 17, 1894 | March 19, 1894 |
| Summers, Martha N. | Williams, Joseph | A2/40 | May 2, 1855 | May 6, 1855 |
| Summers, Martiller | Owens, Jessie | C/82 | February 5, 1874 | February 5, 1875 |
| Summers, Mary | Tatum, J. M. | C/438 | June 27, 1891 | June 27, 1891 |
| Summers, Miss | Bryson, Robert | A2/57 | August 6, 1857 | August 20, 1857 |
| Summers, Nancy E. Miss | Tarpley, R. W. | B/98 | January 8, 1870 | January 11, 1970 |
| Summers, Nola | Simpson, E. A. | E/244 | December 21, 1889 | December 24, 1889 |
| Summers, Rilda Miss | Prater, T. G. | C/390 | June 14, 1887 | June 15, 1887 |
| Summers, Rufus | Odom, Sallie | C/418 | October 11, 1890 | No Return |
| Summers, Sarah Miss | Worley, Arthur | B/102 | May 9, 1970 | May 10, 1870 |
| Summers, Susan | Young, J. C. | C/46 | December 20, 1872 | No Return |
| Summers, Susan | Pullium, Dolly | C/152 | January 17, 1877 | January 18, 1877 |
| Summers, Teresa | Young, Felling M. | A2/40 | April 29, 1855 | Returns Missing |
| Sumnar, Louisa | Vardel, John T. | A2/109 | September 18, 1863 | No Return |
| Sumnar, W. H. | Wilson, Lucinda | A2/107 | March 3, 1863 | No Return |
| Sumner, Wm. G. | Philips, Miss Mary Ann | A2/64 | April 22, 1858 | April 22, 1858 |
| Suthern, Nancy L. Miss | Richerson, Wm. G. | A2/42 | September 27, 1855 | September 27, 1855 |
| Sutten, Lavender | Kirby, Miss Julena | A2/47 | March 15, 1856 | March 16, 1856 |
| Sutton, Adaline Miss | Mullins, Dozier | A/69 | April 26, 1844 | April 26, 1844 |
| Sutton, Elizabeth Miss | McKnight, William W. | A/123 | July 5, 1849 | No Return |
| Sutton, John | Davenport, Mollie | C/250 | July 8, 1880 | No Return |
| Sutton, Margarett Jane Miss | Fite, Daniel | A2/8 | December 23, 1850 | December 25, 1850 |
| Sutton, Mary | Tassey, Alexander | A/29 | May 7, 1840 | May 7, 1840 |
| Swan, Wm. | Haly, Sarah | C/114 | May 29, 1875 | June 3, 1875 |
| Swaner, John | Spangler, Miss Milly | A2/16 | March 11, 1852 | March 16, 1852 |
| Swanford, Bob (col.) | Woodards, Janie (col.) | F/116 | April 17, 1897 | April 18, 1897 |
| Swanger, John | Blackburn, Tennessee | C/424 | December 10, 1890 | December 11, 1890 |
| Swanger, Mary Ann | McFarland, H. R. | C/88 | July 20, 1874 | July 23, 1874 |
| Swanger, Mary Ann | McFarland, W. R. | C/92 | July 20, 1874 | No Return |
| Swanger, Mollie | Duke, Calvin | F/76 | December 14, 1895 | December 14, 1895 |
| Swanger, Tilda | Clendennan, P. C. | C/450 | November 24, 1891 | November 24, 1891 |
| Swanger, W. S. | Duke, Matilda | C/394 | July 16, 1887 | July 16, 18878 |
| Swanger, W. S. | Umbarger, Sarah A. | C/422 | November 2, 1890 | November 5, 1890 |
| Swindell, W. G. | Freeman, Ellar | C/226 | October 30, 1879 | October 30, 1879 |
| Swindle, W. P. | Justice, Elen | C/308 | April 22, 1884 | April 22, 1884 |
| Swoap, W. T. | Gilley, Mary E. | C/328 | March 2, 1885 | March 5, 1885 |
| Swoape, Samuel A. | Moore, Miss Elizabeth J. | A2/123 | April 20, 1865 | April 20, 1865 |

| Groom or Bride | Groom or Bride | Book/Page | Date of License | Date of Marriage |
|---|---|---|---|---|
| Tabour, Charles O. | Spry, Elizabeth | A2/25 | July 18, 1853 | July 19, 1853 |
| Tabour, Nathan C. (Talor) | Lasater, Nancy Ann | A/77 | February 26, 1845 | February 26, 1845 |
| Tabour, Unice E. Miss | Phillips, Samuel | A/125 | July 17, 1849 | No Return |
| Tackett, John O. | Foster, Miss Katharine | A/62 | May 29, 1843 | May 29, 1843 |
| Tallet, Margrett | Vasser, John | C/340 | November 14, 1885 | November 15, 1885 |
| Talley, Ada | Sea, Abb | C/376 | November 25, 1886 | November 25, 1886 |
| Talley, Harriet | Donnell, James | B/18 | February 2, 1870 | February 2, 1870 |
| Talley, Joe (col.) | Talley, Mary (col.) | D/16 | | October 9, 1882 |
| Talley, Laura | Adams, Henry | C/394 | July 9, 1887 | July 10, 1887 |
| Talley, Locky (col) | Mitchell, Henry | E/26 | March 18, 1888 | March 18, 1888 |
| Talley, Maggie | Stephens, E. Jr. | C/318 | November 24, 1884 | November 24, 1884 |
| Talley, Martin | Martin, Mary | E/117 | December 24, 1888 | December 24, 1888 |
| Talley, Mary (col) | Alexander, Will | E/29 | April 15, 1888 | April 15, 1888 |
| Talley, Mary (col.) | Talley, Joe (col.) | D/16 | | October 9, 1882 |
| Talley, Tennessee | Jennings, Nelson | C/198 | September 4, 1878 | Setember 8, 1878 |
| Talley, Vira | Webb, George | C/346 | December 28, 1885 | December 28, 1885 |
| Talley, W. R. | Vinson, Miss Henrietta W. | A2/162 | June 30, 1866 | July 19, 1866 |
| Tally, Amandy | Officer, Ed | C/118 | August 26, 1875 | No Return |
| Tally, Richard | Chumly, Caroline | A2/105 | October 6, 1862 | October 7, 1862 |
| Tapley, Mattie | Miligan, G. L. | F/146 | March 10, 1898 | March 10, 1898 |
| Tarleton, Susan | Dennis, Mat | A2/122 | March 23, 1865 | No Return |
| Tarlton, James W. | Galahare July | A2/60 | December 9, 1857 | December 10, 1857 |
| Tarpley, R. W. | Summers, Miss Nancy E. | B/98 | January 8, 1870 | January 11, 1970 |
| Tarply, James M. | Stephen, Miss Mary J. | A2/150 | May 12, 1866 | No Return |
| Tarwater, Thomas | Mears, M. | A2/28 | October 13, 1853 | October 14, 1853 |
| Tassey, Alexander | Sutton, Mary | A/29 | May 7, 1840 | May 7, 1840 |
| Tassey, Alexander | Campbell, Miss Nancy | A/92 | October 8, 1846 | No Return |
| Tassey, Bettie Jane Miss | Alexander, J. M. | B/68 | August 12, 1868 | August 13, 1868 |
| Tassey, Margarett | White, J. H. | F/128 | August 30, 1897 | August 31, 1897 |
| Tassey, Mollie | Hollansworth, J. B. | F/102 | November 20, 1896 | November 22, 1896 |
| Tate, Ada | Bullard, Willey | F/52 | October 27, 1894 | October 27, 1894 |
| Tate, Amanda Miss | Taylor, Edmund H. | B/68 | August 25, 1868 | August 25, 1868 |
| Tate, Hannah Emaline Miss | McEwen, John Dixson | A/111 | May 25, 1848 | May 25, 1848 |
| Tate, J. B. | Blair, Sarah | F/6 | March 6, 1893 | March 7, 1893 |
| Tate, J. B. | Gunter, Evie | F/126 | August 22, 1897 | August 22, 1897 |
| Tate, Jacob B. | Kersey, Miss Elizabeth | A2/13 | December 30, 1851 | January 3, 1852 |
| Tatum, A. C. | McAdow, Miss Eliza | A2/9 | December 30, 1850 | December 30, 1850 |
| Tatum, Elvia | Stewart, R. C. | C/202 | November 2, 1878 | November 3, 1878 |
| Tatum, Emma | Hayes, John | C/314 | October 12, 1884 | October 12, 1884 |
| Tatum, Julia | Rucker, Wm. | C/314 | September 21, 1884 | September 21, 1884 |
| Tatum, M. E. | Hayes, T. E. | C/76 | December 10, 1873 | December 10, 1873 |
| Tatum, R. F. | Bethell, Miss M. E. | B/40 | February 6, 1867 | February 7, 1867 |
| Tayler, Phebe | Macon, James | F/14 | August 5, 1893 | August 27, 1893 |
| Taylor, A. B. | Moore, Miss E. C. | B/54 | October 28, 1867 | October 29, 1967 |
| Taylor, Adam | Moore, Tennie | F/68 | September 14, 1895 | September 16, 1895 |
| Taylor, Aggie | McFerrin, Joe | C/224 | September 10, 1879 | September 10, 1879 |

| Groom or Bride | Groom or Bride | Book/Page | Date of License | Date of Marriage |
|---|---|---|---|---|
| Taylor, Agnes | Taylor, Allen | B/2 | August 21, 1865 | November 3, 1865 |
| Taylor, Agness | Cannon, Henry | A/3 | May 15, 1838 | May 15, 1838 |
| Taylor, Allen | Taylor, Agnes | B/2 | August 21, 1865 | November 3, 1865 |
| Taylor, Ann | Gannon, S. E. | F/164 | December 29, 1898 | December 29, 1898 |
| Taylor, Annie | Gannon, S. E. | E/328 | December 29, 1898 | |
| Taylor, Barry K. | Cooper, Miss Martha | A2/10 | February 3, 1851 | February 7, 1851 |
| Taylor, Bettie Miss | Moore, J. G. | B/120 | December 15, 1870 | December 15, 1870 |
| Taylor, David | Lyon, Yander | E/62 | August 18, 1888 | August 19, 1888 |
| Taylor, Dedie | Bogle, G. B. | F/154 | August 20, 1898 | August 21, 1898 |
| Taylor, Edmund H. | Tate, Miss Amanda | B/68 | August 25, 1868 | August 25, 1868 |
| Taylor, Eliza | Sullins, Wm. | F/18 | September 12, 1893 | September 14, 1893 |
| Taylor, Elizabeth Miss | Anderson, Elijah | A/37 | April 6, 1841 | April 6, 1841 |
| Taylor, Elizabeth R. Mrs. | Sanford, Thomas B. | A/119 | February 14, 1849 | February 15, 1848? |
| Taylor, Elvira | Fugett, Washington | B/8 | December 8, 1865 | December 8, 1865 |
| Taylor, Frances Miss | Stewart, James | A2/69 | October 21, 1858 | October 21, 1858 |
| Taylor, Francis A. Miss | Williams, R. M. | A2/41 | September 13, 1855 | September 20, 1855 |
| Taylor, George | Taylor, Susan | B/6 | August 26, 1865 | August 26, 1865 |
| Taylor, George | Roberts, Elizabeth | B/6 | August 28, 1865 | August 28, 1865 |
| Taylor, George L. | Anderson, Miss Jane | A/93 | November 2, 1846 | November 2, 1846 |
| Taylor, J. B. | Brage, Miss Georgia | F/62 | April 16, 1895 | May 4, 1895 |
| Taylor, J. R. | Manus, Miss Malissa | B/108 | September 1, 1870 | September 1, 1870 |
| Taylor, James | Wharton, Miss Eliabeth R. | A/96 | January 21, 1847 | January 26, 1847 |
| Taylor, James | New, Maria | B/6 | September 1, 1865 | July 1, 1865? |
| Taylor, James D. | Ferrell, Miss Martha | B/118 | November 28, 1870 | December 1, 1870 |
| Taylor, James T. | Smith, Miss Susan L. | A2/76 | August 16, 1855 | August 16, 1855 |
| Taylor, John M. | McBroom, Manerva | A2/124 | July 18, 1865 | July 18, 1865 |
| Taylor, Julia | Ferrel, Jordon | B/4 | August 22, 1865 | August 28, 1865 |
| Taylor, L. B | Sissom, J. L. | F/4 | February 18, 1893 | February 26, 1893 |
| Taylor, L. E. | Weatherspon, A. B. | C/118 | September 13, 1875 | September 14, 1875 |
| Taylor, Laura (col.) | McFerrin, James (col.) | D/2 | | August 23, 1881 |
| Taylor, Mariah | Fugitt, Wash | C/250 | July 1, 1880 | July 1, 1880 |
| Taylor, Martha | Webb, Samuel | B/6 | September 2, 1865 | September 4, 1865 |
| Taylor, Martha L. Miss | Anderson, William W. | B/44 | April 6, 1867 | April 7, 1867 |
| Taylor, Mary | Stephens, Benj. | C/74 | November 22, 1873 | November 23, 1873 |
| Taylor, Mary J. | Webb, Nelville | C/358 | April 24, 1886 | April 25, 1886 |
| Taylor, Mary J. | Williams, Soloman | D/7 | | November 27, 1881 |
| Taylor, Mary Jane Miss | Cates, Joseph M. D. | A/113 | September 5, 1848 | September 5, 1848 |
| Taylor, Mattie (col.) | Weadon, Tom (col.) | F/114 | March 13, 1897 | March 13, 1897 |
| Taylor, Nancy | Wooderd, George W. | A/4 | July 17, 1838 | July 17, 1838 |
| Taylor, Nannie | Dunn, Daniel (col.) | C/408 | November 26, 1887 | November 27, 1887 |
| Taylor, Nathaniel M. | Henderson, Miss Mary | A/40 | August 25, 1841 | August 26, 1841 |
| Taylor, Richard | Brashears, Nelly | A/78 | May 9, 1845 | May 9, 1845 |
| Taylor, S. E. Miss | Cotter, T. G. | B/122 | December 29, 1870 | December 29, 1870 |
| Taylor, Sallie | Bogle, Isaac | E/260 | January 10, 1890 | No Return |
| Taylor, Sallie | Vasser, John A. | C/252 | July 24, 1880 | July 25, 1880 |
| Taylor, Sarah | Thompson, Jerdon | C/20 | January 20, 1872 | January 20, 1872 |

| Groom or Bride | Groom or Bride | Book/Page | Date of License | Date of Marriage |
|---|---|---|---|---|
| Taylor, Sarah | Taylor, Wm. | C/330 | June 20, 1885 | June 21, 1885 |
| Taylor, Susan | Taylor, George | B/6 | August 26, 1865 | August 26, 1865 |
| Taylor, Virginia P. | Moore, Jessee G. | A2/121 | February 27, 1865 | February 28, 1865 |
| Taylor, W. N. | Cates, Miss Mary | B/84 | August 26, 1869 | August 26, 1869 |
| Taylor, Wesley | Barton, Mary | B/6 | August 28, 1865 | September 3, 1865 |
| Teague, Emaly | Owens, Jeremiah J. | A/50 | July 5, 1842 | July 5, 1842 |
| Teague, M. J. Miss | Mithcel, Thos. P. | A2/80 | July 15, 1857 | July 21, 1857 |
| Teague, Rachel A. Miss | Sullivan, Wm. H. | A2/60 | November 19, 1857 | November 19, 1857 |
| Teague, Roxie Miss | English, Andrew | A2/146 | April 20, 1866 | April 22, 1866 |
| Teague, Sarah A. Miss | Carnahan, John H. | B/74 | December 2, 1868 | December 3, 1868 |
| Teague, W. A. | Thomas, Miss Sarah P. | B/64 | March 16, 1868 | March 17, 1868 |
| Teal, Ann Miss | Young, William | C/386 | March 7, 1887 | No Return |
| Teal, Ed | Summars, Nannie | F/20 | October 17, 1893 | No Return |
| Teal, Ed | Summers, Manie | F/34 | March 17, 1894 | March 19, 1894 |
| Teasley, Matilda Miss | Sullivan, William L. | A/43 | October 30, 1841 | October 31, 1841 |
| Teasley, William | Preston, Miss Lucinda | A/45 | December 23, 1841 | December 23, 1841 |
| Teasly, Thomas | Preston, Miss Rebecca | A/38 | April 12, 1841 | April 18, 1841 |
| Techoble, Elmangy (col.) | Weadon, Hiller (col.) | F/136 | November 8, 1897 | November 8, 1897 |
| Tedder, J. C. | Davis, S. C. | F/74 | November 23, 1895 | November 24, 1895 |
| Tedder, Mary | Travis, Daniel | A/49 | May 19, 1842 | May 19, 1842 |
| Tedder, Mary C. | Mears, James | A/117 | November 14, 1848 | November 14, 1848 |
| Tedder, Melvina Miss | Davenport, J. M. | B/82 | July 5, 1869 | July 18, 1869 |
| Tedder, Thomas | Sauls, Miss Rhoda | A/88 | March 26, 1846 | March 26, 1846 |
| Teddler, M. F. | Wood, W. M. | C/366 | September 11, 1886 | No Return |
| Teel, Elizza | Sumers, George | F/34 | September 8, 1894 | September 19, 1894 |
| Teel, Miss M. E. | Simmons, A. B. | F/50 | November 27, 1894 | November 28, 1894 |
| Teele, Lou | Elams, Rubin L. | C/468 | November 23, 1892 | November 23, 1892 |
| Teeples, | Johnson, Libe | A2/109 | October 8, 1863 | No Return |
| Tembleton, William | Odom, Miss Hanah | B/48 | July 24, 1867 | July 24, 1867 |
| Templeton, Samuel | Patton, Miss Tempa | A2/17 | March 16, 1852 | March 16, 1852 |
| Tenerson, Mary J. Miss | Millikin, Albert G. | A2/75 | August 31, 1854 | August 31, 1854 |
| Tennison, Elizabeth Miss | Todd, James Jr. | A/83 | October 4, 1845 | October 5, 1845 |
| Tennpenny, Colister | Davenport, Nathan | E/234 | November 24, 1889 | November 24, 1889 |
| Tennyson, M. A. Miss | Walkup, J. A. | A2/84 | January 5, 1859 | January 6, 1859 |
| Tenpenney, H. M. | Fann, John L. | F/26 | December 21, 1893 | December 21, 1893 |
| Tenpenny, A. A. | Stroud, Miss Aline | F/110 | January 20, 1897 | January 20, 1897 |
| Tenpenny, A. H. | Harris, J. D. | C/338 | October 10, 1885 | October 11, 1885 |
| Tenpenny, A. G. | Owen, Della | F/112 | February 10, 1897 | February 10, 1897 |
| Tenpenny, Alfred | Hays, Miss France | A/115 | October 18, 1848 | October 18, 1848 |
| Tenpenny, B. A. | Prater, J. H. | C/470 | November 28, 1892 | November 29, 1892 |
| Tenpenny, B. F. | Pittard, Jas. L. | A2/101 | July 28, 1860 | July 29, 1860 |
| Tenpenny, Charleny Miss | McBroom, Alexander D. | A2/49 | August 12, 1856 | No Return |
| Tenpenny, Daniel Jr. | Gaither, Miss Mary Jane | A/72 | September 12, 1844 | September 12, 1844 |
| Tenpenny, David | Sullivan, Mary A. | A2/129 | September 21, 1865 | September 21, 1865 |
| Tenpenny, E. J. | Todd, Margaret | A2/133 | December 16, 1865 | December 17, 1865 |
| Tenpenny, E. J. Miss | Woods, A. U. | C/390 | June 28, 1887 | No Return |

| Groom or Bride | Groom or Bride | Book/Page | Date of License | Date of Marriage |
|---|---|---|---|---|
| Tenpenny, E. J. Miss | Woods, A. H. | C/392 | June 28, 1886 | No Return |
| Tenpenny, Elizabeth Miss | Preston, E. C. | A2/52 | December 16, 1856 | No Return |
| Tenpenny, Emma | Odom, D. F. | C/90 | July 20, 1874 | July 20, 1874 |
| Tenpenny, Emma | Odom, D. F. | C/92 | July 30, 1874 | No Return |
| Tenpenny, Emma Miss | Woods, William | C/392 | June 26, 1887 | No Return |
| Tenpenny, Emma C. Miss | Woods, William D. | C/390 | June 28, 1887 | No Return |
| Tenpenny, Frances | George, Miles B. | B/4 | August 23, 1865 | September 2, 1865 |
| Tenpenny, Frances | Campbell, J. W. | F/10 | June 15, 1893 | June 15, 1893 |
| Tenpenny, J. E. | Higgins, Eula | F/116 | April 30, 1897 | May 24, 1897 |
| Tenpenny, James | Richards, Miss Rebecca | A/71 | July 27, 1844 | July 27, 1844 |
| Tenpenny, James | Burry, Miss Margart | A2/89 | September 17, 1859 | No Return |
| Tenpenny, Jane | Hollis, J. H. | A2/101 | August 14, 1860 | No Return |
| Tenpenny, Jas. | Peeler, Rocksy Ann | F/112 | February 22, 1897 | February 24, 1897 |
| Tenpenny, Jesse A. | Bogle, E. E. | D/7 | | November 21, 1881 |
| Tenpenny, John | Alexander, M. P. | A2/74 | November 3, 1853 | November 3, 1853 |
| Tenpenny, John | Alexander, Miss M. P. | A2/74 | November 3, 1853 | November 3, 1853 |
| Tenpenny, John | Barton, Jane | B/18 | December 23, 1869 | No Return |
| Tenpenny, Joseph W. | Pittard, Miss Mary L. | A2/87 | August 16, 1859 | No Return |
| Tenpenny, Julian Miss | Duboise, James P. | B/48 | July 25, 1867 | July 25, 1867 |
| Tenpenny, Lizzie | Prater, J. H. | E/70 | September 6, 1888 | September 6, 1888 |
| Tenpenny, Mariah | Todd, Jessee A. | A2/105 | October 11, 1862 | October 12, 1862 |
| Tenpenny, Mary J. Miss | Vasser, Alford | B/128 | March 4, 1871 | March 4, 1871 |
| Tenpenny, Maryann | McBorren, Isaac | A2/15 | February 17, 1852 | February 17, 1852 |
| Tenpenny, Mumphard | Hays, Margrett | D/15 | | August 31, 1882 |
| Tenpenny, Nicy J. | Escue, George | C/202 | October 16, 1878 | October 16, 1878 |
| Tenpenny, Orrila | Hoover, O. A. | F/138 | November 17, 1897 | November 17, 1897 |
| Tenpenny, Richard Jr. | Summar, Miss Eunicy | A/100 | July 19, 1847 | July 20, 1847 |
| Tenpenny, Robert | Woods, H. M. | E/91 | October 23, 1888 | October 23, 1888 |
| Tenpenny, S. A. | Woods, J. D. | C/444 | August 17, 1891 | No Return |
| Tenpenny, S. J. | McIntire, Arren | C/288 | August 13, 1883 | August 13, 1883 |
| Tenpenny, Sallie | Smithson, James | C/258 | October 6, 1880 | October 6, 1880 |
| Tenpenny, Saphrona | Prater, Adam | E/153 | December 14, 1888 | December 14, 1888 |
| Tenpenny, Sarah | Vance, Anderson | B/18 | January 27, 1870 | January 27, 1870 |
| Tenpenny, Sibbie Miss | Alexander, W. T. | C/414 | August 6, 1890 | August 6, 1890 |
| Tenpenny, T. B. | Irvine, Myrtle, S. C. | E/206 | September 3, 1889 | September 3, 1889 |
| Tenpenny, Tobias | Owen, Mis Lena | E/133 | February 6, 1889 | February 7, 1889 |
| Tenpenny, Wm. | Morgan, Miss Caroline | A2/65 | July 27, 1858 | July 27, 1858 |
| Tenpeny, J. H. | Lafevers, M. A. | F/30 | January 18, 1894 | No Return |
| Teples, Malvira | Manis, E. D. | A2/113 | March 27, 1864 | March 27, 1864 |
| Terner, Isaac | Vane, Sarrah S. | A2/39 | March 28, 1855 | March 29, 1855 |
| Terry, Drew | Odom, Andrew | C/86 | April 2, 1874 | April 2, 1874 |
| Tettard, Tiner | Travis, Wm. | F/46 | October 14, 1894 | October 14, 1894 |
| Tetters, Fanny | Pitts, Wiley | C/442 | August 5, 1891 | August 6, 1891 |
| Theirs, Isaac | Jones, Mary | A2/27 | August 4, 1853 | No Return |
| Thomas (col.) | Webb, Annie (col.) | F/130 | September 4, 1897 | September 5, 12897 |
| Thomas, A. | Bush, Mariah | A2/103 | November 11, 1860 | No Return |

| Groom or Bride | Groom or Bride | Book/Page | Date of License | Date of Marriage |
|---|---|---|---|---|
| Thomas, A. D. Miss | Curlee, T. G. | B/56 | November 19, 1867 | November 20, 1867 |
| Thomas, Allice | Higgins, Sandy | C/146 | October 21, 1876 | October 22, 1876 |
| Thomas, Amanda E. Miss | Leech, William C. | A/114 | September 12, 1848 | September 12, 1848 |
| Thomas, Anlzo | Sander, Charlotte | F/8 | April 29, 1893 | April 29, 1893 |
| Thomas, Ben | Haley, Betty | F/128 | September 1, 1896 | September 1, 1897 |
| Thomas, Catherine | Moonehan, Axy | F/6 | March 1, 1893 | March 2, 1893 |
| Thomas, Daniel | Farler, Miss Mary | A/71 | August 1, 1844 | August 1, 1844 |
| Thomas, Della | Pitts, Wm | F/14 | August 2, 1893 | September 1, 1893 |
| Thomas, Della | Gann, Thomas | F/72 | October 1, 1895 | October 21, 1895 |
| Thomas, Della | Deberry, Charles | C/468 | November 19, 1892 | November 20, 1892 |
| Thomas, Dorah | Young, V. L. | F/68 | September 14, 1895 | September 15, 1895 |
| Thomas, E. K. | Reed, Miss Jane | A2/2 | April 13, 1850 | No Return |
| Thomas, Ed | Wright, Mary | F/10 | June 12, 1893 | June 12, 1893 |
| Thomas, Ema M. | Johnson, John B. | A2/78 | January 26, 1856 | January 26, 1856 |
| Thomas, Emaliza | McEwin, Jospeh | A/12 | April 6, 1839 | April 7, 1839 |
| Thomas, George W. | Mears, Eliza J. | E/228 | November 2, 1889 | November 2, 1889 |
| Thomas, H. L. | Dennis, T. M. | F/30 | January 24, 1894 | No Return |
| Thomas, Henry N. | Good, Miss Mary A. | A/115 | October 12, 1848 | October 12, 1848 |
| Thomas, J. F. | Maclan, Miss Harriet | A2/73 | March 10, 1859 | No Return |
| Thomas, J. F. | Maclin, Harriet | A2/84 | March 10, 1859 | No Return |
| Thomas, J. W. | Davis, Miss M. E. | B/102 | April 4, 1870 | April 7, 1840 |
| Thomas, James N. | Wimberley, Miss Elizabeth | A/70 | July 20, 1844 | July 21, 1844 |
| Thomas, Jane Miss | Manus, Thomas | A/102 | September 25, 1847 | No Return |
| Thomas, Joel | Hibdon, Miss C. C. | A2/89 | October 19, 1859 | No Return |
| Thomas, John, A. | Aldridge, Millia | A/7 | October 2, 1838 | October 2, 1838 |
| Thomas, Josie | Manus, Thomas E. | E/56 | August 4, 1888 | August 5, 1888 |
| Thomas, Julie | Kennedy, W. C. | D/13 | | April 25, 1882 |
| Thomas, June | Todd, John | B/14 | December 2, 1868 | No Return |
| Thomas, Lucy Jane | Fann, Levi | E/59 | August 11, 1888 | August 11, 1888 |
| Thomas, Margrett | McMahan, J. T. | C/98 | October 23, 1874 | October 24, 1874 |
| Thomas, Margarett Miss | Marcuis, Jacob | A2/17 | June 10, 1852 | June 10, 1852 |
| Thomas, Mary | Underwood, Benj. | C/46 | December 2, 1872 | December 6, 1872 |
| Thomas, Mary | Pendleton, Samuel | A/57 | December 21, 1842 | December 21, 1842 |
| Thomas, Mary J. | Taylor, Brent | C/236 | January 8, 1880 | January 8, 1880 |
| Thomas, Mary Miss | Youngblood, Jonnathan | B/130 | April 20, 1871 | April 20, 1871 |
| Thomas, Maud | Davis, J. A. | E/253 | December 27, 1889 | December 27, 1889 |
| Thomas, Minnie | Manns, Lee | F/134 | October 29, 1897 | October 29, 1897 |
| Thomas, Miss Luda | McMahan, John S. | F/168 | January 24, 1899 | No Return |
| Thomas, Nancy | Lance, James | D/101 | | February 12, 1882 |
| Thomas, Nancy | Mears, Robt, F. | C/316 | November 14, 1884 | November 14, 1884 |
| Thomas, Nelson G. | Wimberlyey, Margarett | A/59 | February 8, 1843 | February 8, 1843 |
| Thomas, Queen E. | Wilburn, T. A. | C/120 | September 15, 1875 | September 16, 1875 |
| Thomas, Rezen F. | Winnett, Miss Eleanor | A2/139 | February 28, 1866 | March 1, 1866 |
| Thomas, Sallie | Wright, Allen | F/12 | July 7, 1893 | July 12, 1893 |
| Thomas, Samuel | Thomas, Sarah | B/4 | August 26, 1865 | August 27, 1865 |
| Thomas, Sarah | Thomas, Samuel | B/4 | August 26, 1865 | August 27, 1865 |

| Groom or Bride | Groom or Bride | Book/Page | Date of License | Date of Marriage |
|---|---|---|---|---|
| Thomas, Sarah F. Miss | Elkins, Silas | B/126 | March 4, 1871 | No Return |
| Thomas, Sarah M. | Johnson, Issac N. | A2/3 | July 26, 1850 | July 30, 1850 |
| Thomas, Sarah Miss | Farley, John Jefferson | A/98 | March 6, 1847 | March 7, 1847 |
| Thomas, Sarah Miss | Knight, James M. | A/119 | January 22, 1849 | No Return |
| Thomas, Sarah P. Miss | Teague, W. A. | B/64 | March 16, 1868 | March 17, 1868 |
| Thomas, Sue | Vance, F. M. | C/336 | September 5, 1885 | September 9, 1885 |
| Thomas, W. C. | McMahan, Lillie | F/152 | July 4, 1898 | July 5, 1898 |
| Thomas, William | Elkins, Miss C. | A2/61 | December 24, 1857 | December 24, 1857 |
| Thomas, William | Williams, Roxanna | A2/125 | August 9, 1865 | August 8, 1865 |
| Thomas, William | McCabe, Miss Mary C. | B/108 | August 25, 1870 | No Return |
| Thomas, Zachariah | Travis, Miss Issabella | A2/6 | October 8, 1850 | October 8, 1850 |
| Thomason, A. J. | Knox, J. F. | F/144 | January 26, 1898 | January 30, 1898 |
| Thomason, J. A. | Bowen, Miss S. T. | B/116 | November 10, 1870 | November 11, 1870 |
| Thompkins, Robert | Gaither, Miss Emma | E/197 | August 3, 1889 | August 4, 1889 |
| Thompson, A. | Burk, Miss Sarah | A2/63 | February 13, 1858 | No Return |
| Thompson, Allen | Bush, Mariah | A2/97 | June 7, 1860 | No Return |
| Thompson, Andrew | Jennings, Esther | E/171 | April 18, 1889 | April 18, 1889 |
| Thompson, Barbary Miss | Smith, John | A/80 | July 10, 1845 | July 10, 1845 |
| Thompson, Barbary Miss | Smith, John | A/81 | July 10, 1845 | July 10, 1845 |
| Thompson, Caroline Miss | Church, Franklin | A/109 | March 21, 1848 | March 21, 1848 |
| Thompson, Dan (col.) | Scruggs, Fannie | F/68 | September 21, 1895 | September 21, 1895 |
| Thompson, Daniel | Black, Sarah | B/4 | August 23, 1865 | August 28, 1865 |
| Thompson, Dianna | Worley, Leoroy | A2/113 | March 26, 1864 | March 27, 1864 |
| Thompson, Eliza | Reddy, Ben | C/206 | December 18, 1878 | December 19, 1878 |
| Thompson, Elizabeth | Milligan, David T. | A/13 | April 13, 1839 | May 9, 1839 |
| Thompson, Elizabeth A. Miss | Wood, E. J. | A2/35 | September 7, 1854 | September 7, 1854 |
| Thompson, Ellen | Rankin, Duglass | C/86 | April 9, 1874 | April 9, 1874 |
| Thompson, Ella | Holt, John | F/126 | August 20, 1897 | August 22, 1897 |
| Thompson, F. | Young, Miss Sarah | A2/27 | August 10, 1853 | No Return |
| Thompson, F. E. | Bynum, J. F. | D/10 | | December 25, 1881 |
| Thompson, F. G. | Cooper, Martha J. | A2/31 | February 20, 1854 | February 20, 1854 |
| Thompson, Fannie (col.) | Vernon, R. L. (col.) | F/80 | January 4, 1896 | January 5, 1896 |
| Thompson, Fanny | Ivy, Bud (col.) | C/444 | August 27, 1891 | August 30, 1891 |
| Thompson, Gideon | Estes, Margarett Ann | A/76 | December 26, 1844 | December 26, 1844 |
| Thompson, Hugh L. | Herrell, Miss Ann E. | A/68 | April 13, 1844 | April 14, 1844 |
| Thompson, James A. | Young, Miss Margaret | A2/131 | November 9, 1865 | November 9, 1865 |
| Thompson, James A. (col) | Towy, Margaret | B/20 | November 9, 1865 | Executed--No Date |
| Thompson, John B. | Ewing, Miss Nancy M. | A2/137 | February 13, 1866 | February 14, 1866 |
| Thompson, John R. | Owen, Kansas | E/128 | January 7, 1889 | January 8, 1889 |
| Thompson, M. J. Miss | Lance, J. L. | A2/69 | November 10, 1858 | November 11, 1858 |
| Thompson, Martha Ann Miss | Cooper, John | A/80 | July 3, 1845 | July 3, 1845 |
| Thompson, Martha Ann Miss | Cooper, John | A/81 | July 3, 1845 | July 3, 1845 |
| Thompson, Mary | Jones, Kit (col.) | C/308 | June 19, 1884 | No Return |
| Thompson, Mattie Z. Miss | Hare, John P. | B/60 | December 25, 1867 | December 25, 1867 |
| Thompson, Nancy | Underwood, Woodson | A2/122 | March 23, 1865 | No Return |
| Thompson, Parilee V. Miss | Youngblood, Wm. | B/110 | September 22, 1870 | September 22, 1870 |

| Groom or Bride | Groom or Bride | Book/Page | Date of License | Date of Marriage |
|---|---|---|---|---|
| Thompson, Sam | Walls, Effie | F/52 | December 24, 1894 | December 25, 1894 |
| Thompson, Samuel | Mitchell, Mattie | B/14 | July 30, 1868 | July 30, 1868 |
| Thompson, Sarah (col.) | McKnight, John (col.) | F/104 | December 15, 1896 | December 17, 1896 |
| Thompson, Sarah | Fletcher, John | C/98 | October 31, 1874 | November 29, 1874 |
| Thompson, Sarah A. | Watson, Riley | C/146 | September 30, 1876 | October 1, 1876 |
| Thompson, Sarah C. Miss | Coleman, Franklin | A/33 | September 30, 1840 | October 1, 1840 |
| Thompson, Sophia | Mitchell, Coleman | C/128 | December 23, 1875 | December 23, 1875 |
| Thompson, T. J. | Nokes, Miss Mary Ann | A2/38 | February 2, 1855 | February 2, 1854? |
| Thompson, T. J. | Mullins, Miss Rebecca | A2/137 | February 15, 1866 | February 18, 1866 |
| Thompson, Talitha | Morris, William | A/99 | May 29, 1847 | May 29, 1847 |
| Thompson, Taylor | Almon, Miss Sarah E. | B/66 | June 10, 1868 | June 11, 1868 |
| Thompson, W. D. T. | Good, Miss Harriet C. | B/96 | December 23, 1869 | Return Not Executed |
| Thompson, William | Worley, Levila | A/31 | July 26, 1840 | July 26, 1840 |
| Thompson, William | Hollis, Miss Paulina | A/82 | July 31, 1845 | July 31, 1845 |
| Thompson, Wm. | Cathy, Miss Sarah S. | A2/50 | October 10, 1856 | October 10, 1856 |
| Throw, J. H. | Stewart, Miss Mattie | B/116 | November 17, 1870 | November 17, 1870 |
| Throwe, W. R. | Lawrence, Sallie | F/24 | December 4, 1893 | December 8, 1893 |
| Thrower, Fanny Miss | Jourdan, John | A/64 | July 25, 1843 | No Return |
| Thrower, John | Webb, Mary | F/114 | March 28, 1897 | March 28, 1897 |
| Thrower, Syntha | Gannon, W. J. | C/406 | November 12, 1887 | November 13, 1887 |
| Thrower, Wm. T. | Keele, Fanny | E/195 | July 27, 1889 | July 28, 1889 |
| Thurston, George W. | Sullivan, Miss Nancy Ruth | A2/10 | February 2, 1851 | February 2, 1851 |
| Thurston, W. J. | Alexander, Dora | F/58 | February 2, 1895 | February 3, 1895 |
| Tiflor, Catherine | Ware, W. N. M. | C/312 | September 13, 1884 | September 14, 1884 |
| Tilford, Nichols C. | Gowen, Miss Julia Y. | A/49 | April 25, 1842 | April 26, 1842 |
| Tindel, E. A. | Sissom, W. J. | C/18 | December 27, 1871 | December 27, 1871 |
| Tindell, Sallie A. | Sissom, J. T. | D/14 | | August 2, 1882 |
| Tinley, Josephus | Simpson, Miss Louisa Jane | A/107 | January 19, 1848 | January 19, 1848 |
| Tinsly, Maud America Miss | Oneal, E. G. | A2/93 | January 2, 1860 | No Return |
| Tittle, Adam | Gann, Miss Cinthia | A/88 | May 2, 1846 | May 3, 1846 |
| Tittle, Adam Jr. | Henderson, Miss Julia Ann | A2/9 | January 4, 1851 | January 5, 1851 |
| Tittle, Ader | Davenport, M. B. | D/16 | | October 22, 1882 |
| Tittle, Anna Lee | Campbell, J. H. | C/404 | October 13, 1887 | October 13, 1887 |
| Tittle, Barbary Ann Miss | Higgins, Isaac | B/38 | January 17, 1867 | January 17, 1867 |
| Tittle, Easter | Tenpenny, John | C/292 | September 6, 1883 | September 6, 1883 |
| Tittle, Elizabeth Miss | Gilly, Amos | A2/31 | February 12, 1854 | February 15, 1854 |
| Tittle, Elza | Youngblood, Callie | F/142 | December 28, 1897 | December 30, 1897 |
| Tittle, H. Y. | Melton, Miss Elizabeth | B/106 | August 19, 1870 | August 21, 1870 |
| Tittle, James | Roberts, Miss E. | A2/35 | September 29, 1854 | No Return |
| Tittle, John | Elkins, Miss Sarah Ann | A2/30 | December 22, 1853 | December 22, 1853 |
| Tittle, John | Northcutt, Miss M. A. | F/58 | February 4, 1895 | February 16, 1895 |
| Tittle, Juia Ann | Nokes, O. B. | C/420 | October 15, 1890 | October 16, 1890 |
| Tittle, Julia Ann | Elkins, John D. | A/17 | September 4, 1839 | September 5, 1839 |
| Tittle, M. D. | Prater, J. D. | C/320 | December 13, 1884 | December 15, 1884 |
| Tittle, Mollie Miss | Bogle, Jas. G. | C/456 | March 12, 1892 | March 2, 1892 |
| Tittle, N. P. | Broyles, J. A. | C/418 | September 16, 1890 | September 18, 1890 |

| Groom or Bride | Groom or Bride | Book/Page | Date of License | Date of Marriage |
|---|---|---|---|---|
| Tittle, Salena Miss | Dirting, John | A/68 | March 5, 1844 | March 28, 1844 |
| Tittle, Sam | Smith, Tinnie | F/148 | March 26, 1898 | March 27, 1898 |
| Tittle, Samuel | Higgins, Miss Locky Jane | A2/56 | June 15, 1857 | June 21, 1857 |
| Tittle, Sarah A. | Mullinix, W. G. | C/128 | December 25, 1875 | December 26, 1875 |
| Tittle, Sarah A. Miss | Herndon, J. M. | A2/54 | February 14, 1857 | February 15, 1857 |
| Tittle, Selina | Duggen, Henry S. | A/14 | June 6, 1839 | June 6, 1839 |
| Tittle, Susan | Milligan, Joel | A/77 | February 26, 1845 | February 26, 1845 |
| Tobbert, J. J. | Moore, Elvira | A2/114 | May 16, 1864 | No Return |
| Tober, Ida S. | Campbell, J. R. | F/130 | September 11, 1897 | September 12, 1897 |
| Tobert, Permeline J. Miss | Sissom, Wm. J. | B/96 | December 14, 1869 | No Retrun |
| Todd, A. J. | Williams, L. E. | D/7 | | December 4, 1881 |
| Todd, Alice E. | Hollis, J. L. | A2/138 | February 28, 1866 | March 1, 1866 |
| Todd, Almarinda | Freeman, Avander | A2/48 | June 6, 1856 | June 15, 1866 |
| Todd, Ann L. | McCabe, James M. | C/216 | June 13, 1879 | June 23, 1879 |
| Todd, Annie | Stroud, Lavander | C/188 | March 23, 1878 | March 23, 1878 |
| Todd, Asa | Todd, Miss S. A. | E/135 | February 8, 1889 | No Return |
| Todd, B. L. | McAdoo, Laura | D/20 | | August 10, 1882 |
| Todd, Bettie (col.) | Beaty, Andy (col.) | F/168 | January 21, 1899 | January 22, 1899 |
| Todd, Bud (col.) | Beaty, Jane | F/136 | November 3, 1897 | No Return |
| Todd, Caroline | Northcutt, William | C/78 | December 25, 1873 | December 25, 1873 |
| Todd, Cora A. | Patton, D. F. | F/142 | January 3, 1898 | January 6, 1897 |
| Todd, David | Philips, Mary | A2/124 | July 1, 1865 | July 8, 1865 |
| Todd, E. J. Miss | Bush, Z. | A2/62 | January 28, 1858 | No Return |
| Todd, Eliza | Herriman, John | C/286 | July 12, 1883 | No Return |
| Todd, Eliza J. Miss | McDougal, John W. | B/102 | April 7, 1870 | April 7, 1870 |
| Todd, Elizabeth | Hollis, John | A/128 | November 19, 1849 | No Return |
| Todd, Elizabeth Miss | Todd, John | A2/146 | October 9, 1866 | October 9, 1866 |
| Todd, G. W. | Wilburn, Bettie | F/26 | December 23, 1893 | December 25, 1893 |
| Todd, Granvill | Scott, Miss Marry Ann | A2/21 | December 15, 1852 | December 15, 1852 |
| Todd, Hiram | Espey, Henrietta | A/32 | August 13, 1840 | August 13, 1840 |
| Todd, Isabella | Gooding, James | C/42 | October 17, 1872 | October 17, 1872 |
| Todd, Ive | Smith, Eliza | F/34 | September 13, 1894 | September 13, 1894 |
| Todd, J. B. | Bragg, M. E. | D/18 | | December 20, 1882 |
| Todd, J. D. | Lasiter, Ann | F/106 | December 17, 1896 | December 23, 1896 |
| Todd, J. H. | Bell, Miss M. E. | A2/96 | May 18, 1860 | May 20, 1860 |
| Todd, J. L. | Henderson, Mary | D/4 | | September 21, 1881 |
| Todd, J. W. | Spicer, Emma | A2/132 | November 25, 1865 | November 25, 1865 |
| Todd, Jaco | Basham, Mattie | F/152 | August 6, 1898 | August 6, 1898 |
| Todd, James | Bogle, Hattie | F/172 | March 12, 1899 | No Return |
| Todd, James A. | Williams F. R. | D/20 | | August 9, 1883 |
| Todd, James H. | McCabe, Miss Cornelia A. | A2/146 | November 1, 1866 | November 1, 1866 |
| Todd, James H. | St. John, Miss Jennie | E/14 | January 26, 1888 | January 26, 1888 |
| Todd, James Jr. | Tennison, Miss Elizabeth | A/83 | October 4, 1845 | October 5, 1845 |
| Todd, James S. | Cox, Miss Jemima | A/92 | October 16, 1846 | October 16, 1846 |
| Todd, Jane Miss | Hoover, Isaac | B/40 | February 6, 1867 | February 7, 1867 |
| Todd, Jemima M. | Ford, James W. | A2/130 | October 20, 1865 | November 1, 1865 |

| Groom or Bride | Groom or Bride | Book/Page | Date of License | Date of Marriage |
|---|---|---|---|---|
| Todd, Jesse | Givens, Miss Mary F. | A/78 | March 14, 1845 | March 16, 1845 |
| Todd, Jessee A. | Tenpenny, Mariah | A2/105 | October 11, 1862 | October 12, 1862 |
| Todd, John | Todd, Miss Elizabeth | A2/146 | October 9, 1866 | October 9, 1866 |
| Todd, John | Thomas, June | B/14 | December 2, 1868 | No Return |
| Todd, John | Bogle, Nancy Ann | F/14 | August 19, 1893 | |
| Todd, John F. | Woods, Caroline | D/9 | | December 25, 1881 |
| Todd, John H. | Morgan, Miss Roxanah | B/66 | May 15, 1868 | May 17, 1868 |
| Todd, John R. | Blansett, Miss Lavisa | A2/23 | January 29, 1853 | January 30, 1853 |
| Todd, L. A. | Brynum, Miss Sallie A. | B/42 | February 28, 1867 | March 3, 1867 |
| Todd, L. M. | Simpson, G. W. | C/118 | September 11, 1875 | September 12, 1875 |
| Todd, M. F. | Irvin, T. N. | C/332 | July 25, 1885 | July 26, 1885 |
| Todd, M. J. | Thomas, J. M. | C/100 | November 26, 1874 | November 26, 1874 |
| Todd, M. T. | Lorance, J. M. | C/24 | February 22, 1872 | No Return |
| Todd, Margaret | Miller, Richard | C/150 | December 4, 1876 | December 5, 1876 |
| Todd, Margarett M. | Robinson, A. W. | C/156 | February 14, 1877 | February 15, 1877 |
| Todd, Martha C. | Jones, T. B. | C/60 | July 7, 1873 | No Return |
| Todd, Martha J | Lemmons, Issac N. | C/34 | August 14, 1872 | August 15, 1872 |
| Todd, Mary | Ruckley, Wiley | C/84 | February 24, 1874 | February 28, 1874 |
| Todd, Mary | Henderson, Nathaniel | C/86 | March 28, 1874 | March 29, 1874 |
| Todd, Mary A. | Stroud, W. P. | C/310 | August 4, 1884 | August 4, 1884 |
| Todd, Mary F. | Thurston, J. M. | C/182 | December 29, 1877 | December 30, 1877 |
| Todd, Minnie | Burk, Samuel | C/380 | January 1, 1887 | January 2, 18867 |
| Todd, Miss Lizzie | Bryan, L. P. | C/382 | January 18, 1887 | January 19, 1887 |
| Todd, Miss Mary Jane | Brandon, James | C/412 | December 2, 1887 | December 2, 1776 |
| Todd, Miss Minnie | Cook, William | C/394 | July 13, 1887 | July 13, 1887 |
| Todd, Mollie | Lyons, Frank | C/38 | September 8, 1872 | September 8, 1872 |
| Todd, Nancy | Sagely, B. L. | C/48 | December 21, 1872 | December 29, 1872 |
| Todd, Nancy | Inglish, W. B. | C/226 | October 29, 1879 | October 30, 1879 |
| Todd, Sarah | McCabe, James A. | C/30 | July 12, 1872 | July 14, 1872 |
| Todd, Sue | Todd, William J. | C/74 | November 22, 1873 | November 23, 1873 |
| Todd, Tennie | James, Wm. | C/202 | October 26, 1878 | October 27, 1878 |
| Toddd, Adeline | Moore ? | C/416 | September 12, 1890 | September 14, 1890 |
| Tolbert, L. N. | Simpson, David | C/18 | December 23, 1871 | December 24, 1871 |
| Tolbert, Mary | Hollis, D. A. | C/370 | October 16, 1886 | No Return |
| Tollier, Tennie | Mitchell, Alexander | C/402 | September 24, 1887 | No Return |
| Todd, L. J. Miss | McKnabb, J. F. | A2/136 | January 20, 1866 | January 31, 1866 |
| Todd, Levi | Vardelle, Mary | A/36 | January 13, 1841 | January 15, 1841 |
| Todd, Locky Jane | Young, Mark L. | A/114 | September 20, 1848 | September 20, 1848 |
| Todd, Locky Jane Miss | Bogle, George R. | A/110 | April 7, 1848 | No Return |
| Todd, M. E. Miss | Brandon, J. A. | B/118 | December 14, 1870 | December 14, 1870 |
| Todd, M. F. | Croughonour, Miss Maleda | A2/79 | May 12, 1856 | May 13, 1856 |
| Todd, Margaret | Tenpenny, E. J. | A2/133 | December 16, 1865 | December 17, 1865 |
| Todd, Margarett | Wilson, Walter | A/55 | November 3, 1842 | November 3, 1842 |
| Todd, Margret Miss | Goad, G. B. | A2/32 | May 6, 1854 | March 5, 1855 |
| Todd, Martha | Allen, E. R. | F/138 | November 27, 1897 | November 28, 1897 |
| Todd, Martha A. | Spicer, James H. | D/101 | | February 7, 1882 |

| Groom or Bride | Groom or Bride | Book/Page | Date of License | Date of Marriage |
|---|---|---|---|---|
| Todd, Martha Miss | Sissom, Calvin | B/114 | October 14, 1870 | October 20, 1870 |
| Todd, Mary | Carter, Jess M. | F/134 | October 2, 1897 | October 3, 1897 |
| Todd, Mary J. Miss | Hoover, Bengamin | B/86 | September 23, 1869 | September 23, 1869 |
| Todd, Mattie | Youree, J. H. | F/100 | October 28, 1896 | No Return |
| Todd, Micajah F. | Cox, Susannah | A/5 | August 22, 1838 | August 22, 1838 |
| Todd, Milton | Bodkins, Miss Rachael C. | A/84 | November 10, 1845 | November 10, 1845 |
| Todd, Miss Cornelia | Vance, Dee | F/166 | January 7, 1899 | January 8, 1898 |
| Todd, Miss S. A. | Todd, Asa | E/135 | February 8, 1889 | No Return |
| Todd, Miss Sarah | Ferrell, J. G. | F/170 | February 10, 1899 | February 12, 1899 |
| Todd, Nancy J. Miss | Knox, William A. | A/127 | September 15, 1849 | September ?, 1849 |
| Todd, Nancy P. | Harper, Joseph P. | A/13 | April 18, 1839 | No Return |
| Todd, Nettie (col.) | Baker, Bill (col.) | F/84 | February 22, 1896 | February 29, 1896 |
| Todd, Ranson | Duncan, Matisa | A2/21 | November 20, 1852 | November 21, 1852 |
| Todd, Rebecca Jane Miss | Jernigan, Andrew J. | A2/85 | April 2, 1859 | ?? 6, 1859 |
| Todd, Robert | Beverly, Miss Jane | A2/72 | January 17, 1859 | No Return |
| Todd, Robert | Beverly, Miss Jane | A2/83 | January 17, 1859 | No Return |
| Todd, S. A. | Neeley, F. F. | D/9 | | December 29, 1881 |
| Todd, S. E. | Lawrance, M. W. | A2/103 | September 19, 1860 | No Return |
| Todd, Sarah | Cooper, Thomas | A2/80 | December 5, 1857 | December 5, 1857 |
| Todd, Sarah J. | Bush, Henry L. | A2/23 | January 4, 1853 | January 6, 1853 |
| Todd, Sarah Miss | Winnett, James | B/60 | December 21, 1867 | December 22, 1867 |
| Todd, T. J. | Creson, M. B. | D/10 | | December 29, 1881 |
| Todd, T. M. | Wilson, Miss Mary J. W. | A2/138 | February 28, 1866 | March 1, 1866 |
| Todd, Vina | Gannon, G. W. | E/178 | May 25, 1889 | May 25, 1889 |
| Todd, W. A. | Elkins, Lora | F/142 | December 30, 1897 | December 30, 1897 |
| Todd, W. L. | McCabe, Miss Mary J. | B/86 | September 9, 1869 | September 9, 1869 |
| Todd, Walter L. | Elkins, Margaret | A2/123 | June 15, 1865 | June 15, 1865 |
| Todd, Wiley | Hayes, Della | E/238 | December 4, 1889 | December 5, 1889 |
| Todd, William F. | Bragg, Miss Julian | B/60 | January 13, 1868 | January 14, 1868 |
| Todd, Wilson | Barnes, Mary J. | A2/103 | October 20, 1960 | No Return |
| Todd, Wm | Ewell, Sarah | A/14 | June 18, 1839 | June 21, 1839 |
| Todd, Wm. C. | Coughanour, E. C. | A2/109 | September 17, 1863 | September 20, 1863 |
| Todd, Wm. F. | Lafevers, Miss Bettie | E/89 | October 17, 1888 | October 17, 1888 |
| Todd, Wm. T. | Sanders, Miss Sarrah A. | A2/37 | December 21, 1854 | December 21, 1854 |
| Todder, Eleanor Miss | West, Benjamin W. | A/33 | September 28, 1840 | September 29, 1840 |
| Tolber, L. G. | Lyon, Miss Sallie | E/42 | June 22, 1888 | June 22, 1888 |
| Tolber, William | Earp, Alice | F/132 | September 18, 1897 | September 23, 1897 |
| Tolbert, Elizabeth B. Miss | Kennedy, M. A. | A/126 | September 7, 1849 | No Return |
| Tolbert, James | Youree, Miss Eliza | E/7 | January 20, 1888 | January 20, 1888 |
| Tolbert, L. J. | Bynum, Elizabeth | A2/134 | January 1, 1866 | January 4, 1866 |
| Tolbert, Matilda | Jernigan, A. M. | E/32 | April 25, 1888 | April 26, 1888 |
| Tolbert, Mollie | Rollens, Dave | F/76 | December 7, 1895 | December 7, 1895 |
| Tolbert, P. J. Miss | Arnold, W. J. | B/110 | September 15, 1870 | September 18, 1870 |
| Tolbert, Parlee Miss | Burke, G. C. | B/70 | September 30, 1868 | No Return |
| Tolbert, Sallie Miss | Dunlap, W. S. | E/25 | March 8, 1888 | March 8, 1888 |
| Tolbert, Silas | McMahan, Frances | E/115 | December 22, 1888 | December 23, 1888 |

| Groom or Bride | Groom or Bride | Book/Page | Date of License | Date of Marriage |
|---|---|---|---|---|
| Tolbert, W. C. | Reed, Lucy | A2/108 | May 8, 1863 | No Return |
| Tolivar, Katharine Miss | Simmons, Isham | A/119 | January 5, 1849 | January 5, 1849 |
| Tompkins, Ella | Know, Mell | F/24 | December 9, 1893 | December 9, 1893 |
| Tort, Susan | Winnett, Norman | A2/64 | April 29, 1858 | April 29, 1858 |
| Tosh, Charles A. | Sullivan, Netter | E/172 | April 25, 1889 | June 25, 1889 |
| Towy, Margaret | Thompson, James A. (col) | B/20 | November 9, 1865 | Executed--No Date |
| Travers, Mary Miss | Warren, Zachariah | A/66 | December 30, 1843 | January 1, 1844 |
| Travis, Angeline | Travis, John | F/110 | February 1, 1897 | February 3, 1897 |
| Travis, Daniel | Tedder, Mary | A/49 | May 19, 1842 | May 19, 1842 |
| Travis, Daniel | Porterfield, Miss Mary | A2/52 | December 30, 1856 | December 30, 1856 |
| Travis, Daniel | Morris, Miss Mary W. | B/126 | February 10, 1871 | February 10, 1871 |
| Travis, Franklin W. | Crop, Martha | A/14 | June 15, 1839 | No Return |
| Travis, Iser | Barrett, J. H. | C/448 | October 12, 1891 | No Return |
| Travis, Issabella Miss | Thomas, Zachariah | A2/6 | October 8, 1850 | October 8, 1850 |
| Travis, J. C. Miss | Holemane, L. | A2/44 | December 11, 1855 | No Return |
| Travis, James | Coulter, Malinda | A/55 | October 29, 1842 | October 29, 1842 |
| Travis, James | Crafte, Miss Martha | A2/15 | February 29, 1852 | No Return |
| Travis, James W. | Wharry, Miss Cyntha Jane | A/116 | November 1, 1848 | No Return |
| Travis, John | Pond, Miss Sarah | A2/68 | October 14, 1858 | October 14, 1858 |
| Travis, John | Travis, Angeline | F/110 | February 1, 1897 | February 3, 1897 |
| Travis, John A. | Alexander, Neomi | A2/110 | December 30, 1863 | December 31, 1863 |
| Travis, Johnson | Holt, Minnerva | A/22 | January 16, 1840 | January 16, 1840 |
| Travis, L. E. | Paschall, S. J. | E/227 | October 31, 1889 | October 31, 1889 |
| Travis, L. F. | Travis, Mary | D/8 | | December 11, 1881 |
| Travis, Lillie E. | Hatchett, V. S. | F/26 | December 23, 1893 | No Return |
| Travis, Malisa | Richards, Jas T. | C/178 | November 24, 1877 | No Return |
| Travis, Martha | Escue, M. L. | C/278 | May 15, 1881 | May 15, 1881 |
| Travis, Martha | Travis, W. A. | F/92 | August 15, 1896 | August 16, 1896 |
| Travis, Martha Jane Miss | Minten, J. G. | A2/71 | December 14, 1858 | December 14, 1858 |
| Travis, Martha M. Miss | Moore, J. G. | A2/52 | January 20, 1857 | January 20, 1857 |
| Travis, Mary | Reed, Ed | E/60 | August 15, 1888 | August 15, 1888 |
| Travis, Mary | Travis, L. F. | D/8 | | December 11, 1881 |
| Travis, Mary | Keele, C. W. | C/336 | September 16, 1885 | September 16, 1885 |
| Travis, Mary J. Miss | Hays, J. C. | A2/55 | February 25, 1857 | No Return |
| Travis, N. L. | Osbon, Harvey | A2/117 | October 31, 1864 | November 2, 1864 |
| Travis, N. F. | Travis, W. D. | C/334 | August 2, 1885 | August 2, 1885 |
| Travis, Nancy | Barrett, Dillard | D/15 | | September 3, 1882 |
| Travis, Plem | Barrett, James | C/446 | September 25, 1891 | September 25 1891 |
| Travis, Polly Miss | Mingle, George | A/105 | November 26, 1847 | November 26, 1847 |
| Travis, Ridy E. | Gannon, John P. | A2/95 | February 23, 1860 | February 23, 1860 |
| Travis, S. D. | Larance, Sarah J. | A2/93 | December 29, 1859 | No Return |
| Travis, S. D. | Travis, Mrs. S. J. | B/118 | December 13, 1870 | December 13, 1870 |
| Travis, S. D. Miss | Davis, J. E. | E/109 | December 18, 1888 | December 18, 1888 |
| Travis, S. J. Mrs. | Travis, S. D. | B/118 | December 13, 1870 | December 13, 1870 |
| Travis, Sal | Barret Levi | C/460 | July 9, 1892 | July 17, 1892 |
| Travis, Sallie | Duggin, M. C. L. | C/400 | September 5, 1887 | No Return |

| Groom or Bride | Groom or Bride | Book/Page | Date of License | Date of Marriage |
|---|---|---|---|---|
| Travis, Sarah M. Miss | Keele, James A. | A2/67 | September 16, 1858 | September 16, 1858 |
| Travis, Susan | Gannon, John | C/446 | October 1, 1891 | October 1, 1891 |
| Travis, Thomas J. | Moody, S. E. | F/10 | May 27, 1893 | May 28, 1893 |
| Travis, W. A. | Travis, Martha | F/92 | August 15, 1896 | August 16, 1896 |
| Travis, Wm. | Bogle, Miss Bunter | E/106 | November 30, 1888 | November 30, 1888 |
| Travis, Wm. | Tettard, Tiner | F/46 | October 14, 1894 | October 14, 1894 |
| Travis, Wm. H. | Vance, Catharine | A/21 | December 26, 1839 | December 26, 1839 |
| Tribble, Elizabeth | Orand, J. M. | A2/107 | February 19, 1863 | No Return |
| Trigg, Amanda Miss | Bush, Willis | A/72 | September 18, 1844 | September 19, 1844 |
| Trimble, Aaron | McKnight, Mary Ann | B/8 | February 17, 1866 | February 18, 1866 |
| Trimble, Milley | McAdoo, Richard | C/310 | July 24, 1884 | No Return |
| Trollinger, Elizabeth M. Miss | Simpson, James | A/97 | February 4, 1847 | February 4, 1847 |
| Trollinger, Matilda | Hall, William J. | A/67 | February 5, 1844 | No Return |
| Trott, Henry | Major, Miss Hannah A. | A/47 | February 15, 1842 | February 15, 1842 |
| Trott, Marthaann | George, James O. | A/5 | August 21, 1838 | August 21, 1838 |
| Truett, Francis | Talley, Thomas | C/248 | June 5, 1880 | June 5, 1880 |
| Truit, John | Owen, M. E. | F/14 | August 4, 1893 | No Return |
| Tubb, John | Parton, Miss Charlotte | B/40 | January 31, 1867 | January 31, 1867 |
| Tubb, John | Sowell, Nettie | F/20 | October 21, 1893 | October 22, 1893 |
| Tubs, Charlotta | Tittle, Adam | C/200 | September 22, 1878 | September 22, 1878 |
| Tubs, James | Mount, Mollie | D/21 | | September 29, 1883 |
| Tucker, Andrin J. | Werley, Mollie | F/32 | February 21, 1894 | February 25, 1894 |
| Tucker, David | Sowell, Sarh Jane | A/68 | February 17, 1844 | February 19, 1844 |
| Tucker, Evaline | Herriman, J. R. | F/146 | March 18, 1898 | March 22, 1898 |
| Tucker, Frances | Fann, H. D. | E/192 | July 24, 1889 | July 25, 1889 |
| Tucker, H. E. | Malard, W. A. | C/246 | April 10, 1880 | April 11, 1880 |
| Tucker, J. D. | McKnight, Ella | F/52 | December 11, 1894 | December 13, 1894 |
| Tucker, Jackson | Bragg, Miss Lizy | A2/17 | May 9, 1852 | May 9, 1852 |
| Tucker, James M. | Exque, Miss Mary R. | A2/7 | November 2, 1850 | November 3, 1850 |
| Tucker, John | Cross, Miss Eliza Issabella | A/121 | October 19,1848 | October 19,1848 |
| Tucker, Katharine Miss | Gaither, Wilson | A/61 | April 8, 1843 | April 9, 1843 |
| Tucker, Lucretia | Davis, Anderson | A2/3 | August 3, 1850 | August 4, 1850 |
| Tucker, Lucretia | Davis, Anderson | A2/4 | August 3, 1850 | August 4, 1850 |
| Tucker, Malissa Miss | Parker, Nathaniel | B/70 | September 3, 1868 | September 3, 1868 |
| Tucker, Ody | Parker, Rachel | F/96 | September 17, 1896 | September 22, 1896 |
| Tucker, Pinkney | Herriman, Miss Mary | B/102 | May 23, 1870 | May 26, 1870 |
| Tucker, Renn | Youngblood, S. B. | C/348 | January 2, 1886 | January 3, 1886 |
| Tucker, Sara | Harris, Ransom P. | A/60 | March 23, 1843 | March 23, 1843 |
| Tucker, Sarah | Lewis, W. C. | C/328 | March 5, 1885 | March 5, 1885 |
| Tucker, Savana | Herriman, George M. | E/49 | August 2, 1888 | August 5, 1888 |
| Tucker, Solomaon | Johnson, Lula | E/366 | November 26, 1898 | |
| Tucker, Thomas | Fann, Mary E. | E/54 | September 18, 1888 | September 18, 1888 |
| Tucker, Thomas | Fann, Mary E. | E/74 | September 18, 1888 | September 18, 1888 |
| Tuples, Martha | Jacobs, W. H. | D/3 | | August 24, 1881 |
| Turner, Allice | Ferrell, T. E. | C/292 | September 17, 1883 | September 20, 1883 |
| Turner, Amandy M. | Espey, W. J. | C/98 | October 19, 1874 | October 20, 1874 |

| Groom or Bride | Groom or Bride | Book/Page | Date of License | Date of Marriage |
|---|---|---|---|---|
| Turner, Bettie | Odom, A. R. | C/218 | June 28, 1879 | June 29, 1879 |
| Turner, C. A. Mrs. | Warrick, Jessee | B/114 | October 27, 1870 | October 27, 1870 |
| Turner, Callie | Tenpenny, John L. | C/474 | December 29, 1892 | December 29, 1892 |
| Turner, Elisabeth | Mitchell, James A. | C/246 | May 8, 1880 | May 9, 1880 |
| Turner, Elizabeth | Philips, James | A/128 | November 27, 1849 | November 27, 1849 |
| Turner, Ellen | Deberry, Jacob | E/96 | November 3, 1888 | November 4, 1888 |
| Turner, G. T. | Edwards, Miss Mary E. | B/86 | September 18, 1869 | September 19, 1869 |
| Turner, Hanah D. Miss | Melton, John M. | B/102 | May 14, 1870 | May 15, 1870 |
| Turner, Ider | Blair, John | C/470 | December 10, 1892 | December 11, 1892 |
| Turner, J. E. | Elledge, Miss Susan | B/122 | December 24, 1870 | December 25, 1870 |
| Turner, J. R. | Hancock, Miss M. P. | A2/63 | February 22, 1858 | No Return |
| Turner, Jennie | Spidell, R. S. | F/32 | February 24, 1894 | February 25, 1894 |
| Turner, M. E. Miss | Youngblood, G. W. | B/114 | November 3, 1870 | November 3, 1870 |
| Turner, M. E. Miss | Brewer, S. A. | B/120 | December 19, 1870 | December 22, 1870 |
| Turner, M. M. C. | Brien, James W. | A2/47 | April 28, 1856 | No Return |
| Turner, Madora | Owenby, E. C. | C/106 | January 15, 1875 | No return |
| Turner, Martha Miss | Adams, Alexander | B/12 | December 21, 1867 | December 21, 1867 |
| Turner, Mary A. Miss | Merritt, James M. | A/130 | December 27, 1849 | January 9, 1850 |
| Turner, Nancy | Craft, Jonathan A. | A2/97 | May 26, 1860 | May 28, 1860 |
| Turner, Pleasant R. | Melton, Miss Sarah F. | B/88 | September 27, 1869 | September 28, 1869 |
| Turner, Sarah Katharine | Mellon, Thomas J. | A2/27 | August 3, 1853 | August 3, 1853 |
| Turner, W. C. | Gilley, Dovie | F/56 | January 15, 1895 | January 16, 1895 |
| Turner, W. H. | Bailey, Miss M. J. | A2/67 | September 29, 1858 | September 29, 1858 |
| Turney, Cleo | Gasay, Hyram | F/8 | April 18, 1893 | April 19, 1893 |
| Turney, Mai | Meares, T. J. | E/384 | October 15, 1898 | |
| Turney, Mai Miss | Meares, T. J. | F/158 | October 15, 1898 | October 23, 1898 |
| Turney, Nancy E. | Keaton, John | C/56 | March 19, 1873 | March 20, 1873 |
| Turney, Peter S. | Hancock, Miss Eliza A. | B/94 | December 11, 1869 | December 12, 1869 |
| Turpen, Nettie | Mathews, Robert | C/436 | May 13, 1891 | May 13, 1891 |
| Tuttle, Martha Miss | Rigsby, William T. | A/129 | November 29, 1849 | November 29, 1849 |
| Tyree, William H. | Batton, Miss Angie | B/92 | November 19, 1869 | November 24, 1869 |
| Umbarger, Sarah A. | Swanger, W. S. | C/422 | November 2, 1890 | November 5, 1890 |
| Underhill, A. E. | Hutcherson, Nancy | A2/126 | August 24, 1865 | August 27, 1864 |
| Underhill, A. O. | Gunter, H. K. | F/50 | November 24, 1894 | December 5, 1894 |
| Underhill, George W. | Ford, Miss Amanda T. | B/66 | June 13, 1868 | June 14, 1868 |
| Underhill, J. H. | Bailey, M. A. | F/60 | March 15, 1895 | March 17, 1895 |
| Underwood, E. D. Miss | Richerson, Serge D. | A2/65 | May 12, 1858 | May 13, 1858 |
| Underwood, Elizabeth | Underwood, Martin | A2/129 | September 19, 1865 | September 19, 1865 |
| Underwood, Emma | Shelton, Everitt | C/440 | July 25, 1891 | July 26, 1891 |
| Underwood, Jacob | McBride, Polly | A/29 | June 8, 1840 | June 8, 1840 |
| Underwood, James | Ratly, Miss Malisa | A2/28 | October 1, 1853 | October 2, 1853 |
| Underwood, Joseph | Isam, R. C. | A2/101 | August 27, 1860 | August 29, 1860 |
| Underwood, Mark L. | Worley, Miss Martha | B/68 | July 23, 1868 | July 26, 1868 |
| Underwood, Martin | Underwood, Elizabeth | A2/129 | September 19, 1865 | September 19, 1865 |
| Underwood, Mary | Lambert, David | A2/110 | July 18, 1863 | No Return |
| Underwood, Mary Miss | Worley, Arthur | B/76 | January 15, 1869 | January 17, 1869 |

| Groom or Bride | Groom or Bride | Book/Page | Date of License | Date of Marriage |
|---|---|---|---|---|
| Underwood, Nancy C. | Soap, Gorge, W. | A2/18 | June 3, 1852 | June 3, 1852 |
| Underwood, Reniah Miss | Richerson, Drew | A2/66 | August 21, 1858 | August 22, 1858 |
| Underwood, Thomas | Herral, Mary | A2/31 | December 27, 1853 | December 28, 1853 |
| Underwood, Thomas | Richardson, Matilda | E/48 | July 28, 1888 | July 28, 1888 |
| Underwood, Wm. B. | Davis, Fannie E. | D/22 | | April 1, 1883 |
| Underwood, Woodson | Thompson, Nancy | A2/122 | March 23, 1865 | No Return |
| Urp, Willie A. | Ford, Wm. J. | C/330 | May 23, 1885 | May 24, 1885 |
| Ursery, Sarrah | Young, J. M. | A2/44 | December 20, 1855 | December 20, 1855 |
| Usselton, Elizabeth Miss | Horn, John | A2/138 | February 26, 1866 | No Return |
| Valentin, Mary Miss | Barrett, J. W. | B/86 | September 9, 1869 | September 9, 1869 |
| Vance, Anderson | Tenpenny, Sarah | B/18 | January 27, 1870 | January 27, 1870 |
| Vance, Catharine | Travis, Wm. H. | A/21 | December 26, 1839 | December 26, 1839 |
| Vance, D. B. | Brewer, Miss Bettie | B/72 | November 22, 1868 | November 23, 1868 |
| Vance, Daniel | Reed, Miss Martha | A2/60 | December 3, 1857 | December 3, 1857 |
| Vance, David | Morgan, Liza E. | A2/115 | August 4, 1864 | August 4, 1864 |
| Vance, David | Blanks | E/151 | December 17, 1888 | December 20, 1888 |
| Vance, Dee | Todd, Miss Cornelia | F/166 | January 7, 1899 | January 8, 1898 |
| Vance, E. R. Miss | Gannan, G. W. | A2/58 | October 1, 1857 | October 1, 1857 |
| Vance, Eliza J. Miss | Mason, J. T. | B/56 | November 27, 1867 | November 28, 1867 |
| Vance, Eliza Miss | Vasser, Alfred | B/68 | July 29, 1868 | July 29, 1868 |
| Vance, Irene (col.) | Martin, John (col.) | F/88 | May 7, 1896 | May 10, 1896 |
| Vance, Isham | Moore, Miss Sarah | A2/156 | May 29, 1866 | May 29, 1866 |
| Vance, J. R. | Richards, N. J. | E/136 | February 8, 1889 | February 8, 1889 |
| Vance, James | Summar, Miss Elizabeth | A2/137 | February 8, 1866 | February 8, 1866 |
| Vance, James | Dobbs, A. S. | E/262 | January 15, 1890 | No Return |
| Vance, James | Davenport, Ona | F/98 | October 3, 1896 | October 6, 1896 |
| Vance, Jennie | Robertson, Aubry | F/118 | May 29, 1897 | May 29, 1897 |
| Vance, John D. | Ashford, Bettie | F/22 | November 21, 1893 | November 22, 1893 |
| Vance, Katharine Miss | Richards, Jesse | A/102 | September 16, 1847 | September 16, 1847 |
| Vance, Richard | Peedon, Elisar | A2/106 | January 6, 1863 | January 6, 1863 |
| Vance, S. A. | Blanks, John C. | C/424 | December 10, 1890 | December 11, 1890 |
| Vance, S. C. | Gaither, R. F. | C/448 | October 17, 1891 | October 22, 1891 |
| Vance, Sallie | Hollis A. L. | F/2 | February 2, 1893 | No Return |
| Vance, Samuel | Elledge, Miss Sarah Ann | A/44 | November 13, 1841 | November 14, 1841 |
| Vance, Sarah | Walcup, R. O. | A2/97 | No Dates Summer 1860 | |
| Vance, Thomas | Armstrong, Miss Mahala | B/40 | February 14, 1867 | February 14, 1867 |
| Vandagriff, Christopher | Viars, Eliza | A/56 | November 19, 1842 | November 19, 1842 |
| Vandagriff, John | McGee, Miss Jane | A2/32 | April 28, 1854 | No Return |
| Vandagriff, Marry A. Miss | Spurlock, Joseph | A2/88 | September 14, 1859 | September 14, 1859 |
| Vandagriff, Mary Jane Miss | Elkins, M. G. | A2/37 | December 7, 1854 | December 7, 1854 |
| Vandagriff, Nancy Miss | Williams, Thomas J. | A/118 | January 3, 1849 | January 4, 1849 |
| Vandagriff, Richard | Francis, Miss Malinda | A2/70 | December 22, 1858 | December 22, 1858 |
| Vandagriff, William | Williams, Lucinda | A/59 | January 12, 1843 | January 12, 1843 |
| Vandagriffe, Mary Miss | Hollinsworth, Charles W. | A/126 | August 17, 1849 | August 19, 1849 |
| Vandagrift, Delie | Hamilton, A. J. | F/168 | January 28, 1899 | January 29, 1899 |
| Vandegriff, Melvina Miss | Williams, Thomas J. | B/84 | July 29, 1869 | July 29, 1869 |

| Groom or Bride | Groom or Bride | Book/Page | Date of License | Date of Marriage |
|---|---|---|---|---|
| Vandegriff, Sarah P | Melton, David | C/90 | July 13, 1874 | No Return |
| Vandegriff, Sarah P. | Melton, David | C/88 | July 14, 1874 | July 14, 1874 |
| Vandell, Bettie | Alexander, W. T. | F/8 | April 13, 1893 | April 13, 1893 |
| Vandergriff, Alexander | King, Alamenta | A/1 | March 20, 1838 | March 27, 1838 |
| Vandergriff, Bettie | George, Rufus | C/466 | October 11, 1892 | October 11, 1892 |
| Vandergriff, Dona | Gannon, S. E. | F/28 | December 27, 1893 | December 27, 1893 |
| Vandergriff, J. B. | JOnes, M. M. | F/24 | December 12, 1893 | December 17, 1893 |
| Vandergriff, John A. | Ferrell, Amanda | E/93 | October 25, 1888 | October 25, 1888 |
| Vandergriff, M. J | Hancock, A. L. | C/26 | April 1, 1872 | April 1, 1872 |
| Vandergriff, Marion | Campbell, Miss Susan | A2/87 | July 16, 1859 | No Reutrn |
| Vandergriff, Nancy A. | Melton, Greenfield | C/136 | March 22, 1876 | No Return |
| Vandergriff, W. J. | Campbell, Rhoda | A2/132 | November 23, 1865 | November 23, 1865 |
| Vandergriff, William | Dillian, Phebe | A/9 | December 13, 1838 | December 15, 1838 |
| Vandergriff, Wm | Haltiman, Eliza | D/4 | | September 18, 1881 |
| Vandergriph, Lucinda | Jones, Pinking | A/21 | January 7, 1840 | No Return |
| Vandygrift, Lucinda | McDengal, J. D. | C/218 | July 19, 1879 | July 20, 1879 |
| Vane, Mary A. | Brandon, Mathew | A2/36 | October 26, 1854 | October 26, 1854 |
| Vane, Sarrah S. | Terner, Isaac | A2/39 | March 28, 1855 | March 29, 1855 |
| VanHooser, Hattie | Gilley, Robt | F/148 | April 23, 1898 | April 24, 1898 |
| Vanhooser, I. W. | Stacy, Mary A. | F/32 | February 28, 1894 | No Return |
| Vanhooser, Nancy | Burger, Sam | E/220 | October 14, 1889 | No Return |
| Vanhoozer, W. J. | Gilley, Miss M. J. | B/100 | February 7, 1870 | February 8, 1870 |
| Vardel, John T. | Sumnar, Louisa | A2/109 | September 18, 1863 | No Return |
| Vardelle, Mary | Todd, Levi | A/36 | January 13, 1841 | January 15, 1841 |
| Varton, Edmund | Stone, Nancy Ann | A/22 | January 9, 1840 | January 9, 1840 |
| Vassar, Ella Miss | Todd, Syney | C/460 | July 16, 1892 | No Return |
| Vasser, Alford | Tenpenny, Miss Mary J. | B/128 | March 4, 1871 | March 4, 1871 |
| Vasser, Alfred | Vance, Miss Eliza | B/68 | July 29, 1868 | July 29, 1868 |
| Vasser, Anney | Borren, Brazell | A2/42 | September 9, 1855 | Returns Missing |
| Vasser, Caswell | West, Miss Mary Jane | A2/6 | September 3, 1850 | September 30, 1850 |
| Vasser, Cyntha Miss | Milligan, James C. | A/35 | December 19, 1840 | December 25, 1840 |
| Vasser, Cynthia | Patrick, Robert | A/50 | July 4, 1842 | July 14, 1842 |
| Vasser, Elizabeth J. Miss | Youngblood, A. J. | B/46 | May 21, 1867 | May 21, 1867 |
| Vasser, J. B. | Irvin, Sarah E. | D/21 | | January 30, 1883 |
| Vasser, James | MaGlocklin, Miss Sarah Jane | A/128 | October 17, 1849 | No Return |
| Vasser, Joshua | Murfrey, Miss Sally Ann | A/100 | June 3, 1847 | No Return |
| Vasser, Joshua Jr. | Summar, Miss Sally | A/73 | October 3, 1844 | September 3, 1844 |
| Vasser, Margrett | Todd, W. P. | C/106 | February 1, 1875 | February 1, 1875 |
| Vasser, Nancy A. | Freeman, William | C/208 | January 1, 1879 | January 1, 1879 |
| Vasser, W. J. | Freeman, Miss Nancy A. E. | B/128 | March 6, 1871 | March 7, 1871 |
| Vasser, William | Arnold, Miss Mariah | A2/37 | November 29, 1854 | November 30, 1854 |
| Vasser, William | -----, Miss Lucinda | A2/73 | May 3, 1852 | May 4, 1852 |
| Vassor, Nan | Williams, Schudder | F/12 | July 18, 1893 | July 19, 1893 |
| Vaughan, H. C. | Odom, F. E. | A2/111 | January 30, 1864 | No Return |
| Vaughan, J. C. | Wherry, Miss L. B. | A2/30 | December 18, 1853 | December 29, 1853 |
| Vaughan, Sallie Ann Miss | Starr, John | B/48 | August 2, 1867 | August 3, 1867 |

| Groom or Bride | Groom or Bride | Book/Page | Date of License | Date of Marriage |
|---|---|---|---|---|
| Vaughn, G. W. | Osborn, H. M. | A2/96 | May 5, 1860 | May 9, 1860 |
| Vaughn, Judie Miss | Peoples, John | B/124 | January 7, 1871 | January 12, 1871 |
| Vaughn, Mary | Webb, Jacob | C/168 | August 25, 1877 | August 26, 1877 |
| Vaughn, Thomas | Mullins, Miss Mahala | A/49 | April 28, 1842 | April 28, 1842 |
| Vaughn, Thomas | Merritt, Miss Catharine | B/74 | December 2, 1868 | December 2, 1868 |
| Vernan, Edy | Hickenbotham, Thomas | C/360 | July 6, 1886 | No Return |
| Vernon, Ann | Barnes, Robert | C/454 | February 1, 1892 | February 1, 1892 |
| Vernon, Eda | Barnes, Stephen (col.) | F/6 | March 18, 1893 | March 18, 1893 |
| Vernon, Elias | Stafford, Charlotte | B/14 | October 16, 1868 | October 16, 1868 |
| Vernon, Lewis (col.) | Smith, Viola (col.) | F/122 | July 31, 1897 | July 31, 1897 |
| Vernon, Maggie | Stewart, Bethell (col.) | C/412 | December 31, 1887 | December 31, 1887 |
| Vernon, R. L. (col.) | Thompson, Fannie (col.) | F/80 | January 4, 1896 | January 5, 1896 |
| Viars, Eliza | Vandagriff, Christopher | A/56 | November 19, 1842 | November 19, 1842 |
| Vicars, Sarah | Summars, R. C. | C/244 | March 6, 1880 | March 8, 1880 |
| Vichers, Maggie | Good, W. M. | E/219 | October 14, 1889 | October 15, 1889 |
| Vickers, William | Summar, Miss Mary Lavisa | B/84 | July 27, 1869 | No Return |
| Vinson, Benjamin | Neely, Miss Sarah | A2/32 | March 15, 1854 | March 15, 1854 |
| Vinson, Benjamin | Neely, Miss Sarah | A2/75 | March 15, 1854 | March 15, 1854 |
| Vinson, Bettie Miss | Hollandsworth, John | B/106 | August 3, 1870 | August 3, 1870 |
| Vinson, Colewall | Higdon, Hettie | F/54 | January 3, 1895 | January 9, 1895 |
| Vinson, Dela | Markum, John B. | D/19 | | December 21, 1882 |
| Vinson, Dollie Miss | Melton, Wm. | C/456 | March 16, 1892 | March 17, 1892 |
| Vinson, F. Buck | Spradley, Fannie | F/64 | July 25, 1895 | July 4,1895 |
| Vinson, Fannie | Melton, Henderson | C/160 | March 24, 1877 | March 27, 1877 |
| Vinson, Henrietta W. Miss | Talley, W. R. | A2/162 | June 30, 1866 | July 19, 1866 |
| Vinson, John Ann | Gilley, James | F/48 | November 17, 1894 | November 18, 1894 |
| Vinson, Luiza Miss | Young, Marling | A2/30 | December 13, 1853 | December 13, 1853 |
| Vinson, Malissie | Butcher, R. J. | F/62 | March 20, 1895 | March 21, 1895 |
| Vinson, Mary Miss | Barrett, Nathan | A2/11 | March 18, 1851 | March 18, 1851 |
| Vinson, Robert | Barrett, Miss Frances L. | B/94 | December 2, 1869 | December 2, 1869 |
| Vinson, Sarah | Barrett, John W. | A/120 | February 20, 1849 | February 20, 1849 |
| Vinson, Sarah M. Miss | Nichols, Daniel A. | A2/55 | March 17, 1857 | No Return |
| Vinson, Thomas J. | Rigsby, Miss Martha J. | B/90 | October 16, 1869 | No Return |
| Vinson, Ursula Ann Miss | Bowen, Samuel | A/103 | October 26, 1847 | October 28, 1847 |
| Vosser, Wm | Jonran, Miss Lucinda | A2/16 | May 3, 1852 | May 4, 1852 |
| Wade, Elizabeth Miss | Franklin, Peter F. | A/128 | October 11, 1849 | October 31, 1849 |
| Wade, Enoch | Keith, Mary | C/416 | September 3, 1890 | September 2, 1890 |
| Wade, Laura | Shepherd, F. H. | C/224 | September 20, 1879 | September 21, 1879 |
| Wade, William | Roberts, Sarrah Jane | A2/40 | July 14, 1855 | Returns Missing |
| Wade, Wm | Keth, Nervie A. | D/101 | | January 30, 1882 |
| Wade, Wm. | Jones, Miss Martha Ann | A2/38 | February 5, 1855 | June 5, 1855 |
| Wadkins, S. Y. | Richardson, B. W. | D/17 | | October 29, 1882 |
| Wadkins, Samantha | Worley, Wm. | D/13 | | August 10, 1882 |
| Walcup, R. O. | Vance, Sarah | A2/97 | No Dates Summer 1860 | |
| Waldon, R. E. | Bonn, A. | A2/95 | March 5, 1860 | No Return |
| Wale, Celisa Jane Miss | Hall, H. B. | A/109 | February 28, 1848 | February 29, 1848 |

| Groom or Bride | Groom or Bride | Book/Page | Date of License | Date of Marriage |
|---|---|---|---|---|
| Wale, J. H. | Blanton, Jane | A2/97 | May 29, 1860 | May 29, 1860 |
| Wale, J. H. | McWhearter, L. H. | C/46 | November 23, 1872 | November 24, 1872 |
| Wales, J. M. | McBroom, Narissie | C/306 | February 29, 1884 | March 2, 1884 |
| Walker, ---- | Higgins, J. L. | D/21 | | April 12, 1883 |
| Walker, Annie Miss | Herrald, J. R | E/18 | February 11, 1888 | February 12, 1888 |
| Walker, Bettie | Reed, William | D/5 | | October 6, 1881 |
| Walker, Bob | Barrett, Clem | F/106 | December 24, 1896 | December 24, 1896 |
| Walker, D. B. | Summar, J. F. | C/342 | November 20, 1885 | November 22, 1885 |
| Walker, Edna | Guimore, Porter | C/466 | September 27, 1892 | September 28, 1892 |
| Walker, Isaac | Moore, Jane | C/80 | January 17, 1874 | January 18, 1874 |
| Walker, J. R. | Morgan, Sarah G. | A2/126 | September 1, 1865 | September 3, 1865 |
| Walker, J. T. | Cantrell, Mary | F/90 | July 15, 1896 | July 15, 1896 |
| Walker, J. W. | House, Bell D. | C/170 | September 17, 1877 | September 18, 1877 |
| Walker, Jeremiah C. | Gilley, Miss Judah F. | A/71 | August 5, 1844 | August 5, 1844 |
| Walker, Kizzie | Higgins, J. L. | C/282 | April 12, 1883 | No Return |
| Walker, Leonard | Adamson, Nancy M. | A/54 | September 12, 1842 | No Return |
| Walker, Mary | Davis, James | E/61 | August 16, 1888 | August 16, 1888 |
| Walker, Mattie | Moody, James | E/131 | January 31, 1889 | January 31, 1889 |
| Walker, Oallie Miss | Saddler, J. W. | F/170 | February 4, 1899 | February 5, 1899 |
| Walker, Sarah | Travis, James | C/92 | August 15, 1874 | August 16, 1874 |
| Walker, Sarah C. | Stewart, Robert | A/20 | December 10, 1839 | December 12, 1839 |
| Walker, W. A. | Melton, Lue | F/120 | July 10, 1897 | July 11, 1897 |
| Walker, W. W. | Wood, Miss L. G. | A2/139 | March 30, 1866 | April 1, 1866 |
| Walker, W. W. | Wood, Miss L. G. | A2/144 | March 30, 1866 | No Return |
| Walkes, Cath | Gann, Munroe | C/242 | December 8, 1879 | December 10, 1879 |
| Walkins, Louisa | Wammack, J. B. | C/160 | March 15, 1877 | March 15, 1877 |
| Walkup, A. O. | Sullivan, Miss Minty | A2/42 | October 9, 1855 | October 9, 1855 |
| Walkup, Bettie | Hall, H. N. | C/192 | May 29, 1878 | May 30, 1878 |
| Walkup, C. N. | Higgins, Miss Margarett | A2/22 | December 27, 1852 | December 25, 1852 |
| Walkup, Emily Miss | Elkins, D. L. | A2/7 | November 29, 1850 | December 1, 1850 |
| Walkup, G. E. | Elrod, S. E. | D/6 | | October 19, 1881 |
| Walkup, Hanar | McKnight, W. A. | C/202 | October 16, 1878 | October 16, 1878 |
| Walkup, J. A | Tennyson, Miss M. A. | A2/84 | January 5, 1859 | January 6, 1859 |
| Walkup, J. A. | Robinson, Sarah E. | C/268 | December 15, 1880 | December 16, 1880 |
| Walkup, J. R. Miss | Peay, Tiendolphus | B/38 | January 16, 1867 | January 16, 1867 |
| Walkup, J. W. | Young, M. A. | C/42 | October 9, 1872 | No Return |
| Walkup, James | Woods, Lula | F/22 | November 4, 1893 | November 5, 1893 |
| Walkup, M. E. | Richards, J. A. | C/90 | June 22, 1874 | June 22, 1874 |
| Walkup, M. F. Miss | Yourie, S. M. | B/38 | January 16, 1867 | January 16, 1867 |
| Walkup, Martha E. Miss | Melton, George G. | A2/74 | January 16, 1854 | January 17, 1854 |
| Walkup, Mary J. Miss | Melton, Joel D. | A2/1 | March 4, 1850 | March 5, 1850 |
| Walkup, Miss Hassie | Mason, R. L. | F/86 | March 10, 1896 | March 17, 1896 |
| Walkup, Nora | Moore, Wm. W. | F/12 | July 19, 1893 | July 20, 1893 |
| Walkup, Rocinda Miss | Perry, J. H. | C/8 | September 7, 1871 | September 7, 1871 |
| Walkup, W. H. | Stone, Sallie | C/152 | December 28, 1876 | No Return |
| Walkup, Willia J. | Hollis, Mary Ann | A/6 | September 8, 1838 | September 9, 1838 |

| Groom or Bride | Groom or Bride | Book/Page | Date of License | Date of Marriage |
|---|---|---|---|---|
| Walkup, Wm. J. | Nichols, Miss Inthy Adaline | A2/27 | August 23, 1853 | August 24, 1853 |
| Wallace, Dovie Matilla | Lowe, John | E/216 | October 5, 1889 | October 6, 1889 |
| Wallace, J. E. | Gaither, Sarah B. | C/266 | December 23, 1880 | December 26, 1880 |
| Wallace, James | Cagwell, Martha | A/31 | July 21, 1840 | July 21, 1840 |
| Wallace, James | Gaither, Jennie | E/127 | January 7, 1889 | January 7, 1889 |
| Wallace, James A. | Miller, Amandy C. | D/13 | | April 16, 1882 |
| Wallace, Jesse | Praton, Florence | F/66 | July 19, 1895 | July 20, 1895 |
| Wallace, Martha A. | Prater, J. H. | C/84 | February 25, 1874 | February 25, 1874 |
| Wallace, Mollie | Mitchel, W. E. | C/270 | January 22, 1881 | January 23, 1881 |
| Wallace, Virginia | Bryson, W. B. | F/156 | September 5, 1898 | September 5, 1898 |
| Wallace, W. H. | Lance, Sarah L. | C/342 | December 5, 1885 | December 6, 1885 |
| Wallace, William | Williams, Miss Millia | B/100 | March 28, 1870 | No Return |
| Wallace, Wm. (Wilburn H.) | Smith, Mary L. | C/40 | October 2, 1872 | October 3, 1872 |
| Wallis, S. R. | Warren, S. A. | A2/80 | March 13, 1857 | March 15, 1857 |
| Walls, Caroline Miss | Conley, James G. | A/33 | October 6, 1840 | October 6, 1840 |
| Walls, Daniel | Connelly, Elizabeth | A/129 | December 6, 1849 | December 6, 1849 |
| Walls, Daniel | Cinly, Miss Dovy | A2/90 | November 12, 1859 | No Return |
| Walls, Dovey | Farley, Patton | C/20 | January 1, 1872 | January 1, 1872 |
| Walls, Effie | Thompson, Sam | F/52 | December 24, 1894 | December 25, 1894 |
| Walls, Elizabeth | Parton, Henry | A2/113 | May 3, 1864 | May 3, 1864 |
| Walls, Henry M. T. | Preston, Miss Sarah | A/110 | April 6, 1848 | April 6, 1848 |
| Walls, James J. | Cummings, Miss Francis | C/406 | November 2, 1887 | November 2, 1887 |
| Walls, Jane | Dobbs, J. T | D/17 | | November 25, 1882 |
| Walls, Martha Miss | Couch, Willis F. | A/123 | June 15, 1849 | June 15, 1849 |
| Walls, Mary | Gann, Willis | C/272 | January 27, 1881 | No Return |
| Walls, Polly Miss | Preston, Eli | A/43 | November 12, 1841 | November 14, 1841 |
| Walls, Rebecca E. | Hill, William T. | C/26 | May 11, 1872 | May 11, 1872 |
| Walls, Sarah | Adams, John | C/208 | December 23, 1878 | No Return |
| Walls, Tip | Pelham, Martha | F/20 | October 14, 1893 | October 14, 1893 |
| Walls, Will | Harris, Miss Mary | C/458 | May 15, 1892 | May 15, 1892 |
| Walton, Henry | Woodard, Miss E. | B/116 | November 9, 1870 | November 10, 1870 |
| Wamach, Robert | Seat, Miss Nancy M. | A2/23 | February 10, 1853 | February 10, 1853 |
| Wamack, Bethena Miss | Mitchell, John F. | A2/75 | November 17, 1855 | November 17, 1855 |
| Wamack, C. B. | Milligan, G. A. | C/214 | March 12, 1879 | No Return |
| Wamack, J. S. | Bogle, Miss E. E. | A2/59 | October 29, 1857 | No Return |
| Wamack, John | Roberts, Lize | C/128 | December 29, 1875 | December 29, 1875 |
| Wamack, Nancy M. | Bogle, W. R. | C/20 | September 25, 1871 | September 27, 1871 |
| Wamack, Patsey Miss | Sewell, Emerson | B/50 | August 3, 1867 | August 4, 1867 |
| Wammack, J. B. | Walkins, Louisa | C/160 | March 15, 1877 | March 15, 1877 |
| Wammack, Thomas | Reed, Lydia A. | A2/124 | July 10, 1865 | July 12, 1865 |
| Wammack, Wm. T. | Wommack, Mandy J. | C/134 | February 26, 1876 | No Return |
| Ward, Caroline Miss | Alexander, J. G. | A2/21 | December 21, 1852 | December 30, 1852 |
| Ward, Gemriah | Gann, Miss Ann | C/456 | March 23, 1892 | March 23, 1892 |
| Ward, James E. | St. John, Miss Mary L. | A/123 | August 2, 1849 | August 2, 1849 |
| Ward, M. E. | Wood, H. W. | C/376 | December 1, 1886 | December 5, 1886 |
| Ward, M. L. | Brandon, Nancy | C/262 | November 13, 1880 | November 14, 1880 |

| Groom or Bride | Groom or Bride | Book/Page | Date of License | Date of Marriage |
|---|---|---|---|---|
| Ward, M. S. | Hodges, Miss Sarah E. | A2/87 | August 17, 1859 | August 17, 1859 |
| Ward, Milton | Patterson, Nancy | A/9 | December 24, 1838 | No Return |
| Ward, Nancy A. Miss | Barrett, Joseph H. | A2/22 | December 23, 1852 | December 23, 1852 |
| Ward, S. J. | Kelly, B. A. | C/194 | July 25, 1878 | July 28, 1878 |
| Ward, W. M. | Miller, M. H. | E/251 | December 27, 1889 | December 29, 1889 |
| Ward, Zachariah | Wheeler, Fannie | E/190 | July 10, 1889 | July 10, 1889 |
| Ware, A. A. | Allen, Jesse | D/17 | | December 4, 1882 |
| Ware, Sallie | Wharton, W. T. H. | A2/95 | March 28, 1860 | March 29, 1860 |
| Ware, W. N. M. | Tiflor, Catherine | C/312 | September 13, 1884 | September 14, 1884 |
| Warley, Jasper | Norman, Alice | C/266 | December 25, 1880 | No Return |
| Warnack, D. D. | Ledford, Mary M. | A2/133 | December 12, 1865 | December 13, 1865 |
| Warren, Alexander | Barkley, Miss Nancy Ann | A2/9 | January 6, 1851 | January 7, 1851 |
| Warren, Arthur | Sullivan, Rebeccah | A/17 | September 5, 1839 | No Return |
| Warren, Benjamin | Curdon, Miss Marry | A2/21 | December 14, 1852 | December 14, 1852 |
| Warren, Elizabeth A. | Prator, Benjamin P. | A/11 | March 9, 1839 | March 10, 1839 |
| Warren, Elvira Miss | Blair, Isaac P. | A/72 | September 7, 1844 | September 8, 1844 |
| Warren, J. K. | Ferrell, Sallie B. | F/80 | January 3, 1896 | January 5, 1896 |
| Warren, J. W. | Hale, Miss L. | A2/46 | February 9, 1856 | February 10, 1856 |
| Warren, Joe | Ferrell, Caroline | E/57 | August 8, 1888 | August 8, 1888 |
| Warren, John | Benfon, Miss Mary E. | A/95 | December 26, 1846 | December 27, 1846 |
| Warren, M. V. | Phillips, William | A2/82 | April 13, 1858 | April 13, 1858 |
| Warren, Margarette Ann Miss | Justice, John B. | A/113 | August 26, 1848 | September 5, 1848 |
| Warren, Martha Miss | Hancock, Richard | A2/34 | August 5, 1854 | August 6, 1854 |
| Warren, Mary | Logan, G. W. | C/254 | August 19, 1880 | August 19, 1880 |
| Warren, Mary Frances Miss | Adamson, Prestly L. | A/82 | July 28, 1845 | July 29, 1845 |
| Warren, Mary Miss | Holder, B. H. | B/44 | April 15, 1867 | April 15, 1867 |
| Warren, Rebecca J. Miss | Cook, Samul | A2/90 | November 15, 1859 | Executed No Date |
| Warren, S. A. | Wallis, S. R. | A2/80 | March 13, 1857 | March 15, 1857 |
| Warren, S. J. Miss | Singleton, H. D. | B/70 | September 2, 1868 | September 2, 1868 |
| Warren, Sallie A. | Bogle, James | F/2 | February 4, 1893 | February 5, 1893 |
| Warren, Sam | Grooms, Tennie | C/206 | November 27, 1878 | November 28, 1878 |
| Warren, Sarahfine Miss | Melton, John | B/44 | March 28, 1867 | March 28, 1867 |
| Warren, Susan Miss | Summar, J. C. | B/100 | March 18, 1870 | No Return |
| Warren, W. H. | Herrald, Miss Sarrah J. | A2/54 | February 4, 1857 | February 5, 1857 |
| Warren, W. M. | Neely, Susan | C/396 | August 4, 1887 | No Return |
| Warren, Wm. | Bailey, Miss Anna | C/450 | December 9, 1891 | December 9, 1891 |
| Warren, Zachariah | Travers, Miss Mary | A/66 | December 30, 1843 | January 1, 1844 |
| Warrick, H. D. | Brewer, Mattie | F/98 | October 3, 1896 | October 4, 1896 |
| Warrick, J. W. | Lynn, Miss Lavisa J. | B/106 | August 20, 1870 | No Return |
| Warrick, Jessee | Turner, Mrs. C. A. | B/114 | October 27, 1870 | October 27, 1870 |
| Warrick, M. E. | Summars, T. J. | C/380 | December 27, 1886 | December 28, 1886 |
| Wasson, B. F. | Oliver, Miss Rebkah | F/166 | January 18, 1899 | January 18, 1899 |
| Waters, Cravin | Farley, Miss Nancy J. | B/120 | December 22, 1870 | December 23, 1870 |
| Waters, Delitha Miss | Faulkenberg, Benjamin | A2/1 | January 24, 1850 | No Return |
| Waters, Edward | Farler, Miss Tabith | B/48 | August 3, 1867 | August 4, 1867 |
| Waters, Gardner | Woods, Callie | C/250 | July 13, 1880 | July 13, 1880 |

| Groom or Bride | Groom or Bride | Book/Page | Date of License | Date of Marriage |
|---|---|---|---|---|
| Waters, Henry | Hailey, Miss Clementine | B/42 | February 27, 1867 | Solemnized, No Date |
| Watkins, Emanuel | Harp, Miss Rachael | A/64 | August 17, 1843 | August 17, 1843 |
| Watson, A. C. Miss | Brown, John A. J. | B/102 | May 28, 1870 | May 29, 1870 |
| Watson, Annie | Hale, James | C/116 | July 29, 1875 | August 1, 1875 |
| Watson, Beulah | Robinson, C. F. | F/72 | October 3, 1895 | October 4, 1895 |
| Watson, E. | Burkette, Joanna | C/468 | November 16, 1892 | November 17, 1892 |
| Watson, Elisabeth | Hollandsworth, John | C/260 | October 20, 1880 | October 21, 1880 |
| Watson, F. E. | Justice, Alice | C/78 | December 30, 1873 | December 30, 1873 |
| Watson, G. M. D. | Woodside, Miss Sarah Elizabeth | B/48 | July 29, 1867 | July 30, 1867 |
| Watson, Geneva | Cox, C. A. | C/20 | December 27, 1871 | December 27, 1871 |
| Watson, J. M. | Owen, Bettie | C/312 | August 14, 1884 | August 14, 1884 |
| Watson, James | Patton, Mary | A/7 | September 25, 1838 | September 26, 1838 |
| Watson, James | Watson, M. E. | B/80 | April 6, 1869 | April 6, 1869 |
| Watson, James N. | McAlexander, Miss Rebecca | A/107 | February 3, 1848 | February 9, 1848 |
| Watson, Jeff | Spurlock, Mary | C/266 | December 4, 1880 | December 5, 1880 |
| Watson, Joel | Barrett, Mary | C/348 | January 11, 1886 | January 11, 1886 |
| Watson, John | Wilsher, Mary | C/44 | October 31, 1872 | No Return |
| Watson, Joseph | Barret, M. L. | E/34 | May 11, 1888 | May 22, 1888 |
| Watson, Joseph T. | King, Nancy C. | C/214 | March 5, 1879 | March 5, 1879 |
| Watson, M. E. | Watson, James | B/80 | April 6, 1869 | April 6, 1869 |
| Watson, M. H. | Owen, James | C/260 | October 30, 1880 | October 30, 1880 |
| Watson, Nancy | Spurlock E. J. | D/12 | | March 5, 1882 |
| Watson, Nancy A. | Butter, J. W. | A2/83 | January 15, 1859 | No Return |
| Watson, Nancy A. | Collins, Frances | C/166 | August 8, 1877 | August 9, 1877 |
| Watson, Nancy A. Miss | Bullen, J. W. | A2/72 | January 15, 1859 | No Return |
| Watson, P. E. Miss | Ridener, L. W. | C/4 | July 28, 1871 | July 28, 1871 |
| Watson, Riley | Thompson, Sarah A. | C/146 | September 30, 1876 | October 1, 1876 |
| Watter, R. J. | Mears, Robert R. | A2/117 | November 2, 1864 | November 3, 1864 |
| Watters, L. | Craft, Bird | C/294 | October 15, 1883 | No Return |
| Watts, Mary Miss | Witherspoon, William E. | A/89 | May 21, 1846 | May 21, 1846 |
| Watts, Milton E. | Porterfield, Miss P. C. | A/52 | August 31, 1842 | September 1, 1842 |
| Weadon, Hiller (col.) | Techoble, Elmangy (col.) | F/136 | November 8, 1897 | November 8, 1897 |
| Weadon, Tom (col.) | Taylor, Mattie (col.) | F/114 | March 13, 1897 | March 13, 1897 |
| Weatherford, S. M. Miss | Pittered, P. H. | B/52 | September 4, 1867 | September 4, 1867 |
| Weatherly, Jesse | McKnight, Nancy | B/12 | November 9, 1867 | November 14, 1867 |
| Weatherly, Jesse | Rucker, July | C/268 | December 8, 1880 | December 9, 1880 |
| Weatherspon, A. B. | Taylor, L. E. | C/118 | September 13, 1875 | September 14, 1875 |
| Weatherspoon, Mary Eliza | Reynolds, John | A/21 | December 23, 1839 | December 24, 1839 |
| Webb, Alsa | Higgins, Mary E. | C/40 | September 25, 1872 | September 29, 1872 |
| Webb, Anni | Lance, J. M. | C/374 | November 10, 1886 | November 11, 1886 |
| Webb, Annie (col.) | Thomas (col.) | F/130 | September 4, 1897 | September 5, 12897 |
| Webb, Bettie | Fugett, Sam | C/170 | September 15, 1877 | No Return |
| Webb, Eliza J. | McGregor, Denton | C/194 | July 30, 1878 | July 30, 1878 |
| Webb, Emer | Woodard, Henry C. | C/234 | December 23, 1879 | No Return |
| Webb, George | Stewart, Mary | C/212 | February 16, 1879 | February 16, 1879 |
| Webb, George | Talley, Vira | C/346 | December 28, 1885 | December 28, 1885 |

| Groom or Bride | Groom or Bride | Book/Page | Date of License | Date of Marriage |
|---|---|---|---|---|
| Webb, Ibbia Miss | Spurlock, Joseph | B/98 | January 18, 1870 | January 18, 1870 |
| Webb, J. B. | Jones, Serena | F/140 | December 16, 1897 | December 17, 1897 |
| Webb, J. C. | Mullins, Sarah | E/248 | December 23, 1889 | December 24, 1889 |
| Webb, J. W. | Satine, Laura | A2/13 | December 25, 1851 | December 25, 1851 |
| Webb, Jacob | Vaughn, Mary | C/168 | August 25, 1877 | August 26, 1877 |
| Webb, Jacob | Barrett, Missie | C/446 | September 20, 1891 | No Return |
| Webb, Jacob | Barns, Polley | D/4 | | September 11, 1881 |
| Webb, Jane | Sullins, Samuel | E/186 | June 24, 1889 | June 24, 1889 |
| Webb, Jesse | Foster, Hannah | C/402 | September 15, 1887 | September 15, 1887 |
| Webb, Julina | Sullins, Joseph D. | C/372 | October 30, 1886 | No Return |
| Webb, Mahaley A. | Webb, Pattrick H. | B/6 | August 28, 1865 | August 28, 1865 |
| Webb, Mary | Thrower, John | F/114 | March 28, 1897 | March 28, 1897 |
| Webb, Mary | Williams, Lewis | C/288 | August 13, 1883 | August 13, 1883 |
| Webb, Mary E. | McFerin, L. B. | A2/120 | February 7, 1865 | February 7, 1865 |
| Webb, Mary L. | McKnight, Joe D. | C/106 | February 1, 1875 | February 4, 1875 |
| Webb, Nannie E. | Thompkin, J. T. | C/104 | January 2, 1875 | January 2, 1875 |
| Webb, Nelville | Taylor, Mary J. | C/358 | April 24, 1886 | April 25, 1886 |
| Webb, Parlee | Wood, Isaac | B/6 | August 28, 1865 | August 28, 1865 |
| Webb, Pattrick H. | Webb, Mahaley A. | B/6 | August 28, 1865 | August 28, 1865 |
| Webb, R. | Paris, D | C/230 | November 15, 1879 | November 16, 1879 |
| Webb, Samantha | Blew, John | B/16 | May 1, 1869 | May 1, 1869 |
| Webb, Samuel | Taylor, Martha | B/6 | September 2, 1865 | September 4, 1865 |
| Webb, Sarah | Fugitt, Nathan | C/138 | May 31, 1876 | June 1, 1876 |
| Webb, Tennessee P. Miss | Williams, Joseph H. | B/58 | December 2, 1867 | December 10, 1867 |
| Webb, Vivan (col.) | Melton, Sandy (col.) | F/104 | December 12, 1896 | December 12, 1896 |
| Webb, W. J. | Stephens, S. E. | C/92 | August 13, 1874 | August 16, 1874 |
| Webber, Albert | Napper, Caroline | C/248 | May 11, 1880 | May 17, 1880 |
| Webber, Benjamin | Ashley, Mary | A2/112 | February 1, 1864 | No Return |
| Webber, Elizabeth E. | Johnson, Richard P. | A/2 | April 14, 1838 | April 20, 1838 |
| Webber, Elizabeth Miss | Gray, William | A/52 | August 4, 1842 | August 5, 1842 |
| Webber, F. M. | Briant, Frances | A2/124 | July 31, 1865 | August 5, 1865 |
| Webber, Henry | Merriman, Roda | D/20 | | March 19, 1883 |
| Webber, J. G. | Baltimore, Mary A. | C/120 | September 16, 1875 | September 17, 1875 |
| Webber, Jane Adaline Miss | Jamison, William A. | B/50 | August 12, 1867 | August 18, 1867 |
| Webber, Jane Miss | Parker, Lorenzo D. | A/35 | November 5, 1840 | No Return |
| Webber, John | Simpson, Cinthy | A2/20 | October 28, 1852 | Return Crossed out |
| Webber, John A. | Finley, Miss Effa | A/87 | February 20, 1846 | February 22, 1846 |
| Webber, Martha L. Miss | Bynum, Wm. | A2/90 | November 2, 1859 | No Return |
| Webber, Mary Miss | Rains, John | A2/5 | September 12, 1850 | September 22, 1850 |
| Webber, Phillip | Worlien, Miss Elisabeth | A2/15 | February 14, 1852 | No Return |
| Webber, Polley | Campbell, W. D. | C/14 | November 27, 1871 | November 27, 1871 |
| Webber, Rebecca | Sissom, Thomas | A/117 | November 14, 1848 | November 14, 1848 |
| Webber, Sarah Miss | Sissom, William | A/69 | June 5, 1844 | June 6, 1844 |
| Weedan, Tennessee E. Miss | Fisher, A. N. | A2/78 | January 22, 1856 | January 22, 1856 |
| Weeden, George (col.) | McKnight, Eller | F/70 | September 11, 1895 | September 12, 1895 |
| Weedon, A. M. | Mathews, Paulina J. P. | A/61 | March 27, 1843 | March 30, 1843 |

| Groom or Bride | Groom or Bride | Book/Page | Date of License | Date of Marriage |
|---|---|---|---|---|
| Weedon, A. M. | Stone, Miss Sarah | A/110 | April 11, 1848 | No Return |
| Weedon, Daniel F. | Rucker, Mariah S. | A/14 | June 6, 1839 | No Return |
| Weedon, J. P. | Wood, W. J. | A2/97 | May 24, 1860 | May 24, 1860 |
| Weedon, Jim (col.) | Spurlock, Sindy (col.) | F/162 | December 10, 1898 | January 2, 1899 |
| Weedon, Jo Miss | Campbell, W. R. | B/124 | January 24, 1871 | January 25, 1871 |
| Weedon, John | Jetton, Julia | B/10 | March 26, 1867 | No Return |
| Weedon, John | Jetton, Julia | B/14 | October 8, 1868 | November 22, 1868 |
| Weedon, John F. | Ferrell, Mary Jane | A/59 | January 31, 1843 | January 31, 1843 |
| Weedon, John F. | Ferrell, Miss Eliza Ann | A/128 | November 12, 1849 | November 13, 1849 |
| Weedon, Martha E. | Brewer, Jesse | A/61 | March 23, 1843 | March 23, 1843 |
| Weedon, Sallie M. Miss | Smith, M. D. | B/80 | March 24, 1869 | March 25, 1869 |
| Weedon, Wesley | Dement, Vina | C/32 | August 12, 1872 | August 12, 1872 |
| Weeks, William | Woods, Miss Mollie | C/450 | November 11, 1891 | November 11, 1891 |
| Weellan, S. E. Miss | Williams, A. M. | A2/58 | October 27, 1857 | October 27, 1857 |
| Welch, M. E. | Barret, B. F. | A2/130 | October 4, 1865 | October 11, 1865 |
| Wells (Webb), John | Brown, Mrs. Sarah P. | A/61 | April 11, 1843 | April 11, 1843 |
| Werley, Mollie | Tucker, Andrin J. | F/32 | February 21, 1894 | February 25, 1894 |
| West, A. W. | Brison, Martha M. | A2/98 | June 26, 1860 | No Return |
| West, A. W. | Harris, Emily | A2/109 | October 7, 1863 | October 7, 1863 |
| West, Amanda | West, Carrol | C/402 | September 23, 1887 | September 23, 1887 |
| West, Amanda | Tenpenny, Wm. | C/426 | December 23, 1890 | December 23, 1890 |
| West, Anna | Smith, J. B. | C/236 | December 28, 1879 | No Return |
| West, Barbey | Lorance, B. B. | C/244 | February 26, 1880 | February 26, 1880 |
| West, Benjamin W. | Todder, Miss Eleanor | A/33 | September 28, 1840 | September 29, 1840 |
| West, Carrol | West, Amanda | C/402 | September 23, 1887 | September 23, 1887 |
| West, Charles | Pendleton, Miss Melinda | A/115 | October 7, 1848 | October 7, 1848 |
| West, Dallas | Smithson, Marisu | C/364 | September 1, 1886 | No Return |
| West, Ester Miss | McCullough, John | C/412 | December 16, 1887 | December 18, 1887 |
| West, Frank | Fann, Mary Ann | E/372 | October 5, 1898 | |
| West, Frank | Morgan, Fani | F/160 | November 5, 1898 | No Return |
| West, Henry | Hoover, Susan | C/232 | November 20, 1879 | November 20, 1879 |
| West, Henry | Womack, Eliza | F/92 | August 20, 1896 | August 20, 1896 |
| West, Henry H. | Craft, Miss Elisabeth | A2/98 | June 29, 1860 | July 1, 1860 |
| West, John | Lemmons, Mahaley | C/300 | January 21, 1884 | January 21, 1884 |
| West, John | Henderson, Rachal | C/340 | November 2, 1885 | No Return |
| West, John A. | Cooper, Rachiel | A2/104 | November 8, 1860 | No Return |
| West, Jourden | Davis, Miss Paralee | A2/82 | August 9, 1858 | August 11, 1858 |
| West, Lucinda Miss | Pendleton, John Jr. | A/101 | August 9, 1847 | August 9, 1847 |
| West, Malinda | Finly, Alex | C/62 | July 21, 1873 | No Return |
| West, Malissa J. Miss | Carmichael, William G. | A2/6 | June 4, 1850 | June 4, 1850 |
| West, Manerva Ann Miss | Allen, Samuel B. | A/45 | December 10, 1841 | December 10, 1841 |
| West, Martha | Bryant, Jas. | C/176 | November 9, 1877 | November 11, 1877 |
| West, Mary E. | Gann, Robert | C/276 | March 5, 1881 | March 5, 1881 |
| West, Mary J. | Bryant, James | C/286 | July 13, 1883 | July 15, 1883 |
| West, Mary Jane Miss | Vasser, Caswell | A2/6 | September 3, 1850 | September 30, 1850 |
| West, Milly | Tittle, Thomas | C/434 | April 6, 1891 | April 7, 1891 |

| Groom or Bride | Groom or Bride | Book/Page | Date of License | Date of Marriage |
|---|---|---|---|---|
| West, Nancy E. Miss | Lewis, J. W. | A2/91 | November 29, 1859 | No Return |
| West, Robt | Petty, Lou | F/138 | November 20, 1897 | November 21, 1897 |
| West, S. A. Miss | Youngblood, J. H. | B/120 | December 21, 1870 | December 22, 1870 |
| West, Sally | Bryson, William | A/5 | August 15, 1838 | August 15, 1838 |
| West, Sarah M. | Sison, J. D. | E/58 | August 10, 1888 | August 11, 1888 |
| West, Sarah M. | Sisson, J. D. | E/77 | August 10, 1888 | August 12, 1888 |
| West, T. F. | Pitman, Amandy | C/28 | June 10, 1872 | June 10, 1872 |
| West, T. F. | Manus, Margrett | E/235 | November 28, 1889 | November 28, 1889 |
| West, Thomas | Lafevers, Maud | F/6 | March 29, 1893 | April 2, 1983 |
| West, Vesta | Spicer, Wm | F/32 | February 28, 1894 | February 28, 1894 |
| West, Willey | Elkins, Lilley | F/80 | January 4, 1896 | January 4, 1896 |
| West, Z. A. Miss | Stacy, W. J. | A2/89 | October 20, 1859 | October 20, 1859 |
| Wetherspoon, Louis F. W. | Harris, Sarah E. | A/31 | August 4, 1840 | No Return |
| Wharrey, Louisa Lavina Miss | Hall, Jonathan | A/44 | December 9, 1841 | December 9, 1841 |
| Wharry, Cyntha Jane Miss | Travis, James W. | A/116 | November 1, 1848 | No Return |
| Wharry, Malvina Ann | McCullough, William W. | A/59 | January 11, 1843 | January 12, 1843 |
| Wharten, Lida | Hearn, H. M. | D/22 | | February 1, 1883 |
| Wharton, Eliabeth R. Miss | Taylor, James | A/96 | January 21, 1847 | January 26, 1847 |
| Wharton, J. H. | Wheeler, Miss M. H. | A2/137 | February 1, 1866 | February 1, 1866 |
| Wharton, Jennie C. | Howel, E. J. | C/150 | December 17, 1876 | December 17, 1876 |
| Wharton, W. T. H. | Kennedy, Miss B. L. | A2/53 | January 24, 1857 | No Return |
| Wharton, W. T. H. | Ware, Sallie | A2/95 | March 28, 1860 | March 29, 1860 |
| Wheeler | Graham, T. N. | B/126 | March 2, 1871 | March 2, 1871 |
| Wheeler, Alice | Campbell, J. W. | C/52 | February 13, 1873 | February 13, 1873 |
| Wheeler, Elizabeth | Mairs, James | D/3 | | June 29, 1881 |
| Wheeler, Fannie | Ward, Zachariah | E/190 | July 10, 1889 | July 10, 1889 |
| Wheeler, Forest | McBroom, Mahala | C/406 | October 9, 1887 | October 10, 1887 |
| Wheeler, M. H. Miss | Wharton, J. H. | A2/137 | February 1, 1866 | February 1, 1866 |
| Wheeler, N. T. | Baird, Miss Mary | B/116 | November 10, 1870 | November 10, 1870 |
| Wheeler, Thomas R. | Barnes, Della | C/188 | March 12, 1878 | March 12, 1878 |
| Wheeling, Bennett | Barrett, Miss Elizabeth | A/131 | December 19, 1849 | December 20, 1849 |
| Wheeling, James M. | Fry, Elizabeth | A2/18 | August 18, 1852 | August 19, 1852 |
| Wheelr, B. F. | Mooneyhen, M. J. | C/340 | November 7, 1885 | No Return |
| Wherry, Frances E. Miss | Mears, John C. | B/34 | December 20, 1866 | December 20, 1866 |
| Wherry, L. B. Miss | Vaughan, J. C. | A2/30 | December 18, 1853 | December 29, 1853 |
| Wherry, Margarett Miss | Hall, Preston | A/127 | September 25, 1849 | |
| Whirley, Etna | Davenport, W. C. | C/472 | December 17, 1892 | December 18, 1892 |
| Whit, Benjamin | Young, Miss Sarah | A2/27 | August 10, 1853 | August 10, 1853 |
| Whit, Martha Anne Miss | Colwell, Andrew J. | A/31 | July 22, 1840 | July 22, 1840 |
| Whitaker, B. A. | Craig, Miss Sue | E/47 | July 11, 1888 | July 12, 1888 |
| Whitamoore, John | Williams, Alma | E/392 | October 3, 1890 | |
| Whitamore, Jesse G. | Spangler, Miss Abigail | A/66 | December 21, 1843 | December 24, 1843 |
| Whitamore, John | Williams, Alma | F/158 | October 3, 1898 | October 5, 1898 |
| Whitamore, William | Duncan, Miss Mary Ann | A2/9 | January 10, 1851 | January 12, 1851 |
| White, George J | Ollivar, Hixie | E/17 | January 30, 1888 | January 31, 1888 |
| White, J. H. | Tassey, Margarett | F/128 | August 30, 1897 | August 31, 1897 |

| Groom or Bride | Groom or Bride | Book/Page | Date of License | Date of Marriage |
|---|---|---|---|---|
| White, Malinda T. Miss | Pearson, Thomas | A/53 | August 31, 1842 | August 31, 1842 |
| White, Melton | Daniel, Lindy | C/134 | February 25, 1876 | February 27, 1876 |
| White, W. J. | Stone, Miss Josaphine | A2/10 | January 28, 1851 | No Return |
| White, Wm. | Barrett, Bettie | E/159 | December 30, 1888 | December 30, 1888 |
| Whitefield, M. C. Miss | Ring, Wm. | A2/35 | September 20, 1854 | September 21, 1854 |
| Whitefield, W. E. | Whitfield, Elizabeth A. | A2/32 | February 23, 1854 | February 23, 1853 |
| Whiteley, Sarah Miss | Peden, James | A/85 | December 27, 1845 | December 27, 1845 |
| Whitfield, Haly | Jarnagin, Cary | A/9 | November 29, 1838 | No Return |
| Whitfield, A. J. | Knox, Miss Jennie | F/176 | May 13, 1899 | No Return |
| Whitfield, Ag | Gaither, Miss Oplia | C/388 | May 7, 1887 | No Return |
| Whitfield, Elizabeth A. | Whitefield, W. E. | A2/32 | February 23, 1854 | February 23, 1853 |
| Whitfield, M. J. | Brown, W. E. | C/94 | September 11, 1874 | September 17, 1874 |
| Whitfield, Marry Ann Miss | Rotty, Jackson | A2/25 | May 21, 1853 | May 22, 1853 |
| Whitfield, Mary J. | Jernigan, L. W. | A2/134 | December 27, 1865 | December 27, 1865 |
| Whitfield, Mathew | Whitfield, Miss Sarah L. | A2/13 | December 9, 1851 | December 9, 1851 |
| Whitfield, Sarah Ann B. | St. John, W. T. | A2/142 | July 28, 1866 | Executed No Date |
| Whitfield, Sarah L. Miss | Whitfield, Mathew | A2/13 | December 9, 1851 | December 9, 1851 |
| Whitlock, Allice | Bryans, Irving | F/106 | December 16, 1896 | No Return |
| Whitlock, Catherine | Hammer, J. N. | F/82 | January 8, 1896 | No Return |
| Whitlock, E. B. | Wilson, Miss Nancy | A2/41 | August 24, 1855 | August 27, 1855 |
| Whitlock, J. H. | Jernigan, Willie E. | F/78 | December 16, 1895 | December 16, 1895 |
| Whitlock, John | Bragg, Miss Sarah | A2/6 | October 24, 1850 | October 24, 1850 |
| Whitsmore, Tabitha Miss | Spangler, Samuel | A/42 | October 14, 1841 | October 14, 1841 |
| Whitt, Em. M. | Mars, Miss May | A2/93 | July 6, 1859 | No Return |
| Whitt, Felix | Morgan, Miss Elizabeth C. | A/90 | August 20, 1846 | August 27, 1846 |
| Whitt, Jonathan | Colwell, Miss Nancy | A/64 | August 4, 1843 | August 7, 1843 |
| Whitt, Sarah Jane Miss | Merrett, John | A2/23 | January 15, 1853 | January 16, 1853 |
| Whittamore, Abagale Miss | Ross, James | A2/139 | March 5, 1866 | March 15, 1866 |
| Whittamore, J. H. | Finley, Malinda | C/198 | September 18, 1878 | September 19, 1878 |
| Whittamore, Newton | Ross, Miss Malinda | A2/138 | February 23, 1866 | February 25, 1866 |
| Whittemic, Simon | Hayes, Louisa F. | A2/94 | February 2, 1860 | No Return |
| Whittemore, Jane | Rackley, Wiley | C/240 | January 21, 1880 | No Return |
| Whittemore, M. E. | Espy, John L. | C/296 | November 10, 1883 | November 18, 1883 |
| Whittemore, Sarah | Brown, Silas N. | F/144 | January 14, 1898 | January 15, 1898 |
| Whittemore, T. L. | Stacy, J. M. | E/121 | December 27, 1888 | December 20, 1888 |
| Whittemore, William B. | Finley, Miss Nancy | A2/145 | September 22, 1866 | September 23, 1866 |
| Whitter, Sammie | Maney, Miss Polly | B/94 | December 13, 1869 | December 13, 1869 |
| Whittiemore, Simeon | Williams, Sallie | C/376 | December 18, 1886 | December 19, 1886 |
| Whorton, Thomas | Ferrel, Miss Elizabeth J. | B/108 | August 24, 1870 | August 25, 1870 |
| Wilburn, Bettie | Todd, G. W. | F/26 | December 23, 1893 | December 25, 1893 |
| Wilburn, T. A. | Thomas, Queen E. | C/120 | September 15, 1875 | September 16, 1875 |
| Wilcher, C. M. | Rigsby, Martha | D/21 | | April 4, 1883 |
| Wilcher, Delila E. Miss | Bogle, John E. | B/104 | July 4, 1870 | No Return |
| Wilcher, Eliza | Stanley, J. C. | F/50 | November 28, 1894 | November 28, 1894 |
| Wilcher, Eliza | Gann, John | F/78 | December 17, 1895 | December 18, 1895 |
| Wilcher, Eliza J. | McGee, J. S. | D/23 | | February 7, 1883 |

| Groom or Bride | Groom or Bride | Book/Page | Date of License | Date of Marriage |
|---|---|---|---|---|
| Wilcher F. C. | Martin, L. B. | C/218 | July 19, 1879 | July 20, 1879 |
| Wilcher, J. A. | Carter, Miss Elizabeth | B/62 | February 13, 1868 | February 13, 1868 |
| Wilcher, J. B. | Milligan, Ruth J. | C/86 | April 8, 1874 | April 9, 1874 |
| Wilcher, Melissa | Higgins, John | C/438 | June 22, 1891 | June 22, 1891 |
| Wilcher, Tina | Adams, W. F. | C/216 | June 22, 1879 | June 22, 1879 |
| Wilcher, W. B. | Jones, Nancy Ann | C/448 | October 14, 1891 | October 15, 1891 |
| Wilcher, William | Clore, Miss Nancy J. | A/38 | May 14, 1841 | May 16, 1841 |
| Wilcher, Wm. B. | Stone, Miss Burnavista | B/88 | September 23, 1868 | No Return |
| Wildman, William | Starr, Miss Nancy | A/95 | January 1, 1847 | No Return |
| Wiley, Fanie | Martin, Bill | C/334 | August 29, 1885 | August 29, 1885 |
| Wiley, Frances Ann Miss | Baird, J. A. | A/72 | August 30 1844 | September 1, 1844 |
| Wiley, Ida (col.) | King, Hence (col.) | D/9 | | December 25, 1881 |
| Wileyford, John | Elam, Francis | C/62 | July 28, 1873 | July 31, 1873 |
| Wilkenson, Ben | Stephens, Clem | C/352 | February 6, 1886 | February 7, 1886 |
| Wilkerson, Martha M. Miss | Reynolds, John A. | A2/16 | April 15, 1852 | April 15, 1852 |
| Willard, Alta | Frances, Jimm | F/68 | September 17, 1895 | September 15, 1895 |
| Willard, Ann | Milligin, Mathew | F/108 | December 30, 1896 | December 30, 1896 |
| Willard, Beverly | Smith, Adaline | A2/107 | April 15, 1863 | No Return |
| Willard, D. B. | Frances, Miss Malissa | B/76 | January 23, 1869 | January 24, 1869 |
| Willard, Eag. | McMillon, Wason | F/92 | August 3, 1896 | August 23, 1896 |
| Willard, Florence | Summer, Charley | F/4 | February 22, 1893 | February 23, 1893 |
| Willard, J. A | Odom, Miss Hanah J. | A2/59 | November 5, 1857 | No Return |
| Willard, John A. | Odom, Nancy | A2/110 | November 21, 1863 | November 22, 1863 |
| Willard, M. A. | Summar, Elizabeth | A2/116 | August 21, 1864 | No Return |
| Willard, M. W. | Odom, D. T. | C/14 | November 16, 1871 | November 19, 1871 |
| Willard, Martha Elizabeth | Ready, William | A/115 | October 12, 1848 | October 12, 1848 |
| Willard, Mattie Miss | Robinson, Robert | C/450 | December 7, 1891 | No Return |
| Willard, Patsy | Mingle, H. L. | F/168 | January 25, 1899 | January 29, 1899 |
| Willard, S. E. | McBroom, Benjamine | C/472 | December 23, 1892 | December 28, 1892 |
| Willard, Sam | Gann, Sarah E. | C/210 | January 4, 1879 | No Return |
| Willard, Virginia | Davenport, H. M. | C/454 | February 1, 1892 | February 3, 1892 |
| Willard, William | Summar, Talitha | A/54 | September 19, 1842 | No Return |
| Willard, Wm. P. | Odom, L. A. | A2/112 | February 12, 1865 | February 17, 1864 |
| Willas, Wiley | McGille, Lillie | C/358 | May 27, 1886 | May 30, 1886 |
| William, Julie A. Miss | Brooks, Wm. | B/112 | September 24, 1870 | September 25, 1870 |
| William, W. L. | McCullough, Angeline | E/46 | July 11, 1888 | July 16, 1888 |
| Williams David | Finley, Rebecca | A2/12 | November 11, 1851 | November 11, 1851 |
| Williams F. R. | Todd, James A. | D/20 | | August 9, 1883 |
| Williams W. M | Green, Catherine | F/126 | August 26, 1897 | August 26, 1897 |
| Williams, A. M. | Weellan, Miss S. E. | A2/58 | October 27, 1857 | October 27, 1857 |
| Williams, Alma | Whitamoore, John | E/392 | October 3, 1890 | |
| Williams, Alma | Whitamore, Johnm | F/158 | October 3, 1898 | October 5, 1898 |
| Williams, Amandy | Cotter, Willie | C/246 | April 4, 1880 | No Return |
| Williams, Annie Miss | Mathews, J. W. | B/118 | December 7, 1870 | December 7, 1870 |
| Williams, B. A. | Bratton, M. F. | C/202 | October 18, 1878 | November 19, 1878 |
| Williams, Benjamin | McCullough, Rada S. | A2/126 | September 4, 1865 | September 7, 1865 |

| Groom or Bride | Groom or Bride | Book/Page | Date of License | Date of Marriage |
|---|---|---|---|---|
| Williams, Berry | Leonard, Miss Cyrena A. | A/105 | November 18, 1847 | November 18, 1847 |
| Williams, Bettie | Duncan, P. B. | E/239 | December 11, 1889 | December 15, 1889 |
| Williams, C. H. | Stacy, Slizabeth | A2/55 | April 18, 1857 | April 17, 1857 |
| Williams, C. H. | Caffy, Daisey | F/32 | February 15, 1894 | February 25, 1894 |
| Williams, Charlie | Moore, Ada Lee | F/174 | April 29, 1899 | April 29, 1899 |
| Williams, D. C. | McKnight, Sallie | C/148 | November 19, 1876 | November 19, 1876 |
| Williams, David | Brown, Mary A. | C/40 | September 21, 1872 | September 22, 1872 |
| Williams, Delila A. Miss | Mathis, Thomas | C/390 | June 9, 1887 | June 13, 1887 |
| Williams, Dennis | Spry, H. A. | C/72 | November 19, 1873 | November 20, 1873 |
| Williams, Dennis | Alexander, Mary | C/178 | November 30, 1877 | December 2, 1877 |
| Williams, Elizabeth | Dean, Noah | A/12 | March 22, 1839 | March 22, 1839 |
| Williams, Frances | Summar, Misa | A2/123 | April 3, 1865 | April 6, 1865 |
| Williams, Frances Miss | Bush, L. P. | B/74 | December 12, 1868 | December 13, 1868 |
| Williams, Freelin | Carter, Roda L. | C/184 | January 12, 1878 | January 13, 1878 |
| Williams, G. W. | Hays, S. E. | C/206 | November 28, 1878 | December 1, 1878 |
| Williams, H. C. | Bush, E. J. | C/226 | October 29, 1879 | October 30, 1879 |
| Williams, Harvey T. | Hollis, Miss Mary E. | A/117 | November 14, 1849 | November 15, 1849 |
| Williams, Howell | Gilither, Tennie | C/254 | August 26, 1880 | August 26, 1880 |
| Williams, Isaac | Hamlet, Miss Nancy | A2/13 | December 18, 1851 | No Return |
| Williams, J. B. | Bynum, Miss Mary C. | B/72 | December 1, 1868 | December 2, 1868 |
| Williams, J. H. | Patton, Mary | F/18 | October 11, 1893 | October 11, 1893 |
| Williams, J. M. | Dodd, Miss A. A. | A2/58 | October 22, 1857 | October 22, 1857 |
| Williams, J. W. | Lewis, Bell | F/2 | February 6, 1893 | February 7, 1893 |
| Williams, James | Petty, Elizabeth Ann | A/76 | January 30, 1845 | No Return |
| Williams, James M. | Brazel, Laura | C/330 | June 16, 1885 | June 18, 1885 |
| Williams, Jane F. | Duke, G. A. | C/102 | December 18, 1874 | December 20, 1874 |
| Williams, Jerusha | Haley, John W. | A/30 | June 12, 1840 | June 14, 1840 |
| Williams, Jesse | Duncan, Polly | A/33 | September 22, 1840 | September 22, 1840 |
| Williams, Jno. R. | Duke, Mary A. | C/96 | October 5, 1874 | October 11, 1874 |
| Williams, John | Smith, Miss Isabela | A2/70 | December 1, 1858 | December 1, 1858 |
| Williams, John | Kuykendall, Miss Telitha F. | A2/138 | February 21, 1866 | February 23, 1866 |
| Williams, John | Smith, Francis | C/200 | October 12, 1878 | October 13, 1878 |
| Williams, John | Duke, Ann | C/312 | August 27, 1884 | August 27, 1884 |
| Williams, John A. | Mullins, Miss Julia Ann | A/130 | December 13, 1849 | December 13, 1849 |
| Williams, John B. | Kerklin, Miss E. J. | A2/60 | November 23, 1857 | November 23, 1857 |
| Williams, Joseph | Summers, Martha N. | A2/40 | May 2, 1855 | May 6, 1855 |
| Williams, Joseph H. | Webb, Miss Tennessee P. | B/58 | December 2, 1867 | December 10, 1867 |
| Williams, Joseph O. | Barratt, Martha J. | A2/120 | February 18, 1865 | February 19, 1865 |
| Williams, Joshua | Batson, Miss Jane | A/98 | March 30, 1847 | March 31, 1847 |
| Williams, Joshua | Murry, Clera M. | C/132 | February 3, 1876 | February 3, 1876 |
| Williams, Josie | Simmons, Andrew | F/142 | December 29, 1897 | December 29, 1897 |
| Williams, Julia | Cawthon, Hyram | F/14 | August 7, 1893 | August 27, 1893 |
| Williams, L. E. | Todd, A. J. | D/7 | | December 4, 1881 |
| Williams, L. W. | Rushing, Martha | C/30 | June 15, 1872 | June 15, 1872 |
| Williams, Laura | Simmons, W. T. | F/56 | January 17, 1895 | January 24, 1895 |
| Williams, Lewis | Webb, Mary | C/288 | August 13, 1883 | August 13, 1883 |

| Groom or Bride | Groom or Bride | Book/Page | Date of License | Date of Marriage |
|---|---|---|---|---|
| Williams, Lewis | Brown, Sarah A. | D/16 | | October 3, 1882 |
| Williams, Lillie | Finley, J. A. | F/120 | July 19, 1897 | July 24, 1897 |
| Williams, Lucinda | Vandagriff, William | A/59 | January 12, 1843 | January 12, 1843 |
| Williams, Lucy J. | Sheriden, John | C/464 | September 8, 1892 | September 8, 1892 |
| Williams, Luraney Miss | King, Jacob A. | A2/92 | October 21, 1867 | October 21, 1867 |
| Williams, M. A. Miss | Gilley, W. P. | C/458 | May 28, 1892 | No Return |
| Williams, M. D. | Hall, J. W. | C/162 | May 31, 1877 | May 31, 1877 |
| Williams, M. E. Mrs. | Mare, M. N. | A2/100 | July 18, 1860 | No Return |
| Williams, M. G. | Phillips, C. E. | C/112 | May 23, 1875 | December 11, 1875 ? |
| Williams, M. J. | Smithson, G. W. B. | C/356 | April 6, 1886 | April 11, 1886 |
| Williams, M. L. Miss | Tedder, J. B. | C/412 | December 5, 1887 | December 11, 1887 |
| Williams, M. T. | Tedder, J. L. | C/406 | August 17, 1887 | August 17, 1887 |
| Williams, Malvina | Gilley, Jessee N. | C/106 | January 19, 1875 | January 21, 1875 |
| Williams, Martha | Woods, Albert | B/2 | August 21, 1865 | August 28, 1865 |
| Williams, Martha C. Miss | Holt, H. N. | B/78 | February 9, 1869 | February 28, 1869 |
| Williams, Mary | Davenport, Hardy | C/256 | September 7, 1880 | September 7, 1880 |
| Williams, Mary | Loftton, R. Y. | F/24 | December 12, 1893 | December 13, 1893 |
| Williams, Mary Ann | Gilley, Williams | F/8 | May 1, 1893 | May 2, 1893 |
| Williams, Mary M. | Duncan, L. H. | C/310 | August 2, 1884 | August 3, 1884 |
| Williams, Mary M. | Cawthon, Burt | C/428 | January 5, 1891 | January 18, 1891 |
| Williams, Mary T. | Simpson, P. M. | C/36 | September 4, 1872 | No Return |
| Williams, Mattie | Lewis, J. O. | F/92 | August 3, 1896 | August 9, 1896 |
| Williams, May J. | Evans, John C. | C/246 | March 31, 1880 | March 31, 1880 |
| Williams, Millia Miss | Wallace, William | B/100 | March 28, 1870 | No Return |
| Williams, Milly | Ewel, Laten | A2/112 | February 22, 1864 | No Return |
| Williams, Mineva | Freeman, William | F/24 | November 28, 1893 | November 28, 1893 |
| Williams, N. C. | Lewis, S. P. | E/209 | September 7, 1889 | September 8, 1889 |
| Williams, N. C. | Parker, A. W. | F/102 | November 14, 1896 | November 15, 1896 |
| Williams, N. E. | Nobles, A. J. | C/434 | April 1, 1891 | April 4, 1891 |
| Williams, Nance E. | Lewis, J. M. | F | August 21, 1893 | No Return |
| Williams, Nancy E. | Reed, J. R. | C/70 | October 20, 1873 | October 21, 1873 |
| Williams, Paralee | Brown, J. N. | F/148 | March 5, 1898 | March 8, 1898 |
| Williams, Parialee | Brown, J. N. | F/114 | March 5, 1897 | No Return |
| Williams, R. H. | Mathis, Miss Clarinda | A2/144 | September 8, 1866 | September 11, 1866 |
| Williams, R. M. | Taylor, Miss Francis A. | A2/41 | September 13, 1855 | September 20, 1855 |
| Williams, Roxanna | Thomas, William | A2/125 | August 9, 1865 | August 8, 1865 |
| Williams, Sallie | Whittiemore, Simeon | C/376 | December 18, 1886 | December 19, 1886 |
| Williams, Sarah | Parker, Thomas | A2/20 | November 19, 1852 | November 23, 1852 |
| Williams, Sarah | Higgins, H. H. | E/1 | January 7, 1888 | January 8, 1888 |
| Williams, Sarah A. | Saddler, J. H. | C/288 | August 11, 1883 | August 12, 1883 |
| Williams, Sarah Miss | King, Martin | A/108 | February 25, 1848 | February 25, 1848 |
| Williams, Schudder | Orr, Linda | C/468 | October 18, 1892 | October 18, 1892 |
| Williams, Schudder | Vassor, Nan | F/12 | July 18, 1893 | July 19, 1893 |
| Williams, Senna J. | Sissom, J. H. | C/118 | August 26, 1875 | August 26, 1875 |
| Williams, Soloman | Taylor, Mary J. | D/7 | | November 27, 1881 |
| Williams, Susan | Heriman, John | A/15 | July ??, 1839 | ?? ??, 1839 |

| Groom or Bride | Groom or Bride | Book/Page | Date of License | Date of Marriage |
|---|---|---|---|---|
| Williams, T. R. | Todd, James A. | C/288 | August 9, 1883 | No Return |
| Williams, Thomas H. | Gray, Nancy E. | A/8 | October 13, 1838 | October 18, 1838 |
| Williams, Thomas J. | Vandagriff, Miss Nancy | A/118 | January 3, 1849 | January 4, 1849 |
| Williams, Thomas J. | Vandegriff, Miss Melvina | B/84 | July 29, 1869 | July 29, 1869 |
| Williams, Thos. | Spry, Isabella | C/42 | October 15, 1872 | October 29, 1872 |
| Williams, W. C. | Harris, Mary | C/20 | January 10, 1872 | January 10, 1872 |
| Williams, W. H. | Bailey, Mollie S. | D/23 | | April 17, 1883 |
| Williams, W. J. | Gray, Jemima E. | A2/132 | December 1, 1865 | December 2, 1865 |
| Williams, W. P. | Patton, Ophie | E/43 | June 26, 1888 | June 26, 1888 |
| Williams, Washington | Messick, Miss Sarah | A/112 | June 10, 1848 | June 11, 1848 |
| Williamsm J. H. | Hail, Mary, F. | C/318 | November 29, 1884 | December 1, 1885 |
| Willird, D. L. Miss | Davenport, B. D. | A2/65 | August 2, 1858 | August 2, 1858 |
| Willis, Temperance Miss | Woodruffe, R. W. | A/65 | September 25, 1843 | September 25, 1843 |
| Willsen, Andrew | Cook, Miss Elizabeth Ann | A2/39 | March 29, 1855 | March 29, 1855 |
| Willson, Bill | Stacy, Roxie | F/2 | January 15, 1893? | No Return |
| Willson, E. Miss | Bogle, J. M. | A2/68 | October 20, 1858 | October 20, 1858 |
| Willson, Elizabeth Miss | Hall, R. | A2/29 | December 2, 1853 | December 4, 1853 |
| Willson, G. W. | Barthen, Sarah | A2/20 | November 19, 1852 | November 19, 1852 |
| Willson, J. | Higgins, Angeline | C/88 | July 18, 1874 | July 19, 1874 |
| Willson, Lucy Miss | Bogle, John F. | A2/71 | January 3, 1859 | January 5, 1959 |
| Willson, Lusey | Bogle, Josiah F. | A2/83 | January 3, 1859 | No Return |
| Willson, M. E. Miss | Devanport, William | A2/81 | January 15, 1858 | January 15, 1858 |
| Willson, S. S. Miss | Devanport, A. H. | A2/50 | October 10, 1856 | No Return |
| Willson, Sarah J. Miss | Summer, Jacob L. | A2/57 | September 25, 1857 | No Return |
| Willson, W. A. | Barett, Miss Martha | A2/59 | November 10, 1857 | November 11, 1857 |
| Wilmoth, Easter Miss | Meritt, Madison | A/41 | September 8, 1841 | September 9, 1841 |
| Wilsher, Charles M. | Cox, Miss Mary N. | A/40 | August 25, 1841 | August 26, 1841 |
| Wilsher, Mary | Watson, John | C/44 | October 31, 1872 | No Return |
| Wilsher, William | Gilley, Emaline | A/95 | December 23, 1846 | December 24, 1846 |
| Wilson, A. B. | Newby, Mattie | F/28 | January 3, 1894 | January 4, 1894 |
| Wilson, A. F. | Smithson, Miss Lavisa J. | A2/138 | February 20, 1866 | No Return |
| Wilson, Amandy | Wilson, John | D/3 | | August 24, 1881 |
| Wilson, Ben. | Hays, Mary J. | C/222 | August 11, 1879 | August 13, 1879 |
| Wilson, Benjamin | Scott, Miss Mary Ann | A/52 | August 6, 1842 | August 7, 1842 |
| Wilson, Benjamin Jr. | Seal, Miss Thursey A. | B/38 | January 19, 1867 | January 22, 1867 |
| Wilson, Betti | Basham, James H. | D/3 | | September 8, 1881 |
| Wilson, Bill | Stacy, Roxie | F/10 | June 15, 1893 | June 19, 1893 |
| Wilson, C. N. | Alexander, A. W. | F/152 | August 1, 1898 | August 3, 1898 |
| Wilson, Callie | Gordon, J. H. | C/326 | February 18, 1885 | February 19, 1885 |
| Wilson, Catherine | Smithson, D. A. | C/146 | October 28, 1876 | October 29, 1876 |
| Wilson, Cynthia A. | Byford, J. W. | C/152 | January 17, 1877 | January 18, 1877 |
| Wilson, Della | Braxton, John | F | August 21, 1893 | No Return |
| Wilson, E. C. | McBroom, John | C/158 | February 24, 1877 | February 25, 1877 |
| Wilson, Elisabeth | Brewer, James | C/262 | November 12, 1880 | No Retrun |
| Wilson, Eliza J. | Pelham, Thomas | C/130 | January 18, 1876 | January 18, 1876 |
| Wilson, Elizabeth | Carr, O. C. | D/6 | | October 27, 1881 |

| Groom or Bride | Groom or Bride | Book/Page | Date of License | Date of Marriage |
|---|---|---|---|---|
| Wilson, Emma | Burchett, F. J. | C/334 | August 3, 1885 | August 5, 1885 |
| Wilson, Emma Miss | Miller, J. | F/80 | December 30, 1895 | December 31, 1895 |
| Wilson, G. M. | Pitman, J. N. M. | C/38 | September 9, 1872 | September 11, 1872 |
| Wilson, H. B. | Young, Sena | A2/109 | September 26, 1863 | October 1, 1863 |
| Wilson, H. W. | Pelham, Mary J. | C/38 | September 12, 1872 | September 12, 1872 |
| Wilson, H. W. | Campbell, Catherine L. | C/204 | November 13, 1878 | November 14, 1878 |
| Wilson, Hattie | Parris, Walter | F/64 | May 3, 1895 | May 5, 1895 |
| Wilson, Hiram | Moon, Miss Martha C. | A/40 | August 10, 1841 | August 15, 1841 |
| Wilson, Isham | Jones, Ada | C/340 | November 13, 1885 | November 15, 1885 |
| Wilson, J. E. | Bottoms, Bettie | E/240 | December 16, 1889 | December 18, 1889 |
| Wilson, J. W. | Odom, R. E. | C/186 | February 11, 1878 | No Return |
| Wilson, J. W. | Herriman, Bettie | C/290 | August 15, 1883 | August 15, 1883 |
| Wilson, James | Hays, Malisa | C/218 | July 10, 1879 | No Return |
| Wilson, James A. | Maddox, Florence | E/63 | August 20, 188 | August 23, 1888 |
| Wilson, James W. | Francis, Miss Martha | A2/8 | December 5, 1850 | No Return |
| Wilson, Jas T. | Woods, Nina Caroline | F/66 | August 10, 1895 | August 11, 1895 |
| Wilson, Jemima Miss | Gann, Nathan | B/64 | March 2, 1868 | March 4, 1868 |
| Wilson, Jennie | Spicer, Henry | F/172 | March 16, 1899 | March 16, 1899 |
| Wilson, Jenny | Masey, R. L. | C/438 | July 3, 1891 | July 5, 1891 |
| Wilson, Joe | Higgins, Angeline | C/90 | July 18, 1874 | No Return |
| Wilson, John | Leigh, Miss Mary | A/132 | February 23, 1850 | February 24, 1850 |
| Wilson, John | Elam, Miss Mary Ann | A2/154 | May 25, 1866 | May 25, 1866 |
| Wilson, John | Wilson, Amandy | D/3 | | August 24, 1881 |
| Wilson, John | Basham, Amandy | D/7 | | November 30, 1881 |
| Wilson, John | Wilson, Sarah | F/98 | October 10, 1896 | October 10, 1896 |
| Wilson, John A. | Kirby, Ellen | C/440 | July 22, 1891 | July 23, 1891 |
| Wilson, John H. | Bush, Sallie | C/136 | March 30, 1876 | March 30, 1876 |
| Wilson, L. D. H. | Muncy, Miss Sarah | B/92 | November 19, 1869 | November 21, 1869 |
| Wilson, L. J. | Akins, W. B. | F/22 | November 18, 1893 | November 18, 1893 |
| Wilson, Laura A. | Brandon, A. J. | C/50 | February 3, 1873 | February 4, 1873 |
| Wilson, Lucinda | Sumnar, W. H. | A2/107 | March 3, 1863 | No Return |
| Wilson, Lillie | Masey, James | C/444 | August 8, 1891 | August 9, 1891 |
| Wilson, M. A. | Rogers, L. R. | C/122 | October 1, 1875 | October 1, 1875 |
| Wilson, M. G. | Hayes, P. | C/346 | December 23, 1885 | December 23, 1885 |
| Wilson, M. J. | Denny, J. A. | E/330 | December 28, 1898 | |
| Wilson, M. J. | Lemay, J. A. | F/164 | December 28, 1898 | No Return |
| Wilson, M. L. | Bryson, E. D. | A2/125 | August 4, 1865 | August 6, 1865 |
| Wilson, M. V. | Odom, Mary | A2/107 | May 13, 1863 | May 13, 1863 |
| Wilson, Margret C. | Lemay, P. W. | C/204 | December 4, 1878 | December ??, 1878 |
| Wilson, Margrett A. | Fugitt, Sam | C/338 | October 17, 1885 | October 18, 1885 |
| Wilson, Mary J. Miss | Stacy, W. J. | C/10 | September 12, 1871 | September 17, 1871 |
| Wilson, Marshall | Basham, Bettie | E/158 | December 27, 1888 | December 27, 1888 |
| Wilson, Martha | Fann, Wm. | A2/114 | June 25, 1864 | June 25, 1864 |
| Wilson, Martha | Lowe, Tobe | F/130 | September 6, 1897 | September 6, 1897 |
| Wilson, Mary J. W. Miss | Todd, T. M. | A2/138 | February 28, 1866 | March 1, 1866 |
| Wilson, Mary Miss | Scott, Henry | A/91 | October 3, 1846 | October 3, 1846 |

| Groom or Bride | Groom or Bride | Book/Page | Date of License | Date of Marriage |
|---|---|---|---|---|
| Wilson, Mattie J. | Canes, Wm. L. | C/352 | February 15, 1886 | February 15, 1886 |
| Wilson, Michael | Bryson, Martha | A/8 | October 16, 1838 | October 16, 1838 |
| Wilson, Mike | Blanks, L. A. | C/332 | July 30, 1880 | August 30, 1885 |
| Wilson, Mike | Alexander, Fannie | F/56 | January 12, 1895 | January 13, 1895 |
| Wilson, Nancy | Stacy, John P. | C/212 | February 6, 1879 | February 8, 1779 |
| Wilson, Nancy | Lyon, Toney | C/340 | October 17, 1885 | October 18, 1885 |
| Wilson, Miss Nancy | Whitlock, E. B. | A2/41 | August 24, 1855 | August 27, 1855 |
| Wilson, P. A | Higgins, E. C. | C/140 | July 29, 1876 | July 30, 1876 |
| Wilson, R. T. | Sullivan | E/114 | December 22, 1888 | December 23, 1888 |
| Wilson, Riley | Rackley, Mary | C/164 | July 17, 1877 | July 17, 1877 |
| Wilson, Robert | Woods, Clem | C/430 | February 18, 1891 | February 19, 1891 |
| Wilson, Rosie | Davenport, R. H. | C/196 | August 28, 1878 | August 29, 1878 |
| Wilson, S. A. | Bassham, Alvis | C/78 | December 31, 1873 | December 31, 1873 |
| Wilson, S. F. | Parsley, John | F/118 | May 31, 1897 | May 31, 1897 |
| Wilson, S. H. | Bogle, Mickey | C/138 | April 27, 1876 | April 28, 1876 |
| Wilson, Saml. B. | Higgins, Nancy E. | C/94 | September 10, 1874 | September 10, 1874 |
| Wilson, Sarah | Wilson, John | F/98 | October 10, 1896 | October 10, 1896 |
| Wilson, Sarah | Justice, J. W. | F/168 | January 21, 1899 | January 22, 1899 |
| Wilson, Sarah E. | Gaither, Joseph | C/120 | September 22, 1875 | September 22, 1875 |
| Wilson, Sarah E. Miss | Winnett, Calvin T. | B/64 | March 20, 1868 | March 21, 1868 |
| Wilson, Sarah F. Miss | Richardson, C. D. | C/396 | August 8, 1887 | August 8, 1887 |
| Wilson, Stephen | Bond, Barthena | C/42 | October 16, 1872 | October 20, 1872 |
| Wilson, Stephen H. | Markum, Sifie | F/34 | September 6, 1894 | September 7, 1894 |
| Wilson, T. A. | Parker, Sarah C. | C/420 | October 14, 1890 | October 15, 1890 |
| Wilson, T. H. | Gann, C. J. | D/21 | | March 21, 1883 |
| Wilson, Tennie | Basham, Isaiah | C/470 | December 17, 1892 | December 18, 1892 |
| Wilson, Tennie | Todd, J. C. | C/244 | March 11, 1880 | March 11, 1880 |
| Wilson, Tennie | Basham, Isaiah | C/470 | Decmeber 17, 1892 | December 18, 1892 |
| Wilson, W. A. | Bogle, S. L. | D/15 | | September 27, 1882 |
| Wilson, W. N. | Alexander, T. A. | F/52 | December 12, 1894 | December 13, 1894 |
| Wilson, Walter | Todd, Margarett | A/55 | November 3, 1842 | November 3, 1842 |
| Wilson, Walter | Craft, Miss Frances | B/102 | May 2, 1870 | May 3, 1870 |
| Wilson, Walter | Lehmay, Martha A. | E/358 | December 3, 1898 | |
| Wilson, Walter | Davis, Lottie | F/146 | February 14, 1898 | February 14, 1898 |
| Wilson, Walter | Lemay, Martha A. | F/162 | December 3, 1898 | December 4, 1898 |
| Wilson, Walter, Jr. | Craft, Rositta | C/126 | December 18, 1875 | December 19, 1875 |
| Wilson, William | Womack, Miss Temperance | A/111 | June 8, 1848 | June 8, 1848 |
| Wilson, William | Bryant, Miss Beet | E/44 | June 28, 1888 | July 1, 1888 |
| Wilson, Willie | Bassham, Jenny | C/430 | January 26, 1891 | January 26, 1891 |
| Wilson, Wm. | Arnold, Emmar | C/282 | May 7, 1883 | February 6, 1884 |
| Wily, H. A. | Shoelford, Miss Mary E. | A2/41 | August 14, 1855 | Return Missing |
| Wimberley, Elizabeth Miss | Thomas, James N. | A/70 | July 20, 1844 | July 21, 1844 |
| Wimberley, G. W. | Stacy, Elizabeth N. | B/94 | November 30, 1869 | December 1, 1869 |
| Wimberley, J. C. | Burch, Jane | A2/122 | March 10, 1865 | March 10, 1865 |
| Wimberley, Margarett | Thomas, Nelson G. | A/59 | February 8, 1843 | February 8, 1843 |
| Wimberley, Martha Miss | Brooks, John R. | A/97 | January 25, 1847 | February 7, 1847 |

| Groom or Bride | Groom or Bride | Book/Page | Date of License | Date of Marriage |
|---|---|---|---|---|
| Wimberley, Polly | Patton, John | A/128 | October 15, 1849 | October 17, 1849 |
| Wimberly, Elizabeth | Merrett, Presley | A2/129 | September 16, 1865 | September 17, 1865 |
| Wimberly, J. E. | Goff, Miss Martha Ann | B/62 | March 5, 1868 | March 8, 1868 |
| Wimberly, Jonathan | Binem, Martha | A2/100 | July 14, 1860 | July 15, 1860 |
| Wimberly, Lyda | Davenport, J. B. | D/18 | | November 7, 1882 |
| Wimberly, Marry Miss | Merritt, Jackson | A2/26 | July 2, 1853 | No Return |
| Wimberly, Mary | Moore, Thomas C. | D/16 | | June 2, 1882 |
| Wimberly, Miss Julian | Lorance, G. R. | B/88 | September 28, 1869 | September 28, 1869 |
| Wimberly, P. A. Miss | Hawkins, Wm. B. | A2/66 | August 18, 1858 | August 18, 1858 |
| Wimberly, Wm. A. | Jones, Sarah T. | D/21 | | January 4, 1883 |
| Wimbley, Elizabeth | Robinson, Jacob | A2/45 | December 29, 1855 | No Return |
| Winaham, Elizabeth Miss | Bowers, William | A/79 | May 28, 1845 | May 28, 1845 |
| Winily, Caroline | Gooding, Robert | A2/100 | July 21, 1860 | July 26, 1860 |
| Winnet, R. M. Miss | Woods, J. K. P. | A2/147 | November 8, 1866 | Solemnized, No Date |
| Winnett, Bettie | Markum, Charles | C/374 | November 16, 1886 | November 17, 1886 |
| Winnett, C. F. | Stroud, N. E. | F/140 | December 22, 1897 | December 23, 1897 |
| Winnett, Calvin T. | Wilson, Miss Sarah E. | B/64 | March 20, 1868 | March 21, 1868 |
| Winnett, Charlotte Miss | Fowler, Jessee | A2/138 | February 20, 1866 | February 21, 1866 |
| Winnett, Deller | Good, Willie | C/304 | February 24, 1884 | February 28, 1884 |
| Winnett, Eleanor Miss | Thomas, Rezen F. | A2/139 | February 28, 1866 | March 1, 1866 |
| Winnett, Elizabeth | Gains, Thomas | C/98 | October 13, 1874 | October 13, 1874 |
| Winnett, F. M. | Gilley, M. E. | C/254 | August 18, 1880 | August 19, 1880 |
| Winnett, James | Todd, Miss Sarah | B/60 | December 21, 1867 | December 22, 1867 |
| Winnett, Jennie Miss | Lance, S. H. | F/88 | May 8, 1896 | May 10, 1896 |
| Winnett, Julia A. | Davenport, Warren | C/80 | January 10, 1874 | January 11, 1874 |
| Winnett, M. C. | Harvell, W. L | C/428 | January 15, 1891 | January 15, 1891 |
| Winnett, Malissie | Jones, Dock | F/92 | August 7, 1896 | August 9, 1896 |
| Winnett, Nannie | Lorance, A. C. | F/148 | April 18, 1898 | April 21, 1898 |
| Winnett, Norman | Tort, Susan | A2/64 | April 29, 1858 | April 29, 1858 |
| Winnett, Norman | Lorance, M. A. | C/192 | May 18, 1878 | May 19, 1878 |
| Winnett, R. J. Miss | Lorance, Wm. W. | B/82 | December 31, 1868 | December 31, 1868 |
| Winnett, Sarah E. | Devenport, John S. | C/40 | October 2, 1872 | October 3, 1872 |
| Winnett, T. J. | Bailey, Miss H. L. | F/90 | June 29, 1896 | June 29, 1896 |
| Winnett, Tabitha | Smith, Harvey | C/146 | October 14, 1876 | October 15, 1876 |
| Winnette, Telia | Davis, E. H. | C/474 | December 29, 1892 | January 1, 1893 |
| Winnett, W. S. | Lorance, Miss N. E. | F/56 | January 1, 1895 | No Return |
| Winnett, Willie | Smithson, Dessie | C/432 | February 25, 1891 | No Return |
| Winnette, Telia | Davis, E. H. | C/474 | December 29, 1892 | January 1, 1893 |
| Wiser, Julian J. Miss | Bankston, James M. | A2/157 | June 15, 1866 | June 17, 1866 |
| Wiser, William | Parker, Miss Vioet | A/65 | November 27, 1843 | November 30, 1843 |
| Witherspoon, D. | McAdow, Miss L. F. | A2/29 | October 18, 1853 | October 18, 1853 |
| Witherspoon, John K. | Alexander, Miss Margarett A. | A/117 | November 21, 1848 | No Return |
| Witherspoon, Lewis E. W. | Robinson, Miss Amanda | A2/7 | October 29, 1850 | October 29, 1850 |
| Witherspoon, Mary M. | Summars, Evert | A/8 | November 22, 1838 | November 22, 1838 |
| Witherspoon, Mary S. Miss | Reynolds, William | A/85 | December 23, 1845 | December 24, 1845 |
| Witherspoon, Septima F. Miss | Porterfield, Leonades F. | A/66 | November 29, 1843 | November 30, 1843 |

| Groom or Bride | Groom or Bride | Book/Page | Date of License | Date of Marriage |
|---|---|---|---|---|
| Witherspoon, Thurza Einaline | Shannon McKnight | A/91 | September 28, 1846 | No Return |
| Witherspoon, William E. | Watts, Miss Mary | A/89 | May 21, 1846 | May 21, 1846 |
| Withrowe, Allen | Bates, Abbie | C/398 | August 16, 1887 | August 17, 1887 |
| Witt, Martin M. | Brown, Miss Manerva J. | A/125 | July 30, 1849 | July 30, 1849 |
| Witter, J. W. | Ferrell, E. T. | E/64 | August 29, 1888 | August 29, 1888 |
| Witty, J. W. | Young, Laura | C/346 | December 22, 1885 | No Return |
| Witty, M. G. | Mazo, B. F. | C/392 | July 1, 1887 | July 3, 1887 |
| Witty, W. W. | Sherley, M. J. | C/58 | April 22, 1873 | April 22, 1873 |
| Witty, W. W. | Melton, Miss Sallie | C/452 | December 11, 1891 | December 12, 1891 |
| Wivite, Robert (col) | Furgerson, Ella | C/380 | January 5, 1887 | January 5, 1887 |
| Womach, L. N. | Rigsby, Willie | C/260 | October 21, 1880 | October 21, 1880 |
| Womach, W. J. | Milligan, Alneeda | E/245 | December 23, 1889 | December 24, 1889 |
| Womack, A. C. | Morgan, J. I. | D/6 | | November 10, 1881 |
| Womack, A. J. | McBroom, M. H. | D/20 | | July 16, 1882 |
| Womack, A. J. | Phillips, J. L. | C/336 | September 17, 1885 | September 17, 1885 |
| Womack, Abram | Wood, Elizabeth | A/83 | September 10, 1845 | September 11, 1845 |
| Womack, Amanda J. Miss | Higgins, Elijah C. | B/106 | August 15, 1870 | August 18, 1870 |
| Womack, Benjamin | Davis, Miss Mary | C/386 | March 3, 1887 | March 3, 1887 |
| Womack, Bery | Miller, Miss Bethany | A2/9 | December 26, 1850 | January 19, 1851 |
| Womack, D. G. | Alread, J. S. | C/286 | July 6, 1883 | July 8, 1883 |
| Womack, D. M. | Rigsby, Deley | D/6 | | November 3, 1881 |
| Womack, Eliza | West, Henry | F/92 | August 20, 1896 | August 20, 1896 |
| Womack, Etta | Jones, W. J. | C/418 | September 23, 1890 | September 28,1890 |
| Womack, Fannie | Hayes, Bud | F/116 | April 5, 1897 | April 7, 1897 |
| Womack, H. B. | Skirlock, M. C. | C/182 | December 24, 1877 | December 25, 1877 |
| Womack, I. Y. | Bogle, B. A. | F/12 | July 21, 1893 | July 24, 1893 |
| Womack, J. A. N. | Womack, P. P. | C/60 | July 12, 1873 | July 12, 1873 |
| Womack, J. B. | Johnson, Callie | F/90 | July 14, 1896 | July 16, 1896 |
| Womack, J. J. | Scott, Miss Eliza | C/430 | February 24, 1891 | March 13, 1891 |
| Womack, James | Bogle, Mollie | C/438 | June 25, 1891 | June 25, 1891 |
| Womack, James Jasper | Parker, Miss July Ann | A2/4 | August 15, 1850 | August 15, 1850 |
| Womack, James M. | King, Martha A. | C/210 | January 25, 1879 | January 26, 1879 |
| Womack, Jo B. | Robertson, Sarah A. | C/182 | January 3, 1878 | January 3, 1878 |
| Womack, John N. | Scott, July Ann D. | A2/2 | April 6, 1850 | April 7, 1850 |
| Womack, John S. | Milligan, Liza A. | C/304 | February 3, 1884 | February 3, 1884 |
| Womack, Julia | Davenport, Gawen | C/428 | January 2, 1891 | January 4, 1891 |
| Womack, L. D. | Davenport, L. C. | D/15 | | September 10, 1882 |
| Womack, Lizzie Miss | Bogle, J. R. | E/179 | June 8, 1889 | June 9, 1889 |
| Womack, Lucinda Miss | Sullens, Richmond | A/127 | September 18, 1849 | September 18, 1849 |
| Womack, M. A. A. Miss | Brandon, John F. | A2/80 | March 14, 1857 | March 15, 1857 |
| Womack, M. J. | Bogle, M. C. | E/134 | February 7, 1889 | February 13, 1889 |
| Womack, M. P. | Marler, M. M. | C/242 | December 27, 1879 | December 27, 1879 |
| Womack, Malisie | St. John, E. B. | F/74 | November 22, 1895 | November 22, 1895 |
| Womack, Margarette | Spradley, W. T. | E/266 | January 31, 1890 | No Return |
| Womack, Martha | Branatt, Munro | C/50 | January 11, 1873 | January 12, 1873 |
| Womack, Martha F. | Davenport, Riley | C/200 | September 27, 1878 | September 28, 1878 |

| Groom or Bride | Groom or Bride | Book/Page | Date of License | Date of Marriage |
|---|---|---|---|---|
| Womack, Mary E. | Davis, T. J. | C/12 | October 21, 1871 | October 21, 1871 |
| Womack, P. P. | Womack, J. A. N. | C/60 | July 12, 1873 | July 12, 1873 |
| Womack, Parlee | Bogle, Robert | C/272 | February 26, 1881 | February 27, 1881 |
| Womack, Sara S. | Davenport, E. H. | E/22 | February 27, 1888 | March 1, 1888 |
| Womack, Temperance Miss | Wilson, William | A/111 | June 8, 1848 | June 8, 1848 |
| Womack, Thomas J. | Collins, Miss A. R. | B/110 | September 14, 1870 | September 15, 1870 |
| Womack, William | Roemines, Miss Eleanor | A/98 | April 9, 1847 | April 11, 1847 |
| Womberly, Martha J. | Lee, Charles | A2/132 | November 16, 1865 | No Return |
| Wommack, Mandy J. | Wammack, Wm. T. | C/134 | February 26, 1876 | No Return |
| Wommack, Y. J. | Davis, R. M. | C/122 | October 16, 1875 | No Date |
| Wommacs, Matilda Miss | More, Howel | A2/16 | March 11, 1852 | March 11, 1852 |
| Wood, Ann Miss | Stephens, Benj. | C/4 | August 3, 1871 | August 3, 1871 |
| Wood, Annie | Rains, E. L. | F/24 | December 11, 1893 | December 17, 1893 |
| Wood, B. F. | Baily, Miss Mary A. | A2/59 | November 3, 1857 | November 5, 1857 |
| Wood, B. F. | Earwood, Caroline | D/10 | | December 4, 1881 |
| Wood, B. F. L. | McCabe, Sarah | C/260 | November 8, 1880 | November 9, 1880 |
| Wood, Callie | Todd, Burton A. | C/264 | November 18, 1880 | No Return |
| Wood, Clem | Holt, Newman | C/254 | August 21, 1880 | August 22, 1880 |
| Wood, E. J. | Thompson, Miss Elizabeth A. | A2/35 | September 7, 1854 | September 7, 1854 |
| Wood, Elizabeth | Womack, Abram | A/83 | September 10, 1845 | September 11, 1845 |
| Wood, Elizabeth Miss | Merritt, Jame | B/50 | August 29, 1867 | August 29, 1867 |
| Wood, Fanny | Newby, George | B/14 | January 16, 1868 | January 16, 1868 |
| Wood, Francis | Gilley, Columbus | C/182 | December 22, 1877 | No Return |
| Wood, H. W. | Ward, M. E. | C/376 | December 1, 1886 | December 5, 1886 |
| Wood, I. E. | Prater, R. B. H. | F/82 | January 13, 1896 | January 14, 1896 |
| Wood, Isaac | Webb, Parlee | B/6 | August 28, 1865 | August 28, 1865 |
| Wood, Isaac | Mount, America O. | C/412 | November 28, 1887 | November 28, 1887 |
| Wood, J. H. | Johnson, Stella | F/126 | August 7, 1897 | August 8, 1897 |
| Wood, James | Sullins, Susan F. | C/184 | January 3, 1878 | January 3, 1878 |
| Wood, James | Lewis, Mary P. | F/26 | December 26, 1893 | No Return |
| Wood, Jerry | Daules (Daubs), Judie | C/70 | November 6, 1873 | November 6, 1873 |
| Wood, Jessee | Wright, Lucy | B/2 | August 22, 1865 | September 3, 1865 |
| Wood, John | Barnes, Harriett | F/18 | October 9, 1893 | October 9, 1893 |
| Wood, John A. | Sanders, Miss Sarah T. | A2/78 | February 21, 1856 | February 22, 1856 |
| Wood, Josephine | Fugitt, Saml. (Col) | C/54 | February 22, 1873 | February 22, 1873 |
| Wood, Josie | Daniel, Robert | E/147 | March 27, 1889 | March 28, 1889 |
| Wood, L. G. Miss | Walker, W. W. | A2/139 | March 30, 1866 | April 1, 1866 |
| Wood, L. G. Miss | Walker, W. W. | A2/144 | March 30, 1866 | No Return |
| Wood, L. P. | Heneger, Z. V. | C/80 | January 28, 1874 | January 28, 1874 |
| Wood, Larry | Sawyers, Elvira | C/170 | September 7, 1877 | No Return |
| Wood, Lue | Holt, Robert | C/248 | June 19, 1880 | June 20, 1880 |
| Wood, M. A. | Batton, P. D. | C/66 | August 30, 1873 | September 2, 1873 |
| Wood, M. E. | Turner, J. G. | C/236 | January 5, 1880 | January 5, 1880 |
| Wood, Margarett Miss | Grizzle, Daniel | A/127 | September 26, 1849 | September 27, 1849 |
| Wood, Marie | Paris, F. M. (col.) | C/456 | March 12, 1892 | March 13, 1892 |
| Wood, Martha H. | St. John, M. E. | A2/106 | October 30, 1862 | October 30, 1862 |

| Groom or Bride | Groom or Bride | Book/Page | Date of License | Date of Marriage |
|---|---|---|---|---|
| Wood, Mary A. | Mahaffa, E. D. | C/142 | August 16, 1876 | August 17, 1876 |
| Wood, Mary E. | Spears, Geo. M. | C/76 | December 22, 1873 | December 22, 1873 |
| Wood, Mary S. Miss | Mears, William | B/114 | October ??, 1870 | October 20, 1870 |
| Wood, Mattie | Hays, J. T. | F/78 | December 17, 1895 | December 18, 1895 |
| Wood, Mattie J. Miss | Freeman, J. H. | A2/67 | September 21, 1858 | No Return |
| Wood, N. C. C. | Phillips, Caroline | C/32 | August 10, 1872 | August 10, 1872 |
| Wood, Nancy Ann | Elledge, William F. | A/18 | October 3, 1839 | October 4, 1839 |
| Wood, Nancy Ann Miss | Cock, John | A2/37 | December 20, 1854 | December 21, 1854 |
| Wood, Parlee Miss | Powel, Peyton | A2/164 | July 18, 1866 | July 18, 1866 |
| Wood, Russ | Roberson, Jane | C/114 | June 24, 1875 | June 24, 1875 |
| Wood, Sarah Miss | Adcock, Leonard | A/43 | October 30, 1841 | October 30, 1841 |
| Wood, Sarah Miss | Holandsworth, Ira | B/106 | June 26, 1870 | June 26, 1870 |
| Wood, Sillie | Gilley, Michiga | C/184 | January 5, 1878 | January 6, 1878 |
| Wood, Susan C. | Elledge, George | C/204 | November 16, 1878 | No Return |
| Wood, Susan E. | Basham, T. G. | C/268 | January 3, 1881 | January 6, 1881 |
| Wood, Tennie Miss | McFerrin, J. A. | B/122 | January 1, 1871 | January 1, 1871 |
| Wood, Thos. O. | Alexander, Martha L. | A2/113 | April 19, 1864 | April 19, 1864 |
| Wood, Violet | Wood, Washington | C/28 | June 11, 1872 | June 11, 1872 |
| Wood, W. J. | Weedon, J. P. | A2/97 | May 24, 1860 | May 24, 1860 |
| Wood, W. J. | Martin, Linnie | C/86 | April 25, 1874 | April 26, 1874 |
| Wood, W. J. | Daniel, Ellen | E/233 | November 23, 1889 | November 24, 1889 |
| Wood, W. M. | Teddler, M. F. | C/366 | September 11, 1886 | No Return |
| Wood, Washington | Wood, Violet | C/28 | June 11, 1872 | June 11, 1872 |
| Wood, Wiley | Stacy, Permlie | C/362 | July 29, 1886 | July 29, 1886 |
| Wood, William T. | Covington, Miss Mary | A2/146 | October 8, 1866 | October 9, 1866 |
| Woodall, Sarah T. Miss | Herndon, James M. | A/96 | January 8, 1847 | January 8, 1847 |
| Woodall, William C. | Oliver, Miss Delia | A/108 | February 21, 1848 | February 21, 1848 |
| Woodard, E. Miss | Walton, Henry | B/116 | November 9, 1870 | November 10, 1870 |
| Woodard, Henry C. | Webb, Emer | C/234 | December 23, 1879 | No Return |
| Woodard, Lucy | Alexander, Sandy | E/155 | November 17, 1888 | November 18, 1888 |
| Woodards, Janie (col.) | Swanford, Bob (col.) | F/116 | April 17, 1897 | April 18, 1897 |
| Wooderd, George W. | Taylor, Nancy | A/4 | July 17, 1838 | July 17, 1838 |
| Wooderd, Henry | Mitchell, Amandy | F/26 | December 23, 1893 | December 23, 1893 |
| Wooderick, Laura | Taylor, Burt (col.) | C/412 | December 30, 1887 | December 30, 1887 |
| Woodroff, Wm | Marlin, Merry Jane | A2/12 | November 22, 1851 | No Return |
| Woodruff, J. W. | Sullivan, Annie | D/9 | | December 29, 1881 |
| Woodruffe, R. W. | Willis, Miss Temperance | A/65 | September 25, 1843 | September 25, 1843 |
| Woods, A. C. | St. John A. L. | C/142 | August 5, 1876 | August ??, 1876 |
| Woods, A. H. | Tenpenny, Miss E. J. | C/392 | June 28, 1886 | No Return |
| Woods, A. U. | Tenpenny, Miss E. J. | C/390 | June 28, 1887 | No Return |
| Woods, Albert | Williams, Martha | B/2 | August 21, 1865 | August 28, 1865 |
| Woods, Alexander H. | Blackwell, Eliza A. | C/214 | March 5, 1879 | March 5, 1879 |
| Woods, Andrew J. | Prator, Miss Eliza J. | B/52 | September 25, 1867 | September 26, 1867 |
| Woods, Andy | Stewart, Mandy | C/154 | February 2, 1877 | February 3, 1877 |
| Woods, Anna (col.) | Dickens, Henry (col.) | D/18 | | November 10, 1882 |
| Woods, B. F. | Jones, Mary F. | E/9 | January 21, 1888 | January 21, 1888 |

| Groom or Bride | Groom or Bride | Book/Page | Date of License | Date of Marriage |
|---|---|---|---|---|
| Woods, B. F. L. | Phillips, M. T | C/140 | July 22, 1876 | July 23, 1876 |
| Woods, B. F. L. | Shelton, L. E. D. | F/74 | November 6, 1895 | November 7, 1895 |
| Woods, Benjamin F. | Philips, Martha | A2/41 | August 22, 1855 | Returns Mixed Up |
| Woods, Callie | Waters, Gardner | C/250 | July 13, 1880 | July 13, 1880 |
| Woods, Caroline | Todd, John F. | D/9 | | December 25, 1881 |
| Woods, Clem | Wilson, Robert | C/430 | February 18, 1891 | February 19, 1891 |
| Woods, D. | Todd, Wm. | C/308 | May 11, 1884 | No Return |
| Woods, Eley | St. John, J. A. | C/382 | January 25, 1887 | January 25, 1887 |
| Woods, Elizabeth Miss | Hendrick, John R. | A2/65 | June 14, 1858 | June ??, 1858 |
| Woods, Ellen | Pearson, Morgan | F/28 | January 6, 1893 | January 7, 1894 |
| Woods, Frank | Mullinax, Harriet | C/156 | February 4, 1877 | February 4, 1877 |
| Woods, G. D. | Cummins, Miss Mary J. | B/126 | February 10, 1871 | No Return |
| Woods, George | Classie Woodley | B/16 | August 20, 1869 | August 20, 1869 |
| Woods, H. M. | Tenpenny, Robert | E/91 | October 23, 1888 | October 23, 1888 |
| Woods, Harritt | Taylor, Park | C/172 | October 11, 1877 | October 11, 1877 |
| Woods, Hatti | Young, Tatum | C/456 | February 13, 1892 | February 14, 1892 |
| Woods, Ida | Smithson, Lee | C/470 | December 17, 1892 | December 22, 1892 |
| Woods, I. M. Miss | Smith, W. R. | F/86 | April 16, 1896 | April 16, 1896 |
| Woods, Isaac | Robinson, Charity | D/21 | | January 16, 1883 |
| Woods, J. D. | Tenpenny, S. A. | C/444 | August 17, 1891 | No Return |
| Woods, J. K. P. | Winnet, Miss R. M. | A2/147 | November 8, 1866 | Solemnized, No Date |
| Woods, J. K. P. | Sternly, Josephine | C/232 | November 29, 1879 | November 30, 1879 |
| Woods, J. V. | St. John, Etter | E/176 | May 6, 1889 | No Return |
| Woods, Jack | Barton, Ann | F/1 | January 7, 1893 | January 7, 1893 |
| Woods, James H. | Smith, Miss Caroline | A2/19 | August 30, 1852 | September 2, 1852 |
| Woods, Joe (col.) | Dieheus, Rebecca | C/454 | February 13, 1892 | No Return |
| Woods, John (col.) | Gilley, Susan | C/420 | October 18, 1890 | October 18, 1890 |
| Woods, Josie | Gann, R. L. | F/106 | December 19, 1896 | December 20, 1896 |
| Woods, Levada | Higdon, G. A. | F/98 | October 1, 1896 | October 1, 1896 |
| Woods, Lula | Walkup, James | F/22 | November 4, 1893 | November 5, 1893 |
| Woods, M. E. | Merrett, Wm | C/216 | May 16, 1879 | May 18, 1879 |
| Woods, M. F. Miss | Prator, G. D. | B/82 | June 2, 1869 | June 6, 1869 |
| Woods, Mary | Lillard, Brist | C/74 | November 23, 1873 | November 25, 1873 |
| Woods, Martha J. Miss | Hart, William T. | B/104 | June 9, 1870 | June 9, 1870 |
| Woods, Mollie Miss | Weeks, William | C/450 | November 11, 1891 | November 11, 1891 |
| Woods, Mollie | Spurlock, John | C/124 | November 19, 1875 | November 20, 1875 |
| Woods, Nathan | Prater, Miss Kessiah | A/74 | November 19, 1844 | November 19, 1844 |
| Woods, Nathan T. | Phillips, Miss Margarett | A2/58 | October 15, 1857 | October 15, 1857 |
| Woods, Newton | Cawthon, W. M. | C/364 | August 18, 1886 | September 2, 1886 |
| Woods, Nina Caroline | Wilson, Jas T. | F/66 | August 10, 1895 | August 11, 1895 |
| Woods, Robt Lee | Heart, Ambie | F/150 | May 14, 1898 | May 15, 1898 |
| Woods, S. E. | Prater, A. M. | C/112 | May 15, 1875 | May 15, 1875 |
| Woods, Sarah | Gann, H. | E/148 | March 30, 1889 | March 31, 1889 |
| Woods, Sarah A. | Bell, Lewis | D/101 | | February 19, 1882 |
| Woods, Sarah B. | Rigsby, William | C/376 | December 18, 1886 | December 18, 1886 |
| Woods, Susan | Roberson, Robert | B/16 | January 2, 1869 | January 3, 1869 |

| Groom or Bride | Groom or Bride | Book/Page | Date of License | Date of Marriage |
|---|---|---|---|---|
| Woods, T. S. | St. John, S. E. | D/22 | | No Date |
| Woods, Thomas J. | Evans, Miss C. E. | A2/26 | August 3, 1853 | August 3, 1853 |
| Woods, W. L. | Sowels, M. E. | C/290 | August 13, 1883 | August 22, 1883 |
| Woods, William | Tenpenny, Miss Emma | C/392 | June 26, 1887 | No Return |
| Woods, William D. | Tenpenny, Miss Emma C. | C/390 | June 28, 1887 | No Return |
| Woodside, Mary Miss | Seal, John | B/62 | February 13, 1868 | February 13, 1868 |
| Woodside, Sallie | Pitman, Lee | C/382 | January 8, 1887 | January 8, 1887 |
| Woodside, Sarah Elizabeth Miss | Watson, G. M. D. | B/48 | July 29, 1867 | July 30, 1867 |
| Woodsides, J. H. | Bethell, Len | C/124 | November 29, 1875 | December 2, 1875 |
| Woodsides, Shela L. | Rich, Alice E. | C/462 | July 23, 1892 | July 24, 1892 |
| Woodward, Lucy | Martin, Mat | C/382 | January 19, 1887 | No Return |
| Woolard, Ella | Brown, Elmore | F/112 | February 13, 1897 | February 13, 1897 |
| Wooton, Doshie | Davis, John | F/92 | August 3, 1896 | August 5, 1896 |
| Wooton, J. M. | Logan, Miss M. | B/32 | December 16, 1866 | December 16, 1866 |
| Wooton, Miss Allie | Rigsby, G. A. | F/62 | April 20, 1895 | April 21, 1895 |
| Wooton, W. E. | Elrod, Daisey | F/72 | October 21, 1895 | October 21, 1895 |
| Worley, Arthur | Underwood, Miss Mary | B/76 | January 15, 1869 | January 17, 1869 |
| Worley, Arthur | Summers, Miss Sarah | B/102 | May 9, 1970 | May 10, 1870 |
| Worley, Clark D. | Haney, Miss Sarah | B/104 | June 18, 1870 | June 19, 1870 |
| Worley, D. B. | Evans, Miss E. A. | B/112 | October 13, 1870 | October 16, 1870 |
| Worley, Eliza | Hooper, David | D/1 | | May 29, 1881 |
| Worley, Isaac C. | Jones, Roxanah | B/82 | December 31, 1869 | December 31, 1869 |
| Worley, Leoroy | Thompson, Dianna | A2/113 | March 26, 1864 | March 27, 1864 |
| Worley, Levila | Thompson, William | A/31 | July 26, 1840 | July 26, 1840 |
| Worley, Martha Miss | Underwood, Mark L. | B/68 | July 23, 1868 | July 26, 1868 |
| Worley, Matilda P. Miss | Cummins, L. T. | A2/146 | October 24, 1866 | October 25, 1866 |
| Worley, Osiah | Elkins, Mary M. J. | C/126 | December 17, 1875 | December 17, 1875 |
| Worley, Sarah Miss | Hale, George | C/434 | April 24, 1891 | April 24, 1891 |
| Worley, Vann | Spurlock, Bettie | C/324 | January 13, 1885 | January 14, 1885 |
| Worley, Wm. | Wadkins, Samantha | D/13 | | August 10, 1882 |
| Worlien, Elisabeth Miss | Webber, Phillip | A2/15 | February 14, 1852 | No Return |
| Wrather, Farmer D. | Brown, Miss Elizabeth | A/120 | February 15, 1849 | February 15, 1849 |
| Wright, Alice | Mitchell, Green | C/126 | December 11, 1875 | December 12, 1875 |
| Wright, Allen | Thomas, Sallie | F/12 | July 7, 1893 | July 12, 1893 |
| Wright, Allen (col.) | Sims, Sarah L. (col.) | D/18 | | December 24, 1882 |
| Wright, Billie Calvin | Jones, Jessie Herbert | E/41 | May 29, 1888 | May 29, 1888 |
| Wright, Calline | Hase, Anthony | C/118 | August 27, 1875 | No Return |
| Wright, Etta | Armstrong, Allen | B/18 | August 3, 1870 | No Return |
| Wright, J. D. | People, Martha | C/42 | October 2, 1872 | October 2, 1872 |
| Wright, Jennie | McClelland, Andrew | F/4 | February 16, 1893 | February 16, 1893 |
| Wright, Joseph | McFerrin, Louisa | B/4 | August 23, 1865 | September 3, 1865 |
| Wright, Lucy | Wood, Jessee | B/2 | August 22, 1865 | September 3, 1865 |
| Wright, Mary | Thomas, Ed | F/10 | June 12, 1893 | June 12, 1893 |
| Wright, Peal | Pinkerton, Jesse | C/470 | November 27, 1892 | November 22, 1892 |
| Wright, T. R. | Duncan, Rebecca A. | C/60 | July 10, 1873 | No Return |
| Wright, William | Hare, Fannie D. | D/7 | | November 27, 1881 |

| Groom or Bride | Groom or Bride | Book/Page | Date of License | Date of Marriage |
|---|---|---|---|---|
| Wright, William B. | Martin, Miss Susan J. | A2/1 | March 1, 1850 | March 3, 1850 |
| Wright, Yandell | Furgerson, Malissa | E/120 | December 26, 1888 | December 26, 1888 |
| Writh, Wingo (col.) | McKnight, Merry | C/412 | December 30, 1887 | December 30, 1887 |
| Wron, Elizabeth | Lamberth, David | A/30 | June 17, 1840 | June 18, 1840 |
| Wyly, Nancy S. Miss | Dunkin, Owen | A2/24 | March 9, 1853 | March 10, 1853 |
| Yancey, Laura | Pitts, William | E/231 | November 9, 1889 | November 15, 1889 |
| Yarbro, Florence | Marris, Samuel B. | F/12 | June 28, 1893 | June 28, 1893 |
| Yates, Joesie | Dixon, James | C/444 | August 27, 1891 | August 27, 1891 |
| Yeargain, F. J. | Grizzle, S. C. | C/212 | February 17, 1879 | February 20, 1879 |
| Yearwood, D. B. | Mitchell, Miss Nancy A. | B/82 | July 24, 1869 | July 27, 1869 |
| York, Antney | Blaire, Millia | B/18 | July 29, 1870 | No Return |
| York, Bertha | Bowren, C. L. | F/110 | January 9, 1897 | January 10, 1897 |
| York, Eliza | Blain, Jonathan T. | A2/104 | November 19, 1860 | No Return |
| York, Elizabeth | Higgins, James | B/18 | January 9, 1870 | January 9, 1870 |
| York, J. N. | Markum, Martha A. | A2/118 | December 17, 1864 | No Return |
| York, Jonathan | Laseter, Miss Mariah | B/62 | February 12, 1868 | February 16, 1868 |
| York, S. E. | Green, E. H. | C/228 | October 25, 1875 | October 25, 1879 |
| York, Sallie | Officer, Martin | C/358 | June 27, 1886 | June 27, 1886 |
| York, Sam | Melton, Susan | C/254 | August 14, 1880 | August 15, 1880 |
| York, Si | Rushing, Ellen | C/26 | May 16, 1872 | May 16, 1872 |
| York, Susan | Patterson, A. B. | C/392 | July 1, 1886 | July 3, 1887 |
| York, Syrilda Miss | Foster, Isaac | B/66 | June 9, 1868 | June 14, 1868 |
| Young, Alexander | Ashford, Miss Mary | A/61 | April 6, 1843 | No Return |
| Young, C. Miss | Alexander, John | B/122 | December 28, 1870 | December 29, 1871 |
| Young, Calvin | Bailey, Mary J. | C/216 | March 30, 1879 | March 30, 18779 |
| Young, Caroline | Bogle, Allen | A2/121 | March 1, 1865 | March 1, 1965 |
| Young, Charity Miss | Cooper, Berry | A/132 | February 23, 1850 | February 23, 1850 |
| Young, Delpha | Bowren, Joseph | A2/19 | September 22, 1852 | September 22, 1852 |
| Young, Dora Miss | Cambel, William | A2/56 | April 6, 1857 | Return not Executed |
| Young, E. J. | Mazy, Miss Louisa A. | B/90 | October 20, 1869 | No Return |
| Young, E. J. Miss | Carrick, Joseph N. | A2/82 | September 9, 1858 | September 8, 1858 |
| Young, E. L. | Miller, July A. | C/234 | December 18, 1879 | December 18, 1879 |
| Young, E. M. | Bogle, Miss A. C. | B/120 | December 14, 1870 | December 14, 1870 |
| Young, Eliza J. | Clendin, Fatt | F/70 | September 6, 1895 | September 6, 1895 |
| Young, Elizabeth | Preston, James | A2/127 | September 11, 1865 | September 11, 1865 |
| Young, Elizabeth Miss | Hall, William J. | A/90 | August 19, 1846 | August 20, 1846 |
| Young, Emma L. | Campbell, W. H. | F/48 | November 5, 1894 | No Return |
| Young, Etta | Richetts, John | C/316 | November 20, 1884 | November 20, 1884 |
| Young, Felling M. | Summers, Teresa | A2/40 | April 29, 1855 | Return Missing |
| Young, Hattie | Patton, Dillard | C/382 | January 25, 1887 | January 26, 1887 |
| Young, I. L | Rigsby, B. A. | F/74 | November 2, 1895 | November 3, 1895 |
| Young, Isaac | Paits, Mary E. | C/208 | January 2, 1879 | January 2, 1879 |
| Young, Isaac | Cummings, Nancy | D/19 | | December 17, 1882 |
| Young, J. A. | Brewis, Media | F/26 | December 26, 1893 | December 28, 1893 |
| Young, J. C. | Summers, Susan | C/46 | December 20, 1872 | No Return |
| Young, J. B. | Neeley, J. G. | C/324 | January 20, 1885 | January 22, 1885 |

| Groom or Bride | Groom or Bride | Book/Page | Date of License | Date of Marriage |
|---|---|---|---|---|
| Young, J. B. | Neeley, J. G. | C/324 | January 20, 1885 | January 22, 1885 |
| Young, J. E. | Schobt, Jane | F/106 | December 19, 1896 | December 20, 1896 |
| Young, J. M. | Ursery, Sarrah | A2/44 | December 20, 1855 | December 20, 1855 |
| Young, James | Herrod, Dora | F/8 | April 28, 1893 | May 1, 1893 |
| Young, James A. | Jaco, T. J. | C/262 | November 22, 1880 | November 20, 1880 |
| Young, James H. | Preston, Miss Martha E. | B/50 | August 10, 1867 | August 11, 1867 |
| Young, Jane Miss | Hammon, John | A/43 | November 1, 1841 | No Return |
| Young, Jane Miss | Rigsby, Thomas | A2/76 | January 12, 1855 | January 14, 1855 |
| Young, John | Mullins, Mrs. Jane | B/104 | June 23, 1870 | June 23, 1870 |
| Young, John A. | Elkins, Stacy C. | A/56 | November 23, 1842 | November 23, 1842 |
| Young, Joseph | Cummins, Miss Adaline | A2/22 | December 22, 1852 | January 3?, 1852 |
| Young, Laura | Ready, T. B | D/15 | | September 14, 1882 |
| Young, Laura | Witty, J. W. | C/346 | December 22, 1885 | No Return |
| Young, Lennie | Smithson, Frasier | F/94 | August 29, 1896 | August 30, 1896 |
| Young, M. A. | Walkup, J. W. | C/42 | October 9, 1872 | No Return |
| Young, M. A. | Davis, W. V. | C/326 | February 4, 1885 | February 5, 1885 |
| Young, Margaret | Rigsby, Thomas | A2/20 | October 9, 1852 | October 10, 1852 |
| Young, Margaret Miss | Thompson, James A. | A2/131 | November 9, 1865 | November 9, 1865 |
| Young, Margarett J. Miss | Mazey, W. W. | B/36 | December 26, 1866 | January 3, 1867 |
| Young, Mark L. | Todd, Locky Jane | A/114 | September 20, 1848 | September 20, 1848 |
| Young, Marling | Vinson, Miss Luiza | A2/30 | December 13, 1853 | December 13, 1853 |
| Young, Marry J. Miss | Reid, Alford | A2/35 | September 28, 1854 | September 28, 1854 |
| Young, Martha A. Miss | Mitchel, E. H. | A2/89 | October 24, 1859 | No Return |
| Young, Martha E. Miss | Mullins, James B. | A2/145 | September 24, 1866 | September 24, 1866 |
| Young, Martha Miss | McFerrin, Burton L. | A/62 | June 1, 1843 | June 1, 1843 |
| Young, Martha Miss | Haley, Allen | A/99 | April 10, 1847 | April 10, 1847 |
| Young, Mary | Preston, James | A2/125 | August 2, 1865 | August 2, 1865 |
| Young, Mary | Carrick, James T. | F/10 | May 15, 1893 | May 16, 1893 |
| Young, Mary A. Miss | Daniel, R. T. | A2/92 | December 17, 1859 | No Return |
| Young, Mary Caroline Miss | Elkins, Leroy Lafayette | A2/79 | April 5, 1856 | April 6, 1856 |
| Young, Matilda J. Miss | McGlothin, W. C. | A2/71 | December 21, 1858 | December 22, 1858 |
| Young, Mollie | Spurlock, Wm. | C/346 | December 23, 1885 | December 24, 1885 |
| Young, Nancy A. | Robinson, Wm. | C/328 | March 10, 1885 | March 12, 1885 |
| Young, Nancy Emaline | Davis, John | A/83 | September 10, 1845 | September 10, 1845 |
| Young, Nancy Frances Miss | Young, Silas H. | B/62 | February 5, 1868 | February 13, 1868 |
| Young, Nancy Francis | Neely, William | D/15 | | September 28, 1882 |
| Young, Nancy J. | Shelton, Thomas | F/74 | November 20, 1895 | November 20, 1895 |
| Young, Nancy T. | Hammons, John J. | A2/124 | July 29, 1865 | July 30, 1865 |
| Young, Nicy C. | Carrick, Thomas M. | C/252 | August 2, 1880 | August 2, 1880 |
| Young, P. A. | King, Miss R. P. | C/412 | December 13, 1887 | December 15, 1887 |
| Young, P. V. | Smithson, Olivia C. | E/338 | December 24, 1898 | |
| Young, P. V. | Smithson, Alma C. | F/164 | December 24, 1898 | December 25, 1898 |
| Young, Polk | Elkins, Eliza | F/20 | November 1, 1893 | November 1, 1893 |
| Young, R. A. Miss | Bell, J. T. | A2/70 | November 24, 1858 | November 25, 1858 |
| Young, R. E. | Mullins, J. B. | A2/99 | July 13, 1860 | Executed--No Date |
| Young, R. W. | Smithson, Cledar | F/150 | May 19, 1898 | May 22, 1898 |

| Groom or Bride | Groom or Bride | Book/Page | Date of License | Date of Marriage |
|---|---|---|---|---|
| Young, Rebeca | Bruce, Robert | C/406 | October 29, 1887 | October 29, 1887 |
| Young, Ruth Miss | Parten, William H. | A/97 | January 26, 1847 | January 27, 1847 |
| Young, Samuel | Murphy, Miss Sarah Jane | A2/88 | September 10, 1859 | No Return |
| Young, Samuel | Mullins, Sarah | A2/115 | July 22, 1864 | No Return |
| Young, Samuel | Jetton, Miss Sarah | B/62 | January 13, 1868 | January 14, 1868 |
| Young, Sarah | Young, Wm | C/358 | May 13, 1886 | May 13, 1886 |
| Young, Sarah A. | Rigsby, Wm. | C/26 | April 18, 1872 | April 18, 1872 |
| Young, Sarah D. | Kerby R. S. | C/330 | March 28, 1885 | No Return |
| Young, Sarah F. | Campbell, Marian F. | C/300 | January 21, 1884 | January 31, 1884 |
| Young, Sarah F. Miss | Carrick, T. A. | B/72 | November 13, 1868 | November 14, 1868 |
| Young, Sarah Miss | Ferrell, William | A/64 | August 1, 1843 | August 1, 1843 |
| Young, Sarah Miss | Thompson, F. | A2/27 | August 10, 1853 | No Return |
| Young, Sarah Miss | Whit, Benjamin | A2/27 | August 10, 1853 | August 10, 1853 |
| Young, Sena | Wilson, H. B. | A2/109 | September 26, 1863 | October 1, 1863 |
| Young, Silas H. | Young, Miss Nancy Frances | B/62 | February 5, 1868 | February 13, 1868 |
| Young, T. M. | Cummins, Sallie | C/148 | November 24, 1876 | November 26, 1876 |
| Young, Tatum | Woods, Hatti | C/456 | February 13, 1892 | February 14, 1892 |
| Young, Thomas | Cambell, Sallie | F/30 | January 28, 1894 | January 28, 1894 |
| Young, Tilford M. | Allen, Miss Nancy V. | A2/90 | November 16, 1859 | No Return |
| Young, V. L. | Thomas, Dorah | F/68 | September 14, 1895 | September 15, 1895 |
| Young, W. E. | Morgan, Miss Lidy E. | B/120 | December 21, 1870 | No Return |
| Young, Willey | Smithson, Emma | F/80 | January 4, 1896 | January 5, 1896 |
| Young, William | Litrell, Miss Jane | A/42 | October 9, 1841 | October 10, 1841 |
| Young, William | Burket, Martha | A2/118 | December 18, 1864 | No Return |
| Young, William | Teal, Miss Ann | C/386 | March 7, 1887 | No Return |
| Young, Wm | Young, Sarah | C/358 | May 13, 1886 | May 13, 1886 |
| Young, Wm. | Parton, Salinda | C/36 | August 31, 1872 | September 1, 1872 |
| Young, Wm. H. | Gaither, Miss Meran L. | A2/53 | January 13, 1857 | January 13, 1857 |
| Young, Wm. H. | Preston, Nancy E. | A2/111 | January 5, 1864 | January 7, 1864 |
| Young, Youffey Miss | Allen, Benjamin F. | A/38 | April 13, 1841 | April 13, 1841 |
| Youngblood, A. J. | Vasser, Miss Elizabeth J. | B/46 | May 21, 1867 | May 21, 1867 |
| Youngblood, Allen | Mairs, Rose E. | C/292 | September 19, 1883 | September 19, 1883 |
| Youngblood, Amandy | Jones, J. | C/170 | September 12, 1877 | September 15, 1877 |
| Youngblood, Arthelia | Farley, Thos H. | C/196 | August 14, 1878 | August 15, 1878 |
| Youngblood, Andrew | Elkins, Miss Rachell J. | A2/56 | April 22, 1857 | April 22, 1857 |
| Youngblood, Archelaus | Hooper, Miss Nancy E. | A/91 | October 5, 1846 | October 6, 1846 |
| Youngblood, Callie | Tittle, Elza | F/142 | December 28, 1897 | December 30, 1897 |
| Youngblood, Elizabeth C. | Fowler, W. J. | C/82 | February 12, 1874 | February 12, 1874 |
| Youngblood, G. W. | Turner, Miss M. E. | B/114 | November 3, 1870 | November 3, 1870 |
| Youngblood, Ibie | Prater, James | F/126 | August 14, 1896 | August 14, 1897 |
| Youngblood, J. H. | West, Miss S. A. | B/120 | December 21, 1870 | December 22, 1870 |
| Youngblood, James H. | Jones, Elizabeth C. | A/66 | December 21, 1843 | No Date |
| Youngblood, James T. | Hollandsworth, Miss N. J. | A2/92 | December 27, 1859 | No Return |
| Youngblood, Joe | Earles, Eva | E/348 | December 21, 1898 | |
| Youngblood, Joe | Earles, Eva | F/162 | December 21, 1898 | December 25, 1898 |
| Youngblood, Johnson | Miller, Carisanda | C/398 | August 25, 1887 | August 25, 1887 |

| Groom or Bride | Groom or Bride | Book/Page | Date of License | Date of Marriage |
|---|---|---|---|---|
| Youngblood, Jonnathan | Thomas, Miss Mary | B/130 | April 20, 1871 | April 20, 1871 |
| Youngblood, Lucy A. | Thomas, J. F. | C/156 | February 15, 1877 | February 15, 1877 |
| Youngblood, M. F. | Fowler, John | C/68 | October 16, 1873 | October 16, 1873 |
| Youngblood, M. J. | Mears, Marcus | C/84 | March 19, 1874 | No Return |
| Youngblood, Martha A. | Prater, T. J. | C/248 | June 11, 1880 | June 16, 1880 |
| Youngblood, Mary E. | McWhirter, S. A. | C/198 | September 14, 1878 | September 15, 1878 |
| Youngblood, M. J. | Youngblood, R. A. | A2/101 | September 2, 1860 | September 2, 1860 |
| Youngblood, Nancy Ann | Spicer, William | A/30 | June 18, 1840 | June 18, 1840 |
| Youngblood, Polly Miss | Hooper, James | A/89 | July 25, 1846 | July 26, 1846 |
| Youngblood, R. A. | Youngblood, M. J. | A2/101 | September 2, 1860 | September 2, 1860 |
| Youngblood, S. B. | Tucker, Renn | C/348 | January 2, 1886 | January 3, 1886 |
| Youngblood, W. J. | Beshears, M. A. | C/434 | April 1, 1891 | April 2, 1891 |
| Youngblood, Wm. | Thompson, Miss Parilee V. | B/110 | September 22, 1870 | September 22, 1870 |
| Youree, Eliza Miss | Tolbert, James | E/7 | January 20, 1888 | January 20, 1888 |
| Youree, G. C. | Laseter, Nancy E. | A2/94 | February 1, 1860 | No Return |
| Youree, G. C. | Lasiter, Miss F. E. | C/456 | March 1, 1892 | No Return |
| Youree, J. A. | Patton, James | C/276 | December 20, 1880 | December 23, 1880 |
| Youree, J. F. | Doak, Miss Birtha | F/110 | February 8, 1897 | February 8, 1897 |
| Youree, J. H. | Todd, Mattie | F/100 | October 28, 1896 | No Return |
| Youree, J. P. | Smith, Maggie E. | C/142 | August 7, 1876 | No Return |
| Youree, R. S. | Doaks, Pheivia | F/138 | December 7, 1897 | December 7, 1897 |
| Youree, Sarah | Thomas, P. J | C/244 | March 11, 1880 | March 11, 1880 |
| Youree, T. W. | Moon, Julie | C/400 | September 6, 1887 | September 7, 1887 |
| Youree, W. E. | Carter, R. R. | C/72 | November 13, 1873 | November 13, 1873 |
| Youree, W. H. | Hollis, Miss M. L. | A2/94 | February 13, 1860 | February 14, 1860 |
| Youree, W. H. | Crage, S. W. | D/22 | | February 12, 1883 |
| Yourie, S. M. | Walkup, Miss M. F. | B/38 | January 16, 1867 | January 16, 1867 |
| Zuarles, Alex | Simmon, Mattie | F/156 | September 12, 1898 | September 14, 1898 |
| Zuarles, Joe | Braswell, Joe | F/154 | August 30, 1898 | August 31, 1898 |
| Zumbro, Elizabeth S. | Bivins, L. M. S. | A2/106 | December 27, 1862 | December 28, 1862 |